U.S. CONFLICTS
IN THE 21ST CENTURY

U.S. CONFLICTS IN THE 21ST CENTURY

Afghanistan War, Iraq War, and the War on Terror

VOLUME 1: A–H

Spencer C. Tucker

Editor

Paul G. Pierpaoli Jr.

Associate Editor

An Imprint of ABC-CLIO, LLC
Santa Barbara, California • Denver, Colorado

Library of Congress Cataloging-in-Publication Data

U.S. conflicts in the 21st century : Afghanistan War, Iraq War, and the War on Terror / Spencer C. Tucker, editor ; Paul G. Pierpaoli Jr., associate editor.

     pages cm

  Includes bibliographical references and index.

  ISBN 978-1-4408-3878-1 (alk. paper) — ISBN 978-1-4408-3879-8 (ebook)   1. United States—History, Military—21st century. 2. Afghan War, 2001–   3. Iraq War, 2003–2011.   4. War on Terrorism, 2001–2009.   I. Tucker, Spencer, 1937– editor.   II. Pierpaoli, Paul G., Jr., 1962– editor.   III. Title: Afghanistan War, Iraq War, and the War on Terror.

  E897.U55   2016

  355.009730905—dc23   2015016739

ISBN: 978-1-4408-3878-1

EISBN: 978-1-4408-3879-8

20 19 18 17 16   1 2 3 4 5

This book is also available on the World Wide Web as an eBook.
Visit www.abc-clio.com for details.

ABC-CLIO
An Imprint of ABC-CLIO, LLC

ABC-CLIO, LLC
130 Cremona Drive, P.O. Box 1911
Santa Barbara, California 93116-1911

This book is printed on acid-free paper ∞
Manufactured in the United States of America

This work is dedicated to the memory of my father,
Colonel Cary S. Tucker, USAR Rtd. (1906–1962),
who served in World War II and the Korean War and whose own scholarship
in military history set me on this long and rewarding journey

Contents

List of Entries

List of Documents

List of Maps

Preface

On the morning of September 11, 2001 (9/11), 19 Islamist terrorists (15 of them citizens of Saudi Arabia), acting under a plan developed by the Al Qaeda terrorist network located in Afghanistan, employed box cutters to seize control of four airliners taking off from three different U.S. cities. The terrorists, who had received some training at U.S. flight schools, then crashed two of the heavily fueled planes into the Twin Towers of the World Trade Center in New York City, collapsing the buildings. They crashed a third plane into the Pentagon in Arlington County, Virginia, causing extensive damage there. Passengers in the fourth airplane, which was evidently headed for the White House in Washington, D.C., alerted by cell phone as to what had occurred in the other airplanes, attempted to take control of their aircraft from the terrorists. In the ensuing melee the plane crashed into a field in Pennsylvania. All those aboard the four aircraft were killed, while casualties at the World Trade Center and Pentagon were heavy. In all, 2,996 people lost their lives (including the 19 hijackers), and more than 6,000 people were injured. This was the worst terrorist attack in U.S. history and represented a greater death toll than that which occurred during the December 1941 Japanese attack on Pearl Harbor.

While a terrorist attack on the United States by Al Qaeda, headed by Saudi national Osama bin Laden, was considered likely, and there had been indicators that this might include attempts to seize control of passenger planes and fly them into buildings, intelligence indicators were simply not acted on. These included reports of the training of would-be pilots from the Middle East only interested in learning about the instruments and piloting passenger-type aircraft in flight as opposed to takeoffs and landings. There was precious little communication and coordination among U.S. agencies such as the Federal Bureau of Investigation, the Central Intelligence Agency, and the National Security Agency.

On September 12, the United Nations (UN) Security Council denounced the attack and called on all member states to assist in apprehending those responsible. President George W. Bush characterized the attacks not as simply "acts of terror" but as "acts of war," and on October 2 the North Atlantic Treaty Organization for the first time in its 52-year history invoked Article 5 of its charter; many member nations, a number of which had lost their own citizens in the Twin Towers, provided assistance. The attacks were immensely costly to the U.S. economy, especially the aviation and insurance industries. Estimates of the total cost run to $3.3 trillion, or $1 million for every $1 spent by Al Qaeda in the operation. The attacks also led to the diversion of considerable funding from other worthy programs to enhance domestic security.

Al Qaeda's responsibility for the attacks was soon established, and in a September 20 televised address to a joint session of Congress, President Bush announced a U.S. "war on terror" that would commence against Al Qaeda but not end "until every terrorist group of global reach has been found, stopped, and defeated." The term "war on terror," which came to be known formally as the Global War on Terror, is actually something of a misnomer. Terror is a tactic, a war-fighting technique. As it has turned out, the "war" waged by the United States and its allies has been almost exclusively against Islamist extremists, who have made their own aims quite clear. They are jihadists embarked on a religious war with the West, intent on eradicating Western influence in the Muslim world, toppling Western institutions everywhere, and establishing a caliphate based on sharia (Islamic law) that would, at the least, embrace all Muslims.

In his September 20 remarks Bush demanded that the Taliban, the radical Islamist regime that held power in Afghanistan, immediately turn over bin Laden, destroy Al Qaeda bases, and expel that organization from its territory or risk military action. The Taliban insisted that the U.S. government first provide proof of Al Qaeda's guilt, which bin Laden denied (he would not admit responsibility until 2004). Ultimately the United States did provide information, passed to the Taliban through Pakistan, but with the Afghan government still intransigent, Bush secured from Congress approval for military operations.

Following a month of planning by the United States and its allies, the Afghanistan War, known as Operation ENDURING FREEDOM, commenced on October 7, 2011. It would be America's longest war, lasting in its combat phase for U.S. forces until the end of 2014, with some 10,800 U.S. forces still in that country in 2015. The Taliban was rather easily ousted from power, with U.S. and allied forces, including the British and Australians, teaming up with the Afghan opposition Northern Alliance. Nonetheless, the military campaign was mishandled in that insufficient resources on the ground were available to secure the capture of key Taliban and Al Qaeda leaders, at first holed up in the caves of the mountains of Tora Bora. Most, including bin Laden, subsequently escaped into the Islamist-dominated Northwest Territories of Pakistan, where they commenced guerrilla warfare against the occupiers.

As U.S. and coalition forces settled in for the long haul, the Bush administration established at the U.S. Guantánamo Bay Navy Base in Cuba a facility to hold and interrogate members of the Al Qaeda organization and Taliban "terrorists." Other so-called black sites beyond the constraints of U.S. law were established in countries allied with the United States. At Guantánamo and these other facilities, prisoners were subjected to coercive interrogation, or what most experts regard as torture. Late in 2014 a U.S. Senate committee released a damning 500-page summary report that confirmed the torture charges raised earlier and confirmed that this had been authorized under a finding by the Bush administration. These methods included the near-drowning experience of waterboarding, repeated numerous times in several cases; physical abuse; and sleep deprivation. The report also concluded that such practices did not in fact obtain useful information and furthermore involved detainees who had no connection to terrorist activity. Nevertheless, defenders of these practices, most notably Bush's outspoken vice president Richard "Dick" Cheney, strongly attacked the report and continued to hold that the practices were justified in view of the September 11 attacks.

Meanwhile, any hopes of bringing the Afghanistan War to a speedy conclusion were dashed by the Bush administration's foolhardy decision to initiate a second war, this time with Iraq, with the Afghanistan War still unwon. Iraq's strongman President Saddam Hussein had long been a thorn in the side of the United States. In August 1990, Hussein had sent his military into Kuwait and quickly seized control of that small oil-rich state. This action had prompted U.S. president George H. W. Bush, George W. Bush's father, to form a powerful international coalition that drove Iraq from Kuwait in the Persian Gulf War of January 1991. But the senior Bush understood what his son did not—that toppling Hussein from power and occupying Iraq would unleash long pent-up sectarian and ethnic tensions that might well spin out of control. It would also split the Arab coalition that had participated in the Persian Gulf War and would strengthen regional rival Iran, now essentially a theocracy ruled by Muslim mullahs. The senior Bush and his successor, President Bill Clinton, intended merely to contain Hussein.

That sectarian tensions in Iraq were explosive was shown at the end of the Persian Gulf War during a Shiite uprising in southern Iraq, which had been encouraged by the United States. There was also an uprising by Kurds in the northern part of the country. Both revolts were put down with great ferocity by Hussein (the Kurds had already experienced the use of poison gas in 1988 that killed thousands).

The policy of merely containing Hussein was continued and involved the established no-fly zones in both southern and northern Iraq to protect the Shias and the Kurds and in Operation PROVIDE COMFORT (March 1991–December 1998), which witnessed an international aid effort for the northern Iraqi Kurdish population. On several occasions during the Clinton years, the United States launched air strikes and cruise missiles to bring Hussein to heel. Although he continued to rule Iraq with an iron fist, he was essentially contained. Iraqis continued to suffer economically thanks to international sanctions, but this did not trouble Hussein, who continued to trumpet Iraq's military prowess.

Part of Hussein's policy of bluff and bluster was an attempt to cow his own restive population, but it was also part of his ongoing effort to restore Iraq's power in the region and to send a strong message to Iran, with which Hussein had fought a very costly and protracted war during 1980–1988. Hussein's policy of bluff included the suggestion that Iraq was bent on acquiring nuclear, chemical, and biological weapons, the so-called weapons of mass destruction (WMD). This was easy to believe, as Iraq had earlier tried to acquire nuclear weapons, only to have its nuclear reactor destroyed in Operation OPERA, an Israeli air strike in June 1981. Neighboring Syria also boasted one of the world's largest stockpiles of chemical weapons, so it seemed quite likely that Iraq might be following suit. Wild stories circulated, including one that Iraq was seeking to purchase yellowcake uranium in Niger. Such stories were trumpeted by Iraqi opposition leaders abroad who were anxious to topple Hussein and rule in his place.

The Bush administration quickly bought into such stories. Bush himself had already, of course, announced the Global War on Terror, and in the course of a speech before Congress on January 29, 2002, he proclaimed the existence of an "axis of evil" consisting of Iran, Iraq, and North Korea. Cheney and a number of other neocons (short for "neoconservatives") urged swift action. Neocons championed an aggressive assertion of democracy worldwide and saw Hussein's regime as a threat to the entire Middle East. Hussein's presumed effort to acquire WMD offered the excuse to topple him and establish in his place a democratic Iraq that would be an engine of change for the entire region. Notable neocons included Defense Secretary Donald Rumsfeld, Deputy Secretary of Defense Paul Wolfowitz, Assistant Secretary of State (later UN ambassador) John Bolton, National Security Council staffer Elliott Abrams, Defense Policy Board Advisory Committee chairman Richard Perle, and Kissinger and Associates managing director Lewis Paul Bremer. Urged on by Cheney, Bush began to build the case for war. The Central Intelligence Agency (CIA) was eager to oblige, given that it was charged only with finding evidence to support the case for war.

On February 5, 2003, widely respected U.S. Secretary of State Colin Powell, who as chairman of the Joint Chiefs of Staff during the 1991 Persian Gulf War had stood squarely against a full-scale invasion of Iraq and regime change, presented the case for war at the UN. The evidence, much of which was provided by the CIA, turned out to be faulty. The case for war was made easier, however, by Hussein's quite deliberate policy of deception and his government's failure to cooperate fully with and indeed its obstruction of UN weapons inspectors.

UN secretary-general Kofi Annan and most UN member states greeted the U.S. case for war with Iraq with great skepticism. Although a handful of other nations did provide military assistance, it was initially essentially a U.S.-British effort. The war, dubbed Operation IRAQI FREEDOM, commenced on March 20, 2003. In its U.S. phase, it would last more than eight years and eight months.

Toppling Hussein in the Iraq War (Operation IRAQI FREEDOM) was the easy part. Although the U.S. plan for a two-pronged invasion—one from the south mounted from Kuwait and the other from the north staged from Turkey—failed to materialize when the Turkish government balked (owing in large part to concerns regarding the Kurds), the southern invasion proved sufficient, accompanied by airlifts of small forces into northern Iraq. Baghdad was taken on April 12. The United States—quite prematurely as it turned out—trumpeted the end of major offensive combat operations in Iraq on May 1, 2003. Hussein was captured on December 13. He was later put on trial by the new Iraqi government and found guilty and was executed in December 2006.

With the Iraqi Army seemingly defeated, the real travail began in the commencement of sectarian violence and insurgency, which became a virtual civil war in Iraq. The truism of Powell's warning that to invade Iraq was "to own it" became fully apparent, despite Defense Secretary Rumsfeld's continued rosy pronouncements. Rumsfeld bears considerable blame for a mismanaged war. Tensions between Rumsfeld and the military leadership dated from the beginning of his tenure at the Department of Defense in early 2001, with his calls for greater civilian control over the military and a slimmer, faster force, which were viewed with mistrust by many senior officers. Rumsfeld's aggressive, abrasive style and insistence that only those who agreed with him occupy senior military posts caused alarm and enmity. Certainly Rumsfeld and much of the Bush team believed that superior U.S. airpower and technology would produce easy victory. Rumsfeld micromanaged the wars in Afghanistan and Iraq, even deciding what units would deploy there and the equipment they could utilize. A key reason for the failure at Tora Bora in Afghanistan was his refusal to allow the 10th Mountain Division to deploy to that country with its organic artillery.

Rumsfeld simply refused to allow the military professionals to run the wars in Afghanistan and Iraq. He rejected the costs in manpower and treasure that were presented by the military as necessary to maintain order in Iraq. Indeed, given that many other powers had contributed financially to ease the strain on U.S. taxpayers in the Persian Gulf War, the neocons believed that Iraq's considerable oil reserves would more than pay for this war. General Eric Shinseki, then army chief of staff, testified before the Senate Armed Services Committee a month prior to the 2003 invasion that occupying Iraq would require "something on the order of several hundred thousand soldiers," an estimate far higher than the figure proposed by Rumsfeld. In sharp public pronouncements, Both Rumsfeld and Wolfowitz, another key invasion planner, rejected Shinseki's estimate.

In all fairness, the belief that airpower is a panacea continues today and is embraced by the Barack Obama administration. Airpower alone has never won wars, and if the coalition now battling the Islamic State of Iraq and Syria (ISIS) is to triumph, it will only be a result of action on the ground supported by airpower. As of early 2015 the commitment was basically only airpower, and it remained unclear where the ground forces would be found.

Bremer also bears much responsibility for the Iraq quagmire. Appointed head of the U.S. Provisional Authority in Iraq, Bremer took two steps that proved disastrous. First, he banned members of Hussein's ruling Baath Party from holding public office. The Baath Party had dominated both the administration and the educational establishment, and many party members were trained bureaucrats rather than ideologues. At one stroke this forced a complete administrative restructuring from the ground up. The other step was to disband the Iraqi Army. This created a security nightmare for the too few U.S. and "coalition of the willing" troops, even as they were joined by other UN-mandated peacekeeping forces. Not appreciated at the time, it also prevented the hollowed-out U.S. military from effectively prosecuting the ongoing Afghanistan War. Military assets that might have won the war there were now shifted to Iraq. The war there was waged by a relatively small force. Even to secure that manpower required deployments in a far from ideal arrangement of U.S. National Guard troops and units of the Army Reserve, Air Force Reserve, Navy Reserve, and Marine Corps Reserve in both wars. Many of these individuals underwent multiple deployments to Afghanistan and Iraq.

As could be predicted, free elections in Iraq brought the majority Shiites to power; they had long chaffed under Hussein's repressive rule, and many of them were determined to exact revenge on the Sunnis, while the minority Kurds also saw the opportunity to assert what amounted to home rule in the Kurdish-dominated region of northern Iraq. The Sunnis, who had been in the drivers' seat under Hussein, now found themselves on the outside looking in, and many of them took to arms. U.S. forces were obliged to retake certain key cities such as Fallujah and Ramadi in the Sunni stronghold of Anbar Province, but Baghdad saw much violence in costly suicide bombings that also occurred throughout the country and exacted a heavy toll on Iraqi civilians. Iraqi Christians also came under persecution. The rising Iraqi insurgency also exacted a dreadful toll on U.S. and coalition forces, which suffered far more casualties after major combat operations had been declared over.

During 2006–2014 the Iraqi government was led by Shiite Nuri al-Maliki, who practiced a divide-and-rule concept of governance that largely repressed and excluded the Sunnis and Kurds from participation. Corruption continued on a considerable scale, and the Iraqi military languished, despite some $18 billion in U.S. assistance and training.

Rumsfeld found himself under mounting pressure, including calls for his resignation from retired U.S. generals, some of whom had held command positions during the war. Rumsfeld and his aides were accused of too often unnecessarily inserting themselves into military decision making, often disregarding advice from military commanders in the field.

A troop surge of 20,000–30,000 men announced by the Bush administration in January 2007 somewhat calmed the situation, but American public opinion had now turned decidedly against the war, abetted by the Abu Ghraib prison scandal, which was made public in 2004. Photographs were released showing what turned out to be poorly trained American military personnel abusing Iraqi prisoners at the American-run facility.

Obama assumed the U.S. presidency in January 2009. He had been strongly opposed to the Iraq War since its onset and was determined to bring the U.S. presence there to an end and shift the focus back on Afghanistan. U.S. forces were gradually withdrawn even as civilian casualties from sectarian violence in Iraq mounted. After the Maliki government rejected a status of force agreement with the United States that would have allowed a residual force to remain there and train the Iraqi military, the last U.S. troops quit that country at the end of 2011, bringing that war to a close, at least as far as the Americans were concerned.

At the same time, new challenges emerged for the United States. Unrest in Tunisia in late 2010 led to a change of government there, and the ripples spread outward, beginning what became known as the Arab Spring. Egypt's iron-fisted president, Hosni Mubarak, was forced from power in Egypt in February 2011, and demonstrations against Muammar Qadaffi of Libya commenced that same month. When Qadaffi sought to quell these with force, it led to a bloody civil war there. Obama was reluctant to involve the U.S. militarily in Libya, but the mounting Libyan government attacks on civilians brought North Atlantic Treaty Organization (NATO) intervention in the form of air strikes, cruise missiles, and naval support. The U.S. role here was largely logistical support. Qaddafi was overthrown in August 2011, although sharp fissures soon appeared, and fighting between rival factions continued into 2015.

Civil war also commenced in Syria in 2011, as demonstrations occurred demanding reforms by the government of President Bashar al-Assad, whose family had long held power. Obama rejected calls that the United States arm the moderate Syrian rebels fighting the repressive Assad regime supported by Iran and Russia, perhaps missing an opportunity to prevent more radical factions from coming to the fore. Obama did subsequently threaten to use force should the Syrian government employ chemical weapons against civilians, but when this occurred he failed to do so on a Syrian agreement that its chemical weapons would be removed and destroyed under the eyes of international inspectors. The Syrian Civil War continues, however, in what is nothing short of a humanitarian catastrophe. By the end of 2014 more than 200,000 had perished in the conflict, and millions more were refugees.

Meanwhile, sectarian violence continued in Iraq; indeed that country experienced some of its heaviest losses since the 2003 U.S. invasion as suicide bombings exacted a frightful toll. New Iraqi elections in 2014 saw Maliki's coalition win the most votes, but this time he did not secure the premiership. Instead, after prolonged wrangling it went to a moderate Shiite, Haider al-Abadi, who promptly promised to lead a "strong and inclusive government," "empower local authorities," and "fight corruption by strengthening the rule of law." He also found himself having to deal with the very real possibility that Iraq would split into three separate states of Kurds, Shiites, and Sunnis.

Much of northern Syria had now come under the control of a radical Islamist group calling itself the Islamic State of Iraq and Syria (ISIS), later simply the Islamic State. Following a June 2014 offensive, ISIS had also secured large swaths of northern Iraq. The fighting displaced more than half a million Iraqis and gave ISIS control of most of the Sunni-dominated Anbar Province, extending to some 60 miles outside of Baghdad and actually threatening the capital itself. When confronted with the fanatical ISIS fighters, many soldiers of the poorly led Iraqi Army simply threw down their weapons and ran. Unlike Maliki, whose reaction was to mobilize Shiite militias, Abadi recognized the need for

reform. He sacked several dozen senior army commanders and revealed to parliament how corrupt and hollowed out the Iraqi military establishment had become. In these desperate circumstances, he also called on the United States to return to Iraq.

Widespread ISIS atrocities against civilians—including the displacement of minority populations, massacres of those refusing to convert to Islam, the enslavement of women, and the beheadings of two American hostages, the images of which were then released over the Internet—led Obama to employ U.S. airpower against ISIS in Iraq; request and secure congressional approval for aid to moderate Syrian rebels, to include small arms and the commitment of 400 personnel to train up to 15,000 moderate opposition forces to take back territory previously lost to ISIS; and form a military coalition of nations against the radical Islamists. This has now grown to some 60 nations, with coalition air strikes against ISIS targets in both Iraq and Syria. By early 2015 it appeared that the ISIS offensive in Iraq was receding and that its large offensive to secure the Syrian town of Kobani on the border with Turkey, which had begun in September 2014, had been blunted in what would be its first major defeat.

The year 2014 brought a new leader in Afghanistan as well. Ashraf Ghani took over the presidency there following a disputed election and the departure of an embittered Hamid Karzai, who left office amid a failed attempt to negotiate with the Taliban and sharp criticism of the United States. On taking office, Ghani promptly signed the status of forces agreement with the United States that Karzai had negotiated but then refused to sign. At the end of 2014 the NATO-led international combat forces departed. Obama, who had planned for a smaller residual U.S. force to train the Afghan military and counter any threats from Al Qaeda, increased that number slightly to 10,800 troops, given growing Taliban military activities. These forces also have authority to conduct air strikes in support of the Afghan military if need be. In early 2015, however, it was by no means clear that the Afghan Army of some 200,000 men, trained by the United States and the International Security Assistance Force, would be any more successful than the new Iraqi Army and would be able to stand against the Taliban.

In 2015, Islamist extremist offensives appeared blunted in three states. In Mali, an Islamist offensive had secured much of the north of that large landlocked African country and threatened to take over the remainder when it was turned back by a French military intervention at the behest of the Mali government. The United States rendered logistical support.

Somalia had descended into chaos and tribalism, with the radical Islamist Al-Shabaab organization threatening a takeover of that failed state. Gangs of Somali pirates seized hundreds of merchant ships transiting the Red Sea and held them and their crews for ransom. This activity finally forced international action, led by the United States, in patrolling and convoying warships of a number of navies, including those of China and Russia. U.S. drone strikes also took out some of the leadership of the Al-Shabaab organization that threatened a takeover of Somalia, and by the end of 2014 troops of member states of the African Union Military joined Somali government forces in driving the Islamists from most of the territory they once had held.

In the Philippines, in March 2014 the government signed a peace accord with the Moro Islamic Liberation Front, the country's largest Muslim rebel group. The United States had been providing material assistance and advising the Philippine Army on counterinsurgency tactics against Islamic rebel groups demanding greater autonomy or independence in the island of Mindanao.

Twenty-first-century relations between the United States and Pakistan have often been stormy, given shadow support by the Pakistani intelligence services for the Taliban in Afghanistan. U.S. drone strikes had continued across the border into Pakistan to take out the Taliban leadership, often bringing a sharp reaction from the Pakistani government, including the torching of supply convoys. Pakistanis expressed great displeasure at the May 1, 2011, killing of bin Laden at his compound in Pakistan at the hands of U.S. commanders without Pakistani government concurrence. Nonetheless, a growing Pakistani civilian death toll from Taliban bombings brought a government military campaign against the northwest tribal areas in June 2014. This registered solid gains. The retaliatory December massacre of 145 children at a school in Peshawar run for dependents of the Pakistani Army brought widespread horror and may well have definitively tipped public opinion in Pakistan against the Taliban.

Yemen was hardly a success story, however. In 2011 its strongman, President Ali Abdullah Saleh, was finally forced from office, but Al Qaeda in the Arabian Peninsula (AQAP), which was responsible for the bombing of the U.S. Navy destroyer *Cole* in October 2000, remained entrenched in what is increasingly regarded as a failed state. U.S. drone strikes have taken out some of the AQAP leadership, but this did not stop it from fomenting a series of attempts to strike the United States and Western Europe. Then, in early January 2015, two members of an apparent AQAP sleeper cell in France attacked the officers of French satirical magazine *Charlie Hebdo*, killing 12 people for its cartoons of the Prophet Muhammad. Later that same month in a major setback for the campaign against AQAP, a coup d'état by Houthi rebels toppled the Somali government and forced the resignation of President Abed Rabbo Mansour Hadi and his government. This left the U.S. campaign against AQAP and Al Qaeda there—even the American presence in Yemen—in jeopardy. The Shiite Houthi rebels, while they oppose AQAP, are supported by Iran and strongly oppose both the United States and Saudi Arabia. The simultaneous death of Saudi king Abdullah bin Abdulaziz al Saud further complicates the regional picture, although new king Salman bin Abdulaziz pledged to continue his brother's policies.

Muslim North Africa remains a major question mark. Unrest continues in Libya, with armed groups utilizing the considerable stocks of weapons seized with the collapse of the Qaddafi regime fighting to control Libya's considerable oil assets. While Tunisia appears at this writing to be a success story, Algeria has seen terrorist organization active, especially in the south of the country.

Iran is a major concern for the United States. Shiite Iran is locked in a major geopolitical power struggle with the more populous Sunni Muslim states, headed by Saudi Arabia. Many observers believe that Iran's clerical leadership is determined that the country acquire nuclear weapons. In mid-2015, international talks were still in progress in an effort to prevent this from occurring, but it was by no means clear that a satisfactory agreement was possible. The threat of Israeli military action is very real. Certainly there is ample proof that Iran has supplied weaponry to the Taliban in Afghanistan, to Hamas in Gaza, to Hezbollah in Lebanon, to the Houthi rebels in Yemen, and to the government side in the Syrian Civil War. Reportedly, this weaponry has included sophisticated missiles.

In 2014 the United States was also forced to respond to the crisis caused by Russian president Vladimir Putin's coup de main in the Russian takeover of the Crimean Peninsula and his intervention in eastern Ukraine in an effort to detach it as well. These moves followed a revolution in Ukraine that ousted pro-Russian president Viktor Yanukovych and saw demands by the majority of the population for closer ties with the European Union (EU). Obama and the EU states chose to rely on sanctions, although Obama requested and received funds from Congress to provide light weapons and training by the American military of a limited number of Ukrainian security forces. Putin had done much to modernize the Russian military, and both Russia and China have sharply increased their defense budgets. Increasingly worrisome is the sharp rhetoric from the Chinese government. It too has asserted its territorial rights, in this case to the energy assets of much of the East China Sea, while Putin insists that Russia has the right to defend (i.e., incorporate) territory inhabited by Russian speakers everywhere.

Nearly a decade and a half of war has proven costly for the United States in terms of both blood and treasure. The Afghanistan War (2001–2014) resulted in 2,356 U.S. military deaths and an additional 20,000 or so wounded. The Iraq War (2003–2011) saw 4,488 U.S. military deaths, with an additional 34,000 wounded. The conflicts resulted in massive deficit spending, made worse by the Bush administration's insistence on simultaneous tax cuts. Huge budget deficits and mounting national debt badly skewed the American economy and were contributing factors to the 2008 financial meltdown and the deep economic recession that ensued. And because of the massive budget deficits created by the Bush administration, the federal government lacked the financial resources necessary to help engineer a robust economic recovery. Thus, the recession—deeper than any since the Great Depression of the 1930s—took years to reverse; in some cases, its effects lingered into 2015.

Many Americans on both sides of the political spectrum have also come to lament the effects of the 21st-century wars on the national psyche as well as constitutional and civil liberties. The establishment of the Transportation Safety Administration has cost the U.S. government and U.S. airlines tens of billions of dollars, and air travel has become more burdensome for millions of Americans. In recent years, reports that the National Security Administration has been collecting substantial information on most Americans, including e-mails and phone records, has raised serious concerns that Americans' constitutional and privacy rights were abrogated by an overzealous national security establishment. In early 2014 the Obama administration, forced to deal with these reports because of WikiLeaks and the activities of Edward Snowden, vowed to protect Americans' basic civic and constitutional rights, but the inherent secrecy behind these issues will make it very difficult—if not impossible—to ascertain whether changes will indeed be made and what the outcome might be.

In February 2014 with the end of the Iraq War and the winding down of the U.S. military presence in Afghanistan, the Obama administration announced plans to reduce the size of the U.S. Army to some 420,00–450,000 personnel, down from a post–September 2011 peak of 575,000.

The plan would also eliminate some weapons systems and retard the procurement of others. These reductions reportedly would leave the U.S. military capable of defeating any enemy but too small for long foreign occupations and would involve greater risk if U.S. forces were asked to carry out two large-scale military actions at the same time. Despite these cuts, as of this writing the U.S. military remains the world's strongest. The Stockholm International Peace Research organization calculated actual 2013 U.S. defense spending at some $640 billion, accounting for more than one-third of the world total. China was second at $188 billion, and Russia was third at $88 billion. Indeed, the U.S. defense budget was larger than the next nine nations combined. As a percentage of gross national product it was considerably higher than that for China, 3.8 percent to only 2.0. (Russia was at 4.8 percent). America's strategic reach and logistical systems remain unmatched, but with major military challenges on a number of fronts, questions abound as to whether the allocation of resources is correct and whether manpower resources will be adequate for the challenges ahead. Certainly, careful attention to these considerations will be essential if a satisfactory outcome is to be achieved.

This encyclopedia treats U.S. military actions in the 21st century, including the September 11, 2001, terrorist attacks on the United States and events of the Global War on Terror as well as the U.S. wars in Afghanistan and Iraq, and—most recently—the campaign against the Islamic State of Iraq and Syria (ISIS). We also address selected military activities involving the United States and North Atlantic Treaty Organization states elsewhere in the world, including Africa and Asia.

The encyclopedia introduction is a comprehensive examination of U.S. policies in the Middle East and Central Asia. The body of the work consists of 663 entries treating countries, overviews of the principal conflicts, leading population centers and regional topography, national leaders and individuals of note, weapons systems, and key battles. There is also a lengthy chronology treating the many events of the years 2000–2014, a glossary, a bibliography, and some 64,000 words of documents and related commentary.

I am, as always, most grateful for the work of associate editor Dr. Paul G. Pierpaoli Jr., who has written many of the entries treating recent events and edited and updated so many others.

Spencer C. Tucker

Introduction

The United States in the Middle East and Western and Central Asia

Until World War I, U.S. involvement in Middle Eastern affairs was both spotty and small-scale. The notable undertakings were two naval wars in the very early years of the 19th century to eradicate the threat posed by the Barbary privateers of the semiautonomous Ottoman Empire states of Morocco, Tunis, Algiers, and Tripoli to American maritime commerce in the Mediterranean. Both ended in U.S. naval victory.

During the remainder of the 19th century, American dealings with the Near and Middle East were largely private and primarily educational or commercial. In 1866 Presbyterian missionaries established the Syrian Protestant College, which later became the American University in Beirut. Other American universities and colleges were founded in Cairo and Istanbul. American businessmen also traded with the region. By the early 20th century, American diplomats sought to ensure that the Ottoman Empire and Morocco granted their country's nationals trading concessions on a par with those accorded to European nations through capitulatory treaties.

Under President Theodore Roosevelt, a strong proponent of an assertive U.S. international posture, in 1906 American representatives played a leading role at the Algeciras Conference, which mediated a diplomatic crisis between France and Germany over the status of Morocco and ended in effectively making the sultanate a French protectorate. Roosevelt's belief in the forthright defense of American interests was also demonstrated in 1904, when a wealthy Greek American resident in Tangier, Ion Perdicaris, was kidnapped by Raisuli, a Moroccan bandit. In a move popular with the American public, Roosevelt dispatched seven battleships and a force of marines to Morocco, demanding that it ensure the safe delivery of "Perdicaris alive or Raisuli dead." Eventually, Perdicaris was released.

World War I brought enhanced, though still limited, American involvement in the Middle East. Before 1914, American oil companies showed little interest in competing with European firms for the right to develop Middle Eastern petroleum sources. The war itself created new uncertainties in the region, promoting Arab nationalism and bringing finish to Ottoman rule over the areas then known as Mesopotamia, Palestine, and Arabia (present-day Iraq, Syria, Jordan, Israel, Saudi Arabia, and the Arab emirates as well as the province of Armenia). In late 1914 the Ottoman Empire allied itself with Germany and Austria-Hungary against Great Britain and France. The latter two powers then encouraged Arab revolts against Ottoman rule, making somewhat ambivalent pledges to recognize the rule of Hussein ibn Ali, sharif of the Islamic territory of the Hejaz, and his three sons, Ali, Feisal, and Abdullah, over Mesopotamia and Arabia. Britain and France also made secret agreements with each other (and with Russia) envisaging the territorial division of Mesopotamia and Palestine between their two empires. In addition, in November 1917 to encourage worldwide Jewish support for the Entente side in the war, the British government issued the Balfour Declaration, promising Jews a national homeland, although not a state, in Palestine.

When the United States entered World War I in April 1917, it declared war only on Germany, leaving the proclamation of a formal state of hostilities with Austria-Hungary until December 1917 and refraining entirely from any declaration of war against the Ottoman Empire. In 1918 President Woodrow Wilson, rather to the distaste of diplomats in the State Department, endorsed the Balfour Declaration in principle, but at the subsequent Paris Peace Conference he made no great effort to press for the establishment of a Jewish homeland. Wilson distrusted the other major Allied powers of Britain, France, and Italy, and he deplored what he perceived as their eagerness to extend their own colonial holdings by annexing former colonies and other territories that had belonged to the Central Powers before 1914. Wilson particularly opposed the secret inter-Allied treaties and agreements regarding the disposition of territories that had been under the control of the Central Powers.

In an effort to pressure the Allies into accepting liberal war aims, on January 8, 1918, Wilson publicly announced his Fourteen Points, an idealistic and wide-ranging set of diplomatic principles for a nonpunitive postwar settlement that included national self-determination and autonomous development for lands that had been part of the Ottoman Empire prior to 1914. Britain and France responded by stating their intention to establish indigenous governments in these areas, regimes that would nonetheless be expected to accept the tutelage and guidance of "more advanced" nations.

American distaste for imperialism led to the creation at the 1919 Paris Peace Conference of a mandate system whereby former colonies of the defeated powers taken over by the victorious powers would fall under the ultimate jurisdiction of the new League of Nations. The British mandates eventually comprised present-day Iraq, Transjordan (now Jordan and the Right Bank occupied by Israel), and Palestine (now Israel), while the French controlled what is now Syria and Lebanon.

In practice, the British and French negotiated this division of the Ottoman spoils with each other, and the League of Nations mandates simply ratified their spheres of influence arrangement. In the early 1920s Britain established monarchies in Iraq and Jordan, each ruled by one of Hussein's sons, and during the 1930s these regimes won increasing autonomy from British supervision. The British and French hoped to induce the United States to join the League of Nations mandatory states and accept a comparable tutelary role over Armenia, but Washington declined the invitation.

European influence extended far beyond the Near East and the Levant. The French controlled Morocco and Tunisia and regarded Algeria as an integral part of France. The British also controlled Aden and dominated Egyptian affairs. They had a maritime presence and exerted influence over the various sheikhdoms and emirates of the Persian Gulf region, and they exchanged the promise of military protection for an alliance with Saudi Arabia. The British and Russians each sought to influence Iran and Afghanistan in what was known as the Great Game.

Between the world wars, the U.S. government held largely aloof from developments in the Middle East and Western Asia, declining to take any position on the situation in Palestine, where growing Jewish immigration and determined Zionist demands for the establishment of a Jewish state met official British resistance and provoked rising Arab resentment, leading on occasion to violent riots. American interests remained largely commercial, with the State and Commerce Departments both eager to exert pressure to encourage and facilitate American oil company access to the Middle East's vast petroleum resources. By the early 1930s, these companies were beginning to explore development of oil concessions in the Persian Gulf area. The Turkish Petroleum Company, later renamed the Iraq Petroleum Company, a consortium that included some American oil companies, had a monopoly on exploration in much of the region, and within this grouping only British nationals could develop oil concessions in the Persian Gulf emirates.

In 1932 Standard Oil of California (SOCAL), a firm outside the consortium that had already broken into this closed shop on oil exploration by establishing a subsidiary—albeit one that included a British member on its board—in the small sheikhdom of Bahrayn (Bahrain), a British quasi protectorate, applied for an exploratory oil license in neighboring Saudi Arabia. Seeking to improve the terms offered him, Saudi king Abdul Aziz encouraged the Iraq Petroleum Company to compete for the concession, and SOCAL eventually outbid its rival. The American firm obtained a 60-year contract that granted it exclusive oil exploration and drilling rights on 360,000 square miles of eastern Saudi Arabia and a preferential option on an adjoining region, territory whose ownership was in dispute between Saudi Arabia and the neighboring emirate of Kuwait. The SOCAL-Saudi agreement was the first major oil concession negotiated by U.S. business in the Middle East.

In 1936 SOCAL merged with the Texas Company (Texaco), and the two established the California Texas Oil Company (CALTEX), acquiring 50 percent interests in each other's operating subsidiaries. The discovery of large quantities of oil in Saudi territory in 1938 brought the negotiation one year later of a new agreement with Saudi Arabia, with the king obtaining higher royalties in exchange for a substantial expansion of the exclusive California Arabian Standard Oil Company (CASOC) concession.

With a major war then imminent in Europe, one that would almost certainly involve the Middle East, Saudi and other Middle Eastern oil fields were seen as a vital strategic prize for which powers on both sides in the impending conflict would be competing.

Such concerns soon led to an allied takeover of Persia (Iran), in which the U.S. government acquiesced. During the 1930s, Shah Reza Pahlavi I of Iran, who resented the fact that the British-dominated Anglo-Iranian Oil Company controlled most of Iran's oil revenues and industry, favored Nazi Germany and staffed much of his government with German advisers. From September 1939 Germany was at war with Great Britain, and in June 1941 German chancellor Adolf Hitler sent his armies against the Soviet Union, which shared a border with Iran. Russia was now a British ally. Anglo-Russian competition for influence in Iran dated back more than a century, but for the war's duration the two nations cooperated there, as they had in the early 20th century when they divided Iran into spheres of influence. Seeking both to deny Iran's oil reserves to Germany and to protect Soviet oil fields in the nearby Caucasus, in the summer of 1941 both British and Soviet officials demanded that the shah expel the 2,000 Germans then resident in Iran. When he refused, British and Soviet military forces jointly occupied Iran, replacing the pro-German shah with his youthful son, Shah Reza Pahlavi II. Soviet forces controlled northern Iran, and the British occupied the southern portion.

In January 1942 the three powers concluded a treaty of alliance against Germany. This permitted British and Soviet armed forces unrestricted use of Iranian military facilities. Although Iranian nationalists resented the alliance, which was forced on them, at their insistence this agreement included clauses whereby both Britain and the Soviet Union pledged to respect the territorial integrity, sovereignty, and political independence of Iran. In addition, it provided that both British and Russian occupying forces would leave no later than six months after hostilities had ended. The treaty went into effect on February 1, 1942.

The Franklin D. Roosevelt administration in the United States welcomed this situation and sent a military mission to Iran. By late 1941 Soviet Russia had become a major recipient of U.S. Lend-Lease assistance, and after Pearl Harbor the two nations were formally allied in war against Germany. The United States sent large quantities of Lend-Lease supplies to

the Soviet Union by sea and through Iran. The U.S. Persian Gulf Command, established for this purpose, handled the Lend-Lease shipments by rail through the Caucasus.

Within the U.S. State Department, moreover, a small group of Middle Eastern experts began to develop more ambitious schemes for U.S. involvement in the region, viewing Iran as a potential test case for the encouragement of democracy and social and economic reforms in developing nations, as envisaged under the August 1941 Atlantic Charter. Such U.S. involvement would also help check the expansion of communist influence in northern Iran. An expanded American role would also enable the United States to provide better protection for its existing oil interests in Saudi Arabia and possibly even help it secure a greater share in Iran's own British-dominated oil industry.

As early as 1939, Shah Reza I had attempted to entice the United States into taking more interest in his country and acting as its patron against other great powers by offering oil concessions to American firms. For similar reasons a sizable group of Iranian politicians, including the young shah, encouraged the growing American interest in their country, which they viewed as a means of countering both British and Russian influence.

In August 1943, Secretary of State Cordell Hull recommended to President Roosevelt a policy of enhanced U.S. involvement in Iran, aimed at building up that country under American patronage, which Roosevelt accepted. Toward the end of the year at the Tehran Conference, Britain, the Soviet Union, and the United States all affirmed their commitment to maintaining Iran's postwar independence and territorial integrity. This switch to a proactive U.S. policy toward Iran marked an important long-term turning point in American involvement in the Near and Middle East. From early 1943 assorted missions, often poorly coordinated, of American experts attempted to guide and direct the wholesale reform of the Iranian military, police, and finances, together with Iran's political and agricultural systems.

In early 1943 the U.S. government also began to demonstrate new and growing interest in the Kingdom of Saudi Arabia. In April 1942 the U.S. State Department appointed a resident vice-consul in Jeddah, the first U.S. physical diplomatic presence in Saudi Arabia. Even so, during 1941 and 1942 the U.S. government turned down suggestions by CASOC that it should give the kingdom official economic aid under Lend-Lease. Within the Washington bureaucracy, however, Secretary of the Navy Frank Knox and his deputy and successor, James V. Forrestal, later to be the first secretary of defense, both considered the region's oil resources a major strategic interest that the U.S. military should be prepared to secure and defend.

In early 1943 the American government began discussions as to whether it might buy out CASOC's Saudi concession as a strategic military and naval oil reserve. In March 1943 the U.S. State Department declared Saudi Arabia eligible for Lend-Lease assistance on unusually generous terms. As another indication of growing official American interest in the kingdom, in April 1943 the American mission in Jeddah was upgraded to a legation with a resident minister.

Official U.S. interest in Saudi Arabia continued to expand, culminating in the negotiation by the Defense Department in early August 1945 of an agreement for the construction of an American air base at Dhahran, a facility that could be used if necessary in providing military protection to American oil interests in the kingdom. Britain regarded all this as an encroachment on its sphere of influence but could not compete with the United States in terms of economic and military assistance and so was forced to acquiesce in the growing U.S. involvement. American officials admitted that the generous budgetary aid for 1945 they offered the Saudi government was a major factor in the successful negotiation that summer of the Dhahran air base agreement, subsequently repeatedly renewed.

By early 1944, concerns about U.S. access to international oil supplies was sufficiently strong to impel the State Department to formulate a policy position that envisaged ensuring equal terms for American access, conserving the Western Hemisphere's oil resources for its own use and discouraging exports of these outside the Western Hemisphere, and facilitating U.S. access to and maximum development of Middle Eastern oil reserves. U.S. officials were also anxious to prevent the transfer of American-owned Middle Eastern oil concessions to nationals of other countries.

The April 1944 guidelines gave striking proof that the U.S. government was fully conscious that petroleum was a valuable and essential international commodity, vital to the effective functioning of its country's civilian and military economies, and that State Department officials were determined, in the interests of national security, to encourage American business interests to obtain and develop to their own and their country's maximum advantage as large a share as possible of global petroleum reserves.

American eagerness to facilitate access to Middle Eastern oil reserves contributed to growing tensions between the United States and the Soviet Union. As it became clear that the defeat of their common enemy of Germany would soon occur, the most important controlling factor

underlying their wartime alliance, the need to destroy Hitler's regime, became ever more irrelevant. In Iran, relations between the two countries became increasingly strained from late 1944 onward, when an Iranian offer of oil concessions in the north of the country to American companies brought Soviet protests. Occupying Russian troops banned Anglo-American forces from their zone of Iran and tightened their own control in the area. The independence promised Iran under the Tehran declaration seemed increasingly in jeopardy.

From the late 1940s onward, the American and Soviet governments competed not just to control Middle Eastern petroleum resources but also to gain international support and ideological loyalty from the patchwork of predominantly Muslim states across the area stretching from North Africa, Arabia, and the Persian Gulf to Afghanistan and Pakistan. As a rule, relatively conservative monarchical or authoritarian regimes leaned toward the United States, while radical nationalist governments tended to align themselves with the Soviets. U.S. support for the creation of the Jewish State of Israel in 1948 and increasingly close ties between those two countries further complicated American relations with Arab states throughout the region, most of whom deeply resented the existence of Israel.

The erosion of the position of European powers in the Middle East led both American and Soviet officials to seek to expand their own influence in the region. One of the earliest Cold War crises now erupted over Iran.

In the autumn of 1945, Soviet officials backed separatist forces in establishing an independent Soviet socialist republic in Iran's northern province of Azerbaijan and encouraged a similar separatist movement in Kurdistan, setting up a puppet state there in early 1946. American and British forces withdrew from Iran on schedule in early 1946, but the Soviets announced their intention to retain some troops in the north of the country. The United States used the forum of the new United Nations (UN) organization to endorse Iranian demands for complete Soviet withdrawal.

After complicated maneuverings between Iranian politicians and Soviet representatives, the Soviets withdrew their forces in exchange for promised oil concessions in northern Iran. With the backing of American advisers, in late 1946 Iranian prime minister Qavam es-Sultanah, who in the interim had successfully negotiated with the United States a substantial package of military, economic, and cultural support, reneged on this bargain, and shortly afterward Iranian forces successfully overturned the Azerbaijani and Kurdish republics.

This episode contributed to growing American distrust of Soviet designs on the Middle East. Simultaneous Soviet demands that the Turkish government accord the Soviet Union special rights over the Dardanelles Straits, which was the only passage for Russian naval and commercial vessels from the Black Sea to the Mediterranean, further confirmed such suspicions. American officials encouraged the Turkish government to refuse these Soviet demands and reinforced their stance by dispatching an American naval squadron to the Mediterranean.

In early 1947 the British government announced that economic difficulties meant that it could no longer continue to provide military or financial assistance to the governments of Greece, then fighting a communist insurgency, and Turkey, raising the specter that Soviet power might move in to fill the vacuum left by Britain's departure. This crisis became the occasion for President Harry S. Truman to announce in February 1947 what became known as the Truman Doctrine, a wide-ranging pledge that the United States would provide assistance to any state threatened by internal or external communist subversion. The geographical proximity of Greece and Turkey to shipping routes along which much Middle Eastern oil was transported alarmed policy makers in Washington and encouraged the United States to provide aid. Both Greece and Turkey subsequently received extensive economic assistance under the Marshall Plan, announced later in 1947. In 1952 the two states simultaneously became members of the North Atlantic Treaty Organization (NATO), tying them firmly into Western defensive alliances.

The American quest for reliable and stable long-term allies in the Middle East itself proved more problematic. One added complication was American support for Israel, which became heavily dependent on American aid, both governmental and private. President Truman's personal inclinations were largely responsible for American endorsement of the new state, a policy that for strategic and diplomatic reasons the State Department and the Defense Department both opposed. Most Arab states, whether conservative or radical, fiercely opposed Israel's very existence. Israel's military success in gaining and retaining previously Arab territories in several short but bitter and hard-fought wars, in 1948–1949, 1956, 1967, and 1973, only deepened Arab resentment. Hostility toward Israel was widespread and intense in Arab countries, Turkey, and Iran, making it difficult and even personally hazardous for Middle Eastern leaders to moderate their stance and seek compromise with Israel.

In 1981, for example, a cell of a radical Islamist group assassinated President Anwar Sadat of Egypt, who, with strong encouragement from U.S. president Jimmy Carter, had negotiated a peace agreement with Israel two years earlier. Repeated American and other outside efforts to broker a final and permanent peace settlement and modus vivendi between Israel and its Arab opponents, including Palestinians from territories seized by Israel in the recurrent Arab-Israeli conflicts, became almost standard fixtures of the late 20th-century and early 21st-century international diplomatic arena but were at best only partially successful. Almost invariably, they fell victim to extremist forces on both sides. Although a Palestinian entity eventually came into existence on lands that Israeli forces had taken in the various wars, throughout the first decade of the 21st century several key issues still remained unresolved, provoking bitter divisions among Israelis, Palestinians, and the broader Arab community.

The two countries that became the strategic linchpins of American alliance policy in the Middle East were Saudi Arabia and Iran, which together with Iraq possessed the bulk of the region's oil reserves. Under Saudi pressure, in 1950 ARAMCO (Arabian-American Oil Company) renegotiated its royalty agreement with the Saudi government so that each party received 50 percent of the profits. In 1951 Saudi Arabia signed a mutual defense agreement with the United States, and from then on a permanent American Military Training Mission was based in the kingdom. Saudi governments upgraded their military forces and placed lucrative armaments orders with American defense companies, goods they paid for with the proceeds from oil sales. In return for loyal support from the conservative Arab kingdom, for decades U.S. governments consistently overlooked the absence of democracy and the disregard for international human rights standards that characterized the Saudi regime. The strong ties that the United States developed with this and other authoritarian Middle Eastern governments meant that the Americans were often perceived as representing illiberal forces opposing change and as the successors to European imperialists.

Such views were reinforced by the close American relationship with another monarchical regime, that of Iran. In 1951, the Iranian government announced its intention of nationalizing the Anglo-Iranian Oil Company; the British, who controlled the refineries, withdrew their technicians and blockaded all exports of Iranian oil, provoking severe economic difficulties within Iran. The government headed by Prime Minister Mohammad Mossadegh stood firm and eventually, after an abortive attempt to replace him by the young shah, Reza Pahlavi II, declared a national emergency and took control of the Iranian military. In alliance with radical Muslims and the nationalist, leftist Tudeh Party, in 1952 Mossadegh implemented nationalist reforms, especially in agriculture, and broke diplomatic relations with the United Kingdom. Britain turned to the United States for assistance, characterizing Mossadegh as a radical who was turning toward communism and steering Iran into the Soviet orbit.

The administration of Republican president Dwight D. Eisenhower, which took office in January 1953, proved sympathetic to the British position and authorized the Central Intelligence Agency (CIA) to assist in spending up to $1 million to remove Mossadegh. CIA agents in Tehran spread rumors and disinformation, and in some cases, acted as agents provocateurs. Economic problems intensified, and Mossadegh suspended parliament and extended his emergency powers. The CIA sought to persuade the indecisive young shah to dismiss Mossadegh, while Mossadegh urged the monarch to leave the country. Eventually in 1953 the shah dismissed Mossadegh, but the latter refused to step down from office, and the shah took refuge in Italy. Major promonarchy and antimonarchy protests were held throughout the country, as Iranians of all political stripes assumed that before long Mossadegh would declare Iran a republic and himself head of state.

Promonarchy forces, heavily funded by the CIA, gained the upper hand, however, and Iranian tanks and troops entered Tehran and besieged the prime minister's residence until Mossadegh surrendered. He was subsequently placed under house arrest, then put on trial for treason and sentenced to three years in prison. General Fazlollah Zahedi, one of the military leaders who arrested Mossadegh, became prime minister, and the shah resumed power.

From then until his overthrow in 1979, the shah was a key U.S. ally in the Middle East. He soon reached an agreement with the British and Americans under the terms of the foreign oil companies still made substantial profits and large amounts of Iranian oil once more flowed to world markets. These revenues, together with several billion dollars in American military and economic assistance, enabled the shah to modernize his country and build a strong military establishment. The 1953 coup also represented the first occasion when the CIA was instrumental in successfully ousting another government. The success of this undertaking subsequently emboldened CIA director Allen W. Dulles and other agency officials to try to orchestrate comparable operations against several other foreign governments that U.S. leaders found unpalatable in Guatemala, Cuba, the Dominican Republic, and Chile.

In addition to its Iranian alliance, the United States attempted to persuade other Middle Eastern states to collaborate against potential Soviet expansionism. In 1955 American diplomats encouraged the establishment of the Baghdad Pact—a grouping of Turkey, Iran, Iraq, Pakistan, and Britain—that established a military liaison with the United States. The objective was to erect a bastion of anticommunist states along the Soviet Union's southwestern frontier. The alliance was originally known as the Middle Eastern Treaty Organization (METO). After Iraq, the only Arab member, withdrew in 1958 in the aftermath of a revolution led by the leftist and Moscow-oriented Baath Party, the United States joined as a full member, and the grouping became the Central Treaty Organization (CENTO). It proved largely ineffective in preventing the spread of Soviet influence in the Middle East. During the 1960s and 1970s, the Soviet Union simply bypassed the CENTO states to develop close military and economic ties with Egypt, Syria, Iraq, Yemen, Somalia, and Libya, establishing bases in Egypt, Somalia, and Yemen.

Although the United States sought to portray its own policies as representing a break with the earlier Western imperialism that many Arab nationalists deeply resented, these efforts were not particularly successful. American dealings with Egypt during the 1950s demonstrated that even when the U.S. government tried to dissociate itself from European colonialism, its policies often proved unconvincing and failed to win over skeptical opponents. In 1952 charismatic young Egyptian Army officer Gamal Abdel Nasser became president of Egypt. He was determined to reverse decades of Western-inflicted humiliation in the Arab world and to overthrow Israel. In 1955 Nasser sought and obtained arms for this purpose from the Soviet bloc, whereupon the United States withdrew promised economic assistance for a major hydroelectric project, the Aswan Dam. Nasser then announced his intention to nationalize the Suez Canal, then still under British and French control, and to use canal revenues to finance the dam project.

Against American advice, in October 1956 the Israelis, British, and French teamed up to attacked Egypt, defeating its army. Nasser then blocked the canal. The British, French, and Israelis thought that a major Egyptian military setback would cause the Egyptian population to rise up and overthrow President Nasser, but this did not occur. Fearing a major oil crisis, permanent Middle Eastern instability, and the further strengthening of both radical nationalism and Soviet influence, Eisenhower demanded that the invaders withdraw their forces, threatening to cease financial support for the beleaguered British currency should they refuse to do so. The crisis left Nasser more popular than ever before not only in Egypt but also in the broader Arab world and the Third World. It also revealed the true balance of power in the post–World War II period and dealt Britain's prestige a devastating blow, marking the end of its imperial age.

During the Suez Crisis, the Soviet Union also threatened to use nuclear weapons against the invaders unless they withdrew. Fearing that this move presaged enhanced Soviet interest in the region, in January 1957 Eisenhower sought congressional authority both to increase economic and military aid to anti-Soviet Middle Eastern states and to deploy American military forces in the region if necessary to oppose overt armed aggression from any nation controlled by international communism. Arab states immediately condemned the Eisenhower Doctrine. Under its auspices, the United States intervened in both Lebanon and Jordan in 1958. The negative responses by the United States to the Arabist trend in the Middle East and U.S. interventions convinced some that the United States was a conservative power wedded to the status quo. Throughout the 1960s, the military-based republican governments in the Middle East tended to turn to the Soviet Union or the Eastern bloc for assistance.

In June 1967, a swift preemptive strike by Israel destroyed the Egyptian Air Force on the ground and initiated a new Arab-Israeli war, which ended in a stunning Israeli victory. The outcome was seen as a terrible defeat by the entire Arab world and created a new wave of misery for the Palestinians of the West Bank and Gaza, who now passed under direct Israeli military rule. The war demonstrated conclusively to the Arab world the unshakeable U.S. support for Israel over the interests of the Palestinians.

The 1967 Arab defeat had far-reaching effects. It encouraged the growth of radical movements whose followers were opposed to the existing Arab governments and willing to engage in acts of terrorism and airline hijackings outside the region. It also discouraged moderate support for state-led Arabism. U.S. Middle East policy makers did not appear to appreciate the profound malaise in the region regarding the 1967 defeat.

From the early 1970s onward, the United States was forced to respond to dramatic changes in the configuration of power in the Middle East. In October 1973 Egypt, Syria, and Iraq launched a surprise attack on Israel. By the second week Israeli forces had largely reversed early Arab successes, leaving Israel's military supplies heavily depleted. The U.S. government resupplied Israel, a move the Arab states deeply resented. In response, Arab members of the Organization of Petroleum Exporting Countries (OPEC), led by Saudi Arabia, cut back on oil production, quickly leading oil prices to quadruple. These policies stoked gathering inflation throughout the Western world, contributing to a major economic downturn that lasted throughout the 1970s. American inability to persuade OPEC, several of whose members were U.S. clients or allies, to moderate its policies contributed to a growing sense that American power was in decline. During the 1960s and 1970s, moreover, Arab states largely obtained control of their own oil industries, either, as with Saudi Arabia, through negotiations with American and other foreign firms or, where more radical states such as Libya or Iraq were concerned, through outright seizure and nationalization.

Developments in the late 1970s greatly disturbed the stability of overall U.S. strategy in the Middle East. A key American ally was driven from power, while Soviet military policies in Afghanistan and the Horn of Africa seemed to herald a menacing expansion of Soviet power in the region. Although Mohammad Reza Shah Pahlavi had tried to modernize his country, his authoritarian policies, persecution of opponents, and the social disruptions caused by his reforms eventually alienated many Iranians and were among the reasons why in late 1978 and early 1979 a large-scale Islamic revolution ended his rule and changed the entire basis of the government in Iran. In a surprising action, radical Iranian students stormed the U.S. embassy in Tehran on November 4, 1979, to protest past American support for the ousted shah, especially his admission to the United States for medical treatment. The students captured 52 Americans and held them hostage. In April 1980 U.S. military forces mounted an ineffectual rescue attempt in which 8 American servicemen died. The entire episode was widely regarded as a major national humiliation for the United States. The hostage crisis was not ended until the inauguration of Republican president Ronald Reagan in January 1981, when the Iranians released the hostages in return for a previously negotiated agreement that the U.S. government would unfreeze blocked Iranian economic assets.

In November 1979, another American ally was shaken when 500 armed Islamic fundamentalists seized the Grand Mosque of Mecca. They had hoped to capture King Khalid and his officials, who were supposed to have been at prayer, but many others were taken hostage. The incident showed that religious militancy was not confined to Iran, for the hostage takers led by Juhayman al-Utaybi refused to give up. Blood could not be shed in the Grand Mosque, but eventually a fatwa was issued that permitted the use of force. The official tally from the incident was 255 dead and another 560 injured before the Grand Mosque was secured.

In Afghanistan, meanwhile, in late December 1979 a Soviet-backed palace coup replaced one leftist president with another. Soviet ground forces and paratroopers promptly entered the country, the beginning of a decade-long war in which 15,000 Soviet troops and almost 1 million Afghans died. In addition, since 1977 many thousands of Soviet and Cuban troops had been stationed in Ethiopia, supporting that nation in a war with neighboring Somalia over the disputed Ogaden territory. Top American officials interpreted these developments as evidence of a systematic effort to enhance Soviet influence in territories bordering the Middle East and to take advantage of the regional destabilization caused by recent events in Iran. These developments, together with skyrocketing oil prices and high inflation and unemployment, contributed to a growing sense of malaise and American impotence in international affairs.

President Jimmy Carter responded by proclaiming in his January 1980 State of the Union address that "business as usual" with the Soviet Union was no longer possible and that the United States would take all measures necessary to defend the Persian Gulf. The president moved to reinstitute containment policies, demanded annual 5 percent increases in military spending, proposed that young American men be compelled to register for a potential draft, and moved to create a Persian Gulf rapid deployment force. He also called for energy policies that would make the United States less dependent on foreign oil. Carter's speech, which effectively reiterated the 1957 Eisenhower Doctrine, also marked a definite break with his earlier efforts toward U.S.-Soviet détente and disarmament, inaugurating several years of deep ideological and strategic antagonism between the two superpowers.

Throughout the 1980s, the Carter and Reagan administrations provided substantial financial support and equipment for the Afghan mujahideen, a collection of Islamist resistance groups that conducted guerrilla warfare against occupying Soviet forces. Antiaircraft missiles proved vital in nullifying the Soviet aviation advantage. The United States also offered neighboring Pakistan funding, logistical backing, and personnel to establish and run military training camps for the mujahideen. Pakistani special forces quietly took part in the war, and their British and American counterparts were also believed to be quietly involved. The war proved to be a lengthy, expensive, and ultimately unwinnable morass for the Soviet Union. In 1985 a new Soviet president, Mikhail Gorbachev, came to power. Gorbachev quickly moved to initiate new policies intended to moderate decades of Cold War hostilities and bring about rapprochement with

Western powers. He removed Soviet forces from the Horn of Africa. In March 1988 he also announced that all Soviet forces would be withdrawn from Afghanistan within 12 months. Although Soviet forces left Afghanistan on schedule, bitter civil war continued in Afghanistan. In the later 1990s the country fell under the control of the radical Islamic Taliban, which allowed it to become a haven for anti-Western Muslim terrorist groups.

Following the 1979 Islamic Revolution in Iran and the ensuing U.S. embassy hostage crisis, relations between the United States and Islamic Iran remained hostile. The American government imposed an embargo on all commercial and financial dealings with Iran by U.S. citizens, air traffic was suspended, and most other contacts entirely or largely halted. In September 1980 President Saddam Hussein of Iraq began a major war against neighboring Iran, seeking to settle long-standing border disputes between the two states and to create Iraqi regional hegemony. The war soon stalemated, and the two countries became bogged down in bloody stalemate. During this conflict, the United States leaned toward Iraq and provided intelligence information. Hussein was able to purchase some military supplies from the United States and other Western powers. In 1982 the United States normalized diplomatic relations with Iraq, which had been broken ever since the 1967 Arab-Israeli war. In 1987 and 1988 American naval forces in the Persian Gulf, deployed there in an effort to protect oil tankers from attack by either belligerent, skirmished repeatedly with Iranian vessels. In July 1988 an American cruiser, the *Vincennes,* shot down an Iranian passenger jet, killing 290, an incident for which the U.S. government later paid Iran almost $132 million in compensation but never apologized.

American policy was nonetheless not entirely consistent. Officials in the Reagan administration, which had publicly stated that it would not pay any ransom to secure the return of American hostages, secretly offered to sell Iran badly needed weaponry. Any monies received were to be used to support operations in Nicaragua by American-backed antigovernment guerrillas, known as the Contras, thereby evading a ban the U.S. Congress had recently imposed on the use of any American government funds for this purpose. The release of American hostages would also constitute part of the purchase price. After these dealings became public in late 1986, Reagan administration officials defended them on the grounds that their contacts and negotiations with relatively moderate Iranian officials had increased the probability that more conciliatory and less anti-American political forces would eventually come to power in Iran. The

Iran-Contra Affair, as it became known, was nonetheless a major political embarrassment for the Reagan administration, casting doubt on its good faith and competence as well as its stated hard-line attitude on terrorism.

The Iran-Iraq War finally ended in 1988 with no decisive victory on either side. Both countries suffered heavy losses of manpower in a war each found economically debilitating and destructive. Believing that this step would not encounter serious opposition, in August 1990 Saddam Hussein sent his forces into and annexed the small, wealthy, and neighboring oil-rich state of Kuwait. Hussein's action alarmed other rich but militarily weak Arab states, most notably Saudi Arabia. This was the first major international crisis since the proclamation earlier that year of the ending of the Cold War between the Soviet Union and the United States. U.S. president George H. W. Bush was instrumental in forging an international coalition, including the NATO powers, Saudi Arabia, and Japan, committed to expelling Iraqi forces from Kuwait and in winning a UN resolution authorizing such action. Hussein attempted to win support from other Arab states by proclaiming his intention of attacking Israel should coalition forces invade, but only the Palestine Liberation Organization supported his efforts. Launched in January 1991, Operation DESERT STORM ended quickly and successfully as Hussein's troops were swiftly driven from Kuwait and pushed back into Iraqi territory.

Bush and his advisers soon decided to halt the invasion of Iraq, however, as they did not wish to alienate their Arab partners in the coalition or deal with the challenges that overthrowing Hussein was likely to bring in its train, and they therefore left the weakened dictator in power but subject to confining UN sanctions and restrictions. Although the United States directly encouraged separatist Kurds in northern Iraq and Shiite Muslims in the south to rise up against Hussein's regime, they received no support from coalition forces, and Hussein's military brutally suppressed the revolts, using poison gas against the Kurds and killing tens of thousands of rebels.

Addressing Congress shortly after the Persian Gulf War had ended, a triumphant Bush promised aid to the Middle East. He then proclaimed that the ending of the Cold War had made it possible for the UN to function as its founders had originally intended so that there was a very real prospect of a new world order, one in which freedom and respect for human rights would find a home among all nations. Critics charged that Bush envisaged that the United States would use its unrivaled military and economic might to dominate the new world order in its own interests. During the 1990s the

principal focus of U.S. international policy was economic, as the American government concentrated on what was termed "globalization," liberalizing trade and investment practices and promoting the spread of free market norms.

President William "Bill" J. Clinton made energetic although only partially successful efforts to reach a permanent resolution of the Palestinian-Israeli impasse, but otherwise the Middle East attracted only sporadic attention. Despite criticism from humanitarian organizations, throughout the 1990s UN sanctions on significant trade with Iraq remained in place, although a program whereby Iraqi oil was exchanged for food was eventually initiated. British and American warplanes bombed potential military targets and enforced no-fly zones in southern and northern Iraq, permitting the Kurds there to enjoy virtual autonomy.

With the ending of the Cold War, the overarching principle of American foreign policy could no longer, as in the past four decades, be the containment of communism. The Reagan administration saw a new enemy in radical Islam.

Harvard University political scientist Samuel P. Huntington claimed that global conflict was inevitable. Basing his ideas on those of historian Bernard Lewis, Huntington suggested that international fault lines would now correspond with differing belief and value systems, such as the Western Judeo-Christian tradition, Islam, and Confucianism, and that major clashes among these civilizations must be anticipated. Many unfamiliar with the Middle East belatedly seized on Huntington's thesis following the events of September 11, 2001.

An Islamic revival had meanwhile shaken the Arab world, fueled in part by the shock of the defeat at the hands of Israel in 1967 but also driven by the failure of nationalist non-Islamist movements. The Islamic Revolution in Iran in 1979 was simultaneously Islamist and nationalist. The new Iranian leader, Ayatollah Ruhollah Khomeini, was hostile to the United States. He and many other Iranians feared that the United States might intervene to reverse the revolution. Certainly the U.S. government opposed the concept of an Islamic government, characterizing it as a medieval theocracy. In Afghanistan, however, throughout the 1980s equally conservative Muslim mujahideen guerrilla forces battling the Russian occupiers received substantial American economic and military aid, which came to an end once the Soviets had left.

During the 1990s Islamic rebels battled Russian rule in Chechnya, but partly because of the failure to reach a comprehensive Israeli-Palestinian settlement, something many Muslims believed was primarily due to American bias toward Israel, militant Islamic antagonism focused increasingly on the United States. As the Soviet-Afghan War wound down in the late 1980s, certain Islamic mujahideen groups involved in that conflict founded a new radical organization known as Al Qaeda; its objective was to continue jihad, or holy war, on other fronts. The most prominent figure in this group, Osama bin Laden, who came from a wealthy Saudi family, used his own financial resources to support its undertakings and could also tap heavily into other Arab sources of funds.

Official Saudi support for American operations during the 1991 Persian Gulf War deeply angered bin Laden, who deployed his organization not just against the United States but also against the Saudi government and other Middle Eastern nations, including Egypt, who were close American associates. Bin Laden issued public proclamations, or fatwas, demanding the expulsion of all foreign troops from Islamic lands and the overthrow of Middle Eastern governments that acquiesced in their presence. Al Qaeda personnel, expelled from Saudi Arabia, found refuge first in Sudan and then in Afghanistan, where a radical Islamic regime, the Taliban, took power in 1996. During the 1990s Al Qaeda claimed responsibility for several terrorist assaults on prominent American targets at home and overseas, including a 1993 truck bomb attack against the World Trade Center in New York; simultaneous 1998 car bombings of U.S. embassies in Kenya, Nairobi, and Dar es Salaam, Tanzania; and a 2000 suicide attack on the American destroyer *Cole* in Yemen. In response, the Clinton administration declared Al Qaeda a terrorist organization and in the summer of 1998 reacted to the embassy bombings with air strikes on Al Qaeda training camps in Sudan and Afghanistan.

In January 2001 President George W. Bush, eldest son of the president who had launched the Persian Gulf War, took office. In the areas of diplomacy and defense, Bush appointed numerous top officials associated with a predominantly Republican think tank venture, the Project for the New American Century. Many of these individuals, including Bush's influential vice president, Richard B. Cheney, a former secretary of defense, believed that the United States had been mistaken in not overthrowing Saddam Hussein in 1991 and had publicly called on Clinton, Bush's predecessor, to drive the Iraqi president from power. They argued that Hussein, who in 1998 expelled UN inspectors charged with monitoring his weapons programs, was determined to regain regional hegemony by developing chemical, biological, and nuclear weapons of mass destruction. Since these

ambitions posed a long-term threat to U.S. strategic interests, affiliates of the Project for the New American Century argued that their country would be morally and legally justified in taking preemptive action to overthrow him and preclude this potential danger.

The Bush administration also sought to prevent Iran from developing nuclear weapons, an ambition clearly cherished by the Iranian government, which though now rather more secular in character than during most of the 1980s and 1990s was nonetheless decidedly anti-American. Initially, the Bush administration accorded combating international terrorism a much lower priority.

The events of September 11, 2001, when two dozen Arab Islamic extremists associated with Al Qaeda hijacked four American airliners and used these to launch suicide attacks on the World Trade Center towers in New York and the Pentagon in Washington, D.C., brought a dramatic change, as the president publicly declared an expansive Global War on Terror. Al Qaeda claimed responsibility for the attacks, in which almost 3,000 civilians died, giving the American public a novel sense of vulnerability to terrorist threats. Bush called on the Taliban government of Afghanistan, which had provided bases and training camps for thousands of Al Qaeda operatives, to surrender bin Laden and his top advisers, but Mullah Mohammed Omar, the Afghan leader, refused, as this would violate tribal and Islamic ethics. In October 2001 the United States and Britain, in collaboration with the forces of anti-Taliban Afghan Northern Alliance warlords, began military hostilities against Afghanistan. By the end of the year they had overthrown the Taliban government and driven Al Qaeda into the rugged mountains of the Afghan-Pakistani border, although coalition forces failed to capture bin Laden.

Afghan representatives subsequently held a traditional *loya jirga* assembly, which chose a Pashtun aristocrat, Hamid Karzai, as Afghanistan's new president. The new leader publicly committed his country to democracy and sought to implement wide-ranging social and economic reforms. Militarily, his regime nonetheless remained heavily dependent on British and American troops, and its authority did not extend far beyond Kabul, the Afghan capital. In 2006 a resurgence by Taliban forces threatened to destabilize the country, a development that many observers blamed on the failure of the U.S. government to concentrate on winning complete victory in Afghanistan. As the last year of Bush's presidential term began, the situation in Afghanistan remained precarious, with many expecting further Taliban territorial gains. One plausible explanation for the diversion of American resources from Afghanistan was the eagerness of the Bush administration at all costs to return to its earlier agenda and launch a second war against Iraq, which began in March 2003.

Throughout 2002, Bush administration officials made the case that Iraq represented the greatest and most pressing international threat to American interests, making it imperative to overthrow Saddam Hussein before he could inflict long-term strategic damage on the United States. In his January 2002 State of the Union address, Bush proclaimed that the three most dangerous external enemies for the United States were Iraq, Iran, and North Korea, who, he declared, constituted an "axis of evil." With support from British prime minister Tony Blair but over strong opposition from such long-term European allies of the United States as France and Germany and to great skepticism from Russia and China, the Bush administration pressured the UN Security Council to endorse resolutions stating that Iraqi weapons programs had equipped that country with formidable armaments whose possession put it in breach of earlier UN demands and constituted ample justification for an outside invasion designed to topple Hussein's government. UN weapons inspectors failed to unearth any quantities of such weaponry, and many foreign governments doubted whether Iraq actually held appreciable stockpiles of banned armaments. Subsequent revelations suggested that Bush and his top advisers, together with their British counterparts, doctored intelligence reports to make it appear that Iraq had acquired far more in the way of stored weapons and production capabilities than was really the case. Supporters of an invasion, notably Vice President Cheney, also claimed that close ties existed between Al Qaeda and other terrorist organizations and Hussein, alleging that the Iraqi president had in some way been involved in the September 11, 2001, attacks. No information tied the Iraqi president to these attacks, and Al Qaeda links were at best tenuous.

Ignoring all internal and external protests and misgivings, the Bush administration eventually proclaimed its determination to move unilaterally against Iraq even if it proved impossible to obtain a UN resolution specifically authorizing this undertaking.

Leading American supporters of war within the administration, notably Paul Wolfowitz, deputy secretary of defense, believed in addition that an invasion of Iraq would give the United States an ideal opportunity to remake the entire Middle East. From this perspective, war against Iraq came to seem almost a magic bullet, an exercise in transformational diplomacy that would recast the whole region. They argued that by removing Hussein and replacing him with a democratic government, one that would bring Iraq the benefits of peace, prosperity, and economic development, the United States would encourage the contagious democratization of all the remaining Middle East. The belief was that the creation of a progressive, stable, flourishing, and affluent Iraq would so impress other states in the region that they would practically automatically seek to establish similar governmental systems themselves, almost painlessly inaugurating a benign era of American-led peaceable economic growth and forward-looking social development throughout the Middle East.

On March 20, 2003, an American-led allied coalition force, to which the British contributed by far the second most sizable contingent, launched a full-scale invasion of Iraq. Military victory was quickly attained, as coalition forces took Baghdad and other major Iraqi cities and toppled statues of Hussein. Major looting and disorder marred the allied triumph, an early indication that coalition forces might have more trouble maintaining civil control than they did winning battles. On May 1, 2003, Bush declared an end to major combat, standing on an American aircraft carrier deck before a banner declaring "Mission Accomplished." In December 2003 American forces captured Hussein, who eventually was brought to trial by the new Iraqi government and executed three years later.

U.S. officials soon discovered, however, that it was far easier to overthrow Hussein's government than to restore peace, order, and stability to Iraq, let alone to establish a democratic government capable of exercising authority and acceptable to all parties in Iraq. Deep ethnic, religious, and political fissures divided the country. While Hussein's regime had been largely secular in outlook, his rule had relied primarily on the country's Sunni Muslim element, while the majority of Iraq's population, who were Shia Muslims, had been largely excluded from power. In addition, the Kurds of northern Iraq sought autonomy if not outright independence and had no wish to be controlled by a government based in Baghdad, the Iraqi capital. In mid-2003 occupying forces disbanded the largely Sunni armed forces so that by default much power on the ground was exercised by various militia groupings, predominantly Shiite but also Sunni organizations. For several years large areas of Iraq were in a state of virtual civil war, characterized by suicide bombing attacks against military, civilian, and religious targets as well as murders, kidnappings, and torture. No foreigners, whether soldiers or civilians, could count on being personally secure, nor could any Iraqis, even in the supposedly most protected areas of Baghdad.

The toll of Iraqi dead and injured was exponentially higher than the casualty figures for the coalition forces, but even those continued to rise inexorably, belying official U.S. claims of success. Only 138 U.S. soldiers were killed in Iraq before Bush declared the end of major combat; by the end of the war in December 2011, 4,425 had died in combat or had been killed by other causes.

What was supposed to be a splendid little war, bringing maximum results at minimum costs, swiftly metamorphosed into a grim quagmire, and it became ever more unclear how the United States could extricate itself from this entanglement. A brief moment of optimism after December 2005, when elections were held in Iraq under the political constitution accepted earlier that year, quickly dissipated, as it became clear that members of most ethnic groups had voted for candidates from their own groups and that Iraq remained bitterly politically divided, with no genuine consensus emerging among the competing parties. Violence escalated, and the government of Prime Minister Nuri al-Maliki was widely perceived as lacking the strength and authority to control and pacify the country.

Bush administration officials alleged that Al Qaeda units had infiltrated into Iraq and charged the Syrian and Iranian governments with supporting Shiite militia forces within Iraq in an effort to promote their own political influence in the country. As casualties continued to rise and with no convincing exit strategy in sight, popular support for the war fell dramatically among the American public and politicians, and in the November 2006 midterm elections George W. Bush's Republican Party lost control of both houses of Congress.

Media revelations, illustrated with dramatic photographs and video footage, that American soldiers had abused Iraqi captives held in Abu Ghraib prison and other facilities circulated widely around the world, discrediting the Bush administration's claims that the Iraqi intervention was designed to uphold human rights and other liberal principles. Throughout the Arab and Muslim world, distrust and antagonism toward the United States soared dramatically. More broadly, the tactics, including the torture of prisoners, which the U.S. government embraced in pursuit of the Global War on Terror, inflicted enormous damage on the country's international reputation.

Massive antiwar demonstrations occurred across Europe and in much of Asia. Even states that had been allies of the United States began to reconsider their support for the war. Several nations that had initially been part of the American-led international coalition and had intervened in Iraq withdrew or reduced their forces. In Spain, the new government that won elections in March 2004, shortly after 191 Spaniards died and almost 2,000 were injured in terrorist bombings of train stations in Madrid, quickly announced that all Spanish troops would leave Iraq. The Labour politician Gordon Brown, who replaced the strongly prowar Tony Blair as British prime minister in July 2007, likewise embarked on a program of gradual British troop withdrawals.

By then, the U.S. government had announced a new strategy in Iraq. In December 2006, an independent bipartisan commission headed by James A. Baker III, former secretary of state during the Persian Gulf War, issued a report urging that the United States should seek to stabilize the situation in Iraq. Its recommendations included temporarily increasing American military forces in Iraq, allowing Iraqi civilian and military officials and forces to take increasing responsibility for running the country themselves, providing greater aid for training and equipment that would enhance their ability to do so, leaving occupying forces only in support roles, and working in collaboration with the UN, the European Union, and other regional governments, including those of Saudi Arabia, Iran, and Syria, to restore and maintain order in Iraq. The Baker Report also urged a renewed effort to bring about a permanent Palestinian-Israeli peace settlement, a recommendation that Bush and Secretary of State Condoleezza Rice sought to implement in late 2007 and early 2008.

The Bush administration did announce a troop surge in January 2007, and by the end of that year the military situation in Iraq had immensely improved as moderate Shiite and Sunni forces began to gain some authority so that full-scale civil war seemed less probable. In general, violence and suicide bombings had decreased by late 2008 but unfortunately resumed in the spring of 2009.

Close cooperation with Iran, the region's most substantial Shiite Muslim power whose relative strength was much enhanced by the weakening of neighboring Iraq and Afghanistan, its former rivals and counterweights, proved more problematic. Ever since taking office, Bush administration officials had sought to prevent Iran from developing nuclear weapons but had only succeeded in obtaining ambiguous commitments from Iranian president Mahmoud Ahmadinejad. In July 2007, the U.S. Congress passed resolutions condemning covert Iranian military involvement in

Iraq, authorizing the use of American force against Iran if deemed necessary to halt its nuclear program. Such strained relations rather precluded close Iranian cooperation with the United States and its allies over Iraq. U.S. ambassador to Iraq Zalmay Khalilzad (2005–2007) encouraged communication between Iraq and Iran, for he believed that the two neighbors could deal productively with such issues at border disputes and pilgrim traffic to Islam's holy cities. Afghan president Karzai also said that his government sought a positive relationship with Iran.

As the American presidential elections approached ever closer in 2008, Middle Eastern policy was in flux. The situation was yet further complicated in the last days of December 2007 by the assassination of former Pakistani prime minister Benazir Bhutto, who recently returned to her country after a decade of exile to contest impending democratic elections there. In Pakistan, a military government headed by former army chief President Pervez Musharraf had held power since 1999. After September 11, 2001, the U.S. government had dropped its earlier objections to Musharraf's authoritarian regime, and Pakistan had become a leading ally in the Global War on Terror, especially with U.S. efforts to extirpate Al Qaeda and its leaders.

Militant Muslim elements nonetheless enjoyed substantial political influence in much of Pakistan and were believed to be possibly responsible, with the connivance of some Pakistani security officials, for Bhutto's death. Following her assassination, riots and disorder convulsed much of Pakistan, bringing fears that a major American ally and regional strategic partner was itself in serious jeopardy of destabilization. Soaring oil prices added still another twist, since a large proportion of the world's petroleum reserves were located in the Middle East. In January 2008 Bush appealed to Saudi Arabia to use its influence in OPEC to reduce the cost of oil, but the response of Saudi officials was unenthusiastic.

As U.S. politicians competed for the Republican and Democratic presidential nominations in 2008, their preferred strategies for approaching the Middle Eastern situation and especially the still-continuing American occupation of both Iraq and Afghanistan remained somewhat vague and unspecific. Most of the candidates stated that they sought the withdrawal of most if not all American troops from Iraq and Afghanistan but would endeavor to accomplish this objective while leaving governments friendly to the United States in power in those countries so as to safeguard American interests.

Having won the November 2008 presidential election, Democratic Party candidate Barack Obama assumed office in January 2009. He pledged a new era in American foreign policy (his speech at Cairo University on June 4, 2009, was especially well received) and especially in the Middle East, which led to his being awarded the Nobel Prize for Peace in 2009. Nonetheless, while pledging to bring to a close U.S. involvement in both the Iraq and Afghanistan Wars, a deterioration in the military situation in Afghanistan early in 2009 forced Obama to send thousands of additional troops to Afghanistan beginning in early 2010. In Iraq sectarian violence continued to exact a heavy toll, but when Premier Maliki rejected a status of forces agreement that would have permitted a residual U.S. force to remain, Obama withdrew all U.S. troops from Iraq in December 2011, bringing the Iraq War to an official close. Sectarian violence continued there and indeed rose, as did the threat from Al Qaeda and other Islamic extremist groups.

U.S. aircraft and warships also took part in a NATO coalition to support rebel forces in the Libyan Civil War (2011) that ultimately removed strongman Muammar Qaddafi from power. Obama was much more reluctant to involve the United States in the ongoing Syrian Civil War (2011–present), but the Syrian government's use of chemical weapons against its own citizens was a prime factor in Obama's decision to help train Syrian rebel forces, a step approved by the U.S. Congress.

Then in 2014, fighters of the self-proclaimed radical Islamic State of Iraq and Syria (ISIS), who had already taken significant territory in Syria during the civil war, seized large stretches of Iraq and even threatened Baghdad. They also committed mass atrocities, including the execution of opponents and the enslavement of women. The threat posed by ISIS led a new Iraqi government to call on U.S. military assistance and prompted Obama to put together a large international coalition of more than 60 nations pledged to defeat ISIS. Soon limited numbers of American forces had returned to Iraq, and U.S. and coalition air forces were bombing ISIS targets.

Fighting continued in Afghanistan, where the Taliban mounted growing numbers of suicide bombings and other attacks. A new government took power under Ashraf Ghani in 2014 and concluded a status of forces agreement with the United States that the Karzai administration had negotiated but then had refused to sign. During 2014, the International Security Assistance Force, which was largely drawn from NATO members, carried out significant reductions in its forces, with the plan to turn over combat operations to the Afghan military by the end of 2014.

Priscilla Roberts

References

Anderson, Terry H. *Bush's Wars.* New York: Oxford University Press, 2011.

Brands, H. W. *Into the Labyrinth: The United States and the Middle East, 1945–1993.* New York: McGraw-Hill, 1994.

Cooley, John K. *Payback: America's Long War in the Middle East.* Washington, DC: Brassey's, 1991.

Goode, James F. *The United States and Iran: In the Shadow of Musaddiq.* New York: St. Martin's, 1997.

Hart, Parker T. *Saudi Arabia and the United States: Birth of a Security Partnership.* Bloomington: Indiana University Press, 1998.

Knights, Michael. *Cradle of Conflict: Iraq and the Birth of Modern U.S. Military.* Annapolis, MD: Naval Institute Press, 2005.

Lesch, David W. *The Middle East and the United States: A Historical and Political Reassessment.* New York: Perseus Books, 2006.

Painter, David S. *Oil and the American Century: The Political Economy of the U.S. Foreign Oil Policy, 1941–1954.* Baltimore: Johns Hopkins University Press, 1986.

Salt, Jeremy. *The Unmaking of the Middle East: A History of Western Disorder in Arab Lands.* Berkeley: University of California Press, 2008.

Yergin, Daniel. *The Prize: The Epic Quest for Oil, Money, and Power.* New York: Simon and Schuster, 1993.

General
Maps

MIDDLE EAST

TOPOGRAPHY OF THE MIDDLE EAST

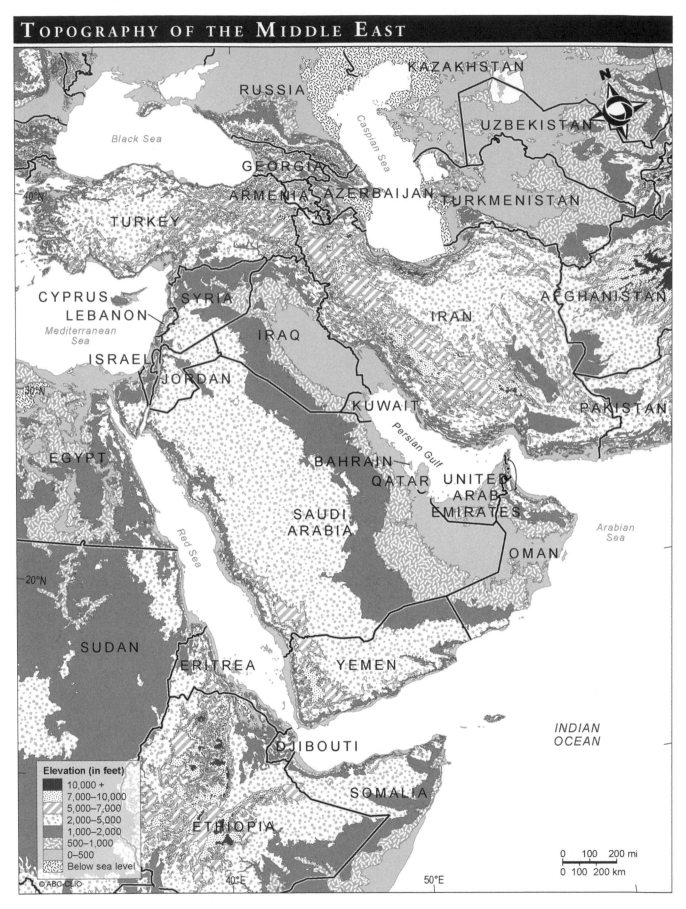

Elevation (in feet)
- 10,000 +
- 7,000–10,000
- 5,000–7,000
- 2,000–5,000
- 1,000–2,000
- 500–1,000
- 0–500
- Below sea level

© ABC-CLIO

0   100   200 mi

0 100 200 km

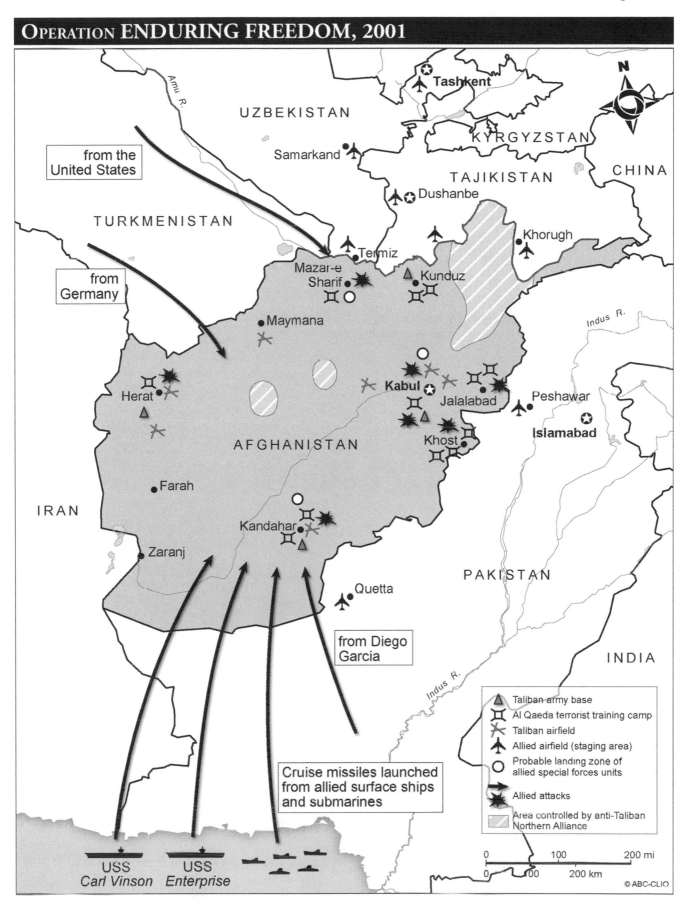

OPERATION ENDURING FREEDOM, 2001

from the United States

from Germany

from Diego Garcia

Cruise missiles launched from allied surface ships and submarines

USS *Carl Vinson*

USS *Enterprise*

Tashkent

UZBEKISTAN

KYRGYZSTAN

Samarkand

TAJIKISTAN

CHINA

Dushanbe

Khorugh

TURKMENISTAN

Termiz

Mazar-e Sharif

Kunduz

Maymana

Kabul

Jalalabad

Peshawar

Herat

Islamabad

Khost

AFGHANISTAN

Farah

Kandahar

Zaranj

IRAN

Quetta

PAKISTAN

INDIA

Amu R.

Indus R.

Indus R.

Legend

△ Taliban army base
✕ Al Qaeda terrorist training camp
✶ Taliban airfield
✈ Allied airfield (staging area)
○ Probable landing zone of allied special forces units
➤ Allied attacks
▨ Area controlled by anti-Taliban Northern Alliance

0   100   200 mi
0   100   200 km

© ABC-CLIO

DISPOSITION OF FORCES ON THE EVE OF THE 2003 IRAQ WAR

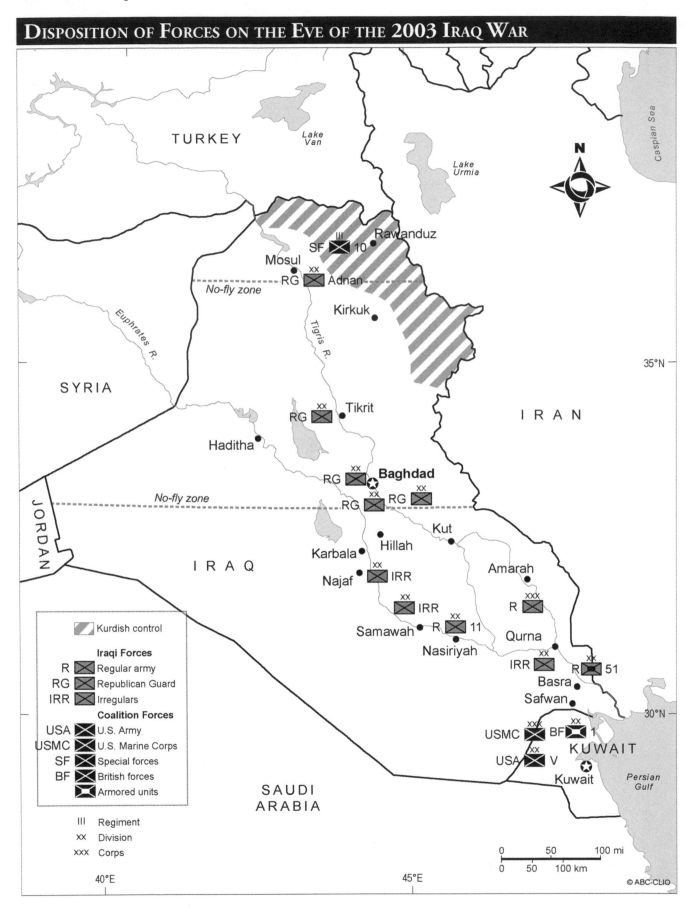

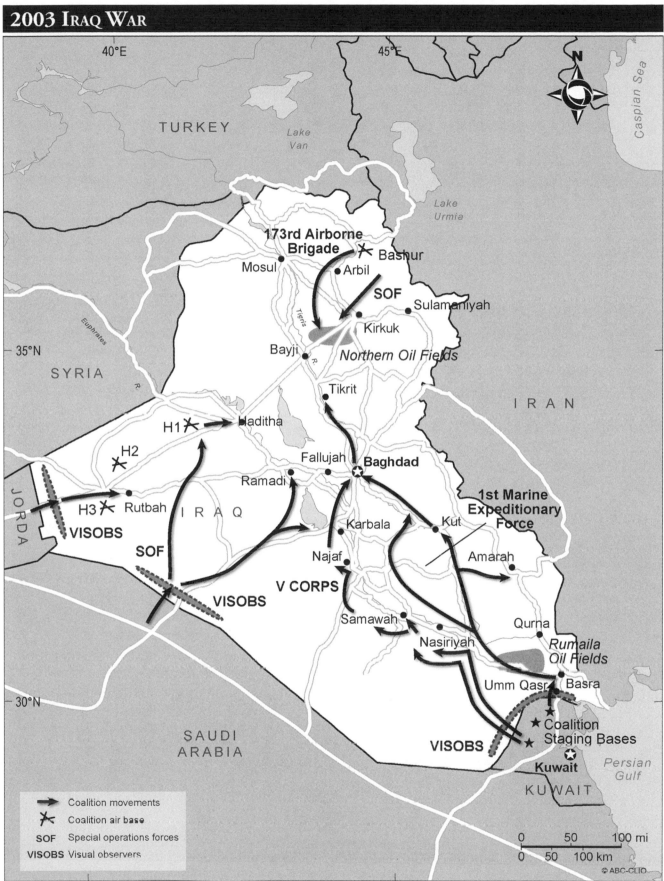

2003 IRAQ WAR

A

Abadi, Haider al- (1952–)

Iraqi engineer, politician, and prime minister of Iraq since September 8, 2014. Haider al-Abadi was born in Baghdad on April 25, 1952. He earned an undergraduate degree in electrical engineering from the University of Technology in Baghdad in 1975 and a PhD in electrical engineering from the University of Manchester in England in 1980. Abadi was active in the Iraqi Dawa Party, having joined in 1967, and in 1977 while a student in London, he was named party head. The Dawa Party was outlawed by Saddam Hussein's Baath Party in 1979, however, and in 1983 Hussein's government revoked Abadi's passport. Abadi chose to remain in London and would not return to Iraq until 2003. He worked as an engineering consultant in both the public and private sectors in England between 1980 and 2003.

When Abadi returned to Iraq in the summer of 2003 after Hussein's ouster following the Anglo-American military invasion, Abadi agreed to serve as minister of communications in the Coalition Provisional Authority (CPA), Iraq's interim government. His tenure, which began on September 1, was a rocky one, however, as he continually clashed with CPA administrator L. Paul (Jerry) Bremer. Refusing to be a mere "rubber-stamp" functionary, Abadi vigorously disagreed with Bremer's policy that all state-owned companies should be immediately privatized prior to elections that would form a new Iraqi government. Abadi left his post on June 1, 2004, several weeks before Bremer left his CPA position.

In January 2005 Abadi agreed to serve as a consultant to the Iraqi government, chiefly on issues relating to reconstruction and infrastructure. In December 2005 running on the Islamic Dawa Party ticket, Abadi won a seat in the Iraqi parliament. In 2007, he was elected deputy leader of the Islamic Dawa Party. Abadi was reelected to parliament in 2010, having now gained a reputation for even-handedness and impartiality. In 2006 and again in 2010, his name had been mentioned as a potential candidate for the Iraqi premiership, which ultimately went to Nuri al-Maliki. Meanwhile, many Iraqis admired Abadi's tough stance toward the continued stationing of coalition troops in Iraq. Indeed, he became one of the chief architects of the Iraqi status of forces agreement with the United States, finally approved in December 2008.

Prime Minister Maliki's tenure quickly turned into disaster. Once U.S. troops left Iraq in late 2011, Maliki, a Shiite Muslim, engaged in a campaign of repression against Iraq's Sunni Muslim population. He alienated large portions of the Iraqi population and permitted the Iraqi military to languish. This aided in the rise of Islamic extremist groups, particularly the Islamic State of Iraq and Syria (ISIS), which began seizing control and unleashing terror over large portions of northern and eastern Iraq by early 2014. Despite the fact that Maliki had lost the support of key international allies, including the United States, as well as the support from many within his own party and government, he stubbornly clung to power until the late summer of 2014.

Finally, with the situation in Iraq steadily deteriorating, Maliki agreed to step down on August 14. Meanwhile, Iraqi president Fuad Masum had nominated Abadi as Maliki's replacement on August 11, a move that was widely hailed as a positive step in the Iraqi government regaining control of its territory. On September 8, 2014, the Iraqi parliament confirmed Abadi's appointment, and he took office that same day.

Abadi, who is a Shiite, vowed to reinvigorate the Iraqi Army and work closely with the new coalition formed to stop and eventually eradicate ISIS. He also pledged more governmental transparency and efforts to bridge the gaping chasm between Iraq's Sunni and Shiite populations.

On November 12, 2014, Abadi announced the removal of 36 senior military commanders in a sweeping move to improve Iraqi Army fighting ability as it attempted to take the offensive and retake territory lost to ISIS. Despite having received more than $35 billion in U.S. training and equipment in the past decade, the Iraqi Army performed abysmally in losing immense swaths of the country to ISIS, with much of the blame for this falling on inept Iraqi military leadership. Abadi also installed 18 other commanders in order to promote professionalism and counter corruption.

PAUL G. PIERPAOLI JR.

See also

Bremer, Lewis Paul; Iraq, History of, 1990–Present; Islamic State in Iraq and Syria; Maliki, Nuri al-; Status of Forces Agreement, U.S.-Iraqi

References

Alawi, Ali A. *The Occupation of Iraq: Winning the War, Losing the Peace*. New Haven Yale University Press, 2007.

"Prime Minister Haider al-Abadi Pledges to Unify Iraq in Fight Against Islamic State." *Wall Street Journal*, September 25, 2014, http://online.wsj.com/articles/prime-minister-haider-al-abadi-pledges-to-unify-iraq-in-fight-against-islamic-state-1411688702.

Abbas, Abu (1948–2004)

Leader of the Palestine Liberation Front (PLF). Abu Abbas, the nom de guerre of Muhammad Zaidan, was born in Safed, Palestine, on December 10, 1948. His family fled to Syria that same year along with 12,000–15,000 Arab residents after the Haganah attacks. In 1968 he joined the Popular Front for the Liberation of Palestine General Command (PFLP-GC) led by Ahmad Jibril. Abbas disagreed with Jibril over the PFLP-GC's strong support for Syria and its failure to criticize Syrian support of the Lebanese Phalangist Party against the Palestine Liberation Organization (PLO) in Lebanon. In April 1977, Abbas and Talat Yaqub left the PFLP-GC to form the PLF.

During the 1970s Abbas advocated armed struggle against Israel, chiefly in the form of attacks mounted from southern Lebanon. He was wounded in fighting during the 1982 Israeli invasion of Lebanon. The following year when the PLF split into three factions, he led the largest pro-Iraqi group. In 1984 he became a member of the PLO Executive Committee.

On October 7, 1985, Abbas masterminded the PLF's most dramatic terrorist action, the hijacking of the Italian cruise ship *Achille Lauro*, which at the time was steaming from Alexandria to Port Said, Egypt. The hijacking resulted in the death of U.S.-born Jew Leon Klinghoffer. Although the Egyptian aircraft carrying Abbas and the other three hijackers to asylum in Tunisia was diverted by U.S. aircraft to a North Atlantic Treaty Organization air base in Sicily, the Italian government allowed the passengers to depart, and Abbas escaped among them.

There was, however, much criticism of Abbas for the PLF's attempted terrorist attack on Nizamim Beach near Tel Aviv on May 30, 1990, which was designed to torpedo the possibility of PLO-Israeli peace talks. Nonetheless, the Israeli government alleged that the PLF had regularly received funding from PLO chairman Yasser Arafat. Indeed, in January 1996 the PLO agreed to provide an undisclosed sum to finance the Leon and Marilyn Klinghoffer Memorial Foundation of the U.S. Anti-Defamation League, in return for which Klinghoffer's daughters dropped a lawsuit brought against the PLO. In 1989 Abbas had supported the PLO's acceptance of United Nations Security Council Resolution 242; therefore, these militant actions betrayed that stance.

Following the 1993 Oslo Accords, Abbas returned to Gaza. He then moved to Iraq. There was a standing U.S. warrant for his arrest, and in 2003 during the U.S.-led invasion of Iraq, he was taken into custody by U.S. forces. He died in Iraq, reportedly of natural causes, on March 8, 2004, while in U.S. custody.

SPENCER C. TUCKER

See also

Global War on Terror

References

Alexander, Yonah. *Palestinian Secular Terrorism*. Ardsley, NY: Transnational Publishers, 2003.

Bohn, Michael K. *The Achille Lauro Hijacking: Lessons in the Politics and Prejudice of Terrorism*. Dulles, VA: Potomac Books, 2004.

Cassese, Antonio. *Terrorism, Politics and Law: The Achille Lauro Affair*. Princeton, NJ: Princeton University Press, 1989.

Nassar, Jamal R. *The Palestine Liberation Organization: From Armed Struggle to the Declaration of Independence.* New York: Praeger, 1991.

Abdel-Rahman, Omar (1938–)

Omar Abdel-Rahman was born in Fayyum, Egypt, on May 3, 1938. He suffered from childhood diabetes, which resulted in blindness when he was 10 months old. By age 11, he had memorized the Koran and devoted himself to preaching the Muslim faith. He graduated in Koranic studies from Al-Azhar University in Cairo. As a professor at the Theological College in Asyut, he gained a large militant following in Cairo's southern slums and villages after speaking out against the government's violations of traditional Islamic sharia laws. Abdel-Rahman became the spiritual leader of the loosely knit, highly militant al-Gama'a al-Islamiyya (Islamic Group) umbrella organization and the Egyptian Islamic Jihad. Both organizations opposed the Egyptian government's policies and preached militant jihad. Islamic Jihad was responsible for the 1981 assassination of Egyptian president Anwar Sadat.

In 1981, Abdel-Rahman and 23 other Islamic militants were arrested in connection with Sadat's assassination. Abdel-Rahman spent three years in Egyptian jails, where he was tortured. Although acquitted of conspiracy in the assassination of Sadat, Abdel-Rahman was expelled from Egypt and went to Afghanistan, where he reportedly made contact with Al Qaeda leader Osama bin Laden. Abdel-Rahman then traveled widely, recruiting mujahideen to fight in Afghanistan against the Soviet Union. Returning to Egypt, he was again arrested in 1989 for inciting antigovernment clashes in Fayyum but was again acquitted.

Abdel-Rahman fled Egypt after being linked to further terrorist attacks on Coptic Christians in northern Egypt and illegally entered the United States in 1990 on a tourist visa obtained in Sudan. He gained permanent U.S. residency as a religious worker in 1991, an action that the U.S. Immigration and Naturalization Service (INS) now says was erroneous. However, Abdel-Rahman's marriage to an American Muslim convert enabled him to avoid deportation, despite Egypt's calls for his extradition and his status as a prominent figure on the official U.S. terrorist list.

In January 1993, Abdel-Rahman was discovered to be actively preaching militant Islamic fundamentalist sermons to thousands of Egyptian, Yemeni, Sudanese, and other Muslim immigrants in New York's mosques. The sheikh's messages, secretly recorded on tape cassettes and funneled to his followers in the Egyptian underground, advocated "the eradication of all those who stand in the way of Islam" because "the laws of God have been usurped by Crusaders' laws. The hand of a thief is not cut off, the drinker of liquor is not whipped, the adulterer is not stoned. Islamic holy law should be followed to the letter."

Abdel-Rahman was arrested in the United States in July 1993 for his suspected involvement in the World Trade Center bombing, but insufficient evidence forced the INS to initially hold him on lesser charges of illegal immigration and polygamy. He was held in a U.S. federal prison while he appealed the deportation order against him and was awarded limited preferential treatment because of his ill health and blindness.

On October 1, 1995, in the largest terrorism trial up to that point in U.S. history, Abdel-Rahman was convicted of 48 of 50 charges, including seditious conspiracy, for leading a four-year terrorist campaign of bombings and assassinations intended to destroy the United Nations building and other landmarks in the New York area. He was also convicted of conspiring to assassinate Egyptian president Hosni Mubarak and of solicitation to attack U.S. military installations. Abdel-Rahman was sentenced to life imprisonment on January 17, 1996. He is currently serving his life sentence at the Federal Administrative Maximum Penitentiary Hospital in Florence, Colorado. Abdel-Rahman is also believed to have ordered the November 1990 assassination in New York of militant Zionist leader Rabbi Meir Kahane. In 2005, members of Rahman's legal team, including lawyer Lynne Stewart, were convicted of facilitating communication between the imprisoned sheikh and members of the terrorist organization al-Gama'a al-Islamiyya in Egypt. They received long federal prison sentences based on their violated obligation to keep the sheikh incommunicado while providing him with legal counsel. In 2012 it was rumored that Egypt's new president, Mohamed Morsi, had begun negotiations with the United States to have the sheikh extradited to Egypt, but Morsi's ouster in July 2013 put an end to such efforts.

Spencer C. Tucker

See also

World Trade Center Bombing; Yousef, Ramzi Ahmed

References

Fried, Joseph P. "Sheik Sentenced to Life in Prison in Bombing Plot." *New York Times,* January 18, 1996.

Hedges, Chris. "A Cry of Islamic Fury Tape in Brooklyn for Cairo." *New York Times,* January 7, 1993.

Kohlmann, Evan F. *Al-Qaida's Jihad in Europe.* London: Berg Publishers/Bloomsbury Academic, 2004.

Lance, Peter. *1000 Years for Revenge: International Terrorism and the FBI.* New York: HarperCollins, 2003.

Macfarquhar, Neil. "In Jail or Out, Sheik Preaches Views of Islam." *New York Times,* October 2, 1995.

Abdullah, Abdullah (1960–)

Afghan physician, politician, and chief executive officer (de facto prime minister) of Afghanistan since September 29, 2014. Abdullah Abdullah was born in September 1960 in Kabul, Afghanistan, to a middle-class family. He is of mixed Pashtun-Tajik ancestry, although he identifies himself primarily as Tajik. After earning a medical degree at Kabul University in 1983, he practiced as an ophthalmologist in Kabul before leaving the country in 1986 during the Soviet-Afghan War (1979–1989). He thereafter practiced at an Afghan refugee hospital in Peshawar, Pakistan. Abdullah eventually became a friend and confidante of Ahmad Shah Massoud, a prominent Afghan mujahideen leader.

In late 1992 after the communist Afghan government fell and was replaced by the Islamic State of Afghanistan, Abdullah was named chief of staff and spokesman for the Afghan defense ministry. In 1996 when the extremist and repressive Taliban took control of most of Afghanistan, Abdullah abandoned his government post and remained loyal to Massoud, who also rejected the Taliban regime. In the winter of 2001—only months before Massoud's September 9, 2001, assassination—Abdullah accompanied Massoud when he went to Brussels to address the European Parliament, urging it to provide aid to the Afghan people and supply anti-Taliban forces with arms and other supplies.

In October 2001 after the U.S.-led campaign against the Taliban had begun, Abdullah was named minister of foreign affairs in the interim government led by Hamid Karzai, which post Abdullah retained until April 20, 2005. In May 2009 Abdullah announced his intention to run for the Afghan presidency as an independent candidate. He placed second in that contest to the incumbent Karzai, which triggered a runoff election. However, after several months of stonewalling by the Karzai government and reports of election fraud, Abdullah declared on November 1 that he was withdrawing from the runoff process, asserting his mistrust in the ability of the Afghan government to hold a fair election. This decision, however, gave Karzai a second presidential term by default.

Abdullah then formed the Coalition for Change and Hope (CCH), a political coalition designed to affect change in the Afghan government and as an opposition force to Karzai's increasingly corrupt and inept regime. The CCH won a plurality of seats during the September 8, 2010, parliamentary elections, which made it the chief opposition party. In 2011 Abdullah broadened the CCH, which was renamed the National Coalition of Afghanistan that same year.

On October 1, 2013, Abdullah announced his candidacy for the Afghan presidency in a national election to be held on April 5, 2014. Like his principal rival, Ashraf Ghani, Abdullah declared his support for the status of forces agreement with the United States slated to take effect on January 1, 2015.

In the election Abdullah won 44.65 percent of the vote, compared to Ghani's 33.9 percent. Because neither candidate won a clear majority, a runoff election was scheduled for June 14. The results of the runoff proved immediately controversial, with allegations of fraud, intimidation, and other electoral malfeasance being issued by both candidates. After months of haggling, which included a direct intervention by U.S. secretary of state John F. Kerry in August, Abdullah and his supporters agreed to a power-sharing arrangement in which Ghani would serve as president while Abdullah became the de facto prime minister (an office, however, that was not constitutionally recognized). The agreement was finalized on September 19, when the Independent Election Commission declared Ghani the winner of the runoff election. The deal mandated that the precise vote totals of the runoff election would not be made public. Both Ghani and Abdullah were sworn into office on September 29, 2014. It remains unclear just how much clout Abdullah will yield in the new government, but as of early 2015, the power-sharing arrangement seemed to be working relatively smoothly.

PAUL G. PIERPAOLI JR.

See also

Afghanistan; Ghani, Ashraf; Karzai, Hamid; Kerry, John Forbes; Status of Forces Agreement, U.S.-Afghan

References

"After Rancor, Afghans Agree to Share Power." *New York Times,* September 21, 2014, http://www.nytimes.com/2014/09/22/world/asia/afghan-presidential-election.html?_r=0.

Barfield, Thomas. *Afghanistan: A Cultural and Political History.* Princeton, NJ: Princeton University Press, 2012.

Abdullah, King of Saudi Arabia (1924–2015)

Saudi crown prince (1982–2005), acting ruler of Saudi Arabia (1995–2005), and king of Saudi Arabia (2005–2015). Abdullah ibn Abd al-Aziz al-Saud was born in Riyadh, Saudi Arabia, on August 1, 1924. He was educated privately, chiefly at the Princes' School in the Royal Court. He became acquainted with governmental and administrative work at a young age and became mayor of Mecca in 1950.

In 1963 Abdullah assumed the post of deputy defense minister and commander of the National Guard. In 1975 he began serving as second deputy prime minister. He became the crown prince as well as first deputy prime minister in 1982 when Fahd ibn Abdul Aziz al-Saud, his half brother, became king.

Abdullah's power increased dramatically after Fahd was incapacitated by a stroke in 1995, becoming the nation's de facto ruler. Abdullah began his formal rule when he ascended the throne on August 1, 2005. A devout Muslim, he was known in Saudi Arabia as a moderate reformer who led a modest lifestyle. The challenges confronting him were not easy, given both rising demands for reform and the activities of radical Islamic groups in the Middle East and within the borders of his own country.

Abdullah walked a diplomatic tightrope following the September 11, 2001, terrorist attacks on the United States. Although he strongly condemned the attacks, critics in the West pointed out that more of the 9/11 terrorists were Saudis than any other nationality and that Saudi Arabia was a major funding source for terrorist networks. He cooperated with international agencies in closing down numerous Islamic institutions and charitable associations, but he also had to take into account the sentiments of Saudi Arabia's very conservative population, which opposed Western criticisms of the kingdom's Islamic lifestyle and laws. Saudi Arabia had nonetheless provided financial support for Islamic educational institutions, including some of the madrasas in Pakistan and Afghanistan that the West claimed were breeding grounds for Islamic fundamentalism in many Islamic nations.

Abdullah was interested in making peace with Israel and devised a plan known as the Arab Peace Initiative in March 2002. It called for the creation of a Palestinian state in the West Bank and Gaza with its capital in East Jerusalem, in return for peace with all Arab states to be formalized in a peace treaty with Israel. Israel would then receive diplomatic recognition and exchange diplomats with all Arab states. Many in the Arab states and Israel opposed the plan, however. In January 2004, Abdullah produced an addendum to his plan that addressed the problem of Palestinian refugees. His plan still met with much skepticism and, in any case, was rejected by Israel.

Abdullah did not fundamentally change the foreign policy of Saudi Arabia and maintained cordial relations with the United States in spite of occasional strains. Having visited

Former Saudi crown prince Abdallah bin Abd al-Aziz Al Saud during a meeting with U.S. Secretary of Defense Donald H. Rumsfeld in Riyadh on April 29, 2003. Abdullah became king in 2005 and ruled Saudi Arabia until his death in 2015. (AP Photo/ Khaled El-Fiqi)

Exporting Countries. In early 2008 while President Bush paid a visit to Riyadh, he pointed out the difficulties that oil prices posed to the United States and the international economy. Abdullah acted to increase output and lower the price, although this action had little impact owing to a variety of other factors. In 2011 Abdullah called for the creation of an Arab common market.

Domestically a cautious reformer, Abdullah introduced somewhat broader freedoms in Saudi Arabia and invested considerable sums from the nation's vast oil wealth in large scale education and infrastructure projects. Critics pointed out that he fell short in gaining greater independence for women.

With the beginning of the Syrian Civil War in 2013, Abdullah supported the Syrian rebels opposing the regime of Bashar al-Assad. Abdullah was critical of President Obama's failure to support the rebels but joined Saudi Arabia to the coalition fighting the terrorist Islamic State of Iraq and Syria. During the last half of 2014 when world oil prices plummeted by more than 40 percent, Abdullah refused to cut Saudi oil output to prop up prices. Many observers opined that he hoped to further damage Iran's already-crippled economy.

After a period of failing health, Abdullah died of pneumonia at age 90 in a Riyadh hospital on January 23, 2015. He was succeeded by his 79-year-old brother, Salman bin Abdulaziz Al Saud, who had served as defense minister since 2011 and has pledged to continue his brother's policies.

PATIT PABAN MISHRA AND SPENCER C. TUCKER

See also

Assad, Bashar al-; Bush, George Walker; INHERENT RESOLVE, Operation; Islamic State in Iraq and Syria; Obama, Barack Hussein, II; Oil; Saudi Arabia; September 11 Attacks; Syrian Civil War; Terrorism

References

Al-Rasheed, Madawi. *A History of Saudia Arabia.* New York: Cambridge University Press, 2002.

Lippman, Thomas W. *Inside the Mirage: America's Fragile Partnership with Saudi Arabia.* New York: Westview, 2005.

Ménoret, Pascal. *The Saudi Enigma: A History.* London: Zed, 2005.

Teitelbaum, Joshua. *The Rise and Fall of the Hashemite Kingdom of Hejaz.* New York: New York University Press, 2001.

Abizaid, John Philip (1951–)

U.S. Army officer and commander in chief of the U.S. Central Command (CENTCOM) from July 7, 2003, to March 16, 2007. John Philip Abizaid was born on April 1, 1951, in Coleville, California, into a Christian Lebanese family who had immigrated to the United States in the 1880s. He graduated from the U.S. Military Academy, West Point, in 1973 and was commissioned as a second lieutenant. Abizaid served initially in a parachute regiment as platoon leader before moving to the Rangers as a company commander.

Abizaid won a prestigious Olmsted Scholarship, which entitled him to study at a foreign university. After a year of training in Arabic, he enrolled in the University of Jordan–Amman in 1978. Political tension in Jordan resulted in the shutdown of the university, however, so Abizaid used the opportunity to train with the Jordanian Army instead. In 1980 he earned a master of arts degree in Middle Eastern studies from Harvard University.

Abizaid led a Ranger company during the U.S. invasion of Grenada in 1983. During the Persian Gulf crisis he commanded the 3rd Battalion, 325th Airborne Infantry Regiment. In 1991 the battalion was deployed in northern Iraq during Operation PROVIDE COMFORT, which immediately succeeded the end of Operation DESERT STORM. Abizaid subsequently studied peacekeeping at Stanford University's Hoover Institution and commanded the 504th Parachute Infantry Regiment of the 82nd Airborne Division before serving as assistant division commander of the 1st Armored Division in Bosnia-Herzegovina. Numerous staff appointments along the way included a tour as a United Nations observer in Lebanon and several European staff tours.

In 1997, Abizaid became commandant of cadets at West Point as a newly promoted brigadier general. There he played a major role in reforming some of the more egregious requirements of the plebe system. Promoted to major general in 1999, Abizaid assumed command of the 1st Infantry Division, which contributed troops to Operation JOINT GUARDIAN, the North Atlantic Treaty Organization campaign in Kosovo.

Abizaid's appointment as director of the Joint Staff brought with it advancement to lieutenant general. In January 2003 he became deputy commander of the U.S. Central Command, which has responsibility for covering 27 countries of the Middle East and Central Asia. During Operation IRAQI FREEDOM, which began in March 2003, Abizaid served as deputy commander (Forward), Combined Force Command. Abizaid succeeded General Tommy Franks as CENTCOM commander when the latter retired in July 2003. At the same time, Abizaid was promoted to full (four-star) general. When he took command of CENTCOM, insurgent violence in Iraq was escalating rapidly. Abizaid had already expressed reservations about poor planning for the postwar era in Iraq and the competence of Pentagon officials in charge of the arrangements. He believed that most Iraqis would not welcome a U.S. occupation of their country and that widespread terrorism and guerrilla activity would likely follow a U.S. invasion.

Abizaid used the opportunity of his first press conference to state that the United States was now fighting a classic guerrilla insurgency in Iraq, an opinion directly opposite the views held by Secretary of Defense Donald Rumsfeld, who bristled at Abizaid's comments. The contradiction quickly made headlines and resulted in Abizaid receiving a private reprimand from Rumsfeld.

Abizaid also disagreed with the decision by Paul Bremer, head of the Coalition Provisional Authority, to disband the Iraqi Army and advocated rehiring select Sunni officers.

Abizaid was also critical of Bremer's de-Baathification policy. In addition, Abizaid realized that the U.S. intelligence apparatus in Iraq was in total disarray. On October 1, 2003, he issued orders reorganizing intelligence operations so that in the future all reports would be passed through a single intelligence fusion center.

During the summer of 2004, Abizaid informed his superiors that a military victory in Iraq was unlikely. Instead of pursuing an elusive victory, Abizaid favored a policy of shifting the burden of the war to Iraqi security forces and minimizing the U.S. presence. Abizaid also supported research into the situation in Iraq and on the Global War on Terror. However, publicly and in interviews with the press he presented an optimistic version of events, despite having privately expressed doubts. In keeping with his public optimism, Abizaid appeared before the Senate Armed Services Committee on March 16, 2006, and gave another positive review of progress in Iraq. During a break in the proceedings, Abizaid approached Congressman John Murtha (D-PA), a former marine who had been highly critical of the Iraq War, and indicated to Murtha that Murtha's views were close to his own.

Abizaid's retirement as head of CENTCOM was announced in December 2006. On March 16, 2007, he was replaced by Admiral William Fallon. On May 1, 2007, Abizaid retired from his 34-year army career to take up a post as research fellow at the Hoover Institution. In 2008, he became a member of the board of directors of RPM International.

PAUL WILLIAM DOERR

See also

Baath Party; Bremer, Lewis Paul; Fallon, William Joseph; Franks, Tommy; IRAQI FREEDOM, Operation; Rumsfeld, Donald; United States Central Command; United States Congress and the Iraq War

References

Gordon, Michael R., and General Bernard E. Trainor. *Cobra II: The Inside Story of the Invasion and Occupation of Iraq.* New York: Pantheon Books, 2006.
Ricks, Thomas E. *Fiasco: The American Military Adventure in Iraq.* New York: Penguin, 2006.
Woodward, Bob. *State of Denial: Bush at War, Part III.* New York: Simon and Schuster, 2006.

Able Danger

A highly classified military intelligence program, the leaders of which have claimed to have identified Muhammad Atta and three other members of the plot to hijack U.S. airliners and use them as weapons well before the September 11, 2001, terror attacks. General Hugh Shelton, the chairman of the Joint Chiefs of Staff, issued a directive in early October 1999 to establish an intelligence program under the command of the U.S. Special Operations Command (SOCOM) of the Department of Defense to be directed specifically against the Al Qaeda terrorist organization and its operatives. The commander of Able Danger was U.S. Navy captain Scott Philpott, who headed a unit of 20 military intelligence specialists and a support staff. The chief analyst of Able Danger was Dr. Eileen Priesser.

The purpose of Able Danger was to identify Al Qaeda members and neutralize them before they could initiate operations against the United States. The data-mining center was located at the Land Information Warfare Activity/Information Dominance Center at Fort Belvoir, Virginia. In the summer of 2000, the Land Information Warfare Activity was transferred to Garland, Texas.

Members of this unit began intelligence operations seeking to identify Al Qaeda operatives both in the United States and abroad. Its computer analysts set up a complex computer analysis system that searched public databases and the Internet for possible terrorist cells. One of the terrorist cells so identified contained the name of Muhammad Atta and three others who were later implicated in the September 11 plot. Atta's name was supposedly placed, along with those of the others, on a chart of Al Qaeda operatives. Lieutenant Colonel Anthony Shaffer, a reserve officer attached to the Pentagon and Able Danger's liaison with the Defense Intelligence Agency as well as others, decided to inform the Federal Bureau of Investigation (FBI) about the threat posed by the Al Qaeda operatives. Three potential meetings with the FBI were postponed because of opposition from military lawyers in the Pentagon. The apparent reason for the opposition from SOCOM was fear of controversy that might arise if it was made public that a military intelligence unit had violated the privacy of civilians legally residing in the United States. Another possible reason was that the lawyers believed that the program might be violating the Posse Comitatus Act, which prohibits employing the military to enforce civil laws.

The leaders of Able Danger then decided to work their way up the military chain of command. In January 2001, the leadership of Able Danger briefed General Hugh Shelton, still the chairman of the Joint Chiefs of Staff, on its findings. Shortly afterward the Able Danger unit was disbanded, its operations ceasing in April 2001. Defense Department lawyers had determined that the activities of Able Danger violated President Ronald Reagan's Executive Order 12333, intended to prevent the Pentagon from storing data about U.S. citizens. A direct order came from the Defense Department to destroy the database; as a result, 2.4 terabytes of information about possible Al Qaeda terrorist activities were destroyed in the summer of 2001. A chart identifying four hijackers, including Muhammad Atta, was produced by Able Danger and presented to the deputy national security adviser, Jim Steinberg, but nothing came of it.

Able Danger was a classified program until its story surfaced shortly after the National Commission on Terrorist Attacks upon the United States, or the 9/11 Commission, issued its report, which stated categorically that the U.S. government had no prior knowledge about the conspiracy that led to the September 11 attacks. Keith Phucas, a reporter for the *Norristown Times Herald* in Pennsylvania, broke the story of Able Danger on June 19, 2005, in an article titled "Missed Chance on Way to 9/11."

When the story about Able Danger became public, it erupted into a political controversy. On June 27, 2005, Representative Curt Weldon (R-PA), the vice chairman of the House Armed Services and House Homeland Security committees, brought the Able Danger issue into the national limelight. In a speech before the House of Representatives, Weldon accused the U.S. government of negligence in its failure to heed the information gathered by Able Danger.

Despite some lapses of information (and a tendency to blame the William J. Clinton administration for the lapses), Weldon summarized many of the features of Able Danger without disclosing its nature as a secret military intelligence initiative run from within the Department of Defense. Weldon also disclosed that the information about Able Danger had been reported to the staff of the 9/11 Commission.

Members of the 9/11 Commission responded to these charges with a series of denials. Lee H. Hamilton, former vice chair of the 9/11 Commission, admitted learning about the Able Danger program but denied hearing anything credible about a possible identification of Atta or other skyjackers in the 9/11 plot. This argument contradicted the testimony of Shaffer that he had communicated Able Danger's findings about Atta in a meeting with the commission's executive director, Philip Zelikov, at Bagram Air Base, Afghanistan, in late 2003. Leaders of the commission then requested and obtained information about Able Danger from the Defense Department, but there had been nothing about Atta in the information provided. They also admitted that Captain Philpott had mentioned something about Atta only days before the final report came out.

This denial of prior knowledge by members of the 9/11 Commission drew the attention of Lieutenant Colonel Shaffer. In an interview on August 15, 2005, Shaffer told the story of Able Danger, and he indicated that he had been at the "point of near insubordination" over the refusal to pursue the information about Atta. Furthermore, Shaffer insisted that he had talked to the staff of the 9/11 investigation in October 2003 in Afghanistan, where his next tour of duty had taken him. Captain Philpott and civilian contractor J. D. Smith confirmed Shaffer's claim about Able Danger's awareness of Atta.

The controversy has continued because the participants have felt left out of the investigation of the events surrounding 9/11. Many of them have placed their careers in jeopardy by countering the government's version. Shaffer had his security clearance revoked by the Defense Intelligence Agency and his personal records of Able Danger destroyed. In September 2006, the Defense Department's inspector general issued a report denying that Able Danger had identified Atta by calling the testimony of witnesses inconsistent. Weldon criticized the report and investigation as incomplete. Although Weldon was an effective spokesperson in Congress who kept the story alive, his defeat in the 2006 elections deprived him of that important forum. Nevertheless, the last word has not been said about Able Danger and about whether information about Atta and others had been stored in a government database.

STEPHEN E. ATKINS

See also

Atta, Muhammad; September 11 Attacks; September 11 Commission and Report

References

Lance, Peter. *Triple Cross: How Bin Laden's Master Spy Penetrated the CIA, the Green Berets, and the FBI—and Why Patrick Fitzgerald Failed to Stop Him.* New York: ReganBooks, 2006.

McCarthy, Andrew C. "It's Time to Investigate Able Danger and the 9/11 Commission." *National Review* (December 8, 2005): 1.

Rosen, James. "Able Danger Operatives Sue Pentagon." *News Tribune* [Tacoma, WA], March 4, 2006, 6.

Rosen, James. "A 9/11 Tip-Off: Fact or Fancy? Debate Still Swirls around Claim That Secret Military Program ID'd Hijackers a Year before Attacks." *Sacramento Bee,* November 24, 2005, A1.

Shenon, Philip. "Officer Says Military Blocked Sharing of Files on Terrorists." *New York Times,* August 17, 2005, 12.

Shenon, Philip. "Report Rejects Claim That 9/11 Terrorists Were Identified before Attacks." *New York Times,* September 22, 2006, A15.

Abouhalima, Mahmud (1959–)

One of the principal conspirators in the 1993 World Trade Center bombing and a devoted follower of the militant Islamist Sheikh Omar Abdel Rahman. Mahmud Abouhalima was born in 1959 in the small town of Kafr Dawar, about 15 miles south of Alexandria, Egypt. Unhappy about his lack of career prospects in Egypt, he left school early, immigrating to Munich, West Germany, in 1981. There he lived among fellow Arabs, working first as a dishwasher and later in a grocery store. Although he disliked Germany, he married a German woman. When his German visa expired, Abouhalima decided to move his family to the United States.

Abouhalima arrived in the United States in 1986. Soon after arriving in New York City, he found a job as a taxicab driver. He became a convert to radical Islam while in the United States. He left New York City in the late 1980s to travel to Afghanistan to fight against the Soviets. Besides gaining combat experience, he became more radicalized. In Afghanistan, he became friendly with expert bomb maker Ramzi Ahmed Yousef. Abouhalima then returned to the United States, determined to carry the religious fight to the secular West.

The arrival of the blind Muslim cleric in New York City in July 1990 gave Abouhalima a spiritual mentor. Most of Abouhalima's nonwork activities revolved around the al-Farouq Mosque and the al-Kifah Refugee Center. Abouhalima became Abdel-Rahman's principal guide and driver. When the militants began to plan terrorist operations, Abouhalima volunteered his services. When El Sayyid Nosair decided to assassinate the Israeli extremist Meir Kahane in November 1990, Abouhalima was to provide his escape transportation. However, a mistake kept Abouhalima from arriving. Nosair shot and killed Kahane and tried to escape but was wounded in the throat and captured. Abouhalima's role in this conspiracy was not discovered by the police until much later.

Abouhalima played a major role in the 1993 World Trade Center bombing, helping Yousef build the bomb. On February 23, 1993, Abouhalima drove a car escorting the bomb van. After the terrorists parked the Ryder van in the underground garage of the World Trade Center, Abouhalima and the others awaited the results of the explosion but were disappointed when the North Tower failed to collapse and fall into the South Tower. The day after the bombing, Abouhalima flew to Saudi Arabia. After a brief stay he decided to visit family in Egypt but, on entering the country in March 1993, was arrested and promptly turned over to Egyptian interrogators. Abouhalima soon confessed to his role in the World Trade Center bombing.

Egyptian authorities subsequently turned Abouhalima over to American authorities for trial. Despite evidence of a large terrorist conspiracy, in keeping with Federal Bureau of Investigation policy Abouhalima and his fellow plotters were tried as criminals. After a five-month trial, on March 4, 1994, Abouhalima was found guilty on all counts. He and his three codefendants each received a sentence of 240 years; Abouhalima is now serving his sentence at a maximum-security federal prison.

STEPHEN E. ATKINS

See also

Abdel-Rahman, Omar; Nosair, El Sayyid; Terrorism; World Trade Center Bombing; Yousef, Ramzi Ahmed

References

Bell, J. Bowyer. *Murders on the Nile: The World Trade Center and Global Terror.* San Francisco: Encounter Books, 2003.

Reeve, Simon. *The New Jackals: Ramzi Yousef, Osama Bin Laden and the Future of Terrorism.* Boston: Northeastern University Press, 1999.

Abu Ghraib

Notorious Iraqi prison facility located about 20 miles west of the Iraqi capital of Baghdad. Known during the regime of Saddam Hussein as an infamous place of torture and execution, Abu Ghraib prison later drew international attention when photographs of inmate abuse and reports of torture at the hands of coalition troops were made public in 2004.

Abu Ghraib, officially called the Baghdad Central Confinement Facility under the Hussein regime, was built by British contractors hired by the Iraqi government in the 1960s. Covering an area of about one square mile, the prison housed five different types of prisoners during the Hussein regime: those with long sentences, those with short sentences, those imprisoned for capital crimes, those imprisoned for so-called special offenses, and foreign detainees. Cells, which are about 51 square feet in area, held as many as 40 people each.

During the 1980–1988 Iran-Iraq War, the Iraqi Baathist regime used the facility to imprison political dissidents and members of ethnic or religious groups seen as threats to the central government. In particular, hundreds of Arab and Kurdish Shiites and Iraqis of Iranian heritage were arrested and housed in the Baghdad Central Confinement Facility; torture and executions became routine. Among the tactics used by prison guards was the feeding of shredded plastic to inmates, and it has been speculated that prisoners were used as guinea pigs for biological and chemical weapons.

U.S. Army Private Lynndie England, who served in the 372nd Military Police Company in Iraq, holds a leash attached to a prisoner at the Abu Ghraib prison in Iraq. Photographs of the torture of prisoners taken by fellow soldiers were made public in early 2004 and caused a furor in the United States and abroad. (U.S. Army)

Although the Iraqi government kept its actions within the complex secret from Iraqi citizens and the international community alike, Amnesty International reported several specific incidents, including the 1996 execution of hundreds of political dissidents and the 1998 execution of many people who had been involved in the 1991 Shiite revolt. The prison, which contained thousands of inmates who were completely cut off from outside communication and held without conviction, was also used to house coalition prisoners of war during the 1991 Persian Gulf War.

With the 2003 U.S.-led Iraq War and subsequent fall of the Hussein government in Iraq, coalition troops took control of Abu Ghraib prison. The U.S. military used the complex for holding Iraqi insurgents and terrorists accused of anti-U.S. attacks, although by 2004 it had released several hundred prisoners and shared use of the facility with the Iraqi government. Because of the disarray in the Iraqi criminal system, many common criminals uninvolved in the war were held at the facility as well.

Abu Ghraib became a household name in April 2004 when the television program *60 Minutes II* aired photographs of prisoner abuse at the hands of U.S. troops. Just two days later, the photographs were posted online with Seymour Hersch's article in the *New Yorker* magazine. The photos, which showed prisoners wearing black hoods, attached to wires with which they were threatened with electrocution, and placed in humiliating sexual positions, sparked worldwide outrage and calls for the investigation and conviction of the military personnel involved.

The abuse was immediately decried by U.S. president George W. Bush and by Defense Secretary Donald Rumsfeld, who on May 7, 2004, took responsibility for the acts occurring during his tenure. The Pentagon, which had been investigating reports of abuse since 2003, launched a further investigation into the incidents documented in the photographs. Previously, detainee abuse had been investigated by U.S. Army major general Antonio Taguba, who had been given digital images of the abuse by Sergeant Joseph Darby in January 2004. Major general Taguba concluded in his 53-page report that U.S. military personnel had violated international law. More than a dozen U.S. soldiers and officers were removed from the prison as a result of the internal investigation.

More details emerged following the *60 Minutes II* broadcast. Photographs that the U.S. government would not allow to be released earlier were circulated in 2006. Most important, it appeared that the senior U.S. military officer, Lieutenant General Ricardo Sanchez, had authorized treatment "close to" torture, such as the use of military dogs, temperature extremes, and sensory and sleep deprivation, thus making it more difficult to locate responsibility for the general environment leading to abuse. However, in addition to charging certain troops and contractors with torture, the United States made an effort to reduce the number of detainees—estimated at 7,000 prior to the scandal's outbreak—by several thousand. However, many argued that the measures taken were not harsh enough to fit the crime, and some demanded Rumsfeld's resignation. Meanwhile, in August 2004 a military panel confirmed 44 cases of prisoner abuse at the facility and identified 23 soldiers as being responsible. The so-called ringleader of the operation, U.S. Army specialist Charles Graner, was convicted and sentenced to 10 years in prison. In January 2005, Abu Ghraib was twice attacked by insurgents attempting to free prisoners held there.

The United States held detainees in the portion of the prison known as "Camp Redemption," built in 2004. In September 2006, the United States handed over control of Abu Ghraib to the Iraqi government. The Iraqi government holds convicted criminals in the older area known as the "Hard Site," although efforts were made to release those who might be innocent.

The terrorist organization Al Qaeda in Iraq claimed responsibility for two coordinated assaults on July 23, 2013, that freed 500–600 militants being held at Abu Ghraib and Taji. This action greatly enhanced the Al Qaeda affiliate's fortunes in Iraq and Syria. At least 26 members of the Iraqi security forces and more than a dozen prisoners died.

JESSICA BRITT

See also

Al Qaeda in Iraq; Bush, George Walker; Hussein, Saddam; Iraq, History of, 1990–Present; Karpinski, Janis; Kurds; Miller, Geoffrey D.; Rumsfeld, Donald; Taguba, Antonio Mario

References

Danner, Mark. *Torture and Truth: America, Abu Ghraib, and the War on Terror.* New York: New York Review Books, 2004.

Graveline, Christopher, and Michael Clemens. *The Secrets of Abu Ghraib Revealed.* Dulles, VA: Potomac Books, 2010.

Greenberg, Karen J., and Joshua L. Dratel, eds. *The Torture Papers: The Road to Abu Ghraib.* Cambridge, MA: Cambridge University Press, 2005.

Strasser, Steven, ed. *The Abu Ghraib Investigations: The Official Independent Panel and Pentagon Reports on the Shocking Prisoner Abuse in Iraq.* New York: PublicAffairs, 2004.

Abu Sayyaf

Islamic insurgent group in the southern Philippine Islands. The name "Abu Sayyaf" comes from Arabic and is loosely translated as "father of swordsmith." Its members also call themselves Al-Harakat Al-Islamiyya (Islamic Movement). Established in 1991 and led by Khadaffy Janjalani until his death in battle with Philippine government forces in September 2006, Abu Sayyaf members seek the establishment of an independent Islamic state in the southern Philippines, where other Islamic organizations—most notably the Moro National Liberation Front and the Moro Islamic Liberation Front—have been active since 1969.

With an estimated 200 fighters and an extended membership of 2,000, Abu Sayyaf is the smallest of the Islamic insurgent groups seeking autonomy or independence for the largely Muslim southern Philippines. It is also the most radical organization, wanting establishment of an Islamic fundamentalist state. Most active in the islands of Jolo and Basilan, it has been involved in bombings, drive-by shootings, kidnappings, and extortion. It is also reportedly involved in drug dealing.

The U.S. government has included Abu Sayyaf on its list of international terrorist organizations, and since 2002 fighting it has been part of the mission of the U.S. military in the Global War on Terror. The U.S. Central Intelligence Agency has dispatched agents to help hunt down Abu Sayyaf leaders, and several hundred U.S. Army Special Forces personnel have been sent to the Philippines to assist Filipino forces in counterinsurgency training.

SPENCER C. TUCKER

See also
Central Intelligence Agency; Global War on Terror

Reference
Banlaoi, Rommel. *Philippine Security in the Age of Terror.* New York: Taylor and Francis, 2010.

Academi

See Blackwater USA

ACHILLES, Operation (March 6–May 31, 2007)

A North Atlantic Treaty Organization (NATO)–led military counterinsurgency operation in Afghanistan during March 6–May 31, 2007. In response to increased Taliban and Al Qaeda activities in the Helmand Province in southwest Afghanistan, NATO sought to expand its area of operations into the region and to disrupt a growing insurgency network there. Over the previous two years the Taliban had launched annual campaigns in the area each spring, and NATO planners wanted to strike the insurgents before they were able undertake another springtime operation. Furthermore, poppy production in the region had expanded dramatically, and Helmand Province was responsible for as much as 40 percent of the world's total heroin production. The NATO action was also designed to suppress the narcotics trade and undermine the power of local warlords, many of whom were allied with the Taliban.

Operation ACHILLES was the largest NATO-led ground offensive in Afghanistan to date. The campaign was a follow-on to Operation VOLCANO of February 2007, during which British forces had dislodged a large Taliban force of approximately 700 fighters in 25 compounds near the Kajaki Dam in the province. The dam was one of two major hydro-electric producers in the country and the major source of irrigation for the region. However, only one of two turbine generation units were operable by the end of 2006, and the facility faced constant attack by the Taliban. An internationally funded $100 million plan to upgrade the plant and add a third turbine had been repeatedly delayed by fighting. One of the specific goals of Operation ACHILLES was to create a secure environment for the dam to be brought up to full operational capacity. British and Australian economic and Provincial Reconstruction Teams were slated to support the military effort.

NATO deployed 5,500 troops during the campaign. The majority were British, with smaller contingents from the United States, Canada, Denmark, and the Netherlands, along with 1,000 troops from the Afghan National Army. ACHILLES would be one of the largest operations undertaken by the Afghan Army and would provide coalition commanders with an assessment of the capabilities of its troops. The NATO-led forces were opposed by approximately 4,000 to 5,000 Taliban fighters. The NATO forces were initially commanded by Dutch major general Ton van Loon; British major general Jonathan "Jacko" Page assumed command of the region on May 1, 2007.

Operation ACHILLES began on March 6, 2007. The NATO-led forces moved into the more lawless northern areas in the province, including Musa Qala, Washir, Nawzad, Sangin Kajaki, and Grishk. Initially, two large Taliban compounds were attacked and captured by coalition forces near Garmsir. A combined Dutch-Afghan group, Task Force Uruzgan, was deployed along the border between the Helmand and Uruzgan Provinces to block the escape route of Taliban forces. In addition, on April 30 NATO and Afghan forces attacked a large Taliban force at Gereshk, killing approximately 130 enemy fighters and forcing the Taliban from the area. Coalition forces employed air assets against the Taliban in Gereshk and surrounding villages.

Civilian casualties from the engagement led to protests among villagers in the region. Reports indicated that as many as 50 civilians were killed in the fighting. This created renewed tensions between the local populace and the NATO-led coalition. Nonetheless, by the end of May Taliban forces had been effectively removed from both Gereshk and Sangin.

The majority of fighting involved small-unit action, with bands of 10–50 Taliban fighters conducting small-scale attacks on coalition forces and posts. In most of these engagements, the NATO forces were able to use a combination of airpower, precision-guided munitions, and artillery to overwhelm Taliban resistance. The Taliban also increasingly resorted to terrorist-style attacks similar to those used in Iraq, including the use of improvised explosive devices to attack convoys and the use of car bombs, especially against Afghan police or civilian targets. During one week in April, 11 NATO troops were killed by roadside bombs, while none died in combat operations.

A leaflet drop over southeastern Afghanistan, part of Operation ACHILLES in March 2007. The leaflets warned the Taliban not to interfere with Coalition operations. (U.S. Department of Defense)

While the main thrust of the campaign was to destroy concentrations of Taliban fighters, the operations also included tactical air strikes and special operations forces' actions against Taliban leaders. On May 13 Mullah Dadullah, the military operational commander of the Taliban and a member of the organization's 10-member central committee, was killed in a raid by NATO forces, becoming the most senior Taliban figure killed in Afghanistan to that point. In addition, coalition air strikes were credited with killing a number of midlevel Taliban leaders during the campaign.

Operation ACHILLES ended on May 31. During the campaign, NATO leaders reported that Afghan troops performed well and undertook a number of missions independent of coalition personnel. Casualties included 19 Afghan National Army troops and 16 NATO soldiers. Taliban casualties were estimated to be between 700 and 1,000. In addition, some 39 Taliban fighters were captured. In order to support the continued presence of Afghan National Army forces, a series of bases were built by NATO engineers, and patrol stations were established throughout the region for NATO and Afghan forces. In an effort to capitalize on the relative success of Operation ACHILLES, NATO launched a series of smaller campaigns and raids throughout the summer. One result was that the Taliban failed to mount an offensive in the spring of 2007. However, ACHILLES was unable to restore large areas of Helmand to Afghan government control, and the campaign did not significantly disrupt the region's poppy production. In addition, in 2008 the Taliban launched renewed attacks on the Kajaki Dam. Nevertheless, in September, British forces were able to deliver the planned third turbine at the hydroelectric plant, and work began on dramatically increasing the facility's power output.

TOM LANSFORD

See also

North Atlantic Treaty Organization; Provincial Reconstruction Teams, Afghanistan; Taliban

References

Bhatia, Michael, and Mark Sedra. *Afghanistan, Arms and Conflict: Armed Groups, Disarmament and Security in a Post-War Society.* New York: Routledge, 2008.

Crews, Robert D., and Amin Tarzi, eds. *The Taliban and the Crisis of Afghanistan.* Cambridge, MA: Harvard University Press, 2008.

Guistozzi, Antonio. *Koran, Kalashnikov and Laptop: The Neo-Taliban Insurgency in Afghanistan.* New York: Columbia University Press, 2008.

Jones, Seth G. *Counterinsurgency in Afghanistan: RAND Counterinsurgency Study No. 4.* Santa Monica, CA: RAND Corporation, 2008.

Mills, Greg. *From Africa to Afghanistan: With Richards and NATO to Kabul.* Johannesburg: Wits University Press, 2007.

Addington, David (1957–)

Attorney, government official in the Ronald Reagan and George H. W. Bush administrations, legal counsel for Vice President Dick Cheney (2001–2005), and Cheney's chief of staff (2005–2009). David Addington was born in Washington, D.C., on January 22, 1957. He attended Georgetown University and earned a law degree from Duke University. Admitted to the bar in 1981, he served as an assistant general counsel for the Central Intelligence Agency (CIA) from 1981 to 1984. During 1984–1987, he acted as counsel for the U.S. House of Representatives' committees on intelligence and international relations. Also in 1987, he served as a special assistant to President Reagan and then as deputy assistant until 1989. During this time, Addington suggested that Reagan's signing statements, or written statements made upon the signing of a bill into law, should exempt the president from wrongdoing in the Iran-Contra Affair.

From 1989 to 1992, Addington was special assistant to Secretary of Defense Cheney. By this time Addington had firmly established his bona fides as a rightist Republican and a war hawk. From 1992 to 1993, he was general counsel for the Department of Defense. Addington had unusual sway over policy matters, and he became a close confidant of both Cheney and the elder Bush. Addington was reportedly deeply involved, along with Cheney, in developing contingency plans for the continuity of the U.S. government in the wake of a nuclear attack or other catastrophe. The plans that Addington envisioned called for a paramount executive in whom most power would be invested and who would work with the "cooperation" of Congress and the courts. Several sources indicate that since that time, Addington has carried with him a copy of the U.S. Constitution. Some have argued that both Addington and Cheney became obsessed by such doomsday scenarios. During 1993–2001, Addington practiced law privately and spearheaded a political action committee that attempted to lay the groundwork for a Cheney presidential campaign, which never panned out.

In 2001, Addington became Vice President Cheney's legal counsel. As such, Addington played a major role in setting policy during the George W. Bush administration, especially in areas pertaining to national security. After the September 11, 2001, attacks, Addington was the principal architect of Bush's numerous signing statements and helped shape U.S. policy concerning enemy combatants and detainees. Addington has consistently argued that the executive branch holds almost unlimited power in wartime, a stance that has angered and concerned Americans on both sides of the political spectrum. In 2002 he helped craft the Justice Department's opinion that in certain cases the torture of detainees during wartime may be justifiable, and he also helped shape the Bush administration's controversial policies at the Guantánamo Bay Detainment Camp. Indeed, Addington's role in national security affairs has been so consistent and central that the magazine *U.S. News and World Report* termed him "the most powerful man you've never heard of." In 2005 when Scooter Libby was indicted for his role in the Valerie Plame Wilson incident, Addington took his place as Cheney's chief of staff.

In 2007 Addington, in reply to a U.S. Senate inquiry on the use of classified information, informed Senator John Kerry that the vice president's office was exempt from the U.S. National Archives' oversight of classified material because of national security imperatives. Prior to that, Addington had called for the elimination of the oversight office. He allegedly was also involved in the Bush administration's controversial activities involving the tapping of phone calls between U.S. citizens and those abroad, which had been pursued without the requisite court orders.

In June 2008 Addington was compelled to testify under a subpoena to the House Judiciary Committee, which relentlessly grilled him about the treatment of enemy combatants and other detainees, the use of torture and questionable interrogation tactics, and the extent of executive powers in wartime. Addington remained firm in his commitment to sweeping executive powers and saw no wrongdoing in regard to detainees and enemy combatants. In 2008, Jane Mayer published *The Dark Side: The Inside Story of How the War on Terror Turned into a War on American Ideals.* The book is a highly critical study of the George W. Bush administration, including an indictment of Addington's central role in what the author sees as the trampling of civil and constitutional liberties.

Addington is currently vice president and director of domestic and economic and policy studies for the Heritage

Foundation, a conservative think tank headquartered in Washington, D.C.

PAUL G. PIERPAOLI JR.

See also

Bush, George Walker; Cheney, Richard Bruce; Global War on Terror; Libby, I. Lewis; Wilson, Valerie Plame

References

Dean, John W. *Worse than Watergate: The Secret Presidency of George W. Bush.* Boston: Little, Brown, 2004.

Mayer, Jane. *The Dark Side: The Inside Story of How the War on Terror Turned into a War on American Ideals.* New York: Doubleday, 2008.

Adl, Sayf al- (1960?–)

Senior Al Qaeda operative, strategic planner, and commando trainer, considered by some to be number three in the Al Qaeda hierarchy. He is currently wanted in connection with the 1998 bombings of U.S. embassies in Dar es Salaam, Tanzania, and Nairobi, Kenya. Sayf al-Adl is a nom de guerre meaning "sword of justice." His identity has been confused with Sayf al-Din al-Ansari, a different jihadist ideologue, but he has also used the names Ibrahim al-Madani and Umar al-Sumali at different times. According to some sources and the Federal Bureau of Investigation, he is Muhammad Ibrahim Makkawi, born in Egypt on April 11, 1960 or 1963, but this point too is disputed. If he is not Makkawi, then that individual was probably killed, and there are some theories that he was a plant possibly connected with the Central Intelligence Agency. Makkawi's history is nevertheless given as that of Adl.

Adl has written that he turned toward Islam in the 1980s. He attained the rank of colonel in the Egyptian Army Special Forces in 1987. That same year, he was arrested along with thousands of other Islamists who were attempting to revive the illegal Jihad Islami (Islamic Jihad) organization, a cell of which had assassinated Egyptian president Anwar al-Sadat in 1981. Adl was allegedly part of a plot to drive a truck bomb and an airplane into the Egyptian parliament building, and he was imprisoned with more than 400 others from Islamic Jihadist operatives.

In 1988, Adl left for Saudi Arabia and was then based in Peshawar, Pakistan, from which he moved into Afghanistan and conducted military training for its operatives near Khost. If Adl is not Makkawi, then he may have traveled to Pakistan a year or two later. In 1992, Adl went to Khartoum and also conducted military training for Al Qaeda in vacant areas of Damazin Farms. He was part of Al Qaeda's expansion into other areas, and by then he was a member of its military committee. Subsequently, he sent an important operative into Somalia to begin activities there. In 1993 and 1994, he was engaged in activities in Somalia and wrote a letter recommending the establishment of an Al Qaeda base in southern Somalia along with a detailed description of the route from there to Nairobi, which featured tourist areas and other local sites. He may have been in Yemen in 1995 before returning to Afghanistan, where he trained commandos at the Mes Aynak camp near Kabul in 1999; he likely remained there until 2001.

During this period, Adl came to know Jordanian militant Islamist Abu Musab al-Zarqawi; helped him establish his training camp, which was near Heart; and provided points of contact for mujahideen coming from Iran into Afghanistan. A split developed among Al Qaeda leaders over the wisdom of attacking U.S. interests, and Adl was reportedly, like the Taliban's Mohammed Omar, opposed to such an operation. However, once the United States attacked Afghanistan after the September 11, 2001, terror attacks, Adl directed Al Qaeda operations there. He led one contingent into Iran with assistance from Gulbuddin Hekmatyar's Hizb al-Islam. From there, Adl planned to move back into Afghanistan to fight, while Zarqawi's group was to move into Iraq. Large numbers of both groups were arrested by Iranian authorities, and it has been asserted that Adl was still in custody or under house arrest in Iran as of 2005 along with others, including the son of Osama bin Laden. Adl was last heard from in a 2005 memoir of Zarqawi solicited by journalist Fuad Husayn.

In Iran, Adl remained active in Al Qaeda's information activities and planning operations, perhaps in the truck bombing of a synagogue in Djerba, Tunisia, and definitely in actions of al-Qaida fi jazirat al-arabiyya (QAP) in Saudi Arabia. That group began publishing an Internet journal, Muaskar al-Battar, in December 2003 to which Adl contributed a regular section, "Security and Intelligence Operations." In 2004, he published an Internet manual on jihadi planning ("The Base of the Vanguard") to which other Al Qaeda members contributed. Although Adl may not initially have approved of attacking the United States, he later provided the strategic rationale for it, arguing that attacking the United States on its own soil was like smashing the head of a snake. Such attacks, he continued, would lead to the emergence of a new and "virtuous" world leadership that would vindicate the downtrodden around the world.

Adl further explained how the United States could reorient its foreign policy objectives, which were costly and would lead ultimately to its defeat. U.S. objectives, as he saw them, included (1) ending the Palestinian intifada (meaning a cessation of all resistance to Israel), (2) gaining control over Hezbollah in Lebanon, (3) forcing Syria to withdraw from Lebanon, (4) promoting successful elections in Iraq, and (5) maintaining security over the oil fields in the Persian Gulf and "maritime crossing points." Jihadists engaged in a lively debate on the impact of 9/11 and the U.S.-led Global War on Terror. Adl's whereabouts remain very much in dispute.

SHERIFA ZUHUR

See also

Al Qaeda; Al Qaeda in Iraq; Al Qaeda in the Arabian Peninsula; Bin Laden, Osama; Dar es Salaam, Bombing of U.S. Embassy; Jihad; Nairobi, Kenya, Bombing of U.S. Embassy; Somalia, International Intervention in

References

Combating Terrorism Center, U.S. Military Academy. "Harmony and Disharmony: Exploiting al-Qa'ida's Organizational Vulnerabilities." West Point, NY: CTC, USMA, February 2006.

Husayn, Fu'ad. *Al-Zarqawi al-jil al-thani l-il-Qa'ida.* Beirut: Dar al-Khayal, 2005.

Zabel, Sarah. "The Military Strategy of Global Jihad." Carlisle Papers. Carlisle, PA: Strategic Studies Institute, October 2007.

Zuhur, Sherifa. *A Hundred Osamas: Islamist Threats and the Future of Counterinsurgency.* Carlisle Barracks, PA: Strategic Studies Institute, U.S. Army War College, 2006.

Afghan Armed Forces

The Afghan armed forces are the military forces of the Islamic Republic of Afghanistan charged with the national defense. They consist of the Afghan National Army (ANA) and the Afghan Air Force. (Being landlocked, Afghanistan has no navy.) The president of Afghanistan, Ashraf Ghani, is the military commander in chief, acting through his minister of defense, currently General Bismillah Khan Mohammadi, in Kabul, the capital city and military headquarters. The Afghan armed forces currently number some 200,000, men with 6,800 of these in the air force. Lieutenant General Sher Mohammad Karimi is chief of staff of the Afghan General Staff. There are seven regional corps commands.

The Afghan army came into being in the 1880s. From the early 1960s to early 1990s it was equipped by the Soviet Union and retains much of that Soviet (Russian) equipment today. It then fragmented into forces of the various warlords between 1990 and 1996 but was reestablished in the period of Taliban rule, assisted by Pakistan. The ANA, also known as the National Army of Afghanistan, was formally established by decree of President Hamid Karzai on December 1, 2002. First trained by the British, it has since received training, equipment, and weapons from the United States and other North Atlantic Treaty Organization (NATO) members formed into the International Security Assistance Force (ISAF). The army has grown in size from an operational strength of 1,750 men in 2003 to 194,000 men in 2014. The basic ANA unit is the *kandak* (battalion), comprising some 600 troops. The ANA also has commando and special forces units. Illiteracy and desertion remain problems.

Afghan soldiers are equipped with the U.S. M116 rifle, the M4 carbine, and the M249 light machine gun. Vehicles include Russian BMP-1 and BMP-2 armored personnel carriers as well as U.S. M113A2 armored personnel carriers, Humvee high-mobility multipurpose wheeled vehicles, and M117 armored security vehicles. Main battle tanks are the T-55 and T-62 Russian tanks, while the principal ANA artillery consists of Soviet 2A18 (D-30) 122-mm and U.S. M114 155-mm howitzers.

With the lack of a regular Afghan army in 2001, coalition forces took the lead in land-based military operations in that country. In January 2003, slightly more than 1,700 soldiers in five *kandaks* had completed a 10-week training course; by June of that year, 4,000 soldiers had been trained.

By March 2007 almost half of the planned army of 70,000 soldiers had been raised, with 46 Afghan battalions operating alongside NATO forces. The ANA has also benefited from genial relations with India, as highlighted by the 2001 Bonn Agreement in which governments of other nations were asked to support the rebuilding of Afghanistan. Deliveries of military goods from other nations commenced in June 2003; India has already contributed 50 4.5-ton trucks, 300 other trucks, 120 jeeps, and 15 ambulances.

Relations with Pakistan have often been difficult, given Pakistani support for the Taliban, and the ANA has sporadically engaged in cross-border fire exchanges with Pakistani troops. On March 2, 2007, the ANA fired rockets on a Pakistani Army border post in the Kudakhel area, while in a separate incident a border clash erupted between Afghan soldiers and Pakistani troops who overnight had seized areas in the border region of Paktika Province in the southeast of the country. Relations between Pakistan and Afghanistan are especially strained over the issue of border security, and President Hamid Karzai accused the Pakistanis of doing too little to restrain Islamist militants. On June 15, 2008, Karzai insisted that Afghanistan retained the right to pursue

Taliban fighters withdrawing into Pakistan's tribal regions after executing attacks in Afghanistan. Shortly thereafter on June 21, 2008, artillery fire from Pakistan was directed at the ANA and NATO troops. Pakistani prime minister Yusuf Raza Gillani responded to Karzai that his country would not allow Afghan troops in its territory, although he stressed that Pakistan wished to maintain friendly ties with Afghanistan.

The ANA has collaborated with coalition forces in a number of military operations. On March 7, 2007, Afghan soldiers captured senior Taliban leader and expert bomb maker Mullah Mahmood near Kandahar. Perhaps the most notable ANA undertaking, however, was Operation ACHILLES, executed during March 6–May 31, 2007, by the ANA and ISAF against Taliban insurgents. Some 1,000 ANA troops joined 4,200 British, 1,000 American, 320 Danish, 300 Canadian, 200 Dutch, and 80 Polish troops in a successful attack on Taliban strongholds in addition to arms and ammunition storage facilities in the Garmsir area in Helmand Province in southwestern Afghanistan.

Another notable operation was STRIKE OF THE SWORD (KHANJAR) during July 2–August 20, 2009, in which 650 ANA soldiers joined 4,000 members of the U.S. 2nd Marine Expeditionary Brigade in the Helmand River Valley. The operation was the largest airlift offensive since the Vietnam War.

The Afghan Air Force was first established in 1924. It has grown in size from 4 aircraft in 2001 to more than 100 currently. Plans call for the United States to expend some $5 billion to increase its size to some 120 aircraft. Types of aircraft flown range from Russian Mil Mi-17 troop-carrying helicopters and Mil M-35 attack helicopters (the helicopters being purchased from Russia, the Czech Republic, and Slovenia) to Lockheed C-130 Hercules and (Swiss) Pilatus PC-12 transport aircraft. U.S. Air Force personnel train its aircrew. The air force command center is located at Kabul International Airport. Lieutenant General Mohammad Dawran is air force chief of staff, while Major Genera Abdul Wahab Wardak in the Afghan Air Force commander.

K. LUISA GANDOLFO AND SPENCER C. TUCKER

See also

ACHILLES, Operation; Bonn Agreement; Ghani, Ashraf; Global War on Terror; International Security Assistance Force; Karzai, Hamid; Pakistan; Taliban

References

Dorronsoro, Gilles. *Afghanistan: Revolution Unending, 1979–2002*. London: C. Hurst, 2003.
Hodes, Cyrus, and Mark Sedra. *The Search for Security in Post-Taliban Afghanistan*. Adelphi Paper 391. Abingdon, UK: Routledge for the International Institute for Strategic Studies, 2007.
Maley, William. *The Afghanistan Wars*. New York: Palgrave Macmillan, 2002.
Rotberg, Robert I. *Building a New Afghanistan*. Washington, DC: Brookings Institution Press, 2007.

Afghanistan

Located in Central and South Asia, landlocked Afghanistan has a population of some 32 million people. Afghanistan is bordered by Iran to the west; Turkmenistan, Uzbekistan, and Tajikistan to the north; China to the northeast; and Pakistan to the east and south. This geographically forbidding nation, almost half of which is more than 6,500 feet in elevation, has some mountains exceeding 16,000 feet and extensive desert regions.

Afghanistan's strategic location has made it the object of international intrigue and intervention throughout its long history. Nineteenth-century Afghanistan was the center of the so-called Great Game, an imperialist rivalry between Britain and Russia. The struggle ended before the turn of the century, however, with the establishment of an independent Afghanistan that divided the regional ethnic groups in the area among Russia, British India, and Afghanistan. As elsewhere in the world, artificial borders mandated by the major European powers brought problems that festered throughout the 20th century.

Afghanistan was neutral in both World War I and World War II. The Cold War that followed World War II saw Afghanistan caught between the Soviet Union, naturally interested in a country on its southern border with ethnic connections to the Soviet Central Asian republics, and the United States, which was fearful of communist expansion. The U.S. containment policy sought to encircle the Soviet Union and communist China with an interlocking system of alliances including the North Atlantic Treaty Organization (NATO), the Central Treaty Organization (CENTO), and the Southeast Asia Treaty Organization (SEATO); thus, Afghanistan found itself wedged between the West and the East.

After 1933, Afghan king Mohammad Zahir Shah tried to enhance his position by dealing with the Soviets as a counter to the British in India. Following World War II, the United States displaced Britain as the principal Western force in Asia, and the Afghan government continued to court the Soviets as a counter to perceived Western imperialism. An agreement with the Soviets in 1950 provided Afghanistan with substantial economic support and promises of oil

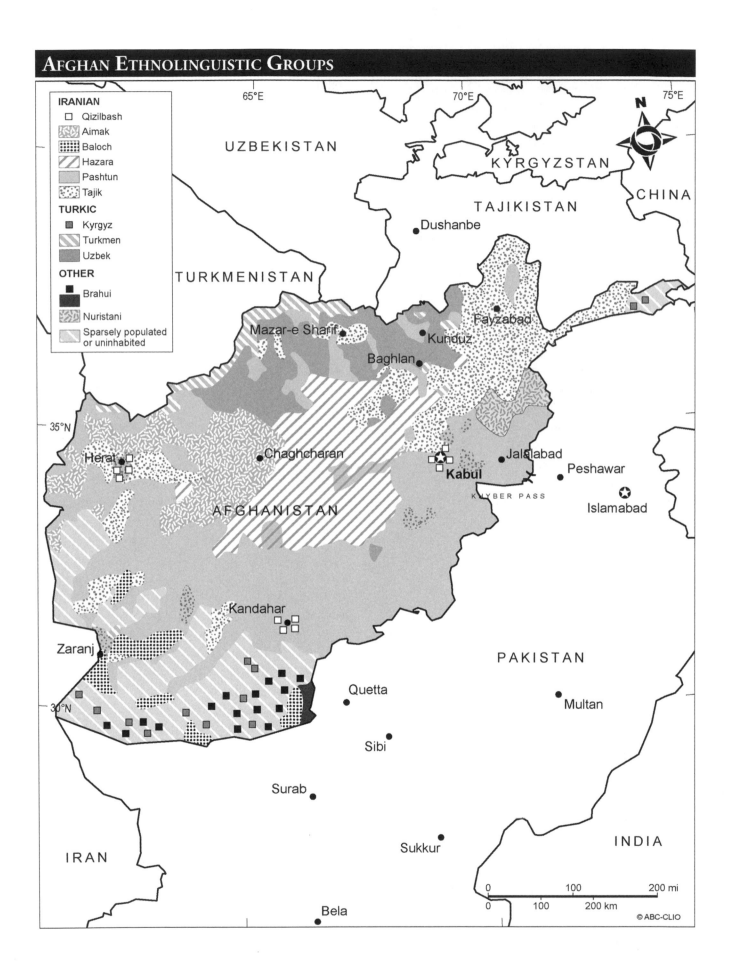

AFGHAN ETHNOLINGUISTIC GROUPS

IRANIAN
- ☐ Qizilbash
- Aimak
- Baloch
- Hazara
- Pashtun
- Tajik

TURKIC
- ■ Kyrgyz
- Turkmen
- Uzbek

OTHER
- ■ Brahui
- Nuristani
- Sparsely populated or uninhabited

UZBEKISTAN

KYRGYZSTAN

TAJIKISTAN

CHINA

Dushanbe

TURKMENISTAN

Mazar-e Sharif

Fayzabad

Kunduz

Baghlan

35°N

Herat

Chaghcharan

AFGHANISTAN

Kabul

Jalalabad

Peshawar

KHYBER PASS

Islamabad

Kandahar

Zaranj

PAKISTAN

Quetta

Multan

30°N

Sibi

IRAN

Surab

Sukkur

INDIA

Bela

65°E   70°E   75°E

0   100   200 mi

0   100   200 km

© ABC-CLIO

shipments, albeit interrupted by disputes over the Pashtun border with Pakistan.

At the time, proponents of containment envisioned an interlocking system of alliances to surround the communist world. The first was NATO, in 1949, securing Western Europe. In 1954 CENTO and SEATO surrounded the southern and eastern flanks of the communist bloc. Never fully realized, the idea was to link the three through multilateral collective security guarantees. CENTO included Pakistan, Iran, Iraq, and the linchpin, Turkey, which was also a NATO member. Pakistan was also a member of SEATO and thus tied to NATO through Turkey. Afghanistan was not a member of any of these organizations.

In 1953 Mohammad Daoud Khan, a member of the Afghan royal family, became prime minister. Daoud secured a Soviet economic development loan of $3 million in 1954 that preceded a 1955 visit by Soviet leaders Nikita Khrushchev and Nikolai Bulganin, who promised another $100 million. The United States refused military aid to Afghanistan but did assist in improving the Kandahar airport. The Soviets then promised military aid and a military aircraft facility at Mazar-e Sharif. For a time, it seemed that Afghanistan was the fortunate beneficiary of Cold War rivalries.

Daoud's tenure ended in 1963, however, when Zahir resumed direct rule. The details of Daoud's fall are not entirely clear, although several factors were involved, including high inflation in the country, continued tensions with Pakistan, popular opposition to Daoud's secular government, and the king's desire to broaden participation in government.

Zahir exercised direct rule for a decade, during which time a leftist political opposition movement gained momentum, led by Babrak Karmal of the People's Democratic Party of Afghanistan. Political unrest and a severe drought resulted in a military coup in 1973 that placed Daoud back in power, now as head of a republic with support from Karmal. Daoud, a moderate leftist, surprised many by seeking U.S. financial aid through Mohammad Reza Shah Pahlavi of Iran. The Soviets were also providing assistance, and Daoud visited the Soviet Union in 1974 and again in 1977.

Daoud continued to endeavor to play the two superpowers against each other and also developed closer ties with both Iran and Saudi Arabia. By 1978, Daoud lost Karmal's support on the Left and the Islamist fundamentalists' support on the Right. That same year, Daoud's government was overthrown. Karmal and Nur Muhammad Taraki now led a new government. It had strong ties to the Soviets. The two Afghan leaders soon split, however, and in 1979 the Soviet Union sent troops to support Karmal. The ensuing Soviet-Afghan War became a quagmire for the Soviets that would not end until 1989.

Meanwhile, local tribal leaders took advantage of the turmoil, as did Islamic fundamentalists who feared that Soviet rule would result in a wholly secular regime. This dynamic forced the Soviets to back Karmal's regime with 150,000 troops and massive military aid. Sensing Soviet vulnerability, the United States provided arms and covert aid to the Afghan mujahideen (holy warriors). The parallel to Vietnam is not without merit. During the Vietnam War the communist powers, principally the Soviet Union and China, provided sufficient aid to the North Vietnamese and their Viet Cong allies to keep the United States bogged down in a protracted struggle until 1973. In Afghanistan the United States, Britain, and Pakistan supplied aid to keep the Soviets pinned down until 1989, when they finally gave up the struggle and withdrew. The Soviet-Afghan War played a sizable role in the collapse of the Soviet Union just a few years later.

After the Soviet exit, Afghanistan was plunged into a long civil war that finally ended in 1996 when the Islamist extremist Taliban regime, supported by Pakistan's intelligence services, came to power. The Taliban cultivated ties with the terrorist Al Qaeda organization. The Taliban established an Islamic fundamentalist regime that severely repressed basic civil liberties and employed barbaric means to "cleanse" Afghanistan of all things secular and Western.

Afghanistan's economy was in shambles, but opposition groups were effectively stymied by the Taliban's heavy-handed rule. The Taliban's fortunes changed after Al Qaeda's terrorist attacks on the United States on September 11, 2001. The George W. Bush administration immediately demanded that the Taliban hand over Al Qaeda leader Osama bin Laden and other Al Qaeda operatives who had sought refuge in Afghanistan or face military reprisal. Having established a close relationship with Al Qaeda, the Taliban leaders refused, and in October 2001 the United States led a small coalition to invade the country and aid the indigenous Northern Alliance, soon defeating the Taliban and ousting it from power. U.S. forces were, however, siphoned off to fight yet another war, an invasion of Iraq pushed by the Bush administration and begun in March 2003.

In 2002 Hamid Karzai, a prominent Pashtun who was viewed favorably by the U.S. government, became interim president of Afghanistan. Elected in his own right in 2004, Karzai had the unenviable task of trying to rebuild his nation, holding Taliban fighters and other Islamic extremists at bay, and maintaining a close working relationship with Washington. In the meantime, Afghanistan's economic problems proved quite intractable, with much of the nation mired in grinding poverty.

Afghanistan is the world's major source for heroin, and Karzai refused to take major measures against opium (poppy) producers, despite much pressure from Washington, because such cultivation provides badly needed revenue for the Afghan economy. Some 11 percent of national revenue is said to come from the opium trade, which is certainly a chief source of income for the Taliban insurgency. This and other issues, especially Karzai's 2007 offer to reach out to moderate elements of the Taliban, led to friction in the U.S.-Afghan relationship.

By 2007 the Taliban insurgency was clearly on the rise, despite the presence of NATO and other allied forces in the country formed that same year into the International Security Assistance Force (ISAF) working with the Afghan National Army. By 2009 with Taliban fortunes sharply on the rise, new U.S. president Barack Obama ordered a troop surge of 30,000 troops to the country, aided by commitments from other nations. At the same time Karzai attempted to open peace talks with the Taliban, which however, rejected the overture. Meanwhile, suicide bombings, assassinations, and small-scale ambushes of Afghan forces in the field increased. Taliban fighters continued to find safe haven in tribal areas of Pakistan, and there was increased combat on the border between the two nations, while the largely Pakistani-based Haqqani Network carried out attacks across Afghanistan. The U.S. government warned Pakistan and accused its government of failing to secure control of the Federally Administered Tribal Areas of northwestern Pakistan.

Karzai, meanwhile, openly criticized the United States and ISAF of air attacks and military operations that invariably produced civilian casualties. He also negotiated with the United States and had an Afghan *loya jirga* (grand assembly) approve a status of forces agreement, only to then refuse to sign it. This stance threatened the departure of all foreign forces aiding the Afghan government. Those forces were scheduled to leave Afghanistan by December 3, 2014.

A hotly disputed Afghan presidential election occurred in 2014, but no candidate secured the necessary majority. This forced a runoff election between leading contenders Abdullah Abdullah and Ashraf Ghani. There was considerable voter fraud, but the Afghan Election Commission finally declared Ghani the winner. For a time Abdullah refused to concede, but U.S. pressure led the two men to work out a power-sharing arrangement in September in which saw Ghani became president, with Abdullah as premier.

Both candidates had declared their support for the status of forces agreement, which was then signed. The withdrawal of ISAF combat forces took place by the end of 2014, with residual forces, including those of the United States, remaining in place to continue training the Afghan Army, which had already assumed responsibility for combat operations against the Taliban, and to provide special support if required. With the outcome uncertain, anti-Taliban United Front (Northern Alliance) groups began regrouping under the political umbrella of the National Coalition of Afghanistan and the military arm of the National Front of Afghanistan. In addition to overcoming the Taliban threat, the government must also deal with widespread corruption, deep ethnic divisions, opium production, and the economy.

How well the 200,000-man NATO-trained Afghan armed forces will fare against the Taliban is unclear, but one possible positive may be the ongoing significant Pakistani Army offensive against the Taliban in the tribal areas of northeastern Pakistan that began in June 2014.

DANIEL E. SPECTOR AND SPENCER C. TUCKER

See also

Afghanistan War; Al Qaeda; Bin Laden, Osama; Ghani, Ashraf; International Security Assistance Force; Karzai, Hamid; North Atlantic Treaty Organization; Pakistan; Taliban; Troop Surge, U.S., Afghanistan War

References

Dupree, Louis. *Afghanistan.* Princeton, NJ: Princeton University Press, 1980.

Hanson, Victor Davis. *Between War and Peace: Lessons from Afghanistan to Iraq.* New York: Random House, 2004.

Hopkins, B. D. *The Making of Modern Afghanistan.* New York: Palgrave Macmillan, 2008.

Hopkirk, Peter. *The Great Game: The Struggle for Empire in Central Asia.* New York: Kodansha, 1992.

Johnson, Robert. *The Afghan Way of War: How and Why They Fight.* New York: Oxford University Press, 2011.

Kagan, Frederick. *Finding the Target: The Transformation of American Military Policy.* New York: Encounter, 2006.

Maley, William. *The Afghanistan Wars.* New York: Palgrave Macmillan, 2002.

Afghanistan Freedom Support Act of 2002

Comprehensive legislation authorizing the provision of economic, democratic, and military assistance to Afghanistan subsequent to the removal of the Taliban from power. The act was sponsored by U.S. senator Charles T. "Chuck" Hagel (R-NE) and passed by Congress on November 14, 2002.

President George W. Bush signed the act into law on December 4, 2002.

The year 2002 witnessed the continuation of decades of violence and conflict in Afghanistan. Fighting against the Soviet Union in the 1980s and civil war during the following decade had wrought human suffering and the destruction of infrastructure throughout the country. The rise of the Taliban to power in 1996 brought further suffering to the Afghan people. These decades of constant conflict spawned the emergence of four intertwining economies. They included a war economy based on arms trafficking, looting, and black market activity; a drug economy focused on the poppy trade; a humanitarian economy driven by drought, poverty, and violence and dependent upon foreign aid for survival; and an agricultural economy that had sustained the country prior to the civil war of the 1990s. Inherent conflicts resonated within this economic mosaic, further prohibiting any chance of stabilization and growth.

Throughout the decades of violence, the United States contributed huge amounts of aid, either directly or via international relief agencies. The 1990s witnessed the United States contributing the largest amount of assistance to Afghanistan than any other foreign provider. However, the emergence of Taliban rule from 1996 to 2001 forced the United States to contribute aid through relief agency intermediaries. Even then, the United States provided $500 million in emergency aid to the Afghan people.

The removal of the Taliban from power in late 2001 during Operation ENDURING FREEDOM and the subsequent formation of an interim government favorable to international assistance providers opened additional and more substantial avenues for the flow of aid. The U.S. complement of humanitarian assistance in fiscal year 2001 amounted to $184.3 million. Fiscal year 2002 appropriations increased to $530 million, and fiscal year 2003 funding amounted to $295.5 million. These allotments did not include military costs incurred through continued U.S. involvement in Operation ENDURING FREEDOM and other military activities.

The most significant U.S. aid legislation in the post-Taliban era, however, was the most far-reaching and targeted other than humanitarian needs, including the negative consequences stemming from the drug economy and Taliban treatment of women. The Afghanistan Freedom Support Act of 2002 authorized two major forms of assistance totaling $3.7 billion over the fiscal year 2003–2006 period. First, the economic and democratic development assistance portion of the act focused on a host of emergency humanitarian needs and economic development aid in the amount of $1.7

billion, including repatriation and resettlement of refugees and Afghans displaced internally in the country as well as basic needs for water, food, health care, and shelter. The economic aid focused on the cultivation of a market economy with the promotion of small industry, the establishment of financial institutions, the development of trade relations with other countries within the region, and reconstruction efforts. Congress also recognized the impact of the drug economy by authorizing $60 million in counternarcotics assistance over a four-year period, to include poppy eradication programs, training of Afghan enforcement agencies in drug interdiction, and the disruption of heroin production.

Assistance for political development to coincide with efforts to stabilize the Afghan economy included a $30 million outlay for national, regional, and local elections. Additional areas of aid focus included the reestablishment of such basic infrastructure elements as transportation, health, sanitation, and urban services and the stabilization and development of the agricultural economy. The act also provided a total of $80 million to Afghan agencies responsible for providing health care and educational services to women and for monitoring of rights for women and children. These provisions augmented the educational and health care benefits embodied in a previous authorization bill, the Afghan Women and Children Relief Act of 2001.

The second major title of the act addressed military assistance for Afghanistan. Congress made it clear that the goal of transitioning to a fully representative government in Afghanistan required U.S. support of a trained Afghan Army and police force dedicated to human rights, civilian control, and a broad representation of Afghan society. Accordingly, $300 million was devoted to the core needs for developing such an army and police force: defense materials, equipment, and services and military and counternarcotics training and education. An additional $1 billion was also authorized to expand the International Security Assistance Force responsible for peacekeeping in Afghanistan and led by the North Atlantic Treaty Organization. Military costs associated with the ongoing Operation ENDURING FREEDOM were not included in the act.

Recommendations made by the U.S. 9/11 Commission prodded Congress in 2004 to promulgate amendments to the 2002 act to strengthen the oversight and monitoring mechanisms of U.S. assistance activities in Afghanistan. The initial act and its subsequent amendments highlighted a U.S. history of active support for Afghanistan and telegraphed a firm U.S. future commitment to the war-torn country.

MARK F. LEEP

See also

Afghanistan; International Security Assistance Force; United States Agency for International Development, Afghanistan

References

Katzman, Kenneth. *Afghanistan: Post-War Governance, Security, and U.S. Policy.* Washington, DC: Congressional Research Service, September 2008.

Margesson, Rhoda, and Johanna Bockman. *Reconstruction Assistance in Afghanistan: Goals, Priorities, and Issues for Congress.* Washington, DC: Congressional Research Service, February 2003.

Afghanistan War (October 7, 2001– December 31, 2014)

On September 11, 2011, the radical Islamist terrorist organization Al Qaeda carried out the largest and most deadly attack in U.S. history. When the Islamic fundamentalist Taliban government of Afghanistan failed to hand over for trial Al Qaeda leader Osama bin Laden and take other steps demanded by the U.S. government, the U.S. and some allied forces invaded Afghanistan. This military action was carried out under "Authorization for the Use of Military Force against Terrorism," legislation passed by the U.S. Congress on September 14 and signed by President George W. Bush on September 18. The Bush administration did not seek a declaration of war and indeed chose to classify Taliban combatants as "terrorists," which placed them beyond protection offered by the Geneva Convention and due process of law. Planning for the invasion had commenced immediately following the September 11 attacks. It was done by the U.S. Central Command (CENTCOM), headed by U.S. Army general Tommy Franks, who also commanded the invasion effort. The U.S. goals in the war were the toppling of the Taliban regime, to include the capture of death of bin Laden and the rooting out of terrorist enclaves in Afghanistan.

Throughout history Afghanistan has posed major challenges for any invader, not the least of which is the physical environment of deserts, high plateaus, and rugged mountain ranges. The plan developed by CENTCOM envisioned the employment of the most advanced military and communications technology in the world in what was certainly one of the world's most primitive battlefields.

Hostilities in what was called Operation ENDURING FREEDOM began on October 7, 2001, with the start of U.S. air strikes against Taliban targets in Afghanistan. These were directed at targets in Kabul, including Kabul Airport, and at Kandahar and Jalalabad. The first ground elements were from the Central Intelligence Agency's (CIA) Special Activities Division, followed by U.S. Army Special Forces. Special forces of the United States and the United Kingdom would play a key role in aiding the Afghan anti-Taliban forces of the Northern Alliance to seize and maintain the battlefield initiative. From the beginning, U.S. forces constituted the bulk of the foreign forces committed.

Cruise missiles from destroyers and cruisers and bombs from Northrop Grumman B-2 Spirit and Boeing B-52 Stratofortress aircraft flying from the United States and British-held Diego Garcia concurrently and quickly reduced the number of viable military targets to include command, control, and communication centers and air bases and antiaircraft sites. On the ground, U.S. and allied special forces (especially those of the United Kingdom and Australia) and CIA operatives would be joined by units of the 10th Mountain Division (Light) and Marine Expeditionary Unit 15 in working with the Northern Alliance. In addition to the United Kingdom and Australia, Canada also supplied forces, while other countries granted overflight permission and allowed the use of their bases.

U.S. carrier-based McDonnell Douglas F/A-18 Hornet aircraft struck Taliban vehicles, while other U.S. aircraft, including Lockheed AC-130 Spectre gunships, answered appeals from Northern Alliance fighters to concentrate on Taliban frontline positions. At the same time, B-52 bombers pummeled the Taliban and Al Qaeda hideouts in the rugged Tora Bora mountain area.

Initial operations went surprisingly well, with some 15,000 members of the Northern Alliance and allied airpower defeating some 45,000 Taliban troops and an estimated 3,000 Al Qaeda fighters. Critical to their success was the American close air support called in by the CIA and special forces teams. Boeing AH-64 Apache attack helicopters of the 101st Combat Aviation Brigade soon joined the fray.

In an effort to win the struggle of hearts and minds, the military campaign was accompanied by large-scale humanitarian assistance, which saw cargo planes dropping food to starving Afghans in remote locations. Indeed, a shortage of food threatened as many as 6 million Afghans with starvation. Logistics problems were immense and prompted the seizure of airfields inside Afghanistan at earlier stages of the campaign.

The Taliban suffered a major defeat with the capture on November 9 of Mazar-e Sharif. It fell to forces of the Northern Alliance assisted by CIA personnel and special forces. The city is home to the Shrine of Hazrat Ali (Blue Mosque) and is a major transportation hub, with two key airports and a road leading into Uzbekistan. Mazar-e Sharif proved to be an important U.S. base in subsequent operations against Kabul and Kandahar. Rumors that some 8,000 Taliban might be planning to counterattack Mazar-e Sharif led to the airlifting of 1,000 members of the 10th Mountain Division there.

Most Taliban forces fled from the Afghan capital of Kabul on the night of November 12, although there was some fighting the next afternoon when coalition forces entered the city. In short order the major cities along the border with Iran had also been taken, including Herat. Pashtun commanders secured Jalalabad and the rest of northwestern Afghanistan, while in northern Afghanistan the Taliban fighters withdrew on Kunduz. It came under siege by November 16. In the Taliban base of southeastern Afghanistan, the prize was the city of Kandahar. Meanwhile, some 2,000 Taliban fighters and members of Al Qaeda, including bin Laden, were holed up in the cave complexes of Tora Bora some 30 miles southwest of Jalalabad. The area came under U.S. bombing on November 16.

Kanduz was taken by November 26. Shortly before its fall, Pakistani aircraft arrived there and evacuated key personnel who had been aiding the Taliban in their fight against the Northern Alliance. On November 25 some 600 Taliban prisoners, who had been moved into the Qala-i-Janghi medieval fortress near Mazar-e Sharif, rose up against their guards and seized half of the fortress, where they secured a cache of small arms and crew-served weapons. Seven days of fighting ensued, and air strikes were called in. Some 50 Northern Alliance troops were killed, as was CIA agent Johnny Michael Spann—the first U.S. fatality of the war.

Kandahar was the last major Taliban stronghold to fall. It was the home of Taliban head of state Mullah Mohammed Omar Mujahi (known in the West as Mullah Omar). Commanding its defense, Mullah Omar ordered his men to fight to the death. Northern Alliance forces as well as fighters under Hamid Karzai and Gul Agha Sherzai converged on the city, cutting it off from resupply, while U.S. marines arrived and set up the first coalition base, known as Camp Rhino, south of Kandahar on November 25. On December 7 Mullah Omar abandoned the city, escaping to the north with others on motorcycles. Kandahar then fell to Guk Agha's forces. Remaining Taliban fighters fled into the mountains or into Pakistan, where they were given safe haven.

Victorious to this point, coalition forces suffered a major failure in the military operation in the mountains of Tora Bora in December, where they endeavored to ferret out members of Al Qaeda, including bin Laden, in its extensive cave base complexes. U.S. aircraft pounded the area, and some 200 Al Qaeda members and an unknown number of tribal fighters were killed. The cave complexes were secured by December 17, but the failure to provide a sufficient number of U.S. troops on the ground as had been requested resulted in the escape of bin Laden and most members of Al Qaeda into Pakistan.

Meanwhile, diplomatic efforts were under way to establish a new Afghan government. Twenty-five prominent Afghans met in Bonn, Germany, and on December 22 they established the Afghan Interim Authority of 30 members, headed by a chairman. It was to last six months, followed by a two-year Transitional Authority and then national elections. One of the provisions of the Bonn Agreement called for establishment of an International Security Assistance Force (ISAF). United Nations Security Council Resolution 1386, adopted unanimously on December 20, set up ISAF. Its task was to assist the Interim Authority in maintaining security in Kabul, later expanded to all Afghanistan. ISAF included forces from 46 nations, although the United States supplied roughly half of its manpower.

Following a *loya jirga* (tribal council), Hamid Karzai was chosen to head the interim government. U.S. forces meanwhile established their headquarters at Bagram Air Base north of Kabul. Another important U.S. base was Kandahar airport, while outposts were established throughout eastern Afghanistan to enable operations against the remaining Taliban.

In early March 2002, ISAF and Afghan forces launched Operation ANACONDA. It was mounted to destroy a Taliban buildup of as many as several thousand fighters in the Shah-i-Kot Valley and Arma Mountain regions. Although Taliban forces sustained heavy casualties, several hundred were able to regroup in the tribal regions of northwestern Pakistan, and by late 2002 the Taliban was again carrying out traditional hit-and-run guerrilla operations against coalition bases, supply convoys, and nongovernmental organizations (NGOs) operating in Afghanistan. Taliban forces were also active in southern Afghanistan.

Meanwhile, the Bush administration had shifted resources. With the Afghanistan War not yet won, the administration opened a larger military effort in the form of war with Iraq in March 2003. There can be little doubt that this decision was costly as far as Afghanistan was concerned, as it both prolonged that conflict and made it much more expensive in the long run. Meanwhile, on August 11, 2003, the North Atlantic Treaty Organization (NATO) assumed command of ISAF, which now included non-NATO members.

While U.S. forces as well as those of other NATO countries and of the new Afghan government responded to the Taliban and Al Qaeda with military offensives and increased numbers of troops, their operations failed to halt the insurgents, who were able to take advantage of the porous Pakistani-Afghan border and regroup, recruit, train, and resupply in the tribal areas of northwestern Pakistan, controlled by the Pakistani Taliban. Their military operations settled into a pattern of avoiding pitched combat with coalition forces who were better armed and supported. Organized into units of 50 or more fighters, they would attack isolated ISAF outposts and bases and then break into smaller groups to escape the reaction forces. They also sought to disrupt coalition ground communications through the destruction or bridges, and they used improvised explosive devices (IEDs) to attack supply convoys and individual vehicles. They frequently employed suicide bombings against government checkpoints and soft targets in the cities. The Islamist fundamentalist Taliban also sought to prevent girls from attending schools and attacked NGOs seeking to improve health care for Afghan citizens.

In early 2006 a multinational force made up largely of British, Australian, Canadian, and Netherlands troops began taking over from U.S. forces in southern Afghanistan. There they established Provisional Reconstruction Teams. The heaviest fighting of the war since the fall of the Taliban occurred in southern Afghanistan as the coalition forces launched Operation MOUNTAIN THRUST in May and Operation MEDUSA in July. NATO carried out numerous other operations later that year and in 2007 aimed at disrupting Taliban offensive operations. Taliban strength was estimated at some 10,000 fighters, of whom 2,000–3,000 were dedicated full-time combatants. Perhaps 10 percent of the full-time fighters were foreign volunteers.

Endemic and widespread Afghan government corruption and tribalism and the opium trade plagued the coalition military effort. At the same time, the Iraq War took first claim on U.S. military resources, even as commanders in Afghanistan sought more manpower. In 2008 there was a sharp increase in U.S. troop strength in Afghanistan, however, with the total jumping from 26,607 in January of that year to 48,250 in June. British troop strength also slightly increased, to 8,030.

On July 13, 2008, the Taliban carried out a spectacular operation, freeing all prisoners held in the Kandahar jail. This raid was a great embarrassment to the Afghan government and ISAF. It released 1,200 men, 400 of them Taliban prisoners.

Tensions between the United States and ISAF with Pakistan also greatly increased. On September 3, U.S. commandoes, traveling by helicopter, raided across the border into Pakistan and attacked three houses in a known Taliban stronghold. The Pakistani government retaliated by suspending NATO truck resupply through that country into Afghanistan. This led to a spate of incidents involving U.S. and Pakistani forces. On September 23, Pakistani forces fired on ISAF helicopters that they said were in Pakistan's airspace, a claim the Pentagon angrily denied. U.S. forces did apparently cross into Pakistani territory in an operation against insurgents in Khyber Pakhtunkwa Province, bringing Pakistani government charges that they had killed 20 innocent civilians. Despite heightened tensions, the United States increased the use of drone strikes against Taliban targets in Pakistan, resulting in some civilian deaths. By early 2009 these strikes had increased 183 percent over 2006. In an effort to ease tensions, Pakistani officials urged that ISAF commit greater resources to policing the Afghan side of the border to prevent the Taliban from crossing into Pakistan, but there was insufficient manpower to accomplish this.

Late that year there were multiple Taliban attacks on supply convoys in Pakistan that included the burning of large numbers of tankers and other cargo trucks and raids on coalition supply dumps in Pakistan. Some 300 trucks and smaller vehicles were destroyed in December alone. Increasing interruption of supplies through Pakistan and the Kyber Pass with the torching of stalled truck convoys led the coalition to establish a northern supply network through Russia and Uzbekistan. Azerbaijan also subsequently provided airport facilities and granted use of its airspace. The first shipments on this route took place in February 2009. By 2011, 40 percent of supplies were arriving by the northern route as opposed to 30 percent through Pakistan.

Hamid Karzai won the scheduled August 2009 presidential election, defeating challenger Abdullah Abdullah amid widespread charges of voter fraud and intimidation. In November Karzai made a public appeal for direct peace talks with the Taliban. In the course of his remarks, he made it clear that the U.S. government opposed such a step.

The resurgence in Taliban operations in Afghanistan led the Bush administration to augment U.S. forces there, which was then substantially increased by the new administration of President Barack Obama. In the course of a December 1, 2009, speech at the U.S. Military Academy, West Point, Obama announced his intention to send some 30,000 more troops to Afghanistan. Despite this, increased use of IEDs by the Taliban led to significantly higher casualties among coalition soldiers, principally Americans. Indeed, 2010 saw the largest number of Taliban attacks in the war to date. Meanwhile the troop surge continued, with some 33,000 additional American troops sent to Afghanistan, then withdrawn by September 2012.

Tensions between the United States and Pakistan again increased on September 30, 2010, when two U.S. helicopter gunships attacking members of the Taliban fleeing into Pakistan fired on several Pakistani border posts and killed two Pakistani soldiers. In retaliation the Pakistan government closed the Torkham border crossing point from Pakistan into Afghanistan, through which a quarter of nonlethal ISAF supplies moved. The Pakistani Taliban then attacked the backed-up supply convoys, destroying some 100 tank trucks. Relations with Pakistan were further strained when on May 2, 2011, in Operation NEPTUNE SPEAR, U.S. Navy SEALs killed Al Qaeda leader Osama bin Laden in his compound in Bilal Town, Abbottabad, Pakistan.

During May 7–9, 2011, there was a major battle for Kandahar, the chief enterprise of the Taliban's spring offensive in which it tried to capture the city. At least eight locations in the city came under attack in what proved to be a major embarrassment for the Afghan government, although the attack was beaten back. Beginning in 2011 also, there were a growing number of so-called insider attacks with members of the Taliban belonging to, or pretending to belong to, the Afghan armed forces and police attacking them and ISAF personnel.

Asserting that sufficient numbers of Afghan soldiers and police were being trained, President Obama announced on June 22, 2011, that 10,000 U.S. troops would be withdrawn by the end of the year, with another 22,000 departing Afghanistan by the summer of 2012. Other nations followed suit. By July 2011, Canadian troops had ended combat operations and shifted to a training role. During a summit meeting in May 2012, leaders of the NATO member states providing military assistance to Afghanistan agreed that most of the 130,000 ISAF forces would depart by the end of December 2014; meanwhile, all combat missions in the country would be turned over to the Afghan Army and security forces in the summer of 2013, with NATO and coalition partners assuming a training role.

Although the security transfer was completed on schedule in June 2013, the Taliban increased its suicide bombings. As violence against Afghan civilians mounted, Karzai chose to place much blame on NATO and, particularly, U.S. troops, sharply criticizing the civilian casualties that often accompanied coalition military operations, especially air strikes.

Although President Karzai negotiated a new status of forces agreement and then secured its approval by the *loya jirga,* he subsequently refused to sign it, leaving open the possibility that all U.S. and ISAF forces would have to quit Afghanistan completely at the end of 2014. The two-stage 2014 Afghan national presidential election, however, brought to power Ashraf Ghani, and he promptly signed the security agreement negotiated earlier, meaning that some U.S. and NATO and other allied forces would remain in a support and training role in Afghanistan in 2015 and beyond.

Meanwhile, violence in Afghanistan was increasing with a large number of Taliban suicide attacks and mounting civilian losses, even in Kabul. The United Nations estimated that 3,000 civilians were killed in the country in 2013, while another 5,500 were injured. These statistics matched those of 2011, which had been the high mark of civilian casualties in Afghanistan since 2001.

In June 2014 the Pakistani Army undertook a major offensive aimed at clearing out the militants in its restive regions bordering Afghanistan. The offensive displaced tens of thousands of people, and in response to army inroads the Pakistani Taliban mounted terror attacks throughout Pakistan, the most spectacular and horrific of which occurred on December 16 when Taliban suicide bombers attacked an army-run school in Peshawar and systematically executed 145 people, 132 of them children. This attack outraged Pakistanis and may have been a turning point in Pakistan, with major consequence for the Afghanistan War.

On October 26, 2014, the United States and Britain officially ended their combat role in Afghanistan when they handed over their last combat bases, camps Leatherneck and Bastion in Halemand Province, to the Afghan Army. President Obama had made winding down the Iraq and Afghanistan Wars a priority and had pledged an end to all U.S. combat operations in Afghanistan with assumption of a purely advisory role after the end of 2014. His administration somewhat reversed course in early December 2014, however, when outgoing U.S. defense secretary Chuck Hagel announced during a surprise visit to Afghanistan that given the still formidable challenge from Taliban insurgents (including a surge in suicide attacks in Kabul in recent weeks), in 2015 the United States would retain up to 1,000 more soldiers than previously planned in the drawdown schedule reported in November. U.S. forces would fall to 10,800 rather than the 9,800 originally planned.

Hagel also announced that the United States would "take appropriate measures against Taliban members who directly threaten U.S. and coalition forces in Afghanistan or provide direct support to al Qaeda." Commander ISAF in Afghanistan U.S. general John Campbell had earlier said that this would include limited air support to Afghan soldiers.

Even as U.S. officials praised the accomplishments of Afghan forces, the high rate of Afghan casualties was seen as unsustainable and has raised serious concerns as the numbers of foreign troops were sharply diminished. Republican members of Congress charged that gains against the Taliban could be lost in much the same way that violence returned to Iraq after the U.S. withdrawal. The NATO-led combat mission in Afghanistan officially ended on December 31, 2014. What the future held for Afghanistan was quite unclear.

SPENCER C. TUCKER

See also

Afghan Armed Forces; Afghanistan; Al Qaeda; ANACONDA, Operation; Bin Laden, Osama; Bush, George Walker; Cameron, David William Donald; ENDURING FREEDOM, Operation, Initial Ground Campaign; ENDURING FREEDOM, Operation, Planning for; Franks, Tommy; Ghani, Ashraf; Hagel, Charles Timothy; Improvised Explosive Devices; International Security Assistance Force; Karzai, Hamid; *Loya Jirga*, Afghanistan; MOUNTAIN THRUST, Operation; Obama, Barack Hussein, II

References

Call, Steve. *Danger Close: Tactical Air Controllers in Afghanistan and Iraq.* College Station: Texas A&M University Press, 2010.

Coll, Steve. *Ghost Wars: The Secret History of the CIA, Afghanistan, and Bin Laden, from the Soviet Invasion to September 10, 2001.* New York: Penguin, 2004.

Cordesman, Anthony H. *The Lessons of Afghanistan: War Fighting, Intelligence, and Force Transformation.* Washington, DC: CSIS Press, 2002.

Dale, Catherine. *War in Afghanistan: Strategy, Military Operations, and Issues for Congress.* Washington, DC: Congressional Research Service, Library of Congress, 2009.

DeLong, Michael, with Noah Lukeman. *Inside CENTCOM: The Unvarnished Truth about the Wars in Afghanistan and Iraq.* Washington, DC: Regnery, 2004.

Girardet, Edward. *Killing the Cranes: A Reporter's Journey through Three Decades of War in Afghanistan.* White River Junction, VT: Chelsea Green Publishing, 2011.

Risen, James. *State of War: The Secret History of the CIA and the Bush Administration.* New York: Simon and Schuster, 2008.

Saideman, Stephen M., ed. *NATO in Afghanistan: Fighting Together, Fighting Alone.* Princeton, NJ: Princeton University Press, 2014.

Stewart, Richard W., and John S. Brown. *Operation Enduring Freedom: The United States Army in Afghanistan, October 2001–March 2002.* Darby, PA: Diane Publishing, 2004.

Woodward, Bob. *Bush at War.* New York: Simon and Schuster, 2002.

Afghanistan War, Causes of

The Afghanistan War was the direct result of the September 11, 2001, terrorist attacks, the worst such event ever committed on U.S. soil. The individuals involved, acting in accordance with a plan concocted by the Al Qaeda terrorist organization based in Afghanistan, had received some flight training in the United States, and on the morning of September 11 they seized control of four fully loaded commercial airliners. They then flew two of these into the Twin Towers of the World Trade Center in New York City and another into the Pentagon in Washington, D.C. Passengers on the fourth aircraft, informed by cell phone of what had transpired on the other three planes, battled with the hijackers, and that plane crashed in a Pennsylvania field before it could reach its target, believed to be the White House. All but one of the 19 terrorists who carried out the deadly attacks were originally from Saudi Arabia, as was the mastermind Osama bin Laden, head of the Al Qaeda Islamic terrorist organization based in Afghanistan, ruled by the fundamentalist Islamic regime of the Taliban.

The death toll of the September 11 attacks surpassed that of the December 7, 1941, Japanese attack on Pearl Harbor. A total of 2,995 people died in the attacks: the 19 hijackers, 246 passengers on the four planes (there were no survivors), 2,605 people in the collapse of the Twin Towers in New York City, and 125 people at the Pentagon, of whom 55 were military personnel. The terrorist actions crippled not only the city and economy of New York City but also the U.S. economy. Particularly hard hit were the airline and insurance industries, both of which suffered billions of dollars of losses.

The immediate aftermath of the attacks saw a widespread outpouring of international sympathy and outrage. Taliban foreign minister Wakil Ahmed Muttawakil was among those condemning the attacks. On September 12, the United Nations (UN) Security Council denounced the attacks and called on all member states to assist in apprehending those responsible. President George W. Bush characterized the attacks not as simply "acts of terror" but as "acts of war." Also, for the first time in its 52-year history, the North Atlantic Treaty Organization (NATO) invoked its collective security mechanism, which states that an attack on any NATO member nation will be treated as an attack on them all.

On September 14, the U.S. government demanded that the Taliban surrender all known Al Qaeda personnel in Afghanistan, provide full information regarding bin Laden and his activities, and expel all terrorists from its territory.

Lieutenant General Mahmud Ahmed, director of the Inter-Service Intelligence (ISI), the Pakistani intelligence services, conveyed these demands to Mohammed Omar (known in the West as Mullah Omar) and the Taliban leadership of Afghanistan. Mahmud reported that the Taliban was waiting for a ruling by a council of clerics to decide the matter. on September 20 President Bush announced in a televised address to a joint session of Congress that the U.S. "war on terror" would begin with Al Qaeda but would not end "until every terrorist group of global reach has been found, stopped, and defeated." Bush demanded that the Taliban immediately turn over bin Laden, destroy its bases, and expel Al Qaeda or risk military action by the United States and its allies.

Also on September 20, a council of more than 1,000 Afghan Muslim clerics issued a fatwa expressing sorrow at the events of September 11, urging bin Laden to leave Afghanistan, and calling on the UN and the Organization of Islamic Cooperation to open an investigation into the events. At the same time, however, it warned the United States against an invasion and stated that should this occur, "jihad becomes an order for all Muslims." The White House promptly rejected this response. Although Secretary of State Colin Powell said on September 23 that the U.S. government would release evidence definitively linking bin Laden to the September 11 attacks, it did so only after the U.S. invasion of Afghanistan.

Bin Laden, meanwhile, in a statement issued on September 17 and in an interview on September 29 denied any involvement in the September 11 attacks; indeed, not until 2004 did he admit responsibility. The Taliban leadership was defiant. It insisted that the U.S. government furnish definitive proof of Al Qaeda's involvement and warned that a U.S. invasion would meet the same result as had befallen the British and Russian militaries. Although Powell did not release this evidence to the press, he did present it to the Pakistani government, which stated that it was sufficient for a court of law. Mahmud also passed the information to the Taliban leadership. Mahmud warned the U.S. government that while the Taliban leadership was weak and divided and might easily be overthrown, the result of any change of government would be chaos in Afghanistan, and "real victory" would come only through negotiations.

On September 28 Mahmud led eight Pakistani clerics to Afghanistan in an effort to get Mullah Omar to accept a ruling by religious leaders from Muslim countries regarding bin Laden. Mullah Omar refused to commit himself. Meanwhile, Washington rejected any negotiations with

the Taliban. Indeed, on September 30 in a memorandum to President Bush, Secretary of Defense Donald Rumsfeld urged that consideration be given to going beyond mere "regime change" in Afghanistan. He concluded that "The USG [U.S. government] should envision a goal along these lines: New regimes in Afghanistan and another key State (or two) that supports terrorism (To strengthen political and military efforts to change policies elsewhere)."

On October 1, Mullah Omar agreed to a proposal by Qazi Hussain Ahmad, head of the Jamaat-i-Islami, the leading Islamic party in Pakistan, that bin Laden be taken to Peshawar, Pakistan, and there held under house arrest until his fate could be decided by an international tribunal. Pakistani president Pervez Musharraf rejected this plan, however, on the grounds that he could not guarantee bin Laden's safety. The U.S. government, meanwhile, continued to reject all negotiation on the matter. Mullah Omar warned that if the U.S. military invaded Afghanistan, the Taliban would simply retreat to the mountains and "continue the fight." On October 5, the Taliban offered to bring bin Laden before an Afghan court as long as the U.S. government could produce "solid evidence" of his guilt.

No other offers were forthcoming, and on October 7 following a month of planning the by U.S. Central Command (CENTCOM) headed by U.S. Army general Tommy Franks, U.S. forces commenced bombing Taliban targets in Afghanistan in what became known as Operation ENDURING FREEDOM. That same day the U.S. State Department sent a message to the Taliban through the Pakistani government that all Al Qaeda leaders were to be handed over or else "every pillar of the Taliban regime will be destroyed." On October 16, the Taliban dropped the condition of evidence proving bin Laden's guilt and offered to send him to a third county in return for a halt to the bombing. Washington rejected this offer, which some Afghan experts believe represented a face-saving formula.

The Bush administration based the decision to go to war on legislation passed by the U.S. Congress on September 14 titled "Authorization for the Use of Military Force against Terrorism." The president signed it on September 18. The Bush administration did not seek a declaration of war and indeed chose to classify Taliban troops as "terrorists" and thus beyond protection offered by the Geneva Convention and due process of law, a position that the U.S. Supreme Court overturned in a 2008 ruling. In 2007 bin Laden asserted that the Taliban had absolutely no knowledge of the plans for the September 11 attacks.

SPENCER C. TUCKER

See also

Afghanistan; Afghanistan War; Al Qaeda; Bin Laden, Osama; Bush, George Walker; ENDURING FREEDOM, Operation, Initial Ground Campaign; ENDURING FREEDOM, Operation, U.S. Air Campaign; Franks, Tommy; Global War on Terror; Musharraf, Pervez; Omar, Mohammed; Powell, Colin Luther; Rumsfeld, Donald; September 11 Attacks; Taliban; United States Central Command

References

Call, Steve. *Danger Close: Tactical Air Controllers in Afghanistan and Iraq.* College Station: Texas A&M University Press, 2010.

Coll, Steve. *Ghost Wars: The Secret History of the CIA, Afghanistan, and Bin Laden, from the Soviet Invasion to September 10, 2001.* New York: Penguin, 2004.

Cordesman, Anthony H. *The Lessons of Afghanistan: War Fighting, Intelligence, and Force Transformation.* Washington, DC: CSIS Press, 2002.

Girardet, Edward. *Killing the Cranes: A Reporter's Journey Through Three Decades of War in Afghanistan.* White River Junction, VT: Chelsea Green Publishing, 2011.

Risen, James. *State of War: The Secret History of the CIA and the Bush Administration.* New York: Simon and Schuster, 2008.

Saideman, Stephen M., ed. *NATO in Afghanistan: Fighting Together, Fighting Alone.* Princeton, NJ: Princeton University Press, 2014.

Stewart, Richard W., and John S. Brown. *Operation Enduring Freedom: The United States Army in Afghanistan, October 2001–March 2002.* Darby, PA: Diane Publishing, 2004.

Woodward, Bob. *Bush at War.* New York: Simon and Schuster, 2002.

Afghanistan War, Consequences of

The name of the U.S.-led military operation in Afghanistan—Operation ENDURING FREEDOM—is correct to the extent that the war has certainly endured. It officially lasted from October 7, 2001, when U.S. forces opened their campaign against the Taliban, to December 31, 2014, when U.S. forces and the coalition International Security Assistance Force ended their combat mission and withdrew most of their forces. The 13-year war was America's longest, but some 10,800 U.S. servicemen remained in country into 2015, serving there with other North Atlantic Treaty Organization (NATO) forces to provide training and other support to the Afghan forces, with the possibility of participation in combat operations to assist the Afghans should that prove necessary.

The greatest negative is that the Taliban insurgency continues, with the fundamentalist Islamist Taliban very much a viable military threat. There also has been only modest progress in ending endemic Afghan corruption that makes Afghanistan, according to one survey, among the world's most corrupt nations (fourth behind only Somalia, North Korea, and Sudan). Electoral fraud is prevalent, and the survival of democratic institutions is very much in doubt in a country that has had scant experience with such and is badly split along tribal lines, with regional warlords holding great power.

Opium production remains a major problem. Afghanistan is the world's leading producer of opium, which is Afghanistan's (and the Taliban's) greatest source of revenue. Despite U.S. taxpayers having spent some $7.5 billion to eradicate it, in 2014 opium production was at an all-time high; reportedly more than half a million acres are devoted to its production, a 36 percent increase over 2012. Drug use within Afghanistan is also growing, posing a severe challenge in a societal sense but also for the economy. According to the special inspector general for Afghanistan reconstruction, some 1.3 million Afghan adults were regular drug users in 2012 in a population of some 32 million.

Serious doubts remain as to whether the 200,000 members of the Afghan armed forces will be able to maintain security now that the NATO and coalition combat forces have largely departed. Even though combat operations have been handed over to the Afghans, the Barack Obama administration has said that U.S. forces may carry out combat operations on their own against the residual forces of the Al Qaeda terrorist network responsible for the September 11, 2001, terrorist attacks on the United States and provide air and other support to Afghan Army units in the field should this prove necessary.

The war has certainly been costly. According to one estimate, through 2014 the Afghanistan War has cost American taxpayers nearly $1 trillion and will probably cost several hundred billion dollars in the future. Owed interest on the debt for this money is already some $125 billion. The cost of deploying one U.S. serviceman to Afghanistan for a year is said to be on the order of $1 million.

Substantial advances have been registered, however, in improving the lives of the Afghan people, as evidenced by the fact that during 2002–2013 an estimated 5.7 million Afghan refugees returned to their homeland, although another 2.2 million remained refugees.

U.S. and other foreign governments as well as nongovernmental organizations have brought great benefits to the Afghan people. Improvements in health care are estimated to have saved hundreds of thousands of lives; much of Afghanistan is rural, but some 65 percent of the population now has access to health care. In 2013 an estimated 8.2

million Afghans were attending school, including 3.2 million girls. This compares with 1.2 million students in 2001, including only 50,000 girls. Certainly the lot of women has greatly improved, at least in the urban areas of the country, and there are even some women in the Afghan Army.

Significant accomplishments have also been registered in the economy and in improving communications, with the population having some 16 million cell phones. Considerable improvements have been registered in both the transportation and energy infrastructure, with the construction and improvement of many roads and bridges. These have opened up for economic development many areas of the country with strategic raw materials. Electrification efforts have also gone forward. The overall gross national product grew at a rate of 4.2 percent in 2013.

No one can predict the future with certainly, but in the case of Afghanistan it would appear that all bets are off.

SPENCER C. TUCKER

See also
Afghanistan War; International Security Assistance Force; Taliban

References
Dale, Catherine. *War in Afghanistan: Strategy, Military Operations, and Issues for Congress.* Washington, DC: Congressional Research Service, Library of Congress, 2009.

DeLong, Michael, with Noah Lukeman. *Inside CENTCOM: The Unvarnished Truth about the Wars in Afghanistan and Iraq.* Washington, DC: Regnery, 2004.

Girardet, Edward. *Killing the Cranes: A Reporter's Journey Through Three Decades of War in Afghanistan.* White River Junction, VT: Chelsea Green Publishing, 2011.

Saideman, Stephen M., ed. *NATO in Afghanistan: Fighting Together, Fighting Alone.* Princeton, NJ: Princeton University Press, 2014.

Afghanistan Warlords

In Afghanistan, warlords traditionally have been military leaders who often served as the de facto government of provinces and cities, usually organized by ethnic or tribal affiliation but sometimes by ideology, as with the mujahideen and Taliban. A warlord system has variously consisted of the collection of taxes and customs duties, the maintenance of private armies and fiefdoms, and the exploitation of the criminal, or underground, economy.

Historically, Afghanistan has been the meeting point of the Indian subcontinent, Central Asia, and the Middle East. Over the course of numerous invasions Afghanistan evolved into a nation comprising numerous ethnic groups: Persian, Pashai, Baluch, Chahar, Tajik, Turkmen, Aimak, Pashtun, Uzbek, Arab, Nuristani, Kirghiz, and Hazara. Of these groups, the Pashtuns emerged as the most dominant both numerically and politically. They represent about 50 percent of the total population; politically, they have constituted the royal family and have often held power. The Tajiks are the second-largest ethnic group, comprising some 25 percent of the population.

Afghan warlords emerged following the end of the British protectorate in 1919. In the aftermath of the Bolshevik Revolution in Russia in 1917 the king of Afghanistan, Amanullah, who ascended the throne in 1919, marked the country's independence by signing a treaty of aid and friendship with Russian revolutionary Vladimir Lenin and declaring war on Britain. In response, the British Royal Air Force bombed the Afghan capital of Kabul, and the British government conspired with conservative religious groups and landowning communities who had grown contemptuous of Amanullah's attempts at secularization and reform. This gave birth to the warlords.

In 1929 Amanullah abdicated following an uprising and civil unrest, and the warlords then competed in earnest for power. The turn of events that led to the abdication of Amanullah marked the first but not final instance in which disgruntled religious and landowning factions would collaborate with Western or Soviet powers to achieve change in Afghanistan.

Afghanistan's new king, Muhammad Nadir Shah, commenced an ill-fated reign that was cut short 4 years later with his assassination in 1933. Muhammad Zahir Shah succeeded to the throne. He ruled for 40 years before he was deposed by his cousin, Mohammad Daoud Khan, in 1973, whereupon Afghanistan was formerly declared a republic. In the meantime, warlords played a sizable role in Afghanistan, especially at the provincial and municipal levels.

From the early 20th century on, the significant role of the warlords in determining the political and religious orientation of Afghanistan indicates not only the deep-rooted nature of warlordism in the country but also an enduring determination to vie for power both internally and with external intervening powers. Nevertheless, warlords of both the mujahideen beginning in the 1980s and the Taliban in the 1990s have demonstrated a willingness to court both Western and Soviet powers to serve national and personal interests. While the "Great Game" in the late 19th century had rendered Afghanistan a buffer between British and

Russian interests, the end of the 20th century brought a pro-active mobilization of the warlords.

The most recent contingent of warlords flourished during the ongoing civil war and Soviet occupation (1979–2001) and amid the ensuing breakdown of central authority. As young military commanders usurped traditional governance structures and bodies of authority, such as the village *shura* or *jirga*, the warlords provided rudimentary public services while exhibiting predatory behavior toward local communities.

While the years 2001 and 2002 provided a period of uncertainty for Afghan warlords, especially after Operation ENDURING FREEDOM began, the Bonn Agreement of 2001 consolidated the position of the warlords not only in their fiefdoms but also within the newly restored power and authority of the state. Yet far from stabilizing the nascent government, led by President Hamid Karzai, the co-option of the warlords hindered state progress in the realms of reform and modernization. While nepotism has threatened the legitimacy of the government, in the eyes of the wider population the warlords have become synonymous with the destruction of the state rather than its renewal. Notable warlords in Afghanistan include Abd al-Rashid Dostum, Gulbuddin Hekmatyar, Mullah Mohammed Omar, Pasha Khan Zadran, Abdul Malik, and the sole female warlord, Bibi Ayesha.

Despite the seemingly negative implications that have arisen from the assimilation of Taliban warlords into the Afghan state, their involvement has been endorsed by the international community, most notably the United States, which has favored the formation of alliances with regional commanders to preserve security and stability until the Afghan National Security Forces are trained and equipped.

Nevertheless, the strategy of placing warlords in government has so far lacked the degree of success that had been anticipated by both Afghanistan and international observers. A significant obstacle has been ongoing competition between the warlords. Between 2002 and 2003, the forces of Rashid Dostum, the leader of the predominantly Uzbek political group Junbish-e Milli-ye-Islami (and after the 2014 Afghanistan elections the nation's vice president), and Ustad Atta Mohammed, a key figure in the Tajik-dominated Jamaat-e-Islami, clashed in northern Afghanistan, despite the fact that both Dostum and Mohammed were prominent allies of the government. While the hostilities between the two groups had been quelled through the intervention of the central government and the international community, skirmishes continue to persist. In October 2006, fighting between two Pashtun clans in Herat killed 32 people and injured many more.

The integration of warlords into the Afghan government has also borne negative security implications. Just as warlords are able to stand in elections, they also find other avenues of political influence open to them. For example, the parliament's standing committees are being dominated by former jihadi commanders, often to the detriment of more qualified individuals. Moreover, the warlords have gained further protection since the passing of a motion on February 1, 2007, that guaranteed immunity to all Afghans who had fought in the civil war, thereby preventing further prosecution of commanders for their involvement in war crimes.

K. LUISA GANDOLFO

See also

Afghanistan; Bonn Agreement; Dostum, Abd al-Rashid; Hekmatyar, Gulbuddin al-Hurra; Karzai, Hamid; Omar, Mohammed; Taliban

References

Dorronsoro, Gilles. *Afghanistan: Revolution Unending, 1979–2002.* London: C. Hurst, 2003.

Hodes, Cyrus, and Mark Sedra. *The Search for Security in Post-Taliban Afghanistan.* Adelphi Paper 391. Abingdon, UK: Routledge for the International Institute for Strategic Studies, 2007.

Rashid, Ahmed. *Taliban: Militant Islam, Oil, and Fundamentalism in Central Asia.* New Haven, CT: Yale University Press, 2001.

Tanner, Stephen. *Afghanistan: A Military History from Alexander the Great to the Fall of the Taliban.* New York: Da Capo, 2003.

Ahmadinejad, Mahmoud (1956–)

Iranian politician and president of Iran (2005–2013). Mahmoud Ahmadinejad was born in Aradan, Iran, on October 28, 1956, although his family moved to Tehran when he still an infant. He received both his undergraduate degree and a master's degree from Iran University of Science and Technology (IUST), where he studied civil engineering. Upon joining the Islamic Revolutionary Guards in 1986, the corps funded study for his PhD, which he received in traffic and transportation engineering and planning. Ahmadinejad became a professor of civil engineering at the school following the completion of his doctorate in 1997.

While at IUST, Ahmadinejad became involved in the 1979 Islamic Revolution as a student representative. He became increasingly religious, advocating that Islam should become the driving political force in Iran. Because of his support of Ayatollah Khomeini and his own strategic location within a key university in Iran, many believe that Ahmadinejad participated in purging the school of dissident students and teachers. The group in which he was involved, the Office for Strengthening of Unity between Universities and Theological Seminaries, claimed responsibility for seizing the U.S. embassy in Tehran in November 1979 and holding more than 50 U.S. citizens hostage for 444 days.

Ahmadinejad's entry into the Revolutionary Guards in 1986 made him an active participant in the Iran-Iraq War, during which he became involved with extraterritorial operations, or attacks implemented outside Iran. Upon the creation of the al-Quds Force within the Revolutionary Guards, Ahmadinejad became a senior commander of the elite group and is said to have masterminded several political assassinations throughout the Middle East.

At the end of the war in 1988, Ahmadinejad engaged in politics. He served as governor of the cities of Maku and Khoy until 1993, when he was made adviser to the minister of Islamic culture and guidance. That same year, he became governor of Ardabil Province in the northwestern part of the country. Despite these positions, Ahmadinejad was a relative unknown before being elected mayor of Tehran on May 3, 2003. While mayor, Ahmadinejad implemented many conservative religious policies, and he became the manager of *Hamshahri,* a daily newspaper based in Tehran.

On June 17, 2005, presidential elections pitted Ahmadinejad against former president Hashemi Rafsanjani, who was reluctantly supported by many liberals and reformists who feared that Ahmadinejad's ultraconservative and populist policies would reverse many reforms instigated by President Mohammed Khatami. After a run-off vote, Ahmadinejad won nearly 62 percent of the vote, easily beating the former president to become president of Iran. Despite allegations that hard-liners had rigged the results, Rafsanjani did not challenge the outcome. Many people boycotted the election entirely and called it a race between extremists. Nevertheless, Ahmadinejad was sworn in as the sixth president of Iran on August 3, 2005.

During his first term as president, Ahmadinejad generally pursued populist economic policies while taking a very hard-line approach to foreign policy. When officials on important government panels or within his cabinet obstructed his plans, he usually had them summarily replaced. Government authority was used to intervene directly in economic affairs, including such tactics as forcing extremely low-interest rates on lending and subsidizing

Mahmoud Ahmadinejad was the hardline president of Iran during 2005–2013. (UN Photo/Paulo Filgueiras)

basic commodities such as food and fuel. Ahmadinejad's government spent liberally and ended up with a very large budget deficit, forcing government efforts such as fuel rationing and increased taxation. Ahmadinejad was accused by domestic and foreign critics of corruption and mismanagement, and Human Rights Watch harshly criticized his first-term government for cracking down on political speech and assembly. Ahmadinejad endured international condemnation on several occasions for remarks or actions widely perceived as blatantly anti-Semitic or supportive of efforts to destroy the State of Israel. He became renowned for denying the Holocaust.

Perhaps the most contentious of Ahmadinejad's policies was his expansion and defense of Iran's nuclear program. Efforts to increase uranium enrichment were actively promoted by Ahmadinejad. Although Iran's government repeatedly claimed that such enrichment was intended solely for peaceful purposes, foreign governments and intelligence services openly questioned whether a nuclear weapons program was also in the works. Coupled with Ahmadinejad's belligerent public stance toward Israel and historical Iranian support for terrorist organizations such as Hezbollah, many, particularly within the U.S. government and the European Union, saw the Iranian nuclear program as a great threat to the region. Iranian insistence on continuing with the nuclear program seriously strained relations with many Western nations, most notably the United States, the United Kingdom, France, and Germany, and brought Iran condemnation and increasingly harsh economic sanctions.

Although Ahmadinejad generally had the support of Ayatollah Ali Khamenei, Iran's supreme leader, the 2009 presidential campaign proved quite contentious. A very strong movement against Ahmadinejad coalesced around reformist candidate Mir-Hossein Mousavi. Extremely high voter turnout on election day, June 12, convinced many that Mousavi had either won the election or come very close to doing so. The official results, however, indicated that Ahmadinejad had won a resounding victory—more than 62 percent of the votes—an outcome that was immediately called into question. Accusations of election rigging were widespread, and most reformists called for an investigation or a new election. Khamenei voiced his support for Ahmadinejad, however, and the election was considered final. Massive protests erupted throughout Iran, which the government eventually quashed violently.

Beginning with the violent crackdown on the protests, Ahmadinejad's second term proved highly problematic, including allegations of corruption even from his patron Khamenei. Outwardly, the president continued with hardline stances on nuclear development plans and occasional provocative statements. In 2012, for example, he claimed that AIDS was a Western plot designed to harm poor countries. Meanwhile, Iran's economy continued to go into a free fall as international sanctions were tightened, and Ahmadinejad antagonized parliament to such an extent that the body considered undertaking impeachment proceedings. By 2012, Khamenei seemed to be losing confidence in and patience with Ahmadinejad but did not intervene to prevent his impeachment or resignation.

Constitutionally limited to two terms by the Iranian Constitution, Ahmadinejad left office in August 2013. His legacy was a troubled one. The Iranian economy was virtually paralyzed, inflation was rampant, budget deficits were high, and government cronyism and corruption were endemic. Ahmadinejad was replaced by a moderate, Hassan Rouhani, who immediately began to seek improved ties with the West and signaled his willingness to engage in multilateral talks concerning Iran's nuclear program. Those negotiations continued into 2015.

JESSICA BRITT

See also
Iran; Rouhani, Hassan

References
Fathi, Nazila. "Iran's President Says Nuclear Work Will Resume." *New York Times,* July 24, 2005.
"A Loyal Liability." The Majalla, December 22, 2010, http://www.majalla.com/eng/2010/12/article55220236.
Slackman, Michael. "Iran's Reformists Link Defeat to a Split from the Poor." *New York Times,* July 7, 2005.
Slackman, Michael. "Winner in Iran Calls for Unity; Reformists Reel." *New York Times,* June 26, 2005.

Airborne Warning and Control System

A modified Boeing 707/320 (known in this configuration as E-3 Sentry) commercial airframe with a rotating radar dome that provides integrated command and control battle management (C2BM), all-altitude and all-weather surveillance, target detection and tracking, and early warning of enemy actions during joint, allied, and coalition operations.

The E-3's radar dome is 30 feet in diameter and 6 feet thick and is positioned 11 feet above the fuselage by two struts. It contains a radar subsystem that permits surveillance from Earth's surface up into the stratosphere, over land or water. The radar, with a range of more than 250 miles and an identification friend or foe (IFF) subsystem, can look down to detect, identify, and track enemy and friendly low-flying aircraft by eliminating ground clutter returns that confuse other radar systems. Major subsystems in the E-3 are avionic, navigation, communications, radar, and passive detection sensors. The mission suite includes consoles that display computer-processed data in graphic and tabular format on video screens.

The radar and computer subsystems on the E-3 Sentry can gather and present broad and detailed battlefield information that includes position and tracking information of potentially hostile aircraft and ships and the location and status of friendly aircraft and naval vessels. The information can be sent to major command and control centers in rear areas or aboard ships and can also be forwarded to the president and secretary of defense in the United States. The Sentry can provide direct information for interdiction, reconnaissance, airlift, and close-air support for friendly ground forces. It also provides information for commanders of air operations so they can gain and maintain control of the air battle and can direct fighter-interceptor aircraft to enemy targets. It can detect threats and control assets below and beyond the coverage of ground-based command and

The E-3 Sentry Airborne Warning and Control System (AWACS) can detect, identify, and track aircraft from great distances and direct fighter-interceptor aircraft to enemy targets. AWACS has been a critical tool for allied forces during the U.S. wars in the Middle East. (U.S. Department of Defense)

control (C2) and can exchange data with other C2 systems and shooters via data links.

As an airborne warning and control system (AWAC), the Sentry can change its flight path to meet changing mission and survival requirements. It can stay aloft for about eight hours without refueling and has in-flight refueling capability to extend its range and on-station time.

The U.S. Air Force began engineering, testing, and evaluating the first E-3 Sentry in October 1975. In March 1977, the 552nd Airborne Warning and Control Wing (now 552nd Air Control Wing), Tinker Air Force Base, Oklahoma, received the first E-3s. The air force currently possesses 33 such aircraft. The North Atlantic Treaty Organization obtained 17 E-3s and support equipment. The United Kingdom has 7 E-3s, France has 4, and Saudi Arabia possesses 5. Japan has 4 AWACS housed on a Boeing 767 airframe.

Between 1977 and 1991, the E-3 Sentry registered numerous significant achievements. Air force E-3s provided surveillance for an ongoing border dispute between North and South Yemen and assumed an ongoing commitment to support the North American Aerospace Defense Command in

defense of North America. In October 1979, E-3s provided surveillance of the Korean Peninsula after the assassination of President Park Chung-hee. In September 1980, U.S. Air Force E-3s began Operation EUROPEAN LIAISON FORCE I, an eight-year deployment to Saudi Arabia during the Iran-Iraq War.

The E-3 Sentry provided airborne surveillance and battlefield management during Operation URGENT FURY, the invasion of Grenada, in November 1983 and for Operation JUST CAUSE, the invasion of Panama, in December 1989. The E-3 Sentry also provided airborne surveillance of the Caribbean Sea and Central America as part of the Department of Defense's participation in counternarcotic operations. In September 1994 the E-3 Sentry supported Operation UPHOLD DEMOCRACY, which ousted Haitian military leaders and returned the elected leader, Jean-Bertrand Aristide, to power.

After the Iraqi invasion of Kuwait in August 1991, E-3s deployed to the Persian Gulf region. When Operation DESERT STORM began on January 17, 1991, four air force Sentries were airborne at all times. A typical DESERT STORM E-3 mission lasted 16 to 18 hours, and each E-3 carried at least two full crews. The Sentries controlled more than 3,000 combat sorties per day and achieved a mission-capable rate of 98 percent. E-3 aircrews flew more than 7,300 combat hours with an average 91.36 percent mission-capable rate. They controlled almost 32,000 strike sorties without losing a single allied aircraft in air-to-air action and controlled 20,400 aerial refueling sorties.

After the Persian Gulf War, E-3s at Incirlik Air Base, Turkey, provided surveillance support for Operation PROVIDE COMFORT and later Operation NORTHERN WATCH, enforcing the United Nations (UN)–sanctioned no-fly zone north of the 36th Parallel in Iraq. E-3 aircraft in Saudi Arabia provided postwar surveillance for Operation SOUTHERN WATCH and guided several air strikes against Iraqi targets in response to Iraqi violations of the no-fly zone imposed by the UN. E-3s of the United States Air Forces in Europe took part in Operation ALLIED FORCE against Serbia, which began on March 24, 1999.

Immediately after the terrorist attacks on the United States of September 11, 2001, air force E-3s were quickly airborne to patrol the airspace over the eastern United States for Operation NOBLE EAGLE, which has continued to the present. For Operation ENDURING FREEDOM, which began on October 7, 2001, U.S. Air Force and Royal Saudi Air Forces E-3s provided air surveillance and battlefield management over Afghanistan.

The air campaign for Operation IRAQI FREEDOM began on March 21, 2003. The U.S. Air Force provided six E-3s, operating from Prince Sultan Air Base, Saudi Arabia, and three from Royal Air Force (RAF) Akrotiri, Cyprus. The RAF also operated nine E-3s from RAF Akrotiri. The E-3s worked closely with the E-8 Joint Surveillance Target Attack Radar System and RC-135 Rivet Joint aircraft throughout IRAQI FREEDOM to direct strike aircraft against emerging ground threats and to keep commanders informed of the current battlefield status. E-3 Sentry crews have provided 24-hour surveillance of battle space in Iraq and Afghanistan.

The worst incident involving an E-3 Sentry occurred on April 14, 1994, during Operation PROVIDE COMFORT. Two McDonnell Douglas F-15 Eagle pilots, under the control of an E-3 Sentry, misidentified two U.S. Army Sikorsky UH-60 Black Hawk helicopters as Iraqi Mil Mi-24 "Hind" helicopters violating the no-fly zone. The two pilots fired missiles at the helicopters, destroying both and killing all 26 military and civilian personnel aboard.

The U.S. Air Force has regularly upgraded the E-3's radar systems, sensors, other electronic equipment, and mission software to improve the aircraft's network-centric capabilities. These modifications allow greater use of AWACS mission data, better access to external web services data, an enhanced suite of battle-management tools, and improved connections to other assets throughout the airborne battle space and with battle managers on the ground.

Since its introduction in the air force inventory, the E-3 Sentry has demonstrated that it is the premier C2BM aircraft in the world through the provision of unrivaled radar surveillance and control and time-critical information on the actions of enemy forces to senior leaders.

ROBERT B. KANE

See also

ENDURING FREEDOM, Operation, U.S. Air Campaign; IRAQI FREEDOM, Operation, Air Campaign; Joint Surveillance and Target Radar System Aircraft; Network-Centric Warfare

References

Donald, David, ed. *US Air Force Air Power Directory*. London: Aerospace Publishing, 1992.

Knights, Michael. *Cradle of Conflict: Iraq and the Birth of Modern U.S. Military*. Annapolis, MD: Naval Institute Press, 2005.

Lambeth, Benjamin S. *Air Power against Terror: America's Conduct of Operation Enduring Freedom*. Santa Monica, CA: RAND Corporation, 2005.

Putney, Diane T. *Airpower Advantage: Planning the Gulf War Air Campaign, 1989–1991*. Washington, DC: Air Force History and Museum Programs, 2004.

Aircraft, Attack and Multipurpose

The late 1960s saw the Middle East become the primary arena of U.S.-Soviet competition, making its conflicts a crucible in which the contending superpowers' air warfare doctrine, tactics, and aircraft were employed, evaluated, and adjusted. While successes in air-to-air combat drew the headlines, strikes delivered by attack aircraft shaped the ground wars of the Middle East. Oil wealth ensured that most nations in the region could afford their choice of aircraft and weapons platforms. Pro-Western countries have generally acquired Western-made aircraft that focused on precision weapons delivery, good range, and, after 1970, maneuverability and defensive countermeasures equipment.

The least expensive and among the most versatile of these aircraft is the single-seat single-engine Douglas (later McDonnell Douglas) A-4 Skyhawk. Originally designed in the 1950s as a light U.S. Navy attack aircraft, the A-4 initially cost less than $1 million each and remains one of the cheapest attack aircraft ever built, even after the addition of several thousand pounds of electronic warning

A U.S. Air Force Fairchild Republic A-10 Thunderbolt II, known affectionately as the "Warthog," in flight over Iraq on December 14, 2006. (U.S. Department of Defense)

and countermeasures equipment as well as new engines. Light, agile, and simple to fly and maintain, once it drops its bombs, its maneuverability is equal to that of the Soviet-designed Mikoyan-Gurevich MiG-17 fighter. It continues to serve as an adversary aircraft in the United States but has not participated in active military operations since 2002.

The twin-engine two-seat Grumman A-6E Intruder was the U.S. Navy's all-weather heavy bomber for most of the last four decades of the 20th century. Entering service in 1963, the Intruder carried a multimode navigation and bomb-aiming radar, an inertial navigation system, and a vast array of electronic warning and countermeasures systems that were operated by the bombardier/navigator. It carried an impressive 18,000 pounds of bombs and other ordnance. By 1984, the A-6E also carried the instrumentation and guidance systems to guide laser and electro-optically guided precision weapons onto targets as well as Harpoon antiship cruise missiles. The A-6E also had a Forward Looking Infrared (FLIR) and Target Recognition and

Attack, Multi-Sensor (TRAM) system. The last A-6s left U.S. Navy service in 2003.

The twin-engine F/A-18 Hornet and F/A-18E Super Hornet have been the U.S. Navy's leading fighter/attack and multipurpose fighter-bomber, respectively, since 2003. The single-seat McDonnell Douglas F/A-18 entered service in 1983. Designed as a low-cost alternative to the F-14A Tomcat, the F/A-18 initially was to appear in two variants: the A-18, to replace the A-7E Corsair attack aircraft, and the F-18 fighter, to supplant the F-4 Phantom aircraft. However, improvements in computer, avionics, and radar technologies enabled the designers to integrate both capabilities into a single airframe. The result was a supersonic fighter/attack aircraft with a top speed of Mach 1.8, carrying a maximum ordnance load of more than 13,700 pounds. It can employ the full range of U.S. aerial weaponry, including the AMRAAM, AIM-9 Sidewinder, HARM, Harpoon, and Maverick missiles as well as guided and unguided bombs. It is also equipped with electronic countermeasures equipment and a single Vulcan 20-mm "Gatling gun" cannon with a firing rate of 3,000 rounds a minute. Its twin GE 404 turbofan engines generate a maximum thrust of 17,400 pounds each, giving the F/A-18 a thrust to weight ratio of .98:1.0 when configured solely for an air-to-air mission and a tactical combat radius of 400 nautical miles with a maximum external load. The F/A-18 was the first U.S. aircraft to employ the now standard multifunction Heads-Up Display (HUD) that greatly improves the pilot's ability to assimilate the vast array of information endemic to modern air operations. It is expected to remain in service through the 2020s.

The Boeing F/A-18E Super Hornet grew of the requirement to replace both the F-14 Tomcat and the A-6E Intruder. Essentially an expanded F/A-18 with a larger wing, a longer fuselage, and more powerful engines, the Super Hornet carries more fuel, ordnance, and improved avionics that enable it to execute a wider range of missions and give it more range. Its GE 414 turbofan engines produce 22,000 pounds of thrust each, allowing the heavier Super Hornet (maximum takeoff weight of 66,000 pounds) a top speed of Mach 1.8. Ordnance load increased to 17,600 pounds, but thrust to weight ratio dropped to 0.93:1.0.

Entering service in 1999, the F/A-18 Super Hornet is truly a multimission aircraft. In addition to its fighter/attack roles, it can be configured as a fleet tanker and air defense suppression aircraft, enabling it to replace the KA-6D as well as the A-6E and F-14s. Both Hornet variants saw extensive action in Operations IRAQI FREEDOM and ENDURING FREEDOM.

The U.S. Marine Corps introduced the Hawker Siddeley vertical/short takeoff or landing (VSTOL) AV-8A Harrier in 1970. It was replaced by the improved AV-8B Harrier II in 1988. The AV-8B carries FLIR, the AN/APG-65 radar, a GAU-12U 25-mm cannon, and, if it uses a short takeoff roll, up to 13,000 pounds of ordnance, including Harpoon, HARM, and Maverick missiles as well as two AIM-120 AMRAAMs. If it takes off vertically, the ordnance load drops to approximately 4,000 pounds. The Harrier II served with U.S. Marine Corps and Italian forces during Operations DESERT SHIELD, DESERT STORM, ENDURING FREEDOM, IRAQI FREEDOM, ODYSSEY DAWN, and UNIFIED PROTECTOR. The AV-8B Harrier II and new variants remain in Italian, Spanish and U.S. Marine Corps service through 2014.

The Fairchild-Republic twin-engine A-10 Thunderbolt II entered U.S. Air Force service in the 1970s. The A-10 was optimized for close air support and antitank attack. It was intended to conduct both deep strikes against Soviet-era mass tank formations and provide close air support to army units on the ground. Its two GE TF-30 GE100 turbofan

engines provide 9,065 pounds of thrust each and are located in armored nacelles high above the tail to protect them from runway rocks, dust and sand, and ground fire. The pilot sits in an armored tub, and the plane's controls also have armor protection.

The A-10 can take multiple direct hits from 23-mm cannon fire and even withstand hits from handheld surface-to-air missiles under some circumstances. It is equipped with a HUD, inertial navigation and precision-guided munitions instrumentation, and infrared and electronic warning and countermeasures systems. Its light wing loading gives it exceptional maneuverability at low speed, and its GAU/8 30-mm cannon can destroy any armored vehicle in service. More important, it can carry up to 16,000 pounds of bombs or missiles.

The A-10 proved devastatingly effective against Iraqi tanks and air defense systems during Operation IRAQI FREEDOM as well as against Taliban units during Operation ENDURING FREEDOM. In fact, A-10s flew 33 percent of combat sorties during Operations IRAQI FREEDOM and ENDURING FREEDOM between 2001 and 2008 and 19 percent after that. It was the close air support aircraft of choice in Afghanistan through 2013, and despite calls for its retirement, the A-10 is being employed against the Islamic State in Iraq and Syria (ISIS) as part of Operation INHERENT RESOLVE through 2015. It is expected to remain in service through at least 2026.

The Lockheed Martin F-117 Nighthawk stealth fighter was the first U.S. stealth aircraft, a harbinger of those entering service across the world today. The single-seat attack aircraft entered service in 1983 and saw extensive combat and contingency operations from 1989 to 2004, participating in Operations JUST CAUSE, DESERT STORM, DESERT THUNDER, ALLIED FORCE, IRAQI FREEDOM, and ENDURING FREEDOM. Newly emerging technologies gave it a radar cross section less than that of a single-engine Piper Cub, making it a very difficult aircraft to detect and track. The F-117A's stealth characteristics and instrumentation made it the key strike asset during all major U.S. bombing operations from 1990 to 2003. F-117s targeted heavily defended critical command centers and air defense systems. Unfortunately, the plane's aging technology, particularly its complicated stealth coatings, required intensive maintenance. The last F-117As were retired from service in August 2008. It has been replaced by the F-22 Raptor.

The Panavia Tornado was the predominant European-built attack aircraft to serve in Operations DESERT STORM, ALLIED FORCE, and ENDURING FREEDOM. Designed and built by a trinational consortium consisting of British, West German, and Italian manufacturers, the twin-engine two-seater Tornado entered service in 1978. Britain also purchased an air defense variant that saw action in Operations IRAQI FREEDOM, ODYSSEY DAWN, and UNIFIED PROTECTOR. Italy employed its IDS (Interdiction/Strike) in Operations DESERT SHIELD, ENDURING FREEDOM, and UNIFIED PROTECTOR. Intended as a supersonic fighter-bomber, the Tornado employs a variable geometry wing to provide good slow speed maneuverability and landing characteristics without compromising supersonic performance. Armament includes a single Mauser BK-27 27-mm cannon, two AIM-9 AAMs, and up to 19,800 pounds of bombs or guided munitions. The Tornado carries a full suite of electronic warning and self-defense countermeasures equipment, an integrated GPS-inertial navigation and digital weapons system, a terrain-following radar, and all-weather guidance systems for the full range of western guided munitions. It remained in service with the air forces of Britain, Germany, Italy, and Saudi Arabia as of the end of 2014.

The 21st century has so far seen no U.S. opponent employ attack aircraft. Afghanistan had about a dozen Soviet-built Su-7s on one airfield in late 2001 when ENDURING FREEDOM began, but none were in flying condition. The Su-7 had two 30-mm cannon in the nose and could carry up to 4,400 pounds of bombs, but its lack of electronic countermeasures equipment and its poor maneuverability made it vulnerable to modern air defense systems.

The Sukhoi Su-25 Frogfoot was the only attack aircraft inside Iraq during Operation IRAQI FREEDOM. The twin-engine single-seat Frogfoot was specifically designed for close air support missions. Like the A-10, its cockpit and critical flight systems were protected by titanium armor. Its two R95Sh nonafterburning turbojet engines provide 18,960 pounds of thrust. Armament includes a 30-mm cannon and up to 9,700 pounds of bombs and guided missiles. It is also equipped with radar warning systems, chaff and flare pods, and a guidance system for the AS-7 Kerry ASM. The Afghan Air Force also had about a dozen Su-25s in its inventory at the beginning of Operation ENDURING FREEDOM, but none were in flying condition. Neither Iraq nor Afghanistan operate the Su-25 today.

Attack aircraft with crews specifically trained in bombing and precision weapons employment have been critical to the conduct of military operations since World War II. Air supremacy nets the military commander little if it does not lead to decisive strikes against key enemy positions or support to forces on the ground or at sea. The success of the United States and of its allies in recent warfare may be attributed in large part to the successful integration and employment of all facets of airpower, of which attack aircraft

play a sizable role. High-technology attack aircraft have constituted a major component of Western airpower and will remain so for many years to come.

CARL OTIS SCHUSTER

See also

Aircraft, Bombers; Aircraft, Electronic Warfare; Aircraft, Reconnaissance, Manned, U.S.; ENDURING FREEDOM, Operation, U.S. Air Campaign; IRAQI FREEDOM, Operation, Air Campaign

References

Gordon, Yefim. *Sukhoi Su-7/-17/-20/-22 Soviet Fighter and Fighter-Bomber Family.* Hersham, Surrey, UK: Ian Allan Publishing, 2004.

Green, William, and Gordon Swanborough. *The Complete Book of Fighters.* New York: Barnes and Noble Books, 1998.

Higham, Robin D., and Stephen Harris. *Why Air Forces Fail: The Anatomy of Defeat.* Lexington: University Press of Kentucky, 2006.

Hunter, Jamie, ed., *Jane's All the World's Aircraft in Service, 2013–2014.* London: Jane's Publishing, 2013.

Jackson, Paul. *Jane's All the World's Aircraft, 2007/2008.* London: Jane's Publishing, 2008.

Kaplan, Robert D. *Hog Pilots, Blue Water Grunts: The American Military in the Air, at Sea and on the Ground.* New York: Random House, 2007.

Smallwood, William L. *Warthog: Flying the A-10 in the Gulf War.* Dulles, VA: Potomac Books, 1993.

Winchester, Jim. *Douglas A-4 Skyhawk.* Yorkshire, UK: Pen and Sword Books, 2005.

Aircraft, Bombers

Middle Eastern air forces have never had large numbers of specialized bombers. Regional opponents were close enough geographically to the fighting that the longer ranges offered by bomber aircraft were not necessary, and none of the combatants seriously envisioned a strategic bombing campaign. Iraq has been the only Middle Eastern country to acquire bombers. These Soviet-built aircraft, however, played no meaningful role in the Persian Gulf War and had been destroyed by Operation IRAQI FREEDOM.

The United States, on the other hand, employed its strategic bombers extensively in conventional roles. The U.S. Air Force used Boeing B-52 Stratofortress, Rockwell B-1 Lancer, and Northrop Grumman B-2 Spirits bombers in Afghanistan in 2001 and against Iraq in 2003. U.S. bombers were especially valued for their heavy payloads and ability to loiter over the target area for long periods. Bombers primarily attacked mobile targets and supported ground troops, however, because there were few strategic targets in Iraq and none in Afghanistan.

Coalition nations in the Middle East Wars did not operate dedicated bombers. The British and French, for example, used fighter aircraft capable of dropping bombs, but these are not considered bombers. Neither Afghanistan nor Iraq possessed any bomber aircraft at century's start or as of 2015.

The United States was the only nation to operate bomber aircraft during the Middle East wars. The oldest of these was the Boeing B-52 Stratofortress, designed in 1948 for intercontinental nuclear strikes on the Soviet Union. Between 1952 and 1962, Boeing built 744 B-52s in numerous variants. During Operations ENDURING FREEDOM (Afghanistan, 2011) and IRAQI FREEDOM (2003), B-52s provided precision close air support to coalition troops. The B-52 weighs 185,000 pounds empty and 265,000 pounds loaded. It has a maximum speed of 650 miles per hour and a 55,773 foot ceiling, and its unrefueled combat radius is 4,480 miles. It has a crew of five. It can carry up to 60,000 pounds of cruise missiles, bombs, and other munitions. It is also considered an effective maritime surveillance and strike platform. A reliable aircraft that is easy to maintain and operate, the B-52 is expected to remain in service into the 2040s, giving it perhaps the longest service life of any aircraft in history.

The Rockwell B-1 resulted from the search for a new manned strategic bomber in the late 1960s. It first entered service in 1985. This swing-wing aircraft was designed to take off and land at low speed while being able to penetrate enemy air defenses at low altitude and supersonic speeds. As America's last remaining swing-wing aircraft, it participated in Operations ENDURING FREEDOM and IRAQI FREEDOM. Powered by four GE F-101 turbofan engines, the B-1B's maximum speed is 950 miles per hour, with a cruising speed of 600 miles per hour and a 60,000-foot ceiling. Unrefueled range is 7,457 miles. The B-1B has a crew of four and is usually armed with 24 2,000-pound Global Positioning Satellite (GPS)–guided bombs. The aircraft weighs 190,000 pounds empty and 477,000 pounds loaded.

The Northrop B-2 Spirit is a flying wing design. It emerged from secret studies in the mid-1970s into stealth technology, the use of shapes and materials to reduce the aircraft's visibility to enemy radar. The B-2 was originally designed to conduct nuclear strikes on the Soviet Union. With the end of the Cold War in 1991, intended production was drastically curtailed from 132 to 21 aircraft. The B-2 was given the capability to deliver conventional precision munitions.

Six B-2s served in Operation ENDURING FREEDOM in 2001, including a mission to Afghanistan that began in Missouri and lasted 44 hours. Four B-2s served in Operation IRAQI FREEDOM in 2003, dropping 583 joint direct-attack munition precision bombs. The B-2 has a maximum speed of 475 miles per hour and a 50,000-foot ceiling. Unrefueled range is 7,457 miles. The B-2 has a crew of two and carries up to 80 2,000-pound GPS-guided bombs. It weighs 100,000 pounds empty and 400,000 loaded.

Manned bombers are expected to remain an integral part of the major world air forces for the foreseeable future.

JAMES D. PERRY

See also

Aircraft, Fighters; Diego Garcia; ENDURING FREEDOM, Operation, U.S. Air Campaign; Iraq, Air Force; IRAQI FREEDOM, Operation, Air Campaign; Persian Gulf War

References

Angelucci, Enzo. *The Rand McNally Encyclopedia of Military Aircraft, 1914–1980.* New York: Military Press, 1983.

Fredriksen, John C. *International Warbirds: An Illustrated Guide to World Military Aircraft, 1914–2000.* Santa Barbara, CA: ABC-CLIO, 2001.

Fredriksen, John C. *Warbirds: An Illustrated Guide to U.S. Military Aircraft, 1915–2000.* Santa Barbara, CA: ABC-CLIO, 1999.

Aircraft, Electronic Warfare

American-led electronic warfare (EW) efforts were critical to the success of the air campaigns in Operations ENDURING FREEDOM (Afghanistan, 2001), IRAQI FREEDOM (Iraq, 2003), ODYSSEY DAWN (Libya 2011), and UNIFIED PROTECTOR (Libya, 2011), rendering enemy air defense and command and control systems ineffective. In campaigns that involved more than destroying radars, command bunkers, and communications, American EW aircraft jammed sensors and communications when required and often allowed enemy systems to operate so that allied intelligence services could glean critical information about operations and intentions. Coalition forces controlled the electronic spectrum during those conflicts and determined whose military forces could use it and when. The phrase "information dominance" characterized their superiority in the movement and use of battlefield information.

Originally developed as part of an effort to defeat large armies in the field, the concept has evolved tactically in the Global War on Terror to attack terrorist groups that have a lower reliance on and less structured use of electronics. Although America's interest and work in EW can be traced back to World War II, it was the Vietnam War (1958–1975), supplemented by lessons learned during the 1973 Yom Kippur War, that drove the United States to make

EW superiority a strategic and tactical imperative. In those wars, EW shortcomings cost aircraft and lives. Therefore, as America's involvement in the Middle East increased, EW aircraft, while not numerous, constituted a key component of its air operations.

Because air defense systems rely most heavily on the electronic spectrum, aircraft have become the most important assets in any EW operation. Jamming radars, data links, and communications systems require intimate knowledge of the equipment and their signals and how they are used. Since 2000, the United States has relied on the U.S. Air Force Boeing RC-135 and the U.S. Navy Lockheed EP-3 Shadow aircraft.

The RC-135, which is also utilized by the Royal Air Force, is based on the C-135 Stratolifter cargo plane, itself derived from the Boeing 707 commercial airframe. Its four CF-801 turbofan engines give it a top speed of 580 miles per hour and a maximum range of more than 3,450 miles. It has a 3-person flight crew and up to 27 mission personnel operating its electronic surveillance equipment. First entering service in 1964, the RC-135 has undergone a number of modifications during the years. Its latest variants are expected to remain in service through 2015.

The Lockheed EP-3 is the U.S. Navy's last remaining electronic surveillance aircraft. Derived from the P-3 antisubmarine warfare (ASW) aircraft, the land-based EP-3 Aries is a four-engine turboprop with a four-person flight crew and up to 24 operator stations. It has a maximum speed of 485 miles per hour and a range of 2,739 miles, with an on-station time of up to 14 hours. First flown in 1969, EP-3s have supported every U.S. contingency and combat operation in the Middle East from 1974 to the present. Two nine-plane squadrons remain in commission through 2014, but the EP-3 is scheduled to be replaced by the MQ-4C Broad Area Maritime Surveillance unmanned aerial vehicle by 2020.

The United States entered the 21st century with only one electronic countermeasures aircraft in service, the EA-6B Prowler, which was also the only such aircraft in Western service. In fact, the Prowler's importance to U.S. and allied air operations is best demonstrated by the fact that missions over Iraq in 2003 and Libya in 2011 were aborted if no EA-6Bs were available. Manufactured by Grumman (now Northrop Grumman Aerospace) and first entering service as an updated EA-6A in 1974, the Prowler is built around a heavily altered A-6 Intruder airframe. Its four-member crew operates a wide variety of advanced jamming and deception equipment. The control systems are operated from the cockpit, but the actual jamming/deception equipment is carried in wing pods. The pod load-out varies with the mission and targeted portion of the electromagnetic spectrum. For example, EA-6Bs operating over Iraq and Afghanistan were configured with systems that jam the frequencies over which terrorists remotely detonate improvised explosive devices. The U.S. Navy currently retains 12 four-plane EA-6B squadrons, and the U.S. Marine Corps has three such squadrons. The EA-6B is being replaced by the EA-18G Growler, with the last EA-6B slated to be completely retired by 2020.

Entering the fleet in 2009, the EA-18G is the fourth major variant of the F/A-18 family. A derivative of the F/A-18F Super Hornet, the 2-seat Growler uses high-speed computer processing and data links to provide the same EW capabilities as the EA-6B in a supersonic (Mach 1.8) platform. Its speed and 1,500-mile range enable it to accompany strikes deep into enemy territory and conduct integral or stand-off electronic jamming and other countermeasures, including air defense suppression using the high-speed antiradiation missile (HARM). The EA-18G has the ability to conduct soft or hard kills of enemy sensor and communications systems.

The first full squadron of EA-18Gs entered service in 2010. Called the Grizzly in fleet service to avoid confusion with EA-6B Prowler in radio communications, the EA-18 first saw action in 2011, participating in both Operation ENDURING FREEDOM and Operation ODYSSEY DAWN.

CARL OTIS SCHUSTER

See also

Aircraft, Bombers; Aircraft, Fighters; Aircraft, Helicopters; Aircraft, Reconnaissance, Manned, U.S.; Aircraft, Suppression of Enemy Air Defense; IRAQI FREEDOM, Operation

References

Fabey, Michael. "Growler Passes Milestone C." *Aerospace Daily,* July 19, 2007.

Gunston, Bill. *An Illustrated Guide to Spy Planes & Electronic Warfare Aircraft.* New York: Arco Publishing, 1983.

Hewson, Robert. *Jane's Air-Launched Weapons, 2001.* London: Jane's Publishing, 2002.

Jackson, Paul, et al. *Jane's All the World's Aircraft, 2005–06.* London: Jane's Publishing, 2005.

Olsen, John. *Strategic Air Power in Desert Storm.* London: Frank Cass, 2003.

Tripp, Robert. *Lessons Learned from Operation Enduring Freedom.* Santa Monica, CA: RAND Corporation, 2004.

Aircraft, Fighters

The aircraft design requirements, aerial combat tactics and air operations of today have been shaped by lessons learned from the Vietnam War and the many Middle East conflicts of the Cold War era. The latter also shaped perceptions about which manufacturers produced the most advanced and effective designs. Much of this was due to the Middle East conflicts being the primary fighter combat arena during the Cold War and in the years immediately afterward. These eventually shaped global perceptions of which superpower's doctrine and equipment was superior, and they have shaped arms market preferences ever since. However, the 21st century's early years have been noteworthy for the absence of aerial combat in the various conflicts in which the United States and its allies have entered. The primary state protagonists of the early 21st century, Afghanistan and Iraq, had few or no operational fighter aircraft in service at century's start. The nonstate actors (e.g., terrorist groups) had no aviation assets at all. This has resulted in U.S. and allied fighter aircraft being employed more in attack aircraft roles than in traditional fighter operations.

The fighters flown by the Western powers provide a wide range of aerial performance characteristics, including low-speed maneuverability and acceleration, while increasingly focusing on combat systems that have eased pilot workload and expanded awareness of the three-dimensional battle space. Improvements in computer technology and radar antenna designs have also enhanced combat systems so that such aircraft are equally capable in air-to-air and air-to-ground combat. That, combined with intensive training and a more flexible doctrine, has made Western fighters truly multirole platforms. The primary American fighter platforms of the 21st century—the General Dynamics F-16 Fighting Falcon, the McDonnell Douglas F-15 Strike Eagle, the McDonnell Douglas F/A-18 Hornet, and the Lockheed Martin F-22 Raptor—all incorporate those design features.

The Douglas F-15 and the F-16 were the high-mix replacement for the F-4 Phantom. Incorporating the lessons learned in the Vietnam War, the F-15 has the 20-mm Vulcan nose cannon that has become the standard for all U.S. fighter aircraft (F-15, F-16, F/A-18 and F-22). It also employs a lift-body design to reduce wing loading and enhance maneuverability. Its radar has both a look-up and a look-down intercept capability. It also has internal radar warning and infrared detection systems. Its two Pratt and Whitney F-100 engines provide a maximum thrust of 23,770 pounds each, giving the F-15 a top speed of Mach 2.5 and thrust to weight ratio of 1.0:1.0 when configured for an air-to-air mission. As of 2008, the F-15 has the enviable record of having downed 104 enemy aircraft without suffering a loss. In the attack role, the F-15A-D models can carry a maximum load of 16,000 pounds. F-15a are expected to remain in service to 2020.

The two-seat F-15E Strike Eagle is an enlarged F-15 with a more comprehensive electronic warfare suite. Designed to execute long-range missions without requiring an electronic warfare (EW) aircraft escort, the F-15E grew out of the requirement to replace the General Dynamics F-111 Aardvark. The F-15E employs a larger, stronger, and heavier airframe than the F-15A-D and has a greater fuel capacity. The radar is more powerful and more jamming resistant, and it can be configured for low-level terrain following missions by the flick of a switch. A second crewman was added to manage the EW equipment. It also has more powerful F-100 229 turbofans. Their 29,000 pounds of thrust each enable the Strike Eagle to achieve a top speed of Mach 2.4 and a thrust to weight ratio of 0.93:1.0 with a normal mission load. The plane's maximum ordnance load is 23,000 pounds, and it has a tactical combat radius of 1,000 nautical miles. The F-15E Strike Eagle is expected to remain in service through 2025.

General Dynamics' single-seat single-engine F-16 Fighting Falcon is the U.S. Air Force's low-mix replacement for the F-4 Phantom. The first fighter aircraft to employ fly-by-wire technology, the F-16 has evolved into a very capable multirole aircraft. Its GE F-110 turbofan generates 28,600 pounds of thrust. The plane's top speed is Mach 2.2, and its thrust to weight ratio is 1.0:1.0 when configured for air-to-air missions. The Falcon's maximum ordnance load is 17,000 pounds, and it has a tactical radius of 295 nautical miles.

The U.S. Navy/U.S. Marine Corps F/A-18 Hornet initially entered service to replace the A-7 Corsair attack aircraft. The newest of the fighter aircraft, the single-seat F-22 Raptor, incorporates stealth technologies that make this aircraft very difficult to detect and engage. The F-22 is also the world's first supersonic stealth aircraft. Even its radar is stealthy.

Designed under the U.S. Air Force's Advanced Tactical Fighter program, the twin-engine air superiority F-22 fighter entered service in 2005. Its frequency-changing AN/APG-77's radar antenna is shaped to minimize the radar cross section and its transmission signal changes more than 1,000 times a second to defeat electronic interception and identification. It employs signal coding and pulse compression to defeat jamming and facilitate target identification, respectively. Its three internal weapons bays ensure that the F-22's radar cross section remains minimal even when armed. The centerline bay carries six medium-range air-to-air missiles (AAMs) or 4,000 pounds of bombs. The two outer bays each contain one AIM-9 Sidewinder short-range AAM. However, it also has four hard points on the wings for drop tanks or up to 5,000 pounds of bombs each. Maximum ordnance load is about 12,000 pounds.

The F-22's Pratt and Whitney F-119 PW-100 turofan engines with thrust vectors provide a maximum thrust of 35,000 pounds each, giving the plane a thrust to weight ratio of 1.16:1.0 at its maximum flight weight of 64,480 pounds and almost unmatched maneuverability at any speed. It has a top speed of Mach 2.25 and a tactical radius of 410 nautical miles. The plane's electronic warning systems have also made a good signals intelligence platform. Unfortunately, maintenance and systems problems limited the F-22's early operations. The plane first saw combat in Operation INHERENT RESOLVE, the coalition effort against the Islamic State of Iraq and Syria (ISIS) in late 2014.

America's fighter aircraft were employed to great effect during Operations ENDURING FREEDOM (Afghanistan, 2001–2014), IRAQI FREEDOM (Iraq, 2003–2011), ODYSSEY DAWN and UNIFIED PROTECTOR (Libya, 2011), and INHERENT RESOLVE (Iraq and Syria, 2014–). The lack of aerial opposition freed the pilots to focus on ground-attack missions and the suppression of ground-based air defense systems.

CARL OTIS SCHUSTER

See also

Afghanistan War; Aircraft, Bombers; Aircraft, Electronic Warfare; Aircraft, Reconnaissance, Manned, U.S.; Aircraft Carriers; ENDURING FREEDOM, Operation, U.S. Air Campaign; INHERENT RESOLVE, Operation; IRAQI FREEDOM, Operation; Libyan Civil War

References

Higham, Robin D., and Stephen Harris. *Why Air Forces Fail: The Anatomy of Defeat.* Lexington: University Press of Kentucky, 2006.

Hunter, Jamie, ed. *Jane's All the World's Aircraft in Service 2013–2014.* London: Jane's Publishing, 2013.

Jackson, Paul. *Jane's All the World's Aircraft, 2007/2008.* London: Jane's Publishing, 2008.

Aircraft, Helicopters

Whether in warfare or in humanitarian pursuits, helicopters have constituted a key component of virtually every U.S. military operation since the Vietnam War (1958–1975). They give ground forces unprecedented mobility, almost regardless of terrain, and have proven critical in providing logistical support to isolated outposts. Given their importance in military operations, helicopters will remain a ubiquitous presence on America's battlefields and those of its allies for years to come.

The primary U.S. transport helicopters employed in the 21st century include the twin-rotor Boeing CH-46E Sea Knight and Boeing CH-47 Chinook and single-rotor Sikorsky CH-53D Sea Stallion and Sikorsky UH-60 Black Hawk. The U.S. military operates two attack helicopters, both single-rotor units: the U.S. Marine Corps Bell AH-1S Cobra and the U.S. Army's AH-64 Apache. Additionally, the United States has introduced a hybrid helicopter-aircraft, the twin-engine Bell MV-22 Osprey. Faster and farther ranged than traditional helicopters, it promises to revolutionize American amphibious operations.

The Sikorski CH-53E is America's longest-ranged and most powerful pure helicopter. Early models could carry up to 32 fully armed troops or lift 12,000 pounds of cargo; the latest variant, the CH-53E Super Stallion, can lift up to 16,000 pounds of cargo and transport it more than 100 nautical miles. It can also refuel in flight from Lockheed Martin KC-130 Hercules tankers, giving it almost unlimited range.

The first CH-53A Sea Stallion entered U.S. Marine Corps service in 1967, and the latest variant, the CH-53E Super Stallion, is expected to remain in use well beyond 2020. The Super Stallion's powerful lift capability has proven particularly useful in the thin air and high altitudes of Afghanistan. U.S. Air Force combat search-and-rescue and other special operations detachments employ specially modified Sikorsky HH-53 Pave Low helicopters, equipped with armor, refueling probes, and special electronic warning and countermeasures equipment as well as 7.62-mm electronic Gatling guns and other armament. U.S. Air Force transport helicopter squadrons received the standard CH-53C. The U.S. Navy modified the Sea Stallion for minesweeping, giving it the designation RH-53 (later MH-53). Like their U.S. Marine Corps counterparts, the air force and navy variants will remain in service until 2020.

The CH-46 Sea Knight has been the U.S. Navy and U.S. Marine Corps standard transport helicopter since 1964. Current models can transport up to 26 fully equipped troops or 5,000 pounds of cargo. Armament is optional but can include two M-60 7.62-mm or Browning M-2 .50-caliber machine guns. The U.S. Navy retired the last of its UH-46s in 2004, but the U.S. Marine Corps plans to retain its Sea Knights until they can be replaced by Bell Helicopter's MV-22 Osprey.

The final U.S. Marine Corps Vietnam War–era helicopter, the Bell AH-1 Cobra (models AH-1J and AH-1T thru AH-1Z Super Cobras) attack helicopter has been the backbone of that service's attack helicopter force since 1969. The Super Cobra variants presently in service have a top speed of 218 miles per hour, are equipped with a 3-barreled 20-mm cannon in a nose turret, and can carry two AIM-9 infrared-guided air-to-air missiles in addition to a normal load of

A Sikorsky UH-60 Black Hawk helicopter flies past one of former president Saddam Hussein's palaces in Tikrit, Iraq. (U.S. Department of Defense)

8 AGM-65 Maverick and AGM-114 guided air-to-surface missiles.

By 2000, the U.S. Army had five helicopters in its inventory: the Hughes OH-6 Cayuse light observation helicopter, the Bell OH-58 Kiowa reconnaissance and observation helicopter, the Boeing Ch-47 Chinook Heavy Lift and UH-60 Black Hawk transport helicopters, and the Hughes/McDonnell Douglas AH-64 Apache attack helicopter. Of these, the OH-6 was the oldest, having entered service in 1966. In the 1980s, the OH-6A was modified for special forces transport and attack and was assigned to the army's elite 160th Aviation Battalion as MD Helicopter's MH-6C Little Birds and AH-6Cs, respectively. They were still serving with the battalion during the wars in Afghanistan (2001–2014) and Iraq (2003–2011). The MH-6 can carry up to six soldiers, while the AH-6 is armed with two 7.62-mm miniguns, two .50-caliber GAU-19 machine guns, four AGM-114 Hellfire missiles, and two 70-mm rocket pods.

The OH-58 Kiowa began to replace the OH-6 in 1985. Essentially a more robust version of the venerable Bell 206 Jet Ranger, the single-rotor OH-58 was equipped with a sensor mast above its rotor so it could detect, track, and designate targets while remaining hidden below the tree line. The OH-58C was also equipped with an infrared suppression and countermeasures system. It was also the first U.S. Army helicopter to carry radar warning equipment.

The armed OH-58D Kiowa Warrior served with U.S. Army Air Cavalry units throughout the Afghanistan War and the Iraq War, where the flexibility provided by its universal weapons pod enabled local commanders to tailor its weapons load to specific missions. In addition to a minigun and a 40-mm grenade launcher, the Kiowa Warrior can carry a load of AGM-114 Hellfire missiles, two Hydra 7-tube 70-mm rocket pods, a M-296 .50-caliber machine pod, or four AIM-92 Stinger air-to-air missiles. Despite the upgrade, the helicopter's primary employment is in armed scouting and reconnaissance.

The AH-64 Apache has been the army's attack helicopter since the 1980s. The single-rotor two-seat Apache was designed originally by Hughes Aircraft, which was subsequently purchased by McDonnell Douglas. The two-person crew compartment and fuel tanks are armored against 23-mm antiaircraft fire, and the helicopter carries a 30-mm chain cannon for antitank engagements. Additionally, it is equipped with a helmet-mounted display that enables the gunner to aim its weapons by turning his head toward the target. The Apache is equipped with the Global Positioning System (GPS), electronic and infrared sensing systems, and infrared suppression and countermeasures equipment. During Operation Iraq War, the Apache went beyond its originally intended antitank role to air defense suppression, where its low-altitude all-weather capabilities and advanced electronic sensor suite enabled it to destroy key portions of Iraq's radar network. Its versatility and robustness have made it a popular weapons system. The British Army operates a license-built Westland variant, while the Dutch Air Force owns 30 Apaches, which have deployed in 6-aircraft detachments to Iraq, Djibouti, and Afghanistan.

The twin-rotor Boeing CH-47 Chinook and single-rotor Sikorsky UH-60 Black Hawk are the U.S. Army's primary cargo and troop transport helicopters. The Chinook has been in service since 1962, enjoying many upgrades during its long years of service. The CH-47D constitutes the mainstay of the U.S. Army and British Army heavy helicopter transport squadrons in 2015 and is expected to remain in service to 2020. With a maximum lift capacity of 26,000 pounds, it can transport a 155-mm howitzer, its 11-man crew, and up to 30 rounds of ammunition over 100 nautical miles in a single lift. Its navigation systems include GPS and instrumentation for all-weather flying. It has a terrain-following radar to support nap-of-the-earth flying in poor visibility.

The U.S. Air Force flies the CH-47, designated the HH-47. There is also a specially modified MH-47E serving with the army's 160th Special Operations Aviation Regiment. The MH-47E has in-flight refueling capability, infrared suppression systems, and electronic warning equipment. It has a greater fuel capacity and range than the MH-47D. Other upgraded versions, the CH-47F and MH-47G, entered production in 2007. The newest models have received upgraded avionics, more robust engine transmissions, and improved high-altitude performance as a result of lessons learned from operations in Afghanistan.

The UH-60 Black Hawk is the army's most numerous transport helicopter. A maritime variant, the Sikorsky SH-60 Sea Hawk, also serves with the U.S. Navy. The Black Hawk entered service in 1979 and replaced the UH-1 as the army's light transport helicopter by 1989. The Black Hawk can carry up to 11 passengers or 6,000 pounds of cargo slung below the fuselage. Its command and control version is designated the EUH-60C. The MH-60K and MH-60L direct-action penetrator variant equips the 160th Special Operations Aviation Regiment.

The MH-60s have in-flight refueling capabilities, special navigation systems, infrared warning, suppression and countermeasures equipment, and electronic sensor systems. The MH-60L mounts a 30-mm chain gun, an M134D minigun, and 70-mm rocket pods. U.S. Army Black Hawks saw action in both Afghanistan and Iraq. The Australia Army also employed the Black Hawk in these two wars. Black Hawks will remain the primary troop transport aircraft for the U.S. Army and the U.S. Navy through 2020.

The latest addition to America's vertical aviation fleet, the Bell/Boeing MV-22 Osprey, entered U.S. Marine Corps service in 2007 after a 26-year development process. The U.S. Air Force accepted its first Ospreys a year later, designating them the CV-22. The air force employs them in special operations squadrons, where they will replace CH-53s in the search-and-rescue role.

A hybrid design that combines the vertical flight characteristics of a helicopter with the high transit speed and long range of a turboprop aircraft, the MV-22 uses a tilt-rotor design with the engines mounted on the wing tips. For vertical operations its engines are pointed directly skyward, but they can be tilted 45 degrees for short takeoff and landing operations or horizontally for conventional landings and takeoffs as well for normal flight cruising. The MV-22 is to replace the CH-46. Each of its two Rolls-Royce Allison T406 turboshaft engines generates 6,160 horsepower. The engines are interconnected so that one engine can run both rotors in the event of an engine failure. Maximum cargo capacity is 32 fully equipped troops or 20,000 pounds of cargo internally or 15,000 pounds on an external sling. Maximum speed is 351 miles per hour, with a range of 979 miles. Armament includes up to two M2 .50-caliber or M-60 7.62-mm machine guns. Kits are being developed so the Osprey can be configured for tanker operations.

The once ubiquitous Bell/Textron UH-1 Iroquois "Huey" light utility helicopter was America's first gas turbine-powered military helicopter. Entering production in 1963, it was the army's primary troop transport helicopter during the Vietnam War but today is flown only by America's allies. Italy produced a license-built version known as the Augusta-Bell 204 that served with the North Atlantic Treaty Organization (NATO)–led International Security Assistance Force (ISAF) in Afghanistan.

The single-rotor Sikorsky SH-3 Sea King left U.S. Navy service in 2003 but, like the various UH-1 variants, soldiers on in the British and Italian navies. Its missions range from antisubmarine warfare, fleet logistics, and troop transport to search and rescue. In lieu of the normal load of dipping sonar and 1–2 Mark 46 antisubmarine torpedoes, British Sea Kings are also equipped to carry two Sea Eagle antiship cruise missiles. For combat search-and-rescue missions, the Sea King can carry an M-60 7.62-mm machine gun slung in the cargo door. The Italian and British navies plan to retire their Sea Kings by 2016.

The single-rotor Aerospatiale SA-332 Super Puma is a medium-lift transport helicopter that serves with the French military services and those of over a dozen other countries. Derived from the SA-330 Puma that entered service in 1968, the Super Puma is the French Army's primary troop transport helicopter. The U.S. Coast Guard also uses the Super Puma for search-and-rescue operations. It has more powerful engines and better avionics than the SA-330 and can carry more cargo (24 troops or 6,000 pounds of cargo). Dutch Super Pumas served in Afghanistan and Iraq through 2008. France deployed its Super Pumas to Afghanistan in 2002 as part of ISAF operations until the French withdrew in 2010.

Two Soviet-era helicopters deserve mention. The Mil Mi-8 (known as the Hip in its NATO designation) entered service in 1967 and still operates in Afghanistan and parts of East Africa. It carries up to 24 passengers or 6,600 pounds of cargo. In addition to serving in the Afghan Air Force, the Hip is often employed by leasing companies that support United Nations commands and activities in remote areas.

The Mil Mi-24 (known by its NATO reporting name of Hind) was developed to fulfill a variety of roles. Derived from the Mi-8, it entered service in 1974–1974 and combines both reduced size and increased power, providing improved maneuverability and performance. It can carry a wide variety of weapons. Its more slender fuselage makes its suitable as a gunship, although it can still accommodate a crew of four and a maximum of eight armed troops. It has a maximum speed of 208 miles per hour and range of 280 miles. The Mi-24 has a tricycle landing gear with retractable main units and a semiretractable nose unit.

The Mil-24 saw wide service during the Soviet invasion of Afghanistan (1979–1989) and the Iran-Iraq War (1980–1988) as well as a great many other world conflicts. Widely exported, a number remain in service in several dozen countries worldwide, including Afghanistan and Iraq.

Its large helicopter inventory has enabled the United States to conduct vertical envelopment operations that far exceed those of any other nation. In addition to serving as logistics carriers and troop transports, U.S. helicopters have conducted air defense suppression missions and close air support platforms during the Afghanistan War and the Iraq War. Its ability to deliver troops, equipment, and weapons quickly and directly onto an objective has made the helicopter an indispensable platform for tactical operations in the difficult terrain and complex political environment where most of today's conflicts are being fought.

Carl Otis Schuster

See also

Afghanistan War; Enduring Freedom, Operation, U.S. Air Campaign; International Security Assistance Force; Iraqi Freedom, Operation, Air Campaign; Iraq War

References

Bernstein, Jonathon. *AH-64 Units of Operation Enduring Freedom and Iraqi Freedom.* Oxford, UK: Osprey, 2005.

Hunter, Jamie, ed. *Jane's All the World's Aircraft in Service 2013–2014.* London: Jane's Publishing, 2013.

Jackson, Paul, ed. *Jane's All World Aircraft, 2001–2002.* London: Jane's Publishing, 2002.

Jackson, Paul. *Jane's All the World's Aircraft, 2007/2008.* London: Jane's Publishing, 2008.

Jackson, Robert, ed. *Helicopters: Military, Civilian and Rescue Rotorcraft.* Berkeley, CA: Thunder Bay Press, 2005.

Pretty, Ronald T. *Jane's Weapons Systems, 1972–73.* London: Jane's Publishing, 1973.

Aircraft, Reconnaissance, Manned, U.S.

Manned aircraft are some the best platforms for reconnaissance gathering, thanks to their ability to peer into or fly across international borders. Reconnaissance aircraft are capable of carrying a variety of cameras as well as sensors that can locate and record electronic emissions from various communications and intelligence sources. The United States utilized manned aircraft for these missions during its 21st-century wars while completing a transition from planes dedicated exclusively to tactical photographic reconnaissance to a system of pods that could be added to any fighter. At the same time, the United States increased its use of unmanned aerial vehicles (UAV) for reconnaissance duties.

The 1991 Persian Gulf War was the last war in which the United States employed manned aircraft variants dedicated exclusively to tactical photographic reconnaissance. The 21st century has seen the manned aircraft's reconnaissance role increasingly giving way to UAVs, particularly for imagery intelligence missions. However, manned aircraft still dominate signals and radar imaging intelligence missions. Signals intelligence collection and radar imaging are radio-frequency–intensive missions that create radio-frequency interference problems with the UAVs' control systems, or the UAVs' control frequencies are close to the signals intended to be collected. Imaging radars employ powerful pulse-compression signals and computer processing to create three-dimensional near–photographic-quality images of a target area. Signals intelligence is a critical component of electronic warfare and modern warfare's reliance on information dominance.

The oldest American aerial reconnaissance aircraft in service and perhaps the most famous such aircraft ever developed is the long-serving Lockheed U-2 Dragon Lady. The prototype first flew in 1955, and variations of the aircraft still flew in 2015. After 1994, the U.S. Air Force initiated an extensive modernization program for the U-2 series, resulting in the current designation of U2-S. The U-2 is powered by a single General Electric F-118–101 engine and has a reported speed of greater than 400 miles per hour and a range in excess of 7,000 miles. The aircraft provides photographic and imaging radar reconnaissance from very high altitudes. The U-2 has served with the U.S. Air Force in the Afghanistan War (2001–2014) and the Iraq War (2003–2011) and in North Atlantic Treaty Organization operations during the Libyan Civil War (2011) as well as in support of Combined Joint Task Force Africa and its efforts to monitor terrorist activity in East Africa. U-2s have also been involved in measuring nuclear activity and tracking radioactive pollution surrounding various countries' illicit nuclear programs and following Japan's Fukushima nuclear accident. The U-2 is scheduled for retirement as sufficient numbers of MQ-4 UAVs enter service in the 2015–2016 time frame.

At the onset of the Afghanistan War, the U.S. Navy utilized Grumman F-14 Tomcat aircraft carrying the Tactical Aviation Reconnaissance Pod System (TARPS) as its primary manned tactical photographic reconnaissance platform and the Lockheed EP-3 Orion for signals intelligence

(SIGINT) missions, while the U.S. Air Force relied heavily on the U-2 for manned photographic reconnaissance and the Boeing RC-135 in the SIGINT role.

With F-14s leaving service, the navy introduced the Shared Reconnaissance Pod (SHARP) on Boeing (McDonnell Douglas) F/A-18 Hornet aircraft as a replacement for TARPS during Operation IRAQI FREEDOM in 2003. The U.S. Air Force continued to rely on the U-2. Because of the lack of U.S. Air Force aircraft dedicated exclusively to manned tactical photographic reconnaissance, the Royal Air Force assumed an important role in these lower-level missions. In 2004, the U.S. Air Force deployed the Theater Airborne Reconnaissance System (TARS) on General Dynamics F-16 Fighting Falcon aircraft supporting ongoing military operations in Iraq.

The single-seat single-engine F-16 entered service with the U.S. Air Force in 1978 as an air superiority fighter but has evolved into a multirole aircraft. F-16s carrying SHARP reconnaissance pods took to the air over Iraq in 2003. A year later F-16s began to carry the Theater Airborne Reconnaissance System (TARS) pods. TARS is an under-the-weather system housed in a pod that is attached to the centerline underneath the aircraft. The system includes digital cameras that eliminate the need for film processing and speed the process between taking the pictures and analyzing them. A recorder housed in the pod can store more than 12,000 images.

The U.S. Navy introduced the twin-engine Boeing (McDonnell Douglas) F/A-18 Hornet to service in 1983, initially as a multirole replacement for the A-7 Corsair. It has since replaced the now retired F-14 as well. During the Iraq War, the U.S. Navy flew F/A-18s carrying SHARP. The SHARP system, developed by Raytheon and mounted in a pod underneath the aircraft, houses medium- and high-altitude cameras. The pods are capable of transmitting real-time images directly from the aircraft to a monitoring station. Although designed primarily for the F/A-18 E and F models, the pod can be carried by other aircraft.

Although UAVs increasingly dominate aerial reconnaissance in modern warfare, manned aircraft retain an important role in scenarios where SIGINT collection, radar imaging, or platform survival is the primary consideration.

TERRY MAYS AND CARL OTIS SCHUSTER

See also

Aircraft, Bombers; Aircraft, Electronic Warfare; Aircraft, Fighters; Aircraft, Tankers; ENDURING FREEDOM, Operation, U.S. Air Campaign; IRAQI FREEDOM, Operation, Air Campaign; Libyan Civil War

References

Birkler, John. *Competition and Innovation in the U.S. Fixed-Wing Military Aircraft Industry.* Santa Monica, CA: RAND Corporation, 2003.

Fredriksen, John C. *International Warbirds: An Illustrated Guide to World Military Aircraft, 1914–2000.* Santa Barbara, CA: ABC-CLIO, 1999.

Hunter, Jamie, ed. *Jane's All the World's Aircraft in Service 2013–2014.* London: Jane's Publishing, 2013.

Jackson, Paul. *Jane's All the World's Aircraft, 2007/2008.* London: Jane's Publishing, 2008.

Aircraft, Suppression of Enemy Air Defense

The advent of integrated air defense involving a vast array of surface-to-air missiles (SAMs) and antiaircraft artillery has made suppressing an enemy's air defenses a critical component of any bombing campaign, particularly during the opening phases. The basic principle is that integrating fighter-interceptors, SAMs, and antiaircraft artillery provides defense in depth and enables the air defense commander to employ his force components to comparative advantage.

Fighters engage incoming enemy aircraft either beyond the range of SAMs or, if enemy fighters are more numerous, behind the SAMs to intercept targets of opportunity. The SAMs provide general area defense, primarily against high- and medium-altitude aircraft. Antiaircraft artillery is then employed for close-in and point defense to attack low-altitude enemy bombers flying along predicted routes or those diving to lower altitudes to escape SAM intercepts.

Theoretically, an IAD forces the attacking aircraft to maneuver and evade nearly the entire time they are over enemy territory. During the Vietnam War (1958–1975), the Democratic Republic of Vietnam's IAD system inflicted heavy losses on U.S. fighter-bombers operating over North Vietnam, while Egypt's IAD nearly halted Israeli air operations during the Yom Kippur War of 1973. In both cases, integrated air defense inflicted such losses that suppression of enemy air defense (SEAD) missions now constitute nearly 30 percent of the sorties launched during an air campaign's first week and 5–10 percent of those during the remainder of a campaign. Integrated air defense also gave rise to a class of aircraft and weapons specifically designed to suppress them.

There are two methods of suppressing enemy air defenses. One is through electronic warfare (EW), often called the "soft kill" option. EW consists of jamming and deception of enemy communications networks and radars. The other means is the physical destruction or damage (i.e., "hard kill"). Aircraft engaged in hard-kill missions are known as SEAD aircraft. Typically, they are modified fighter or attack aircraft that have had their air intercept or bombing systems replaced by an onboard electronic sensor and targeting system that can detect, identify, and locate an enemy threat radar. In some cases, the aircraft simply carry wing pods with that capability. SEAD aircraft also carry antiradiation missiles designed to home in on enemy radar emissions and fly down the beam to destroy the antenna and any nearby supporting equipment.

Today, virtually every fighter, attack, and EW aircraft can carry the antiradiation missile and other armaments used to execute a hard kill of an air defense system. For example, the U.S. Navy and U.S. Marine Corps Boeing EA-18G Growler and the Northrop Grumman EA-6B Prowler aircraft and McDonnell Douglas F/A-18 Hornet are all equipped to carry and launch the high-speed antiradiation missile (HARM) used to destroy air defense radars and command systems. The aircraft operate in pairs, with the "hunter" guiding the "killer" to the target. The EA-18 included SEAD missions among its capabilities on entering service in 2010. With the retirement of the EA-6B at the end of 2014, all U.S. SEAD-capable aircraft are now supersonic.

The U.S. Air Force's McDonnell Douglas F-15E Strike Eagle can also conduct SEAD, which the U.S. Air Force calls Wild Weasel missions. However, the air force also employs two squadrons of specially designed aircraft for SEAD. Derived from the General Dynamics Block 50 F-16C that entered production in 1994, the F-16CJ is a single-seat supersonic single engine fighter that can carry the HARM targeting system in a wing pod and up to two HARMs. It first saw combat in the late 1990s but played a major role in 2003 in Operation IRAQI FREEDOM (2003–2011) and in NATO operations during the Libyan Civil War of 2011. The U.S. Air Force retained two operational and one training squadron, each with 24 aircraft, in service through 2012.

America's NATO allies also have SEAD aircraft, but Italy is the only nation that has employed its SEAD aircraft in combat operations in the 21st century. The Royal Air Force uses Panavia Tornado GR4's carrying four air-launched antiradiation missile missiles, while the Italian Air Force employs the Tornado ECR. The Tornado is a family of twin-engine aircraft jointly developed by the United Kingdom, Germany, and Italy. The Royal Air Force GR4 is a modification of the reconnaissance variant of the Tornado in which electronic targeting pods replace the normal reconnaissance systems. The two-man crew consists of a pilot and a sensor systems operator. The Royal Air Force acquired 30 GR4s, some of which are upgraded GR1s. The Italian Tornado ECR is unique in that it is the only European aircraft specifically designed for SEAD missions. First entering service in 1990, it is equipped with an emitter-locator sensor system and can carry up to four AGM-88 HARMs. Italy employed four ECRs in the NATO intervention in the Libyan Civil War of 2011.

Not all SEAD missions require aircraft specifically designed to attack enemy air defense systems. During the Persian Gulf War and the Iraq War, the United States employed Boeing AH-64 Apache helicopters firing Hellfire missiles to take out Iraqi radars located along that country's border. Then U.S. Air Force and U.S. Navy attack aircraft employed the electro-optically guided GBU-15 bombs, laser-guided Paveway bombs, and AGM-154 joint standoff weapons against air defense positions. Such weapons are quite accurate and provide the stand-off distance required to ensure the attacking aircraft's survival.

As an air campaign progresses, SEAD aircraft increasingly are used in direct support of specific strikes or to conduct area denial missions to attack any remaining air defense systems. Typically, if the early SEAD operations are successful, mobile air defense systems are all that remain after the air campaign's first week.

A nation's ability to suppress enemy air defenses may spell the difference between success and failure in an air warfare operation or campaign. More often, SEAD effectiveness determines the attackers' combat loss rate and bomber effectiveness. Even if the enemy air defenses don't down many attacking aircraft, the need to evade engaging missiles and artillery and dedicate aircraft to SEAD missions reduces the number and accuracy of the weapons delivered on target. Thus, suppressing enemy air defenses will no doubt remain a critical mission for some time to come. The development of microminiaturization and high-speed and high-capacity computer systems suggests that future SEAD missions will involve fighter, attack, or EW aircraft equipped with plug-in or pod systems and stand-off weapons. Barring development of an air defense system requiring highly detailed and unique technologies to be defeated, the days of specialized SEAD aircraft may be at an end.

CARL OTIS SCHUSTER

See also

Aircraft, Attack and Multipurpose; Aircraft, Electronic Warfare; Aircraft, Fighters; ENDURING FREEDOM, Operation, U.S. Air Campaign; IRAQI FREEDOM, Operation, Air Campaign; Libyan Civil War

References

Davies, Steve. *F-15E Strike Eagle Units in Combat, 1990–2005.* Oxford, UK: Osprey, 2005.

Gunston, Bill. *An Illustrated Guide to Spy Planes & Electronic Warfare Aircraft.* New York: Arco Publishing, 1983.

Hewson, Robert. *Jane's Air-Launched Weapons, 2001.* London: Jane's Publishing, 2002.

Jackson, Paul, et al. *Jane's All the World's Aircraft, 2005–06.* London: Jane's Publishing, 2005.

Knight, Michael, ed. *Operation Iraqi Freedom and the New Iraq.* Washington, DC: Washington Institute for Near East Policy, 2004.

Tripp, Robert. *Lessons Learned from Operation Enduring Freedom.* Santa Monica, CA: RAND Corporation, 2004.

Aircraft, Tankers

For military aircraft, fuel means range, speed, and in many cases survival. Thus, tanker aircraft—that is, fuel carrying aircraft specially designed to refuel other aircraft in midair—are considered mission essential. Aerial refueling extends the range or time on station of other aircraft and allows them to take off with a larger payload than would normally be possible. Additionally, knowing that tankers are available enables pilots to operate their aircraft at higher power settings, providing the greater speed, climb, and maneuvering characteristics that can make the difference between victory and defeat in combat.

There are two types of tanker aircraft refueling. In the first, the tanker aircraft's tail-mounted boom is guided into a receptacle on the receiver aircraft. In the other, the tanker aircraft trails a basketlike drogue on the end of a hose, and the receiver aircraft guides a probe into the drogue. Both methods are complex and require considerable training to execute safely.

Few air forces have purchased significant numbers of tankers, either because of anticipated short ranges for combat operations or because their political leaders are focused entirely on combat aircraft and have given little thought to what is required to maximize their combat aircraft's capabilities. The United States has the world's largest fleet of tanker aircraft, enabling it to extend the range and power of all aspects of its air operations from logistical transport through reconnaissance and combat sorties. There are a number of different aircraft in the U.S. tanker inventory.

The Lockheed KC-130J is a C-130 Hercules transport variant that refuels fixed-wing aircraft or helicopters via two wing-mounted drogue pods. It has four turboprops. Fuel capacity is 61,364 pounds with external tanks. The U.S.

A McDonnell Douglas F-15C Eagle undergoing in-flight refueling from a Boeing KC-135R Stratotanker. (U.S. Airforce/to/Tech. Sgt. Angelique Perez)

Marine Corps is the primary American user of the KC-130, but it is also popular among U.S. allies. The KC-130J has a cruising speed of 362 miles per hour, a ceiling of 30,000 feet, and a maximum range with external tanks of 4,920 miles. The U.S. Marine Corps KC-130s is expected to remain in service through the 2030s.

The Boeing KC-135 Stratotanker replaced the KC-97 and took its name. It is based on the Boeing 707 commercial airframe, which also became the basis for the RC-135 strategic reconnaissance and E-3A airborne warning and control system (AWACS) aircraft. The KC-135 has four turbofans and transfers up to 200,000 pounds of fuel via boom or drogue. Cruise speed is 530 miles per hour, ceiling is 50,000 feet, and range is 3,450 miles. It is scheduled to remain in service through 2040.

The McDonnell Douglas KC-10 Extender, derived from the commercial DC-10 passenger jetliner, entered service in 1981. Fifty-nine remain in service. The KC-10 can transfer up to 342,000 pounds of fuel via boom or drogue. Fifteen can provide fuel from a centerline boom and two wingtip drogue pods simultaneously. All can carry cargo and passengers as well as fuel and can be refueled themselves, extending their time on station. They have three turbofan engines. Cruise speed is 619 miles per hour, ceiling is 42,000 feet, and range is 4,400 miles. They too are expected to remain in service through 2040.

Tankers are critical to American power projection and have been heavily involved in every U.S. military operation, whether of a humanitarian or combat nature, since the 1960s. In the first three months of Operation ENDURING FREEDOM in Afghanistan (2001–2014), 60 tankers flew 13,625 sorties to support strike aircraft that often needed two refuelings each way to complete their missions. In the opening stage of Operation IRAQI FREEDOM in 2003, 319 tankers offloaded 450 million pounds of fuel in 9,700 sorties. The aerial offensive would have been very different in nature, if indeed possible at all, without aerial refueling. U.S. tankers also provided over 75 percent of the tanking missions in Operation UNIFIED PROTECTOR, the North Atlantic Treaty Organization intervention in the Libyan Civil War of 2011, and are playing a key role in Operation INHERENT RESOLVE (Iraq and Syria, 2014–present), the coalition battle against the Islamic State of Iraq and Syria (ISIS).

The British operated their own Vickers VC10 tankers. Converted from VC10 transports, the VC10 has four turbofans. Four K.3, 5 K.4, and 11 C.1K models remain in service.

The K.3 and K.4 tankers transfer fuel from three hose/drogue units (one unit in the centerline, two pods under each wing). The C.1K model has two underwing pods only. The C.1K and K.4 models transfer up to 155,000 pounds of fuel, and the K.3 transfers up to 176,000 pounds. Cruise speed is 580 miles per hour, ceiling is 38,000 feet, and range is 4,720 miles. British tankers participated in Operations ENDURING FREEDOM, IRAQI FREEDOM, and UNIFIED PROTECTOR. The Royal Air Force intends to replace 20 of its tankers by 2020, with one based on the Airbus A330–200 airframe, a large commercial jetliner.

JAMES D. PERRY AND CARL OTIS SCHUSTER

See also

ENDURING FREEDOM, Operation, U.S. Air Campaign; IRAQI FREEDOM, Operation, Air Campaign; Libyan Civil War

References

Angelucci, Enzo. *The Rand McNally Encyclopedia of Military Aircraft, 1914–1980.* New York: Military Press, 1983.
Fredriksen, John C. *Warbirds: An Illustrated Guide to U.S. Military Aircraft, 1915–2000.* Santa Barbara, CA: ABC-CLIO, 1999.
Gething, Michael, and Bill Sweetman. "Air to Air Refueling Provides a Force Multiplier for Expeditionary Warfare." *International Defence Review* (January 11, 2006): 5–11.

Aircraft, Transport

Transport aircraft move personnel, supplies, and weapons when speed is required or when ground or sea transport is impossible. Strategic airlifts use large aircraft to move troops and cargo over intercontinental distances. Tactical airlifts use smaller aircraft to move troops and cargo within a theater of operations. In 21st-century wars, the United States has been the primary user of the strategic airlift. Nations in the Middle East have tended to employ tactical airlifts.

U.S. Transport Aircraft

Airlift is essential to U.S. power projection. In fact, the United States maintains the largest air transport force in the world, numbering more than 600 aircraft, making it the only country whose air force truly has global reach. From 2001 to 2004, U.S. transports carried 464,239 tons of cargo and passengers to support Operation IRAQI FREEDOM in Iraq and Operation ENDURING FREEDOM in Afghanistan. Many Middle Eastern countries have acquired U.S. transport aircraft since 1945.

Boeing C-17 Globemaster III

The U.S. Air Force operates 150 Boeing C-17 Globemaster aircraft. Entering service in 1995, the C-17 can carry 170,900 pounds of cargo, 102 paratroops, or an armored fighting vehicle. It has four turbofan engines, a cruising speed of 517 miles per hour, a 45,000-foot ceiling, and a 2,760-mile unrefueled range.

Boeing 707–320

The four-turbofan Boeing 707-320 can transport up to 215 passengers or 63,380 pounds of cargo. It first entered service in 1958 as an airliner. It cruises at 605 miles per hour and has a 39,000-foot ceiling and a 5,755-mile range. Israel purchased 29 707-320 airliners beginning in 1973 and converted them to transports, tankers, and intelligence aircraft. Iran operates 14 707-3J9C transports acquired in the 1970s.

Boeing 747

Boeing built more than 1,400 four-turbofan 747 "Jumbo Jets" from 1970 to 2006. They serve many airlines. The 747-100 carries up to 452 passengers or 30 pallets of cargo. Cruising speed is 555 miles per hour at 35,000 feet, with a 6,100-mile maximum range. Iran operates 11 747 transports acquired in the 1970s (three converted to tankers). Saudi Arabia operates four 747s for communications and VIP transport.

Lockheed C-5 Galaxy

The U.S. Air Force operates 126 C-5 Galaxy aircraft acquired between 1969 and 1989. The C-5 can carry 270,000 pounds of cargo, including 73 passengers and a tank or armored fighting vehicle. The C-5 has four turbofan engines, a cruising speed of 500 miles per hour, a 41,000-foot ceiling, and a 2,473-mile unrefueled range.

Lockheed C-130 Hercules

Lockheed built more than 8,000 of these four-turboprop tactical transports in more than 40 variants from 1956 onward. The latest version (C-130J) carries 92 troops, 64 paratroops, 74 litters, or 42,000 pounds of cargo. The C-130J has a cruising speed of 417 miles per hour, a ceiling of 28,000 feet, and a range with maximum payload of 2,382 miles. During the Persian Gulf War, 145 C-130s operated in theater, flying 46,500 sorties and moving 209,000 personnel and 300,000 tons of supplies. In Operation IRAQI FREEDOM (2003), 124 C-130s flew 2,203 missions, moving 9,662 people and 12,444 tons of supplies.

Many foreign nations operate the C-130. Britain purchased 66 C-130K (equivalent to the C-130E) in 1966, 30 of which were "stretched" into the C-130H-30 configuration in 1980. Britain also ordered 25 C-130J planes in 1994. British

Hercules aircraft served in Operations DESERT STORM and DESERT SHIELD in 1990–1991 and in Afghanistan (2001) and Iraq from 2003 to the present. Today, 44 remain in service.

Israel acquired 13 C-130E and 11 C-130H Hercules aircraft during 1971–1976. Four C-130H serve as tankers and 2 C-130E as electronic intelligence aircraft. Egypt purchased 23 C-130H transports and 2 EC-130H electronic intelligence aircraft in 1974 and 3 C-130H-30 transports in 1990. Jordan bought 4 C-130B in 1972. Jordan also purchased 5 C-130H aircraft in 1978 that remain in service. Iran purchased 20 C-130E and 40 C-130H planes during 1965–1974. Some 15–20 remain in service. Saudi Arabia received 54 C-130E/H aircraft from 1965 to 1992. Seven C-130E, 29 C-130H, 7 KC-130H, and 5 C-130H-30 aircraft remain in service. Kuwait bought two C-130E in 1970, four C-130H-30 in 1983, and four C-130J in 2004.

The C-130E has a cruising speed of 368 miles per hour, a ceiling of 23,000 feet, and a range—with a 45,000-pound maximum payload—of 2,422 miles. The C-130H cruising speed is 374 miles per hour. Ceiling is 33,000 feet, and range with a 36,000-pound maximum payload is 2,356 miles.

The Civil Reserve Air Fleet

Forty U.S. airlines have agreed to provide airlift to the Defense Department during emergencies. This Civil Reserve Air Fleet (CRAF) numbers 1,364 aircraft, including the Boeing 707 and 747, Douglas DC-8 and DC-10, and Lockheed L-1011. CRAF flew two-thirds of the passengers and one-fourth of the cargo to Saudi Arabia during Operation DESERT SHIELD and moved 254,143 troops and 11,050 tons of cargo to Kuwait before Operation IRAQI FREEDOM.

The following American-built transports are no longer in U.S. service, but some still operate in Middle Eastern air forces.

Aero Commander

This light transport with a twin-piston engine first flew in 1948. The 690 model seated 7 to 11 passengers and had a maximum speed of 330 miles per hour, a 31,000-foot ceiling, and an 853-mile maximum range. The Iranian Air Force obtained 8 of the 500 models, 6 of the 680 models, and 15 of the 690 models in the 1970s. Some 10 of the 690 models remain in service.

Douglas C-47 Skytrain

Douglas built an astounding 10,123 Skytrains after 1935. The C-47 served with distinction in World War II. As a civilian airliner it was known as the DC-3. Some remain in service today. The C-47, with two piston engines, carries 28 troops or 6,000 pounds of cargo. Cruising speed is 207 miles per hour, with a 23,200-foot ceiling and a 2,125-mile range. Israel acquired 34 from 1948 to 1960 but retired them in 2001.

Lockheed C-141 Starlifter

The U.S. Air Force procured 284 Starlifters from 1964 to 1982, retiring the last in 2006. The C-141B carried 200 troops, 155 paratroops, 103 litters, or 68,725 pounds of cargo. With four turbofan engines, C-141 cruising speed was 500 miles per hour, ceiling was 41,000 feet, and unrefueled range was 2,500 miles.

Russian and Soviet Transports

Russia has continued the Soviet practice of employing air transports to supply its clients with weapons, ammunition, and equipment. Syria is Russia's only ally in the Middle East and has received weapons ammunition via Russian Il-76 and An-124 transport aircraft. The Soviets also sold many transports to their Middle Eastern clients during the Cold War, and a number of these remain in service to this day.

Antonov An-22

The An-22 is an enlarged twin-tail An-12. Sixty-five were produced between 1965 and 1976. Some remain in service in Russia and have been used to transport weapons and ammunition to Syria and Iran. The An-22 has four turboprops and can carry 180,000 pounds cargo and 29 passengers. Maximum speed is 460 miles per hour, with a 24,600-foot ceiling and a 3,100-mile range.

Antonov An-74

This twin-turbofan design carries 52 passengers or 10 tons cargo. Capable of short takeoff/landing from rough airfields, the An-74 has cruising speed of 440 miles per hour, a l33,136-foot ceiling, and an 2,980-mile range. Iran ordered 10 An-74TK-200 planes in 1997, and 6 remain in service as of the end of 2014.

Antonov An-124

This four-turbofan design can carry up to 150 metric tons of cargo. It has a crew of six, a top speed of 537 miles per hour, and a maximum range of 3,231 miles. Capable of taking off from unprepared or primitive airfields, it resembles the U.S. C-5 Galaxy externally but has a shorter fuselage and a larger wingspan and can carry up to 25 percent more cargo. However, the lack of pressurization in the cargo compartment has limited its passenger capacity to 88 people in a pressurized upper compartment. It is rarely used to carry passengers. Intended as a strategic lift aircraft for the defunct Soviet Union, its low operating costs and large cargo capacity have given it new lift as a leased commercial air transport. The North Atlantic Treaty Organization leased several for logistics support to its International Security Assistance Force in Afghanistan from 2003 to 2014. Production continues in both Russia and the Ukraine, with the AN-124 in wide use to move outsized cargo throughout the world, including the Middle East.

Ilyushin Il-76

Still in production, the Il-76 somewhat resembles the U.S. C-141. It has four turbofan engines and carries 88,185 pounds cargo. Cruising speed is 497 miles per hour with a 50,850-foot ceiling and a 2,265-mile range. Syria purchased four in 1980 and still flies them. Iraq bought 33 from 1978 to 1984, but most were destroyed in the 1991 Persian Gulf War. Fifteen escaped from Iraq to Iran during that war, and Iran has operated them since.

Yakovlev Yak-40

The Yak-40 has three turbofans and carried 32 passengers. It cruised at 342 miles per hour, with a 22,965-foot ceiling and a 901-mile range. Syria operated eight from 1976 onward.

Tupolev Tu-143

The twin-turbofan Tu-143B-3 carries 72 passengers. Cruising speed is 550 miles per hour, with a 39,010-foot ceiling and a 1,174-mile range. Syria operated five from 1983 onward.

Royal Air Force Transports

The Royal Air Force significantly reduced its airlift capacity after the end of the Cold War. It employed Tristar, VC10, and four leased C-17 transports to support its forces in Afghanistan and Iraq from 2001 to 2006.

Lockheed L1011 Tristar

The Royal Air Force operates nine American-built Tristars obtained between 1982 and 1989. Three C.2/2A models are pure cargo aircraft, two K.1 aircraft are tankers, and four KC.1 aircraft can switch between tanker and cargo roles. The C.2/2A transports 266 passengers, and the KC.1 in cargo mode transports 160 passengers or 44 tons of cargo. Tristars have three turbofans. Cruise speed is 605 miles per hour, ceiling is 42,000 feet, and range is 5,998 miles.

Vickers VC10

The Royal Air Force obtained 14 VC10 C.1 transports during 1966–1968. Thirteen were converted into dual-capable cargo/tanker aircraft from 1992 to 1996, and 10 remain in service. They can carry 150 passengers or 45,000 pounds of cargo. The VC10 has four turbofans. Maximum speed is 580 miles per hour, ceiling is 38,000 feet, and range is 7,210 miles.

Other Transport Aircraft

Fokker F.27 Friendship

This Dutch-built twin-turboprop plane is used worldwide. It carries 28 passengers and has a cruising speed of 300 miles per hour, a 32,600-foot ceiling, and a 912-mile range. The Iranian military obtained 19 F.27–400M and 7 F.27–600 models from 1971 to 1983. Ten remain in service.

Iran-140

This Antonov-designed twin-turboprop is built in Iran. The Iran-140 carries 60 passengers or 13,000 pounds of cargo. It has a cruising speed of 328 miles per hour, a 23,622-foot ceiling, and a 1,304-mile range. The Iranian military now operates 45 of them.

James D. Perry and Carl Otis Schuster

See also

Afghanistan War; Aircraft, Tankers; International Security Assistance Force; Iraq War; Persian Gulf War

References

Angelucci, Enzo. *The Rand McNally Encyclopedia of Military Aircraft, 1914–1980.* New York: Military Press, 1983.

Bickers, Richard Townshend. *Military Air Transport: The Illustrated History.* London: Osprey, 1998.

Donald, David. *The Complete Encyclopedia of World Aircraft.* New York: Orbis Publishing, 1997.

Williams, Nicholas M. *Aircraft of the Military Air Transport Service.* London: Midland Publishing, 1999.

Aircraft Carriers

Naval airpower has played an important role in the Middle East over the past decades. Although U.S., British, and French aircraft carriers played important roles throughout the second half of the 20th century, discussion here is limited to their roles in Operations Enduring Freedom and Iraqi Freedom and Operation Unified Protector (North Atlantic Treaty Organization operations during the Libyan Civil War). All these operations saw extensive naval involvement, including naval airpower.

The U.S. Navy Nimitz-class aircraft carrier *John C. Stennis*, conducting operations in the Arabian Sea on February 21, 2007. (U.S. Navy)

French and American aircraft carriers were traditional large-deck or conventional takeoff and landing (CTOL) carriers. That is, these aircraft were launched and recovered (landed on the carrier) by traditional or conventional means (e.g., steam-powered catapults for launch and recovered by using an arresting wire to stop the plane within the flight deck's length.) The advantage of the system is that it enables the carrier to handle high-performance aircraft. The disadvantage is that it requires a large and expensive ship to do it. The French nuclear-powered CTOL carrier displaces more than 40,000 tons and carries a 40-plane air wing, while U.S. aircraft carriers typically displacc 104,000 tons full load (the Nimitz class) and have an air wing of up to 90 aircraft.

Other allied nations deployed smaller vertical/short takeoff and landing (VSTOL) carriers, displacing under 30,000 tons, with air wings of under 25 helicopters and lower-performance McDonnell Douglas/BAE/Boeing AV-8 Harrier VSTOL aircraft. Although their striking power is less than that of their CTOL counterparts, the VSTOL carriers are ideally suited for sea control and sanctions enforcement missions in support of naval operations before and during the outbreak of hostilities.

The United States entered the 21st century with only one conventionally powered aircraft carrier in service, USS *Kitty Hawk* (CV-63). Displacing a little over 82,000 tons and commissioned in 1956, it embarked 76 aircraft and participated in Operations ENDURING FREEDOM and IRAQI FREEDOM. It was decommissioned in 2008. The bulk of the U.S. Navy aircraft carriers supporting Operations IRAQI FREEDOM and ENDURING FREEDOM and all those supporting UNIFIED PROTECTOR were nuclear-powered Nimitz-class units. At more than 90,000 tons displacement, their greater size enables them to carry a larger crew (approximately 6,500 total personnel) and more aircraft (90 versus 72–76) than the older carriers. They are powered by two nuclear reactors, giving them a top speed exceeding 34 knots.

In addition to their air wings, U.S. Navy carriers have extensive command, control, communications, computer, and intelligence (C4I) systems. These systems and their tactical flag command centers enable them to act as fleet flagships: a floating headquarters for a joint task force commander. The combination of ship's sensors, AWACS aircraft, and the capacity to integrate inputs from national and other service component assets enable these ships to monitor the battle space around them out to nearly 400 nautical miles. One improvement introduced with the Gerald Ford class (CVN-78, commissioned on November 9, 2013) is electromagnetic pulse catapults. Less maintenance intensive and more powerful, compact, and energy efficient than the steam catapults they replace, their reliance on electricity also reduces ship construction costs and frees up space and weight for other purposes.

Following the September 11, 2001, terrorist attacks on the United States, the U.S. Navy deployed three carriers for Operations ENDURING FREEDOM: the *Enterprise* (CVN-65), *John C. Stennis* (CVN-70), and *Theodore Roosevelt* (CVN-71). They conducted long-range strike operations as part of the coalition strategic and operational air campaign throughout the fighting in Afghanistan and during Operation IRAQI FREEDOM in 2003, but no U.S. aircraft carriers participated in Operation UNIFIED PROTECTOR.

Italy and France provided aircraft carriers in support of the related coalition naval operations. Italy deployed its 14,000 VSTOL carrier *Garibaldi* for Operations IRAQI FREEDOM and UNIFIED PROTECTOR. Commissioned in 1985, it can carry an air wing of 16 aircraft, usually an equal mix of AV-8 Harriers and helicopters. It is also equipped with 8 OTOMAT long-range antiship cruise missiles and 48 Aspide short-range surface-to-air missiles as well as three 40-mm Oto Melara automatic cannon. A sonar suite and antisubmarine torpedo tubes round out its nonaviation armament. Additionally, it can embark a commando company and related helicopter contingent in lieu of a typical air wing. The *Garibaldi*'s primary role in both operations was sea control, a mission for which it was ideally suited. Its Harrier aircraft also proved to be useful quick-response attack assets.

France deployed its nuclear-powered aircraft carrier *Charles De Gaulle* during the early days of Operations ENDURING FREEDOM and UNIFIED PROTECTOR. Commissioned in May 2001 and displacing 43,000 tons at full load, it is the world's only non-U.S. nuclear-powered aircraft carrier and the largest European aircraft carrier. Its two 30-milliwatt nuclear reactors' power steam turbines drive two propellers, giving it a top speed of 27 knots. However, the reactors have proven troublesome, often causing the ship to terminate operations early. It has two steam catapults and can carry an air wing of up to 40 aircraft. Its defensive armament includes eight 20-mm close-in weapons systems and four 8-cell and two 6-cell surface-to-air missile launchers. Many observers

believe that this carrier will be eclipsed by the Royal Navy's Queen Elizabeth–class carriers that are expected to enter service by 2019. With an expected displacement exceeding 60,000 tons, they are expected to have four catapults and embark an air wing of 60–72 aircraft. Current plans call for France to receive the second unit or the two countries will share the ship, rotating crews as required.

Although some observers believe that the day of the aircraft carrier is at an end, the fact that four nations have six units under construction as of the end of 2014 suggest that they will be in service for the foreseeable future.

CARL OTIS SCHUSTER

See also

IRAQI FREEDOM, Operation, Coalition Naval Forces; Libyan Civil War; United States Navy, Afghanistan War; United States Navy, Iraq War

References

Holmes, Tony. *U.S. Navy Hornet Units of Operation Iraqi Freedom*, Parts 1–2. Oxford, UK: Osprey, 2004, 2005.

Network Centric Warfare in the U.S. Navy's Fifth Fleet: Task Force 50 during Operation Enduring Freedom. Washington, DC: Center for Naval Analysis, 2003.

Saunders, Stephen, ed. *Jane's Fighting Ships, 2004–2005*. London: Jane's Information Group, 2005.

Air Defenses in Iraq, Iraq War

Before the U.S.-led invasion of Iraq in March 2003, the Iraqi air defense system was a major concern for coalition planners. The system included elements of the defenses used in the 1991 Persian Gulf War, during which 39 coalition aircraft were downed. Overall, however, the Iraqi air defenses proved to be largely ineffectual in the Persian Gulf War, and the coalition achieved rapid and complete air supremacy. The Iraqi air defense system was badly degraded by damage in 1991, an ongoing arms embargo, and continued sporadic attacks by U.S. and British aircraft over more than a decade of enforcing the no-fly zones.

Following the 1991 Persian Gulf War, the arms embargo on Iraq made it difficult for Saddam Hussein to replace weapons that had been destroyed in the fighting or had become outmoded. Iraq's air defenses continued to be based on the Soviet model, with radar and observers providing information to a central command in real time. The central commanders were then able to determine the best mix of surface-to-air missiles (SAMs), antiaircraft artillery (AAA), and fighter aircraft to deal with the threat. The system was known as Kari, French for "Iraq" spelled backward. The system employed technology from the 1980s and had been developed by French companies. Computers and equipment came from both European and Soviet sources.

Iraq's central National Air Defense operations center was located in central Baghdad. It received data from four independent Sector Operations Centers (SOCs), which covered different parts of Iraq. The first sector, headquartered at Taji Military Camp in northern Baghdad, covered central and eastern Iraq as well as the capital. This SOC controlled most of the SAMs and AAA. Prior to 2003, many weapons had been removed from other parts of Iraq and concentrated in the capital area. The region included the most sensitive targets, such as presidential palaces and factories where weapons of mass destruction could be produced. The SOC also controlled many individual radar sites and an electronic countermeasures unit.

The second SOC covered western Iraq, including the Jordanian and Syrian borders. The third SOC was headquartered near Talil Air Base and covered southern Iraq. This SOC was most often in action against allied aircraft covering the southern no-fly zone. The fourth SOC was based near Kirkuk and covered the northern part of the country. Its SAM batteries engaged aircraft in the northern no-fly zone.

A separate SOC was also established during the 1990s in Baghdad. It was controlled by the Republican Guard and was armed with some of the most modern SAMs available. Other lightweight SAMs were employed by Republican Guard and regular Iraqi Army units and were not integrated into the Kari system. Instead, these weapons were individually aimed and posed a deadly threat to coalition aircraft, especially those flying at low altitudes and relatively slow speeds. These weapons shot down a number of allied helicopters during the March 2003 invasion.

Most radar used by the Iraqis had been supplied by the Soviets, although some French, Italian, and Chinese radars had been integrated into the system. Different sets included such surveillance radars as the Soviet P-15 Flat Face (NATO designation) or P-15M(2) Squat Eye and the French Thompson-CSF Volex, which were not mobile. Other radars included target tracking and guidance radars, which were usually mounted on vans or trailers and could be moved to avoid coalition targeting. Some jamming and electronic countermeasure equipment was also available, along with thermal imaging telescopes and laser range finders that coalition countermeasures could not block. Even so, most of the equipment in 2003 was the same that had been in place in 1991.

Most of the SAMs available to Saddam Hussein's forces were introduced during the 1950s and 1960s. Some SA-2s

and SA-3s were built by Iraqi factories, but most sources of missile replacements were cut off after the Persian Gulf War in 1991. More recent area defense SAMs included the SA-6, SA-8, SA-9, SA-13, and a few French-made Roland VIIs. While some had been upgraded since 1991, most remained obsolete. The SAMs were supplemented by over 4,000 antiaircraft guns ranging in size from 12.7-mm to 57-mm. Fighter aircraft from the Iraqi Air Force played little role in Iraq's air defenses.

During the 1991 Persian Gulf War, the coalition had attacked Kari's communications nodes. Since then, the Iraqis had improved communications with greater use of optical fiber links, along with continued use of underground bunkers to protect command and communication nodes.

Following the Persian Gulf War, the United States, Great Britain, and France established no-fly zones in southern and northern Iraq. Fighter planes patrolled these areas to prevent Iraqi aircraft from attacking Kurd and Shiite dissidents. After losing several fighters to the allies in 1992 and 1993, the Iraqi Air Force no longer sent aircraft to challenge the patrols. However, the Iraqi Air Defense Command periodically harassed allied patrols with SAM attacks, especially after Operation DESERT FOX in 1998. For the next five years, Iraq's radar and missile sites targeted allied aircraft and tried to shoot them down. In response, allied aircraft were allowed to respond with missiles and bombs. When the Iraqis learned to position their SAMs in population centers, the allies responded with attacks on fixed air defense installations, such as radar sites or communication centers.

Denied access to new technology, the Iraqis developed tactics to improve their chances against allied aircraft. By observing Serbian tactics in Kosovo that brought down several U.S. aircraft, they learned how to quickly turn radars on and off to prevent allied countermeasures from locking on while still allowing a quick launch by SAMs. The Iraqis also improved their use of decoys and hidden deployment of weapons. More incidents of Iraq launching missiles and using radar to lock onto allied aircraft were reported after 1998.

Hussein encouraged attacks on allied aircraft by offering $5,000 to any unit that shot down a U.S. aircraft and $2,500 to any soldier who captured a downed pilot. In response, however, the allies began to target air defense targets in the no-fly zones more intensively, especially from late 2001 to early 2003. Although the number of Iraqi provocations declined, the number of air attacks on air defense sites increased dramatically during that time. In September 2002, for example, a raid by over 100 U.S. aircraft on air defense sites in western

Iraq was not intended to protect aircraft patrolling the no-fly zone. Instead, it opened the way for U.S. special forces to fly from Jordan into northern Iraq. By the time U.S. and British forces moved into Iraq on March 20, 2003, Iraqi air defenses had already been seriously degraded.

The allies took Iraqi air defenses seriously during Operation IRAQI FREEDOM. The main targets of the early air strikes were the command centers in Baghdad. Tactics were similar to those used in 1991. Stealth aircraft and cruise missiles made up the first wave, to weaken air defenses at little risk to pilots. Extensive use of drones forced the Iraqis to turn on their radars, allowing allied aircraft to destroy them. Although the Iraqis fired over 1,660 radar-guided SAMs during the invasion, they failed to down any allied aircraft. Another 1,224 AAA incidents involving centrally controlled Iraqi batteries were reported by the allies, with no effect as well. A complete lack of involvement by Iraqi fighters pleasantly surprised the allies. Most Iraqi Air Force aircraft were hidden in residential or agricultural areas to prevent their destruction. After the first few days of the operation, strategic air defenses declined in activity. Allied suppression missions and the lack of SAMs had done their job.

The most effective Iraqi air defenses during the war were the individually aimed SAMs and AAA. These weapons were locally controlled and were most effective against low-altitude targets. On March 24, for example, the U.S. Army 11th Aviation Brigade attacked the Republican Guard Medina Mechanized Division deep behind Iraqi lines. One McDonnell Douglas/Boeing AH-64D Apache was shot down, and 33 were so badly shot up that they were rendered unserviceable for some time. A total of 7 U.S. aircraft were shot down by locally controlled Iraqi air defenses.

In the end, Iraq's air defenses in 2003 were far too obsolete and limited to prevent the allies from striking at targets that they were determined to hit. Even so, however, the Iraqi defenses in certain areas, such as around Baghdad, were so dense that they continued to pose a threat to low-flying allied aircraft until the collapse of Hussein's regime. All of the aircraft lost to Iraqi defenses were helicopters or ground attack aircraft, indicating that determined Iraqi defenders remained dangerous.

TIM J. WATTS

See also
Antiaircraft Guns; Antiaircraft Missiles, Iraqi; IRAQI FREEDOM, Operation, Air Campaign; Missiles, Surface-to-Air

References
Cordesman, Anthony H. *The Iraq War: Strategy, Tactics, and Military Lessons.* Westport, CT: Praeger, 2003.
Keegan, John. *The Iraq War: The Military Offensive, from Victory in 21 Days to the Insurgent Aftermath.* New York: Vintage, 2005.
Ripley, Tim. *Air War Iraq.* Barnsley, UK: Pen and Sword, 2004.

AirLand Battle Doctrine

In the development of military doctrine, victory in war is usually followed by a period of complacency and stagnation, while defeat spurs a period of critical self-examination and robust internal debate that often leads to dramatic doctrinal innovations. This was true for the United States following the Vietnam War. For the U.S. military, the trauma of the loss in Vietnam was compounded by the unexpected lethality of modern weapons witnessed in the short but violent 1973 Yom Kippur (Ramadan) War. That in turn led to an increasing recognition that the North Atlantic Treaty Organization (NATO) could not rely on battlefield nuclear weapons to offset the overwhelming numerical advantage of the Warsaw Pact in any future war on the European continent.

Working through the problem, American military thinkers identified two types of wars that the United States could face in the future: a heavy mechanized war in Europe or a light infantry war in some other part of the world. Although the mechanized war in Europe was the least likely scenario, it was also the most dangerous. U.S. military doctrine had to be revised to be able to defeat America's strongest and most dangerous enemy.

Initially, the sights of the American military were fixed at the tactical level—"Win the First Battle"—with little consideration beyond that. There also was recognition that the next major conflict would be a "Come as You Are War." Under the direct guidance of General William E. DePuy, the first commander of the newly established U.S. Army Training and Doctrine Command (TRADOC), the initial expression of this doctrinal rethinking was the 1976 edition of *FM 100-5, Operations.* The new manual introduced the notion of active defense, a highly questionable substitute for the tested defensive concepts of mobile defense and defense in depth. In focusing on the lethality of modern weapons, the new doctrine stressed the effects of firepower by devoting the preponderance of space to a discussion of its effects. The new *FM 100-5* did not ignore maneuver, but it did relegate that element of combat power to the mere function of movement to deliver firepower rather than gain positional advantage.

The 1976 edition of *FM 100-5* was wildly controversial even before it had been fully distributed to the field. The critics of DePuy's doctrine rejected it as too mechanical, too dogmatic, and too mathematically deterministic. Nonetheless, DePuy's efforts were a major contribution to the post–Vietnam War U.S. Army, because for the first time in many years, officers were again thinking and writing about doctrine. The resulting debate fueled a renaissance in American military thinking.

The immediate reactions to the 1976 edition resulted in the notion of follow-on forces attack, which in turn led to recognition of the operational depth of the battlefield. That led directly to the final acceptance by the American military and NATO of the concept of the operational level of war, as distinct from the tactical or the strategic. The Soviets had formally recognized this level of warfare as early as the 1920s and had aggressively worked to define and expand the theory of operational art ever since. The West had long rejected the concept as little more than yet another crackpot element of Marxist thinking, but the Soviets had been right all along on this point.

The principal guiding force behind the development of AirLand Battle Doctrine was General Donn A. Starry, who assumed command of TRADOC in July 1977. Working directly under Starry, Major General Donald R. Morelli, TRADOC's deputy chief of staff of doctrine, closely supervised the team of doctrine writers, which included Lieutenant Colonels Leonard D. Holder, Huba Wass de Czega, and Richard Hart Sinnerich. Classical German military thought had a great deal of influence on the development of the new doctrine. Even in the 1976 edition of *FM 100-5,* General DePuy had instructed the doctrine writers to study carefully the current capstone doctrinal manual of the West German Bundeswehr. That manual, *HDv 100/100, Truppenführung* (Command and Control in Battle), was based closely on the manual of the same name first introduced in 1932 with which the German Army fought World War II. Through the influence of the German manual, such standard German doctrinal concepts as *Auftragstaktik* (mission orders) and *Schwerpunkt* (center of gravity) became firmly embedded in American military thinking. Another major influence that was specifically mentioned in that edition was Basil Liddell Hart's book *Strategy,* one of the most important books written about the indirect approach in warfare.

The 1982 edition of *FM 100-5* marked the U.S. military's first formal recognition of the operational level of war and introduced the concepts of AirLand Battle and Deep Battle. AirLand Battle doctrine took a nonlinear view of combat. It enlarged the battlefield area, stressing unified air and ground operations throughout the theater. It recognized the nonquantifiable elements of combat power and restressed that maneuver was as important as firepower. Most significantly, the doctrine emphasized the human element of war, "courageous, well-trained soldiers and skillful, effective leaders." An undercurrent to this last theme, of course, was the fact that the United States had only recently abolished conscription and was then in the process of building an all-volunteer professional army. The AirLand Battle doctrine identified the keys to success in war, which included indirect approaches, speed and violence, flexibility and reliance on the initiative of junior leaders, rapid decision making, clearly defined objectives and operational concepts, a clearly designated main effort, and deep attack.

Depth was one of the keys. A commander had to fight and synchronize three simultaneous battles: close, deep, and rear. The deep battle, of course, would be the enemy's rear battle, and vice versa. A well-coordinated attack deep in an enemy's rear area might in fact prove decisive. This marked the first recognition in American military doctrine that the battle might not necessarily be decided along the line of contact.

One of the most controversial features of the 1976 edition of *FM 100-5* had been the elimination of the venerable Principles of War, first adopted by the U.S. Army in the early 1920s. The 1982 edition restored the Principles of War but then went one step further by introducing the Four Tenets of AirLand Battle: initiative, depth, agility, and synchronization. Initiative is the ability to set the terms of the battle by action and was identified as the greatest advantage in war. Depth has components of time, space, and resources. Agility is the ability to act faster than the enemy to exploit his weakness and frustrate his plans. Synchronization ensures that no effort will be wasted, either initially or as operations develop.

Some critics complained that the Four Tenets of AirLand Battle were unnecessary additions to the Principles of War or were ultimately an attempt to replace them. But as other analysts pointed out, the Four Tenets were for the most part combinations of two or more of the Principles of War. Synchronization, for example, combined economy of force and unity of effort. Initiative combined offensive, maneuver, and surprise.

The 1982 *FM 100-5* was a major milestone in American military thought, but it was far from a perfect document. After its release to the field the debate continued, and the doctrine writers continued to refine the document. The 1986 edition of *FM 100-5* contained no significant changes or innovations, but it presented a far better discussion of the doctrine and corrected some of the minor errors in the 1982 edition. Some errors still remained, however. The 1986 edition used the German concept of *Schwerpunkt* interchangeably as either the center of gravity or the decisive point. As defined originally by 19th-century Prussian military strategist Carl von Clausewitz, however, the center of gravity and the decisive point (*Entscheidungsstelle*) were two distinct and separate concepts. The confusion was not corrected until the 1993 edition of *FM 100-5*, which stated clearly that "Decisive points are not centers of gravity, they are the keys to getting at the centers of gravity."

NATO never fully embraced the AirLand Battle doctrine, and ironically neither did the U.S. Air Force. In any event, the new doctrine never had to be used in an actual war against the Warsaw Pact on the plains of Northern Europe. AirLand Battle, however, greatly concerned the Soviets and was just one more element of pressure in the 1980s that eventually contributed to the collapse of the Soviet Union. The overwhelmingly successful prosecution of the Persian Gulf War (Operation DESERT STORM) in 1991 was based on the 1986 edition of *FM 100-5*, which was arguably the single best official articulation of American war-fighting doctrine ever published.

The 1993 edition of *FM 100-5* actually shifted the emphasis away from operations and conventional war fighting toward strategy and operations other than war. Even the term "AirLand Battle" was dropped in favor of "Army Operations," but that was more the result of bureaucratic infighting between the U.S. Army and the U.S. Air Force. A new edition of *FM 100-5* in 1998 was supposed to shift the emphasis back to operational art, but the final coordinating draft caused considerable internal controversy. The new manual was finally issued in June 2001, under a new numbering system, as *FM 3-0 Operations*. Although the term "AirLand Battle" is no longer officially in use, the U.S. Army continues to train and operate in accordance with its principles, and its precepts were used again during the initial invasion of Iraq in 2003 during Operation IRAQI FREEDOM.

DAVID T. ZABECKI

See also

IRAQI FREEDOM, Operation; United States Air Force, Iraq War; United States Army, Iraq War

References

Naveh, Shimon. *In Pursuit of Military Excellence: The Evolution of Operational Theory.* London: Frank Cass, 1997.

Nomjue, John L. *From Active Defense to AirLand Battle: The Development of Army Doctrine, 1973–1982.* Fort Monroe, VA: United States Army Training and Doctrine Command, 1984.

Zabecki, David T., and Bruce Condell, eds. and trans. *Truppenführung: On the German Art of War.* Boulder, CO: Lynne Rienner, 2001.

Ajuba, Nigeria, Mall Bombing (June 25, 2014)

Bombing of an upscale shopping mall by Boko Haram insurgents in Wuse, a well-to-do suburb of Nigeria's capital, Ajuba, on June 25, 2014. The bombing resulted in 21 deaths and wounded at least 60 others. The explosion seemed purposely timed to inflict maximum casualties. It occurred close to rush hour, when the mall was quite busy; at the same time, many Nigerians inside the mall had begun congregating around large-screen televisions, which were about to begin showing a World Cup soccer match between Nigeria's national team and that of Argentina.

Several witnesses claimed that someone on a motorcycle or power scooter had left a parcel close to the epicenter of the blast and then fled. The bomb blast was so powerful that only body parts of those killed remained. Immediately after the explosion, security guards and Nigerian police apprehended a suspect near the scene of the crime attempting to escape on a motorized bike; he was shot and killed. A second suspect was later taken into custody and questioned, but Nigerian authorities have remained tight-lipped about their investigation.

Although Boko Haram did not take direct credit for the bombing, most authorities presume that the radical Islamist group was behind the attack. Indeed, the mall bombing fit a predictable pattern of such attacks, which Boko Haram had begun as early as 2008. In April 2014 alone, two separate bombings in Abuja attributed to Boko Haram killed or wounded scores of people.

Established in 2002, Boko Haram has engaged in a bloody insurgency chiefly in northeastern Nigeria but also in portions of Cameroon, Chad, and Niger. Over the last half dozen years, it has engaged in a steadily accelerating and expanding campaign of terrorism and violence. The group hopes to rid society of all traces of Western influence and create an Islamic state in Nigeria based strictly on sharia law. In recent years Boko Haram, which is a largely decentralized organization that lacks a strong chain of command, has been led by Abubakar Shekau and Momodu Bama.

Boko Haram is uncompromising in its beliefs and goals and has bombed or attacked government facilities, Christian churches and organizations, schools, malls and marketplaces, and police stations. It has also engaged in the abduction of Westerners and Nigerian schoolchildren and has assassinated Islamic leaders believed to have been co-opted by the Nigerian government. The group also employs child soldiers and suicide bombers. It should be noted that the vast majority of Nigeria's Muslim population does not support Boko Haram and is fiercely critical of its tactics. Nigeria is almost evenly divided between Muslims, who predominate in the north, and Christians, who are most numerous in the south.

The organization is strongest in Nigeria's northeastern states, where the government has declared a state of emergency. The Nigerian government has claimed to be winning the war against Boko Haram, but in reality it has had little success in suppressing Boko Haram or its activities, which became ever bolder during 2014 and into 2015. Between 2002 and the end of 2013, it is estimated that more than 10,000 people died in violence perpetrated by Boko Haram; another 90,000–100,000 people were internally displaced. The violence in Abuja was particularly troubling because it seemed to indicate that Boko Haram was becoming more active in central Nigeria.

In the days after the Abuja bombing, Nigerian security forces raided two Boko Haram camps, in the process killing at least 100 Islamic militants. Both raids occurred in the northeastern portion of Nigeria.

PAUL G. PIERPAOLI JR.

See also
Boko Haram; Sharia

References
"Nigeria: Abuja Bomb Blast in Wuse District Kills 21."
    BBC News, June 25, 2014, http://www.bbc.com/news/
    world-africa-28019433.
"Nigeria Militant Camps Raided after Abuja Bombing Killed 21."
    Bloomberg, June 27, 2014, http://www.bloomberg.com
    /news/2014-06-27/nigeria-militant-camps-raided-after
    -abuja-bombing-killed-21-1-.html.
Pham, J. Peter. "Boko Haram's Evolving Threat." Africa Security
    Threat, April 2012, http://africacenter.org/wp-content
    /uploads/2012/04/AfricaBriefFinal_20.pdf.

Alec Station

U.S. government–sanctioned Central Intelligence Agency (CIA) unit charged with the mission of hunting down and capturing or killing Al Qaeda leader Osama bin Laden. In late 1995 two members of the William J. Clinton administration, National Security Advisor Anthony (Tony) Lake and National Coordinator for Counterterrorism Richard Clarke, met with the head of the CIA's Counterterrorism Center (CTC) to discuss the need for a unit to concentrate solely on bin Laden. Soon afterward, CIA director George Tenet approved just such a unit. The plan called for Alec Station to run for only a couple of years before merging completely with the CTC, but as bin Laden became a greater and greater threat, Alec Station continued its operations for more than a decade.

When the CIA began Alec Station on January 8, 1996, bin Laden was mostly known as a financier of terrorism. Soon afterward it became apparent that he had declared open warfare against the United States and its allies, and the campaign against him was then stepped up. Michael Scheuer, a veteran CIA agent, was placed in charge of the program when it was founded. Although the formal title of the program was the Usama Bin Laden Issue Station, it soon took the name Alec Station, after Scheuer's adopted Korean son, Alec.

Alec Station functioned as a subunit of the CIA's CTC. Sponsors of this program set it up as an interagency unit running agents from both the CIA and the Federal Bureau of Investigation (FBI). The plan was for this unit to fuse intelligence disciplines into one office that included operations, analysis, signals intercepts, overhead photography, and covert action.

As the unit developed, its strength lay in analysis. It began as a small unit with a staff of only about 15 analysts, mostly young women. Alec Station, not considered a choice assignment, was a low-profile operation and was at first housed outside Langley, Virginia, until it moved to the CTC.

By 1998 Scheuer was convinced that bin Laden posed an ongoing danger to the United States but had difficulty convincing his superiors, partly because of his difficult personality; he managed to alienate even those who agreed with him. After learning that bin Laden had attempted to acquire nuclear materials, Scheuer had difficulty convincing his superiors to accept the information and use it to inform others in the government. Scheuer, believing that bin Laden constituted a clear and present danger, became increasingly frustrated by the lack of action taken toward the Al Qaeda leader.

Scheuer also had difficulties with the FBI. Although Alec Station had been set up as an interagency operation, the FBI often refused to share information with the CIA. The most intransigent member of the FBI in this regard was John O'Neill, the FBI's top counterterrorism expert. O'Neill possessed a notebook captured from an Al Qaeda operative that he refused for a year to turn over to Alec Station. In another instance, an FBI agent was caught raiding CIA files with the intent of taking their contents back to the FBI. Scheuer claimed that Alec Station sent 700–800 requests for information to the FBI but never received answers to any of them.

Alec Station planned to capture bin Laden after he moved to Afghanistan in May 1996. For the first time the CIA knew where bin Laden and his family lived, in the Tarnak Farm compound 12 miles outside Kandahar. Beginning in 1997, plans were made with Afghan tribal leaders to kidnap bin Laden and take him to an Arab country or the United States for trial. The CIA even staged four rehearsals for the operation in late 1997 and early 1998. Then on May 29, 1998, Tenet, the head of the CIA, called off the operation. Scheuer's reaction was swift. He complained that the CIA had enough intelligence against bin Laden and Al Qaeda to eliminate both, and he could not understand why the U.S. government had failed to take the chance to do so. The Clinton administration responded that it feared collateral damage and any negative publicity that might follow a less than perfect operation.

It was only after the bombings on August 7, 1998, of the two U.S. embassies in Tanzania and Kenya that the attention of the Clinton administration was redirected toward bin Laden. This resulted in the August 20, 1998, U.S. missile attacks on an Al Qaeda training camp in Afghanistan near Khost and on the El Shifa pharmaceutical plant in Khartoum, Sudan, in which 79 Tomahawk cruise missiles were fired from U.S. Navy ships in the Arabian Sea. However, warnings from Pakistani sources likely made certain that bin Laden escaped the missiles, and the Sudanese plant proved to be a harmless pharmaceutical factory. Several other plans were made to either capture or kill bin Laden, but they were cancelled each time because of one difficulty or another. Most cancellations were caused by a lack of confidence in intelligence sources and information.

The most promising opportunity came in February 1999. CIA agents learned that bin Laden was going to join a number of sheikhs from the United Arab Emirates at a desert hunting camp in Helmand Province, Afghanistan. Satellite pictures identified the camp on February 9. CIA operatives confirmed bin Laden's presence and requested a missile strike. Over the next several days the Clinton administration debated a missile strike before learning that members of the United Arab Emirates royal family were also present at the camp. Because of foreign policy complications with the United Arab Emirates (a provider of gas and oil

supplies) nothing happened, and Scheuer was furious. His e-mails expressing his unhappiness traveled around government circles.

Tenet removed Scheuer from his position as head of Alec Station in the spring of 1999. The CIA claimed that Scheuer's inability to work with superiors and the FBI led to his dismissal. His critics within the agency claimed that he had a vendetta against bin Laden. CIA analysts at Alec Station blamed O'Neill for the firing of Scheuer because the dispute had reached the level of the agency heads of the CIA and FBI. Scheuer's replacement was a key assistant on Tenet's staff and a Middle East specialist, but he lacked Scheuer's drive. By this time, Alec Station had grown from 12 analysts to 25. Most of these analysts were women, something that hurt their credibility in the male-dominated CIA. There was also a feeling in the CTC that others in the CIA ridiculed members of Alec Station for their zeal in tracing the actions of bin Laden.

The status of Alec Station became more precarious after September 11, 2001. Some of the criticism directed against the CIA for failing to uncover the September 11 plot descended on Alec Station, and Scheuer reappeared as a senior analyst at the station after September 11. Members of Alec Station adamantly insisted that little if any connection existed between Iraqi dictator Saddam Hussein and Al Qaeda, something they communicated to Tenet. However, this stance made them enemies in the George W. Bush administration, which wanted the CIA to provide justification for the invasion of Iraq and the overthrow of Hussein. Those in the CIA who opposed the invasion became administration enemies. Personnel were soon transferred out of Alec Station until only 12 analysts remained. Scheuer protested this action, resigning from the CIA on November 12, 2004. Not long afterward, the CIA disbanded Alec Station entirely.

STEPHEN E. ATKINS

See also

Al Qaeda; Bin Laden, Osama; Bush, George Walker; Central Intelligence Agency; Tenet, George John

References

Coll, Steve. *Ghost Wars: The Secret History of the CIA, Afghanistan, and Bin Laden, from the Soviet Invasion to September 10, 2001.* New York: Penguin, 2004.

Scheuer, Michael. *Imperial Hubris: Why the West Is Losing the War on Terror.* New York: Brassey's, 2004.

Tenet, George. *At the Center of the Storm: My Years at the CIA.* New York: HarperCollins, 2007.

Wright, Lawrence. *The Looming Tower: Al-Qaeda and the Road to 9/11.* New York: Vintage Books, 2007.

AL-FAJR, Operation

See Fallujah, Second Battle of

Al-Ittihad al-Islami

Al-Ittihad al-Islami (Islamic Unity, AIAI) was the precursor to the later Somali Islamic Courts Union and the current Islamist Al-Shabaab movement. Indeed, it has been suggested that the AIAI, which was alleged to have had links to Al Qaeda, provided the basis for the wider network of violent Islamists presently active in the Horn of Africa and East Africa.

The AIAI developed during the 1980s as a loose movement of generally educated Somalis, many of whom had worked or studied in the Middle East and opposed the repression and control of the regime of Siad Barre, then president of Somalia. They believed that the only way to rid the country of its endemic corruption and clan factionalism was through the institution of a rigid theocratic order based on a strict interpretation of Islam.

Following the collapse of the Barre regime in 1991, Al Qaeda leader Osama bin Laden is thought to have funded and supported the AIAI as a conduit through which to gain an operational foothold in the Horn of Africa. Some experts continue to believe that the 1993 killings of Belgian, Pakistani, and U.S. military personnel associated with the United Nations Operation in Somalia II mission in Somalia had nothing to do with warlord General Mohammad Farah Aideed but was in fact the work of Al Qaeda and the AIAI.

By the mid-1990s, along with a power base in Bosaaso and the Puntland region of Somalia, the AIAI had also become active among the Somali population in the Ogaden region of eastern Ethiopia and the wider Somali diaspora in Kenya. It is believed that at its height the group had around 1,000 active members. Despite attending a February 1995 peace conference for the Somali nation, the AIAI was later linked to a number of terrorist attacks, including two hotel bombings in Ethiopia and the attempted assassination of Ethiopian minister of transport and communications Abdul Majid Hussein in 1996. In 1999 the group was implicated in the murder of an American aid worker near the Kenyan-Somali border. Perhaps more significantly, U.S. officials have claimed that elements of the AIAI cooperated with the Al Qaeda cell responsible for the August 1998 twin suicide bombings of the U.S. embassies in Nairobi, Kenya, and Dar es Salaam, Tanzania. At the time, these attacks were among the most lethal directed against American interests, leaving 224 people dead and thousands of others wounded.

In the aftermath of the September 11 terrorist attacks, the AIAI's finances, together with the group's leaders, Hassan Dahir Aweys and Hassan al-Turki, were sanctioned under U.S. Executive Order 13224. The action was based on the group's suspected links to Al Qaeda, which purportedly included the establishment of joint training camps in various parts of Somalia. Following the onset of the U.S. invasion of Afghanistan (Operation ENDURING FREEDOM) and the U.S.-led Global War on Terror, many AIAI members dispersed across the Gulf of Aden to the tribal areas of Yemen, and the organization claimed to have dissolved itself. That said, AIAI's legacy has had and continues to have a significant bearing on events in Somalia. One of the main leaders of the Islamic Courts Union, which seized the capital city of Mogadishu in June 2006, was Hassan Aweys. More important was the "career" trajectory of Turki, who went on to lead Al-Shabaab—then the youth movement of the Islamic Courts Union and currently one of the main terrorist-insurgent threats in the country.

RICHARD WARNES

See also

Al Qaeda; Al-Shabaab

References

Gunaratna, Rohan. *Inside Al Qaeda.* New York: Columbia University Press, 2002.

Rabasa, Angel. *Radical Islam in East Africa.* Santa Monica, CA: RAND, 2009.

Rotberg, Robert, ed. *Battling Terrorism in the Horn of Africa.* Washington, DC: Brookings Institution Press, 2005.

Al Jazeera

The most popular news agency in the Arab world and its first large nongovernment-operated news network. Founded in 1996, Al Jazeera (Jazira) has become well known for its willingness to report on topics that are controversial in both the Middle East and in the Western media. Al Jazeera is based in Qatar but is staffed by an international body of reporters. It claims to be the only uncensored news agency in the Middle East. However, its commitment to presenting material and interviews that countered U.S. foreign policy in the Middle East and at times were sharply critical of Middle Eastern leaders or governments made it a focus of displeasure for the U.S. government, which banned its reporters from Iraq during the 2003–2011 Iraq War.

The Arabic term *al-jazeera* (the island) is a colloquial reference to the Arabian Peninsula. Its origins are rooted in a response to the censorship and control in the Arab media on the part of political commentators and reporters and the recognition of the new market available through satellite television.

Although popular with many in the region, the British Broadcasting Corporation (BBC) has discontinued much of its programming there in recent years. Many of the journalists employed by the BBC were eager to continue broadcasting and, together with Sheikh Hamad bin Thamer al-Thani, approached the emir of Qatar for money to establish a new network. Thani, a cousin of Emir Sheikh Khalifa bin Hamad al-Thani, convinced the Qatari ruler to provide a grant of $150 million. This became the start-up money for Al Jazeera. The network continues to receive financial assistance from Qatar and is further funded by advertising revenue and by distributing its exclusive news feeds.

Despite the subsidy from Qatar, Al Jazeera set out to maintain a strict independence from censorship, which was previously almost unknown in the region. Al Jazeera chose as its corporate motto "the right to speak up." It also proclaimed to the world that it sought in its reporting "objectivity, accuracy, and a passion for truth."

Broadcasting via satellite since November 1996, Al Jazeera quickly became the most watched media outlet in the Arab world. Unfettered by the official censorship of government-sponsored news reporting, Al Jazeera has earned a reputation among its audience as a network committed to presenting multiple sides of any debate.

Al Jazeera became the first major news outlet in the Arabic-speaking Middle East to regularly present interviews with official Israeli spokesmen as well as with banned Islamist organizations and feminist groups. Al Jazeera has also been open in its critique of events that illustrate dictatorial or authoritarian actions by the governments of Saudi Arabia, Egypt, Syria, and Iraq. Such diversity of opinion and outspoken criticism of oppression made Al Jazeera a popular force in the latter part of the 1990s and again during the Arab Spring that commenced in 2010. It was in 2001, however, when Al Jazeera captured the attention of news audiences far beyond the Arabic-speaking world.

When the terror attacks of September 11, 2001, were carried out against the United States, Al Jazeera broadcast footage of Osama bin Laden and Sulayman Abu Ghaith praising the carnage. For many in the West who were otherwise unfamiliar with Al Jazeera, the network was now immediately seen as a mouthpiece for Al Qaeda. Al Jazeera vehemently rejected this charge, stating that it had merely presented news footage obtained in the interest of showing all sides in a major story. Nevertheless, the broadcast initiated a new barrage of attacks, particularly by the U.S. government, against Al Jazeera. These were exacerbated by Al Jazeera's coverage of Iraqi resistance activities to the American military presence, which the U.S. government presented as an insurgency carried out mainly by foreign elements.

Although news organizations around the world have purchased the rights to broadcast the footage from Al Jazeera, the George W. Bush administration was extremely critical of the network. The administration was outraged when Al Jazeera broadcast scenes of suffering experienced by Afghan civilians in the wake of the November 2001 invasion of their country by U.S. military forces, claiming that it sponsored the perpetuation of terrorist ideals. News organizations throughout the world, however, were impressed with the unparalleled quality of the Afghanistan War coverage by Al Jazeera. Indeed, its feeds were widely purchased for rebroadcast.

The stakes against Al Jazeera in the United States were raised even higher in early 2003. In the run-up to the March 2003 invasion of Iraq, Al Jazeera was accused of being connected to Iraqi spies by a former Iraqi opposition organization known as the Iraqi National Congress. As a consequence, the U.S. Central Intelligence Agency declared Al Jazeera to be an organ of anti-American propaganda. Al Jazeera's stock was banned from the New York Stock Exchange, and its reporters were ejected from the trading floor. Ironically, the Saddam Hussein regime also tossed out of Iraq Al Jazeera's main reporter at the time, claiming that he was a spy for the United States. In response, Al Jazeera launched a searing editorial attack on an Iraqi government that tried at every turn to thwart free reporting from the country.

Under attack from both the United States and Iraq in the days before the launch of the Iraq War, Al Jazeera became a symbol for what some see as hypocrisy in both Iraq and the United States in regard to a free press.

As the invasion of Iraq progressed in 2003 and the occupation of Iraq took hold, Al Jazeera continued to provide some of the world's most controversial and in-depth reporting, and its feeds were rebroadcast on every continent. Despite its headquarters in Baghdad and Kabul being bombed by U.S. forces and pressure being exerted by Washington on the Qatari government to shut it down, Al Jazeera's reporting on Afghanistan and Iraq continued to be the most comprehensive in the world. In fact, it has often been the only reporting to focus on the heart-wrenching experiences of local people coping with disaster. Al Jazeera continued to broadcast controversial missives from insurgents, including footage of Westerners held hostage, until the Iraqi Interim Government, with U.S. encouragement, banned the network from the country in September 2004.

The 2003 launch of Arabic- and English-language websites for Al Jazeera was plagued with controversy. Hackers repeatedly interrupted service on the English-language site, and several Internet service providers cancelled contracts with Al Jazeera when the network refused to remove controversial content. In 2005 an undeterred Al Jazeera planned to launch an international English-language satellite network based in Kuala Lumpur. Through extreme adversity and international controversy, Al Jazeera continues to be one of the most watched news networks in the world, promoting itself as one of the only truly free voices in the Middle East.

In 2011 when Egypt was wracked by massive street protests, Al Jazeera consistently featured the most detailed reporting available on the events there. Even Secretary of State Hillary Clinton acknowledged the power of Al Jazeera in 2011, claiming that the West was losing the "information war" to the news network. In more recent years, Al Jazeera has diversified, even providing an all-sports network. During the Syrian Civil War, Al Jazeera again garnered controversy. The Bashar al-Assad government claimed that the network was antiregime and supportive of the rebels and the Muslim Brotherhood. Some rebel groups, meanwhile, claimed that Al Jazeera was not shedding as much light as it could on the excesses and atrocities of the Assad regime. In recent years, Al Jazeera has captured praise from Americans, including journalists and politicians.

NANCY L. STOCKDALE

See also

Bin Laden, Osama; September 11 Attacks; Terrorism

References

Al Jazeera English Home Page. http://english.aljazeera.net/ HomePage.

el-Nawawy, Mohammed, and Adel Iskander. *Al Jazeera: The Story of the Network That Is Rattling Governments and Redefining Journalism.* Boulder, CO: Westview, 2003.

Miles, Hugh. *Al Jazeera: How Arab TV News Challenges America.* New York: Grove, 2005.

Allawi, Ayad (1944–)

Iraqi politician who served as prime minister of Iraq's appointed interim government that assumed the governance of Iraq on June 28, 2004. He held the premiership until April 7, 2005. Allawi was born into a well-to-do family in Baghdad on May 31, 1944. His father and uncle were physicians. His father was also a member of Iraq's parliament, and his grandfather had participated in the negotiations that granted Iraq its independence in 1932. The family had commercial and political ties to both the British and the Americans.

Allawi graduated from the American Jesuits' Baghdad College, an intermediate and senior-level preparatory school, and entered the Baghdad University College of Medicine in 1961, the same year he joined the Baath Party, met future Iraqi dictator Saddam Hussein, and became active in the Iraqi National Students' Union. Allawi organized strikes and other activities against the government of Abd al-Karim Qasim. On February 8, 1963, Qassim was overthrown in a Baathist coup, which resulted in General Ahmed Hassan al-Bakr becoming prime minister. Allawi was eventually placed in charge of the central security office at the presidential palace and was given the nickname "palace doctor."

Although unproven, there are charges that Allawi participated in intense interrogations and torture that led to the deaths of trade union officials, students, and political leaders. Allawi was arrested on these charges but was released after Bakr intervened. Allawi participated in the July 17, 1968, coup that made Bakr president and excluded all but Baathists from government positions. Bakr then pressured the minister of health Ezzat Mustafa to expedite Allawi's graduation from the college of medicine.

Opposition to Allawi grew within the government, and he was sent to Beirut in 1971 before moving to London in 1972 to head the Baath National Students Union and to pursue advanced medical studies. Allawi left the Baath Party in 1975 and supposedly began working for MI6, the British foreign intelligence service. In 1976, he earned a master's of science in medicine from London University. Allawi's name was placed on an assassination list in 1978 after Iraqi president Saddam Hussein failed to convince him to rejoin the Baathists. In February 1978, Allawi and his wife were attacked by an ax-bearing intruder in their Surrey home, but escaped serious injury. Allawi earned a doctorate in medicine in 1979 from London University before being certified as a neurologist in 1982.

In 1979, Allawi had begun gathering alienated former Iraqi Baathists together into a group that grew into a Hussein opposition party. It was formalized in December 1990 as the Iraqi National Accord (INA). The INA received backing from Britain, the United States, Jordan, Saudi Arabia, and Turkey. It fomented dissent among the disaffected in

Iraq and committed acts of terror and sabotage in that country in an attempt to bring down the Hussein regime. Allawi and the INA were recruited by the U.S. Central Intelligence Agency (CIA) after the Persian Gulf War (1990–1991) and paid $5 million in 1995 and $6 million in 1996. The CIA supported the INA's 1996 failed military coup, code-named Dbachilles, which led to the execution of many Iraqis and to the confiscation or destruction of approximately $250 million of Allawi family assets.

The INA and Allawi gathered intelligence establishing the alleged existence of weapons of mass destruction in Iraq that formed the core of the MI6 dossier released in September 2002. This dossier formed a major part of the rationale for the 2003 U.S.- and British-led coalition invasion of Iraq in March 2003. On July 13, 2003, Allawi was appointed by Coalition Provisional Authority administrator Paul Bremer to the 25-member Iraqi Governing Council (IGC), where he served as minister of defense and assumed the rotating presidency for October 2003. Allawi resigned as head of the IGC security committee in April 2004 over alleged concerns about U.S. tactics used to subdue the 2004 Fallujah insurgency.

The coalition-led IGC transferred authority to the Iraqi Interim Government, with Allawi as the appointed interim prime minister, on June 28, 2004. During his tenure in this position, he created a domestic spy agency named the General Security Directorate to counter the Iraqi insurgency, closed the Iraqi office of the television network Al Jazeera, attempted to marginalize radical Shiite cleric Muqtada al-Sadr and his militia, and assumed the power to declare martial law. Allawi tried to draw Baathists who had not committed criminal acts during Hussein's rule into the government and considered pardoning insurgents who surrendered their weapons. Allawi stepped down as premier on April 7, 2005, the day Islamic Dawa Party leader Ibrahim al-Jaafari was elected to lead the transitional Iraqi National Assembly.

Allawi's INA won just 25 seats in the December 2005 elections establishing the permanent Iraqi National Assembly. This placed the party a distant third in the assembly, with only 14 percent of the vote. His party fared far better in the 2010 elections, however, capturing the largest plurality of votes (24.7 percent), giving it more seats than any other bloc or party. Allawi retains his dual British citizenship, and his wife and children reside in the United Kingdom for security reasons.

RICHARD M. EDWARDS

See also
Bremer, Lewis Paul; Iraq, History of, 1990–Present

References
Allawi, Ali. *Winning the War, Losing the Peace: The Occupation of Iraq.* New Haven, CT: Yale University Press, 2006.
Keegan, John. *The Iraq War: The Military Offensive, from Victory in 21 Days to the Insurgent Aftermath.* New York: Vintage, 2005.
Polk, William R. *Understanding Iraq: The Whole Sweep of Iraqi History, from Genghis Khan's Mongols to the Ottoman Turks to the British Mandate to the American Occupation.* New York: Harper Perennial, 2006.

Al Qaeda

Al Qaeda is an international radical Islamic organization, the hallmark of which is the perpetration of terrorist attacks against Western interests in the name of Islam. In the late 1980s, Al Qaeda (the Arabic term *qaeda* means the "base" or "foundation") fought against the Soviet occupation of Afghanistan. The organization is, however, best known for the September 11, 2001, terrorist attacks in the United States, the worst such attacks in the history of that nation. The founding of Al Qaeda, which consists chiefly of Sunni Muslims, is shrouded in controversy. Research from a number of Arabic scholars indicates that Al Qaeda was created sometime between 1987 or 1988 by Sheikh Abdullah Azzam, a mentor to Osama bin Laden. Azzam was a professor at Jeddah University in Saudi Arabia. Bin Laden attended Jeddah University, where he met and was strongly influenced by Azzam.

The group Al Qaeda grew out of the Afghan Service Bureau, also known as the Maktab al Khidmat lil-mujahidin al-Arab (MaK). Azzam was the founder of the MaK, and bin Laden funded the organization and was considered the deputy director. This organization recruited, trained, and transported Muslim soldiers from any Muslim nation into Afghanistan to fight the jihad (holy war) against the Soviet armies in the 1980s. Sayyid Qutb, a philosopher of the Muslim Brotherhood, developed the credo for Al Qaeda, which is to arm all Muslims in the world and overthrow any government that does not support traditional Muslim practice and Islamic law.

Following the mysterious death of Sheikh Azzam in November 1989, bin Laden took over the leadership of Al Qaeda. He continued to work toward Azzam's goal of creating an international organization consisting of mujahidin (soldiers) who will fight the oppression of Muslims throughout the world. Al Qaeda actually has several goals: to destroy Israel, rid the Islamic world of the influence of Western

Al Qaeda leader Osama bin Laden (second from left) and his top lieutenant, Ayman al-Zawahiri (second from right), shown at an undisclosed location with two other men in this image, broadcast by Al Jazeera on October 7, 2001. (AP Photo/Al Jazeera)

civilization, reestablish a caliphate form of government throughout the world, fight against any government viewed as contrary to the ideals of Islamic law and religion, and aid any Islamic groups trying to establish an Islamic form of government in their countries.

The organization of Al Qaeda follows the *shura majlis*, or consultative council form of leadership. The emir general's post has been held by bin Laden, who was succeeded by Ayman al-Zawahiri upon bin Laden's death in May 2011. Several other generals are under the emir general, and then there are additional leaders of related groups. There are 24 related groups as part of the consultative council. The council consists of four committees—military, religious-legal, finance, and media. Each leader of these committees was personally selected by bin Laden or Zawahiri and reported directly to them. All levels of Al Qaeda are highly compartmentalized, and secrecy is the key to all operations.

Al Qaeda's ideology has appealed to both Middle Eastern and non–Middle Eastern groups who adhere to Islam. There are also a number of radical Islamic terrorist groups associated with Al Qaeda that have established a history of violence and terrorism in numerous countries in the world today. Nevertheless, Al Qaeda continues to be the central force of world terrorism because it represents a symbol of opposition to Western domination.

Bin Laden was able to put most of the radical Islamic terrorist groups under the umbrella of Al Qaeda. Indeed, its leadership has spread throughout the world, and its influence penetrates many religious, social, and economical structures in most Muslim communities. Today, the upper-echelon leadership of Al Qaeda continues to elude American intelligence and Western armies in Afghanistan and Pakistan. The membership of Al Qaeda remains difficult to determine because of its decentralized organizational structure. By early 2005, U.S. officials claimed to have killed or taken prisoner two-thirds of the Al Qaeda leaders behind the September 11 attacks. However, some of these prisoners have been shown to have had no direct connection with the attacks. Al Qaeda has continued to periodically release audio recording and videotapes, some featuring bin Laden himself, to comment on current issues, exhort followers to keep up the fight, and prove to Western governments that it is still a force with which to be reckoned.

Despite the decimation of Al Qaeda's core leadership in Afganistan and Pakistan, it continues to be a major threat. According to experts, the organization moved from a centralized organization to a series of local-actor organizations forming a terrorist network. Al Qaeda in Iraq was decimated by the end of the Iraq War in 2011, but it has regained control of many of its former staging areas and the ability to launch weekly waves of multiple car bomb attacks. On May 1, 2011, bin Laden was killed in an attack mounted by U.S. special forces on his compound in Pakistan. President Barack Obama called it the "most significant achievement to date" in the effort to defeat Al Qaeda.

In July 2013, however, more than 1,000 people were killed in Iraq, the highest monthly death toll in five years. Most of the attacks were led by Al Qaeda and its affiliates. That same year in Syria, Al Qaeda affiliate Jabhat al Nusra, a combat force that has been fighting with some success against the regime of Syrian dictator Bashar al-Assad, rose to prominence. The force reports directly to Al Qaeda leadership. Between 2009 and 2013 in Libya, Al Qaeda–affiliated terror groups have been blamed for scores of attacks, many of them including civilians. Indeed, Al Qaeda has been blamed for the September 11, 2012, attack on the U.S. consulate in Benghazi that left the U.S. ambassador and 3 other Americans dead. In Yemen, Al Qaeda leaders in strongholds in the country's south have not been vanquished by a Yemeni military backed by U.S. forces and drone strikes. Al Qaeda affiliates in Iraq, Syria, Yemen, and West Africa have dramatically expanded their operating areas and capabilities and appear poised to continue their expansion.

By early 2014, a resurgent Al Qaeda had secured much of Iraq's Anbar Province, including Fallujah, and was making significant headway in Afghanistan, often colluding with a resurgent Taliban. Al Qaeda has also successfully established itself in parts of Lebanon, Egypt, Algeria, and Mali. By early 2014, the Obama administration had begun shipping Hellfire missiles and other weaponry to Prime Minister Nuri al-Maliki's government in Iraq to help suppress the growing insurgency there, which at the end of 2014 was dominated by Al Qaeda. In regard to Afghanistan, the West remains concerned that if the Afghans continue to stall on a status of forces agreement, which would leave some foreign troops in the country after the anticipated withdrawal of the NATO/ISAF force in December 2014, the nation might well descend into complete chaos.

This might permit Al Qaeda and the Taliban to reestablish complete control there.

HARRY RAYMOND HUESTON II

See also

Afghanistan; Al Qaeda in Iraq; Al Qaeda in the Arabian Peninsula; Al Qaeda in the Islamic Maghreb; Bin Laden, Osama; Islamic Radicalism; Jihad; Mubarak, Hosni; Muslim Brotherhood; Salafism; September 11 Attacks; Taliban; Terrorism

References

Bergen, Peter L. *Holy War, Inc.* New York: Touchstone, 2002.

Gunaratna, Rohan. *Inside Al Qaeda.* New York: Columbia University Press, 2002.

Hueston, Harry R., and B. Vizzin. *Terrorism 101.* 2nd ed. Ann Arbor, MI: XanEdu, 2004.

Al Qaeda in Iraq

Al Qaeda in Iraq (al-Qa'ida fi Bilad al-Rafhidayn, AQI) is a violent Sunni jihadist organization that has taken root in Iraq since the 2003 Anglo-American–led invasion of that nation. The U.S. government has characterized the AQI, sometimes referred to as Al Qaeda in Mesopotamia, as the most deadly Sunni jihadist insurgent force now in Iraq. Other sources and experts argue that this designation is exaggerated, as the group is among more than 40 similar organizations, and that the claim was made symbolically to rationalize the idea that coalition forces are fighting terrorism in Iraq and thus should not withdraw precipitously.

Opponents of the continuing U.S. presence in Iraq have argued that the 2003 invasion sparked the growth of Salafi jihadism and suicide terrorism in Iraq and its export to other parts of the Islamic world. The AQI first formed following the invasion and toppling of the Iraq regime, under the name Jama'at al-Tawhid wa-l Jihad (Group of Monotheism and Jihad) under Abu Musab al-Zarqawi.

Zarqawi had fought in Afghanistan in the 1980s and 1990s, and upon traveling to Jordan he organized a group called Bayt al-Imam with the noted Islamist ideologue Abu Muhammad al-Maqdisi (Muhammad Tahir al-Barqawi) and other veterans of the war in Afghanistan. Zarqawi was arrested and imprisoned but was released in 1999. Returning again to Afghanistan and setting up camp in Herat, he reportedly took charge of certain Islamist factions in Kurdistan, from there moving into Iraq and sometimes into Syria. Once Mullah Krekar, the leader of the Kurdish group Islamist Ansar al-Islam, was deported to the Netherlands in 2003, certain sources claim that Zarqawi led some 600 Arab fighters in Syria.

Jama'at al-Tawhid wa-l Jihad was blamed for, or took credit for, numerous attacks, including bombings of the Jordanian embassy, the Canal Hotel that killed 23 at the United Nations headquarters, and the Imam Ali mosque in Najaf. Jama'at al-Tawhid wa-l Jihad is also credited with the killing of Italian paramilitary police and civilians at Nasiriyah and numerous suicide attacks that continued through 2005. The group also seized hostages and beheaded them. A video of the savage execution of U.S. businessman Nicholas Berg, murdered in Iraq on May 7, 2004, reportedly by Zarqawi himself, was followed by other killings of civilians.

The AQI has targeted Iraqi governmental and military personnel and police because of their cooperation with the American occupying force. The AQI's recruitment videos have highlighted American attacks and home searches of defenseless Iraqis and promise martyrdom. Estimates of AQI members have ranged from 850 to several thousand. Also under dispute have been the numbers of foreign fighters in relation to Iraqi fighters. Foreign fighters' roles were first emphasized, but it became clear that a much higher percentage (probably 90 percent) of fighters were Iraqi: members of the Salafi jihadist, or quasi-nationalist jihadist, groups.

In October 2004 Zarqawi's group issued a statement acknowledging the leadership of Al Qaeda under Osama bin Laden and adopted the name al-Qa'ida fi Bilad al-Rafhidayn. The Iraqi city of Fallujah, in western Anbar Province, became an AQI stronghold. U.S. forces twice tried to capture the city, first in the prematurely terminated Operation VIGILANT RESOLVE from April 4 to May 1, 2004. The Fallujah Guard then controlled the city. U.S. military and Iraqi forces conquered the city in Operation PHANTOM FURY (FAJR) during November 7–December 23, 2004, in extremely bloody fighting.

Zarqawi formed relationships with other Salafist jihad organizations, announcing an umbrella group, the Mujahideen Shura Council, in 2006. After Zarqawi was reportedly at a safe house in June 2006, the new AQI leader, Abu Ayyub al-Masri, announced a new coalition, the Islamic State of Iraq, that included the Mujahideen Shura Council.

Al Qaeda, along with other Sunni Salafist and nationalist groups, strongly resisted Iraqi and coalition forces in Baghdad, Ramadi, and Baqubah and continued staging very damaging attacks into 2007. However, by mid-2008 U.S. commanders claimed dominance over these areas. Nevertheless, the AQI was acknowledged to still be operative southeast of Baghdad in Jabour, Mosul, Samarra, Hawijah, and Miqdadiyah. The United States believed that the AQI's diminished presence was attributable to the Anbar Awakening, which enlisted numerous tribes, including some former AQI members, to fight Al Qaeda. The Americans further believed that the AQI had been diminished because of the troop surge strategy that began in early 2007. From then until his death on May 1, 2011, bin Laden had urged the mujahideen to unify in the face of these setbacks.

The AQI has strongly influenced other jihadist groups and actors, particularly through its Internet presence. In sparking intersectarian strife in Iraq, the group has also badly damaged Iraq's postwar reconstruction efforts and tapped into the intolerance of many Salafi groups as well as other Sunni Iraqis and Sunni Muslims outside of Iraq who have been threatened by the emergence of Shia political parties and institutions that had suffered under the Baathist regime of Saddam Hussein. Iraq's Al Qaeda affiliate claimed responsibility for the July 23, 2013, jailbreak from the infamous Abu Ghraib prison that unleashed 500 to 600 militants into an already unstable region and boosted the group's resurgent fortunes in Iraq and Syria. The prisoners were freed in two coordinated assaults in which fighters used suicide bombs and mortars to storm the two top security prisons on Baghdad's outskirts at Abu Ghraib and Taji. Both were once run by the U.S. military and housed the country's most senior Al Qaeda detainees. At least 26 members of the Iraqi security forces and more than a dozen prisoners were killed.

The scale of the attacks against the heavily guarded facilities reinforced an impression building among many Iraqis that their security forces are struggling to cope with a resurgent Al Qaeda since U.S. forces withdrew in December 2011, taking with them much of the expertise and technology that had been used to hold extremists at bay. Iraqis' fears about a resurgent Al Qaeda were further vindicated when the group took control of Fallujah and Ramadi and much of Anbar Province by January 2014. Meanwhile, car bombings, kidnappings, and other violence perpetrated by Al Qaeda and allied groups accelerated rapidly during 2013 and into 2014.

SHERIFA ZUHUR

See also

Al Qaeda; Bin Laden, Osama; Fallujah, Second Battle of; Masri, Abu Ayyub al-; Zarqawi, Abu Musab al-

References

Brisard, Jean-Charles, and Damien Martinez. *Zarqawi: The New Face of al-Qaeda.* New York: Other Press, 2005.

Burns, John, and Melissa Rubin. "U.S. Arming Sunnis in Iraq to Battle Old Qaeda Allies." *New York Times,* June 11, 2007.

Congressional Research Service. *Iraq: Post-Saddam Governance and Security, September 6, 2007.* Report to Congress. Washington, DC: U.S. Government Printing Office, 2007.

"In Motley Array of Iraqi Foes, Why Does U.S. Spotlight al-Qaida?" *International Herald Tribune,* June 8, 2007.

Al Qaeda in the Arabian Peninsula

Underground Muslim militant group based in Saudi Arabia that is loosely affiliated with Osama bin Laden's and Ayman al-Zawahiri's transnational Al Qaeda network. Al Qaeda in the Arabian Peninsula (al-Qaida fi Jazirat al-Arabiyya, AQAP) was organized in 2001–2002 and emerged publicly in 2003 when it carried out a series of deadly bombings against the Saudi government and expatriate residences in the kingdom's major cities, including the capital city of Riyadh and the key Red Sea port city of Jeddah. The group came under attack in 2004 and 2005 during a series of arrests and shoot-outs with Saudi police and soldiers. These shoot-outs resulted in the deaths of several top AQAP leaders and operatives including its founder, Yusuf Salah Fahd al-Uyayri (Ayiri) (d. 2003) and his two successors, Abd al-Aziz bin Issa bin Abd al-Muhsin al-Muqrin (d. 2004) and Salah al-Alawi al-Awfi (d. 2005).

AQAP's primary goal was to overthrow the House of Saud, the kingdom's ruling family, that is seen as corrupt and anathema to the "pure" society that the group's members and other unaffiliated and nonmilitant opponents of the monarchy seek to establish. The monarchy is harshly criticized by both the opposition and many of its own supporters among the ranks of the kingdom's official religious scholars (*ulama*) as being too closely aligned with foreign powers, such as the United States, to the detriment of Saudi interests and social values. AQAP members proved to be adept users of the Internet, creating websites and widely read online publications such as the Internet magazine *Sawt al-Jihad* (Voice of Jihad).

Despite a series of small-scale attacks on Europeans and Americans in the kingdom during 2002 and early 2003, Saudi authorities did not acknowledge the existence of AQAP as a fully operational group until May 12, 2003. On that day, the group carried out three simultaneous suicide vehicle bombings at the Hamra, Vinnell, and Jedewahl housing compounds used by foreign (mainly Western) expatriates. The attacks killed 35 people, including 9 of the terrorists, and wounded 200 others. According to senior U.S. diplomats and Saudi intellectuals, this attack drove home to Crown Prince Abdullah (now King Abdullah) the need to vigorously combat homegrown Saudi radicalism.

In response to the attacks, hundreds of suspects were arrested by Saudi authorities, many of them with ties to AQAP and to the resistance in Iraq, although many were also probably figures from the nonmilitant religious opposition whom the authorities wished to silence under the guise of combating terrorism. Al-Uyayri (or Ayiri), AQAP's founder and first leader, was killed in June 2003 at the height of this sweep by Saudi authorities. He was succeeded by Abd al-Aziz al-Muqrin.

On November 3, 2003, Saudi security forces had a shoot-out with AQAP operatives in the city of Mecca, the location of the Kaba, Islam's holiest shrine, that resulted in the deaths of 2 militants and the capture of a large weapons cache. Five days later AQAP launched a successful suicide bombing attack against the Muhayya housing complex in Riyadh, which was home to many non-Saudi Arab expatriate workers; the attack killed 18 people and wounded scores of others.

The group continued to launch attacks on Saudi and foreign targets, including a Riyadh government building on April 21, 2004, and an oil company office in Yanbu on May 1 that resulted in the killing of five Western workers. AQAP suffered another setback on March 15, 2004, when Khalid Ali bin Ali al-Haj, a Yemeni national and senior AQAP leader, was killed in a shoot-out with Saudi police along with his companion, AQAP member Ibrahim al-Muzayni. The group retaliated with a host of deadly attacks on expatriates, killing in 2004 Herman Dengel (a German) on May 22, BBC cameraman Simon Cumbers on June 6, Robert Jacob (an American) on June 8, Kenneth Scroggs (an American) on June 12, Irish engineer Tony Christopher on August 3, British engineer Edward Muirhead-Smith on September 15, and Laurent Barbot (French) on September 26.

The most widely publicized attack, however, was the June 12, 2004, kidnapping and June 18 beheading of Paul M. Johnson Jr., an American employee of U.S. defense contractor Lockheed Martin. His kidnappers demanded the release of all detainees held by Saudi authorities, which was denied. The beheading was filmed and released on websites associated with and sympathetic to AQAP. That same day, Muqrin was killed by Saudi security forces during a raid on an AQAP safe house. Meanwhile, on May 29 the group succeeded again in successfully carrying out attacks on three targets in the city of Khobar, taking hostages in oil business offices and housing complexes associated with foreign companies. Saudi police and soldiers stormed the buildings the next day and rescued many of the hostages but not before the attackers had killed 22 others. Shortly after this attack, the U.S. Department of State issued a statement that urged U.S. citizens to leave the kingdom. The year was capped off with a spectacular attack on December 6 on the U.S. consulate in Jeddah in which 5 consulate employees, 4 Saudi national guardsmen, and 3 AQAP members were killed.

The Saudi government waged a successful campaign against AQAP throughout 2004 and into 2005, killing dozens of the group's members and nearly wiping out its senior leadership. In April 2005 several senior operatives were killed in a shoot-out in Rass, and in August Saudi security forces killed Muqrin's successor and AQAP leader Salah al-Alawi al-Awfi in the holy city of Medina. Other members were arrested.

Most of the group's members remain at large, and Saudi and foreign intelligence agencies continue to warn that AQAP poses a threat. The Saudi government has responded with antiterrorist measures, such as conferences and public pronouncements, a highly structured in-prison counseling program designed to de-radicalize detainees, and the Sakinah program that analyzes and engages Internet postings. In 2007 and 2008, Saudi security forces detained and imprisoned hundreds of people, some of them suspected militants and others in a variety of incidents, including those planning an attack during hajj, the annual Islamic pilgrimage to Mecca.

On September 30, 2011, a U.S. drone attack in Yemen resulted in the death of Anwar al-Awlaki, one of the group's leaders, and Samir Khan, the editor of *Inspire,* its English-language magazine. Both men were U.S. citizens. AQAP claimed responsibility for the May 21, 2012, suicide attack at a parade rehearsal for Yemen's Unity Day, killing more than 120 people and injuring 200 others. The attack was the deadliest in Yemeni history.

The pace of U.S. drone attacks quickened significantly in 2012, with over 20 strikes in the first five months of the year, compared to 10 strikes during the course of 2011. During 2013, targeted killings by U.S. drones and special forces increased in number, thanks in part to the erection of secret U.S. bases in the Horn of Africa and the Arabian Peninsula. Meanwhile, on October 4, 2012, the United Nations 1267/1989 Al Qaeda Sanctions Committee and the U.S. State Department designated Ansar al-Sharia as an alias for Al Qaeda in the Arabian Peninsula.

In the summer of 2013, in response to news that AQAP was planning an offensive against U.S. diplomatic posts abroad, the American government temporarily closed more than two dozen embassies and legations as a precaution. This corresponded with an uptick in U.S. drone attacks, which now began to target lower-level AQAP members and other militant jihadists.

CHRISTOPHER PAUL ANZALONE

See also

Al Qaeda; Global War on Terror; Saudi Arabia; Terrorism; Yemen

References

Al-Rasheed, Madawi. *Contesting the Saudi State: Islamic Voices from a New Generation.* Cambridge: Cambridge University Press, 2006.

Cordesman, Anthony H., and Nawaf Obaid. *Al-Qaeda in Saudi Arabia: Asymmetric Threats and Islamist Extremists.* Washington, DC: Center for Strategic and International Studies, 2005.

Murphy, Caryle. "Saudi Arabia Indicts 991 Suspected Al Qaeda Militants." *Christian Science Monitor,* October 22, 2008.

Riedel, Bruce, and Bilal Y. Saab. "Al Qaeda's Third Front: Saudi Arabia." *Washington Quarterly* 21 (2008): 33–46.

Zuhur, Sherifa. "Decreasing Violence in Saudi Arabia and Beyond." In *Home Grown Terrorism: Understanding and Addressing the Root Causes of Radicalisation among Groups with an Immigrant Heritage in Europe,* Vol. 60, edited by Thamas M. Pick, Anne Speckard, and B. Jacuch, 74–98. NATO Science for Peace and Security Series. Amsterdam: IOS Press, 2010.

Zuhur, Sherifa. *Saudi Arabia: Islamic Threat, Political Reform and the Global War on Terror.* Carlisle Barracks, PA: Strategic Studies Institute, 2005.

Al Qaeda in the Islamic Maghreb

An Algeria-based clandestine jihadi organization founded on January 24, 2007, that employs terrorist tactics in support of Islamist ideology. Al Qaeda in the Islamic Maghreb (Tanzim al-Qaida fi Bilad al-Maghrib al-Islamiyya, AQIM) seeks to overthrow the Algerian government and establish an Islamic state. AQIM symbolizes Algeria's continuing political instability, North Africa's increasing vulnerability to militant Islam, and Al Qaeda's little-discussed ability to expand not by diffusing or splintering into local cells but rather by skillfully drawing established organizations into its sphere of influence. AQIM draws its members from the Algerian and local Saharan communities, including clans in Mali as well as Moroccans. AQIM has been branded a terrorist organization by the United Nations (UN), the United States, Russia, and a number of other countries.

AQIM's origins lie in Algeria's modern history. The French-Algerian War (1954–1962) freed Algeria from French colonialism and led to rule under the wartime resistance movement, the National Liberation Front (Front de Libération Nationale, FLN). In 1989, however, militant Muslim opponents of the FLN regime formed the Islamic Salvation Front (Front Islamique du Salut, FIS). In the early 1990s the FLN manipulated and canceled elections to prevent the FIS from ascending to power, sparking a bloody civil war. This conflict radicalized and fragmented the opposition, with extremists gathering in the Armed Islamic Group (Groupe Islamique Armé, GIA), a faction bent on utterly destroying the FLN regime and installing a Muslim state under sharia (Islamic law) through indiscriminate terrorist attacks against moderates and foreigners. The FLN weathered the storm, and as the civil war reached a horrendously violent stalemate, a new Islamist group—the Salafist Group for Preaching and Combat (Groupe Salafiste pour la Prédication et le Combat, GSPC)—superseded the GIA by denouncing the widely detested violence against civilians. Founded in 1998, the GSPC would adopt the Al Qaeda moniker a decade later.

The transition from the GSPC to AQIM was the result of a political dilemma facing Algerian Islamists and deft diplomacy by Al Qaeda operatives. The GSPC's first leader, Hassan Hattab (aka Abu Hamza), kept the popular promise to attack only government officials and forces, hoping to regain the far-reaching support for Muslim militancy enjoyed by the FIS. But building a broad backing was slow going, and time suggested that the FLN could withstand a conventional insurgency. Impatient elements within the GSPC forced Hattab's resignation in 2004. His successor, Nabil Sahraoui (aka Abu Ibrahim Mustafa), enjoyed only a brief reign before Algerian soldiers located and eliminated him in June 2004. Abdelmalek Droukdal (aka Abu Musab Abd al-Wadoud) has run the organization since, overseeing its radicalization, renaming, and return to GIA tactics.

Al Qaeda worked to influence the GSPC from its inception. It helped to fund Muslim militants in Algeria in the early 1990s but refused to fully endorse the GIA, despite experiences that so-called Afghan Arabs in the two organizations shared while fighting the Soviets in Afghanistan in the 1980s. In 1998 Al Qaeda leader Osama bin Laden welcomed the advent of the GSPC, a group manned in part by Al Qaeda trainees who tied their renunciation of terrorism to an international jihadi agenda.

The new ideology harnessed the GSPC to Al Qaeda, and 12 days after the terror attacks of September 11, 2001, U.S. president George W. Bush labeled the GSPC a terrorist organization and froze its assets. This confrontation with the West—along with defections after 2000 of the halfhearted adherents, thanks to the Algerian government's amnesties for repentant civil war insurgents—further sharpened the GSPC's anti-Western extremist edge.

In 2002 Al Qaeda sent an emissary to Algeria for meetings with sympathetic figures within the GSPC. Two years later Chadian forces captured a key GSPC regional commander moving through the Sahara, and his colleagues decided to pressure Chad's ally, France, for his release. They reached out to Al Qaeda for assistance, and an obliging Abu Musab al-Zarqawi, head of Al Qaeda in Mesopotamia (Iraq), agreed to support the GSPC by kidnapping French citizens as bargaining chips. The plan did not materialize, but the congenial link remained, and after 2004 the GSPC's new hard-line leaders ultimately developed the link. Al Qaeda, for its part, grew increasingly interested in the GSPC after 2005, when the attempt to forge an affiliate terrorist network in Morocco had failed. Al Qaeda's strategists came to recognize that within North Africa, a critical region supplying long-standing Muslim immigrant communities to nearby Western Europe, only Algeria lacked a pervasive security apparatus capable of rooting out terrorist cells. The two organizations issued cordial statements throughout 2005, and by late 2006 a formal merger between Al Qaeda and the GSPC was announced, with the latter's name change coming the following year.

Since this merger, AQIM has grown more powerful and dangerous. Al Qaeda is probably funneling resources into AQIM, supplementing funds that the Algerian organization can gather on its own through the European financial network it inherited from the GIA. In return, AQIM is internationalizing its purview. Some fear that it could make Europe an area of operations, and it forwent expansion—remaining at several hundred active members—in order to send newly trained North African recruits to fight in Iraq. The Al Qaeda–AQIM alliance has been most pronounced in terms of tactics. The GSPC initially acquired conventional weaponry for guerrilla ambushes, false checkpoints, and truck bombs against military and government targets. With Al Qaeda's help and encouragement, AQIM executes impressive terrorist attacks featuring suicide bombers and civilian casualties. Since December 2006, AQIM has bombed not only the Algerian prime minister's office and an army outpost but also foreign oil-services contractors and UN staff.

AQIM has declared its intention to attack European and American targets. One of the best-armed and most well-financed terrorist organizations, AQIM raises most of its funds through kidnapping and holding individuals for ransom. It is believed to have secured more than $50 million in this fashion during the past decade. One of its leaders, Oumar Ould Hamaha (who was killed in northern Mali in 2014), put it this way: "The source of our financing is the Western countries. They are paying for jihad."

In December 2012 one of AQIM's commanders, Mokhtar Belmokhtar, split off from AQIM and took his brigade with him, executing the In Amenas hostage crisis a month later after France had begun Operation SERVAL, its military intervention against Islamists in Mali. The hostage crisis began on January 16, 2013, when Belmokhtar and his men took more than 800 people hostage at the Tigantourine gas facility near In Amenas in southern Algeria. After four days Algerian special forces attacked the site, endeavoring to free the hostages. At least 39 foreign hostages were killed along with an Algerian security guard, as were 29 Islamists. A total of 685 Algerian workers and 107 foreigners were freed. Three Islamist militants were captured.

BENJAMIN P. NICKELS

See also

Al Qaeda; Al Qaeda in Iraq; Bin Laden, Osama; Global War on Terror; Terrorism

References

Gunaratna, Rohan. *Inside Al Qaeda: Global Network of Terror.* New York: Berkley Publishing Group, 2003.

Hansen, Andrew, and Lauren Vriens. "Al-Qaeda in the Islamic Maghreb (AQIM) or L'Organisation Al-Qaïda au Maghreb Islamique (Formerly Salafist Group for Preaching and Combat or Groupe Salafiste pour la Prédication et le Combat)." Council on Foreign Relations, Backgrounder, July 31, 2008, www.cfr.org/publication/12717.

Hunt, Emily. "Islamist Terrorism in Northwestern Africa: A 'Thorn in the Neck' of the United States?" Washington, DC: The Washington Institute for Near East Policy, Policy Focus #65, February 2007, www.washingtoninstitute.org/templateC04.php?CID=266.

Ibrahim, Raymond. *The Al Qaeda Reader.* New York: Doubleday, 2007.

Stora, Benjamin. *Algeria: A Short History.* Ithaca, NY: Cornell University Press, 2004.

Al-Quds Mosque

Mosque in Hamburg, Germany, where leaders of the September 11 operation worshipped and planned the attack. It was located in a poorer section of Hamburg on Steindamm Street. The al-Quds Mosque was situated above a body-building gym near Hamburg's central railway station. This location, close to cheap transportation, made it attractive to expatriate Muslims. Al-Quds was one of the few Arab Sunni mosques; most of others in Hamburg were Shiite or Turkish Sunni. It was small, holding at most 150 people at prayer time. These small mosques were good places for Islamist extremists to cultivate and recruit members.

Al-Quds was an extremist mosque because of the preaching of its leading cleric, Mohammed al-Fazazi. The founders of the mosque had been Moroccans, and most of its clerics, including al-Fazazi, were Muslims. He preached there constantly. Fazazi believed that Western civilization was the enemy of the Muslim world, and he believed in martyrdom. He was quoted in 2000 as saying that "who[ever] participates in the war against Islam with ideas or thoughts or a song or a television show to befoul Islam is an infidel on war footing that shall be killed, no matter if it's a man, a woman, or a child." It was these ideas that attracted Muhammad Atta to Islamist extremism and later to Al Qaeda. Fazazi spent considerable time with the young men in his congregation talking with them about jihad, holy war, and martyrdom. Later, Fazazi's involvement in bombings in Morocco and Spain led to a 30-year prison sentence in Morocco.

The al-Quds Mosque remained a place where it was possible to recruit others susceptible to the appeal of Fazazi and, later, Al Qaeda. Atta taught religious classes at the al-Quds Mosque, but his hard-line position alienated all but those who thought as he did. All of the members of the Hamburg Cell were recruited at the al-Quds Mosque, including Marwan al-Shehhi and Ramzi ibn al-Shibh. In August 2010 growing concerns that the site was again serving as a gathering place for Islamic extremists led German security authorities to close the mosque.

STEPHEN E. ATKINS

See also

Atta, Muhammad; Hamburg Cell; Shibh, Ramzi Muhammad Abdallah ibn al-

References

Corbin, Jane. *Al-Qaeda: The Terror Network That Threatens the World.* New York: Thunder's Mouth, 2002.

McDermott, Terry. *Perfect Soldiers: The 9/11 Hijackers: Who They Were, Why They Did It.* New York: HarperCollins, 2005.

Vidino, Lorenzo. *Al Qaeda in Europe: The New Battleground of International Jihad.* Amherst, NY: Prometheus Books, 2006.

Al-Shabaab

Extremist jihadist terrorist group operating in Somalia. Al-Shabaab began as the hard-line youth militia of the Islamic Courts Union (ICU), which briefly took control of Mogadishu, Kismayo, and other areas of southern Somalia in June 2006. When a combination of Ethiopian and Somali Transitional Federal Government (TFG) troops forced the ICU to withdraw from Mogadishu in December 2006, Al-Shabaab reconstituted itself as an independent organization and in early 2007 initiated an insurgency in an attempt to gain control of the country. It has since been engaged by TFG troops as well as military forces from the African Union Mission to Somalia (AMISOM), formed at the behest of the United Nations (UN) in February 2007. AMISOM has included several anti–Al-Shabaab militia groups within Somalia as well as military contingents from Uganda, Burundi, Kenya, Djibouti, Ethiopia, Sierra Leone, Ghana, and Nigeria. AMISOM has sometimes been aided in its anti–Al-Shabaab operations by Australia and the United States. Many Western nations have labeled Al-Shabaab a terrorist organization.

Originally led by Aden Hashi Farah "Ayro," Al-Shabaab has used assassinations, bombings, and more recently suicide attacks to target TFG forces, AMISOM peacekeepers, the UN, and foreign nationals. Since September 2014, Ahmed Umar has headed the group. Al-Shabaab's declared intention is to establish a caliphate in Somalia based on a strict Wahhabi interpretation of Islam.

Formally called Harakat al-Shabaab al-Mujahideen, or Movement of Warrior Youth, Al-Shabaab overran Kismayo in August 2008 and by the summer of 2010 had seized most of southern and central Somalia, including much of the capital, Mogadishu. Numbering between 4,000 and 6,000 members, Al-Shabaab appears to be divided into three commands: the Bay and Bokol, South Central and Mogadishu, and Puntland and Somaliland. An affiliate group also exists in the Juba Valley. The group funds itself mainly through charitable donations raised in areas it controls. Al-Shaabab has perpetrated dozens of terror attacks targeting AMISOM troops, TFG troops, and many civilians. Its specialties include the employment of suicide bombers, car and truck bombs, kidnapping, intimidation, and hit-and-run attacks. The group has also been involved in the widespread massacre of elephants, from which ivory is harvested from their tusks. It is believed that a significant portion of Al-Shabaab's funding in recent years has been derived from the illicit ivory trade.

In addition to these domestic attacks, there is increasing concern that Al-Shabaab has forged close links with foreign extremists, many of whom are thought to be based in Somalia and helping with the training of the group's members. Fears were further heightened in February 2010 when Al-Shabaab formally declared its organizational and operational allegiance to Al Qaeda. More recently, Al-Shabaab is believed to have forged informal alliances with Al Qaeda in the Islamic Maghreb as well as Boko Haram, the latter of which is a militant Islamist group operating chiefly in northeastern Nigeria.

Moreover, by 2008 or so, it appeared that Al-Shabaab had made a conscious strategic decision to export terrorism. Al-Shabaab has been linked to a 2009 plot to attack the Holsworthy Barracks in Australia, efforts aimed at recruiting Americans to carry out bombings on U.S. soil, and the attempted assassination in January 2010 of Danish cartoonist Kurt Westergaard, who created controversy in the Muslim world by drawing pictures depicting Muhammad wearing a bomb in his turban. Most seriously, the group claimed responsibility for the July 11, 2010, suicide bombings in Kampala, Uganda, which killed 74 people and wounded another 70, as well as an attack against a bus station in Nairobi, Kenya, on November 31, 2010, that left 3 people dead and injured 39. Al-Shabaab justified the strikes as retaliation for Ugandan and Kenyan support of the AMISOM mission in Somalia.

In August 2011, TFG and AMISOM troops managed to retake all of Mogadishu, which was a major reversal for Al-Shabaab. Meanwhile, a significant drought has caused widespread social and economic disruption in Somalia. That development has apparently caused a rift among some Al-Shabaab members, who disagree over how to attract new members and argue over the group's primary mission. By August 2014, Al-Shabaab had suffered a series of military reversals, as TFG and AMISOM forces gradually retook more and more territory once held by the rebel group. That same month, the Somali government announced a major military campaign to flush out remaining Al-Shabaab strongholds from the countryside.

On September 1, 2014, a U.S. drone strike against a small rebel-held village between the towns of Dhaab Tubaako and Haaway targeted a meeting of Al-Shabaab leaders to discuss an ongoing joint offensive by Somali and African Union troops against their strongholds in the country's south. The strike killed six Al-Shaabab members, including the organization's leader, Ahmed Abdi Godane. The same day, AMISOM announced that its military forces had liberated several important towns from the terrorists in the Middle Shabelle and Hiiran regions. The Somali government also issued a blanket 45-day amnesty for all Al-Shabaab members in an effort to eviscerate the organization and convince members to engage in peace talks with the TFG.

On December 25 Al-Shabaab launched an attack on the African Union base in Mogadishu. Nine people died, including three African Union soldiers, in the attack on the complex, which also houses UN offices and Western embassies. Al-Shabaab said that the attack was aimed at a Christmas party and was in retaliation for the killing of the group's leader Godane.

On December 27, 2014, Zakariya Ismail Ahmed Hersi, who had a $3 million reward on his head, surrendered to

Somali police in the Gerdo region. Hersi was one of eight top Somali leaders for whom the Barack Obama administration had offered a reward of $33 million and may have fallen out with those Al-Shabaab loyal to Ahmed Abdel Godane.

Although Al-Shabaab attacks continued, some observers have suggested that the organization has been substantially weakened and might soon splinter into competing factions or dissolve altogether.

RICHARD WARNES AND PAUL G. PIERPAOLI JR.

See also

Al Qaeda; Al Qaeda in the Islamic Maghreb; Boko Haram; Global War on Terror; Terrorism

References

Landler, Mark. "After Attacks in Uganda, Worry Grows over Group." *New York Times,* July 13, 2010.

"Pentagon Confirms Death of Terror Leader." Garowe Online, September 5, 2014, http://www.garoweonline.com/page/show/post/292/pentagon-confirms-death-of-somalia-terror-leader.

Rabasa, Angel. *Radical Islam in East Africa.* Santa Monica, CA: RAND, 2009.

Yusuf, Huma. "Somali Militant Group Al Shabab Aligns with Al-Qaeda." *Christian Science Monitor,* February 4, 2010.

Alusi, Mithal al- (1954–)

Iraqi politician and member of the Iraqi parliament. Mithal al-Alusi was born into a prominent Sunni professorial family in Anbar Province in 1954. A Baath Party member who was not allied with Saddam Hussein's regime, in 1976 Alusi, while studying in Cairo, was sentenced to death in absentia for trying to organize a plot against Hussein's regime. Alusi lived in exile for a time in Syria and then settled in the Federal Republic of Germany (West Germany), where he became a businessman. Convicted of hostage-taking by a Berlin court, he was sentenced to prison for three years but appealed the conviction and did not serve the full sentence.

Alusi returned to Iraq in 2003 following the overthrow of Hussein and was appointed the director of culture and media at the Higher National Commission for De-Baathification. Alusi is a strong proponent of close Iraqi ties with the United States, the United Kingdom, Turkey, and Israel. In September 2004 after a public visit to Israel, Alusi was expelled from his post and from the Iraqi National Congress of Ahmed Chalabi. Alusi was also indicted by the Central Criminal Court on a charge of having had contact with an enemy state.

Alusi then formed a new political party, the Democratic Party of the Iraqi Nation, to contest the January 2005 Iraqi elections. Receiving only 4,500 votes, it failed to win representation in the Council of Representatives. In February 2005 Alusi's car was ambushed in Baghdad. His two sons and a bodyguard were killed in the attack, although he escaped. Asad al-Hasimi, then minister of culture, was convicted of the crime and sentenced to death in absentia. In December 2005 the Mithal al-Alusi List coalition of small parties ran in the national elections and won only .3 percent of the popular vote. This was sufficient, however, to secure one seat, which Alusi took.

In September 2008 Alusi again visited Israel and spoke as a member of the audience at a conference on counterterrorism, during which he praised Israel and called for the normalization of relations with the Jewish state. On his return to Iraq, the National Assembly voted to revoke his parliamentary immunity and ban him from travel abroad. At the same time, a government minister threatened to indict Alusi again on the charge of having visited a country that is considered an enemy of Iraq. Alusi appealed to the Supreme Federal Court, which overturned the revocation of his immunity and declared that since no Iraqi law bars such travel, no crime had been committed.

In March 2010, Alusi lost his seat in parliament in that year's national elections. He promptly alleged that the election returns had been rigged against him and his party, claiming that the ballot irregularities had been the work of conservatives as well as operatives from Iran and Saudi Arabia. In April, Iraq's Supreme Court ordered a recount, which was completed in May 2010. The recount showed no fraud or vote tampering, and the court upheld the election results.

SPENCER C. TUCKER

See also

Baath Party; Hussein, Saddam; Iraq War

References

Fox, Robert. *Peace and War in Iraq, 2003–2005.* Barnsley, UK: Leo Cooper, 2005.

"Iraq May Execute MP for Israel Visit." *Jerusalem Post,* September 22, 2008.

"Iraq Seeks to Prosecute Legislator for Israel Trip." *Reuters,* September 14, 2008.

Packer, George. *The Assassins' Gate: America in Iraq.* New York: Farrar, Straus and Giroux, 2005.

Ambush Alley

A stretch of road, including two bridges, located at the edge of Nasiriyah, Iraq. The road gained its nickname "Ambush Alley" in March 2003 during the initial stages of Operation

IRAQI FREEDOM because of two incidents. The first was the ambush of the U.S. Army 507th Maintenance Company on March 23. A convoy element of the company blundered into an Iraqi ambush, resulting in several Americans being killed or wounded and several more, including Private Jessica Lynch, being captured.

The second more notable incident also occurred on March 23. In this engagement, Iraqi forces attacked a unit of U.S. marines seeking to capture two bridges over the Saddam Canal and the Euphrates River and the roadway between them. The ensuing battle became the costliest single engagement for American forces during the initial invasion of Iraq. It eventually involved the bulk of Task Force Tarawa, including the 1st and 3rd Battalions of the 2nd Marine Regiment; Alpha Company, 8th Tank Battalion; and Marine Aircraft Group 29.

The marine mission had seemed straightforward. Invasion planners recognized that the two bridges and the road between them represented a vital supply artery on the road to Baghdad. Once the bridges and the road were secured, the way would be open for the Americans to drive north toward Kut and from there to Baghdad.

Neither the marine field commanders entrusted with the capture of the bridges—Lieutenant Colonel Rick Grabowski, the commander of the 1st Battalion, 2nd Marine Regiment, and his immediate superior, Colonel Ronald Bailey, the commander of the regiment—nor the senior U.S. military leadership expected any difficulty here. Nasiriyah lay in one of the areas of Iraq considered by U.S. authorities to be less hostile to coalition forces. Senior U.S. commanders believed that the Shia population, traditionally hostile to the Iraqi regime, would welcome them. The U.S. leadership believed that the Iraqi regular army soldiers in the city, mostly from the 11th Infantry Division, were second rate and would flee or blend into the civilian population as soon as the Americans approached.

Based on these assumptions and the perceived need to capture the two bridges quickly, Grabowski planned to take the Southern Euphrates Bridge with Alpha Company. Bravo Company would then cross the bridge onto Route Moe (Ambush Alley), turn immediately to the east, and push to the Northern Saddam Canal Bridge with close artillery, air, and armored support. Charlie Company, 1st Battalion, 2nd Marines, was to move through Alpha and Bravo's lines and seize the Northern Saddam Bridge. The tank company was included in the initial attack, but some of its M1 Abrams tanks were refueling, so the initial attacks were launched without armored support.

As the marines approached the Southern Euphrates Bridge, Iraqi forces on both sides of the road opened fire on Alpha Company. Shortly thereafter, Charlie Company also reported that it was taking fire from the area around the Saddam Bridge. Bravo Company, following Alpha Company near the southern bridge, was soon pinned down by heavy fire from automatic weapons and rocket-propelled grenades. The marines were trapped in narrow streets surrounding the bridges, where it was difficult to bring their supporting arms to bear. Although they held the southern bridge, their foothold was tenuous.

The fighting involved U.S. efforts to relieve the embattled 1st Battalion and secure the road. The greatest difficulties proved to be getting armored support and reinforcements to the marines through the narrow streets and coordinating air support. The process proved to be costly. The marines faced a maze of Iraqi roadblocks. A field south of the Euphrates Bridge that seemed promising as a route for the tanks proved to be a sewage disposal bog that would not support heavy tanks. Mounting casualties made medical evacuation urgent, but it was impossible to get medevac helicopters to the marine positions because of intense ground fire. In the early afternoon, an air strike by two Fairchild-Republic A-10 Thunderbolt II ground attack aircraft went awry and struck Charlie Company's position instead of the Iraqis.

By the evening of March 23 the 2nd Marine Regiment had seized both bridges, and the firing from the Iraqi positions had slackened. But the marines still had not completely secured Ambush Alley. It would take another two days to completely clear the roadway.

The events at Nasiriyah shook the marines. The official casualty count was 18 dead and 55 wounded, but many American officers privately thought that the count was much higher. Despite many acts of heroism, the Ambush Alley fight was not an impressive beginning to IRAQI FREEDOM. The intelligence on Iraqi strength and fortifications here was faulty, and the marine plan, which involved coordination among multiple commands, was too complicated. The tactics the Iraqis used at Nasiriyah indicated that they would not use conventional tactics but would fight using ambush and hit-and-run tactics. The Battle of Ambush Alley portended the nature of the fighting for the rest of the initial Iraq invasion and the ensuing Iraqi insurgency.

WALTER F. BELL

See also

Fedayeen; IRAQI FREEDOM, Operation; Lynch, Jessica; United States Marine Corps, Iraq War

References

Gordon, Michael R., and General Bernard E. Trainor. *Cobra II: The Inside Story of the Invasion and Occupation of Iraq.* New York: Pantheon Books, 2006.

Pritchard, Tim. *Ambush Alley: The Most Extraordinary Battle of the Iraq War.* New York: Ballatine Books, 2007.

American Airlines Flight 11

American Airlines Flight 11 was a Boeing 767-223ER that was the first aircraft to crash into the World Trade Center complex in New York City on September 11, 2001, striking the North Tower. The pilot of the aircraft was John Ogonowski, a 52-year-old Vietnam veteran from Massachusetts, and its first officer was Thomas McGuinness. Flight 11 departed from Boston's Logan International Airport nearly 14 minutes late, at 7:59 a.m., bound for Los Angeles International Airport. It carried slightly more than half its capacity of 181—81 passengers and a crew of 11—and had a full load of 23,980 gallons of aviation fuel at takeoff, which was routine.

The leader of the terrorist team and its designated pilot on board Flight 11 was Muhammad Atta. Atta and other members of the hijack team—Satam al-Suqami, Waleed al-Shehri, Wail al-Shehri, and Abdul Aziz al-Omari—had bought first-class seats, which research conducted on other flights convinced them gave them the best opportunity to seize the cockpit and gain control of the aircraft. Two of the hijackers sat near the cockpit, and two sat near the passenger section. Atta sat in 8D from whence he could command both teams.

The hijackers had little trouble passing through checkpoint security. American Airlines security checkpoints at Logan International Airport were operated by a private company, Globe Security, which operated these checkpoints under a contract with American Airlines. Because American Airlines desired that passengers be harassed at checkpoints as little as possible, the hijackers had no difficulty in passing through the checkpoints carrying box cutters and mace.

Instructions had been given by Al Qaeda trainers to the hijackers to seize the aircraft by force within 15 minutes of takeoff. Around 8:14 they did so, killing two attendants and a passenger, Daniel Lewin, immediately. Lewin, formerly an officer in the elite Sayeret Matkal unit of the Israeli military, was seen as a threat. The hijackers, who had apparently identified him as a potential air marshal, killed him as soon as possible. To allay suspicions, the hijackers lulled the passengers and crew into a false sense of hope by giving the impression that the plane would land safely and that the passengers would be used as hostages, a successful tactic of hijackers in the past.

Smoke rises from the Pentagon minutes after the hijacked jetliner American Airlines Flight 11 crashed into the building at approximately 9:30 a.m. on September 11, 2001. (United States Marine Corps)

Air traffic controllers received information from the cockpit via Ogonowski's radio, over which they heard a conversation between the pilot and a hijacker in the cockpit that made it evident that a hijacking was in progress. More ominously, they also learned from a hijacker's comment about plans to seize control of other aircraft. This information was the first indication of a plot to hijack numerous aircraft in flight.

The first concrete information about the hijacking came from Betty Ong, a flight attendant on Flight 11, who contacted the American Airlines Flight Center in Fort Worth, Texas, and related that two flight attendants had been stabbed and that another was on oxygen. A passenger, she said, had been killed, and the hijackers had gained access to the cockpit, using some type of mace-like spray to neutralize the crew.

Once the hijackers gained control of the aircraft, they took precautions to control the passengers, securing the first-class section by intimidation, mace and pepper spray, and threats to detonate a bomb. The rest of the passengers, in coach, were led to believe that a medical emergency had occurred in the first-class section. The hijackers also told the passengers that the aircraft was returning to the airport. Another attendant, Madeleine Sweeney, contacted authorities and confirmed Ong's earlier message to the American Flight Services Office in Boston. She reestablished communication and was in fact on the line when the aircraft approached the North Tower of the World Trade Center. By the time the passengers realized what was happening, it was too late to do anything. Many hurriedly called their loved ones and said goodbye either by talking with them or by leaving messages.

The aircraft crashed at about 378 miles per hour between the 94th and 98th floors of the North Tower. The crew, passengers, and hijackers all died instantly from the force of the explosion and the fire that accompanied it. The force of the explosion alone shattered the aluminum wings and fuselage of the aircraft into pieces the size of a human fist.

The impact of the crash and the prolonged burning of aviation fuel weakened the structure of the North Tower, trapping those people above the 98th floor, who had no chance of escape. Those threatened by fire and smoke began to jump from the building. The North Tower collapsed on itself shortly after the South Tower fell.

STEPHEN E. ATKINS

See also

Atta, Muhammad; September 11 Attacks

References

Atkins, Stephen E. *The 9/11 Encyclopedia.* 2nd ed. Santa Barbara, CA: ABC-CLIO, 2011.

Aust, Stefan, et al. *Inside 9/11: What Really Happened.* New York: St. Martin's, 2001.

Bernstein, Richard. *Out of the Blue: The Story of September 11, 2001, from Jihad to Ground Zero.* New York: Times Books, 2002.

Craig, Olga. "At 8:46 AM, the World Changed in a Moment." *Sunday Telegraph* [London], September 16, 2001, 14.

The 9/11 Commission Report: Final Report of the National Commission on Terrorist Attacks upon the United States. New York: Norton, 2004.

Trento, Susan B., and Joseph J. Trento. *Unsafe at Any Altitude: Failed Terrorism Investigations, Scapegoating 9/11, and the Shocking Truth about Aviation Security Today.* Hanover, NH: Steerforth, 2006.

American Airlines Flight 77

American Airlines Flight 77, a Boeing 757-223, was the third aircraft seized by hijackers on September 11, 2001. It left Dulles International Airport near Washington, D.C., at 8:20 a.m., bound for Los Angeles International Airport with 58 passengers and a crew of 6. The pilot was Charles Burlingame, and the first officer was David Charlebois. Because of problems at the security gate, the flight was 10 minutes late taking off. The security checkpoint at Dulles International Airport was operated by Argenbright Security under a contract with United Airlines. Passenger screeners at Dulles International Airport were 87 percent foreign-born and mostly Muslim. Three of the hijackers failed the metal detector test but, after passing hand-wand screening, were permitted to enter the aircraft. There was no indication that any of them were carrying prohibited weapons.

The five-person terrorist team was led by Hani Hanjour, who was also the team's designated pilot. Other members of his team were Nawaf al-Hazmi, Salem al-Hazmi, Khalid al-Mihdhar, and Majed Moqued, who had all bought first-class tickets to gain better access to the aircraft's cockpit. The hijackers used knives and box cutters to gain control of the cockpit sometime between 8:51 and 8:54 a.m., after which Hanjour turned the aircraft around and headed for Washington, D.C. Like the hijackers of American Airlines Flight 11, the hijackers of Flight 77 calmed passengers by convincing them that the plane would land, after which they would be used as hostages.

Although by this time it was known that other aircraft had been seized and turned into flying bombs, authorities in Washington, D.C., were slow to respond. Two passengers, Renee May and Barbara K. Olson, the wife of U.S. solicitor general Theodore Olson, made phone calls reporting the hijacking. She made two calls to her husband, giving him details of the hijacking. He told her the news of the two aircraft crashing into the World Trade Center.

By this time the Dulles air controllers were aware of an approaching unauthorized aircraft coming at high speed toward Washington, D.C. They had been able to obtain a visual confirmation from a military transport, a C-141, as the hijacked aircraft headed toward the Pentagon. Between 9:37 and 9:40 a.m., Flight 77 crashed at 530 miles per hour into the ground at the base of the west side of the Pentagon, killing all passengers. Although much of the crash site contained recently renovated unoccupied offices, the explosion and the resulting collapse of parts of the five-story building killed 125 people. The explosion did its greatest damage to the three outer rings of the Pentagon, but the two inner rings sustained damage as well.

STEPHEN E. ATKINS

See also

Hazmi, Nawaf al-; Mihdhar, Khalid al-; September 11 Attacks

References

"Accounts of Survivors." Tools for Coping with Life's Stressors, http://www.coping.org/911/survivor/pentagon.htm.

Atkins, Stephen E. *The 9/11 Encyclopedia.* 2nd ed. Santa Barbara, CA: ABC-CLIO, 2011.

Aust, Stefan, et al. *Inside 9/11: What Really Happened.* New York: St. Martin's, 2001.

Bernstein, Richard. *Out of the Blue: The Story of September 11, 2001, from Jihad to Ground Zero.* New York: Times Books, 2002.

The 9/11 Commission Report: Final Report of the National Commission on Terrorist Attacks Upon the United States. New York: Norton, 2004.

Trento, Susan B., and Joseph J. Trento. *Unsafe at Any Altitude: Failed Terrorism Investigations, Scapegoating 9/11, and the Shocking Truth about Aviation Security Today.* Hanover, NH: Steerforth, 2006.

Amos, James F. (1946–)

U.S. Marine Corps general and commandant (2010–2014). Born on November 12, 1946, at Wendell, Idaho, James F. "Jim" Amos graduated from the University of Idaho in 1970, then joined the U.S. Marine Corps and qualified as an aviator. Assignments to fighter squadrons followed, where Amos flew the McDonnell Douglas F-4 Phantom. In 1985 he assumed command of Marine Air Base Squadron 24. After transitioning to the McDonnell Douglas/Boeing/Northrop F/A-18 Hornet, he joined Carrier Air Wing 8 on the *Theodore Roosevelt.* In May 1996 Amos assumed command of Marine

Aircraft Group 31. In August 2002 he took command of the 3rd Marine Aircraft Wing, and almost immediately he began planning for conflict in Iraq.

Amos's wing included more than 370 aircraft for operations against Iraq in Operation IRAQI FREEDOM and thus constituted a substantial part of the coalition air assets for the campaign. Marine aircraft were especially important in the ground support effort. Amos strongly supported the concept of the marine air-ground task force, which held that aircraft played an integral role in the support of ground forces. He was determined that his pilots facilitate the ground advance.

To carry out the close support of marine ground forces, Amos worked closely with Major General James Mattis, commanding the 1st Marine Division. Amos also developed a good working relationship with U.S. Air Force lieutenant general Michael Moseley, the air component commander, who had wide latitude in the employment of his air assets. Amos also received naval cooperation.

Marine Bell AH-1 Cobra gunships were based on land, where they were closer to the fighting and able to support the marines quickly. The vertical takeoff and landing (VTOL) McDonnell Douglas/Boeing/BAE Systems AV-8B Harrier fighter-bombers were on amphibious ships offshore. These ships in effect became light aircraft carriers and provided support to the Harriers until they could be based ashore. The marine ground forces also relied on Amos's aircraft for much of their supplies. Mattis was determined to move fast and deep, and his vehicles could carry only a limited amount of ammunition, fuel, food, and water. For resupply, the marines depended on Amos's Lockheed C-130 Hercules transport planes.

When the invasion of Iraq began on March 20, 2003, Amos employed his aircraft aggressively. The Cobras were charged with destroying Iraqi units immediately in front of the marine spearheads, while the Harriers and Hornets were used in deeper missions to cut off Iraqi forces that might threaten the marine advance. To provide greater ability to respond to the needs of the ground forces, U.S. Marine Corps doctrine called for a combat pilot to be detailed to each infantry company as a forward air controller. Amos went even further and provided an extra flight officer to each battalion. As the troops advanced and captured Iraqi airfields, the Cobras were moved forward to decrease flight time.

The 3rd Marine Air Wing played an important role in the success of the marine advance on Baghdad. By the end of the organized fighting in late April, Amos's aircraft had flown 9,800 sorties. They had dropped 2,200 precision-guided bombs and 2,300 gravity bombs, a total of 6.24 million pounds of ordnance. During the advance Amos was often near the front, inspecting the effectiveness of the air effort and gauging the needs.

In July 2004 Amos was advanced to command the II Marine Expeditionary Force based at Camp Lejeune, North Carolina. He reorganized training facilities to be more like those encountered in Iraq and Afghanistan. He also built simulated forward-operating bases similar to those used by the marines in those countries. A road network suitable for training to deal with ambush and improvised explosive device attacks followed. Amos also worked on such projects as improving safety among marine motorcycle riders by organizing clubs and rodeos, and he provided recognition and support for wounded marines by sponsoring the Wounded Warriors Battalion.

Amos's achievements were recognized in July 2008, when he was selected as the 31st assistant commandant of the U.S. Marine Corps, and again in June 2010, when he was chosen as the 35th commandant of the U.S. Marine Corps, the first Marine Corps aviator to hold that position. In 2011 when the Barack Obama administration announced an end to the "don't ask, don't tell" policy toward gays in the military, Amos initially opposed the move. However, after the integration of openly gay service men and women into the armed forces was begun, he stated that the new policy had proven to be a "nonevent" and that he no longer had qualms about the decision. Amos retired on October 17, 2014.

TIM J. WATTS

See also

Iraq War; Moseley, Teed Michael; Obama, Barack Hussein, II; United States Marine Corps, Iraq War

References

Gordon, Michael R., and General Bernard E. Trainor. *Cobra II: The Inside Story of the Invasion and Occupation of Iraq.* New York: Pantheon Books, 2006.

Murray, Williamson, and Robert H. Scales Jr. *The Iraq War: A Military History.* Boston: Belknap, 2003.

ANACONDA, Operation (March 1–18, 2002)

A U.S.-led coalition campaign against the Taliban and Al Qaeda in Afghanistan during March 1–18, 2002. The offensive was part of Operation ENDURING FREEDOM and took place in the Shah-i-kot Valley in Paktia Province in eastern Afghanistan. Although the December 2001 Battle of Tora Bora had routed most of the Taliban and Al Qaeda from the region, by February 2002 insurgents and foreign fighters had begun to return to the Shah-i-Kot Valley and the Arma Mountains and were initiating new attacks on coalition forces. In response, the allies launched Operation ANACONDA in an effort to dislodge the insurgents and prevent a more significant enemy offensive from unfolding in the spring. The coalition was also responding to reports that senior insurgent leaders, including Taliban leader Mullah Mohammed Omar and Al Qaeda leader Osama bin Laden, may have been present in the area.

Operation ANACONDA began on March 1, 2002, after special operations forces from the United States, Australia, Denmark, Germany, the Netherlands, New Zealand, and Norway had been inserted into the region and had established forward observation posts. These were followed by a ground assault that included elements of the U.S. Army's 10th Mountain Division and the 101st Airborne Division as well as the Canadian Army's Princess Patricia's Light Infantry, the British Royal Marines, and Afghan National Army forces. The United States furnished about 1,200 troops, the Afghan National Army furnished 1,000 troops, and the other coalition partners furnished 200 troops. Aircraft from the United States, the United Kingdom, and France provided air support. U.S. Army major general Franklin Hagenbeck had command of the operation.

The difficult terrain in the region complicated the operation. The mountains ranged up to 12,000 feet and were dotted with caves and ravines, which provided hiding places for insurgent forces. The valley floor was between 7,000 and 8,000 feet in elevation. Temperatures during the offensive ranged from 60°F during the day to as low as 0°F at night.

The offensive suffered from a number of intelligence errors. Planners estimated the total number of insurgents at around 250; however, there were actually about 1,000, under the command of Saifur Rahman Monsoor of the Taliban. In addition, coalition officers underestimated their opponents' firepower. The insurgents were equipped with heavy machine guns, mortars, and artillery. One result was that the allied ground forces did not begin the operation with significant artillery support. Instead, they relied on mortars and airpower. Intelligence reports also falsely indicated that the majority of the enemy was on the valley floor, when most were actually in heavily fortified bunkers and caves in the mountains.

Reports also indicated the presence of some 800 civilians in the valley, although there were actually none. In an effort to minimize civilian casualties, the original plans called for the Afghan National forces to enter the valley from the west on March 2, supported by airpower and special operations forces, and help differentiate between the Taliban and Al Qaeda and the civilians. Planners expected the insurgents to flee before the advancing Afghans while U.S. and coalition conventional forces blocked their escape routes to the east and south. Most of the conventional forces were transported into the valley by helicopter.

The allied Afghan column was soon halted by heavy insurgent fire during its advance, and the coalition had to shift tactics. Allied special operations forces coordinated air strikes by bombers, Lockheed AC-130 Spectre gunships, and cruise missiles on Taliban and Al Qaeda positions. The coalition used more than 3,500 aerial bombs and cruise missiles during the offensive. The coalition also used 2,000-pound thermobaric bombs against caves and bunkers. Supported by airpower, the coalition ground forces were redeployed and advanced into the mountains. On March 4 a U.S. helicopter carrying Navy SEALS came under fire near the peak of Takur Ghar, and one SEAL fell from the aircraft; he was killed. The SEALs were to be inserted on the peak but found that the Taliban had a significant concentration of forces, including heavy machine guns and rocket-propelled grenades. During the subsequent rescue attempt, another helicopter was hit and crashed. In the ensuing firefight, seven U.S. troops were killed before the rescue mission was concluded. Although intense combat continued following the incident, the Taliban and Al Qaeda began to withdraw from the region.

On March 12, U.S. and Afghan forces initiated an advance through the valley and met little organized resistance. Operation ANACONDA officially ended on March 18, although there continued to be minor skirmishes in the region for the next month. During the operation, the coalition lost 15 killed and 82 wounded. The majority of the casualties were Americans, including 8 killed and 72 wounded. The Taliban and Al Qaeda lost between 300 and 400 killed; however, the majority of the enemy forces were able to escape.

TOM LANSFORD

See also

Aircraft, Helicopters; Al Qaeda; Bin Laden, Osama; Casualties, Operation ENDURING FREEDOM; North Atlantic Treaty Organization; Omar, Mohammed; Takur Ghar, Battle of; Taliban; Tora Bora; United Kingdom Forces in Afghanistan

References

Hersh, Seymour. *Chain of Command: The Road from 9/11 to Abu Ghraib*. New York: HarperCollins, 2004.

MacPherson, Malcolm. *Roberts Ridge: A Story of Courage and Sacrifice on Takur Ghar Mountain, Afghanistan*. New York: Bantam Dell, 2008.

Naylor, Sean. *Not a Good Day to Die: The Untold Story of Operation Anaconda*. New York: Berkley Trade, 2006.

Anbar Awakening, Iraq War

A U.S. operation to obtain or regain the loyalties of Sunni Arab tribes of Anbar Province, Iraq, that began in the provincial capital of Ramadi in September 2006. Tribal sheikhs who had been marginalized or who sought revenge against Al Qaeda in Iraq (AQI) began cooperating with U.S. forces to root out the AQI network from the province. The Anbar Awakening restored a degree of order to a region that appeared on the verge of slipping irrevocably under insurgent control. It is credited as being a major factor in the diminution of violence in Iraq, which began in earnest in 2007.

That the Sunni tribes of Anbar would serve as the catalyst for such a transformative development was a carefully planned movement, based on the sentiments expressed by U.S. ambassador Zalmay Khalilzad and General David Petraeus as well as others that the Sunni population must be granted a stake in the outcome. However, the province's recent engagement in violent opposition to the U.S.-led coalition and differences with the new Iraqi government were obstacles to be surmounted. Anbar, the largest of Iraq's 18 provinces with its predominantly Sunni population, became a hotspot of insurgent activity following the fall of Baghdad in 2003. Disaffected sheikhs and their tribal followers gravitated to the insurgency, driven by anger at seeing their lands occupied by foreign soldiers, resentment over the loss of jobs and prestige, and distrust of the new Shiite-dominated political order, among other things. The porous border that Anbar shared with Syria at the far western end of the province also provided an easy point of entry for fighters from other nations, who filtered into Fallujah, Ramadi, and the smaller population centers along the upper Euphrates River. Many joined the organization founded by Jordanian extremist Abu Musab al-Zarqawi, which evolved into the AQI.

Tribal insurgents had formed an alliance of convenience with AQI jihadists in Anbar, and the AQI itself was actually an overwhelmingly Iraqi, not foreign, organization. By the middle of 2006, the insurgency had grown so strong that Anbar outpaced even Baghdad in terms of the number of violent incidents, with 30–40 attacks occurring daily in the province. Conditions in Ramadi were particularly grim: public services were negligible, and the Iraqi security presence was almost nonexistent, enabling insurgent fighters to operate freely in most sections of the city. A classified assessment completed by the U.S. Marine Corps in August 2006 concluded that the province was all but lost to the insurgency.

Yet the AQI laid the groundwork for its own demise by demanding control of the insurgency and reducing Anbar's tribal chiefs to subordinate status. AQI operatives punished in brutal fashion any who opposed them, with bombings and murders that targeted not only the sheikhs but also their family members and supporters. The vicious tactics used by the AQI to cow the tribes also alienated them and opened up a rift within the insurgency. In what in retrospect can be seen as a precursor to the Anbar Awakening movement, several tribes around Ramadi in January 2006 formed the al-Anbar People's Council, a breakaway group that sought to distance itself from the AQI while continuing to resist the coalition. The council collapsed soon thereafter after seven of its members were assassinated and a suicide bomber killed dozens at a police recruiting event.

The demise of the al Anbar People's Council demonstrated that the Ramadi tribes lacked the strength and cohesion to stand up against the AQI on their own. A few months later, the sheikhs gained a powerful new benefactor when Colonel Sean MacFarland arrived with the U.S. Army's 1st Brigade Combat Team to take charge of Ramadi's security. MacFarland and his brigade had deployed first in January 2006 to Tal Afar, the city in northern Iraq that had been pacified the previous year by Colonel H. R. McMaster in what was widely hailed as a textbook counterinsurgency operation. Moving to Ramadi in June 2006, MacFarland was determined to apply some of the same counterinsurgency practices that had proven so effective at Tal Afar.

As one of the first steps in his plan to win back the city, MacFarland launched an outreach program aimed at gaining the trust and support of Ramadi's leaders. Among the earliest to respond was a charismatic young sheikh of relatively junior stature named Abd al-Sattar Buzaigh al-Rishawi. His record was far from clean, however: he was reputed to be a smuggler and highway bandit who had cooperated with the AQI in the past. More recently, however, he had lost his father and three brothers to the AQI's campaign of terror against the tribes, so he was receptive to American overtures. With Sattar's help in gathering recruits, MacFarland was able to begin the process of rebuilding Ramadi's embattled police force, which numbered only about 400 at the beginning of his tour. The sheikh also assisted with MacFarland's efforts to persuade other tribal leaders to shift their allegiance from the AQI to the coalition.

Sattar expanded his opposition to the AQI into a full-fledged movement after AQI agents bombed one of the new Iraqi police stations that had been set up in the city and murdered the sheikh whose tribesmen were staffing the post. In response, Sattar convened a meeting of over 50 sheikhs and MacFarland at his home on September 9, 2006. At the gathering, Sattar announced the launching of the Anbar Awakening, an alliance of tribes dedicated to expelling the AQI from the region. Initially, only a handful of tribes signed on to the movement. However, over the next few months the movement acquired new converts in and around Ramadi once those related to Sattar saw that MacFarland was committed to using his troops to protect the tribes that rejected the AQI. The American commander also supported the tribes' efforts to defend themselves through the organization of armed tribal auxiliary groups, later known as Concerned Local Citizens or Sons of Iraq. MacFarland arranged for militia members to receive training and ensured that as many as possible were incorporated into the Iraqi police force. By the end of 2006, some 4,000 recruits had been added to police ranks.

The AQI did not allow itself to be swept aside by the Anbar Awakening movement without a fight. Violence levels in Anbar peaked in October 2006 and remained high through March 2007. But the movement acquired its own momentum, spreading from Ramadi and gaining adherents in Fallujah and other parts of the province throughout 2007. Insurgent activity dropped sharply after March, a trend that reflected not only the diminishing strength of the AQI but also the fact that once sheikhs joined the Anbar Awakening, they directed their followers to cease all attacks on American troops. Sattar himself was killed in a bombing outside his Ramadi home on September 13, 2007, a mere 10 days after he had met with President George W. Bush at a military base in Anbar. Nonetheless, Sattar's death did not reverse or slow the progress that had been made in the province, nor did it diminish local support for the Awakening Councils and their militia offshoots, which had sprouted up in Sunni areas outside of Anbar.

On September 1, 2008, Anbar completed its own remarkable turnaround from the most volatile region in Iraq to a more stable environment, and security for the province was officially transferred to the Iraqi government.

Growing tensions between the Awakening Councils and the government over late pay and a lack of jobs led in March 2009 to an uprising in the Sunni-dominated Fahdil section of Baghdad and the disarmament by Iraqi and U.S. troops of the Awakening Council there. The government retained a number of members of the Fahdi Council but subsequently announced that the 150 members of the council would be offered jobs in the Iraqi security forces.

Unfortunately, after the withdrawal of U.S. and coalition troops from Iraq in 2011, Anbar Province was convulsed by a renewal of sectarian and insurgent violence. By early 2014, Islamist groups, including the AQI, had seized control of both Fallujah and Ramadi, and by the spring of that year the Iraqi government no longer controlled Anbar Province. The Iraqi government has been largely helpless in stemming these developments. By late 2014, the Islamic State of Iraq and Syria (ISIS) controlled Anbar, and the U.S. government began carrying out air strikes there in an attempt to assist the Uraqi government. With Anbar virtually lost, the future of Iraq remained very much in question.

JEFF SEIKEN

See also

Al Qaeda in Iraq; Iraq, History of, 1990–Present; Islamic State in Iraq and Syria

References

Lubin, Andrew. "Ramadi: From the Caliphate to Capitalism." *Proceedings* 134 (April 2008): 54–61.

McCary, John A. "The Anbar Awakening: An Alliance of Incentives." *Washington Quarterly* 32 (January 2009): 43–59.

Smith, Major Niel, and Colonel Sean MacFarland. "Anbar Awakens: The Tipping Point." *Military Review* (March–April 2008): 41–52.

West, Bing. *The Strongest Tribe: War, Politics, and the Endgame in Iraq.* New York: Random House, 2008.

Anglo-American Alliance

One of the most potent and enduring strategic partnerships of modern times, which evolved into a multifaceted strategic relationship based on the solid foundation of common heritage, culture, and language as well as shared values, vision, and interests. Because of its paramount strategic importance, the Middle East played an extremely important role in the evolution of the Anglo-American alliance. Despite sporadic disagreements, most notoriously during the 1956 Suez Crisis and the Yom Kippur (Ramadan) War of 1973 when American and British priorities diverged in the overall course of the Cold War and beyond, Anglo-American relations were generally harmonious, and both powers complemented each other's role in the region. This trend only gained momentum in the post–Cold War world, when new major challenges and threats, particularly the risk of the proliferation of weapons of mass destruction and international

terrorism, stimulated common Anglo-American security concerns and mutual recognition of the need for close strategic cooperation in the region.

There were also several other important factors dealing with the American and British postures in the Middle East and U.S.-UK relations that contributed to the further development of the alliance. Politically and diplomatically, both powers needed each other in the Middle East. For the United States, the solid and stable alliance with Britain had a special value in this volatile and unpredictable region, where changing calculations of self-interest too often motivated many other American partners. Also, the alliance with Britain—one of the major powers and a permanent member of the United Nations (UN) Security Council—enhanced U.S. global leadership and gave American interests in the Middle East an additional international legitimacy. Moreover, despite their withdrawal from empire in the 1950s, 1960s, and 1970s, the British still retained close contacts with many regimes in the Middle East, and their expertise in local culture and traditions was of great advantage in dealing with Muslim countries, particularly during the 1991 Persian Gulf War, the Global War on Terror, the Afghanistan War (2001–2014), and the Iraq War (2003–2011). These connections allowed a division of labor within the alliance: the British were indispensable at international coalition-building efforts, while the Americans could concentrate more on strategic and military planning and preparations.

Militarily, the alliance provided the British with critically important access to American high technology, particularly in reconnaissance and surveillance. At the same time, Britain's experiences of providing a long-term military presence in the Middle East, particularly in special operations, counterinsurgency, urban warfare, and pacification of hostile populations, were made available for the Americans.

Intelligence was another area of particularly fruitful cooperation between the United States and the United Kingdom. The degree of intelligence sharing and reciprocity in intelligence-gathering operations is unlikely equaled between any other two countries in the world. Recently, the intelligence services of both countries have been actively involved in gathering information about terrorist activities, particularly Al Qaeda, and the risk of the proliferation of weapons of mass destruction in the Middle East.

The close personal relations between American presidents and British prime ministers, who as a rule came to depend on each other, have also been of much importance for the development of the Anglo-American alliance. Many

British prime ministers, particularly Margaret Thatcher and Tony Blair, kept extraordinarily high profiles in Washington, frequently setting the very agenda of the alliance with much eloquence and persuasiveness and even personifying the alliance internationally. For example, just prior to the 1991 Persian Gulf War, Thatcher convinced President George H. W. Bush that he must not shy away from using military force if Iraqi president Saddam Hussein did not quit Kuwait within the time span set by the UN.

There was also a strong inclination in both capitals to reassert and solidify the special relationship in any international turmoil, including in the Middle East, on the basis of an almost axiomatic assumption that in case of crisis and/or war, both partners must stand shoulder to shoulder together. On the British side, that trend is frequently supplemented by the belief that a firm commitment to sharing military burdens with America and providing Washington open-ended unqualified support would make Britain the most trusted American ally. In so doing, London believes that it can influence the way in which America exercises its might, and this elevates Britain to the status of pivotal global power, greatly multiplying its real weight in international affairs.

The removal of the Taliban from power in Afghanistan in late 2001 and the rapid military overthrow of the Saddam Hussein regime in Iraq in 2003 signified the culmination of the ongoing Anglo-American strategy in the Middle East, which included the victory in the Persian Gulf War and cooperation in policing of the no-fly zones in the Iraqi sky in its aftermath as well as military collaboration in Operation DESERT FOX in 1998. Diplomatically, the U.S.-UK partnership was instrumental in securing UN backing for the occupation and rebuilding of Iraq, in the promotion of the two-state solution for the Israeli-Palestinian problem, and in Libya's renunciation of its weapons of mass destruction program.

At the same time, the evolution of the Afghanistan War and the Iraq War into protracted insurgencies revealed some underlying problems and complexities in the Anglo-American alliance. Once more, these demonstrated the power asymmetry between the partners whereby close security ties are of much more importance for London than for Washington. There are also differences in the decision-making process and in implementation of security policies in both countries as well as differences in the command and control systems and structures of their respective militaries. Moreover, the British Army found itself underequipped and overstretched by deployments in two very complex combat zones. Furthermore, the British public was not enamored of the alliance and protested their nation's involvement in

Iraq, while Tony Blair was exceedingly unpopular in most parts of the Middle East because of his close ties with American president George W. Bush.

Turning to the specific issues of the Anglo-American partnership, there were also some initial strategic disagreements between the parties on the priorities of the Global War on Terror. For example, the United States sought a military defeat of the terrorists and the states that support and harbor them, while Britain also suggested a continuing active search for the resolution of the Arab-Israeli conflict, which it believed was fanning the flames of terrorist sentiment. In setting the aims of the Iraq War, Britain's primary concern was to prevent Saddam Hussein from acquiring weapons of mass destruction, while the United States was also seeking immediate regime change in the country. The British also paid much more attention than the United States did to the efforts to secure UN sanctioning of the Iraq War and the Iraqi occupation and reconstruction efforts in the country. The British, concerned about the threat of chaos in Iraq after the victory, did not support the U.S.-promoted de-Baathification program.

In Afghanistan, the British supported the anti-Taliban factions among the dominating Pashtun tribes, while the United States supported the rival Northern Alliance. Additionally, there was a growing critique on the part of the U.S. military about British combat performance against the insurgencies in Iraq and Afghanistan. These included complaints about the institutional arrogance of the British military command, its overconfidence in its own counterinsurgency experiences, and its general inflexibility.

The aforementioned trends and developments have complicated the achievement of stability in the Middle East and within the alliance. Emphasizing Britain's modest military resources and its strong desire to achieve a UN mandate for military action, the most active proponents of interventions in Afghanistan and Iraq in the George W. Bush administration—Vice President Dick Cheney, Secretary of Defense Donald Rumsfeld, and Undersecretary of Defense Paul Wolfowitz—were rather skeptical about the values of British contributions to Afghanistan and Iraq. On the British side, there was wide and sustained popular and political criticism about following the American lead, particularly in Iraq. Indeed, the Iraq War proved to be hugely unpopular. Critics emphasized that the war isolated Britain from other European countries, damaged its international stance, and, instead of providing Britain with a voice in American decisions, turned the country into a de facto silent vassal and strategic hostage of the United States. In this atmosphere,

Tony Blair maintained his desire to stay with America until the end by risking his own political future.

Blair resigned in 2007, suffering from historically low approval ratings. He was succeeded by Labour Party leader Gordon Brown, who was less comfortable with coddling the Americans. Nevertheless, he and President Barack Obama, who took office in January 2009, enjoyed a relatively cordial relationship, as both men agreed on the need to wind down the war in Iraq as quickly as possible. By July 21, 2009, all but 400 British service members had been withdrawn from Iraq, and the Brown government announced across-the-board decreases in defense spending amid the building economic recession that had begun in 2008. In 2009 three Londoners—Tanvir Hussain, Assad Sarwar, and Ahmed Abdullah Ali—were convicted of conspiring to detonate bombs disguised as soft drinks on seven airplanes bound for Canada and the United States. The massively complex police and MI5 investigation of the plot involved more than a year of surveillance work conducted by over 200 officers in both countries. By the end of 2011, all coalition forces, including British and American, had withdrawn from Iraq.

In May 2010, Brown was succeeded as prime minister by David Cameron, leader of the Conservative Party. This change slightly strained Anglo-American relations, chiefly because Obama and Cameron were on opposite sides of the political divide. This strain became more apparent after the WikiLeaks scandal that began in 2011. In May 2011 Obama made his first official state visit to Great Britain, during which he praised the British government and reaffirmed the Anglo-American alliance. In 2013, the Americans and British closed ranks after leaks by former U.S. defense contractor Edward Snowden revealed that their two countries had jointly engaged in widespread spying against mutual allies. Regardless of these issues of contention, the British have proven to be unfailing partners with the United States. Indeed, in all three conflicts—the Persian Gulf War, the Afghanistan War, and the Iraq War—Britain provided far more troops than any other nation besides the United States.

PETER J. RAINOW

See also

Afghanistan War; Blair, Tony; Brown, James Gordon; Bush, George Walker; Cameron, David William Donald; Cheney, Richard Bruce; Global War on Terror; Hussein, Saddam; Iraq War; Obama, Barack Hussein, II; Rumsfeld, Donald; Snowden, Edward Joseph; Taliban; WikiLeaks; Wolfowitz, Paul

References

Coughlin, Con. *American Ally: Tony Blair and the War on Terror.* New York: Ecco, 2006.

Dumbrell, John. *A Special Relationship: Anglo-American Relations from the Cold War to Iraq.* New York: Palgrave Macmillan, 2006.

Naughtie, James. *The Accidental American: Tony Blair and the Presidency.* New York: PublicAffairs, 2004.

Shawcross, William. *Allies: The U.S., Britain, and Europe in the Aftermath of the Iraq War.* New York: PublicAffairs, 2005.

Annan, Kofi (1938–)

Ghanaian diplomat and seventh secretary-general of the United Nations (UN), from 1997 to 2006. Kofi Atta Annan was born on April 8, 1938, in the Kofandros section of Kumasi, Ghana, to a prominent chieftain of the Fante tribe. His father was the elected governor of the Ashanti Province of Ghana when it was a British colony known as the Gold Coast. Kofi Annan studied at the University of Science and Technology in Kumasi before going to the United States to attend Macalester College in Minnesota, where he earned a degree in economics in 1961. He attended graduate school in Geneva during 1961–1962 and received a master of science degree in management from the Massachusetts Institute of Technology in 1972. Annan first joined the UN in 1962 at the World Health Organization. Except for a brief stint from 1974 to 1976 as Ghana's director of tourism, Annan has spent his entire career with the UN, having been posted in Europe, Africa, and the United States. His admirers have described him as a man of quiet elegance with a powerful yet understated speaking style.

Annan had a remarkably varied UN career, focusing not only on management and administrative functions but also on refugee issues and peacekeeping. He rose steadily through the UN administrative hierarchy, first as the assistant chief of its programs planning, budget, and finance department and then as the head of human resources. He also served as security coordinator, director of the budget, chief of personnel for the Office of the United Nations High Commissioner for Refugees, and administrative officer for the Economic Commission for Africa. On March 1, 1993, he became the undersecretary-general for peacekeeping operations. Annan distinguished himself in that role as a clear-speaking diplomat and skillful negotiator, despite the failure of a UN peacekeeping operation in Somalia in 1994 and the much-criticized decision not to intervene during the Rwandan genocide of the same year. Annan attracted U.S. attention by negotiating the release of Western hostages held by Iraq prior to Operation DESERT STORM and securing the safety of some 500,000 Asian workers trapped in Kuwait during the Persian Gulf War.

Annan was appointed secretary-general by the UN General Assembly on December 17, 1996, for a term that began on January 1, 1997. He was the first UN leader to have risen to the post through the UN organizational structure and was the first black African to serve in the post. As secretary-general, Annan emphasized his commitment to engaging UN member states in a dialogue about the best use of peacekeeping forces, preventive diplomacy, and postconflict peace building. He hoped to bring the UN closer to the world's people and achieve a consensus among member states as to the role the UN should play in its many fields of endeavor. The United States, the world organization's largest single contributor, hoped that with his administrative skills Annan would be able to reform the organization by cutting the budget, eliminating redundant suborganizations, and pioneering a new way to manage the UN in the post–Cold War era.

On June 29, 2001, Annan was reappointed secretary-general of the UN for another five-year term to begin officially in January 2002. In addition, on October 12, 2001, the Norwegian Nobel Committee announced that Annan and the UN were the 100th winners of the Nobel Peace Prize for their work in advancing world peace and security, which has included steps to eradicate international terrorism. The Nobel committee also praised Annan for his effective management of the UN and his continued dedication to eradicating HIV/AIDS.

Annan's tenure was not always free from controversy, however. On September 16, 2004, when he publicly termed the March 2003 Anglo-American–led invasion of Iraq illegal and in violation of the UN Charter, it strained his already testy relationship with the George W. Bush administration. In the run-up to the Iraq War, Annan had repeatedly urged that military force not be taken against Iraq. In addition, in December 2004, reports of graft and corruption in the UN's Oil-for-Food Programme affected Annan. In particular, Annan's son Kojo was alleged to have received payments from the Swiss company Cotecna Inspection SA, which had in turn received a lucrative contract in the program. Annan appointed an inquiry into the matter, and although he was personally exonerated of any illegal activity, the investigative committee found fault with the UN's management structure and recommended the appointment of a UN chief executive officer to prevent future financial oversights and potential conflicts of interest.

In addition to his regular UN posts, Annan also carried out a number of special assignments. He served as special representative of the UN secretary-general to the former Yugoslavia from November 1995 to March 1996, coordinating the UN's role in maintaining peace following the Dayton Agreement (1995). He has also contributed to the work of the Appointment and Promotion Board and the secretary-general's Task Force for Peacekeeping, and he has served as chairman of the Board of Trustees of the United Nations International School in New York and as governor of the International School in Geneva.

In December 2006 Annan completed his second term as secretary-general of the UN and was succeeded by Ban Ki Moon in January 2007. In his last major speech as secretary-general on December 11, 2006, at the Harry S. Truman Presidential Library in Independence, Missouri, Annan urged the United States to return to the multilateralism typified by the Truman administration and asked that the United States maintain its commitment to human rights, even in the Global War on Terror. The Bush administration took a dim view of the speech.

Annan returned to Ghana in 2007, and some pundits opined that he might become a candidate for head of state. He has been involved in numerous African and international organizations and was named president of the Global Humanitarian Forum in Geneva, Switzerland. He has also been engaged in efforts to quell civil unrest in Kenya and serves on the board of directors of the United Nations Foundation.

In February 2012, Annan was appointed the UN–Arab League peace envoy to Syria in an effort to mediate an end to that nation's bloody civil war. He quickly hammered out a six-point peace plan, which both the Syrian government and the rebels rejected. In August 2012 Annan resigned as envoy to Syria, citing irreconcilable difference among the warring parties and his disappointment with the UN Security Council, which seemed unwilling to involve itself in the crisis. The following month he published his memoir, *Interventions: A Life in War and Peace.*

PAUL G. PIERPAOLI JR.

See also

Ban Ki Moon; Somalia, International Intervention in; Syrian Civil War; United Nations

References

Annan, Kofi. *Interventions: A Life in War and Peace.* New York: Penguin 2012.

Annan, Kofi. *The Quotable Kofi Annan.* New York: United Nations Department of Public Information, 1998.

Meisler, Stanley. *Koffi Annan: A Man of Peace in a World of War.* New York: Wiley, 2007.

Traub, James. *The Best Intentions: Kofi Annan and the UN in the Era of American World Power.* New York: Farrar, Straus and Giroux, 2006.

Ansar al-Islam

A radical Kurdish Islamist separatist movement formed in 2001 in northern Iraq (Kurdistan). The U.S. government has held that the group was founded by Mullah Krekar, with assistance and funds from Al Qaeda leader Osama bin Laden. The complicated history of Ansar al-Islam (Supporters of Islam) dates back to the Islamic Movement in Kurdistan, formed in 1987 of various factions, some of whom had trained and fought in Afghanistan. Some others apparently returned to Kurdistan after the fall of the Taliban in late 2001, which was the basis of U.S. arguments that the group had links to Al Qaeda, a claim also made by its enemies in the larger Kurdish factions.

The Islamic Movement in Kurdistan fought with the Popular Union of Kurdistan (PUK) and eventually had to retreat to the Iranian border before returning to its base in Halabja. In 2001 the group splintered, and various new groupings formed the Jund al-Islam in September of that year, declaring jihad on those Kurdish parties that had left the Islamic path. The PUK fought Jund al-Islam, which dissolved and renamed itself Ansar al-Islam in December 2001 under the leadership of Amir Mullah Krekar, also known as Najmuddin Faraj Ahmad. Since then, however, Krekar has been living in Norway and has faced various indictments and deferred deportation for supporting terrorism.

While still operating under the name of Jund al-Islam, Ansar al-Islam tried to quash non-Islamic practices. It banned music, television, and alcohol; imposed the veil on women and beards on men; closed schools and employment to women; and tried to force a minority religious group called the Ahl al-Haqq to convert and then drove its members out of their villages. Ansar al-Islam also cracked down on the Naqshabandi Sufis. The group also pursued individuals, and some were held and tortured. The group's strict Salafi stance makes it akin to various Sunni nationalist resistance groups that developed after 2003 and accentuates its differences with the principal Kurdish political factions.

The struggle between the PUK and Ansar al-Islam has also involved human rights violations, the assassination of the governor of Arbil, and fighting that has continued for years. In December 2002 Ansar al-Islam forces took two PUK outposts and killed about 50 people; more than half of these reportedly died after they had surrendered. On the other hand, Ansar al-Islam prisoners have been mistreated by the PUK.

When the invasion of Iraq occurred in March 2003, Ansar al-Islam mounted various small attacks and carried out actions against those it called "collaborators" with the Americans, including civilians. The group carried out a much larger attack during 2004, when its suicide bombers attacked the PUK and Kurdistan Democratic Party (KDP) headquarters and killed 109 people, among them the KDP's deputy prime minister, Sami Abd al-Rahman. In 2005 Ansar al-Islam assassinated Sheikh Mahmud al-Madayini, an aide to Grand Ayatollah Sayyid Ali Husayn al-Sistan, in Baghdad.

In 2003 fighters from Ansar al-Islam joined with other Sunni Salafi fighters in the central region of Iraq, forming Jamaat Ansar al-Sunna (formerly Jaysh Ansar al-Sunna). But the Ansar al-Islam elements returned to their earlier name in 2007. Also in 2007, the Ansar al-Sunna, along with Ansar al-Islam, the Islamic Army of Iraq, and the Army of the Mujahideen, formed a new grouping called the Jihad and Reformation Front. In any event, it remains unclear what links Ansar al-Islam has to Al Qaeda in Iraq, and there is some evidence to suggest that it might have received aid from Iran. The group continues to battle more secularist Kurdish groups, and in March 2009 it kidnapped and beheaded three Kurdish truck driver hostages to punish them for cooperating with the Americans. Ansar al-Islam is currently one of the insurgent groups waging war against the Iraqi government. Since the beginning of the Syrian Civil War in 2011, the group has also been active in that conflict. Its fighting units operate under the banner of Ansar al-Sham.

SHERIFA ZUHUR

See also
Al Qaeda; Al Qaeda in Iraq; Bin Laden, Osama; Iraq, History of, 1990–Present; Syrian Civil War

References
"Ansar al-Islam in Iraqi Kurdistan." Human Rights Watch Backgrounder, www.hrw.org/legacy/backgrounder/mena/ansarbk020503.htm.

Stansfield, Gareth R. V. *Iraqi Kurdistan: Political Development and Emergent Democracy.* New York: Routledge, 2003.

Wong, Edward. "The Reach of War: Violence, Militants Show the Beheading of 3 Kurdish Hostages." *New York Times,* March 22, 2009.

Anthrax

Anthrax (Bacillus anthracis) is a bacteriological disease that can manifest itself in cutaneous, pulmonary, and gastrointestinal forms. If not treated aggressively with antibiotics within the first 48 hours after the appearance of symptoms, the disease is almost always fatal. Symptoms may include a rash, swelling of the lymph nodes, and/or flu-like malaise. Anthrax has been a favorite among developers of biological weapons because it is hardy and easy to turn into a weaponized form. When subjected to extremes of temperature, anthrax bacteria encapsulate themselves into a hard shell called a spore, which although dormant can remain infectious for up to 50 years. Therefore, areas infected with anthrax through the use of a delivery system become uninhabitable for 50 years.

The Japanese Army began experimentation with anthrax as a potential weapon in 1936 with the establishment of Unit 731, commanded by Lieutenant Colonel Ishii Shiro. This biowarfare unit refined a weapons-grade anthrax powder. Tests conducted by the Japanese resulted in the deaths of thousands of Chinese during the Sino-Japanese War (1937–1945).

Following World War II, the Soviet Union began large-scale production of biological weapons. The Soviets created an antibiotic-resistant superstrain of anthrax with an unlimited shelf life. Their vast biowarfare conglomerate known as Biopreparat produced hundreds of tons of anthrax. In 1979 Soviet weapons-grade anthrax leaked from a production facility with faulty air filters into the city of Sverdlovsk. Sixty-four people died, and hundreds more were infected. Soviet weapons-grade anthrax has also been sold on the black market, most notably to South African biowarfare specialist Dr. Wouter Basson, who headed South Africa's Project Coast, to develop biological weapons. Basson used anthrax to infect a region of eastern Zimbabwe suspected of harboring guerrillas during 1978–1980. The region remains infectious to this day.

The United States began development of a biowarfare program based at Fort Detrick in Maryland and the Dugway proving ground in Utah shortly after World War II using captured Japanese doctors and research. The United States employed a plague bomb of Japanese design during the Korean War, according to recent research by York University (Toronto) professors Stephen Endicott and Edward Hagerman. In 1969 President Richard Nixon renounced biological weapons research, and U.S. programs for other than defensive measures (i.e., on vaccines and cures) ceased.

The Israelis have developed a biological warfare capability in response to threats from Arab nations that were once clients of the Soviet Union. Countries such as Iraq and Egypt were believed to be developing biowarfare capabilities with Soviet help in the 1970s. The Israelis responded by starting their own advanced program based at Nas Zion in southern Israel, developing strains of weaponized anthrax as the primary agent. They are believed to have developed missile warheads, artillery rounds, and other means for delivering biowarfare agents. The Israelis also warned Dr. Basson and other biowarfare researchers against supplying such technology to Libya (Basson met with Muammar Qaddafi in the 1980s) and other Arab states.

As with Israel's nuclear weapons program, little is known of their biological warfare preparations. Israeli defense policy clearly calls for retaliation in kind should a biowarfare attack be launched on the Jewish state. There is also the Samson Option, a doomsday scenario that calls for the widespread release of anthrax or nuclear weapons in the event Israel is on the verge of being overrun by enemies. U.S. Army planners have had to take this into account when planning assistance strategies for Israel in such a military emergency. U.S. soldiers would need to be equipped with chemical-biological-radiological apparatus if entering such a war zone.

It should also be noted that in 1993 the Japanese religious cult/terrorist group Aum Shinrikyo released aerosolized anthrax spores in the city of Kameido, Japan, but their dispersal method failed, and the attack was not successful. They then switched to nerve gas (sarin), with the horrific results of the 1995 Tokyo subway attack. Some of the anthrax cultures Aum used are believed to have originated at Biopreparat.

In the fall of 2001 just days after the September 11, 2001, terrorist attacks against the United States, several anthrax attacks occurred in New York City; Washington, D.C.; and Florida. These attacks, carried out via mail (anthrax spores had been placed in envelopes and mailed), caused great concern throughout the country, which was still reeling from the effects of the September 11 attacks. The envelopes were sent to news organizations and two U.S. senators (Patrick Leahy and Tom Daschle). The attacks killed 5 people, sickened 17 others, and precipitated near panic throughout much of the U.S. population. Since then there have been several other anthrax scares, but none has caused the damage done in 2001. The 2001 attacks preyed on Americans' feelings of fear and uncertainty following the worse foreign attack on America soil since the December 1941 assault on Pearl Harbor. The attacks also demonstrated how relatively easy anthrax could be used as a weapon of terror.

Rod Vosburgh

See also
Arab-Israeli Conflict, Overview; Global War on Terror; Qaddafi,
  Muammar

References
Alibek, Ken. *Biohazard: The Chilling True Story of the Largest
  Covert Biological Weapons Program in the World: Told from
  Inside by the Man Who Ran It.* New York: Random House,
  1999.
Guillemin, Jeanne. *Anthrax: The Investigation of a Deadly Out-
  break.* Berkeley: University of California Press, 1999.
Harris, Robert, and Jeremy Paxman. *A Higher Form of Killing:
  The Secret History of Chemical and Biological Warfare.* New
  York: Random House, 2002.
Mangold, Tom, and Jeff Goldberg. *Plague Wars: The Terrifying
  Reality of Biological Warfare.* New York: St. Martin's, 1999.

Antiaircraft Guns

Antiaircraft guns remain a major defense against attack aircraft. During Operation IRAQI FREEDOM as in Operation DESERT STORM, the Iraqi air defense system was based on the Soviet doctrine of integrating aircraft, surface-to-air missiles (SAMs), and antiaircraft guns. The guns took primary responsibility for point defense of key targets. Neither the United States nor its allies employed antiaircraft guns in a defensive capacity during either of the wars with Iraq. Also, because of the virtual absence of Afghan aircraft during Operation ENDURING FREEDOM, antiaircraft weapons were not deployed to Afghanistan.

Iraqi antiaircraft guns fell into two categories: artillery and small arms. The former had calibers exceeding 20 millimeters, while the latter consisted of 14.5-mm and smaller guns. All were crew-served weapons and offered the advantages of being relatively cheap to purchase and requiring little training to operate. Most Iraqi antiaircraft guns were manned by conscripts. By 1990, Iraq had more than 7,500 antiaircraft artillery pieces and several hundred light antiaircraft weapons; when properly employed, they could be deadly for aircraft flying below 10,000 feet.

The largest Iraqi antiaircraft artillery piece was the Soviet-built KS-19 100-mm gun. Designed at the end of World War II and entering Soviet service in the late 1940s, the KS-19 served in four gun batteries. Some estimates claim that several hundred guns were placed around Baghdad alone from 1980 through 2003. The KS-19 fired a 33-pound shell out to a maximum range of 60,000 feet with a maximum ceiling of more than 42,000 feet. However, its slow rate of fire (8–12 rounds per minute) and traverse placed it at a disadvantage against high-speed maneuvering aircraft. Its primary purpose was to disrupt incoming air raids. Less than a dozen such batteries remained in Iraqi service in 1990.

Iraq's most numerous antiaircraft artillery piece was the 57-mm S-60, which was structured in six-gun batteries centered on a single Flap Wheel (North Atlantic Treaty Organization designation) conical scan fire-control radar. The S-60 required a crew of six and theoretically fired up to 120 rounds per minute. However, as a practical matter, loader fatigue and barrel heating limited the rate of fire to 60 rounds per minute or less. Moreover, a typical engagement against a tactical jet aircraft was less than a minute. The S-60's maximum effective range and ceiling were 40,000 feet and 13,000 feet, respectively, but few engagements were initiated at ranges beyond 20,000 feet or altitudes above 5,000 feet. Although each weapon was capable of engaging targets independently, the most common practice was for all the battery's guns to fire on the target being tracked by the Flap Wheel radar. Independent firing was conducted only when the fire-control radar was jammed or out of action. Moreover, the maximum effective range dropped to 13,000 feet when using optical fire control. The self-propelled variant, the ZSU-57/2, consisted of two 57-mm guns mounted on a tracked chassis. Lacking a data link or ability to receive fire-control radar inputs, each ZSU-57/2 fired independently.

Iraqi air defenses also included several hundred 37-mm guns and 23-mm guns. Organized into four gun batteries, the 37-mm used visual fire control, with each gun firing independently, although battery commanders could direct all guns to concentrate on a single target. The guns were loaded via 5-round clips, and a well-trained crew could fire up to 240 2-pound shells a minute, although the typical engagement against a jet aircraft lasted less than 30 seconds. The 37-mm had a maximum effective range of 2,500 yards and a theoretical ceiling of 10,000 feet, but tactically they rarely were used against targets flying above 3,500 feet and ranges beyond 4,000 feet.

The guns most feared by coalition pilots were the Soviet-built self-propelled ZSU-23/4 guns, which served with Iraqi armored divisions and as mobile air defense platforms in and around critical facilities. Organized into four-unit platoons, each ZSU-23/4 was equipped with a jam-resistant fire-control radar, high rates of fire (1,000-plus rounds per minute per gun), and high traverse rates that enabled it to engage the fastest and most maneuverable tactical aircraft. The ZSU-23/4 consisted of a quadruple mount of 23-mm automatic cannon on a tracked carriage. Its relatively small size and mobility made it hard to detect prior to an engagement. However, the limited range (under 10,000 feet) and ceiling (under 8,200 feet) confined it to the point-defense role; furthermore, the advent of precision-guided ordnance allowed coalition fighters to attack from outside these weapons' effective range.

Iraqi forces were also equipped with ZPU-23/2, ZPU-14, and individual 14.5-mm guns. All fired individually and were most effective against slow-moving observation aircraft and helicopters. The ZPU-23/2 consisted of two 23-mm guns installed on a collapsible towing mount that could be quickly transitioned into a firing platform. The ZPU-14 was lighter and consisted of four 14.5-mm machine guns mounted on a wheeled transport mount. The ZPU-14 had proven particularly effective against helicopters during the Vietnam War; however, it was all but useless against coalition aircraft employing fire and forget guided munitions fired from outside its maximum effective range of 2,000 yards.

U.S. Arab allies were equipped with the same antiaircraft guns as the Iraqis except that they did not possess the 100-mm K-19. However, the United States and its other allies used few antiaircraft guns, assigning them to provide point air defense to ground units and mobile tactical headquarters. The only antiaircraft gun system employed by the U.S. Army was the M163 Vulcan system, which consisted of the Vulcan 20-mm Gatling cannon mounted on an M-113 chassis. The ammunition was delivered to the gun via 1,000-round powered belts. The Vulcan's rate of fire was 3,000 rounds a minute, and under optical fire control it could engage targets within a range of 8,000 feet and an altitude of 3,000 feet.

The Saudi Arabian Army also employs the M-163 with its mobile units and the Bofors 40-mm L-70 around key facilities. Unlike the Vulcan, the Bofors could use radar fire control, which generally focused the fire of an entire four-gun battery against a target. Its 2-pound shells came with a proximity and contact fuse to ensure target destruction, while the Vulcan's smaller 1-pound shell had only a contact fuse. The Bofors could engage incoming aircraft individually using optical fire control, but that was the exception, not the rule. The Bofors fired up to 240 rounds a minute and had a maximum engagement range of 11,500 feet and a ceiling of 8,000 feet. However, it could also be used against ground targets, which it could engage at ranges beyond 32,000 feet. The other gun in Saudi service was the Oerlikon-Buhrle twin 35-mm Skyguard system that the Royal Saudi Air Force used for airfield defense. Its rate of fire approaches 550 rounds per minute per barrel, and its maximum range against an incoming aerial target is approximately 13,000 feet. As with the Bofors, the Oerlikon can engage targets individually or via concentrated battery fire.

The virtual absence of an enemy air threat precluded the United States or its allies from employing their antiaircraft guns in an air defense role during any of the modern Middle East wars, but Iraq employed large numbers of antiaircraft guns to provide low-level point defense and attack-disruption defense of its tactical units and key facilities. They were integrated effectively into a complex air defense system that relied on SAMs for area and high-altitude air defense coverage, supplemented by interceptor aircraft. The system employed tactics and systems that had proven highly effective against Western air tactics during the Vietnam War, but the introduction of large numbers of precision stand-off weapons and superior coalition electronic warfare tactics exposed the obsolescence of Iraq's tactics and systems. Aircraft deceived and evaded the SAMs and launched their weapons from outside the antiaircraft guns' effective range. Although their large numbers precluded coalition pilots from ignoring the guns' presence, new tactics and weapons had reduced them to a battlefield nuisance.

The ZPU series guns saw widespread use in the Libyan Civil War, mounted in technical pickup trucks, and in the ongoing Syrian Civil War. In Afghanistan, the Taliban has secured through Pakistan ZPU series heavy machine-gun systems able to destroy low-flying helicopters as well as inflict significant damage in ground-use applications. In 2009 the International Security Assistance Force destroyed four such systems in a single month in Helmand province. One of the systems was mounted in the back of a pickup truck. Creating newspaper headlines by downing coalition aircraft remains a high Taliban priority.

CARL OTIS SCHUSTER

See also

Afghanistan War; Aircraft, Electronic Warfare; Aircraft, Fighters; Aircraft, Suppression of Enemy Air Defense; Air Defenses in Iraq, Iraq War; Antiaircraft Missiles, Iraqi; Bombs, Precision-Guided; Libyan Civil War; Missiles, Air-to-Ground; Syrian Civil War

References

Isby, David. *Weapons and Tactics of the Soviet Army*. London: Arms and Armour Books, 1984.

Lynch, Kristin. *Supporting Air and Space Expeditionary Forces: Lessons from Operation Iraqi Freedom*. Washington, DC: RAND Corporation, 2004.

U.S. General Accounting Office. *Operation Desert Storm Evaluation of the Air War: Report to Congress*. Washington, DC: U.S. Government Printing Office, 1996.

Antiaircraft Missiles, Iraqi

Air defense missiles constituted the most significant component of Iraq's integrated air defense system during its three major conflicts since 1980. Iraq used radar-guided surface-to-air missiles (SAMs) for medium- to high-altitude and area air defense and man-portable infrared-guided SAMs for tactical air defense and to complement its antiaircraft artillery systems. Since the most common tactic to evade radar-guided SAMs involved a high-speed roll and dive to lower altitudes, the integration of guns, missiles, and fighter aircraft into a layered defense in depth theoretically provided an almost impenetrable barrier to air attack. Aircraft that successfully avoided radar-guided SAMs found themselves flying through a gauntlet of intense antiaircraft fire supplemented by infrared-guided SAMs, the intensity of which increased as the attacking aircraft approached their target. Those that made it past the target pulled up into the sights of waiting fighter aircraft. Fighters escorting the attack aircraft had to penetrate the same gauntlet to engage enemy interceptors.

Although it did not lead to high scores among the defending pilots, it was a system that had inflicted heavy losses on U.S. aircraft over North Vietnam in the 1960s. The United States and its coalition allies learned from that conflict, however, and possessed the electronic warfare equipment and weapons to defeat the system during Operations DESERT STORM and IRAQI FREEDOM.

Most Iraqi air defense missiles were Soviet-built, with the venerable SA-2 Guideline (the missile and radar designations are those of the North Atlantic Treaty Organization) and its supporting Fan Song radar being the oldest and longest-ranged weapon in service. Developed in the 1950s, the SA-2, with a range of 27 nautical miles, had enjoyed great success during the Vietnam War but was at best obsolete by 1990. Although it could engage aircraft operating at altitudes of up to 89,000 feet, its radar was easily defeated, and only a highly trained crew could employ its electro-optical guidance and electronic counter-countermeasures features effectively. Also, its minimum range of 4–5 nautical miles and its minimum altitude of 3,280 feet made it all but useless against low-flying targets. The SA-3 Goa was newer and longer-ranged. Introduced in Soviet service in 1963, the Goa, with a range of 22 nautical miles, used the Flat Face radar for guidance. It had an operational engagement ceiling of 59,000 feet and enjoyed better tactical mobility than the SA-2. The SA-2 and SA-3 were deployed around major Iraqi cities.

Iraq also deployed a wide range of Soviet mobile SAM systems, including the SA-6 Gainful, SA-9 Gaskin, and SA-12. Of these, the Gainful was the best known, having inflicted heavy losses on the Israeli Air Force when first employed during the October 1973 Yom Kippur War. Mounted on a tracked chassis, the Gainful was a medium-ranged SAM supported by a robust Straight Flush fire-control radar that was difficult to deceive. Introduced into Soviet service in 1970, the SA-6 deployed in four transporter-erector-launcher batteries supported by a single fire-control radar. The missile has a maximum range of 13.2 nautical miles and an operational engagement ceiling of 39,000 feet.

The SA-9 Gaskin was a much shorter-ranged SAM mounted on a wheeled vehicle that carried two pairs of ready-to-fire missiles. The Gaskin was infrared-guided (IR), but unlike most IR missiles, it could engage an incoming target provided the aircraft was not obscured coming by the sun. Normally deployed in proximity to the ZSU-23/4 mobile antiaircraft gun, the SA-9 dated from 1966 and had a maximum range of 4.4 nautical miles and a ceiling of 20,000 feet. The SA-9 had little impact on allied air operations in either of the Persian Gulf conflicts.

The newest mobile SAM in the Iraqi inventory was the short-ranged radar-guided SA-8 Gecko. Carried in six-missile canisters mounted atop a wheeled transporter-erector-launcher-and-radar (TELAR), the SA-8 was employed with Iraqi Army units in the field. Its six-wheeled TELAR was amphibious and was equipped with a frequency agile fire-control radar and alternate electro-optical guidance that made it particularly difficult to defeat electronically. Its normal engagement range was 1.1–5 nautical miles against targets flying between 100 and 16,500 feet. The most common tactics employed against the SA-8 were to use antiradiation missiles against its radar or fly above its engagement envelope.

The remaining SAMs in Iraqi service were man-portable. Of these, the Soviet-built IR-guided SA-7 Grail, SA-14 Gremlin, SA-16 Gimlet, and SA-18 Grouse were the most numerous. The SA-7 was the shortest ranged, reaching out only about 10,000 feet and effective only against slow-moving targets flying away at altitudes below 4,000 feet. The SA-14 was an improvement on the SA-7, providing greater range (3.7 nautical miles) and a limited capability for head-on engagements. The SA-16 incorporated an identification friend or foe (IFF) feature and a more effective IR counter-countermeasures capability. The SA-18 was a simplified and more reliable improvement of the SA-16. The Gimlet and Grouse can engage a target from any aspect; they have a maximum range of 3.1 miles and a ceiling of 15,700 feet. Their performance is comparable to the U.S. FIM-92A Stinger.

The last SAM in Iraqi service was the French-built Roland. The Iraqis used the Roland for airfield defense. The radar-guided Roland had a maximum operational range of 5 nautical miles and an engagement ceiling of 17,100 feet. Its rapid acceleration and high speed made it an ideal air defense weapon. However, in the hands of inexperienced or poorly trained operators, it proved vulnerable to jamming and other electronic countermeasures. Also, the Iraqi missile crews had to operate the system from exposed positions, making them vulnerable to enemy attack, a factor that inhibited the weapon's effectiveness.

Coalition superiority, in terms of both numbers and technology, and superior tactics all but negated Iraq's integrated air defense system in both the Persian Gulf War and the Iraq War. Its SAMs achieved only limited success in the few opportunities that the air campaign presented to them. Allied air defense suppression systems, antiradiation missiles, and well-orchestrated electronic countermeasure operations blinded Iraqi radars, destroyed their command and control systems and communications networks, and inflicted heavy losses on SAM batteries. Although Iraq nominally possessed a modern integrated air defense system, its weapons, sensors, and communications networks were outdated, and its operators were poorly trained for war against a well-trained opponent equipped with third- and fourth-generation aircraft and precision-guided weapons.

Man-portable SAMs, many of them dispersed in the region from Libyan stocks following the civil war in that country, remain a formidable threat to low-flying attack planes and helicopters and there are major concerns that the Islamic State of Iraq and Syria (ISIS) will secure them. Keeping them from the Taliban in Afghanistan is also a major priority, as such weapons extracted a considerable toll on Soviet helicopters during the Soviet-Afghan War. Thus far the United States has rejected appeals for such weapons from forces fighting the Bashar al-Assad regime in Syria.

CARL OTIS SCHUSTER

See also

Aircraft, Electronic Warfare; Air Defenses in Iraq, Iraq War; Antiaircraft Guns; Antiradiation Missiles, Coalition; Bombs, Precision-Guided; IRAQI FREEDOM, Operation, Air Campaign; Islamic State in Iraq and Syria; Missiles, Surface-to-Air; Syrian Civil War

References

Blake, Bernard, ed. *Jane's Weapons Systems, 1988–89 (Jane's Land-Based Air Defence)*. London: Jane's 1988.
Cooper, Toni, and Farzad Bishop. *Iran-Iraq War in the Air, 1980–1988*. Atglen, PA: Schiffer Military History, 2000.
General Accounting Office. *Operation Desert Storm: Evaluation of the Air War; Report to Congress*. Washington, DC: U.S. Government Printing Office, 1996.
Hallion, Richard P. *Storm over Iraq: Air Power and the Gulf War*. Washington, DC: Smithsonian Institution Press, 1997.
Lynch, Kristin. *Supporting Air and Space Expeditionary Forces: Lessons from Operation Iraqi Freedom*. Washington, DC: RAND Corporation, 2004.

Antiradiation Missiles, Coalition

Missiles designed chiefly to defeat enemy radar by honing in on and jamming or destroying radio emission sources. Antiradiation missiles (ARMs) constitute one of the most important weapons in any effort to suppress enemy air defenses (SEAD). ARMs rose out of the Vietnam War in response to North Vietnam's extensive use of surface-to-air missiles (SAMs). Early ARMs were modifications of existing air-to-air and air-to-ground missiles, with a receiver to hone in on a SAM's acquisition or tracking radar. Early ARMs could be defeated by simply turning the radar off briefly, activating a similar radar nearby, or employing multiple radars against the target aircraft. However, by 1990 when Iraq invaded Kuwait, technology had advanced considerably, providing coalition forces with technologically advanced ARMs that could mask their launch, remember the radar's location, and, in some cases, effectively shut down an air defense sector by loitering over it for hours, waiting to attack the first SAM system to activate its radar. ARMs also now had the range to be launched from outside the SAM's engagement range. These weapons proved devastating to Iraq's integrated air defense networks, which many observers had considered one of the world's most effective.

The American-made Raytheon AGM-88 high-speed antiradiation missile (HARM) was the most widely employed of the coalition antiradiation missiles. Developed as a replacement for the Vietnam War–era AGM-45 Shrike and AGM-78 standard ARM, the AGM-88 entered service in 1985. It was supersonic (Mach 2.5) and was equipped with inertial guidance and a computer that captured the enemy radar's location and characteristics. The aircraft's fire-control system fed the radar's information into the missile computer before launch, enabling the computer to guide the HARM onto the radar even if the operators turned it off or tried to draw the missile away by remote jamming or activating a similar radar nearby. A smokeless rocket engine made it all but impossible to detect HARMs visually, and a range of 57 nautical miles enabled the SEAD aircraft to launch HARMs from far outside the Iraqi SAM envelope. American Grumman A-6 Intruder, Ling-Temco-Vought A-7 Corsair II, Grumman EA-6 Prowler, McDonnell Douglas F-4 Phantom II, Lockheed-Martin F-16 Fighting Falcon, and Boeing A/F-18 Hornet aircraft employed HARMs during Operation DESERT STORM and, except for the F-4s, in Operation IRAQI FREEDOM as well. The HARM's most famous employment in DESERT STORM was its accidental use against a Boeing B-52 Stratofortress when the bomber's tail gunner mistakenly targeted a SEAD aircraft, which then engaged what it thought was an Iraqi antidefense radar. The B-52 suffered only slight damage to its tail, and there were no injuries.

British Aerospace's air-launched antiradiation missile (ALARM) was the only other antiradiation missile to see service in DESERT STORM and IRAQI FREEDOM. Employed by both the Royal Air Force and the Royal Saudi Air Force, the ALARM entered service in 1990 and is carried by Panavia GR4 Tornado and F3 Tornado aircraft. Like the HARM, it is a supersonic (Mach 2.1) missile that can be launched from outside most SAM envelopes (range of 50.1 nautical miles). However, it has a major advantage over HARM in that it can loiter over a target area, waiting for the enemy to activate their radars. Once it detects a radar, it ejects the warhead, which then makes a guided parachute descent onto the radar. ALARM proved particularly effective against mobile SAM systems because it could be employed almost as a search-and-destroy weapon over suspected SAM deployment areas. Unfortunately, ALARM's length (15 feet) limits its employment to larger tactical aircraft such as the Tornado, although some Sepecat Jaguar aircraft have been modified to carry it.

Antiradiation missiles are the ultimate in precision-guided weapons. With small warheads designed to destroy only the enemy's radar antennas, they inflict little to no collateral damage, and yet they cripple the enemy's ability to direct and employ their air defense system. The coalition's extensive use of antiradiation missiles all but destroyed Iraq's air defense commanders' ability to employ their SAMs, while allied jamming and strikes on Iraqi surveillance radars and command and control systems blinded those commanders. Within days of the start of both wars, Iraq's air defense forces could capture only glimpses of the coalition air campaign, forcing them to fire almost at random. Even then engagements proved short-lived, as emanating a radar signal almost always resulted in antenna destruction by an ARM.

CARL OTIS SCHUSTER

See also
Aircraft, Bombers; Aircraft, Electronic Warfare; Aircraft, Fighters; Aircraft, Suppression of Enemy Air Defense; Antiaircraft Guns; IRAQI FREEDOM, Operation, Air Campaign; Missiles, Air-to-Ground; Missiles, Surface-to-Air

References
Hewson, Robert. *Jane's Air-Launched Weapons, 2001.* London: Jane's, 2002.
Knight, Michael, ed. *Operation Iraqi Freedom and the New Iraq.* Washington, DC: Washington Institute for Near East Policy, 2004.
Tripp, Robert. *Lessons Learned from Operation Enduring Freedom.* Santa Monica, CA: RAND Corporation, 2004.

Antitank Weapons

Because of the large number of tanks and armored vehicles that saw service in both the Persian Gulf War and the Iraq War, antitank weapons played a critical role. Although initially equipped with large numbers of Soviet- and Russian-designed tanks and other weapons, the Iraqi Army only managed to knock out a small handful of American tanks. In the Iraq War, U.S. forces lost 9 tanks to friendly fire and 2 to mines, and 13 were damaged by various forms of Iraqi antitank fire (5 of those were severely damaged). Crew casualties from Iraqi fire were 1 killed and 13 wounded. The Iraqi Air Force played virtually no role in both wars, so whatever rotary and fixed-wing antitank aircraft they may have had in their inventory were largely irrelevant. The primary Iraqi antitank weapons were limited to antitank guided missiles (ATGMs) and shoulder-fired infantry weapons. In Afghanistan the Taliban had no armored vehicles, and their antitank weapons were limited primarily to shoulder-fired infantry weapons, recoilless rifles, and mines. The majority of the weapons considered here are therefore American systems.

Despite their armor and armament, tanks and other armored vehicles are not invulnerable. They can be defeated by land mines, aircraft, artillery, other tanks, rockets, guided missiles, and a wide range of infantry weapons. The various categories of tank kills are a function of the damage done to the tank combined with the tactical situation. A mobility kill, called an M-kill in current U.S. doctrine, occurs when the tank's power train or running gear have been damaged to the point where the tank cannot move. The tank may still be able to fire its weapons, but its inability to maneuver severely degrades its combat value. A firepower kill, called an F-kill, occurs when the tank's main gun or its fire-control optics and electronics have been severely damaged. A catastrophic kill, called a K-kill, occurs when the tank completely loses its ability to operate. It can neither move nor fire. A K-kill

A U.S. Army pilot inspects an AGM-114A Hellfire antitank missile loaded on a Boeing AH-64A Apache helicopter. (AP Photo)

usually means that the tank has been totally destroyed and often also means that the tank crew has been killed.

Whether fired by artillery, aircraft, another tank, or infantry weapons, the warheads of all antitank rounds are classified as either kinetic energy or chemical energy. Most main battle tanks are capable of firing both types of rounds through their main guns. The three basic types of chemical energy (i.e., explosive) warheads are high explosive (HE), high-explosive antitank (HEAT), and high-explosive plastic (HEP).

Tanks can be defeated by a blast from conventional HEs but only if the charge is large enough and close enough. HE projectiles delivered by artillery or air require a direct or very close hit, which usually exceeds the circular probable error of all but the most advanced precision-guided munitions (PGMs).

The most common and effective chemical energy projectile, the HEAT round, has a shaped-charge warhead that relies on the Munroe Effect to burn a hole through the tank's

armor in the form of an expanding cone. What actually kills the tank crew is the semimolten armor of their own tank. HEAT round detonations can also set off fuel and ammunition fires and secondary explosions.

HEP rounds, also called high-explosive squash head rounds, carry a charge of plastic explosive that upon impact spreads over the outer surface of the armor before detonating. Unlike a HEAT round, the HEP round does actually penetrate the tank's armor. When the HEP charge explodes, it knocks off chunks of armor of a corresponding size, called spall, inside the tank, causing havoc for the crew and the internal components. HEP rounds are generally ineffective against most modern tanks because the internal compartments are equipped with spall liners, protecting the crew, ammunition, fuel, and equipment.

Nonexploding kinetic energy rounds are very heavy and dense and are fired at an extremely high velocity. The most common is some form of sabot round in which an outer casing falls away as soon as the round leaves the gun's muzzle. On impact the sabot punches its way through the target's armor. The effect inside the tank is usually even more catastrophic than that caused by a HEAT round. Tungsten and depleted uranium are two heavy and dense materials widely employed as sabots.

Because kinetic energy rounds require a flat line-of-sight trajectory and an extremely high velocity, they must be fired from a gun as opposed to a howitzer and from a very heavy platform. Thus, only tanks and antitank artillery can fire sabot rounds. A tank's most vulnerable area to a sabot round is at the slip ring, where the turret joins the main hull. Smaller nonsabot kinetic energy rounds are fired from rotary or fixed-wing aircraft armed with special antitank machine guns that deliver a high volume of fire to defeat the target's armor, usually from above, where the armor is the weakest.

Chemical energy rounds do not require a heavy launching platform and are thus ideal for infantry antitank weapons, which include rocket launchers, recoilless rifles, and ATGMs. The best way to defeat a HEAT warhead is to cause it to detonate prematurely, which will prevent the Munroe Effect from forming properly on the outer skin of the tank's armor. Something as simple as a mesh outer screen mounted on the side of a tank with a few inches of stand-off distance will cause that premature detonation. Reactive explosive armor, also called appliqué armor, mounted on the tank's integral armor is also relatively effective against HEAT rounds but not at all effective against sabot rounds. Each element of reactive armor contains a small explosive charge that detonates when it is hit, causing the impacting HEAT round to detonate prematurely and spoiling the Munroe Effect. Finally, the sloped surfaces of the tank's armor can cause the HEAT round to deflect, which also will spoil the Munroe Effect. Sloped armor surfaces can also deflect sabot rounds in certain instances.

Although common in World War II, purpose-built antitank artillery fell into disuse in the years following 1945. By the 1960s the Soviet Union, West Germany, and Sweden were among the few remaining countries still building antitank artillery. Most armies came to regard the tank itself as the premier but certainly not the only antitank weapon.

The antitank rifle first entered service in World War I. Today it is known as the antimaterial (antimatériel or equipment) rifle. Essentially a large-caliber high-velocity rifle firing special armor-piercing ammunition, it is designed to operate against enemy equipment, such as thin-skinned and lightly armored vehicles. The weapon may also be used for long-range sniping. Antimaterial rifles are often favored by special operations military units.

The U.S. Army Browning M-2 .50-caliber machine gun, which can be fired in single-shot mode, fits in this category. The Austrian Steyr 25-mm antimaterial rifle, with a claimed effective range of 1.2 miles, features both a muzzle brake and a hydropneumatic sleeve to reduce recoil. It has a bipod, and the weapon can be broken down for ease of transport by its crew. Among other such weapons is the South African Mechem NTW-20. This 20-mm bolt-action rifle features a 3-round side-mounted box magazine. There is also a 14.5-mm model. To reduce recoil, the NTW-20 uses a hydraulic double-action damper along with a double baffle muzzle brake. Among other such weapons are the U.S. Armalite AR-50 and Barretta M-82A1, both of which fire the 12.7-mm (.50-caliber) North Atlantic Treaty Organization (NATO) round; the British Accuracy International AW50F, firing the 12.7-mm (.50-caliber) NATO round; the Hungarian Gerpard M-1(B) and M-2(B) 12.7-mm rifles, which with an interchangeable barrel can also fire the .50-caliber round; and the Russian KSVK 12.7-mm rifle. A number of these or similar weapons have been used in the various Middle East wars.

In the years following the Vietnam War, both the Americans and the Soviets developed special antitank machine guns for attack aircraft. Although the kinetic energy rounds fired by such weapons are far lighter than the sabot rounds fired from tanks, the high rate of fire from the machine guns produces multiple impacts in a concentrated area on the target that chews into the tank's armor. Attacking from above, the aircraft target the top of the tank, where the armor is generally the thinnest.

Entering service in 1977, the American GAU-8/A Avenger is a 30-mm seven-barrel electrically driven Gatling gun. It fires both armor-piercing incendiary (API) and HE incendiary rounds, usually in a four-to-one mix. The API round weighs a little less than one pound and carries a depleted uranium penetrator. The GAU-8/A has a cyclic rate of fire of 3,900 rounds per minute. The Russian GSh-6–30 30-mm aircraft automatic cannon is a very similar weapon, except that it is gas-operated rather than electrically driven. Entering service in 1998, the U.S. M-230 Chain Gun also fires a 30-mm antitank round. Having only a single barrel, its rate of fire is only 625 rounds per minute, but it is considerably lighter than the GAU-8/A.

Purpose-built antitank mines first appeared in the last years of World War I and figured prominently during World War II. Most modern antitank mines use an HE charge to produce M-kills by blowing off the tread or damaging the road wheels. Some mines are designed to produce K-kills by attacking the underside of the tank, where the armor is thin. Although sometimes command detonated by either wire or remote control, most use pressure or magnetically triggered detonators that react to vehicles but not ground personnel.

The improvised explosive device (IED) is a variation on the antitank mine that has produced a high percentage of American and allied casualties during the Iraq War since 2003 and increasingly in Afghanistan. An IED is any locally fabricated explosive charge coupled with a detonating mechanism. Deadly to personnel, most IEDs initially could only damage unarmored and lightly armored vehicles. If the base explosive charge is large enough—for example, an artillery projectile buried in the road—the resulting explosion could do serious damage to a tank. In recent years, however, IEDs have become more sophisticated, especially with the appearance of explosively formed penetrators (EFPs). The EFP works on the same principle as the shaped charge, effectively transforming the IED from a simple HE to a HEAT weapon. An EFP has a cylindrical-shaped charge capped by a concave metal disk pointed inward. When detonated, the metal disk, often made of copper, becomes a bolt of molten metal that can penetrate the armor on most vehicles in Iraq. An IED with an EFP is difficult to detect and counter because it is effective at standoff distances up to 164 feet.

Recoilless rifles and recoilless guns (smoothbore) were developed during World War II primarily as antitank weapons. Firing HE and HEAT projectiles similar to conventional artillery, a recoilless rifle is essentially a long tube, similar to a modern rocket launcher. Unlike the latter, however, the recoilless rifle has a breech mechanism. Also unlike conventional artillery, that breech has large exit vents, and the ammunition shell casings are perforated. When fired, almost all of the propellant blast escapes from the rear of the weapon. The resulting forward inertial force, however, is still sufficient to launch the projectile. The neutralization of almost all recoil eliminates the need for a standard gun carriage and a recoil system. Although most recoilless rifles are fired from some sort of vehicle or ground mount, some of the smaller calibers can be shoulder fired in the same manner as an infantry rocket launcher.

Recoilless rifles were widely used in Korea and Vietnam, but they were phased out of service in most armies as antitank rockets and guided missiles became more sophisticated from the 1970s on. Nonetheless, Taliban forces in Afghanistan have used a number of recoilless rifles, most of them captured from Soviet forces in the 1980s. The most common is the 82-mm B-10, which first entered service in 1950.

Although it has a maximum range of 2.7 miles, its maximum effective range is only 1,640 feet. The most modern of the Taliban's recoilless antitank weapons is the 73-mm SPG-9. Designed initially for Soviet airborne units and entering service in 1962, it has a maximum effective range of 2,624 feet.

The first effective shoulder-fired infantry antitank weapons were free-flight rockets with HEAT warheads, entering service during World War II. All subsequent antitank rocket systems are derived from two basic designs, both introduced in 1942. The German Panzerfaust was an inexpensive single-shot lightweight weapon that could be fired by one man. The Panzerfaust consisted of a very simple small-diameter disposable launcher preloaded with a three-foot-long finned projectile with an oversized warhead that extended outside of the muzzle of the launching tube. The hollow tube concentrated the escaping gases away from the gunner and made the firing recoilless. Pulling the trigger ignited a small charge of black powder inside the tube, driving the projectile toward its target. The projectile exploded on impact. The Panzerfaust was the prototype upon which the subsequent Soviet/Russian family of rocket-propelled grenade (RPG) antitank weapons was based.

The first U.S. antitank rocket was the 2.36-inch bazooka, which consisted of a rocket and launcher operated by a two-man crew of gunner and loader. The launcher was a reloadable aluminum tube with a shoulder stock and a hand grip that contained a trigger assembly with an electric generator. When the gunner squeezed the trigger, it generated an electric current through the wires to ignite the solid fuel in the rocket. Unlike the Panzerfaust, the entire antitank rocket was launched from inside the bazooka's firing tube. The Germans reverse-engineered captured bazookas to produce the significantly up-gunned 88-mm Panzerschreck. Except for the RPG family of weapons, the bazooka is the prototype for all other modern shoulder-fired infantry antitank rockets.

The Soviet RPG-7 is one of the most widely produced shoulder-fired infantry antitank weapons in the world. It is one of the principal weapons of choice of Afghan and Iraqi insurgents. It is also widely used by Afghan and Iraqi police and military forces loyal to the national governments. First entering service in 1961 and used extensively by the Viet Cong and the North Vietnamese Army against American armored vehicles in Vietnam, the RPG-7 consists of a steel launching tube 40-mm in diameter and 37 inches long. Depending on the exact type of projectile, the protruding warhead can be anything from 83-mm to 105-mm. Most RPG-7 ammunition has a range up to 2,952 feet, and the most effective warhead has a tandem HEAT charge capable of penetrating 600-mm to 700-mm of rolled homogeneous armor (RHA).

The only shoulder-fired free-flight rocket antitank weapon used by U.S. forces today is the Swedish-built AT-4. Similar in operating principle to the World War II–era bazooka, the AT-4 fires an 84-mm projectile with a HEAT warhead to a maximum effective range of 984 feet. The resulting blast can penetrate up to 400-mm of RHA. Unlike the earlier bazooka, the AT-4 is not reloadable. The launcher and projectile are manufactured and issued as a single unit of ammunition. The entire system weighs 14.75 pounds.

ATGMs first started to appear in the late 1960s and represented a vast improvement on the early unguided antitank rockets. ATGMs vary widely in size and type, from individual shoulder-fired missiles to crew-served missiles and to those launched from ground vehicles and from aircraft. Unlike unguided systems, missiles have the great advantage of standoff capability.

First-generation guided missiles were manually controlled during flight. Once the missile was fired, the gunner guided it to the target by means of a joystick or similar device. Second-generation antitank missiles only required that the gunner keep the sight on the target. Guidance commands for the missile were transmitted either by radio or by wire. Third-generation antitank missiles operate by laser painting or marking of the target on a nose-mounted TV camera. They are known as fire-and-forget missiles.

Antitank missiles generally carry a hollow-charge or shaped-charge HEAT warhead. Tandem warhead missiles are designed specifically to defeat reactive or spaced vehicle armor, while top-attack antitank missiles are designed to strike from above against the more lightly armored tops of tanks and armored fighting vehicles (AFVs).

The 9K11 Malyutka, known by its NATO designation as the AT-3 Sagger, was the Soviet Union's first man-portable ATGM and probably the most extensively produced ATGM in history. It was widely used by Iraqi forces in both the Persian Gulf War and the Iraq War. Entering service in September 1963, it was the standard model for all subsequent first-generation ATGMs. Some 25,000 Saggers were produced yearly by the Soviet Union alone in the 1960s and 1970s. It was also manufactured by other Soviet bloc countries as well as the People's Republic of China. The Sagger has been widely exported to the Middle East, including Afghanistan, Algeria, Egypt, Iran, Iraq, Libya, and Syria. Guided to its target by means of a joy stick and wire, the Sagger has a launch weight of some 24 pounds with a warhead of 5.5 pounds. It

has a minimum range of 1,640 feet and a maximum range of 1.8 miles. At maximum range, it takes the missile about 30 seconds to reach its target. The Sagger can be fired from a portable suitcase launcher; from armored vehicles, such as the Soviet BMP-1 or BRDM-2; or from attack helicopters, including the Mi-2, Mi-8, and Mi-24.

The U.S.-made BGM-71 tube-launched optically tracked wire-guided (TOW) missile is a second-generation ATGM. TOWs were first produced by Hughes Aircraft Company and are now produced by Raytheon Systems Company. More than 500,000 TOWs have been manufactured, and they are employed by more than 45 nations. The TOW is designed to attack tanks, AFVs, bunkers and fortifications. First entering service in 1970, the TOW underwent a number of modifications, the most recent of which is the TOW-2B of 1991. The first use of the TOW in combat came in May 1972 during the Vietnam War. It also saw wartime service with the Israeli Army against Syrian forces and in the Iran-Iraq War (1980–1988). The TOW-2B first saw combat in 2003 during the Iraq War.

The TOW-2B missile weighs 49.8 pounds (64 pounds with carrier) and has an explosive filler of some 6.9 pounds. The missile is 5.8 inches in diameter and 48 inches in length. It has a minimum range of 213 feet and a maximum range of 2.3 miles. TOW missiles can be ground fired from a tripod by a crew of four or, more usually, from both wheeled and tracked vehicles, including the M-1/ M-3 Bradley, the M-966 HMMWV, and the M-1134 Stryker. TOWs also are mounted on attack helicopters. The missile operates on command line-of-sight guidance. The gunner uses a sight to locate the target and, once the missile is fired, continues to track the target through the sight, with guidance commands transmitted along two wires that spool from the back of the missile. The TOW-2B attacks the target from the top, and its double warheads explode downward when the missile is just above the target. A bunker-buster variant is designed to defeat bunkers, field fortifications, and buildings.

The Soviet Union's second-generation man-portable 9K111 Fagot (NATO designation AT-4 Spigot) ATGM entered service in 1972. Designed to replace the Sagger, the Spigot has a minimum range of 246 feet and a maximum range of 1.5 miles in a flight time of 11 seconds. Fired from a ground-mount folding tripod, the entire system in firing configuration weighs some 74 pounds, with the missile itself weighing 25.3 pounds and the warhead 5.5 pounds.

The M-47 Dragon was an American antitank infantry weapon that was fired from the gunner's shoulder but stabilized in front by a ground bipod. First fielded in 1975, it was used in the 1991 Persian Gulf War and was retired from service in the late 1990s. The improved Dragon II entered service in 1985, and the Super-Dragon entered service in 1990. At one time the Dragons were supplied to Iran, and the Iraqis captured some Dragons during the Iran-Iraq War and put them into service. The 140-mm wire-guided missile carried a HEAT warhead capable of penetrating 450-mm of RHA and defeating Soviet T-55, T-62, and T-72 tanks. The Dragon's maximum effective range was 3,280 feet. The launcher itself was expendable, but the sights could be removed after firing and reused. The Dragon's most significant drawback was that its tracking system required the gunner to remain kneeling and exposed to enemy fire while tracking the missile to the target.

The Dragon was replaced by the man-portable FGM-148 Javelin, a third-generation system. A joint venture of Texas Instruments (now Raytheon Missile Systems) of Dallas, Texas, and Lockheed Martin Electronics and Missiles (now Missiles and Fire Control) of Orlando, Florida, the Javelin entered service with the U.S. Army and U.S. Marine Corps in 1996. Designed for a two-man crew, the Javelin has a minimum range of 246 feet and a maximum effective range of 1.5 miles, more than twice that of the M-47 Dragon.

The Javelin system consists of a missile in a disposable launch tube, a reusable command launch unit (CLU) with triggering mechanism, an integrated day/night sighting device, and target-acquisition electronics. The missile weighs 49.5 pounds and is 5 feet 9 inches in length. Fins deploy when the missile is launched. The Javelin employs a small thermal imaging TV camera and sophisticated computer guidance system in its seeker section. To fire the missile, the gunner places a cursor over the selected target. The CLU then sends a lock-on-before-launch signal to the missile. The missile's infrared guidance system and onboard processing guide it after launch. The Javelin is designed for top attack and has a dual 8.5-pound warhead capable of defeating all known armor. U.S. forces used the Javelin in both the Afghanistan War and the Iraq War, and British forces also fielded the Javelin in 2005.

The AGM-65 Maverick is an American air-to-ground missile designed to destroy not only armored vehicles but also ships, air defense and artillery emplacements, and logistics nodes. Entering service in 1972, the missile weighs between 462 and 670 pounds, depending on the warhead. The 125-pound shaped-charge warhead has a point-detonating fuse, and the 300-pound HE penetrator has a delay-action fuse. The missile itself has a maximum effective range of 17 miles. The missile has an onboard infrared television camera with which the aircraft pilot or weapons systems officer locks onto the target before firing. Once launched, the Maverick tracks its target automatically, making it a fire-and-forget system. Fired primarily from fixed-wing aircraft, the Maverick was used extensively in both the Persian Gulf War and in the Iraq War.

The AGM-114 Hellfire entered service in 1984. It was designed specifically as an antitank weapon, primarily for launch from attack helicopters, although it can be fired from some fixed-wing attack aircraft and can even be ground launched. The missile weighs 106 pounds, including the 20-pound warhead. It has a maximum effective range of 4.9 miles. The initial versions of the Hellfire were laser-guided, but the more recent variants have been radar-guided. The Hellfire has been used in the Persian Gulf War, the Afghanistan War, and the Iraq War. Between 2001 and 2007 U.S. forces fired more than 6,000 Hellfires in combat.

Although direct-firing antitank artillery guns have been phased out of service by most armies since the 1950s, the increasing technical sophistication of artillery ammunition has given a new antitank role to indirect-firing field artillery. Most American antitank field artillery rounds are 155-mm, fired by either the M-198 towed howitzer or the M-109 family of self-propelled howitzers. Special antitank warheads also exist for the M-270 multiple-launch rocket system (MLRS) and the army tactical missile system (ATACMS), which use the same self-propelled launcher system as the MLRS. The most current version of the M-109 howitzer, the Paladin M-109A6, entered service in 1999 and fires to a maximum range of 13.6 miles. The United States used the M-109A6 in the Iraq War, and the armies of the United States, Britain, Egypt, and Saudi Arabia all used earlier versions of the M-109 in the Persian Gulf War. The M-270 MLRS, which entered service in 1983, was developed jointly by the United States, Britain, Germany, and France. It fires 12 free-flight rockets to a maximum range of 26.1 miles. The MLRS launcher also can fire 2 MGM-140 ATACMS projectiles at a time. Operational in January 1991 and first fired in combat during the Persian Gulf War, the guided missiles have a range of 102 miles.

The improved conventional munitions (ICM) artillery round entered service for the U.S. 105-mm howitzer in 1961 and was first fired in combat in the Vietnam War. The projectile was a cargo-carrying round that burst in the air over the target, dispersing a number of unguided antipersonnel submunitions. In common terms, the ICM was an artillery version of a cluster bomb. In the early 1970s the United States developed a projectile for the 155-mm howitzer that carried submunitions designed to work against either personnel or tanks. Called a dual-purpose ICM (DPICM), the M-483 155-mm projectile carries 88 submunitions capable of penetrating 65-mm of RHA. Each M-42 or M-46 bomblet carries a HEAT shaped charge, designed to attack a tank's relatively thin top armor. The DPICM warhead for the MLRS rocket carries 644 M-77 submunitions, each capable of penetrating 100-mm of RHA. The ATACMS MGM-140 missile warhead carried 950 M-74 submunitions that are classified as antipersonnel/antimaterial (APAM). They are effective against thin-skinned tactical vehicles but not against armored vehicles. The most significant drawback to DPICMs is the 2–5 percent dud rate of the submunitions, which has caused unintended casualties as friendly forces have moved into a target area after the firing. During the 1991 Persian Gulf War, DPICMs acquired the nickname "Steel Rain."

Like DPICM artillery ammunition, family of scatterable mines (FASCAM) rounds are also cargo-carrying projectiles that burst in the air above the target area and disperse unguided submunitions. FASCAM rounds can be emplaced remotely, deep in an enemy's rear, by either field artillery or aircraft. FASCAM projectiles were initially developed for both the 155-mm and 8-inch howitzers and carried either antipersonnel mines (called area denial munitions [ADAMs]) or antitank mines (called remote antiarmor mines [RAAMs]). The 8-inch howitzer was retired from the American arsenal after the Persian Gulf War. The 155-mm M-741 projectile carries nine M-73 antitank mines, which are preset to self-destruct 48 hours after they have been emplaced. The M-741 projectile carries nine M-70 antitank mines, with a preset self-destruct time of 4 hours.

Unlike many antitank mines, the FASCAM RAAMs are designed to achieve a K-kill rather than just an M-kill. Each 3.75-pound M-70 and M-73 mine contains slightly more than 1 pound of RDX (cyclonite) explosive. When the mine is detonated by its magnetically induced fuse, a two-sided Miznay-Shardin plate creates a self-forging fragment that becomes a superdense molten slug that punches through the tank's relatively thin underarmor. The principle is very similar to that of the explosively formed penetrators used in some IEDs. The first artillery-delivered FASCAM minefield in combat was fired by the 5th Battalion, 11th Marines, during the Battle of Khafji (January 29–February 1, 1991).

The first PGM for field artillery weapons was the American M-712 Copperhead, a 155-mm fin-stabilized terminally guided projectile specifically designed to engage tanks and other hardened targets. In order for the Copperhead round to hit a tank directly, an observer must have the target under observation and be close enough to "paint" it with a laser-designator during the terminal leg of the projectile's trajectory. This requires that the round be below cloud cover long enough for it to lock onto the target and have sufficient time to maneuver to impact. The observer can be either a forward observer on the ground or an aerial in a helicopter. Unmanned aerial vehicles (UAVs) equipped with television cameras and laser designators can also be used to guide the Copperhead round to its target. The Copperhead was fired in combat for the first time during the Persian Gulf War.

The U.S. sense and destroy armor (SADARM) system is based in a cargo-carrying artillery round similar to the DPICM projectile except that it carries smart submunitions. The 155-mm M-898 round carries two submunitions that are released 3,280 feet above the target area. Specially designed parachutes slow the descent of the submunition and cause it to swing in a circle. As it descends, its millimeter wave radar and infrared telescope sensors sweep the area below about 492 feet in diameter. When the sensors acquire a target, the explosive charge triggers at the right time, sending an explosively formed penetrator through the top armor of the tank. SADARM rounds were fired in combat for the first time during the Iraq War. The divisional artillery of the U.S. 3rd Infantry Division fired 108 rounds and achieved 48 vehicle kills.

Purpose-built ground-attack aircraft first appeared in the final year of World War I, and during World War II the British, Soviets, and Germans all developed fixed-wing aircraft specifically designed to attack tanks. During the Vietnam War the United States first started using helicopters in a ground-attack role, and during North Vietnam's 1972 Easter Offensives American helicopters firing TOW missiles attacked tanks for the first time.

The first American purpose-designed attack helicopter was the AH-1 Cobra, which entered service in 1967. The U.S. Army retired the Cobra in 1999, but the U.S. Marine Corps still flies the AH-1W Super Cobra, which can mount an antitank armament of eight TOW or eight Hellfire missiles. The U.S. Army's AH-64 Apache entered service in 1983 and saw significant service in the Persian Gulf War. It has also seen significant service in the Afghanistan War and the Iraq War. Specifically designed as a tank killer, the AH-64's primary armament is the M-230 Chain Gun. Depending on its specific mission, each AH-64 can carry up to 16 Hellfire antitank missiles and 1,200 rounds of 30-mm ammunition.

A number of American fixed-wing ground-support aircraft are capable of carrying antitank armament, but like the AH-64 Apache, the A-10 Thunderbolt II, universally known as the "Warthog," was specifically designed as a tank killer. Its primary armament is the GAU-8/A Gatling gun, which weighs 4,029 pounds and accounts for some 16 percent of the aircraft's unladen weight. The A-10 carries 1,174 rounds of 30-mm ammunition. When configured for a specific antitank mission, the A-10 can carry four AGM-65 Maverick missiles.

UAVs were initially designed as reconnaissance platforms. Their sophisticated onboard sensor systems and long dwell times over target areas made them critically valuable assets in finding enemy tanks. But some UAVs also have sufficient lift to carry 106-pound AGM-114 Hellfire missiles in addition to their sensor packages. Although not originally designed as attack platforms, both the MQ-1B Predator and the MQ-9 Reaper have carried and successfully launched Hellfires.

DAVID T. ZABECKI AND SPENCER C. TUCKER

See also

Aircraft, Helicopters; Armored Warfare, Persian Gulf and Iraq Wars; Improvised Explosive Devices; Missiles, Air-to-Ground

References

Gander, Terry J. *Anti-Tank Weapons*. Marlborough, UK: Crowood, 2000.

Ripley, Tim. *Tank Warfare*. Drexel Hill, PA: Casemate, 2003.

Weeks, John S. *Men against Tanks: A History of Anti-Tank Warfare*. New York: Mason/Charter, 1975.

Members of the antiwar movement Code Pink: Women for Peace rally against the Iraq War on the National Mall in Washington, D.C., on January 27, 2007. (Shutterstock.com)

Antiwar Movement, Iraq War

There was little opposition to the U.S. invasion of Afghanistan in 2001, following as it did the Al Qaeda–directed terrorist attacks of September 11. The Iraq War (2003–2011), however, saw substantial antiwar demonstrations and protests, including widespread use of the Internet. Anti–Iraq War demonstrations occurred in the United States, Europe, and the Middle East.

Although lacking the types of civil disobedience tactics accompanying the Vietnam War (1958–1975), opposition was no less intense. Antiwar groups began protests even before military action began in March 2003. Groups such as Americans Against War With Iraq, NOT IN OUR NAME, United for Peace and Justice, and ANSWER insisted that the George W. Bush administration's plans for war would lead to the killing of thousands of U.S. soldiers and Iraqi soldiers and civilians and would have a negative effect on Middle East stability. They also contended that the rush to war was generated by imperialistic concerns based on oil interests, that it would violate international law without United Nations (UN) approval, that it would only breed more terrorism, that Iraqi president Saddam Hussein was not in consort with Al Qaeda, and that Iraq did not possess weapons of mass destruction. Rallies and demonstrations continued prior to the war.

In the third week of January 2003 a group of 50 volunteers from various nations, led by former Persian Gulf War veteran Kenneth O'Keefe, headed to Baghdad to act as human shields against possible impending U.S. air strikes. Eventually, between 200 and 500 human shields made their way to Iraq and remained there during the shock-and-awe bombing campaign in March.

On February 15, 2003, between 100,000 and 250,000 people marched in New York City, making it the largest political demonstration the city had seen since the anti–nuclear proliferation movement of the early 1980s. On March 9 some 3,000 pink-clad women activists marched around the White House to oppose the impending war. This group called itself

CODEPINK. On March 15 the last massive demonstrations before the war began occurred when tens of thousands of protestors participated in antiwar rallies from Portland, Oregon, to Los Angeles to Washington, D.C.

Once the war commenced on March 20, 2003, the antiwar protests grew in number. The antiwar coalitions that appeared were composed of people from all walks of life. They included the elderly, former veterans of past wars, school-age students, college students, and people of all races, ethnicities, and religious backgrounds. Indeed, opposition to the Iraq War cut across race, gender, and economic lines. One of the more unique forms of protest later copied by other antiwar groups was initiated by a Quaker peace group, the American Friends Service Committee (AFSC). Calling it "False Pretenses," the AFSC created a memorial by placing 500 pairs of boots at the Federal Building Plaza in Chicago, symbolizing the number of soldiers who had been killed at that point in the war. Other antiwar activists built mock coffins and stretched them out on busy streets.

One antiwar group that captured the national media's attention was Grandmothers against the War. Primarily a local coalition in New York City, 17 grandmothers, ranging in age from 49 to 90, were arrested on October 17, 2005, when they attempted to enlist in the military at the Times Square recruiting station. Their action inspired other elderly women to take up the cause in Chicago, San Francisco, and Los Angeles.

The actions of Cindy Sheehan also served as a lightning rod for the antiwar movement when, in August 2005, she coducted a 26-day vigil outside President Bush's ranch at Crawford, Texas. Sheehan's son had been killed in Iraq in 2004. Her most dramatic act of civil disobedience occurred during the 2006 State of the Union address, when she was forcibly removed from the House chamber sporting a T-shirt that read "2,245 Dead. How Many More?" In March 2006 Sheehan was arrested for allegedly blocking a door leading to the U.S. mission in the UN in New York City. She was also one of the founders of the Gold Star Families for Peace, an organization dedicated to helping families who had lost relatives in the Iraq War and to bringing an end to U.S. involvement in Iraq. Sheehan became the most recognizable antiwar protester in the United States and appeared on numerous television programs and in many rallies around the country.

From 2002 to 2007, large antiwar demonstrations took place in cities and towns throughout the nation. On January 28, 2007, an antiwar rally in the nation's capital saw thousands of peaceful protestors gather to listen to Hollywood celebrities such as Jane Fonda, Sean Penn, Danny Glover, Susan Sarandon, and Tim Robbins condemn the war.

The antiwar demonstrations were remarkable for their discipline and adherence to the principle of nonviolent civil disobedience. In 2007, apart from visible protests, the National War Tax Resistance Coordinating Committee estimated that between 8,000 and 10,000 Americans refused to pay some or all of their federal taxes to support the war.

One of the unique aspects of the anti–Iraq War movement has been its online organization. Cyberactive antiwar groups such as Americans Against Escalation in Iraq, MoveOn. org, Win Without War, and WHY WAR? have effectively mobilized opposition at the grassroots level through use of the Internet. Use of online activism has emerged as a force for organizing, raising money, and influencing politicians through blogs (web logs) and e-mail messages. These organizations represent the new wave in protest movements, one aimed at influencing votes in Congress rather than just street theater and mass demonstrations. The Internet was also responsible for increasing membership in antiwar organizations such as Veterans for Common Sense, Operation Truth, and Iraq Veterans against the War.

The strength of the anti–Iraq War protests lay in their sophistication and perspective. Certainly, the Internet clearly aided organizational efforts and awareness of the issues. One important difference between the Iraq War protest movement and protests during the Vietnam War is that the former avoided attacking or demonizing the troops and instead concentrated their displeasure on the political leadership. This was seen in the slogan of "Support the Troops: Bring Them Home!"

Overwhelming general antiwar sentiment in Europe—impossible to separate from a pervasive anti-American sentiment—was an important reason why so few members of the North Atlantic Treaty Organization powers made major manpower commitments to forces fighting the Taliban in Afghanistan.

CHARLES FRANCIS HOWLETT

See also
IRAQI FREEDOM, Operation; Sheehan, Cindy Lee Miller

References
Chomsky, Noam. *Hegemony or Survival: America's Quest for Global Dominance.* New York: Metropolitan Books, 2003.

Cortright, David. "The Movement and the 2003 War in Iraq." In *The Movement,* edited by Randy Scherer, 146–152. Farmington Hills, MI: Greenhaven, 2004.

Gardner, Lloyd, and Marilyn Young, eds. *Iraq and the Lessons of Vietnam: Or, How Not to Learn from the Past.* New York: New Press, 2007.

Johnson, Chalmers. *Nemesis: The Last Days of the American Republic.* New York: Henry Holt, 2007.

Miller, Christian T. *Blood Money: Wasted Billions, Lost Lives, and Corporate Greed in Iraq.* New York: Little, Brown, 2006.

Ryan, Claes G. *America the Virtuous: The Crisis of Democracy and the Quest for Empire.* New Brunswick, NJ: Transaction Books, 2003.

Sheehan, Cindy. *Peace Mom: A Mother's Journey through Heartache to Activism.* New York: Atria, 2006.

Arabian Gulf

See Persian Gulf

Arab-Israeli Conflict, Overview

Jewish-Muslim tensions in the Middle East as expressed in the Arab-Israeli conflict are at the core of conflict in the modern Middle East. This is responsible for much of the involvement of the United States in the region. The unflagging U.S. support for Israel is in large part motivated by political considerations driven by demographics. While their population of some 13.9 million worldwide in 2013 makes Jews one of the world's smaller religious minorities, the United States had 6.8 million Jews, even more than that of Israel, with some 6.1 million.

Resolving the Arab-Israeli conflict, however, has defied the best efforts of every American president since Harry S. Truman. It remains the Gordian Knot of international diplomacy. The long history and intricacies of the conflict and the policies and costs to the states involved warrant a full discussion of its roots and history here.

The Arab-Israeli wars are usually said to have begun either with the Arab-Jewish Communal War (1947–1948) or the Israeli War of Independence (1948–1949). The Arab-Israeli Wars extend to the present, however, as a number of the Arab states, most notably Syria, have yet to sign peace treaties with Israel.

Beginning the conflict in 1948 or even 1947 gives a false impression, however, of the true duration of the hostilities. There had been earlier episodes of violence and armed clashes in Palestine between Arabs and Jews, especially in the 1920s and 1930s. These events were sparked by Arab fears over significant Jewish immigration to and land purchases in Palestine. Animosity found expression in the Arab riots of 1920 and the Arab Revolt of 1936–1939.

Of course, strife was hardly new to this region. Palestine has been a battleground since the beginning of recorded history. History's first reliably recorded battle took place here in 1457 BCE at Megiddo, at the head of present-day Israel's Jezreel Valley. When Egyptian forces under the command of Pharaoh Thutmose III decisively defeated a Canaanite coalition under the king of Kadesh, the Canaanites withdrew to the city of Megiddo and the Egyptians brought it under siege. Certain fundamentalist Christians identify Megiddo as the site of Armageddon, where according to the book of Revelation the final great battle between good and evil will take place.

With its location on the eastern Mediterranean coast, ancient Palestine formed an important communication route between larger empires such as Egypt, Assyria, Babylon, and Persia. As such, it was destined for a stormy existence. These empires as well as Alexander the Great, the Seleucid Empire, the Romans, the Byzantines, the Abbasid caliphate, the Tartars, the Mongols, the Mamluks, the Ottoman Turks, and finally the British all fought for control of Palestine. Sometime around 1200 BCE the Jews established and then maintained an independent Jewish state there. Ultimately more powerful states prevailed, and the Jews were largely expelled from their own land by the occupiers in what became known as the Diaspora. Jews settled in most of the world's countries and on almost every continent.

In the 19th century, nationalism swept Europe. Sentiment for a national state also touched the Jews, many of whom longed for a state of their own, one that would be able to protect them from the persecutions (pogroms) that occurred in the late 19th and early 20th centuries, most notably in Russia but also in Poland and even in more tolerant Western societies, such as France. Zionism, or the effort to reestablish a Jewish state in Palestine, attracted a great many Jews—both religious and nonreligious—and a number of them went to Palestine as immigrants.

During World War I, the British government sought to win the support of both Arabs and Jews in the war against the Central Powers, which included the Ottoman Empire. While at the same time supporting the Arab Revolt against the Ottomans, the British government issued the Balfour Declaration of November 1917. It pledged establishment of a Jewish homeland in Palestine. In retrospect, British policies were at once shortsighted and contradictory and certainly helped sow the seeds of even more Arab-Jewish enmity when the war ended in 1918.

After the war both Britain and France secured League of Nations mandates. France obtained Syria and Lebanon, while Britain took control of Palestine, Jordan, and Iraq.

Increasing Jewish immigration, however, as well as ongoing Jewish purchases of Arab land increasingly inflamed Arab leaders in Palestine as well as leaders such as King Abdullah of Jordan and Ibn Saud of Saudi Arabia, who feared that if immigration could not be halted, the growing Jewish minority in Palestine would become a majority. In what became an increasingly violent atmosphere, the British government found it impossible to please both sides. London, worried about its overall position in the Middle East with the approach of a new world war, increasingly tended to side with the Arabs. This meant restrictions on both Jewish immigration and land purchases in Palestine, but this came at precisely the time when German leader Adolf Hitler challenged the post–World War I status quo in Europe and was carrying out a fervent anti-Semitic policy.

Finding it impossible to secure agreement between the two sides, London announced plans for the partition of Palestine. The Arabs rejected this partitioning, insisting on independence for Palestine as one state under majority (Arab) rule. Concerned about their overall position in the Middle East, the British then withdrew from their pro-Zionist policy and in May 1939 issued a white paper that severely restricted the immigration of Jews to Palestine and forbade the purchase of Arab lands in Palestine by Jews.

Following World War II, Jews in Palestine conducted a campaign against the British policy there that mixed diplomatic campaign with armed struggle. Finding it more and more difficult to contain the growing violence in Palestine, coupled with the support of President Harry S. Truman's administration in the United States for the Jewish position, London turned the future of Palestine over to the new United Nations (UN). On November 29, 1947, the UN General Assembly voted to partition the British mandate into Jewish and Arab states. The Arabs of Palestine, supported by the Arab League, adamantly opposed the partition, and the first of four major wars began following news of the UN vote. The first war of 1947–1949 contains two identifiably separate conflicts: the Arab-Jewish communal war of November 30, 1947–May 14, 1948, which included volunteer forces from other Arab states as well as Palestinian Arabs, and the Israeli War of Independence, which began on May 15, 1948, a day after the ending of the British mandate and with the founding of the State of Israel. The war ended with the last truce agreement with Syria on July 30, 1949. The three other conflicts ensued in 1956 (the Sinai War, or Suez Crisis), 1967 (the Six-Day War), and 1973 (the October War, Yom Kippur War, or Ramadan War). In these four major conflicts, Israeli forces eventually triumphed. Each threatened to bring about

superpower intervention, and the four wars also had profound implications throughout the Middle East and beyond. Beyond these wars, however, were ongoing terrorist attacks against Israel; cross-border raids, some of them quite large; a successful Israeli air strike on the Iraqi Osiraq nuclear reactor (1981); large Israeli incursions into southern Lebanon in 1982 and in 2006; and armed conflict between Israel and Hamas in Gaza (2008–2009, 2012, and 2114).

The 1948 war began following the announcement of the UN General Assembly's endorsement of Resolution 181 on November 29, 1947, calling for the partition of Palestine into Jewish and Arab states. While Jewish authorities in Palestine accepted the resolution, the Arabs—including the Palestinians and the Arab League—rejected it. In response to passage of the UN resolution, Arabs began attacking Jews throughout Palestine, and the incidents expanded so that from December 1947 to April or May 1948 an intercommunal war raged between Jewish and Arab residents of Palestine.

The Jewish community in Palestine then numbered some 600,000 people, while there were more than 1.2 million Palestinians. Palestinian numerical advantage counted for little on the battlefield, however. The Palestinians had no national institutions of any kind, let alone a cohesive military. They were fragmented with divided elites and were unprepared for the violence, expulsions, and loss of their property. Perhaps only 5,000 took part in the fighting against the Jews. These essentially guerrilla forces were poorly trained, inadequately equipped, and ineffectively organized.

The Arab League pledged support to the Palestinians but, through its Military Committee, actually usurped the conflict from the Palestinians. The Military Committee and the mufti Haj Amin al-Hussayni argued over the conduct of the war as each sought to control operations. The Military Committee failed, however, to provide the Palestinians with the money and weapons that the Arab rulers had pledged and sent its own commanders to Palestine to oversee the war. Such internal conflicts further weakened the overall Arab effort.

The Jews, on the other hand, were much better equipped and more organized. Jewish society was both Western and industrialized, having all the institutions of a modern state. In fact, structurally the establishment of the Jewish state required only the formal transformation of prestatehood institutions to government entities, parliament, political parties, banks, and a relatively well-developed military arm, known as the Haganah.

The Haganah was organized during the civil war as a full-fledged army, with 9 brigades totaling some 25,000

An Israeli bomb explodes in Rafah, a city in the southern Gaza Strip on January 14, 2009. Israeli forces launched an assault on Gaza beginning on December 27, 2008, seeking to punish the Hamas militant group controlling Gaza for rocket attacks on southern Israel. (AP Photo/Eyad Baba)

conscripts. By May 1948 there were 11 brigades, with nearly 35,000 men. With Jewish forces having taken the offensive in early April 1948, the Palestinians had no chance but to counterattack and by early May had been defeated.

During this time, and even before the Jews' final campaign, hundreds of thousands of Palestinians were driven from or fled their homes and became refugees. By the end of the war, there would be 750,000 to 1 million or more Palestinian refugees. Many of them escaped from the battle zone, but others were forcibly expelled and deported by Jewish forces during the actual fighting.

On May 15, 1948, with the formal establishment of the State of Israel, Israeli forces secured control over all the territory allocated to it by the UN in addition to a corridor leading to Jerusalem and the Jewish part of Jerusalem, which according to the Partition Resolution was to have been internationalized. With the official termination of British rule in Palestine on May 14, 1948, David Ben-Gurion, Israel's first elected prime minister, declared the establishment of the State of Israel. This declaration was followed by the advance

of four Arab armies toward Palestine with the goal of extinguishing Israel.

The resulting war was in many respects primitive. Some 35,000 Israeli soldiers faced 35,000–40,000 Arab soldiers. Both sides were subjected to a UN Security Council arms embargo, but it was the Arabs who suffered the most from this. The Arab armies secured their weapons from Britain to Egypt, while Jordan and Iraq, which had no access to other markets, were forced into this arrangement under treaties with Britain. With the embargo in place, the Arabs were unable to replace damaged or destroyed weapons, and they had only limited access to ammunition. While the Jews received no military equipment from the West, they did manage in early 1948 to sign a major arms contract with the Czech government, purchasing various weapons but mostly small arms and ammunition.

Despite an initial effort to create a unified command structure, the movements of the four Arab armies on Palestine were not coordinated. In April 1948 General Nur al-Din Mahmud, an Iraqi officer, was appointed by the Arab

League to command the Arab forces, but each Arab army acted in isolation. At the last minute Lebanon refrained from participation in the war. Syrian and Iraqi forces fought in the northern part of Israel, the Jordanian Arab League fought in the central sector, and the Egyptian Army fought in the southern sector.

In this initial stage, the Israelis were concentrated along the road to Jerusalem. Both the Jordanians and the Israelis completely misread the other's intentions. The Israelis assumed that the Arab Legion planned to invade Israel, and the Jordanians feared that the Israelis intended to drive the Arab Legion from the West Bank.

In fact, all the Israelis sought was to bring the Jewish part of Jerusalem under Israeli control and, toward that end, to gain control over the road from the coast to Jerusalem. The Israelis feared that the Arab Legion would cut off and occupy all Jerusalem, and to prevent this they reinforced the Jewish part of the city. Fierce fighting ensued between Israeli and Jordanian forces that ended with the Jordanians repulsing the Israeli troops and holding on to bases in the Latrun area, the strategic site along the Tel Aviv–Jerusalem road.

Israeli-Jordanian fighting ended when the Israeli government acknowledged its inability to drive out Jordanian forces who blocked the road to Jerusalem and when the two governments realized that the other posed no risk. In November 1948 Jewish and Jordanian military commanders in Jerusalem concluded an agreement that formalized the positions established with the de facto cease-fire of the previous July.

With the end of the fighting with Jordan, the Israelis launched the final phase of the war. In a two-stage operation in October and December 1948, the Israeli Army drove Egyptian forces from the Negev. The Israeli effort to force out the Egyptians along the coast was only partially successful, however. The Egyptians remained in the Gaza Strip. Indeed, the Gaza Strip remained under Egyptian control until 1967.

Concurrent with the October operations in the south, other Israeli troops stormed the high ground in central Galilee, controlled by the Arab League's Arab Liberation Army. After brief fighting, the Israelis occupied all of Galilee. In early January 1949 a cease-fire came into effect, and shortly thereafter negotiations on armistice agreements began.

The second major confrontation between Israel and the Arabs was the Sinai War, or Suez Crisis, of October 1956. This time, France, Britain, Israel, and Egypt were involved in the fighting. The Israeli-Egyptian portion of the war, which in Israel was known as Operation KADESH, was part of a larger picture.

During 1949–1956, there was constant unrest along the Israeli-Egyptian demarcation line as well as between Israel and Jordan. Infiltrators regularly crossed the border from the Egyptian-controlled Gaza Strip, from the Sinai, and from the West Bank. Some were Palestinian refugees seeking to return to their homes or to visit relatives who remained inside Israel, some hoped to harvest their fields on the Israeli side of the border, some came to steal, and a few were bent on launching terrorist attacks against Israeli targets.

These infiltrations had an enormous impact on Israel. Economic damage mounted, and border-area residents, many of them newly arrived immigrants, were unprepared for the challenge. Israel feared the political implications of the infiltrations, which were thousands per month. Consequently, Israeli security forces undertook harsh measures against the infiltrators, regardless of the motives for crossing the border. Israeli soldiers often ambushed infiltrators, killing them and launching reprisal attacks. As a result, tensions along the Israeli borders increased, chiefly along the frontiers with Jordan and Egypt.

While the cross-border tensions provided the background context, the war occurred for two main reasons. First, Egyptian president Gamal Abdel Nasser had absorbed a large number of Palestinian refugees in Egypt and was responsible in a legal sense for those in the Gaza Strip. Rather than allowing the Palestinians free rein to attack Israel, he sought to support their cause while at the same time limiting the Israeli response to their actions in unspoken rules of engagement, which the Israelis hoped to overturn. Nasser was a fervent Arab nationalist who also aspired to lead and unite the Arab world, a potentiality that deeply troubled Prime Minister Ben-Gurion. Ben-Gurion attributed the Arab defeat in 1948 to a great extent to their divisions, and he was justifiably fearful of a unified Arab world under Nasser's leadership. The third immediate reason for the war was the Egyptian-Soviet arms arrangement (normally referred to as the Czech Arms Deal), announced in September 1955. The agreement assured Nasser of the modern weapons that Ben-Gurion was certain Nasser intended to use in an all-out attack against Israel.

Israeli fears were mitigated by an arms agreement with France, completed in June 1956 one month before Nasser nationalized the Suez Canal on July 26. The latter provoked an acute international crisis that culminated with the 1956 war. Shortly after the beginning of the crisis, France invited Israel to take part in planning a joint military attack on Egypt.

For Israel, while there was no specific reason for such an offensive move, fear of Nasser's intentions seemed sufficient justification. Tensions between Israel and Egypt since 1949, and especially since 1954, had significantly diminished. In the summer of 1956, exchanges of fire along the armistice line had largely ceased. More important, Nasser, expecting a fierce Anglo-French reaction to the nationalization of the Suez Canal, reduced the Egyptian troop deployment along the Israeli-Egyptian border to reinforce the Suez Canal.

Egypt had blockaded the Strait of Tiran, closing it to Israeli ships, but that by itself could not be reason for war, as there was no Israeli commercial maritime transportation along that route. Nevertheless, Ben-Gurion feared that Nasser was planning to unite the Arab world against Israel, and thus the invitation from two major powers to take part in a combined military effort was too much to resist. In a meeting at Svres, France, during October 22–25, 1956, French, British, and Israeli negotiators worked out planning for the war.

According to the plan, Israel would begin the conflict, landing parachutists a few miles east of Suez. France and Britain would then issue an ultimatum to both parties to remove their military forces from the canal. Expecting an Egyptian refusal, French and British forces would then invade Egypt to enforce the ultimatum. In the meantime, Israeli forces would storm the Sinai Peninsula. Their goal was to join up with the parachutists in the heart of the Sinai and to open the Strait of Tiran.

The agreement with the British and French was the determining factor in the Israeli plan of attack. Instead of storming the Egyptian positions in front of them, a paratroop battalion was dropped on October 29 at the eastern gates of the Mitla Pass, some 30 miles east of the Suez Canal. Simultaneously, the paratroop brigade, commanded by Lieutenant Colonel Ariel Sharon, moved into the Sinai to join up with the battalion waiting deep in the Sinai. Other Israeli forces had to wait until the Anglo-French attack on Egypt began.

Israeli commanders in the field were unaware of the agreement with the British and the French. Fearing for the parachute brigade and seeking a resolute and decisive victory over Egyptian forces, Major General Assaf Simhoni, commander of the Israeli Southern Command, ordered his forces to move ahead. The Israeli armored brigade stormed the Egyptian positions, with the remainder of the forces ensuring the defeat of the Egyptians.

Israeli forces completed the occupation of the Sinai and the Gaza Strip within three days. During the fighting, nearly 170 Israeli soldiers were killed and 700 were wounded. The Egyptians suffered thousands of deaths, far more wounded, and more than 5,500 taken prisoner.

Israel did not long enjoy the territorial achievements it gained in the war. Under enormous pressure from the United States and the Soviet Union, Israel was forced to remove its troops from the Sinai and the Gaza Strip. However, the terms of the Israeli evacuation of the Sinai aimed to provide it with the security it was lacking: UN observers were deployed along the armistice demarcation lines to ensure that they would not be crossed by infiltrators. One result of the stationing of UN forces was the nearly complete cessation of infiltration from the Gaza Strip to Israel. It was also agreed that the Sinai would be demilitarized, removing with that the threat of an Egyptian surprise attack against Israel. The Dwight D. Eisenhower administration provided assurances that it would no longer allow closure of the Strait of Tiran. Finally, the performance of Israeli forces in the war marked a dramatic change in the history of the Israel Defense Forces (IDF). The IDF went from being an unsophisticated infantry-based army to an efficient, modernized, and mechanized military force. The lessons of the Sinai War certainly paved the way toward the Israelis' impressive achievement in the Six-Day War of June 6–11, 1967.

While the immediate cause of the Six-Day War may be unclear, the long-term catalysts are more obvious. On May 15, 1967, Nasser sent his army into the Sinai. This set the stage for a dramatic three weeks that culminated in an Israeli attack and the total defeat of Egyptian, Jordanian, and Syrian forces. It also resulted in the loss of territories by these three Arab countries.

Tensions along the Israeli-Syrian and Israeli-Jordanian borders formed the long-term cause of the 1956 war. There were three issues of contention. The first was the Israeli-Syrian struggle over the sovereignty of several pieces of land along their mutual border. According to the Israeli-Syrian armistice agreements, these areas were demilitarized. The Syrians insisted that sovereignty of the areas was undecided, while the Israelis believed that because the areas were on their side of the international border, they were under Israeli sovereignty. Consequently, Israel insisted that it had the right to cultivate the controversial pieces of land, to Syria's dismay. In a number of instances the Syrians tried, by armed force, to prevent Israeli settlers from farming the land. The second point of controversy lay in Syrian attempts to prevent Israel from diverting water from the Jordan River. Encouraged by the Arab League, the Syrians had tried since 1964 to divert the headwaters of the Jordan River inside Syria. Israel reacted fiercely to this, and until the Syrians finally abandoned the project, many clashes took place between the two nations' armed forces. The third issue was the continuing grievances of the Palestinians. Their desire to regain their land and find a solution for their displaced refugees was an ever-present theme in the politics of the neighboring Arab states and the Palestinian refugee community.

During 1957–1964 Palestinian engineer and nationalist Yasser Arafat established Fatah, a political organization dedicated to liberating Palestine within the rubric of the Palestine Liberation Organization (PLO), also established in that year by the Arab League to provide a political representative body for the Palestinians. During the next few years other militant, political, and representative Palestinian organizations were established. In January 1965 Fatah planted a bomb near an Israeli water-pumping station. The Israelis defused the bomb, but Fatah celebrated this as the first Palestinian terrorist attack. Palestinian attacks continued throughout 1965, 1966, and 1967. Despite the relatively low scale of the attacks, Israel responded aggressively, blaming Jordan for funding the terrorists and Syria for harboring and encouraging them.

The extent and ferocity of Israeli-Syrian clashes increased during 1967, culminating in an aerial battle between Israeli and Syrian forces that took place in April 1967. Israeli pilots shot down six Syrian aircraft during one of the dogfights. In the course of a public address, IDF chief of staff Lieutenant General Yitzhak Rabin threatened war against Syria.

A month later in May 1967, Nasser ordered his forces into the Sinai. The reasons for this action are in dispute. The common assumption is that Moscow warned both the Egyptian and Syrian governments that Israel was massing military forces along the Israeli-Syrian border and planning to attack Syria. Because Egypt and Syria were bound by a military pact signed on November 4, 1966, Nasser sent his army into the Sinai to force the Israelis to dilute their forces in the north and to forestall what he assumed was an imminent attack on Syria.

The Israelis responded to Nasser's Sinai action with the calling up of IDF reserve forces. Nasser subsequently increased Israeli concerns when he ordered the UN observers along the Israeli-Egyptian border to concentrate in one location. UN secretary-general U Thant responded by pulling UN forces out of the Sinai altogether. Next, Nasser again closed the Strait of Tiran, yet another violation of the agreements that had led to the Israeli withdrawal from the Sinai in 1957. Besides that, Jordan and Egypt signed a military pact on May 30, 1967. This further increased the Israeli sense of siege.

Israeli military doctrine called for preemptive strikes in case of a concentration of Arab forces along its borders. All that was necessary was U.S. permission, and the Lyndon B. Johnson administration gave that in early June. The war began at dawn on June 5, 1967, with preemptive Israeli air strikes on Egyptian and then Syrian, Jordanian, and Iraqi air bases. The purpose of the attack was to neutralize the Arab air forces and remove the threat of air strikes on Israel. This would also, at a later stage, allow the Israeli Air Force to provide close air support to its forces on the ground.

Catching the vast bulk of the Egyptian aircraft on the ground while their pilots were at breakfast, some 250 Israeli aircraft destroyed the backbone of the Arab air forces within an hour, and by the end of the day the Egyptian Air Force has been almost completely wiped out. More than 300 of a total of 420 Egyptian combat aircraft were destroyed that day. The Israelis then turned to destroy the far smaller Syrian and Jordanian Air Forces.

About an hour after the start of the air raids against Egypt, at about 8:30 a.m. Israeli time, the IDF launched its ground offensive. Three Israeli divisions attacked Egyptian forces in the Sinai and within four days had destroyed the Egyptian army in the Sinai and occupied the peninsula.

Israeli operational plans were initially restricted to the Egyptian front. The IDF high command had developed plans to take the fighting to the Syrian and Jordanian fronts, but on the morning of June 5 it had no wish to go to war with these two Arab states.

There were, however, unexpected developments. As the Israeli troops stormed into the Sinai, Jordanian artillery shelled the suburbs of Jerusalem and other targets in Israel. The Israeli government hoped that Jordan's King Hussein would stay out of the fray and refrain from engaging in serious fighting. That did not happen. Jordanian troops stormed the UN headquarters in Jerusalem, inducing fears that the next step would be an attempt to take over Israeli-held Mount Scopus, an enclave within eastern Jerusalem, a Jordanian-held territory. To prevent that, Israeli forces moved ahead to secure a road to Mount Scopus, and the Jerusalem area became a battlefield. In addition, Israeli troops moved into the northern West Bank, from which long-range Jordanian artillery was shelling Israeli seaside cities. A full-fledged war was now in progress that lasted two days and ended with the complete Israeli victory over Jordanian forces. In what would be a momentous development, Israeli forces then occupied the West Bank and eastern Jerusalem.

In the north, Syrian forces began to move westward toward the Israeli border but did not complete the deployment and, for unknown reasons, returned to their bases. For five long days the Syrians shelled Israeli settlements from the

Golan Heights overlooking the Jordan River Valley. Hoping to avoid a three-front war, the Israelis took no action against the Syrians, despite the heavy pressure imposed on them by the settlers who had come under Syrian artillery fire. It was only in the last day of the war, with the fighting in the south and center firmly under control, that Israeli troops stormed the Golan Heights, taking it after only a few hours of fighting.

The end of the war saw a new Middle East in which Israel controlled an area three times as large as its pre-1967 territory. It had also firmly established itself as a major regional power. Israel also found itself in control of nearly 2 million Arabs in the West Bank, many of whom were refugees from the 1948–1949 war. The 1967 Six-Day War, known as the Naksa in the Arab world, was considered an utter defeat not only for the Arab armies but also for the principles of secular Arab nationalism as embodied in their governments. The defeat led to a religious revival.

Militarily, the 1967 Six-Day War marked a major military departure. First, it was a full-fledged armor war in which both sides, but chiefly the Egyptians and Israelis, deployed hundreds of tanks. Second, Cold War imperatives were clearly evident on the battlefield, with Israel equipped with sophisticated Western weapons and enjoying the full political support of the United States, while the Egyptians and the Syrians had the military and political support of the Soviet Union.

The next major Arab-Israeli conflict occurred six years later: the 1973 Yom Kippur War, also known as the War of Atonement and the Ramadan War. The years between 1967 and 1973 were not peaceful ones in the Middle East. Nasser refused to accept the results of the Six-Day War and rejected Israeli terms for negotiations of direct peace talks that would end in a peace agreement in return for giving up the Sinai. The Jordanians and the Syrians, as well as the rest of the Arab world, also rejected Israel's terms, instead demanding compliance with UN Resolution 242 (November 22, 1967) that called for the "withdrawal of Israeli armed forces from territories occupied in the recent conflict" and the "termination of all claims or states of belligerency and respect for and acknowledgment of the sovereignty, territorial integrity, and political independence of every state in the area."

UN Resolution 242 became the main reference for any agreement in the region, but it has never been enforced. The Israelis argue that it called for the withdrawal of Israeli armed forces from "territories occupied" and not from "the territories occupied," and thus it need not return to all the pre–June 6, 1967, lines as the UN has instead argued. Tel Aviv held that this was a matter for discussion with the Arab states involved. In addition, the resolution was not tied to any demand for the parties to begin direct peace talks, as Israel consistently required. The result was stalemate.

Israel launched settlement endeavors and placed Jewish settlers in the occupied territories, seeking to perpetuate with that its hold on the territories, while the Arab side again resorted to violence. The first to endorse violence were the Palestinians. Disappointed by the Arab defeat and because of the stances of various Arab governments, some of the Palestinians changed their strategy, declaring a revolution or people's movement in 1968–1969. Prior to 1967 they had used terror attacks as a trigger that might provoke war, which they hoped would end in an Arab victory. Now they decided to take their fate into their own hands and launch their own war of liberation against what they called the Zionist entity. The result was a sharp increase in the extent and ferocity of Palestinian terrorist attacks on Israel and increasing tensions between the Arab states and the Palestinians.

In 1968 the Palestinians internationalized their struggle by launching terrorist attacks against Israeli and Jewish targets all over the world. Nasser now also decided to take a path of aggression. Frustrated by his inability to bring about a change in Israel's position, he began a campaign under the slogan of "What was taken by force would be returned by force." Following low-level skirmishes along the Suez Canal and adjoining areas, from June 1968 Egyptian forces began shelling and raiding Israeli troop deployments across the canal. The Israelis responded with artillery fire and retaliatory attacks. The violence escalated as Israel struck deep inside Egypt with its air force. Before long, this midlevel-intensity conflict became known as the War of Attrition. It continued until 1970.

With the growing intensity of Israeli air attacks on Egypt, pilots from the Soviet Union took an active part in the defense of Egypt. The increased involvement of the Soviet military in the conflict deeply worried both the Israelis and the United States. Through the mediation of U.S. secretary of state William Rogers, a cease-fire agreement was concluded in August 1970, and the fighting subsided. However, shortly after the signing of the agreement, the Egyptians began placing surface-to-air (SAM) batteries throughout the Suez Canal area.

During 1970–1973, Rogers and UN mediator Gunnar Jarring introduced peace plans that were rejected by both the Israelis and the Egyptians. Following Nasser's death in September 1970, his successor, Anwar Sadat, was determined to change the status quo. Toward that end, he acted on two fronts: he called for a gradual settlement that would lead to Israeli withdrawal from the Sinai without a full peace agreement, and he expelled the Soviet advisers brought in by Nasser and resumed negotiations with the United States, which Nasser had ended in 1955.

The failure of Sadat's diplomatic efforts in 1971 led him to begin planning a military operation that would break the political stalemate along the Israeli-Egyptian front. Sadat believed that even a minor Egyptian military success would change the military equilibrium and force a political settlement that would lead to a final settlement. In devising his plan, he carefully calculated Israeli and Egyptian strengths and weaknesses. He believed that Israel's strength lay in its air force and armored divisions, well trained for the conduct of maneuver warfare. Egyptian strengths were the ability to build a strong defense line and the new SAM batteries deployed all along the canal area and deep within Egypt. Sadat hoped to paralyze the Israeli Air Force with the SAMs and hoped to counter the Israelis' advantage in maneuver warfare by forcing them to attack well-fortified and well-defended Egyptian strongholds.

In an attempt to dilute the Israeli military forces on the Sinai front, Sadat brought in Syria. A coordinated surprise attack on both the Syrian and Egyptian fronts would place maximum stress on the IDF. But above anything else, the key to the plan's success lay in its secrecy. Were Israel to suspect that an attack was imminent, it would undoubtedly launch a preventive attack, as in 1967. This part of the plan was successful.

Israeli ignorance of effective deceptive measures undertaken by Egypt contributed to Israel's failure to comprehend what was happening. One deception consisted of repeated Egyptian drills along the canal that simulated a possible crossing. The Israelis thus became accustomed to large Egyptian troop concentrations at the canal and interpreted Egyptian preparations for the actual crossings as just another drill. Even the Egyptian soldiers were told that it was simply a drill. Only when the actual crossing was occurring were they informed of its true nature. Even with the actual attack, however, the real intent of Egyptian and Syrian forces remained unclear to the Israelis, and they initially refrained from action.

Beginning at 2:00 p.m. on October 6, 1973, Egyptian and Syrian artillery and aircraft, and later their ground forces, launched major attacks along the Suez Canal and the Golan Heights. On the Israeli-Egyptian front, Egypt amassed a force of nearly 800,000 soldiers, 2,200 tanks, 2,300 artillery pieces, 150 SAM batteries, and 550 aircraft. Egypt deployed along the canal five infantry divisions with accompanying armored elements supported by additional infantry and armored independent brigades. This force was backed by three mechanized divisions and two armored divisions. Opposing this force on the eastern bank of the Suez Canal was one Israeli division supported by 280 tanks.

This Israeli force was no match for the advancing Egyptian troops. The defenders lacked reinforcements, as reserves were called on duty only after the outbreak of the war. They also did not have air support, as Egyptian SAMs proved to be deadly effective against Israeli aircraft.

The attacking Egyptians got across the canal and swept over the defending Israelis. It took less than 48 hours for the Egyptians to establish a penetration three to five miles deep on the east bank of the Suez Canal. They then fortified the area with more troops. Two divisions held the seized area, which was defended also by the SAM batteries across the canal. With that, the Egyptians had achieved their principal aims and a psychological victory.

The Israelis rushed reinforcements southward and launched a quick counteroffensive on October 8 in an attempt to repel the invading Egyptians troops. Much to Israeli surprise, it was a failure. Undermanned, unorganized, and underequipped Israeli troops—largely a tank force insufficiently supported by infantry and artillery—moved against a far bigger and more well-organized and well-equipped force protected by highly effective handheld antitank missiles. The Egyptians crushed the Israeli counteroffensive.

Following this setback, the Israeli General Staff decided to halt offensive actions on the Suez front and give priority to the fighting in the north on the Golan Heights, where in the first hours of the war little stood between massive numbers of invading Syrian armor and the Jewish settlements. Syria deployed two infantry divisions in the first line and two armored divisions in the second. This force had 1,500 tanks against only two Israeli armored brigades with 170 tanks. The Syrian forces swept the Golan Heights, crushing the small Israeli forces facing them. The few Israeli forces there fought desperately, knowing that they were the only force between the Syrians and numerous settlements. The Israeli forces slowed the Syrians and bought sufficient time for reserves of men and tanks to be brought forward. The Syrians also had an ineffective battle plan, which played to Israeli strengths in maneuver warfare. After seven days of fighting, Israeli troops thwarted the Syrian forces beyond the starting point of the war, across the pre–October 1973 Purple Line, and then drove a wedge into Syrian territory. Only then did the IDF again turn to the Egyptian front, where the goal remained driving Egyptian troops from the Sinai.

Sadat also overruled his ground commander and continued the advance. This took his forces out of their prepared defensive positions and removed them from the effective SAM cover on the other side of the canal, working to the Israelis' advantage. Israeli troops also located a gap between the two Egyptian divisions defending the occupied area that had gone unnoticed by the Egyptian command. Israeli forces drove through the gap and crossed the canal. The IDF hoped to achieve two goals. The first and most immediate goal was to create a SAM-free zone over which Israeli aircraft could maneuver free from the threat of missile attack. The second goal was to cut off Egyptian troops east of the canal from their bases west of the canal. After nearly a week of fighting, the Israelis accomplished almost all of their objectives. Nonetheless, Soviet and U.S. pressure led to a cease-fire before the Israelis could completely cut off the two Egyptian divisions in the east from their bases.

Neither the Soviets nor the Americans wanted to see the Egyptians completely defeated. They also assumed that the Egyptian achievement would allow progress in the political process, just as Sadat had wanted. As a result, the war ended with Israeli and Egyptian forces entangled, the latter on the eastern side of the canal and the former on Egyptian soil.

Syrian president Hafez al-Assad's chief motivation in joining Sadat in the war against Israel was to recapture the Golan Heights. Assad had no diplomatic goals and no intention of using the war as leverage for a settlement with Israel. The fighting in the north with Syria ended with the IDF positioned only about 25 miles from Damascus, while no Syrian forces remained within Israeli-held territory. It was only in 1974, after a disengagement agreement, that Israeli forces withdrew from Syrian territory beyond the Purple Line.

The 1973 war in effect ended in 1977 when Sadat took the bold step to visit Israel. On September 17, 1978, following a dozen days of secret negotiations at Camp David, the U.S. presidential retreat in Maryland, where they were hosted and prodded by President Jimmy Carter, Begin and Sadat signed in Washington the Camp David Accords. The two men were later awarded the Nobel Peace Prize. The Camp David Accords led directly to the 1979 Egypt-Israel Peace Treaty. The Palestinians had not been a party to the Camp David Accords, however, and turmoil continued, chiefly from the unresolved Palestinian problem at the root of the Arab-Israeli conflict. Militant Palestinians refused to recognize the existence of the State of Israel, while Israel refused to treat with the Palestinian leadership. Terrorist attacks

against Israel continued, and with a sharp increase in such attacks against the northern settlements from Lebanon, the Israeli government ordered IDF invasions of southern Lebanon in 1978 and 1982. The first invasion of 1978 was extremely costly in terms of civilian loss of life for the Lebanese, who were unable to mount an armed response to the Israelis. The Israelis also began to involve themselves in the ongoing civil war in Lebanon in order to further their own objectives.

Following increasing Palestinian rocket attacks from southern Lebanon, the Israelis began a large-scale invasion (Operation PEACE FOR GALILEE) there on June 6, 1982. Its stated goals of the operation were halting rocket attacks from that area against northern Israel and eliminating the Palestinian fighters there. Ultimately, Israel committed some 76,000 men and a considerable numbers of tanks, artillery, and aircraft to the operation. Minister of Defense Ariel Sharon and Prime Minister Menachem Begin had more ambitious goals, however. They hoped to also destroy the PLO and other Palestinian resistance in Lebanon altogether and to dismantle its political power. They also sought to force Syria from Lebanon and to influence Lebanese politics.

Begin and Sharon informed the cabinet that their goal was merely to eradicate PLO bases in southern Lebanon and push back PLO and Syrian forces some 25 miles, beyond rocket range of Galilee. Once the operation began, however, Sharon changed the original plan by expanding the mission to incorporate Beirut. Within days, the IDF advanced to the outskirts of Beirut. The PLO merely withdrew ahead of the advancing IDF on West Beirut. Sharon now mounted a broader operation that would force the PLO from Beirut, and for some 10 weeks Israeli artillery shelled West Beirut, killing both PLO members and scores of civilians. Fighting also occurred with Syrian forces in the Bekáa Valley area, but most of this combat was in the air. Not until June 2000 did Israel withdraw all its forces from southern Lebanon.

Israel achieved none of its goals in the invasion of Lebanon except for the eviction of the PLO from Beirut to Tunis and the deaths of many Palestinians and Lebanese. The Lebanese political scene was more turbulent than ever, and the PLO was certainly not eliminated. The Lebanese saw Israel as an implacable enemy, and an even more radical Islamic resistance took up hostilities against Israeli occupying troops and their Lebanese allies. That resistance eventually grew into Hezbollah, backed by Syria and Iran.

In December 1987 Palestinians began a protest movement, now known as the First Intifada, against Israeli rule in an effort to establish a Palestinian homeland through a series of demonstrations, improvised attacks, and riots. This intifada produced widespread destruction and human suffering, yet it also helped strengthen the Palestinian sense of popular will and made statehood a clear objective. It also cast much of Israeli policy in a negative light, especially with the deaths of Palestinian children, and thus helped rekindle international efforts to resolve the Arab-Israeli conflict. It also helped return the PLO from its Tunisian exile. Finally, it cost the Israeli economy hundreds of millions of dollars. The First Intifada ended in September 1993 with the signing of the historic Oslo Accords and the creation of the Palestinian National Authority (PNA).

Following torturous negotiations, the Israelis and Palestinians reached limited agreement at Oslo in September 1993 in the so-called Declaration of Principles. This eventually led to the establishment of the PNA and limited Palestinian self-rule in the West Bank and the Gaza Strip. Nonetheless, the agreement was not fully implemented, and mutual Palestinian-Israeli violence continued, placing serious obstacles in the path of a general Arab-Israeli peace settlement.

With the advent of rightist Likud Party governments in Israel in the late 1990s, the Israeli-Palestinian peace process was essentially put on hold. Many politicians in Likud—but especially Prime Minister Benjamin Netanyahu—rejected the so-called land-for-peace formula. In the summer of 2000, U.S. president Bill Clinton hosted talks at Camp David between Israeli prime minister Ehud Barak and PLO chairman Yasser Arafat in an attempt to jump-start the moribund peace process. After 14 days of intense negotiations, the summit ended in an impasse, when Arafat rejected the arrangement hammered out. The failure of the talks led to bitter recriminations on both sides that the other had not negotiated in good faith.

Not surprisingly, the Palestinians lost hope in the negotiation process following the failure of the Camp David talks. Their frustration was heightened by their belief that Israel—and not the Palestinian side—had sabotaged the peace process. A new dimension to Palestinian outrage was added when Likud Party chairman Ariel Sharon visited the Temple Mount (Haram al-Sharif) on September 28, 2000. His presence there ignited Palestinian anger that began as a stone-throwing demonstration. Before long, a full-blown Palestinian uprising, known as the Second (Al-Aqsa) Intifada, was under way. The uprising resulted in the deaths of many Israelis and Palestinians.

In recent years, momentous changes within the PLO and the PNA have wrought more uncertainty for both the Palestinians and the Israelis. Arafat's death in November 2004 resulted in a sea change within the Palestinian leadership. In January 2005 Mahmoud Abbas, like Arafat a member of Fatah, was elected president of the PNA. In the meantime, terror attacks against Israelis and Israeli interests continued, and Abbas seemed powerless to stop the violence. Just a year after he ascended to the presidency, he suffered a stinging reversal when the Islamist party and organization Hamas won a majority of seats in the January 2006 Palestinian legislative elections. This led to the appointment of a Hamas prime minister. The United States and certain European government entities refused to deal with the Hamas-led government and cut off all funding to the Palestinians. As violence continued to occur and the lack of foreign aid hobbled the PNA, Abbas threatened to call for early elections if Hamas would not submit to a coalition-led government. However, Abbas lacked the authority to do so under the PNA's own guidelines, and he was serving as president only because Hamas wanted a unity government.

With increasing violence that included the kidnapping of an Israeli soldier in Gaza and a cross-border raid mounted by Hezbollah from Lebanon in July 2006 that killed three IDF soldiers and captured two others, the cabinet of Israeli prime minister Ehud Olmert again attacked southern Lebanon as well as Gaza. The fighting along the Israel-Lebanese border raged for 32 days between mid-July and mid-August. The incursion was largely limited to artillery and to air strikes that nonetheless included sections of Beirut and key bridges and lines of communication. Finally, some IDF ground troops were also sent in. Hezbollah responded by launching thousands of rockets into Israel. A great deal of Lebanese infrastructure that had been rebuilt since 1982 was destroyed in the countering Israeli strikes, and Israeli's hopes that it might influence Lebanese politics again proved illusory. Indeed, Hezbollah, whose ability to launch rockets into northern Israel appeared undiminished despite the strikes, appeared to have strengthened its position in Lebanese politics and also to have gained prestige in the Arab world for seemingly fighting toe-to-toe with the IDF.

In early 2007 and in 2008, there were renewed calls for a concerted effort to jump-start the peace process. Instead, a truce concluded between Israel and the Hamas government in Gaza in June 2008 broke down in November following Israeli assassinations of Hamas leaders in violation of the truce and Israeli's refusal to loosen the economic boycott. In December 2008 Israel launched an offensive against Gaza. This occurred just before the inauguration of new U.S. president Barack Obama and the holding of Israeli elections. The outgoing Olmert government claimed that it had to attack

Gaza to control rocket fire into southern Israel, which had killed three civilians. The punishing Israeli attacks left much of the Gaza Strip in ruins, with damages estimated at $2 billion. Egypt has hosted talks between Hamas and Fatah aimed at a national unity government and a possible prisoner exchange with Israel, which demanded the release of hostage Gilad Schalit. Meanwhile, President Obama appointed former senator George Mitchell as U.S. special representative to the Middle East, but it was unclear if negotiations would be a priority for the new rightist Israeli government under Prime Minister Benjamin Netanyahu and Foreign Minister Avigdor Lieberman, who took office on April 1, 2009, and whether efforts at a lasting peace in the Middle East would be any more successful now than in the past.

Despite the fact that another major war has not occurred, peace remains elusive. Beginning in the winter of 2013, new U.S. secretary of state John F. Kerry made a major effort to jump-start the moribund Palestinian-Israeli peace process and produce a comprehensive peace settlement. The first of such meetings began in late July 2013. Those talks yielded no results, however. Clearly, the way forward is exceedingly difficult, and a lasting peace deal will not come easily, as neither side completely trusts the other. Israel has also been peripherally involved in the ongoing Syrian Civil War, as it has launched several air strikes against targets within Syria, mainly supply convoys of armaments that the Israelis claim were being supplied by Iran and Russia. With good reason, the Israelis feared that some of these arms were intended for Hezbollah in Lebanon and would be deployed against Israel.

Then, in the summer of 2014 after Hamas launched rockets against Israel from the Gaza Strip, Israel engaged in a 50-day (July 8–August 26) intense air war and ground incursion against Gaza. The fighting ended in a truce in late August 2014, but more than 2,100 Palestinians died during the conflict, while Israel suffered 66 military and 6 civilian dead.

Netanyahu criticized U.S. peace efforts, went ahead with the construction of additional Jewish housing in East Jerusalem and the West Bank in defiance of U.S. and UN appeals, and appeared to reject a two-state solution by stating that Israel would never accept the unilateral recognition of a Palestinian state as presented by the Palestinian Authority to the UN. Such policies have, however, brought increasing international isolation for Israel and sharply deteriorated relations with both Western Europe and the United States.

In a major sign of Israel's growing isolation, in December 2014 the conference of the Fourth Geneva Convention, which governs the rule of war and military occupation practices, ruled that the Israeli practice of constructing Jewish settlements in East Jerusalem and the West Bank is in violation of its responsibilities as an occupying power. It called for "all serious violations" to be investigated and those responsible for breaches to be brought to justice.

On December 2, 2014, hoping to strengthen his domestic position, Netanyahu fired his cabinet and called for new elections to take place in March 2015, in advance of the date mandated by law. On December 23, however, Netanyahu's own foreign minister Avigdor Lieberman denounced Netanyahu's "status quo" approach toward the Palestinians and warned that Israel risked a "diplomatic tsunami" in alienating the European Union, which is Israel's chief trading partner in both exports and imports. Lieberman concurred with many observers that Israel "must reach a diplomatic agreement—not because of the Palestinians or the Arabs, but because of the Jews."

The Arab effort to achieve an independent state of Palestine suffered rebuff in the UN Security Council on December 30, 2014, when that body rejected a resolution demanding an end to the Israeli occupation within three years. The Obama administration had made clear its opposition to the draft resolution and continued to insist on a negotiated peace agreement between Israel and the Palestinians with no imposed timetable. The United States would have used its veto if necessary, but this proved unnecessary, as the resolution failed to receive the minimum nine "yes" votes required for adoption by the 15-member council. The resolution received eight "yes" votes and two "no" votes (the United States and Australia), with five abstentions. On January 1, 2015, the Netanyahu government retaliated by refusing to hand over $127 million in tax revenues it collects for the Palestinian Authority. This is the bulk of the monthly $160 million budget for the Palestinian Authority; unable to pay salaries or provide services for the 2.5 million Palestinians in the West Bank and 1.8 million in Gaza, the Palestinian Authority would have to shut down. This move certainly exacerbated tensions, already high.

By 2015, it was by no means clear what impact these moves or the upcoming Israeli elections would have on that nation's political scene and the peace process, but a final settlement of the Arab-Israeli conflict appeared to be as elusive as ever.

DAVID TAL AND SPENCER C. TUCKER

See also

Arab League; Iraq, History of, 1990–Present; Israel; Syria

References

Barker, A. J. *Arab-Israeli Wars.* New York: Hippocrene, 1980.

Bell, J. Bowyer. *The Long War: Israel and the Arabs since 1946.* Englewood Cliffs, NJ: Prentice Hall, 1969.

Gelvin, James L. *The Israel-Palestine Conflict: 100 Years of War.* New York: Cambridge University Press, 2005.

Hammel, Eric. *Six Days in June: How Israeli Won the 1967 Arab-Israeli War.* New York: Scribner, 1992.

Herzog, Chaim. *The Arab-Israeli Wars: War and Peace in the Middle East from the War of Independence to Lebanon.* Westminster, MD: Random House, 1984.

Herzog, Chaim. *The War of Atonement: October, 1973.* Boston: Little, Brown, 1975.

Oren, Michael B. *Six Days of War: June 1967 and the Making of the Modern Middle East.* Novato, CA: Presidio, 2003.

Reiter, Yitzhak. *National Minority, Regional Majority: Palestinian Arabs versus Jews in Israel.* Syracuse, NY: Syracuse University Press, 2009.

Taylor, Alan R. *The Superpowers and the Middle East.* Syracuse, NY: Syracuse University Press, 1991.

Tucker, Spencer C., ed. *The Encyclopedia of the Arab-Israeli Conflict.* 4 vols. Santa Barbara, CA: ABC-CLIO, 2008.

Arab League

The Arab League, also called the League of Arab States, is a voluntary organization of Arabic-speaking nations. It was founded at the end of World War II with the stated purposes of improving conditions in Arab countries, liberating Arab states still under foreign domination, and preventing the formation of a Jewish state in Palestine.

In 1943 the Egyptian government proposed an organization of Arab states that would facilitate closer relations between the nations without forcing any of them to lose self-rule. Each member would remain a sovereign state, and the organization would not be a union, a federation, or any other sovereign structure. The British government supported this idea in the hopes of securing the Arab nations as allies in the war against Germany.

In 1944 representatives from Egypt, Iraq, Lebanon, Yemen, and Saudi Arabia met in Alexandria, Egypt, and agreed to form a federation. The Arab League was officially founded on March 22, 1945, in Cairo. The founding states were Egypt, Iraq, Lebanon, Saudi Arabia, Transjordan (now Jordan), and Syria. Subsequent members include Libya (1953), Sudan (1956), Tunisia (1958), Morocco (1958), Kuwait (1961), Algeria (1962), South Yemen (1967, now Yemen), Bahrain (1971), Oman (1971), Qatar (1971), the United Arab Emirates (1971), Mauritania (1973), Somalia (1974), Palestine (1976, which the Arab League regards as an independent state), Djibouti (1977), and Comoros

(1993). In July 2013 these 21 states and Palestine constituted some 359 million people.

The original goals of the Arab League were to liberate all Arab nations still ruled by foreign countries and to prevent the creation of a Jewish state in Palestine as well as to serve the common good, improve living conditions, and guarantee the hopes of member states. In 1946 Arab League members added to their pact a cultural treaty under which they agreed to exchange professors, teachers, students, and scholars in order to encourage cultural exchange among member nations and to disseminate Arab culture to their citizens.

The Arab League's pact also stated that all members would collectively represent the Palestinians so long as Palestine was not an independent state. With no Palestinian leader in 1945, the Arab states feared that the British would dominate the area and that Jews would colonize part of Palestine. In response to these fears, the Arab League created the Arab Higher Committee to govern Palestinian Arabs in 1945. This committee was replaced in 1946 by the Arab Higher Executive, which was again reorganized into a new Arab Higher Executive in 1947.

The State of Israel was declared on May 14, 1948. The next day Egypt, Iraq, Lebanon, Saudi Arabia, Syria, and Transjordan responded with a declaration of war against Israel. Yemen also supported the declaration. Secretary-General Abdul Razek Azzam Pasha declared that the Arab League's goal was to conduct a large-scale massacre and extermination. Although King Abdullah of Jordan (he officially changed the name of Transjordan to Jordan in April 1949) claimed to be the legitimate power in Palestine, the Arab League did not wish to see Jordan in control of the area and thus established its own government on behalf of the Palestinians, the All-Palestine State of October 1, 1948. The mufti of Jerusalem, Haj Amin al-Husseini, was its leader, and Jerusalem was its capital. Although ostensibly the new government ruled Gaza, Egypt was the real authority there. In response, Jordan formed a rival temporary government, the First Palestinian Congress, that condemned the government in Gaza. The Arab-Israeli war ended in 1949, with Jordan occupying the West Bank and East Jerusalem and Egypt controlling Gaza.

In 1950 the Arab League signed the Joint Defense and Economic Cooperation Treaty, which declared that the members of the league considered an attack on one member country to be an attack on all. The treaty created a permanent military commission and a joint defense council.

During the 1950s, Egypt effectively led the Arab League. In 1952 a military coup in Egypt nominally headed by

General Muhammad Naguib overthrew King Faruq, but within two years Colonel Gamal Abdel Nasser assumed rule of the nation. A strong proponent of Arab unity, he called for a union of all Arab nations, including Palestine. Nasser ended the All-Palestine government in Palestine, formed the United Arab Republic with Syria, and called for the defeat of Israel.

In 1956 Nasser nationalized the Suez Canal, precipitating the Suez Crisis that brought an Israeli invasion of the Sinai followed by short-lived British and French invasions of Egypt. U.S. economic and political pressures secured the withdrawal of the invaders. Far from toppling Nasser as the British, French, and Israeli governments had hoped, these pressures both strengthened Nasser's prestige in the Arab world and raised the stature of Pan-Arabism and the Arab League.

In the 1960s the Arab League pushed for the liberation of Palestine, and in 1964 it supported the creation of the Palestine Liberation Organization (PLO), which was dedicated to attacks on Israel. Following the Six-Day War of 1967, which ended in extensive territory losses for Egypt, Jordan, and Syria, the Arab League met at Khartoum that August and issued a statement in which its members vowed not to recognize, negotiate with, or conclude a peace agreement with Israel. Egypt also agreed to withdraw its troops from Yemen.

The Arab League suspended Egypt's membership in 1979 in the wake of President Anwar Sadat's visit to Jerusalem and agreement to the 1978 Camp David Peace Accords. The league also moved its headquarters from Cairo to Tunis. When the PLO declared an independent State of Palestine on November 15, 1988, the Arab League immediately recognized it. Egypt was readmitted to the league in 1989, and the headquarters returned to Cairo.

During the prelude to the 1991 Persian Gulf War the Arab League condemned Iraq's invasion of Kuwait, passing a resolution on August 3 demanding that Iraq withdraw its troops. The league also urged that the crisis be resolved within the organization itself and warned that the failure to do so would invite outside intervention. Although somewhat ambivalent about forcing the Iraqis to withdraw by military force, the Arab League did vote—by the narrowest of margins—to allow Syrian, Egyptian, and Moroccan forces to send troops as part of building an international coalition. In the 1990s the Arab League also continued its efforts to resolve the Israeli-Palestine dispute in the Palestinians' favor.

In March 2002 the Arab League adopted the Arab Peace Initiative, a proposal presented by Saudi Arabia for resolving the Arab-Israeli conflict. This offered full normalization of relations with Israel in return for an Israeli withdrawal from all occupied territories; Israeli recognition of a Palestinian state in the West Bank and the Gaza Strip, with East Jerusalem as its capital; and a "just solution" of the Palestinian refugee question. It has continued to endorse the initiative at other summit meetings.

In 2003 the Arab League voted to demand the unconditional removal of U.S. and British troops from Iraq. The lone dissenting voice was the small nation of Kuwait, which had been liberated by a U.S.-led coalition in the 1991 Persian Gulf War. In 2013 the Arab League suspended Syria from membership because of the Syrian government's role in the ongoing Syrian Civil War.

In addition to the Syrian Civil War and the Gordian knot of the continuing Arab-Israeli problem, major foreign policy issues include the efforts of the United States, the Russian Federation, the European Union states, and now China to expand their influence in this oil-rich region, the desire of the European Union to halt illegal immigration from North Africa, and growing Iranian regional influence and its support of the Shia Muslims. The Turkish government is also increasingly as odds with both Syria and Iraq over control of the waters of the Tigris and Euphrates Rivers, while tensions have increased between Spain and Morocco over the Melilla and Ceuta dispute.

AMY HACKNEY BLACKWELL

See also

Iraq War; Syrian Civil War

References

Hourani, Albert. *A History of the Arab Peoples.* Cambridge, MA: Harvard University Press, 1991.

Smith, Charles D. *Palestine and the Arab-Israeli Conflict: A History with Documents.* 6th ed. New York: Bedford/St. Martin's, 2006.

Toffolo, Chris E., and Peggy Kahn. *The Arab League.* London: Chelsea House, 2008.

Arab Spring (December 18, 2010–Present)

The Arab Spring is a wave of prodemocracy uprisings that swept through North Africa and the Middle East beginning in December 2010. The protest movements—a mixture of both violent and nonviolent activities—were spurred mainly by dissatisfaction with local governments and economic inequalities that seemed to deepen after the global

Egyptians protesting in front of an army tank in Cairo's Tahrir Square on January 29, 2011. Tens of thousands of people filled the city's main square to demand that president Hosni Mubarak leave office after nearly 30 years in power. (AP Photo/Ahmed Ali)

economic downturn in 2008. Essentially, the Arab Spring was propelled by a frustrated population contending with oppressive leaders, government corruption, and high levels of unemployment. The grassroots uprisings have had differing levels of success in each of the Arab nations.

On December 17, 2010, a Tunisian street vendor named Mohamed Bouazizi set himself on fire in the provincial city of Sidi Bouzid to protest police confiscation of his unregistered cart and vegetables. He died two weeks later, but the next day his act of self-immolation set in motion what would be the first of the Arab Spring's major movements, the Tunisian Revolution (2011). Angry about what happened to Bouazizi and frustrated with the lack of jobs in Tunisia, among other issues, hundreds of disgruntled young adults took to the streets in Sidi Bouzid on December 18, destroying shop windows and automobiles in their wake. The rioting gained momentum and soon spread throughout the country. By mid-January, autocratic Tunisian leader Zine El Abidine Ben Ali had lost control of the national military and dissolved his police state in favor of a more democratic process.

The success of the Tunisian protest movement encouraged civil dissidence in other parts of the Arab world. In early January 2011, an Egyptian man set himself on fire outside of a parliamentary building in Cairo after loudly criticizing the government. The Egyptian government was perhaps even more restrictive than that of Tunisia and had outlawed any form of public protest or demonstrations. However, despite government control over most media, people began connecting through such social media outlets as Facebook to orchestra massive demonstrations.

Although the government eventually cut Internet and text messaging services, the seed was sown. Some 20,000 people gathered in Tahrir Square in Cairo on January 25, calling for an end to government repression in what was the beginning of the Egyptian Revolution (2011). After a bloody standoff between the military and a crowd of demonstrators that swelled to the millions, Egyptian leader Hosni Mubarak, encouraged to do so by the U.S. government, stepped down as president on February 11.

The Arab Spring demonstrations did not stop with Egypt. Soon, disgruntled citizens in other countries were stepping forward to voice their grievances against authoritative rule. Through most of 2011, prodemocracy protests ensued in such nations as Libya, Yemen, Bahrain, and Syria.

The results were not nearly as swift as what had occurred in Tunisia and Egypt. In Libya, dictator Muammar Qaddafi implemented a brutal crackdown on protests that began in February. However, the protests soon turned to an all-out rebellion. Over the next several months, rebel forces grew in scope and power until they controlled all of eastern Libya. As Qaddafi's military began forcibly taking back territories, the United Nations stepped in to call a no-fly zone in order to protect Libyan residents from air attacks called by their own leader. Aided by Western militaries, the Libyan rebels began setting up a transitional government in August 2011, but it was not until his death by rebel forces on October 20 that Qaddafi truly gave up all power.

In Yemen, large-scale protests began peacefully in February 2011 but turned ugly by early February as police and military led a violent crack down on the demonstrators. Protests continued despite this hard-line stance, and longtime president Ali Abdallah Salih eventually agreed to leave office in November 2011 in exchange for immunity from prosecution over the violent tactics employed to quell the protests. Prodemocracy, antigovernment protests in Bahrain were complicated by religious tensions between the majority Shiite Muslim population and the Sunni Muslim ruling class.

Having lived with political uncertainty and strife since its independence in 1946, Syrian citizens were inspired to take matters into their own hands by the events that unfolded in Tunisia and Egypt. In March 2011, demonstrators took to the streets in what was a remarkably peaceful protest against the government. But the peace was not to last. Soon, Syrian President Bashar al-Assad violently retaliated with military force and martial law. Civil war erupted, and the United Nations had called for Assad to face charges of crimes against humanity.

At the end of the year several nations, including the United States, formally recognized a rebel umbrella organization, the Syrian National Council, as the legitimate government of the people. However, Assad maintained his fight for power. Violent unrest and armed clashes continued. In August 2014 the United Nations placed the death toll from the Syrian Civil War during March 2011–March 2014 at more than 191,000 people.

In addition to these major uprisings, protests and demonstrations also took place in such states as Morocco, Iraq, Iran, and Jordan. Although the Arab Spring has brought with it powerful democratic change in much of the Arab world, the political future of many of these nations still remains uncertain.

TAMAR BURRIS

See also

Assad, Bashar al-; Mubarak, Hosni; Shia Islam; Sunni Islam; Syria; Syrian Civil War; Yemen

References

Brownlee, Jason, Tarek Masoud, and Andrew Reynolds. *The Arab Spring: The Politics of Transformation in North Africa and the Middle East.* Oxford: Oxford University Press, 2013.

Dabashi, Hamid. *The Arab Spring: The End of Postcolonialism.* New York: Palgrave Macmillan, 2012.

Haddad, Bassam, Rosie Bsheer, and Ziad Abu-Rish, eds. *The Dawn of the Arab Uprisings: End of an Old Order?* London: Pluto, 2012.

Lesch, David W. *Syria: The Fall of the House of Assad.* New Haven, CT: Yale University Press, 2011.

Armored Warfare, Persian Gulf and Iraq Wars

The U.S. Army's overwhelming success against Soviet-equipped Iraqi divisions during the 1991 Persian Gulf War marked the culmination of a long-developed doctrine of armored warfare, the hallmarks of which were speed, maneuver, and high technology. With a few notable exceptions, U.S. armored doctrine following the 1950–1953 Korean War anticipated set-piece battles to defend the plains of Central Europe from a Soviet incursion. In the 1970s, catalyzed by the effectiveness of wire-guided antitank weapons used during the 1973 Yom Kippur (Ramadan) War and the burgeoning requirement to modernize and compete against new Warsaw Pact tanks, the U.S. armor community prepared to fully modernize its equipment, training, and doctrine. By 1982 the army had fielded the turbine-powered M-1 Abrams main battle tank; established a state-of-the-art desert training facility at Fort Irwin, California; and published the newly developed AirLand Battle doctrine.

The 1991 Persian Gulf War (Operation DESERT STORM) served as a crucible to test the new doctrine. In particular, AirLand Battle focused on deep-attack offense to extend operational commanders' view of the modern battlefield in both distance and time. It viewed deep attack, the concept of engaging an enemy in close and rear actions simultaneously, as an indispensable requirement in defeating follow-on echelons in Europe. AirLand Battle also focused on the importance of maneuver and close coordination with heavy forces. Armored combined-arms teams became the key instruments of combat power: the M-1 and M-1A1 Abrams main battle tanks would be supported by mechanized infantry, self-propelled artillery, and mechanized combat engineers. Additionally, AirLand Battle emphasized the importance of initiative, adapting the German Army principle of *Auftragstaktik* (mission tactics). Under this principle, American commanders were to continue to press an enemy on the offensive, even in the absence of higher orders, to take advantage of developing tactical situations.

U.S. armor units effectively employed AirLand Battle against the Iraqi Army in 1991. In the opening salvo of the war, an aerial bombing campaign that began in January and lasted more than a month attempted to destroy Iraqi command and control facilities and follow-on echelon forces. Armor units, supported by mechanized infantry, engineers, and coordinated indirect artillery fire, decisively destroyed Iraqi units during four days of offensive operations in February 1991. Massed coalition units conducted a frontal attack across the eastern edge of the Iraqi-Saudi border, while heavy elements of VII Corps engaged in a deep attack from the west, encircling rear and escaping Iraqi units in a maneuver later nicknamed the "Hail Mary." The M-1A1's advanced thermal targeting systems, capable of destroying targets at long ranges while on the move, provided mass firepower and shock effect.

In 1993 the U.S. Army developed a revised doctrine known as Full-Dimensional Operations to anticipate post–Cold War challenges and incorporate lessons learned from the Persian Gulf War. In it, the army attempted to enlarge the doctrinal scope of AirLand Battle by including a section on operations other than war, introducing joint terms, and expanding its scope to encapsulate strategic operations. The doctrine acted as the foundational document during peace-keeping operations in Bosnia and Kosovo and during the next eight years of the army's transformation.

As part of the armor community's force modernization, M-1A2 tanks and other vehicles were retrofitted with new digital battle command systems to increase situational awareness on the battlefield. However, the difficulties in deploying Task Force Hawk in the early days of the Kosovo conflict made clear the difficulty of deploying heavy Cold War equipment. Under the leadership of U.S. Army chief of staff General Eric Shinseki, the army established an immediate ready force in Europe and attempted to decrease reliance on tanks by establishing a lighter objective force capable of quick deployment using Stryker wheeled vehicles via Stryker Brigades. Commensurate with these objectives, in 2001 the army published a revised doctrine known as Full-Spectrum

Operations, which provided the foundation for rapid deployment in response to global threats and for sustained military campaigns and revealed the growing importance of stability and support operations. This doctrine also anticipated that adaptive enemies would seek asymmetric advantages and attempt to pull troops into urban combat.

Strategic doctrine used during the Iraq War (Operation IRAQI FREEDOM) can be divided into two primary periods: the initial 2003 attack lasting from March 20 to May 1, 2003, and subsequent full-spectrum operations thereafter. While the operational strategy used in the 1991 Persian Gulf War can be described as overwhelming force, the 2003 action constituted overmatching power. Under the touted umbrella of shock and awe, American planners intended to overwhelm Iraqi military and government systems by conducting the main ground and air offensive at the same time rather than preparing objectives with a lengthy preinvasion air campaign. Thus, Iraqis were placed on the horns of a multipronged dilemma, defending against rear and forward attacks while maintaining command and control.

To counter the significantly fewer armored vehicles and soldiers employed during the 2003 invasion, American commanders increased combat power by augmented use of special operations forces, speed in movement, and electronic reconnaissance to precisely identify and target enemy locations. Rather than seizing and holding the entire theater, coalition units intended initially only to control key terrain and supply lines as armored U.S. Army V Corps units conducted a blitzkrieg-type movement to Baghdad.

Doctrinally, V Corps, commanded by Lieutenant General William Scott Wallace, adhered to conventional AirLand Battle tenets in executing its initial offensive operations in Iraq. Although the total number of coalition troops employed in 2003 was significantly smaller than in 1991, as directed by AirLand Battle principles, helicopter and artillery units engaged the enemy simultaneously in close and rear actions by conducting deep-strike attacks, while combined-arms units conducted offensive operations using fire and maneuver to seize Baghdad. This proven conventional doctrine allowed V Corps units to occupy Baghdad and remove the Baathist regime from power in just three weeks.

Under the army's 2001 Full-Spectrum Operations doctrine, coalition forces were capable of transitioning smoothly from combat to stability and support operations. Although army planners realized that the operation's post-hostility phase would entail a rolling transition to stability and support operations, the coalition force's numbers were insufficient when compared historically with similar postconflict scenarios, including recent deployments in Bosnia and Kosovo. As sectarian and insurgent violence increased over the ensuing years, coalition troops were forced to counter asymmetric warfare to oppose amplified guerrilla and decentralized attacks. Increasingly, armored units were forced to fight in urban terrain alongside infantry and engineer units.

Actions to quell the 2004 Shia uprisings in Sadr City provide an example of armored employment within the Full-Spectrum Operations doctrine. In this suburban district of Baghdad, U.S. armor units negotiated the gridlike pattern of streets using a box pattern and moved slowly up streets, with weapon systems focused outside of the box. This formation created an artificial set of interior lines, allowing tanks and Bradleys to take advantage of independent thermal viewers to identify targets. Tankers moved with their hatches closed to prevent casualties from enemy sniper fire and removed unnecessary equipment from the top of the tanks to allow Bradleys to kill targets who attempted to climb onto the tanks. As insurgents increasingly used more powerful improvised explosive devices (IEDs) against coalition forces, tanks led the box formation to reduce casualties.

Commensurate with Full-Spectrum Operations, armored units in Iraq faced a wide variety of missions, including route clearance, reconnaissance and surveillance patrols, traffic control points, and raids. To enhance the Abrams' survivability and lethality in urban environments, Tank Urban Survivability Kits were fielded to add armored gun shields and reactive armor tiles to counter antiarmor weapons, and a tank infantry phone was included to communicate with ground troops. Despite disadvantages in urban terrain, including the Abrams' inability to elevate weapons far enough to fire at upper floors of buildings from close range and their vulnerability to light and medium antiarmor weapons when not supported by light infantry, tanks provided decisive support and protection throughout the spectrum of operations in Iraq.

WILLIAM E. FORK

See also

AirLand Battle Doctrine; Antitank Weapons; Bradley Fighting Vehicle; IRAQI FREEDOM, Operation, Ground Campaign; M1A1 and M1A2 Abrams Main Battle Tanks; Stryker Brigades

References

Biddle, Stephen. "Victory Misunderstood: What the Gulf War Tells Us about the Future of Conflict." *International Security* 21(2) (Fall 1996): 139–179.

Blackwell, James A. "Professionalism and Army Doctrine: A Losing Battle?" In *The Future of the Army Profession*, edited by Don M. Snider and Lloyd J. Matthews, 325–348. Boston: McGraw-Hill, 2005.

Bourque, Stephen A. "Hundred-Hour Thunderbolt: Armor in the Gulf War." In *Camp Colt to Desert Storm: The History of U.S. Armored Forces*, edited by George F. Hofmann and Donn A. Starry, 497–530. Lexington: University Press of Kentucky, 1999.

Chiarell, Peter, Patrick Michaelis, and Geoffrey Norman. "Armor in Urban Terrain: The Critical Enabler." *Armor* (June–October 2004): 7–9.

DeRosa, John P. J. "Platoons of Action: An Armor Task Force's Response to Full-Spectrum Operations in Iraq." *Armor* (November–December 2005): 7–12.

Fontenot, Gregory, et al. *On Point: The United States Army in Iraqi Freedom.* Annapolis, MD: Naval Institute Press, 2005.

Murray, Williamson, and Robert H. Scales Jr. *The Iraq War: A Military History.* Cambridge, MA: Belknap, 2005.

Swain, Richard M. "AirLand Battle." In *Camp Colt to Desert Storm: The History of U.S. Armored Forces*, edited by George F. Hofmann and Donn A. Starry, 360–402. Lexington: University Press of Kentucky, 1999.

Tucker, Terry. "Heavy Armor: The Core of Urban Combat." *Armor* (May–June 2005): 4, 49.

Arnett, Peter (1934–)

Acclaimed foreign correspondent and television journalist. Born on November 13, 1934, in Riverton, New Zealand, Peter Arnett left college to become a journalist. Subsequently, he worked for newspapers in New Zealand and Australia. In June 1962, the Associated Press sent Arnett to Saigon. In August of that year near the Mekong Delta, he first witnessed combat, an experience that led him to question U.S. involvement in the war.

Arnett's coverage of the Vietnam War established him as a high-profile reporter. His commitment to getting the real story, no matter the danger, won him the admiration of his peers and the respect of soldiers. Journalist David Halberstam once remarked that Arnett was the "gutsiest" man he had ever known, labeling him the consummate combat reporter.

Arnett's candor created controversy, however. In 1963 Premier Ngo Dinh Diem of the Republic of Vietnam (South Vietnam), who was upset with Arnett's coverage of the South Vietnamese government's treatment of Buddhist monks, threatened him with expulsion from the country. On July 23, 1963, members of the South Vietnamese secret police accosted Arnett on a Saigon street and began to beat him; a colleague interceded, saving Arnett from possible serious injury. The Diem regime then demanded that Arnett leave the country; only after the John F. Kennedy administration intervened on his behalf was he allowed to remain in South Vietnam.

Arnett's forthright style also caused tension with the U.S. military establishment. On several occasions officials attempted to convince him to report a more sanitized version of the war. Because he refused to compromise the accuracy of his stories, Arnett was targeted by the Lyndon B. Johnson administration for surveillance. Military officials also sought to limit his access to combat, but Arnett's many connections with men in the field negated those efforts.

Arnett developed a penchant for covering difficult and revealing stories. In 1966 his dedication earned him a Pulitzer Prize for International Reporting. During the 1968 Tet Offensive, Arnett reported the now-infamous statement of an American officer who said that U.S. forces had to destroy the village of Ben Tre in order to save it. That same year Arnett quoted John Paul Vann, U.S. chief of the civilian pacification program, who opined that the initial U.S. troop withdrawals from Vietnam would consist of "nonessentials." That statement led readers to question the veracity of the Richard M. Nixon administration's promised troop reductions. In 1972 Arnett witnessed the release of the first American prisoners of war in Hanoi, and in 1975 he covered the fall of Saigon to communist forces.

Arnett believes that newsmen do not deserve much of the negative criticism they have received for their coverage of the war. He maintains that journalists merely report events and do not make policy decisions.

In 1981 Arnett joined the Cable News Network (CNN); he was with the network until 1998. During the 1991 Persian Gulf War, Arnett became well known for his "Live from Baghdad" reports. In the opening hours of the war, he was the only Western reporter airing live as air-raid sirens blared in the background and bombs exploded in the distance. Later, Arnett's reports on Iraqi civilian casualties from the fighting earned him the enmity of the U.S. military and the White House. One of the most controversial reports was about the bombing by coalition forces of the Abu Ghraib Infant Formula Production Plant. Arnett was insistent that it had produced only baby formula and that it was not associated with the production of biological weapons, as a U.S. Air Force spokesman and later even General Colin Powell claimed. Two weeks after the war began, Arnett conducted an uncensored interview with Iraqi president Saddam Hussein.

In 1994 Arnett published *Live from the Battlefield: From Vietnam to Baghdad, 35 Years in the World's War Zones,*

about his wartime reporting. In late March 1997 in eastern Afghanistan, Arnett secured the first-ever television interview with Al Qaeda leader Osama bin Laden. In 1998 CNN fired Arnett under pressure from the U.S. Defense Department over Arnett's claim that the United States had employed sarin nerve gas on American troops who had defected in Laos during the Vietnam War.

In late 2001 Arnett reported on the Afghanistan War (Operation ENDURING FREEDOM) for HDNet. In 2003, reporting for *National Geographic Explorer* and NBC television, Arnett covered the beginning of the Iraq War (Operation IRAQI FREEDOM). He again sparked controversy by giving an interview to state-controlled Iraqi television, in the course of which he stated, "The first war plan failed because of Iraqi resistance. Now they are trying to write another war plan. Clearly, the American war planners misjudged the determination of Iraqi forces." NBC and National Geographic promptly dismissed him for what they called a gross error in judgment. Less than 24 hours later Arnett was hired as a correspondent for the British tabloid *Daily Mirror,* which had opposed the invasion of Iraq.

Arnett retired from active reporting in 2007 and moved to Los Angeles. Since then, he has taught at China's Shantou University. The Southern Institute of Technology, in his native New Zealand, has named its journalism school in Arnett's honor.

DEAN BRUMLEY

See also

Afghanistan War; Al Qaeda; Bin Laden, Osama; Iraq War

References

Arnett, Peter. *Live from the Battlefield: From Vietnam to Baghdad, 35 Years in the World's War Zones.* New York: Simon and Schuster, 1994.

Halberstam, David. *The Best and the Brightest.* New York: Penguin, 1983.

Prochnaw, William. "If There's a War, He's There." *New York Times Magazine,* March 3, 1991.

Sheehan, Neil. *A Bright Shining Lie: John Paul Vann and America in Vietnam.* New York: Random House, 1988.

ARROWHEAD RIPPER, **Operation (June 19–August 19, 2007)**

Multi-National Force–Iraq assault against Al Qaeda in Iraq and other insurgents in and around the Iraqi city of Baquba during June 19–August 19, 2007. Baquba is located about 30 miles northeast of Baghdad. As a result of the Baghdad Security Plan developed in early 2007 and the American troop surge that accompanied it, Al Qaeda in Iraq and other Sunni forces withdrew from some areas of Baghdad and began operating in Diyala Province.

The insurgents, who belonged to the Khalf al-Mutayibin group, established a strong presence in Diyala Province and especially in Baquba, a city of some half million people. They made it the capital of their self-proclaimed "Islamic State of Iraq." Al Qaeda was determined to create havoc for the newly formed government of Iraq and to kill coalition troops attempting to gain control of the province.

On June 19, 2007, 10,000 U.S. soldiers, along with more than 1,000 Iraqi police and Iraqi military personnel, launched ARROWHEAD RIPPER, an operation north of Baghdad to clear the region of Al Qaeda militants. Three U.S. brigades participated in the opening days of ARROWHEAD RIPPER: the 1st Cavalry Division's 3rd Brigade Combat Team, commanded by Colonel David Sutherland; the 2nd Infantry Division's 4th Stryker Brigade Combat Team, commanded by Colonel John Lehr; and the 2nd Infantry Division's 3rd Stryker Brigade Combat Team, commanded by Colonel Steven Townsend.

For security reasons, Iraqi leaders were not included in the initial planning of ARROWHEAD RIPPER, but as the operation progressed, the Iraqi 2nd Brigade and the 5th Iraqi Army Division played sizable roles. By the operation's end, the Iraqi 5th Army Division had particularly distinguished itself.

The operation began with a night air assault by Colonel Townsend's 3rd Stryker Brigade Combat Team, which led the effort to clear Baquba. As the operation unfolded, it quickly became apparent that Al Qaeda units, estimated to number more than 1,000 fighters, had dug in to stay. However, news sources reported that the leadership had fled in advance of the operation. In addition to Iraqi security forces (army and police), "concerned citizens" groups—also referred to as Iraqi police volunteers—cooperated with U.S. military personnel and Iraqi security forces in rooting out insurgents. The citizens' movement hoped to restore a measure of peace to the war-torn region. It was instrumental in finding and exposing the safe houses where Al Qaeda militants were hiding.

Fighting was fierce throughout Diyala Province but especially in Baquba, where Al Qaeda had essentially taken control of the city. Multinational troops, going house to house to capture or kill Al Qaeda insurgents, met heavy resistance in the early stages of the battle. As troops entered neighborhoods, they found schools, businesses, and homes booby-trapped with homemade improvised explosive devices (IEDs). The heaviest fighting during the operation occurred within the first four weeks.

American commanders had always believed that Al Qaeda was its own worst enemy, particularly in the way that it treated the locals. Thus, American leaders had anticipated help from citizens in the province, and when these citizens began to pass information as to the whereabouts of insurgents, it was clear that they were ready for Al Qaeda and its operatives to leave their province.

An important goal of ARROWHEAD RIPPER was to prevent insurgents fleeing Baquba from escaping and reorganizing elsewhere. The attacking forces therefore set up a series of blocking posts to the northwest of Baquba in the Khalis corridor and south of the city near Khan Bani Saad to deny insurgents passage through these areas.

Coalition and Iraqi forces also conducted operations to disrupt enemy lines of communication and deny Al Qaeda any areas of safe haven. Following the initial push that cleared Baquba of insurgents, coalition forces began to reposition and destroy Al Qaeda positions northeast of Baquba in the Diyala River Valley. In spite of their attempts to contain Al Qaeda forces inside the area to prevent them from reorganizing elsewhere, many of the insurgents escaped capture and fled.

During the operation, which ended on August 19, the Al Qaeda leader in Baquba was killed, along with more than 100 other insurgents. An additional 424 suspected insurgents were taken prisoner. A total of 129 weapons caches were captured or destroyed, and some 250 IEDs were found and rendered inoperable, including 38 booby-trapped houses, which the military refers to as house-borne IEDs, and 12 vehicle-borne IEDs. Coalition casualties included 18 Americans killed and 12 wounded, 7 Iraqi army personnel killed and 15 wounded, 2 allied Iraqi militiamen killed, and 3 Iraqi police killed. Civilian casualties in the province were not accurately recorded, but an estimated 350 were killed, and many more were wounded. However, it was unclear if civilian casualties were a direct result of Multi-National Force–Iraq military actions or Al Qaeda members simply killing civilians who had helped their enemies.

One reason for the success of the operation was the newly formed Diyala Operations Center, established to coordinate coalition activities in the province. Through it, coalition forces, local police, the Iraqi military, and citizen informants sympathetic to the American military were all linked to one headquarters location. This enabled planners and leaders of the operation to react quickly to any situation, a scenario that the insurgents had not anticipated.

The surge in American troop strength in Iraq combined with operations such as ARROWHEAD RIPPER forced Al Qaeda insurgents out of the cities of the Diyala Valley and broke their ability to sustain day-to-day attacks on coalition troops in the area. Success was also achieved in enabling government ministries to provide fundamental goods and services such as food, fuel, and displaced-persons services to Diyala Province. This enabled the local and national Iraqi governments to show that they could provide for their people and thus raise confidence in government authorities.

The U.S. troop surge begun in early 2007 and operations such as ARROWHEAD RIPPER had great success in the Diyala Valley, with normal life beginning to reemerge by the end of the offensive. Schools, hospitals, and businesses were reopened in the relatively safer environment that came about as a result of the operation.

RANDY JACK TAYLOR

See also
Al Qaeda in Iraq; Iraq, History of, 1990–Present; Troop Surge, U.S., Iraq War

References
Bensahel, Nora. *After Saddam: Prewar Planning and the Occupation of Iraq.* Skokie, IL: RAND Corporation, 2008.
Miller, Debra A. *The Middle East.* Detroit: Greenhaven, 2007.
Radcliffe, Woodrow S. *The Strategic Surge in Iraq: Pretense or Plan for Success?* USAWC Strategy Research Project. Carlisle Barracks, PA: U.S. Army War College, 2007.
Simon, Steven, and Council on Foreign Relations. *After the Surge: The Case for U.S. Military Disengagement from Iraq.* New York: Council on Foreign Relations, 2007.
Simons, G. L. *Iraq Endgame? Surge, Suffering and the Politics of Denial.* London: Politico's, 2008.
Woodward, Bob. *The War Within: A Secret White House History, 2006–2008.* New York: Simon and Schuster, 2008.

Article 51, United Nations Charter

Self-defense clause contained in the charter of the United Nations (UN). Article 51 of the UN Charter guarantees the principle of self-defense by its members, whether through individual or collective security. The article falls under Chapter VII, which is titled "Actions with Respect to Threats to the Peace, Breaches of the Peace, and Acts of Aggression." It states that "nothing in the present charter shall impair the inherent right of individual or collective self-defense if an armed attack occurs against a Member of the UN, until the Security Council has taken measures necessary to maintain international peace and security." Further, it stipulates that "measures taken by Members in the exercise of this right of self-defense shall be immediately reported to the Security Council and shall not in any way affect the authority and responsibility of the Security Council under the present Charter."

The origins of Article 51 can be traced to the concerns shared by a number of Latin American countries in response to the veto power of the Security Council on actions taken by a regional body. In particular, the foreign ministers of Brazil, Colombia, and Cuba were concerned about the prospect of an outside power attacking the Western Hemisphere and then using the veto power of a Security Council member to prevent any collective action. The governments of Latin America were concerned that the Security Council might abrogate the 1945 Act of Chapultepec, which guaranteed the mutual defense of the Latin American republics in the event of an attack, whether by an outside power or by another state within the Western Hemisphere.

The Chapultepec agreement originally applied to concerns over Argentina, which had a military government that was sympathetic to the Axis powers. With World War II concluded, the concern now shifted to growing Cold War tensions. Not only did the Chapultepec agreement seem endangered, but it appeared that the long-standing Good Neighbor policy and even the 1823 Monroe Doctrine would be swept away by the UN Charter. In particular, the Latin American nations were concerned about the infiltration of Soviet influence in the Western Hemisphere. Such concerns even reached prominent American officials such as Senator Arthur Vandenburg, who worried that any provisions that would not protect the Western Hemisphere could lead to a Senate rejection of the UN Charter.

The problem of regionalism and regional defense was solved through the creation of three UN articles. Article 51 enshrined the principle of self-defense. Article 52 allowed the creation of regional bodies and defensive organizations, and Article 53 allowed the Security Council to work through regional agencies. Despite earlier fears, Article 51 maintained long-standing hemispheric agreements such as the Chapultepec agreement. Indeed, both individual and collective security were enshrined. Through Article 51, the United States and the Soviet Union were able to establish such regional security agreements as the North Atlantic Treaty Organization and the Warsaw Pact. The United States used Article 51 as justification for the Vietnam War; although the Republic of Vietnam (South Vietnam) was not a member of the UN, it had the right of collective defense, and the United States had taken up that cause.

In the Middle East, Article 51 permitted the creation and existence of such international defense organizations as the 1955 Baghdad Pact, which morphed into the Central Treaty

Organization (CENTO) after the 1958 Baathist coup in Iraq that deposed the monarchy there. Iraq promptly withdrew from the Baghdad Pact and began to align itself with the Soviet bloc. After that the organization became adopted the name CENTO, and the United States became an associated partner in the organization. Throughout the various Middle East wars since the end of World War II, Article 51 has been invoked by a number of nations under attack. The Israelis have repeatedly referenced it in regard to defensive measures taken against outside aggression, whether it is from nation-states or nonstate entities. Indeed, in the Israeli-Hezbollah War that broke out in July 2006, Israel invoked Article 51 as its legal justification for attacking Hezbollah positions in southern Lebanon. Many nations have argued, however, that Israeli reprisals were out of proportion to the Hezbollah actions against Israel, and were therefore not within the legal scope of Article 51. Clearly, there seems to be sufficient room within Article 51 to allow support for either side of the issue.

DINO E. BUENVIAJE

See also

United Nations

References

Goodrich, Leland, and Edvard Hambro. *Charter of the United Nations: Commentary and Documents.* 2nd and rev. ed. Boston: World Peace Foundation, 1949.

Schlesinger, Stephen C. *Act of Creation: The Founding of the United Nations.* Boulder, CO: Westview, 2003.

Weiss, Thomas G., et al., eds. *The United Nations and Changing World Politics.* Boulder, CO: Westview, 1997.

Articles 41 and 42, United Nations Charter

Provisions that enable the United Nations (UN) Security Council to undertake specific measures to contain aggression and maintain peace. Articles 41 and 42 of the UN Charter established the enforcement power of the Security Council within the mechanism of the UN Charter. These articles are part of Chapter VII of the charter, titled "Action with Respect to Threats to the Peace, Breaches of the Peace, and Acts of Aggression." Article 41 authorizes the Security Council to enact nonmilitary measures to deter acts of aggression, such as "complete or partial interruption of economic relations and of rail, sea, air, postal, telegraphic, radio, and other means of communication and the severance of diplomatic relations." Article 42 authorizes the

Security Council to enact military measures, should Article 41 prove inadequate, such as "demonstrations, blockade, and other operations by air, sea, or land forces of Members of the United Nations."

Articles 41 and 42 were a direct result of the shortcomings of the League of Nations, the predecessor organization to the UN. World War II essentially witnessed the complete failure of the League of Nations to preserve peace. There were two significant factors that contributed to the league's demise: the failure of the United States to ratify the League of Nations Covenant and the organization's lack of enforcement powers. President Franklin D. Roosevelt, who had been an early supporter of the League of Nations, hoped to create an organization to succeed it that would not contain any of its flaws.

The United States had chosen not to join the League of Nations because of the language contained in Article 10 of the League of Nations Covenant, which obligated members "to undertake to respect and preserve, as against external aggression, the territorial integrity and existing political independence of all Members of the League." Some American officials believed that this concept of collective security appeared to endanger the sovereignty of the United States. Article 16 of the Covenant furthermore enjoined its members to participate in protecting other members suffering from aggression. These two articles were soon proven meaningless, however, during Italy's invasion of Ethiopia in 1935. The invasion occurred with virtual impunity.

Unlike Articles 10 and 16 of the League of Nations Covenant, Articles 41 and 42 of the UN Charter gave the Security Council the sole prerogative of deciding what situations would involve the use of force. One reason the League of Nations failed was that it did not have any such mechanism to deliberate in situations that might have required the use of force. Also, the language of Article 16 proved to be the league's undoing by placing an obligation on its members to intervene with nonmilitary measures. Article 41 differs in language by using the words "call upon" rather than "obligate." By placing the responsibility on the Security Council in determining what kinds of measures should be taken, the UN maintained its credibility rather than allowing each individual member to decide what kinds of actions to take.

Article 42 specifically placed military and other security measures in the hands of the Security Council. Under the League of Nations, it was impossible to find a consensus among the members to devote their armed forces toward enforcement. Thus, through Article 42 a system was devised whereby national military forces would be placed under international jurisdiction but only for specified objectives. As a result of these measures, the UN has maintained a credibility that the League of Nations could not uphold.

The UN, largely through Articles 41 and 42, has been heavily involved in the Middle East since 1945. Most of its work has come in the form of peacekeeping, monitoring, and enforcement. Some of its actions here include the UN Observation Group in Lebanon, dispatched in 1958 to ensure that no illegal infiltrations of personnel or materials made their way into Lebanon after the uprising there that same year. In November 1956 following the Suez Crisis and the Sinai Campaign, the UN established the First UN Security Force, whose job was to oversee the withdrawal of French, Israeli, and British forces from Egypt, and then to maintain a buffer zone between Egyptian and Israeli troops. This lasted until June 1967. In October 1973, following the Yom Kippur War, the Second UN Emergency Force was dispatched to the Middle East to enforce the cease-fire between Israel and Egypt. UN forces also created and maintained a buffer zone between the two nations, which lasted until July 1979. In August 1988, the UN established the UN Iran-Iraq Military Observer Group, which was charged with enforcing the terms of the cease-fire after the Iran-Iraq War (1980–1988). The UN Iraq-Kuwait Observation Commission, in operation from April 1991 to October 2003, was charged with deterring any aggression between the two nations and monitoring the demilitarized zone.

Ongoing UN activities in the Middle East include an observation force in the Golan Heights, first created in 1974, to supervise the cease-fire and withdrawal agreements made between Syria and Israel. The UN Interim Force in Lebanon, dispatched in 1978, continues the struggle to enable the Lebanese government to assert control over its territory and keep Israeli troops from occupying Lebanese lands. The UN Truce Supervision Organization, in existence since 1948, continues to monitor truces, observe military movements, enforce cease-fires, and perform other peacekeeping responsibilities in the region. Articles 41 and 42 have also been invoked numerous times during Middle Eastern conflicts to effect embargoes, blockades, and economic sanctions against aggressor states. For example, after the Iraqi invasion of Kuwait in August 1990, the UN Security Council almost immediately passed Resolution 660, which condemned the Iraqi attack and demanded an immediate withdrawal. Just a few days later the Security Council passed Resolution 661, which slapped international economic sanctions on Iraq. After more diplomatic wrangling while Iraq still occupied Kuwait, the UN passed Resolution 678 in November 1990. This resolution gave the Iraqis a firm deadline of January 15, 1991, to withdraw entirely from Kuwait. It also authorized "all necessary means" to implement and enforce Resolution 660, which was a de facto authorization for the use of force. When Iraq refused to leave Kuwait, an international coalition led by the United States forcibly expelled him. Indeed, the 1991 Persian Gulf War was an almost textbook case of the effectiveness of the UN and of Articles 41 and 42, specifically.

The same cannot be said, however, of the 2003 Anglo-American–led coalition that invaded Iraq and ousted Iraqi dictator Saddam Hussein from office. Although the UN had passed a number of resolutions entreating Hussein to cooperate with UN weapons inspectors, it had not passed a clear-cut measure that specifically authorized force, as it had done in 1991. The United States continued to push the case for war, however, citing "clear" evidence that the Iraqis were concealing weapons of mass destruction. Thus, the United States and its allies went to war with Iraq in March 2003 lacking any pretense of UN authorization. This engendered bitter condemnations from many nations, including old allies of the Americans and British. UN secretary-general Kofi Annan termed the invasion "illegal" in September 2004. The lack of international support bedeviled the Anglo-American war in Iraq, as did reports that no weapons of mass destruction were found in Iraq, even after many months of careful hunting by military professionals.

DINO E. BUENVIAJE AND PAUL G. PIERPAOLI JR.

See also

Annan, Kofi; Arab-Israeli Conflict, Overview; IRAQI FREEDOM, Operation; United Nations; Weapons of Mass Destruction

References

Goodrich, Leland, and Edvard Hambro. *Charter of the United Nations: Commentary and Documents.* 2nd rev. ed. Boston: World Peace Foundation, 1949.

Nothedge, F. S. *The League of Nations: Its Life and Times, 1920–1946.* Leicester, UK: Leicester University Press, 1986.

Riggs, Robert Egwon. *The United Nations: International Organization and World Politics.* Chicago: Wadsworth Publishing, 1993.

Artillery

During the last quarter of the 20th century, artillery underwent a number of significant and large technological advances. If a World War II artilleryman had moved 25 years into the future, he would find very little changed in a typical field artillery battalion of the Vietnam War. But a Vietnam War–era artilleryman moving 25 years into the future would have encountered bewildering changes in the typical field artillery battalion of the Persian Gulf War. Moving ahead another 15 years to the Iraq War and the Afghanistan War, our artilleryman from the mid-1960s would find himself almost completely lost.

The fundamental mechanical design of the guns of the 21st century is still based on the same principles as those of the preceding century, but electronics and digitization have completely altered artillery fire planning, fire control, fire direction, the terminal effects of the ammunition, and the manner in which the guns are operated. Through the late 1960s radios and telephones were the only pieces of electronic equipment in a typical firing battery. Today, individual guns are equipped with computers, Global Positioning Systems (GPS), inertial navigation systems, and digital links to various data and command and control systems. Cannons are still the backbone of field artillery, but over the course of the last 30 years artillery rockets and guided missiles have become more sophisticated and widely used.

Field artillery cannon systems are towed or self-propelled (SP). A towed system consists of a cannon and a prime mover, usually a truck that tows the cannon. SP weapons are cannon mounted integrally on a motor carriage, usually tracked, to form self-contained gun platforms. Self-propelled artillery has a higher ground mobility and ability to keep pace with fast-moving mechanized units. Lighter towed artillery has higher air mobility, especially when transported by helicopter.

Towed guns rely on their prime movers to carry ancillary equipment such as aiming collimators, tools, communications equipment, and other fire-control items. The prime mover also typically carries a small amount of ready ammunition, but the majority of the gun section's basic load of projectiles, propellant, and fuzes is carried on a separate ammunition truck.

SP guns likewise carry only a few rounds of ready ammunition on board, with the remainder of the basic load carried in a tracked ammunition vehicle. In many modern SP systems the specially designed ammunition vehicle, such as the American M-992A2 field artillery ammunition supply vehicle, is equipped with an automatic ammunition feed system that connects directly with the onboard hydraulic loader-rammer system of the SP gun. This produces loading speeds and efficiency far greater than the manual systems on almost all towed guns.

The primary light artillery piece in 21st-century warfare has been the American M-119A2 and M-119A3 105-mm

U.S. Marine Corps artillery outside of Fallujah, Iraq, firing against an insurgent position, November 11, 2004. (U.S. Department of Defense)

towed howitzer, which are adaptations of the British L-119 light gun. First entering British service in 1975, the M-119 was adopted by the Americans in 1989. Used by the U.S. Army and Royal Artillery in both Iraq and Afghanistan, the L-119/M-119 has a range of 13,700 meters with standard ammunition and 19,500 meters firing rocket-assisted projectiles (RAP). Entering service in 2013, the M-119A3 variant mounts a digital fire-control system and an inertial navigation system. The system weighs 4,590 pounds.

At the start of the 21st century the primary American medium towed howitzer was the 155-mm M-198, used by both army and marine units in Iraq. The system weighs 15,770 pounds and has a range of 22,400 meters with conventional ammunition and 30,000 meters firing RAP rounds. The M-198 entered service in 1979, but over the course of the succeeding 35 years it was never upgraded to keep pace with emerging technology.

Introduced in 2005 as a replacement for the M-198, the initial M-777 towed 155-mm howitzer had a conventional optical fire-control system. The M-777A1 and M-777A2 variants quickly followed, adding digitization upgrades and inertial navigation systems. Firing the same ammunition as the M-198, the M-777A2 has a range of 24,700 meters with conventional ammunition, and 30,000 meters with RAP rounds. Fired in combat in both Iraq and Afghanistan, the M-777A2 weighs only 7,540 pounds.

At the start of the 21st century the forces of Iraq and Afghanistan were armed largely with Soviet-era weapons. The primary artillery piece was the D-30 122-mm towed howitzer. Introduced into Soviet service in 1963, the D-30 has a maximum range of 15,400 meters with conventional ammunition, and 21,900 meters with RAP rounds. The system weighs 7,080 pounds. The American-trained Afghan National Army still uses the D-30, and from 2010 to 2013 the U.S. Army Project Manager for Towed Artillery Systems assumed the responsibility for supplying the Afghans with 204 refurbished D-30s, along with the necessary operational and maintenance training. The Syrian Army also uses the D-30.

During both U.S.-led wars in Iraq the Iraqi Army was armed with the South African G-5 155-mm towed howitzer, a variant of the excellent Canadian GC-45 howitzer. The gun was designed in the 1970s by Dr. Gerald Bull, the brilliant but controversial Canadian ordnance engineer. In the late 1980s Bull was recruited by Saddam Hussein with the lure of almost unlimited R&D funding to design and build Project Babylon, a 350-mm supergun with a range of 1,000 kilometers. Bull was assassinated in a Brussels hotel room in March 1990, most likely by Israel's Mossad.

The GC-45/G-5 introduced a radical advance in artillery ballistics technology. Bull's great innovation was the development of the Extended Range, Full Bore (ERFB) projectile and the accompanying cannon bore technology capable of firing such ammunition. GC-45 howitzer reversed the normal rifling concept by firing a shell with small fins that rode in the grooves in the bore, as opposed to using a slightly oversized projectile that was forced into the lands between the grooves. The result was a significant increase in muzzle velocity and range. The South African G-5 howitzer, which was based on the GC-45, can fire an ERFB high-explosive (HE) projectile to a maximum range of 30,000 meters and an ERFB RAP round to 50,000 meters. The Iraqi Army bought some 100 of the South African G-5 version and more than 200 of the GHN-45 version, manufactured in Austria. During the Persian Gulf War and the Iraq War, those guns outranged all other guns in the Allied coalition arsenal.

The American M-109 family of 155-mm howitzers is the most widely used SP artillery piece in history. Since it was first introduced in 1963, it has been in service with 33 armies and remains to this day in service with almost all of them. The M-109 has a lightly armored enclosed turret around its firing platform, providing greater protection for the gun crew.

Firing the same 155-mm ammunition as the M-198 and M-777, the original M-109 model had a relatively short barrel, which fired the 97-pound HE projectile to a maximum range of 14,600 meters. The only piece of electronic equipment on the original M-109 was a telephone. Introduced in 1973, the M-109A1 had a longer barrel, which extended the maximum range to 18,100 meters. Introduced in the 1990s, the M-109A6 "Paladin" is capable of firing an RAP round to a maximum range of 30,000 meters. With its automated loading system, the Paladin requires a crew of only four, a significant reduction of the M-109's original crew of eight. The Paladin's sophisticated navigational and automatic fire-control systems give it the ability to halt from the move and fire within 30 seconds. The U.S. Army used the M-109A6 in both Iraq and Afghanistan. In November 2014, the U.S. Army announced the awarding of the contract to produce the initial 18 of a planned 66 of the upgraded M-109A7 Paladins, which will have improved electronic and hydraulic systems.

Up through the 1990s the British Royal Artillery used the American M-109 series of SP howitzers. Rather than adopt the M-109A6 Paladin, however, the British in 1993 instead introduced their own design, the AS-90. Firing the standard NATO 155-mm ammunition, the AS-90 has a maximum range of 24,700 meters. The Royal Artillery used the AS-90 in Iraq but not in Afghanistan.

Like the British, the German Bundeswehr used the American M-109 series for many years. But in the 1990s the Bundeswehr too developed its own 155-mm SP howitzer. Entering service in 1998, Germany's 155-mm Panzerhaubitze 2000 (Armored Howitzer, or PzH-2000) is the most technologically advanced tube artillery system in service today. A tracked SP system with a fully enclosed armored turret, it has an automated ammunition feed and loading system and state-of-the-art GPS onboard fire control. The PzH-2000 has an impressively high rate of fire. It is capable of firing a burst mode of 3 rounds in 9 seconds and 10 rounds in 56 seconds. It has a sustained rate of fire of 10 to thirteen rounds per minute. It carries an onboard basic load of 60 rounds, and two cannoneers can reload all 60 shells and propellant charges in less than 12 minutes. The maximum range is 30,000 meters for conventional HE rounds and 40,000 for RAP rounds.

The PzH-2000 was fired in combat for the first time by the Dutch Army in August 2006, against Taliban targets in Kandahar Province, Afghanistan. In July 2010 German troops assigned to the International Security Assistance Force in Kunduz Province fired three PzH-2000s in support of recovery operations for a damaged vehicle. That was the first time in the history of the Bundeswehr that it fired heavy artillery in combat.

The American 8-inch (203-mm) howitzer had the reputation of being history's most accurate artillery piece. It first entered service in 1940 as the M-1 towed howitzer. It fired a 200-pound HE projectile to a maximum range of 16,800 meters. Its extremely small circular probable error made it an ideal weapon for destructive fire against hardened targets. In 1963 the gun and its carriage were mounted on a tracked chassis and designated the M-110 SP howitzer. Its biggest disadvantage was that its open firing platform left the gun crew exposed to enemy small-arms fire and shell fragmentation.

In the 1970s the 8-inch gun was upgraded with a longer barrel and redesignated the M-110A1 and was further modernized a few years later as the M-110A2. The long-barrel 8-inch gun could fire conventional HE rounds to a range of 25,000 meters and a RAP round out to 30,000. The M 110 was phased out of U.S. Army service immediately following the Persian Gulf War, a move that many artillerymen still consider to have been serious a mistake. It was used by more than 20 armies and still remains in service with a few to this day.

Virtually all the types of artillery ammunition that were in service at the end of World War II are still in service today and account for the majority of the rounds fired. In the last 40 years, however, a number of technologically sophisticated specialized rounds have entered service.

Artillery ammunition is classified generally as fixed, semifixed, or separate-loading. Most direct-fire guns, such as tank guns and antitank guns, fire fixed ammunition, whereby the projectile, fuze, propellant charge, and primer are supplied as a single unit. The propellant charge is packaged in a metal shell casing canister made of brass or steel, which has a primer in its base and the projectile mounted on its top. After firing, the empty casing must be ejected from the firing chamber of the gun.

Semifixed ammunition is similar to fixed except that it does not come prepackaged with a fuze, which gives the firing battery the flexibility of selecting the fuze to match the target. The point-detonating fuze produces a surface or delayed subsurface burst. The time and proximity fuzes produce airbursts over the target. The propellant inside the shell casing canister also comes packaged in separate increment

bags, which the gun crew can remove as necessary to achieve the required charge for the range to the target. As with fixed ammunition, the empty shell casing canister must be removed from the gun after firing. Most light artillery, typically 105-mm or smaller, fires semifixed ammunition.

Almost all medium and heavy artillery pieces, 120-mm or larger, fire separate-loading ammunition, in which the projectile, fuze, propellant, and primer all come separately and are combined as required by the firing crew. Separate-loading propellant charges do not come packaged in a shell casing canister. The number of powder bags representing the required propellant charge is loaded directly into the cannon's breech chamber, immediately behind the projectile, and are completely consumed during the firing process.

The standard artillery projectiles for the last 75 years have been high explosive (HE), illumination, and smoke. Fired with either a point-detonating or an airburst fuze, the HE round produces both blast and fragmentation effects. The fragmentation is popularly but incorrectly called shrapnel, which is a reference to a type of artillery round that became obsolete after World War I. Illumination rounds are used to provide light over a target area during periods of darkness. Detonated at a high airburst, the shell deploys a parachute flare that lasts up to a minute. Smoke rounds have the exact opposite tactical purpose of obscuring battlefield observation, either to screen friendly movements or to prevent enemy observation.

Introduced during the Vietnam War, the Improved Conventional Munition (ICM) round was an air-detonated shell that rained antipersonnel submunitions (cluster bomblets) down on the target area. In the mid-1970s the ICM round was replaced by the Dual-Purpose Improved Conventional Munition (DPICM), designed for both antipersonnel and antitank fire. The DPICM submunitions carry a shaped charge that attacks the top deck of a tank, where the armor is the thinnest.

Lethal chemical artillery rounds were introduced during World War I and used extensively during that war. Although banned following World War I, Iraq made extensive use of chemical weapons during its 1980–1988 war with Iran. During the 1991 Persian Gulf War and the early stages of the 2003–2011 Iraq War, there was serious concern that Iraq would use chemical weapons. Although some allied troops were exposed to chemicals in both wars, they were not extensively used. More recently, evidence points strongly to the use of lethal chemicals by the regime of Bashar al-Assad in the Syrian Civil War that started in 2011. In the early 1990s the United States completely renounced the use of toxic chemical weapons, ceased new production, and started destroying existing stockpiles. The final stocks of American chemical artillery projectiles are scheduled to be destroyed by 2017.

First developed in the early 1950s, nuclear artillery projectiles were low-yield battlefield tactical weapons. Most American, British, and Soviet medium and heavy field artillery systems were capable of firing such projectiles. In 1991 U.S. president George H. W. Bush made the unilateral decision to eliminate nuclear field artillery, withdrawing some 1,300 forward-positioned nuclear shells from U.S. forces in Europe. The Soviet Union followed suit in 1992. The United States destroyed its last nuclear artillery round, a W-79 warhead, in late 2003.

The American M-712 "Copperhead" was history's first precision-guided artillery projectile. Entering service in 1982, the 155-mm round was designed specifically to kill tanks. Once the round was fired, it was guided during the terminal leg of its trajectory by a forward observer using a laser target designator (LTD) to mark the target. U.S. Army artillery units fired some 90 Copperheads during the Persian Gulf War and also used the round in 2003 during the opening phase of the Iraq War.

In 2008 the M-712 Copperhead was replaced by the M-982 "Excalibur," history's first fire-and-forget precision-guided artillery projectile. While the Copperhead had to be steered into the target by an observer close enough to see it and mark it with an LTD, the 155-mm Excalibur is precision-guided by an onboard GPS and an inertial measurement unit. The extended-range version of the round can fire up to 40,000 meters. It has been used in both Iraq and Afghanistan, with 92 percent of the rounds fired hitting within 4 meters of the target, a phenomenal level of precision for artillery. The Excalibur can be fired from the M-198, the M-777, the M-109A6, the British AS-90, and the German PzH-2000.

Field artillery rockets were used extensively by all sides during World War II. German and Soviet multiple-rocket launcher systems were particularly effective. During the first three decades of the Cold War, however, only the Soviets continued to develop and field such systems. That changed in 1983 when the United States, the United Kingdom, Germany, and France introduced the jointly developed M-270 multiple-launch rocket system (MLRS). The M-270 is a fully tracked, fully automated launcher with an onboard GPS and computerized fire-control system and a crew of three. Each launcher carries 12 rockets in two six-pack launch pod containers. The rockets can be fired singly or ripple-fired in one

minute. The M-26 rocket is a free-flight (unguided) system that carries 644 DPICM submunitions. The M-26A1 version of the rocket has a range of 45,000 meters. The M-270 was first fired in combat during the Persian Gulf War, and it was used by both the U.S. Army and the Royal Artillery during the Iraq War.

Entering service in the late 1980s, the M-39 (formerly the MGM-140) army tactical missile system (ATACMS) is a guided surface-to-surface missile fired from the M-270 MLRS launcher. Each M-270 can carry and launch two ATACMS. The M-39A1 version of the missile has a range of 300,000 meters. U.S. Army artillery units fired 32 ATACMS missiles during the Persian Gulf War and more than 450 during the Iraq War.

Upgraded in 2006 as the M-270A1, the newer version of the MLRS launcher is capable of firing the M-30 guided MLRS (GMLRS) missile. Essentially the same size as unguided M-26 rocket, the GPS-guided M-30 carries 404 submunitions. The M-31 missile carries a 200-pound HE warhead and has a range of up to 70,000 meters. In 2011 the Royal Artillery deployed the GMLRS to Helmand Province in Afghanistan, where it quickly acquired the nickname "70-km sniper."

The M-142 High Mobility Artillery Rocket System (HIMARS) is a wheeled lighter-weight launcher capable of carrying and firing a single pod of six M-26 MLRS rockets, six M-30/M-31 GMLRS missiles, or one M-39 ATACMS missile. The system is mounted on a U.S. Army family of medium tactical vehicles five-ton truck. Introduced in 1998, the M-142 HIMARS was used in 2007 by the 2nd Battalion, 14th Marines, in Anbar Province, Iraq. It has also been used in Afghanistan by the International Security Assistance Force.

The first decade of the 21st century was a difficult period for American field artillery. The United States entered both the Iraq War and the Afghanistan War with inadequate artillery support, owing largely to the simplistic and naive belief held by many of the Pentagon's senior leaders that the shock and awe generated by airpower, special operations forces, and electronic warfare made old-fashioned fire and maneuver tactics obsolete. That, however, turned out to be just another variation of the same old "airpower can do it all" siren song heard so often during the 20th century. When the 10th Mountain Division deployed to Afghanistan in early 2002 it did not take its M-119 105-mm howitzers, supposedly because they took up too much space. The idea was to depend on infantry mortars, attack helicopters, and tactical air support for all the division's fire support requirements. That turned out to be a mistake. The division needed its organic field artillery, with its 24-hour all-weather capability, during the March 1–18, 2002, Operation ANACONDA. In the years following, the United States and its various coalition partners all deployed their heaviest artillery systems to both Iraq and Afghanistan.

In Iraq following the end of conventional military operations in 2003 against the main Iraqi Army, the follow-on counterinsurgency operations generally required less artillery. U.S. Army artillery units deployed to Iraq spent much of their tours of duty driving trucks, guarding convoys, securing perimeters, and even fighting as infantry. By 2007–2008 there was a great deal of concern across the field artillery branch that the complex technical and tactical skills necessary to produce rapid, coordinated, and effective fire support were eroding rapidly. Morale within the Field Artillery branch suffered accordingly. Fortunately, since the end of major combat operations in Iraq, the pendulum finally seems to be swinging the other way.

DAVID T. ZABECKI

See also

Afghanistan War; Iraq War

References

Bailey, Jonathan. *Field Artillery and Firepower*. Annapolis, MD: U.S. Naval Institute Press, 2004.

Gudmundsson, Bruce. *On Artillery*. Westport, CT: Praeger, 1993.

Hogg, Ian. *Twentieth-Century Artillery*. New York: Barnes and Noble, 2000.

Assad, Bashar al- (1965–)

President of the Syrian Arab Republic (2000–present) and head of the Syrian Baath Party. Bashar al-Assad was born in Damascus, Syria, on September 11, 1965. His father was Hafiz al-Assad, strongman and president of Syria from 1971 to 2000. The Alawi sect to which the Assads belong encompasses approximately 12 percent of the Syrian population. Bashar al-Assad's older brother, Basil, was more popular among the Syrian public than was Bashar before he was killed in an automobile accident in 1994.

Beginning in the mid-1980s, the Bashar al-Assad studied medicine at the University of Damascus, training in ophthalmology at the Tishrin Military Hospital and then the Western Eye Hospital in London. After Basil's death, Assad enrolled in the military academy at Homs. He became a colonel in the Syrian Army in 1999.

Although Syria is a republic, President Hafiz al-Assad groomed Basil, then Bashar, as his successor, although he never openly declared this intent. Bashar al-Assad's acquisition of both military and Baath Party credentials was imperative to his legitimacy, but most observers believed that the senior power brokers in the Syrian government assented to Assad's succession as a matter of convenience. In 2000, he was elected secretary-general of the Baath Party and stood as a presidential candidate. The People's Assembly amended the Syrian Constitution to lower the minimum presidential age to 35, and Assad was duly elected president for a 7-year term. A general referendum soon ratified the decision.

A reform movement emerged during the first year of Assad's rule, which was dubbed the Damascus Spring. Some Syrians hoped that their young president—who had announced governmental reforms, an end to corruption, and economic liberalization—would open Syria to a greater degree. Indeed, reformers hoped to end the State of Emergency Law, which allows for the abuse of legal and human rights, and issued public statements in 2000 and 2001. Political prisoners were released from the notorious Mezze Prison, and certain intellectual forums were permitted. However, by mid-2001 the president reined in the reformists, some of whom were imprisoned and accused of being Western agents.

Under Bashar al-Assad, Syria opened somewhat in terms of allowing more media coverage than in the past, although censorship remained a contentious issue. Cellular phones are prevalent, and Syria finally allowed access to the Internet, whereas under Hafiz al-Assad, even facsimile machines were prohibited. Economic reform and modernization received top priority under Bashar al-Assad. Job creation, the lessening of Syria's dependence on oil revenue, the encouragement of private capital investments, and the mitigation of poverty have been the key goals in the economic sphere. The government created foreign investment zones, and private universities were legally permitted, along with private banks. Employment centers were established after 2000, and Assad announced his support of an association with the European Union. However, these changes were too gradual to instill much confidence in Syrian modernization.

Syria's relations with Iraq had improved prior to the change of regime in that country in April 2003, and relations between Syria and Turkey were also less tense than in the past. However, the United States showed great irritation with evidence that foreign fighters were crossing into Iraq from Syria and that former Iraqi Baathists were using Syria for funding purposes. The ensuing 2004 sanctions against Syria under the Syria Accountability Act, first enacted by the U.S. Congress in 2003, discouraged investors and the modernization of Syria's banking systems. More important, this situation provided a lever to force Syria out of Lebanon, finally put in motion after the assassination of former Lebanese prime minister Rafic al-Hariri.

Syria adamantly and consistently opposed the American presence in Iraq after the Anglo-American invasion there in March 2003, and the country's own Islamist movement reemerged. Assad also had to deal with a huge influx of Iraqi refugees to Syria, who posed an additional burden on the economy. Further, Assad did not wish to encourage radical Islamists in Syrian territory and made efforts to contain them.

In terms of the Arab-Israeli situation, Assad inherited a hard-line position toward Tel Aviv along with sympathies toward the Palestinian cause during the Second (al-Aqsa) Intifada and its aftermath. Yet internally, the public saw the president as promoting an honorable peace for Syria, deemed necessary for further economic development. This did not mean that Syria and Israel were any closer to a peace agreement, but Syria would also most likely seek to avoid war, as during the Israeli invasion of southern Lebanon in 2006. Syria and Israel engaged in an exploration of peace talks, and by the end of 2008 there were signs that a Syrian-Israeli rapprochement was in the offing, although Israel's war against Hamas in Gaza, which began in late 2008, threatened to suspend further negotiations.

Other important changes came with the shift in Syria's position in Lebanon. When Hariri was assassinated in a bombing in February 2005, suspicions fell on Syria. Anti-Syrian Lebanese demonstrated, as did such pro-Syrian groups such as Hezbollah. The United Nations inquiry into Hariri's death as well as comments by former Syrian vice president Abdul Halim Khaddam implicated Syrians at the highest level and pro-Syrian elements in Lebanon intelligence services in the assassination. The Syrian government fought hard to postpone establishment of a tribunal to investigate Hariri's death but to no avail. Syrian troops finally withdrew from Lebanon in April 2005, thereby ending a long period of direct and indirect influence over the country. Additional important Lebanese figures were assassinated, including Pierre Gemayel, founder of the Kataeb Party. Lebanon was a key economic asset for Syria because of highly favorable trade terms, smuggling, and the absorption of large numbers of Syrian laborers. The U.S. government continued to charge Assad with aiding and bolstering Hezbollah in Lebanon, but Syria viewed the organization as a wholly Lebanese entity.

President Assad was reelected to another seven-year term in 2007. Nevertheless, many Western nations and some Arab nations continued to pressure Assad to curtail relations with Iran and to crack down on terrorism said to be funded or supported by various elements within Syria. Assad had taken pains to improve relations with his Arab neighbors, but his pro-Iranian policies and interference in Lebanese affairs have led to tensions with such countries as Saudi Arabia, and Syria has sided with a new group joined by Qatar. Although considerable differences remained over security issues and water rights, there was speculation in early 2009 that Assad was nearing a peace treaty with Israel that would result in the restoration of the Golan Heights to Syria.

On January 26, 2011, protests began in Syria fueled by popular demands for political reforms, the reestablishment of civil rights, and an end to the state of emergency that has been in effect in the country since 1963. Protests that occurred on March 18–19 were the largest in the country in decades, and Syrian authorities responded with force. In May 2011, U.S. president Barack Obama signed an executive order imposing sanctions on Assad, hoping to pressure him into moving toward a democratic system. Members of the European Union followed suit, as did other nations, particularly Turkey, the government of which has called for international action to oust Assad from power.

Although Assad has utilized U.S. public relations firms and endeavored to project a positive image, nothing has come of his frequent promises of dialogue and pledges of reform as he continues to blame the violence, which grew into full-scale civil war on a small number of "terrorists." President Vladimir Putin of Russia has been a strong supporter of Assad, in part because Russia has Mediterranean bases in Syria. Both Russia and Iran continue to support Assad in international bodies such as the United Nations and through weapons deliveries. Although the fighting had already been under way for some time, in July 2012 the International Committee of the Red Cross officially declared Syria to be in a state of civil war, with the death toll from the fighting reportedly having climbed to nearly 20,000 people.

The United Nations subsequently confirmed that the Assad regime employed poison gas in March and August 2013, killing a large number of innocent civilians. This finding led the Obama administration to threaten military intervention, which forced Assad to agree to surrender his country's large stockpile of chemical weapons and see them destroyed. In August 2014 the United Nations announced that the death toll from the Syrian Civil War during March 2011–March 2014 was more than 191,000 people. Many more have fled the country.

Joining the fight against the Assad regime has been the extremist Islamic State of Iraq and Syria (ISIS), which is determined to carve out an Islamist state under strict sharia law in Iraq and Syria. By far the most effective group fighting the Syrian government, by 2014 ISIS controlled much of northern Syria as well as wide stretches of northern Iraq.

Although Assad was reelected to another presidential term in 2014, following the capture of four key Syrian government military bases in Raqqa province in September 2014 and the massacre of Syrian government troops by ISIS at one of them in September, he has come under increasing criticism from his Alawite base of support. Criticism from among the Alawites is fueled in large part by the disproportionate casualties of soldiers killed from Alawite areas as well as the deteriorating Syrian economic situation and endemic corruption. There is now considerable question as to how long Assad can remain in power.

SHERIFA ZUHUR AND SPENCER C. TUCKER

See also

Biological Weapons and Warfare; Iran; Putin, Vladimir Vladimirovich; Syria; Syrian Chemical Weapons Agreement; Syrian Civil War

References

Darraj, Susan Muaddi. *Bashar al-Assad.* New York: Chelsea House, 2005.

George, Alan. *Syria: Neither Bread nor Freedom.* London: Zed Books, 2003.

Lesch, David W. *Syria: The Fall of the House of Assad.* New Haven, CT: Yale University Press, 2011.

Leverett, Flynt. *Inheriting Syria: Bashar's Trial by Fire.* Washington, DC: Brookings Institution Press, 2005.

Assange, Julian (1971–)

Founder and editor in chief of WikiLeaks, a whistle-blowing website dedicated to sharing classified information by covertly acquiring and posting documents on the Internet. A citizen of Australia, Assange lives, works, and travels all over the world. Since WikiLeaks began operating in 2006, he was primarily known within a few technology and journalism circles; however, he gained worldwide attention when over the course of 2010 WikiLeaks began posting classified material taken from U.S. military and diplomatic reports.

Julian Paul Assange was born on July 3, 1971, in Townsville, Australia. When Assange was 1 year old, his mother married the director of a theater company, and the family moved often, living in 37 different places by the time

Assange was 14. Constant travel made Assange's education inconsistent, and he studied largely on his own. When Assange's mother left her husband and became involved with another man, that relationship did not end well. Feeling threatened, Assange's mother took her two sons to live on the run from the time Assange was 11 until he was 16. For a time the family lived across from an electronics shop, and Assange learned to write as well as crack computer programs. In 1987 he got a modem for his computer and began exploring the computer networks that were in place before websites. Soon, Assange took on the nickname Mendax (from *splendide mendax,* a phrase from Horace meaning "nobly untruthful") and became known as a skillful programmer and hacker. Eventually, he and two other hackers formed a group called the International Subversives. Together they broke into computer systems in Europe and North America, intending, they claimed, to look around but not to cause damage.

The International Subversives continued intruding into secure networks until 1991, when Australian federal police finally tracked down and arrested Assange. He was charged with 31 counts of hacking and related crimes. Assange eventually pleaded guilty to 25 of the charges and paid a fine.

For the next decade, Assange struggled over the custody of his son, traveled, worked various jobs, and attended university classes for periods at a time. He also wrote an essay titled "Conspiracy as Governance" outlining his theory that since illegitimate governments are necessarily secretive, revealing state secrets is a tactic for undermining illegitimate governments. These ideas eventually led Assange to develop the WikiLeaks website, which purports to leak classified information in order to enact political change. Describing itself as "the uncensorable Wikipedia for untraceable mass document leaking and analysis," WikiLeaks posted its first document in December 2006. Since then, Assange, his team, and anyone with access to the website have posted documents from all over the world, including information pertaining to the Kenyan presidential election in 2007; the U.S. detention center at Guantánamo Bay, Cuba; the U.S. rules of engagement for the Iraq War; and the North Atlantic Treaty Organization's war plans for Afghanistan. Today, the primary server for WikiLeaks is located in Sweden, where Internet anonymity is protected by law; however, volunteers and equipment are stationed around the world in order to distribute risk and prevent attacks on the system.

Assange came into the spotlight in a new way in April 2010, when WikiLeaks garnered worldwide attention for posting a video of a U.S. Apache helicopter attacking a dozen people in Baghdad, Iraq, including what turned out to be civilians, reporters, and children. When WikiLeaks posted U.S. military reports and diplomatic cables in July and November 2010, respectively, Assange became an even more controversial figure. Praised by some as a hero of government transparency, Assange has also been condemned by some Americans as a saboteur of U.S. interests. Often highly secretive and hardly ever stationary, Assange added to the controversy by avoiding the press and the Swedish authorities, who wanted him for questioning on sexual assault charges, in the days after the U.S. diplomatic cables were released. Finally appearing in a British court on December 7, Assange denied the allegations against him, claiming that the charges were fabricated in order to discredit WikiLeaks.

Since 2010, Assange has been both vilified and lionized for his efforts to bring clandestine, controversial issues and incidents to light. The U.S. government seriously considered indicting him in absentia for espionage, but so far no charges have been brought against him. Assange's actions clearly influenced Edward Snowden, a U.S. defense contractor employee who in 2013 leaked thousands of top-secret documents and computer data detailing the extent to which U.S. national security and intelligence agencies have snooped on U.S. citizens as well as citizens of other nations, including foreign leaders. Some have lauded Assange's work, including Daniel Ellsberg, who leaked the Pentagon Papers to the American press in the early 1970s. Assange has also garnered a number of prestigious awards for his work. In 2012, he sought and received asylum from the Ecuadorian government. Assange was taken into the Ecuadorian embassy in Great Britain in June 2012, where he has continued to live since that time. Should he attempt to leave the embassy compound, he will be subject to arrest and extradition to Sweden to answer to sexual offense charges. After that, he may be subject to extradition to the United States to face charges of computer hacking and espionage.

SPENCER C. TUCKER

See also

Afghanistan War; Guantánamo Bay Detainment Camp; Snowden, Edward Joseph

References

Khatchadourian, Raffi. "No Secrets: Julian Assange's mission for total transparency." *New Yorker*, June 7, 2010.

Lagan, Bernard. "International Man of Mystery." *Sydney Morning Herald*, April 10, 2010.

"Profile: Julian Assange, the Man behind Wikileaks." *Sunday Times*, April 11, 2010.

Atef, Muhammad (1944–2001)

Head of the terrorist organization Al Qaeda's military operations during the planning and implementation of the September 11, 2001, terror attacks on the United States. At that time Atef was number three in the Al Qaeda hierarchy, behind Osama bin Laden and Ayman al-Zawahiri. Atef made numerous decisions about the planned attack of September 11 from the beginning, assisting Khalid Sheikh Mohammed in the final stages of the plot.

Muhammad Atef was born in 1944 in Menoufya, Egypt, in the Nile Delta, about 35 miles north of Cairo. His birth name was Sobhi Abu Sitta. After graduating from high school, he served his required two years of military service in the Egyptian Army. Reports that Atef was a policeman in Egypt have been denied by the Egyptian government, but nearly all sources state that he was.

Atef became an Islamist extremist early in his career, and in the late 1970s he joined an Egyptian terrorist organization, the Egyptian Islamic Jihad. Evidently a low-ranking member, he did not meet with its leader, Ayman al-Zawahiri, while both were in Egypt. Despite Atef's involvement in this group, he escaped arrest after the crackdown on extremists that followed the assassination of Egyptian president Anwar Sadat in 1981.

In 1983, Atef left Egypt for Afghanistan to fight with the mujahideen (holy warriors, freedom fighters) against the Soviet forces. There he first met Zawahiri, who then introduced him to bin Laden. Atef and bin Laden became close friends. Atef also became acquainted with Abdullah Azzam and admired him greatly, but in the subsequent battle between Azzam and Zawahiri for bin Laden's support, Atef supported Zawahiri. In 1999 Egyptian authorities sentenced Atef to a seven-year prison term in absentia for his membership in the Egyptian Islamic Jihad, but he never returned to Egypt.

Atef's close personal relationship with bin Laden made him an important member of Al Qaeda. When bin Laden founded Al Qaeda, Atef was a charter member. Ubaidah al-Banshiri was Al Qaeda's head of military operations, and Atef assisted him. Atef was active in organizing Somali resistance to the American military presence in 1992, but some evidence suggests that his stay there was not entirely successful. He also served as bin Laden's chief of personal security. Banshiri's death in a boating accident in Africa allowed Atef to replace him in 1996. From then until his death in 2001, Atef was in charge of military operations for Al Qaeda. All military operation came under his oversight, but he always remained subordinate to bin Laden, even after bin Laden's eldest son married one of Atef's daughters in January 2001.

Atef was aware of the September 11 plot from its beginning. Khalid Sheikh Mohammed had apparently outlined the plan to bin Laden and Atef as early as 1996. Bin Laden finally agreed on the basics of the plot in 1998, and it was Atef's job to search Al Qaeda's training camps for suitable candidates for a martyrdom mission that required operatives to live unnoticed in America. Once the members of the Hamburg Cell were picked and recruited by bin Laden, Atef explained to Muhammad Atta, Ramzi Muhammad Abdallah ibn al-Shibh, Ziyad al-Jarrah, and Marwan al-Shehhi the outlines of the plot.

Al Qaeda avoided having its leaders at a single site except for particularly special occasions, a policy prompted by fears of American assassination of Al Qaeda's leaders. Bin Laden announced that in case of his death or capture, Atef would succeed him as head of Al Qaeda. Once the United States began military operations against the Taliban and Al Qaeda in Afghanistan in October 2001, it became even more important for Al Qaeda's leaders to be at separate locations. On November 18, 2001, Atef was at a gathering in Kabul when a U.S. Predator unmanned aerial vehicle fired Hellfire missiles, killing him and those with him—something for which the United States had been offering a $5 million reward. The loss of Atef was a blow to Al Qaeda, but he was soon replaced as military commander by Abu Zubaydah.

STEPHEN E. ATKINS

See also

Al Qaeda; Atta, Muhammad; Bin Laden, Osama; Hamburg Cell; Jarrah, Ziyad al-; September 11 Attacks; Shehhi, Marwan Yousef Muhammad Rashid Lekrab al-; Zawahiri, Ayman al-

References

Bergen, Peter L. *The Osama bin Laden I Know: An Oral History of Al Qaeda's Leader.* New York: Free Press, 2006.

Dawoud, Khaled. "Mohammed Atef: Egyptian Militant Who Rose to the Top of the al-Qaida Hierarchy." *The Guardian,* November 19, 2001, 1.

Athens, Greece, Attack on U.S. Embassy (January 12, 2007)

On January 12, 2007, members of the Epanastatikos Agonas (Revolutionary Struggle, EA) fired a small antitank rocket at the heavily fortified U.S. embassy in Athens. The attack, which occurred at 5:58 a.m., shattered windows but caused no injuries. Dozens of police cars immediately surrounded the building and cordoned off all roads in the area, including a major boulevard in front of the mission.

Greek officials doubted that the attack was the work of foreign or Islamic terrorists and instead pinned the likely responsibility on extreme left-wing radicals seeking to hit a highly iconic target: the huge American seal on the front of the embassy. The round narrowly missed the symbol, punching through a window a few feet above and landing in a bathroom on the building's third story.

Shortly after the attack, a call was made to Greek authorities claiming credit for the strike in the name of the EA. According to a subsequent statement sent to the weekly *Pontiki,* the group said that the action had been carried out to protest U.S. policy in Iraq and the Middle East. In response, Panayiotis Stathis, a spokesman for the Greek Public Order Ministry, said that the attack was a violent act aimed to provoke public opinion and disturb the government's relations with Washington.

Terrorism expert Maria Bossis went further, asserting that the attack was a deliberate attempt by the EA to assert itself as the "boss" among the plethora of left-wing terrorist entities that had emerged following the demise of the Epanastatiki Organosi 17 Noemvri (Revolutionary Organization 17 November) in 2003.

The EA first surfaced in 2003 with a minor bombing outside an Athens courthouse. The group made headlines again with a triple bombing on a police station, again in the capital, that took place just three months before the city hosted the 2004 Olympic Games. Subsequent actions included an attempted assassination of the minister of culture (and former minister of public order) Giorgos Voulgarakis on May 30, 2006 (he was not injured); the bombing of the U.S. embassy in 2007; and a shooting attack on police guarding the Ministry of Culture building in Athens on January 5, 2009 (critically wounding one). The weapon used in the second incident was linked to two previous acts of violence against law enforcement, one on April 30, 2007, that targeted another police station and one on December 23, 2008, on a bus transporting members of the riot squad. The European Union added the EA to its list of designated terrorist organizations. Two years later, the United States formally designated the group as a foreign terrorist organization.

DONNA BASSETT

See also

Global War on Terror

Reference

Fisher, Ian Anthee Carassava, "U.S. Embassy in Athens Is Attacked." *New York Times,* January 12, 2007.

Atta, Muhammad (1968–2001)

Commander of the Al Qaeda terrorist team that hijacked four American jetliners that were then used to attack the United States on September 11, 2001. Muhammad al-Amir Awad al-Sayyid Atta was born on September 1, 1968, in the village of Kafr el-Sheikh in the Egyptian Delta and had a strict family upbringing. His father was a middle-class lawyer with ties to the fundamentalist Muslim Brotherhood. Atta's family moved to the Abdin District of Cairo in 1978 when Atta was 10. His father, who had a dominating personality, insisted that his children study, not play; thus, Atta's family life allowed him few friends.

After attending high school, Atta enrolled in Cairo University in 1986. At his graduation in 1990, his grades were not good enough to admit him to graduate school. On the recommendation of his father, he planned to study urban planning in Germany. In the meantime, he worked for a Cairo engineering firm.

Atta traveled to Hamburg, Germany, in July 1992 to begin studies there. During his courses he interacted very little with fellow students, earning a reputation as a loner. His classmates also noted his strong religious orientation. He traveled to Turkey and Syria in 1994 to study old Muslim quarters. After receiving a German grant, Atta and two fellow students visited Egypt to study the old section of Cairo, called the Old City. Up to this point in his life, Atta appeared to be an academic preparing for a career as a teacher at a university.

In 1995, however, Atta became active in Muslim extremist politics. After a pilgrimage to Mecca, he initiated contact with Al Qaeda recruiters. Atta was just the type of individual sought by Al Qaeda: intelligent and dedicated.

After returning to Hamburg to continue his studies, Atta attended the al-Quds Mosque, where his final recruitment to radical Islam took place. There Atta met radical clerics who steered him toward an Al Qaeda recruiter. Muhammad Haydar Zammar, a Syrian recruiter for Al Qaeda, convinced Atta to join that organization. Several of his friends, Ramzi Muhammad Abdallah ibn al-Shibh, Marwan al-Shehhi, and Ziyad al-Jarrah, also joined Al Qaeda at this time. Atta became the leader of the so-called Hamburg Cell of radical Islamists.

In 1998 Atta left for Kandahar, Afghanistan, to receive military and terrorist training at the Al Qaeda training camp at Khaldan. He so distinguished himself during the training that Al Qaeda leaders decided to recruit him for a future suicide mission. Atta ranked high in all the attributes of an Al Qaeda operative—intelligence, religious devotion, patience,

and willingness to sacrifice. Atta, Jarrah, and Shehhi met and talked with Osama bin Laden in Kandahar. Bin Laden asked them to pledge loyalty to him and accept a suicide mission. They agreed, and Muhammad Atef, Al Qaeda's military chief, briefed them on the general outlines of the September 11 operation. Then Atta and the others returned to Germany to finish their academic training.

Atta was a complex individual, deeply affected psychologically. He held the typical conservative Muslim view that relations with the opposite sex were not permitted outside of marriage. Atta also held strong anti-American views, disturbed as he was by the Americanization of Egyptian society.

After Atta finished his degree in 1999, Al Qaeda's leaders assigned him the martyrdom mission in the United States, a mission planned by Khalid Sheikh Mohammed. Atta arrived in the United States on June 2, 2000. His orders placed him in charge of a large cell, but he, Jarrah, and Shehhi were the only members of it who knew the details of his mission. Several times Atta flew back and forth between the United States and Germany and Spain to coordinate the mission. Members of his cell arrived in the United States at various times. Atta and key members of the cell received orders to take pilot lessons to fly large commercial aircraft.

Most of Atta's time was spent in pilot lessons in Florida. Before he could qualify for training on large commercial aircraft, Atta had to learn to fly small planes. Most of his flying instruction took place at Huffman Aviation in Sarasota, Florida. Next, he began to use simulators and manuals to train himself to fly the larger aircraft.

Atta gathered most of the members of his cell together in Florida for the first time in early June 2001. He organized the cell into four teams, each of which included a trained pilot. Throughout the summer of 2001, each team rode as passengers on test flights in which they studied the efficiency of airline security and the best times to hijack an aircraft. They discovered that airline security was weakest at Boston's Logan International Airport and decided that the best day for hijacking would be a Tuesday. They also decided that first-class seats would give them better access to cockpits. Although the teams tried to remain inconspicuous, the film actor James Woods reported suspicious behavior by one of the teams on a flight. He reported his suspicions to the pilot and a flight attendant, who passed this on to the Federal Aviation Administration, but nothing came of his report.

Atta selected two airlines—American Airlines and United Airlines—that flew Boeing 757s and 767s, aircraft

Two men, identified as hijackers Muhammad Atta, right, and Abdulaziz Alomari, center, pass through airport security in this September 11, 2001 photo from the surveillance tape at Portland International Jetport, Maine. (AP Photo)

that hold the most aviation fuel because they are used for long flights. These aircraft were also equipped with up-to-date avionics, making them easier to fly.

Atta called for a leadership meeting in Las Vegas, Nevada, in late June 2001. Atta, Ziyad Jarrah, Hani Hanjour, and Nawaf al-Hazmi then completed plans for the September 11 operation. Atta and Jarrah used a local Cyberzone Internet Café to send e-mails to Al Qaeda leaders abroad.

Atta then traveled to Spain via Zurich, Switzerland, to update his handlers on his final plans and receive last-minute instructions. He met with Al Qaeda representatives in the resort town of Salou on July 8, 2001, receiving his final authorization for the September 11 mission. Atta was given final authority to determine the targets and date of the operation. Several times bin Laden had attempted to push the plan forward, but Atta had refused to carry out the mission before he was ready and was backed by Khalid Sheikh

Mohammed in this decision. Atta flew back to the United States and, despite an expired visa, had no trouble getting into the country.

Atta issued final instructions about the mission on the night of September 10, 2001. One-way tickets for flights on September 11 had been bought with credit cards in late August. Atta had made arrangements to have the cell's excess funds transferred back to Al Qaeda on September 4. He traveled to Portland, Maine, with Abd al-Aziz al-Umari, and they stayed in South Portland. They caught a 5:45 a.m. flight out of Portland International Airport, but Atta's luggage arrived too late to make American Airlines Flight 11 from Logan International Airport. At 7:45 a.m., Atta and Umari boarded American Airlines Flight 11. Soon afterward, Atta phoned Marwan al-Shehhi, who was aboard United Airlines Flight 175, also at Logan International Airport, to make sure everything was on schedule.

Atta commanded the first team. Approximately 15 minutes after takeoff his team, using box cutters as weapons, seized control of the aircraft. Atta redirected the aircraft toward New York City and the World Trade Center complex, where it crashed into the North Tower of the World Trade Center at about 8:45 a.m. Members of the other teams carried out their attacks successfully except for the one flight lost in Pennsylvania, where the passengers—informed of what had happened with the other three hijacked airplanes—fought the hijackers. Atta, along with the plane's entire crew and all passengers, died instantly when the airliner slammed into the North Tower of the World Trade Center. The North Tower collapsed less than two hours later.

STEPHEN E. ATKINS

See also

Bin Laden, Osama; Hamburg Cell; Jarrah, Ziyad al-; Mohammed, Khalid Sheikh; September 11 Attacks; Shehhi, Marwan Yousef Muhammed Rashid Lekrab al-; Shibh, Ramzi Muhammad Abdallah ibn al-

References

Fouda, Yosri, and Nick Fielding. *Masterminds of Terror: The Truth behind the Most Devastating Terrorist Attack the World Has Ever Seen.* New York: Arcade, 2003.

McDermott, Terry. *Perfect Soldiers: The 9/11 Hijackers; Who They Were, Why They Did It.* New York: HarperCollins, 2005.

Miller, John, Michael Stone, and Chris Mitchell. *The Cell: Inside the 9/11 Plot, and Why the FBI and CIA Failed to Stop It.* New York: Hyperion, 2002.

Sageman, Marc. *Understanding Terror Networks.* Philadelphia: University of Pennsylvania Press, 2004.

AVALANCHE, **Operation (December 2–26, 2003)**

A joint U.S.-Afghan offensive undertaken in December 2003 and the largest coalition military operation in Afghanistan since the fall of the Taliban regime in late 2001. The campaign was designed to counter the growing threat by Taliban and Al Qaeda fighters to Afghan reconstruction efforts and end insurgent attacks on humanitarian and aid workers in the eastern and southern provinces of Afghanistan. Operation AVALANCHE was also designed to disrupt the cycle in which the Taliban and Al Qaeda insurgents used the winter months to regroup and reequip in order to launch offenses in the spring. In addition to identifying and destroying rebel bases, coalition forces sought to interdict supply and transport lines between Afghanistan and Pakistan. Finally, the

Afghans were preparing for a broad-based political convention, known as a *loya jirga,* and there were concerns that the Taliban and Al Qaeda would launch strikes to disrupt the meeting.

Operation AVALANCHE involved about 2,000 U.S. troops and an equal number of Afghan National Army soldiers. On December 2, ground forces began moving into areas around Khost, supported by artillery units at forward operations base Salerno. The base received incoming rocket fire during the operation, but the eight 107-mm rockets failed to cause significant damage or casualties. On December 3, 500 airborne troops of the U.S. 501st Parachute Infantry Regiment were deployed outside of Khost near the border with Pakistan. There they conducted searches and interdiction operations. A second major assault was undertaken on a Taliban complex in Paktia on December 4. Following an aerial bombardment, U.S. forces captured a weapons cache, including small arms, mortars, howitzers, and ammunition, but they failed to apprehend Mullah Jalani, a local Taliban leader. Subsequent smaller operations throughout the region resulted in minor skirmishes and the capture of additional weapons and equipment.

During the operation, coalition forces killed 10 Taliban fighters and captured approximately 100 suspected insurgents. Coalition forces also uncovered dozens of weapons caches and seized small arms, ammunition, mines, rocket-propelled grenades, howitzers, and explosive-making materials. Two Afghan National Army soldiers were killed during AVALANCHE, but no U.S. troops died. U.S. officials reported that their Afghan allies, part of the then 7,500-man Afghan National Army, exceeded expectations during the operation. The *loya jirga* began its deliberations on December 14, without incident.

Operation AVALANCHE was notable for the attention focused on civilian casualties caused by the coalition. For instance, during the bombing of Paktia, 6 Afghan children and 2 adults perished. The civilian casualties led to regional protests against coalition forces and warnings by Afghan officials that such losses undermined popular support for the government and its coalition allies. The following day, 9 children were killed during a mission to capture the Taliban leader Mullah Wazir in Ghazni. The operation involved air units and about 100 ground forces. It failed to apprehend the leader and led to further condemnation because of the loss of civilians, including a call by United Nations secretary-general Kofi Annan for a full investigation of the incident. The operation was essentially over by December 26.

TOM LANSFORD

See also
Afghanistan; Afghanistan War; Al Qaeda; Annan, Kofi; North Atlantic Treaty Organization; Taliban

References
Feickert, Andrew. *U.S. and Coalition Military Operations in Afghanistan: Issues for Congress.* Washington, DC: Congressional Research Service, 2006.
Guistozzi, Antonio. *Koran, Kalashnikov and Laptop: The Neo-Taliban Insurgency in Afghanistan.* New York: Columbia University Press, 2008.
Jones, Seth G. *Counterinsurgency in Afghanistan: RAND Counterinsurgency Study No. 4.* Santa Monica, CA: RAND Corporation, 2008.

"Axis of Evil"

The term "axis of evil" was coined by President George W. Bush in his State of the Union address on January 29, 2002, to describe regimes that in his words sponsor terrorism. He identified Iran, Iraq, and North Korea as threatening the security of the United States. Conceived by presidential speechwriter David Frum, the phrase "axis of evil" was originally intended to justify the invasion of Iraq but came to be used by political neoconservatives to criticize Secretary of State Colin Powell's position on the Bush Doctrine. The doctrine clarified U.S. policy to allow for a preemptive war against terrorists, unilateral military action, and U.S. measures to remain the sole military superpower in the world.

The origin of the phrase "axis of evil" can be traced to December 2001, when head speechwriter Mike Gerson tasked David Frum to articulate the case for dislodging the government of Saddam Hussein in a few sentences, which were to be included in the 2002 State of the Union address. Frum originally intended to use the phrase "axis of hatred" but changed it to "axis of evil" to match the theological tone adopted by President Bush after September 11, 2001. Frum expected his speech to be edited, but "axis of evil" was retained, and the text of the speech was read nearly verbatim by President Bush, a controversial move that was seen in some quarters to be dangerously undiplomatic.

Usage of the phrase "axis of evil" was ultimately meant to suggest links between terrorists and nations that, according to neoconservatives, threatened the United States and its allies. Criteria for inclusion in the "axis of evil" were that the included countries be "rogue states" or nations that allegedly supported terrorist groups that sought chemical, biological, and/or nuclear weapons with which to attack the United States.

Keith A. Leitich

See also
Bush, George Walker; Neoconservatism; September 11 Attacks

Reference
Cha, Victor D. "Korea's Place in the Axis." *Foreign Affairs* 81(3) (May–June 2002): 79–92.

Aziz, Tariq (1936–2015)

Iraqi foreign minister (1983–1991) and deputy prime minister (1979–2003). Tariq Aziz was born on April 1, 1936, into a Chaldean Catholic family in Tell Kaif, Iraq. Originally named Michael Yuhanna, Aziz was the only Christian in a position of power during Saddam Hussein's 34-year dictatorship. While in college Yuhanna changed his name to Tariq Aziz, which means "glorious past," in order to avoid hostility regarding his religious heritage.

In 1957, Aziz joined the Baath Party and worked with Saddam Hussein to generate propaganda against the pro-Western Iraqi monarchy. After receiving his bachelor's degree in English literature in 1958 from the Baghdad College of Fine Arts, Aziz continued to produce Baath Party propaganda in addition to working as a journalist. From 1963 to 1966 he was both editor in chief of the Baath Party's newspaper, *al-Thawra* (The Revolution), and director of the Arab Baath Socialist Party's press office in Damascus, Syria. When the British-imposed Hashimite monarchy came to an end in 1958, the Baath Party continued to seek power in Iraq. After an unsuccessful coup in 1963, the party finally gained power in 1968.

From 1974 to 1977, Aziz served as a member of the Regional Command, the Baath Party's highest governing unit. In 1979, Iraqi dictator Saddam Hussein named him deputy prime minister. Aziz's primary role was to explain and justify Iraq's policies to global audiences. With his effective communication skills, he became known around the world for his eloquent diplomatic discourses.

In 1980, Aziz was wounded in an assassination attempt initiated by the Iranian-backed Shiite fundamentalist group al-Da'wah Islamiyyah (the Islamic Call). Members of the group threw a grenade at him in downtown Baghdad, killing several Iraqis in the process. The attack was one of several that Hussein blamed on the Iranian government, which was part of his justification for his September 1980 invasion of Iran that produced the Iran-Iraq War (1980–1988).

In 1984, just a year after being named foreign minister, Aziz secured the restoration of diplomatic relations with the United States after a 17-year interruption. The United States had chosen to support Iraq as a buffer to Iran's Islamic fundamentalist extremism.

When Iraq invaded Kuwait in August 1990, Aziz ardently supported the military action. He stated that the invasion was justified because of Kuwait's cheating on oil production quotas, which was driving down the price of oil, and because of Kuwait's alleged slant-drilling into Iraqi oil fields. During the subsequent Persian Gulf War (1991), Aziz enjoyed a substantial international profile and was seen by the media as the chief Iraqi spokesperson. After the war he took on more responsibility as deputy prime minister, which forced him to relinquish the foreign ministry portfolio. Nevertheless, he retained a high profile in the government. Aziz now monitored the Iraqi media. In this position he also conducted Iraq's negotiations with United Nations (UN) weapons inspectors.

In his public remarks, Aziz blamed the United States, rather than the UN, for the economic sanctions that followed the Persian Gulf War, believing that they were implemented as a result of U.S. domestic policies. In 1997 he supported the expulsion of U.S. citizens from Iraq who were working for the UN Special Commission.

In February 2003 as tensions over Iraq's alleged illegal weapons programs were about to boil over into war, Aziz spoke with Pope John Paul II about the Iraqi government's desire to cooperate with the international community, notably on disarmament. In response, the pope insisted that Iraq respect and give concrete commitments to abide by UN Security Council resolutions. The Iraqis did not heed the advice. On March 19, 2003, at the beginning of the Anglo-American–led invasion of Iraq, there were reports that Aziz had been killed. They were proven false when Aziz later held a press conference. He surrendered to coalition forces on April 24, 2003.

Aziz, who was charged with crimes against humanity in connection with the murder of hundreds of Kurds in 1982, also testified as a defense witness before the Iraq Special Tribunal set up by the Iraqi Interim Government in May 2006. He testified that the crackdown against the Kurds had been fully justified because of attacks against him and others in the regime. He also reiterated his loyalty to his old comrade Saddam Hussein.

On March 11, 2009, Aziz was sentenced to 15 years in prison for his role in the 1992 summary executions of 42 merchants accused of fixing food prices. Then on October 26, 2010, the Iraqi High Tribunal sentenced him to death. This sentence sparked condemnation from a number of Iraqis as well as the Vatican, the Russian government, the UN, the European Union, and Amnesty International.

Assigned to death row, Aziz reportedly suffered from depression and ill health and had requested a speedy execution to end his "misery." He died of natural causes in al-Hussein Hospital in the city of Nasiriyah on June 5, 2015.

CHARLENE T. OVERTURF

See also

Baath Party; Baker, James Addison, III; Hussein, Saddam; Iraq, History of, 1990–Present; IRAQI FREEDOM, Operation; Kurds

References

Farouk-Sluglett, Marion, and Peter Sluglett. *Iraq since 1958: From Revolution to Dictatorship.* London: I. B. Tauris, 2001.

MacKey, Sandra. *The Reckoning: Iraq and the Legacy of Saddam Hussein.* New York: Norton, 2002.

B

Baath Party

Political party that currently dominates Syria and was the leading party in Iraq from 1968 to the end of Saddam Hussein's regime in 2003. The Baath Party (IIizb al-Baath al-Arabi al-Ishtiraki) also had branches in Lebanon, Jordan, the Sudan, Yemen, Mauritania, and Bahrain and enjoys support from some Palestinians. The Arabic word *baath* means "renaissance" or "resurrection." The party's fundamental principles have been Arab unity and freedom from imperialist control for all Arab states, personal freedom for Arab citizens, and support for Arab culture. The party also supported Arab socialist policies intended to eliminate feudalism but not private property. The Arab Socialist Baath Party of Syria explains its ideology as "national (Pan-Arab), socialist, popular and revolutionary," and its founding charter and constitution identifies its commitment to the "Arab Nation, the Arab homeland, the Arab citizen, the Arab people's authority over their own land and the freedom of the Arab people."

The Arab Baath Party, as it was originally called, grew out of an ideological and political movement in Syria, founded in 1940 in Damascus with the goal of revitalizing the Arab nation and society. The principal founders of the Baath movement and party were Syrian intellectuals Michel Aflaq, a Greek Orthodox Christian; Salah al-Din al-Bitar, a Sunni Muslim who studied at the Sorbonne in the early 1930s; and Zaki al-Arsuzi. The Arab Baath Party accepted Arabs of all religious backgrounds and ethnic groups.

The first Arab Baath Party Congress was held on April 4–6, 1947. Abd al-Rahman al-Damin and Abd al-Khaliq al-Khudayri attended that congress and on their return to Iraq founded a branch of the party there. This evolved into a small group of about 50 individuals, mainly friends and associates of Fuad al-Rikabi, who took control of the group in 1951. The Baathists in Iraq joined with other organizations that were in opposition to the monarchy. Baathism spread more slowly in Iraq than in Syria, with its candidates losing out to Communist Party candidates in many elections in the 1960s.

Meanwhile in Syria, in 1954 Aflaq and Bitar joined forces with Akram al-Hawrani, a populist leader who headed the Socialist Party. They adopted the name Arab Socialist Baath Party. The Baath Party found its greatest strength in Syria and Iraq, although it had branches all over the Arab world.

The Baath Party came to power first in Iraq and then in Syria in coups d'état in 1963. The coup in Iraq did not last out the year, however, during which time 10,000 leftists, Marxists, and communists were killed, 5,000 of these from the Iraqi Communist Party. Three years later, the Syrian and Iraqi parties split. Each was subsequently plagued by factionalism. Some disputes occurred as a result of Syria's union with Egypt in the United Arab Republic; others concerned a possible union of Syria and Iraq or ties with the Soviet Union and local communist parties as well as the Syrian Socialist Nationalist Party in Syria.

Rivalries between different factions of the Syrian Baath Party led to an interparty coup in 1966 followed by another one four years later that brought General Hafiz al-Assad to power. He headed a pragmatic faction that gained control of the military in contrast to a "progressive" faction that had pushed a more pervasive socialism and nationalizations and a harder line regionally. Asad remained in office until his death in 2000. His son, Bashar al-Assad, assumed leadership of the Syrian Baath Party and remains the president of Syria, although his leadership of the party and of Syria has been sorely tested by the ongoing Syrian Civil War, which began in 2011.

Saddam Hussein joined the Iraqi Baath Party at the age of 21 in 1956 and steadily rose in the party's ranks, first as a consequence of the Iraqi Revolution of 1958 and then as an assassin in the U.S.-backed plot to do away with President Abd al-Karim Qasim. Later after the Baath Party had regained power in a 1968 coup, Hussein served as vice chairman of the Revolutionary Command Council and later as president and secretary-general of the Baath Party.

The Baath parties of Iraq and Syria operated in associations in schools, communities, and the army and had workers' and women's associations, such as the General Association of Iraqi Women (al-Ittihad al-amm li-nisa al-Iraq). While the party ostensibly sought to expand membership to comprise a "mass party," in fact membership was tightly controlled. Nonetheless, party members wielded considerable power. Average Syrians and Iraqis could hardly conclude any official business without the intercession of a party member. In the military and in academia, it was nearly impossible to advance or be promoted without being a party member. In Iraq, the party claimed 1.5 million members, or about 10 percent of the country's population, in the late 1980s; however, only about 30,000 were bona fide party cadres. In Syria, Assad opened up membership so that by 1987 it was at about 50,000 people, and there were also some 200,000 probationary party members.

The Baath parties of both countries did not tolerate political challenges of any other group or party. They strongly opposed the Islamist movements that arose in each nation. Despite the dictatorial nature of the Iraqi governments in this period, one notable accomplishment, in part facilitated through the party, was the serious effort to modernize the economy and society by promoting literacy, education, and gender equality. As a result, by the 1970s Iraq had a fairly high level of education. Hussein's disastrous war with Iran and then his invasion of Kuwait, which prompted war with the United States and a coalition of states, had a profoundly negative impact on the country and its economy.

The U.S.-led invasion of Iraq in March 2003 and the overthrow of Saddam Hussein led to an immediate ban of the Baath Party, the so-called de-Baathification, under U.S. and coalition occupation forces. Iraqis also attacked Baath Party offices all over the country. Some critics of the U.S. occupation policies in Iraq claim that U.S. administrator L. Paul Bremer's decision, approved by Washington, to bar all Baathists from government posts hopelessly hamstrung the government and fueled the Iraqi insurgency, which included some bitter and disenfranchised Baathists. Iraqi prime minister Nuri al-Maliki continued enforcing the ban on the Baath Party and extended rehiring only to those who were able to prove that they were forced to join the party. A related controversy emerged over the transfer of the Baath Party records to the Hoover Institution at Stanford University via an agreement with the Iraq Memory Foundation and with permission of Maliki. The seizure of these documents (which could reveal the precise status of connections with the party) has been protested by, among others, the director of the Iraq National Library and Archive and the acting Iraqi minister of culture.

In Syria, the Baath Party has had a great impact. Changes in landholding and commercial policies in the 1960s displaced earlier elites, but suppression of the Sunni merchants and Islamists, even after the Hama massacre, led to an Islamist revival that challenged Baath Party primacy. Although President Assad promised democratic reforms in 2005, virtually no change occurred. Since the civil war began in 2011, survival of Assad's regime has trumped any efforts to reform Syria's political or economic systems.

In Lebanon, Bahrain, and other countries, the Baath Party retains a small presence. In Lebanon it held two seats in parliament in the 1990s, and the Iraqi branch also had a link in a group within the Palestinian Fatah organization. The Sudanese Baath Party operates underground as part of the opposition to the Sudanese regime and publishes a journal, *al-Hadaf*.

STEFAN BROOKS AND SHERIFA ZUHUR

See also

Assad, Bashar al-; Bremer, Lewis Paul; Hussein, Saddam; Iraq, History of, 1990–Present; Syria; Syrian Civil War

References

Batatu, Hanna. *Old Social Classes and New Revolutionary Movements of Iraq.* London: Al-Saqi Books, 2000.

Committee against Repression and for Democratic Rights in Iraq, ed. *Saddam's Iraq: Revolution or Reaction?* London: Zed Books, 1986.

Devlin, John F. *The Ba'th Party: A History from Its Origins to 1966.* Stanford, CA: Hoover Institution Press, 1976.

Heydemann, Steven. *Authoritarianism in Syria: Institutions and Social Conflict, 1948–1970.* Ithaca, NY: Cornell University Press, 1999.
Hinnebusch, Raymond. *Syria: Revolution from Above.* Florence, NY: Routledge, 2001.
Tripp, Charles. *A History of Iraq.* Cambridge: Cambridge University Press, 2007.

Bacevich, Andrew John (1947–)

Retired U.S. Army officer and scholar who has been sharply critical in op-ed articles and books of U.S. foreign and military policies since the end of the Cold War. Born on July 5, 1947, in Normal, Illinois, Andrew John Bacevich graduated from the U.S. Military Academy, West Point, in 1969. Commissioned in the army, he was deployed in Vietnam from July 1970 until July 1971. Thereafter, he held a number of staff and command positions in both the United States and Western Europe. Bacevich was deployed to Iraq during the 1991 Persian Gulf War. The following year, he retired from the service at the rank of colonel. Bacevich earned both an MA and a PhD in U.S. diplomatic history and international relations from Princeton University and taught at West Point, Johns Hopkins University, and Boston University.

From 1998 until 2005, Bacevich was director of the Center for International Relations at Boston University; he is currently the George McGovern Fellow at Columbia University's School of International and Public Affairs. Since 2004, Bacevich has published several books examining U.S. military and foreign policy; he has been invariably critical of both and has argued that the myriad problems associated with them transcend politics and are in fact fueled by bipartisan misperceptions and misunderstandings about diplomacy, the use of force, and war itself.

Bacevich was an outspoken critic of the George W. Bush's post-9/11 advocacy of preventative/preemptory war (the so-called Bush Doctrine) and repeatedly excoriated the administration for what he considered its wrongheaded decision to invade Iraq in 2003. He was even more critical of the subsequent occupation of the country; indeed, Bacevich termed the Iraq War a "catastrophic failure." In May 2007 his son Andrew, a first lieutenant in the U.S. Army, was killed by an improvised explosive device in Iraq.

Bacevich traces the militarization of American foreign policy as far back as the Woodrow Wilson administration (1913–1921) and blames both Republican and Democratic administrations during the last century for a number of needless military interventions that did not serve the best interests of the United States. In his 2005 *The New American Militarism,* Bacevich argues that since the end of the Cold War in 1991, American policy makers have come to be overly reliant on military power because both they and the American public in general "overestimate" the utility of military force in international affairs. Bacevich went on to elaborate that U.S. popular culture romanticizes war, leading many Americans to develop unrealistic conceptions about war and combat.

Although Bacevich supported Barack Obama's 2008 presidential bid, he has since become sharply critical of President Obama's war policies. Indeed, Bacevich has charged that Obama pursued a troop surge in Afghanistan in 2010 out of narrow political interests instead of cultivating a greater understanding of the conflict in Afghanistan, which would have demonstrated that a continuation of the war was not in the country's best interest. More recently, Bacevich has stated his strong doubts that the U.S. bombing campaign against the Islamic State in Iraq and Syria (ISIS), which began in August 2014, will result in a more peaceful or stable Middle East.

PAUL G. PIERPAOLI JR.

See also

Bush, George Walker; Bush Doctrine; Improvised Explosive Devices; IRAQI FREEDOM, Operation; Islamic State in Iraq and Syria; Obama, Barack Hussein, II; Persian Gulf War

References

Bacevich, Andrew J. "Even If We Defeat the Islamic State, We'll Still Lose the Bigger War." *Washington Post,* October 3, 2014, http://www.washingtonpost.com/opinions/even-if-we-defeat-the-islamic-state-well-still-lose-the-bigger-war/2014/10/03/e8c0585e-4353-11e4-b47c-f5889e061e5f_story.html.
Bacevich, Andrew J. *The New American Militarism: How Americans Are Seduced by War.* New York: Oxford University Press, 2005.
Bacevich, Andrew J. *Washington Rules: America's Path to Permanent War.* New York: Macmillan, 2010.

Badr Organization

Paramilitary wing of the Supreme Islamic Iraqi Council (SIIC), also referred to as the Supreme Islamic Council in Iraq, that was known for decades as the Supreme Council for the Islamic Revolution in Iraq (SCIRI), a Shia political party founded in Tehran, Iran, in November 1982 by Iraqi exiles led by Ayatollah Muhammad Baqir al-Hakim. The Badr Organization (Faylaq Badr), which is also commonly referred to as the Badr Corps, the Badr Brigade(s), and the Badr Army, was named after the Battle of Badr, fought between the Prophet Muhammad and the first Muslims against a larger and more well-equipped armed force commanded by his Meccan opponents. The Badr Organization is led by Hadi al-Amiri, a high-ranking SIIC official and an ally of its political leaders, Abd al-Aziz al-Hakim and his son, Sayyid Ammar al-Hakim. Abd al-Aziz is the youngest brother of Muhammad Baqr, who was assassinated by a massive car bombing probably carried out by the organization headed by the Jordanian Abu Musab al-Zarqawi (1966–2006), and a son of Grand Ayatollah Sayyid Muhsin al-Hakim (1889–1970), the most influential and widely followed Shia religious leader in Iraq from 1955 until his death.

The Badr Organization's origins lay in armed units, numbering several thousand men at most, made up of Iraqi Arab exiles trained and equipped with assistance from the Iranian government. These units were named after Ayatollah Sayyid Muhammad Baqr al-Sadr (1935–1980), a prominent Iraqi Arab Shia religious scholar and opposition leader who was executed by the ruling Iraqi Baath Party along with his sister, Amina bint Haydar al-Sadr (also known as Bint al-Huda), in April 1980. Both Muhammad Baqr and Abd al-Aziz al-Hakim were students of Baqr al-Sadr, who was a student of their father, Muhsin al-Hakim. The two brothers along with their other brother, Muhammad Mahdi, were early members of the Islamic Dawa Party (Hizb al-Da'wa al-Islamiyya), which was originally founded by Shia religious scholars (*ulama*) in the southern Iraqi shrine city of Najaf.

The Iranian Revolutionary Guard Corps (IRGC), an armed force dedicated to the protection and preservation of the Iranian revolutionary system, was the key source of training and military equipment for SCIRI's paramilitary wing. This militia was renamed after the Battle of Badr (1982–1983) during the Iran-Iraq War (1980–1988). Badr drew its membership from the tens of thousands of Iraqi Arabs, the majority of them Shia political activists and anti-Baath operatives, who fled to Iran in the late 1970s and 1980s, particularly following the execution of Ayatollah Muhammad Baqr al-Sadr and his sister in April 1980.

After the start of the Iran-Iraq War following Iraq's invasion of western Iran in September 1980, Badr also recruited members from among Iraqi prisoners of war, since many Iraqi soldiers were Shia conscripts who had no love or loyalty for Iraqi president Saddam Hussein. Prisoners of war who wished to join Badr were first required to repent for their membership in the Iraqi Army because it was regarded as an instrument not of the Iraqi nation but of the Iraqi Baath Party. Abd al-Aziz al-Hakim served as Badr's commander from its founding in 1982–1983 until he and his brother Muhammad Baqr returned to Iraq in May 2003 following the collapse of the Iraqi Baathist regime in the wake of the U.S.- and British-led invasion of the country. Despite its Iraqi identity and membership, Badr's leadership was split between Iraqi Arabs such as Abd al-Aziz al-Hakim and IRGC officers, who were largely responsible for the military training of Badr's recruits. Badr included infantry, armored, artillery, antiaircraft, and commando units and maintained ties to activists and small units in Iraq.

The Badr Organization was actively involved in the Iran-Iraq War, primarily in northern Iraq (Iraqi Kurdistan). Following the capture of Haj Omran, villages in northeastern Iraq, by Iranian forces in 1983, Badr units were stationed there, and Muhammad Baqr al-Hakim visited them and prayed on what was termed "freed Iraqi soil." The participation of Badr paramilitary fighters on the side of the Iranians during the war was not welcomed by all Iraqi Shias and was widely criticized by some of SCIRI's political rivals in the Iraqi Shia community.

Badr also carried out bombings and attacks on Iraqi Baath officials and offices during the 1980s and 1990s and sent units across the Iran-Iraq border in March–April 1991 to aid the uprisings in southern and northern Iraq among the Shia and Kurdish populations. These uprisings, encouraged by the U.S. government, were brutally crushed by Baath security forces and the Republican Guard after the United States refused to aid the rebels. The United States was reportedly fearful of empowering Iraq's Shia population, heeding alarmist talk from their Sunni Arab allies and reacting warily to the appearance of Badr fighters in southern Iraq, many of whom carried portraits of Iran's late revolutionary leader, Grand Ayatollah Ruhollah Khomeini, and banners calling for the formation of an Islamic republic in Iraq.

Following the collapse of Saddam Hussein's Iraqi Baath government in April 2003, the SCIRI and Badr leaderships returned to Iraq from exile, mainly from Iran, in May 2003. Muhammad Baqir al-Hakim was welcomed in southern Iraq by tens of thousands of his supporters. According to the Hakims and SIIC/Badr officials, the Badr Organization fielded some 10,000 paramilitary fighters upon their return to Iraq. Abd al-Aziz al-Hakim subsequently claimed that Badr, in addition to its regular fighters, could call upon tens of thousands of other reservists, although this claim seems to be highly exaggerated.

The United Iraqi Alliance (UIA), a loose coalition of mainly Shia political parties, was swept into power in the December 2005 national elections. SCIRI and the Islamic Dawa Party were the two dominant political parties in the UIA. Bayan Jabr, a SCIRI official, was selected by Abd al-Aziz al-Hakim to head the Iraqi Ministry of the Interior in the 2005–2006 transitional government. Jabr oversaw the infiltration of the Iraqi security forces, police, and special commando units, all of which fall under the Interior Ministry. Badr members, both inside and outside of the national security forces, engaged in gun battles with rival Shia parties, particularly the Sadr Movement led by Muqtada al-Sadr, and in a series of operations in Basra and other southern Iraqi cities and towns in the spring and summer of 2008, which were aimed at weakening the Sadr Movement's political and paramilitary structure in southern Iraq before the 2009 elections. Badr members have also been blamed for carrying out sectarian killings and ethnic cleansing of Sunni Arabs in southern and central Iraq as well as in the capital city of Baghdad.

More recently, the Badr Organization separated itself from the armed militia units as it tried to gain more political support and legitimacy. Although the military units have continued to be active in certain areas of Iraq, their activity has diminished significantly since 2012. Beginning in early 2014, Badr militia units began battling Islamic extremists tied to the Islamic State of Iraq and Syria (ISIS).

CHRISTOPHER PAUL ANZALONE

See also

Baath Party; Hakim, Abdul Aziz al-; Hakim, Muhammad Baqir al-; Hussein, Saddam; Iran; Iraq, History of, 1990–Present; Islamic Dawa Party; Sadr, Muqtada al-; Shia Islam; Sunni Islam; Supreme Iraqi Islamic Council; United Iraqi Alliance

References

Jabar, Faleh A. *The Shi'ite Movement in Iraq*. London: Saqi Books, 2003.

Marr, Phebe. "Democracy in the Rough." *Current History* (January 2006): 27–33.

Samii, A. William. "Shia Political Alternatives in Postwar Iraq." *Middle East Policy* 10 (May 2003): 93–101.

Baga Massacre (April 16–17, 2013)

Massacre involving Nigerian civilians that occurred on April 16–17, 2013, in the village of Baga, Nigeria. The event unfolded when fighting broke out between the Nigerian military and members of Boko Haram, an extremist Islamic rebel group that the Nigerian government has been fighting since early 2009. The massacre, perpetrated by the Nigerian military, claimed the lives of at least 200 civilians, many of them children and the elderly. Several hundred more were wounded. Baga is a small fishing town on the shore of Lake Chad, not far from the Niger and Chad borders. At the time of the killings, Boko Haram fighters controlled parts of Baga and some of the surrounding countryside.

On the night of April 16, several Boko Haram insurgents fired on a small detachment of Nigerian soldiers at a military outpost on the outskirts of Baga; one of the soldiers was killed, and another one was wounded. Outraged by the attack, Nigerian military officials called in heavily armed reinforcements. Some soldiers arrived on the scene in armored vehicles. The military contingent swept quickly into Baga that same night, firing indiscriminately and setting many houses and business on fire. The rationale for the assault was to "flush out" the rebels; however, the result instead was mass civilian casualties and much destruction of property. When the dust and smoke cleared the next day, as many as 2,000 houses and businesses had been destroyed. Villagers who attempted to escape the blazes were often shot and killed; others sought refuge in Lake Chad, but they too were gunned down. Others escaped into the adjacent bush. A number of survivors eventually managed to make their way to safety, but they were now homeless.

The Nigerian military blamed the Boko Haram rebels for the atrocity in Baga, but that is in sharp contrast to what eyewitness villagers say happened on the night of April 16–17. Indeed, this incident was not an isolated event; since the government went to war with the Boko Haram insurgents, the military has pursued a scorched-earth policy, and civilians have been routinely killed or wounded. This was, however, the worst loss of civilian life since the campaign began some four years previously. The military attempted to keep journalists out of Baga after the massacre and claimed that only 6 civilians died in the fighting. Meanwhile, military officials claim that 30 rebels were killed, which has never been substantiated.

The violence in Baga provoked outrage within Nigeria as well as in the international community. The Nigerian National Assembly planned to conduct an investigation, and the military conducted its own inquiry, although neither effort reached any irrefutable conclusions. Nigerian allies threatened to reduce or withdraw support for Nigeria's campaign against Boko Haram, including the United States. Much more remains to be done before a completely accurate account of the events in Baga comes to light, but it seems all but certain that the Nigerian military was complicit in the massacre. Nigerian president Goodluck Jonathan ordered another inquiry, but the commission charged with carrying it out has yet to complete its work.

PAUL G. PIERPAOLI JR.

See also
Boko Haram

References
Dixon, Robyn. "Dozens Killed in Gun Battles in Northern Nigeria." *Los Angeles Times,* April 18, 2013, http://www. latimes.com/news/world/worldnow/la-fg-wn-nigeria-gun-battles-20130422,0,3590693.story.
Nossiter, Adam. "Massacre in Nigeria Spurs Outcry Over Military Tactics." *New York Times,* April 18, 2013, http://www. nytimes.com/2013/04/30/world/africa/outcry-over-military-tactics-after-massacre-in-nigeria.html.

Baghdad, Battle for (April 5–April 10, 2003)

Climactic battle of the 2003 Anglo-American invasion of Iraq that ended with the fall of the Iraqi capital and the collapse of Saddam Hussein's government. American planners before the war operated under the assumption that removing Hussein from power would very likely require some kind of ground attack on Baghdad. What everyone from President George W. Bush on down wanted to avoid, however, was grueling urban warfare that would devastate the city and lead to heavy casualties on all sides, the civilian populace included. To avoid being drawn into a costly city fight, the U.S. Army developed a plan to isolate Baghdad first, with the 3rd Infantry Division encircling the city from the west and the I Marine Expeditionary Force enveloping it from the east. Once a rough cordon had been established around Baghdad, the Americans intended to employ a combination of air strikes, armored and mechanized infantry raids, special forces incursions, and other small-scale operations to whittle away at the city's defenses and Baath Party control of the government, ideally reducing one or both to the breaking point.

The army never got the opportunity to test its operational concept for taking Baghdad, however, as the plan was scrapped once elements of the 3rd Infantry Division reached the outskirts of Baghdad just a little over two weeks into the campaign. By April 4, 2003, the division had secured two of the three objectives on its half of the cordon west of the Tigris River: Saddam International Airport (Operation LIONS) and the crucial highway junction just south of the city (Operation SAINTS). The third area (Operation TITANS) controlled the roads heading northwest out of Baghdad and remained in Iraqi hands. Meanwhile, the 1st Marine Division, which had a more difficult approach to the capital through the populated center of the country, was involved in fierce fighting with Republican Guard armor, Iraqi militia, and foreign irregulars and had yet to reach either of the two objectives on its side of the Tigris. Rather than wait for the encirclement of Baghdad to be completed, the 3rd Infantry Division commander, Major General Buford Blount, decided to begin probing the city's defenses immediately.

The recent battles on the approach to the city suggested to Blount that Iraqi resistance was beginning to crumble, while the latest intelligence reports indicated that Baghdad was not the heavily fortified, stoutly defended death trap that some were expecting. In fact, the opposite proved to be true, as Hussein's paranoia had played directly into American hands. His fears of a coup had prevented him from undertaking military preparations of any kind in Baghdad, and he had entrusted defense of the capital to a relatively small cadre of loyal troops—the three brigades of the Special Republican Guard—supported by the irregulars known as Fedayeen Saddam.

Blount launched his first foray into Baghdad on April 5, sending an armored battalion from the 2nd Brigade Combat Team on a thunder run (or reconnaissance in-force) from the SAINTS area into the city center and then out to the airport. The column of 29 Abrams tanks, 14 Bradley fighting vehicles, and assorted other vehicles met with a hail of small-arms fire, rocket-propelled grenades, and mortar fire from the many hundreds of Iraqi fighters who took up positions along its route. A lucky shot from a rocket-propelled grenade disabled one of the American tanks, and it had to be abandoned. Otherwise, the thickly armored Abrams and Bradleys were able to withstand multiple hits, and while the crews were exhausted at the end of the 140-minute mission, the vehicles themselves needed only minor repairs before again being ready for action.

The outcome of the April 5 thunder run confirmed Blount's suspicion that Baghdad's defenses were brittle. While the members of the 2nd Brigade Combat Team battalion received a day to catch their breath, Blount employed the 3rd Brigade Combat Team to tighten his grip on the city perimeter. On April 6 the brigade advanced to take control of objective TITANS, an area that included the Highway 1 bridge across the Tigris, a crucial point of entry and exit from the capital. This move triggered an intense battle with Iraqi tanks and infantry seeking to regain control of the crossing. The Iraqi attack began on the evening of April 6 and continued into the next morning before it was finally broken up by a combination of concentrated artillery fire, direct fire, and low-level strafing attacks by Fairchild-Republic A-10 Thunderbolts flying close air support.

U.S. Army personnel take up position in a Baghdad intersection near a portrait of Iraqi president Saddam Hussein, April 9, 2003. (AP Photo/John Moore)

The conclusion of the battle for the Tigris bridge to the northwest coincided with the launching of the second thunder run. Intended to be a limited raid much like the first, the April 7 thunder run developed into something altogether different, an armored strike into the heart of downtown Baghdad. Colonel Dave Perkins, the commander of the 2nd Brigade Combat Team, took all three of his maneuver battalions on the mission. Blount and his superiors up the chain of command expected Perkins to pull back to the city's edge at the end of the thunder run. Instead, Perkins made the daring decision to lead his two armored battalions into the center of Baghdad and remain there. The battalions met with strong resistance on their drive into the city and afterward had to fend off repeated attacks by small bands of Iraqi fighters once they established their defensive perimeters in the downtown area. But it was the trailing infantry battalion, assigned the vital task of protecting the brigade's supply line into Baghdad, that found itself engaged in some of the heaviest and most desperate fighting. The battalion was assailed not only by Republican Guard and Fedayeen Saddam troops but also by hundreds of Syrian volunteers who had arrived in Iraq only days earlier. Despite some tense moments, the battalion kept the roadway open so that supply vehicles could reach the units parked downtown.

The thunder run of April 7 struck the decisive blow in the Battle for Baghdad. On the same day, the marines breached the Iraqi defenses along the Diyala River and began their advance into east Baghdad. Fighting continued on April 8, especially in the downtown area and in the 3rd Brigade Combat Team's sector at TITANS. By April 9, however, resistance within the city had become generally disorganized and sporadic as increasing numbers of Iraqi fighters put down their weapons and melted into the general populace. The Baathist regime also dissolved, and some governing officials returned home. Others, most notably Saddam Hussein and his two sons, Uday and Qusay, slipped out of the capital and sought refuge elsewhere, leaving Baghdad to troops of the U.S. Army and the U.S. Marine Corps. Baghdad was considered secured by April 10.

Casualty figures are not terribly reliable, but it is believed that the coalition suffered 34 dead and at least 250 wounded. Iraqi dead have been given as 2,300 killed but were undoubtedly higher. There is no estimate of Iraqi wounded.

JEFF SEIKEN

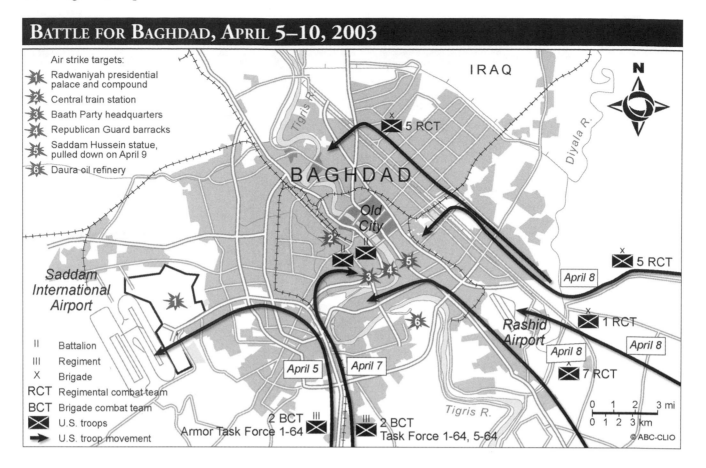

BATTLE FOR BAGHDAD, APRIL 5–10, 2003

Air strike targets:
1. Radwaniyah presidential palace and compound
2. Central train station
3. Baath Party headquarters
4. Republican Guard barracks
5. Saddam Hussein statue, pulled down on April 9
6. Daura oil refinery

II   Battalion
III   Regiment
X   Brigade
RCT   Regimental combat team
BCT   Brigade combat team
U.S. troops
U.S. troop movement

See also

Baghdad, Iraq; Blount, Buford, III; Hussein, Saddam; IRAQI FREE-DOM, Operation; IRAQI FREEDOM, Operation, Ground Campaign

References

Fontenot, Gregory, et al. *On Point: The United States Army in Iraqi Freedom.* Annapolis, MD: Naval Institute Press, 2005.

Gordon, Michael R., and General Bernard E. Trainor. *Cobra II: The Inside Story of the Invasion and Occupation of Iraq.* New York: Pantheon Books, 2006.

Zucchino, David. *Thunder Run: The Armored Strike to Capture Baghdad.* New York: Grove, 2004.

Baghdad, Iraq

Baghdad, established in 762 C.E. by Abbasid caliph al-Mansur, straddles the Tigris River and its tributary, the Diyala. The city is located at 33"18' North latitude and 44"36' East longitude some 130 feet above sea level in east-central Iraq. Baghdad's climate typically consists of hot, dry summers and cool winters. With a 2014 population of approximately 7.24 million people, Baghdad is the second-largest city in Southwest Asia (behind Tehran, Iran) and the second-largest city in the Arab world (behind Cairo, Egypt). The population of Baghdad constitutes slightly more than one-fifth

of the country's people. The name "Baghdad" also refers to the small province that surrounds the city, 1 of 18 in Iraq. Iraq's capital city is ethnically Arab, with small Kurdish and Turkoman minorities.

Baghdad is the center of Iraq's power infrastructure, with power lines webbing outward in all directions. During the 1991 Persian Gulf War, this power infrastructure was severely damaged by the U.S.-led coalition air strikes against the city in retaliation for Iraq's August 1990 annexation of Kuwait. Baghdad is also the air, road, and railroad center of Iraq, including Baghdad International Airport, several major highways, two primary railroads, two key oil pipelines, and one major gas pipeline. Baghdad is Iraq's foremost center of oil refining, food-processing plants, textile mills, tanneries and leather production, cement companies, metal-product manufacturers, and tobacco processing. The local economy is augmented by way of Baghdad's famous bazaars that showcase jewelry, utensils, rugs, cloth, leather, and felt.

Until the invasion of Iraq in March 2003, military installations in the area included air bases, barracks, bunkers, the Iraqi Air Force headquarters, the Republican Guard headquarters, and the Ministry of Defense. Key political buildings included various presidential palaces, the National Assembly, and the Baath Party headquarters. Baghdad is also home to three universities: the University of Baghdad, the University of Technology, and al-Mustansiriyah University.

Portions of Baghdad were heavily damaged during the Persian Gulf War of 1991. Transportation, communication, sanitation, and power-generating centers were all affected to varying degrees. President George H. W. Bush halted coalition troops, however. They were not allowed to proceed to Baghdad, and Iraqi dictator Saddam Hussein was left in power.

In the war's aftermath, Hussein, now far weaker militarily and economically, attempted to rebuild Baghdad. But the extent of the damaged international economic sanctions and Hussein's own spending priorities meant that this proceeded only in piecemeal fashion. Spending on Hussein's palaces and on projects glorifying the regime and Hussein himself continued unabated, however.

In March and early April 2003, Baghdad was bombed heavily during the Iraq War (Operation IRAQI FREEDOM). By April 9 coalition forces had taken the city, and the widely televised toppling of Hussein's statue in Firdaws Square signaled the end of his oppressive regime. Baghdad saw more damage in the extensive looting immediately following the city's fall.

The conquerors soon established the Coalition Provisional Authority in a three-square-mile area (known as the Green Zone) in central Baghdad from which it governed the nation. Democratic elections commenced in 2004, and a new constitution was drafted. Sadly, Baghdad experienced significant violence from both terrorist actions and Sunni and Shia sectarian violence. With Baghdad spiraling out of control in massive car bombings and scattered random executions and the coalition military effort in Iraq seemingly in jeopardy, in 2007 President George W. Bush authorized an increase of more than 22,000 troops in Baghdad to restore order. The U.S. troop surge managed to significantly reduce violence and unrest in Baghdad, and the last American troops exited Iraq in December 2011.

Since 2011, however, Iraq has experienced a growing sectarian- and radical Islamic–based insurgency that has claimed thousands of lives, many of them civilian. The unrest and instability have greatly affected Baghdad and were made far worse by the anti-Sunni policies of the Iraqi government under Prime Minister Nuri al-Maliki. The violence slowed reconstruction efforts in the city and hampered the growth of the capital's economy. Recent studies indicate that Baghdad is among the world's least hospitable places and ranked last (221) of all major cities in terms of overall quality of living. By early 2014, a potent insurgency carried out by the Islamic State of Iraq and Syria (ISIS) threatened

Baghdad itself, coming within 100 miles of the capital. Maliki's successor, Haider al-Abadi, who took office in late September 2014, has pledged a potent defense against ISIS and has vowed to maintain control over all of Baghdad by any means necessary.

DYLAN A. CYR AND PAUL G. PIERPAOLI JR.

See also

Abadi, Haider al-; Bush, George Walker; Green Zone in Iraq; Iraq, History of, 1990–Present; IRAQI FREEDOM, Operation; Islamic State in Iraq and Syria; Maliki, Nuri al-; Persian Gulf War

References

Cohen, Saul B., ed. *The Columbia Gazetteer of the World,* Vol. 1. New York: Columbia University Press, 1998.

Pax, Salam. *The Baghdad Blog.* London: Grove Atlantic, 2003.

The World Guide: An Alternative Reference to Countries of Our Planet, 2003/2004. Oxford, UK: New Internationalist Publications, 2003.

Baghdad Ministry of Justice and Provincial Council Building Bombings (October 25, 2009)

On October 25, 2009, two suicide bombings near the center of Baghdad, Iraq, killed some 160 people and wounded more than 720 others. The attacks occurred within 15 minutes of each other (at 10:15 and 10:30 a.m.) and targeted the Justice Ministry, the Ministry of Municipalities and Public Works, and the Provincial Council; the blasts also destroyed the medical clinic that was part of the only Anglican church in Iraq. They occurred at the height of a Sunni Muslim terrorist campaign that was primarily designed to impress upon the Iraqi population two things: first, that the Shiite Muslim–led government of Prime Minister Nuri al-Maliki could not provide adequate public safety as American military forces prepared to withdraw from the country, and second, that his administration did not have the required sense of direction and purpose as the January 2010 national elections neared.

The strikes cost roughly $120,000 to implement and took the form of vehicle-borne improvised explosive devices (IEDs) that consisted of a minivan and a 26-seat day care bus. The operation itself was both strategically and tactically significant. Not only were the devices constructed and deployed in the most secure part of Iraq—the heavily fortified Green Zone—but the bombings were also executed at a time when it had become increasingly difficult to conduct any type of attack. Overall, it was the deadliest act of terrorism in the country since a series of vehicle-borne IEDs had killed 500 people in northern Iraq in August 2007.

The mastermind behind the operation was Manuf al-Rawl. He had already been implicated in a series of explosions on August 19, 2009, that struck Iraq's finance and foreign ministries and left 122 people dead. He was captured in a raid on March 11, 2010, and later confessed that the October bombings were designed to compound the destabilizing effects of the earlier ones. In the end, however, the withdrawal of U.S. troops continued unabated, and Maliki, who had staked his political future on a pledge to bring peace to Iraq, was elected to a second term in January 2010. As it turned out, however, the security situation in Iraq deteriorated rapidly after the last American troops left Iraq in December 2011, and in September 2014 Maliki was forced to resign his office.

Indeed, the attacks probably did more to hurt the Sunni cause than to advance it. One of the government buildings hit was the Justice Ministry. At the time it was attempting to reduce the number of inmates in Iraq's chronically overcrowded prisons. The attacks halted this process and served to further backlog outstanding criminal cases. Both of these developments generated considerable dissatisfaction among the Sunnis, who make up only 20 percent of the population but 80 percent of those in jail.

The day after the explosions, Al Qaeda in Iraq (AQI) posted a message on the Internet taking credit for the attacks. The group is a Sunni umbrella association of semi-autonomous terrorist organizations made up mostly of Iraqis. It was forged in the aftermath of the 2003 Anglo-American invasion to overthrow Saddam Hussein and, according to U.S. intelligence sources, has a largely foreign leadership. At the zenith of the Iraqi insurgency, the AQI effectively governed large parts of the country and, in common with the Taliban in Afghanistan, was able to operate, recruit members, and raise funds openly. By 2010, however, nearly three-quarters of the AQI's top commanders had been eliminated, and as a result of brutality and indiscriminate violence it had lost much of its original internal backing.

PETER CHALK

See also

Al Qaeda; Al Qaeda in Iraq; Baghdad, Iraq; Green Zone in Iraq; Maliki, Nuri al-; Shia Islam; Sunni Islam

References

Hafez, Mohammed. *Suicide Bombers in Iraq: The Strategy and Ideology of Martyrdom.* Washington, DC: United States Institute of Peace, 2009.

United States Government. *The Resurgence of Al Qaeda in Iraq and Syria.* New York: Progressive Management, 2014.

Baghdadi, Abu Bakr al- (1971?–)

Iraqi jihadist, terrorist, and militant leader of the Islamic State (formerly the Islamic State of Iraq and Syria) since 2010. Abu Bakr al-Baghdadi was born Ibrahim al-Badari on the outskirts of Sammara, Iraq, probably in 1971. He received undergraduate and graduate degrees—including a PhD in Islamic studies—from the Islamic University of Baghdad. Very little is known about Baghdadi prior to the Anglo-American invasion of Iraq in 2003.

Shortly after the fall of Saddam Hussein's regime in early April 2003, Baghdadi cofounded a militant Islamist group known as Jamaat Jaysh Ahl a-Sunnah wa-i-Jamaah (JJASJ). It was committed to expelling all foreign troops from Iraq and establishing sharia law in the country. Although the details of Baghdadi's activities remain rather murky until 2010, the U.S. Defense Department claims that he was incarcerated as a "civilian internee" at Camp Bucca (near Umm Qasr, Iraq) for much of 2004. He was released after a review board deemed him "unremarkable."

In 2006, JJASJ merged with the Mujahideen Shura Council (MSC), and Baghdadi served on its sharia committee. Later that same year, the MSC was renamed the Islamic State of Iraq (ISI), which functioned essentially as Al Qaeda's Iraqi satellite and was also referred to as Al Qaeda in Iraq. On May 16, 2010, Baghdadi assumed leadership of ISI. He immediately stepped up the group's terror activities in Iraq, including at least 23 attacks south of Baghdad during March and April 2011 alone. Upon learning of Al Qaeda leader Osama bin Laden's death at the hands of U.S. commandos in May 2011, Baghdadi pledged to perpetrate more acts of violence to avenge bin Laden's death. True to his word, Baghdadi engineered a spectacular series of suicide attacks throughout Iraq in the remainder of the year. In October 2011, the U.S. State Department listed Baghdadi as a designated global terrorist and offered a $10 million reward for his capture or death.

The departure of U.S. troops from Iraq in December 2011 seemed only to strengthen ISI's influence and reach. Meanwhile, the civil war that had begun in Syria earlier that year caught Baghdadi's attention. Before long, ISI had begun to extend its operations into Syria and was training and arming its militants so they could wage war against both the regime of Bashar al-Assad as well as other antigovernment rebels who did not subscribe to ISI's radical views. In 2013, Baghdadi changed the name of ISI to the Islamic State of Iraq and Syria (ISIS), in recognition that his reach now included swaths of Syria as well as Iraq. He also announced that the

Syrian jihadist group Jabhat al-Nusra had allied with ISIS and would be formally incorporated into Baghdadi's organization. Meanwhile in Iraq, the ineffectual and corrupt government of Nuri al-Maliki appeared unwilling and certainly unable to stop ISIS's advance.

During 2013 and into 2014, ISIS made frighteningly rapid progress in capturing large portions of western and northern Iraq and northeastern Syria. By January 2014, ISIS had taken virtually all of Iraq's Anbar Province and appeared poised to advance on Baghdad. In the process, ISIS was also unleashing a violent holy war against any individuals who refused to accede to its demands. In February 2014 Al Qaeda severed all ties to ISIS, signaling that Baghdadi's campaign was too radical even for it. Fueled by money from wealthy private citizens in Qatar and Saudi Arabia as well as oil revenue from captured wells and refineries, Baghdadi envisions imposing a worldwide Islamic caliphate under his personal direction.

On June 19, 2014, Baghdadi declared himself caliph of the Islamic State. Many Islamic nations, including those in the Middle East, are aghast with Baghdadi's audacity and merciless violence. And many Islamic scholars and religious leaders deem the activities of ISIS as nothing more than apostasy. In the late summer of 2014, the Barack Obama administration began assembling a multinational coalition aimed at defeating Baghdadi's organization. U.S. air strikes against ISIS in Iraq began in August; they were expanded into Syria the following month. Baghdadi's whereabouts remain unknown, although there were reports that he may have been injured in a coalition air attack and sought refuge in Mosul, Iraq, in late September 2014.

PAUL G. PIERPAOLI JR.

See also

Al Qaeda; Islamic State in Iraq and Syria; Maliki, Nuri al-; Syrian Civil War

References

Andress, Carter, with Malcolm McConnell. *Victory Undone: The Defeat of Al Qaeda in Iraq and Its Resurrection as ISIS.* New York: Regnery Publishing, 2014.

"Injured ISIS Leader Abu Bakr Al-Baghdadi Flees Syria to Escape U.S. Air Strikes." International Business Times, October 1, 2014, http://www.ibtimes.co.in/injured-isis-leader-flees -syria-abu-bakr-al-baghdadi-arrives-mosul-after escaping -us-airstrikes-610361.

"20 Facts about Baghdadi, the Elusive ISIS Leader." The Fiscal Times, September 9, 2014, http://www.thefiscaltimes.com /Articles/2014/09/09/20-Facts-About-Baghdadi-Leader-ISIS.

Bahrain

Middle Eastern country consisting of an archipelago of more than 30 islands located in the Persian Gulf. As of 2014 no accurate count of the number of islands was possible, as Bahrain continues to create artificial islands off its coast for economic and tourism purposes. Bordered on the west by the Gulf of Bahrain and by the Persian Gulf on the north, east, and south, Bahrain is also about 20 miles from both Qatar to the south and Saudi Arabia to the west. A causeway connects Saudi Arabia with the Bahraini island of Umm al-Nasan. Bahrain's area is just 274 square miles, with only five of the islands being permanently inhabited. Bahrain's topography consists of low desert plains and a low central escarpment, with a climate ranging from hot and humid summers to temperate winters.

Officially known as the Kingdom of Bahrain, the nation's capital is Manama. Bahrain's population is approximately 1.35 million people, with 63 percent of Bahraini descent, 19 percent Asian, 10 percent Arab, 8 percent Iranian, and a smattering of other nationalities. Islam is practiced by 85 percent of the population, and 70 percent of the Muslim population is Shia. The remaining 15 percent practice Bahai, Christianity, and other religions. Arabic, English, and Farsi are the most commonly spoken languages in Bahrain.

Politically, the country consists of a constitutional monarchy ruled by Emir Khalifa bin Hamad al-Thani. Bahrain is a member of the Gulf Cooperation Council (GCC), a collective security organization consisting of six countries on the western side of the Persian Gulf, the Arab League, the United Nations (UN), the Organization of Islamic Conference, the Organization of Arab Petroleum Exporting Countries, and other international organizations.

Throughout Bahrain's history various empires have occupied the country, including those of Babylon, Assyria, Portugal, and Safavid Iran. Portuguese forces captured Bahrain in 1521 and controlled the country until 1602, when Bahrainis overthrew Portuguese forces on the island. Iran's Safavid Empire quickly conquered Bahrain the same year and maintained control until 1717, a fact used by Iran to make repeated claims on Bahraini territory. In 1783 the Khalifa clan, led by Ahmad ibn Mohammed al-Khalifa, invaded and conquered Bahrain and has led the country since that time.

In 1820 Bahrain signed a treaty with Britain promising that it would not engage in piracy. Britain agreed to provide military protection for Bahrain and official recognition of the Khalifa family as the ruling party of Bahrain. In exchange, Bahrain agreed not to cede its territory to any country except

Britain and not to establish foreign relations with other nations without British consent. Meanwhile, English advisers encouraged the Khalifa rulers to adopt a series of social reforms for the country.

Standard Oil Company of California's discovery of oil reserves in 1932 created significant changes, as Bahrain became an early leading exporter of petroleum. Bahrain allied itself with Britain during World War II, providing oil to the Allies as well as serving as a staging point for protecting British colonies and oil-production facilities in Asia and Africa.

After India acquired its independence on August 15, 1947, British interests in the Persian Gulf region diminished, eventually leading to the decision in 1968 to withdraw from the treaties signed with Persian Gulf states during the 1800s. Initial attempts to unite Bahrain with other Persian Gulf states failed, and on August 15, 1971, Bahrain declared its full independence. By 1973 Bahrain's oil reserves were diminishing, while the price of oil was dramatically increasing. Looking for an alternative source of revenue, Bahrain established a robust banking industry to replace Lebanon's banking industry, which had suffered from the long Lebanese Civil War (1975–1990). Bahrain soon became the banking center of the Middle East.

Although a national assembly was elected in 1973, it quarreled with Emir Isa bin Salman al-Khalifa, who ruled from 1961 through 1999, over implementation of a security law. He responded by dissolving the assembly in 1975 and passed the law by decree. Despite his actions, Bahrain is quite liberal and tolerant compared to most other Islamic nations in the region. In 1981 Iran attempted to encourage Bahrain's large Shia population to foment a revolution in Bahrain. Although some Bahraini Shias staged a coup d'état in 1981, it did not succeed. Iran's interference in Bahraini affairs encouraged the nation to establish collective security agreements that created the GCC and improved relations with the United States.

Periodic violent acts against the government have included attacks by external and internal sources. The Islamic Front engaged in terrorist attacks against Bahraini targets in the county. Political dissent within the kingdom grew during the 1980s and 1990s, as citizens lacked the opportunity to actively participate in the governing of the country. The Bahrain Freedom Movement (BFM), formed by Bahraini dissidents who wanted an Iranian-styled Islamic republic established, also engaged in bombings and other terrorist acts. Bahraini security forces reacted strongly against the BFM.

Emir Isa ibn Salman al-Khalifa's death in 1999 initiated a series of changes, as his son Khalifa bin Hamad al-Thani took a chance on reforming Bahraini society, initiating a series of social and political reforms including the resumption of constitutional rule. Hamad al-Thani agreed to concessions limiting legislative power to the lower house of parliament in the National Action Charter that was designed to restore constitutional government yet reversed his decision with the 2002 constitution. In 2002 he agreed to hold parliamentary elections in which both men and women could vote and run for office, although no woman won a seat. Several parties, including the major religious party al-Wifaq National Islamic Society, boycotted the election.

Presently, there are 12 political parties in the country (6 are Islamic, and 6 are secular). The 2006 elections resulted in the Shia-associated al-Wifaq National Islamic Society winning 17 seats, while the Salafi al-Asalah party won 8 and the Sunni Al-Minbar Islamic Society won 7. The remaining parties and candidates won a combined 8 seats. Although 18 women ran, just 1 captured a seat in parliament. After the 2010 elections, al-Wifaq remained the largest party in parliament. However, when 18 al-Wifaq representatives resigned from parliament to protest the government crackdown on Arab Spring protesters, a new snap election was held in late September 2011. All of the 18 new candidates and winners in that contest were independents.

Although the United States had sent ships to the region during the 1800s, Washington had little interest in Bahrain until 1949, when the United States began leasing British bases in Bahrain. The United States has maintained at least a minimal force in Bahrain since that time. Bahrain's role in America's conflicts in the Middle East can be divided into two parts. The first is marked by its willingness to allow U.S. forces to use Bahraini territory and facilities for launching military operations against Iraq, first during the 1991 Persian Gulf War and next during Operation IRAQI FREEDOM. Bahrain was also used as a base during Operation ENDURING FREEDOM. The U.S. Naval Forces Central Command operates out of Manama. Army and air force units operating in Bahrain include the 831st Transport Battalion, located at Mina Sulman, and the Air Mobility Command, which has a detachment at Muharraq Airfield. Additionally, the Sheik Isa Air Base serves as a military airfield for various U.S. military aircraft.

Bahrain was also actively involved militarily in the Persian Gulf War and in providing limited military assistance in Operations ENDURING FREEDOM and IRAQI FREEDOM. In 1991 Bahrain sent a small contingent of 400 troops to serve in the coalition as part of the Joint Forces Command East. Additionally, the Bahraini Air Force, employing F-16 Fighting

Falcon and F-5 Tiger II fighters, engaged in defensive sorties in the region and launched offensives against Iraqi assets. The Bahraini Navy dispatched forces to assist in ENDURING FREEDOM and in the larger Global War on Terror. Bahrain also provided some limited forces in a strictly support role for Operation IRAQI FREEDOM and to help the Iraqi government stabilize the country.

Beginning in early 2011 amid the larger Arab Spring movement, Bahrain witnessed a series of sometimes violent uprisings, many of them involving the Shia majority, who sought to depose the ruling Sunni minority and institute a more democratic regime. Initially, the government permitted the mass antigovernment rallies. Violent clashes occurred in mid-February, however, and the Bahraini government decided to quash the rebellion. The government promptly declared a state of emergency and requested help from Saudi Arabia and other Persian Gulf nations. Periodic and largely peaceful demonstrations continued, however, but there were several incidents of violence during 2012 and 2013. By 2014, Bahrain's government had come under withering criticism by human rights groups and many democratic governments for its heavy-handed response to the continuing protests. These have included mass arrests, strict censorship, and even reports of torture. It is estimated that between February 2011 and November 2014 nearly 200 people had died in the uprising, with more than 2,700 injured.

WYNDHAM E. WHYNOT

See also

Arab Spring; IRAQI FREEDOM, Operation; Persian Gulf War

References

Congressional Quarterly. *The Middle East*. 10th ed. Washington, DC: CQ Press, 2005.

Ochsenwald, William, and Sydney Nettleton Fisher. *The Middle East: A History*. 6th ed. New York: McGraw-Hill, 2004.

Palmer, Michael. *Guardians of the Gulf: A History of America's Expanding Role in the Persian Gulf, 1833–1992*. New York: Free Press, 1992.

Spencer, William J. *The Middle East*. 11th ed. Dubuque, IA: McGraw-Hill/Contemporary Learning Series, 2007.

Winkler, David. *Amirs, Admirals & Desert Sailors: Bahrain, the U.S. Navy, and the Arabian Gulf*. Annapolis, MD: Naval Institute Press, 2007.

Baker, James Addison, III (1930–)

U.S. politician, influential Republican adviser, secretary of the treasury (1985–1988), and secretary of state (1989–1992). Born on April 28, 1930, in Houston, Texas, to a wealthy local family, James Addison Baker III studied classics at Princeton University, graduating in 1952. After two years in the U.S. Marine Corps, he went on to earn a law degree from the University of Texas at Austin in 1957. That same year he began his legal career with a corporate law firm in Houston, where he practiced until 1975.

Baker first entered politics in 1970, working for George H. W. Bush's unsuccessful U.S. senatorial campaign. Beginning in 1975, Baker spent a year as undersecretary of commerce in the Gerald Ford administration. Baker then managed Ford's unsuccessful 1976 presidential campaign. After managing Bush's unsuccessful bid for the Republican presidential nomination in 1980, Baker became a senior adviser to President Ronald Reagan's 1980 campaign after Bush withdrew from the race.

From 1981 until 1985, Baker served as White House chief of staff. In 1984 he successfully engineered Reagan's reelection campaign. Reagan subsequently appointed him secretary of the treasury in 1985. In 1988 Baker resigned from the treasury and managed Vice President George H. W. Bush's presidential campaign and was rewarded by being appointed secretary of state in 1989. In that role, Baker helped reorient U.S. foreign policy as the Cold War ended. He was involved in negotiations that led to the reunification of Germany and the dismantling of the Soviet Union. Baker also presided over negotiations before and after the successful Persian Gulf War. In 1992 Bush named Baker White House chief of staff and manager of his reelection campaign. Bush lost that election to Democrat Bill Clinton.

After leaving government service in 1993, Baker joined the Houston-based law firm of Baker Botts and become senior counselor to the Carlyle Group, a corporate banking firm in Washington, D.C. In 2000 he served as President-elect George W. Bush's transition adviser during the controversial Florida ballot recount following the November presidential election. In 2004 Baker served as the personal envoy of United Nations secretary-general Kofi Annan in seeking to reach a peaceful solution to the conflict over the western Sahara. In 2003 Baker was a special presidential envoy for President George W. Bush on Iraqi debt relief.

Beginning in March 2006, Baker cochaired, along with former U.S. Democratic representative Lee Hamilton, the 10-person bipartisan Iraq Study Group, charged with recommending changes to deal with the deteriorating situation in the Iraqi insurgency. The group presented its report to President George W. Bush and Congress in early December 2006. Among its recommendations was a strong call for a major drawdown of U.S. troops in Iraq. In January 2007

Bush did just the opposite, implementing a troop surge in Iraq that temporarily subdued the Iraqi insurgency. After the withdrawal of U.S. troops from Iraq in late 2011, however, the insurgency was reenergized. Baker continued to advise the Bush administration on an ad hoc basis until the January 2009 inauguration of President Barrack Obama.

JOHN DAVID RAUSCH JR.

See also

Bush, George Walker; Iraq Study Group; Persian Gulf War

References

Baker, James A., III, with Thomas M. DeFrank. *The Politics of Diplomacy: Revolution, War, and Peace, 1989–1992.* New York: Putnam, 1995.

Gwynne, S. C. "James Baker Forever." *Texas Monthly* 31 (December 2003): 150–173.

Baker-Hamilton Commission.

See Iraq Study Group

Bandar bin Sultan, Prince (1949–)

Saudi Arabian military official, ambassador to the United States (1983–2005), and since October 16, 2005, secretary-general of the Saudi Arabian National Security Council. Prince Bandar bin Sultan bin Abdulaziz Al-Saud was born in Taif, Saudi Arabia, on March 2, 1949, the son of Crown Prince Sultan bin Abdul Aziz, the deputy prime minister, minister of defense and aviation, and inspector general of Saudi Arabia. Prince Bandar graduated from the Royal Air Force College at Cranwell, England, in 1968. He was then commissioned a second lieutenant in the Royal Saudi Air Force.

During the 1970s Bandar studied in the United States at the Air Command and Staff College at Maxwell Air Force Base in Montgomery, Alabama, and at the Industrial College of the Armed Forces at Fort McNair in Washington, D.C. Throughout the 1970s, Bandar commanded fighter squadrons at three different Saudi bases and held major responsibilities in the Royal Saudi Air Force's modernization program, known as Peace Hawk. In 1980 he earned a master's degree in international public policy from Johns Hopkins University.

During his military career, Bandar consistently strove to modernize the Royal Saudi Air Force. Intent on purchasing the most modern technology, in 1978 he successfully lobbied the U.S. Congress to approve the sale of F-15 fighter aircraft to Saudi Arabia. In 1981 he secured approval of the sale of the U.S. airborne warning and control system (AWACS) to Saudi Arabia. In 1982 Bandar was assigned as the Saudi defense attaché to the United States at the rank of lieutenant colonel.

In 1983 Bandar became the ambassador to the United States. During his long tenure as Saudi ambassador to the United States, he rose to be the dean of the diplomatic corps in Washington, D.C. He strongly supported the Saudi Arabian government's decision to permit U.S. staging areas in Saudi Arabia during the 1991 Persian Gulf War. In the aftermath of the September 11, 2001, terrorist attacks on the United States, Bandar worked hard to convince the American public and government of Saudi Arabia's friendship with the United States and of its commitment to the Global War on Terror.

Bandar has repeatedly denied allegations that the Saudi government supported the activities of Osama bin Laden and supports other Islamic terrorists. Bandar also supported the U.S.-led offensive against Iraq's Saddam Hussein regime in March 2003. It is said that Bandar has promoted overtures to Israel and argued for the U.S.-urged harder line toward Hamas. Nevertheless, frequent criticism of Bandar and Saudi foreign policy has circulated in the American media. Director and author Michael Moore, in his film *Fahrenheit 9/11* (2004), strongly criticized the close relationship between the Bush family and the Saudi royal family, especially President George W. Bush's and Vice President Dick Cheney's relationship with Bandar.

From July 2012 until April 2014, Bandar also served as director general of the Saudi General Intelligence Agency. There have been rumors that he was asked to vacate this post because he had differences of opinion with U.S. policy makers, including Secretary of State John F. Kerry, in regard to the ongoing Syrian Civil War.

MICHAEL R. HALL

See also

Bin Laden, Osama; Bush, George Walker; *Fahrenheit 9/11;* Global War on Terror; IRAQI FREEDOM, Operation; Moore, Michael; Persian Gulf War; Saudi Arabia; September 11 Attacks

References

Bond Reed, Jennifer. *The Saudi Royal Family.* New York: Chelsea House, 2002.

International Business Publications. *U.S.-Saudi Diplomatic and Political Relations Handbook.* Washington, DC: International Business Publications, 2005.

Posner, Gerald L. *Secrets of the Kingdom: The Inside Story of the Secret Saudi-U.S. Connection.* New York: Random House, 2005.

Ban Ki Moon (1944–)

South Korean diplomat and eighth secretary-general of the United Nations (UN) (2007–present). Ban Ki Moon was born on June 13, 1944, in the village of Chungju in the province of North Chung-cheong in what is today the Republic of Korea (South Korea). As a teenager he spent several months in the United States. During that time he won a speech contest, and the grand prize was a trip to Washington, D.C., to meet President John F. Kennedy. Ban later credited the trip with sparking his interest in a diplomatic career. In 1970 he graduated from Seoul National University, where he earned a degree in international relations. He later studied public administration at Harvard University's John F. Kennedy School of Government, where he earned a master's degree in 1985.

At the time of his 2006 election as secretary-general, Ban's diplomatic career had spanned more than 30 years. His first position was as South Korea's vice-consul to New Delhi, India, in 1972. He also served at the UN as part of South Korea's permanent observer mission during 1978–1980. In 1980 he was promoted to director of the South Korean Foreign Ministry's UN division. He worked as director of the UN's International Organizations and Treaties Bureau in South Korea's capital, Seoul, and was consul-general at the South Korean embassy to the United States. In the 1990s Ban served in the South Korean government as director-general of the American Affairs Bureau and as an assistant to the foreign minister. He was also vice chair of the South-North Joint Nuclear Commission.

Ban returned to the UN in May 2001 to serve as chief of the UN General Assembly president's cabinet and as South Korea's UN ambassador. Then in January 2004, South Korean president Roh Moo Hyun named Ban as the nation's foreign affairs and trade minister. Ban almost immediately faced several crises, most notably the kidnapping of a Korean worker by Iraqi terrorists in June 2004 and the deaths of many South Koreans in the tsunami of December 2004. In 2005 Ban successfully navigated meetings with the Democratic People's Republic of Korea (North Korea) on nuclear disarmament. In September of that year, the two nations signed a joint statement on denuclearization. Ban remained foreign minister until taking his post at the UN in January 2007.

In February 2006 Ban announced his candidacy for UN secretary-general and traveled around the world to campaign for the post. Based on the UN's informal tradition of rotating the position of secretary-general among regions, outgoing secretary-general Koffi Annan's replacement was fairly certain to be an Asian. Ban faced competition from Shashi Tharoor of India and Prince Zeid al-Hussein of Jordan, but several factors made him the front-runner. First, South Korea is largely seen as a UN success, having emerged from the devastating Korean War into a democratized economic power. Second, many hoped that Ban's experiences in dealing with North Korea would aid the UN in resolving that nation's nuclear ambitions. And third, Ban had the support of the United States, one of the five permanent members of the UN Security Council with veto power over candidates for secretary-general. Ban's candidacy was approved by the Security Council's permanent members on October 9, 2006, and his name was then sent to the 192 members of the General Assembly, which officially elected him secretary-general on October 13. Ban was sworn in as secretary-general on December 14 and officially took over the post on January 1, 2007.

Ironically, the day of Ban's election witnessed the troubling announcement that North Korea had tested a nuclear weapon, prompting Ban to make denuclearization his first priority as secretary-general. Other prominent issues that he laid out included reform of the UN's vast bureaucracy, the cessation of continued warfare and famine in several regions of Africa, the international AIDS crisis, and unrest in the Middle East.

UN observers noted that Ban would most likely be "more secretary than general." Colleagues in the South Korean foreign service referred to him as "the bureaucrat" for his workaholic tendencies and facile administrative skill. Mild mannered, quiet, and modest, Ban has been criticized as uncharismatic. But he attributes his low-key personality to Asian culture, and he has defended his abilities. To many observers, Ban was the secretary-general candidate with whom Security Council members could live but who was not everyone's first choice. Either way, Ban has so far encountered little opposition in the UN, despite the difficulty he has faced. Even though he has continuing concerns about North Korea's nuclear program and nuclear proliferation, he has generally deferred to the Security Council in these matters, just as he has with Iran's nuclear ambitions. He has urged the UN to take a larger role in Iraq to help the Iraqi people reinvigorate their social, political, and economic institutions and has pledged to do more to bring to an end the ongoing Palestinian-Israeli conflict. In March 2008, however, he criticized the Israeli government for its plans to build new housing in a West Bank settlement, calling these incompatible with Israel's earlier commitment to peace, including the so-called Road Map to Peace.

Ban oversees more than 9,000 employees and a budget of some $5 billion. His first five-year term ended in December 2012, at which time he was elected to a second five-year term.

Ban has been criticized by some for the UN's rather tepid response to the ongoing Arab Spring movement that began in late 2010. In 2012, he named former UN secretary-general Kofi Annan as a special UN representative to Syria, but that mission to end the civil war there failed before year's end. To date, the Syrian conflict continues, but the UN has been unable to broker a cease-fire or peace deal during the bloody struggle. In September 2013, the UN agreed to oversee the eradication of Syria's chemical weapons arsenal, the result of a U.S.-Russian initiative to prevent the need for air strikes against the government of Syrian president Bashar al-Assad, which reportedly used chemical weapons against its own people.

PAUL G. PIERPAOLI JR.

See also

Annan, Kofi; Arab Spring; Syrian Chemical Weapons Agreement; Syrian Civil War; United Nations

References

Baehr, Peter R., and Leon Gordenker. *The United Nations: Reality and Ideal.* 4th ed. New York: Palgrave Macmillan, 2005.

Meisler, Stanley. *Koffi Annan: A Man of Peace in a World of War.* New York: Wiley, 2007.

Banna, Sabri Khalil al-

See Nidal, Abu

Barno, David William (1954–)

U.S. Army officer, commander of Combined Forces Command–Afghanistan, and the highest-ranking American commander in Afghanistan from October 2003 to May 2005. Born on July 5, 1954, in Endicott, New York, David William Barno attended the United States Military Academy, West Point, graduating in 1976. He earned a master's degree from Georgetown University in national security studies. During his army career, he also graduated from the United States Army Command and General Staff College and the United States Army War College.

Upon his commissioning in the U.S. Army in 1976, Barno served as a junior officer and company commander in the 25th Infantry Division. After attending the infantry officer advanced course, he assumed duties as a logistics officer in the 1st Battalion, 75th Ranger Regiment. During Operation URGENT FURY, the U.S. invasion that ousted the leftist government of Grenada in October 1983, Barno commanded a ranger company. In Operation JUST CAUSE, the U.S. invasion of Panama to depose dictator Manuel Noriega in December 1989, Barno served as the operations officer for the 2nd Battalion, 75th Ranger Regiment. During his career he served in Korea, Thailand, the Philippines, and New Zealand as well as the continental United States.

During the 1990s Barno held several commands, including a parachute infantry battalion in the 82nd Airborne Division; the 2nd Battalion, 75th Ranger Regiment; and the Warrior Brigade. In July 1997 he served as the chief of the Joint Training and Doctrine Division at the Joint Warfighting Center. Following his promotion to brigadier general in 2000, he became the assistant division commander for operations for the 25th Infantry Division. Thereafter, he served as the deputy director for operations for the Untied States Pacific Command.

At the time of the September 11, 2001, terrorist attacks on the United States, Barno commanded the United States Army Training Center and Fort Jackson in South Carolina. In January 2003 Barno, now a major general, deployed to Tazar, Hungary, for three months, where he commanded Task Force Warrior. Task Force Warrior was an army training unit created to prepare free Iraqi forces before Operation IRAQI FREEDOM began in March 2003. Working closely with the State Department, Task Force Warrior trained a small number of Iraqi volunteers to assist American and coalition civil-military units in their language skills and knowledge of Iraq.

In September 2003 Barno visited Afghanistan to receive briefings on what would become his next command. He assumed responsibility for U.S. military operations in Afghanistan in October 2003. Now a lieutenant general, he created a new military command structure, designated Combined Forces Command–Afghanistan, and established a counterinsurgency strategy for the country. Responsible for a region covering Afghanistan, southern Tajikistan and Uzbekistan, and parts of Pakistan, Barno worked closely with representatives from the U.S. Department of State, the United Nations, the North Atlantic Treaty Organization, the International Security Assistance Force (Afghanistan), and the government of Afghanistan to coordinate counterinsurgency efforts across that country.

Barno shifted the focus of military operations from the primary goal of killing the enemy to reaching and aiding the Afghan people. His counterinsurgency strategy aimed to deny sanctuary to the enemy, support Afghan security forces, engage Afghanistan's neighbors, promote reconstruction and good governance, and create area "ownership" whereby military commanders could learn about and be responsible for specific regions.

Barno served as the assistant chief of staff for installation management before retiring from the army on June 1, 2006, as a lieutenant general. He subsequently accepted the position of director of the Near East South Asia Center for Strategic Studies at the National Defense University at Fort McNair in Washington, D.C., which post he held until 2009. In May 2010 Barno joined the Center for a New American Security as a senior fellow and adviser. He also serves as a consultant on Afghanistan, counterinsurgency operations, and the Global War on Terror for government agencies and other organizations.

LISA MARIE MUNDEY

See also

Combined Forces Command, Afghanistan; International Security Assistance Force

References

Barno, David W. "Fighting 'The Other War': Counterinsurgency Strategy in Afghanistan, 2003–2005." *Military Review* (September–October 2007): 32–44.

Combat Studies Institute, Contemporary Operations Study Group. *A Different Kind of War: The United States Army Operation Enduring Freedom (OEF), September 2001–September 2005.* Fort Leavenworth, KS: Combat Studies Institute Press, 2009.

Rasanayagam, Angelo. *Afghanistan: A Modern History.* London: I. B. Tauris, 2005.

Basra, Battle of (March 23, 2003–April 7, 2003)

Battle fought between British and Iraqi forces during the Iraq War (2003–2011) at the Iraqi city of Basra (Basrah) in southeastern Iraq near the Shatt al-Arab waterway and the Persian Gulf. The battle began on March 23 and ended with the British capture of the city on April 7. At Basra, the British pursued a strategy considerably different from that followed by their American coalition partners during the invasion of Iraq. While this British strategy sharply limited loss of life, it also allowed many Iraqi soldiers and officials to escape and fight in the subsequent insurgency.

Basra is Iraq's main port and its second-largest city, with a current population of about 3.2 million. The city and its

Iraqi civilians fleeing the city of Basra in southern Iraq during Operation IRAQI FREEDOM, March 28, 2003. (AP Photo)

environs hold significant petroleum resources, and the oil refinery at Basra has a daily production rate of approximately 150,000 barrels. Agricultural commodities also represent an important component to Basra's economy. Products such as millet, wheat, barley, dates, and corn are produced in the area's rich soil. Livestock are also an important part of the agricultural sector here. In addition, Basra is home to Iraq's petrochemical sector.

During the opening days of the Iraq War, British forces, supported by U.S. marines and offshore coalition naval units, seized the Faw Peninsula and the deepwater port of Umm Qasr. British forces then took over occupation of the Rumailah oil fields from American units that were needed elsewhere. The next major task for the British then became the capture of Basra.

To achieve the capture of Basra, the British deployed the 1st Armored Division, commanded by Major General Robin Brims. Iraqi forces in the city were commanded by General Ali Hassan al-Majid, otherwise known as "Chemical Ali" for his role in the Iraqi nerve gas attack on the Kurdish town of Halabja in 1988. Ali commanded a mixed force of Iraqi regulars and Baathist militia.

Brims decided upon a unique strategy for the taking of Basra, which would limit civilian deaths and mitigate physical damage to the city's buildings and infrastructure. The population of the city was made up primarily of anti–Saddam Hussein Shias. Basra had suffered greatly during President Hussein's suppression of the 1991 southern Shia rebellion that had followed the 1991 Persian Gulf War. Brims did not want to destroy the city and did not want to inflict needless casualties on the civilian population and thereby turn its people against the coalition.

Brims thus ordered the 1st Armored Division to surround Basra beginning on March 23, but he did not place the city under siege. He allowed anyone who wanted to leave Basra to do so, hoping to encourage desertion among Iraqi conscripts, which did occur. Brims also avoided the use of indirect artillery fire against Iraqi positions in Basra, thereby minimizing civilian casualties. Ali's strategy was to draw the British into battle in the narrow city streets of Basra where the British advantage in armor would be nullified, but Brims refused to engage in street fighting.

Frustrated, the Iraqis attempted to provoke the British into launching a major attack on the city. Ali sent out a column of Soviet-built T-55 tanks to attack the British on the evening of March 26. However, the T-55s were outranged by the 120-mm guns of the British Challenger tanks of the Royal Scots Dragoon Guards, resulting in the destruction of 15 T-55s without loss to the British.

On March 31 British reconnaissance, intelligence, and sniper teams began infiltrating the city, gathering intelligence, sniping at Iraqi officers and Baathist officials, making contact with anti-Hussein resistance circles, and directing artillery and air strikes. Beginning in early April, the British initiated a series of devastating yet limited raids against Iraqi positions using Warrior armored vehicles equipped with 30-mm cannon and capable of speeds of more than 50 miles per hour.

On April 5 an American F-16 fighter-bomber dropped two satellite-guided Joint Direct Attack Munition (JDAM) bombs on a building thought to be Chemical Ali's headquarters. The building was destroyed, and initially Ali was reported killed. He in fact survived the bombing and was not captured until after the war, but reports of his death were widely believed by Iraqi defenders, whose morale now plummeted.

A probe by the British into northern Basra on the morning of April 6 proved highly successful. Brims decided that the time had come to move into Basra in force. At 11:00 a.m. on April 6, he ordered British troops into the city. Despite heavy fighting, most of the city was under British control by nightfall. The British suffered only three soldiers killed. Some additional fighting continued the next day, but by the evening of April 7 the battle was officially over, and Basra was secure.

Because the British were not assigned the task of assaulting Baghdad and overthrowing Hussein's regime and were facing a population that they believed was sympathetic, the British could adopt a strategy at Basra that differed markedly from the strategy followed by the Americans in their drive to Baghdad. Loss of life was minimized, and further damage to the city's infrastructure was avoided. However, many of the Baathists who were allowed to escape from Basra must have certainly joined the postwar Sunni insurgency. Basra also experienced a wave of immediate postwar looting and violence similar to what also took place in Baghdad.

After the fighting stopped, the Multi-National Division under British command engaged in security and stabilization missions in the Basra Governorate and surrounding areas. Despite these pacification efforts, in mid-2006 Basra had seen several violent confrontations between secular Iraqis and Shiite Muslims in the area.

In September 2007 the British troops occupying Basra were withdrawn to the city's airport, part of a plan to

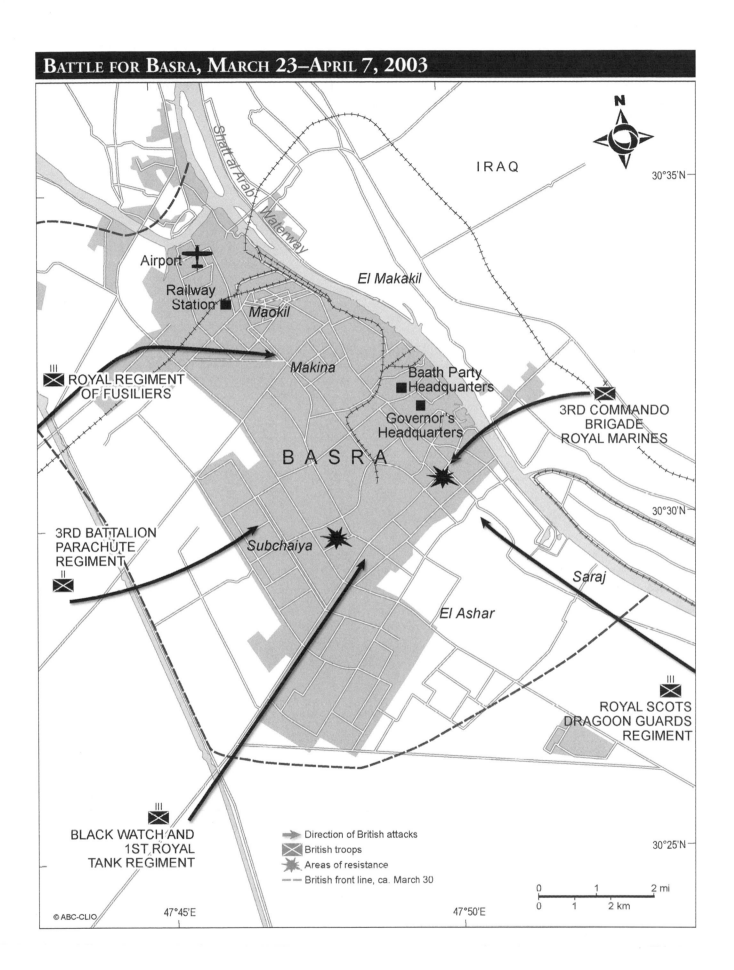

BATTLE FOR BASRA, MARCH 23–APRIL 7, 2003

IRAQ

30°35'N

Airport

El Makakil

Railway
Station

Maokil

Makina

III

ROYAL REGIMENT
OF FUSILIERS

Baath Party
Headquarters

Governor's
Headquarters

3RD COMMANDO
BRIGADE
ROYAL MARINES

B A S R A

30°30'N

3RD BATTALION
PARACHUTE
REGIMENT

Subchaiya

Saraj

II

El Ashar

ROYAL SCOTS
DRAGOON GUARDS
REGIMENT

III

III

BLACK WATCH AND
1ST ROYAL
TANK REGIMENT

30°25'N

→ Direction of British attacks

British troops

Areas of resistance

– – – British front line, ca. March 30

0   1   2 mi

0   1   2 km

© ABC-CLIO

47°45'E

47°50'E

gradually return occupied areas of Iraq over to Iraqi control. In December 2007 British troops withdrew entirely from Basra, including the airport. In the spring of 2008, the Iraqi Army initiated an offensive in Basra to rid the city of fighters associated with the Mahdi Army. Since the withdrawal of coalition troops from Iraq in December 2011, Basra remained relatively stable and through 2014 escaped any direct threat from the Islamic State of Iraq and Syria (ISIS).

PAUL WILLIAM DOERR AND CHARLENE T. OVERTURF

See also

Hussein, Saddam; IRAQI FREEDOM, Operation; Majid al Tikriti, Ali Hassan al-; Shia Islam; Sunni Islam

References

Gordon, Michael R., and General Bernard E. Trainor. *Cobra II: The Inside Story of the Invasion and Occupation of Iraq*. New York: Pantheon Books, 2006.

Keegan, John. *The Iraq War: The Military Offensive, from Victory in 21 Days to the Insurgent Aftermath*. New York: Vintage, 2005.

Benghazi, Attack on U.S. Consulate (September 11–12, 2012)

On the night of September 11–12, 2012, in the immediate aftermath of the Libyan Civil War, as many as 150 Islamic militants stormed the U.S. diplomatic consulate at Benghazi, Libya. Armed with rocket-propelled grenades, machine guns, hand grenades, and other weapons, the mob breached the main gates of the compound and later fired mortars at a nearby consular annex, where staff had taken refuge. Four Americans were killed in the attack: U.S. ambassador to Libya J. Christopher Stevens; security personnel Tyrone S. Woods and Glen Doherty, both former U.S. Navy SEALS; and foreign service officer Sean Smith. While details of the attack still remain murky, it was captured by surveillance cameras and witnessed by the surviving guards.

Initially, the attacks were said to have been a spontaneous response to an anti-Muslim film produced in the United States. The film had already led to protests in Benghazi, Cairo, and other Muslim cities. However, the attacks were subsequently described by the Barack Obama administration as intentional and preplanned. In the investigation that followed, the U.S. State Department reported that the attacks were carried out by a North African branch of Al Qaeda as well as an extremist militia called Ansar al-Sharia. In the meantime, as the November 6 presidential election approached, Republicans sharply criticized the Obama

administration for its handling of the attack and suggested that it had purposely obfuscated details of the incident for political reasons.

Beginning in late 2010 and progressing well into 2011, popular uprisings throughout the Arab world overthrew governments in Egypt, Libya, Yemen, and Tunisia. In Libya, Muammar Qaddafi lost power in late 2011 to rebel forces aided by air support from the North Atlantic Treaty Organization. Western nations hoped that the new leadership in Libya would usher in a new democratic government. However, after Qaddafi's ouster Libya remained very unstable, despite having adopted an interim government and parliament.

After the fall of the Qaddafi government, the Obama administration approved reopening U.S. diplomatic missions in Tripoli and Benghazi. However, in the months prior to the attack, intelligence had reportedly reached the Obama administration that security in Libya was faltering. Extremist groups connected to Al Qaeda were training in the mountains near Tripoli, and there had been attacks on a British diplomatic motorcade and the Red Cross. In an e-mail to the State Department, Stevens told officials that he was nervous about the lack of appropriate security in Benghazi. In the week before the attack, in fact, there was a car bombing in Benghazi, and the Libyan government issued security warnings for the area. The State Department responded to these warnings by increasing the fortification of the U.S. compound in Benghazi, but it is not clear that the government received direct warnings of a specific threat. Stevens's e-mail was later cited by Republicans who criticized the Obama administration's handling of the security threats in Libya.

Ansar al-Sharia, the militant group that has taken credit for the attack, was training openly near Benghazi. The group's location was so well known, in fact, that local citizens had stormed it in protest after the attack.

The U.S. compound in Benghazi is a collection of buildings surrounded by high concrete walls. Security at the compound included five diplomatic security officers and four members of a local militia provided by the Libyan government. A rapid response team was housed at an annex facility approximately one mile away. The timeline of events, according to the State Department, indicates that the attack took place over a relatively short period of time on September 11 and 12.

Sometime around 9:40 p.m. on September 11, 2012, security agents reported hearing loud noises and gunfire at the front gate of the compound, and cameras showed an armed group entering it. Calls were made to officials at the

U.S. embassy in Tripoli as well as officials in Washington and Libya, and the quick reaction force at the nearby annex was also alerted.

Armed security personnel promptly took Stevens and Smith to a safe room inside the compound's main residence building. Attackers then stormed that building. The attackers were unable to break into the room in which Stevens and Smith had sought refuge, so they lit fires around it with diesel fuel. The smoke made breathing nearly impossible. Other members of the U.S. security team returned and pulled Smith out, but he had died from smoke inhalation. They were not able to find Stevens in the smoke-filled building. With security forces unable to hold the perimeter, the decision was made to evacuate the compound and retreat to the nearby annex facility.

Between 4:00 and 5:00 a.m. on September 12, a six-man security team from the embassy in Tripoli arrived at the annex, after being told that a search for Stevens at the compound would be futile. The annex was then hit by mortar fire, killing Woods and Doherty. After the mortar attacks, the decision was made to evacuate all remaining personnel to Tripoli, with the last plane leaving around 10:00 a.m.

In the hours after the initial attack on the compound, locals found Stevens, who had tried to escape the smoke, and took him to the closest medical center. There he was pronounced dead due to smoke inhalation.

On September 12, Obama used the word "terror" to describe the attack in his first public statement but did not specifically label the incident as planned terrorist attacks. Republican presidential candidate Mitt Romney argued that the failure to do so immediately showed weakness and that the situation had been mishandled.

On September 16, U.S. ambassador to the United Nations Susan Rice stated on several television news shows that the events at the compound were the result of spontaneous protests. However, at the same time, new intelligence reports were asserting that this was not the case. In her remarks, Rice was using the Obama administration's talking points based on preliminary intelligence assessments, but because the administration also conveyed what it learned from the newer intelligence reports, it seemed to shift its explanation of the attacks. This led to sharp criticism from congressional Republicans and Romney in what many described as a purely political attack.

Congressional Republicans immediately called for an investigation into the Obama administration's handling of the event. They questioned why the attacks were not immediately labeled as terrorism and why the administration allegedly ignored calls for increased security at the consulate in Benghazi.

On September 26, 2012, Secretary of State Hillary Rodham Clinton announced that the attacks were planned by militant groups with Al Qaeda ties. The events in Benghazi clearly demonstrated that Libya was still very unstable and that its government did not have complete control of the country.

On October 10, Charlene Lamb of the State Department stated that she had not approved increased security for Benghazi despite the increase in violence because she wanted local Libyan forces to be trained for security purposes. On October 15, Clinton officially took the blame for the security oversights. At a Senate hearing in mid-December, Senator John Kerry (D-MA) said that Congress also must accept blame for the attacks, as it had not approved increased funding for embassy security.

In January 2013, Clinton was called to the U.S. Senate to testify about the administration's handling of the attack. The White House and intelligence officials maintained that they were searching for the people behind the attack. The one person held in connection with the attacks was picked up at an airport in Turkey and sent to his native Tunisia, where he was later released because of lack of evidence.

The Benghazi attacks led to an ongoing internal investigation as well as more congressional testimony from top State Department officials. While some say that the investigations and attacks from Republicans were merely political, others claim that the investigations were necessary to understand what went wrong and how to improve diplomatic security.

Numerous and overlapping investigations were launched by the U.S. Senate, the U.S. House of Representatives, the State Department, and the Federal Bureau of Investigation, among other government entities. The general consensus was that the attack was preventable but had not required a lot of preplanning and had been the product of organized terror organizations operating within Libya at the time. Some still question the Obama administration's handling of the incident after it occurred, but no unbiased, irrefutable evidence has yet been offered to suggest a purposeful cover-up. In August 2013 the U.S. government filed numerous charges against as yet unnamed participants in the attack, and in June 2014 U.S. special forces apprehended Ansar al-Sharia leader Ahmed Abu Khattala in Libya. He was charged with masterminding the attack, although he denies any involvement in it.

On November 21, 2014, following nearly two years of hearings and investigation, the Republican-led House Select

Committee on Intelligence released its long-awaited report on the Benghazi attack. The report found that the U.S. military and Central Intelligence Agency (CIA) had responded appropriately during the attacks and had "ensured sufficient security" and "bravely assisted" the night of the attacks. The panel also found no intelligence failure prior to the attacks. The committee also concluded that there was no evidence that the military had been ordered, as some had charged, to stand down during the attacks. It also determined that "appropriate US personnel made reasonable tactical decisions that night," and it dismissed claims that the CIA was involved in arms shipments or other unauthorized activities.

DANIEL KATZ

See also

Central Intelligence Agency; Clinton, Hillary Rodham; Libya; Libyan Civil War; Obama, Barack Hussein, II; United States, National Elections of 2012

References

"Clinton Says Benghazi Is Her Biggest Regret." *Washington Post,* January 22, 2014, http://www.washingtonpost.com/blogs/post-politics/wp/2014/01/27/clinton-says-benghazi-is-her-biggest-regret/.

"Review of the Terrorist Attacks on U.S. Facilities in Benghazi, Libya." U.S. Senate Select Committee on Intelligence, January 15, 2014, http://www.intelligence.senate.gov/benghazi2014/benghazi.pdf.

"U.S. Officials: CIA Ran Benghazi Consulate." UPI, November 2, 2012, http://www.upi.com/Top_News/US/2012/11/02/US-officials-CIA-ran-Benghazi-consulate/UPI-44771351839600/.

Berghdal, Bowe, Release of (May 31, 2014)

The release of U.S. Army sergeant Bowe Robert Berghdal on May 31, 2014, following his 59-month ordeal as a prisoner of war in Afghanistan proved highly controversial and called into question the Barack Obama administration's conduct of the ongoing Global War on Terror. Berghdal, who was 23 years old at the time of his capture by the Taliban-allied Haqqani Network, graduated from infantry school at Fort Benning, Georgia, in late 2008 and deployed to Afghanistan as a corporal in May 2009 (he was promoted to sergeant during his captivity).

Berghdal was taken captive on the night of June 30, 2009, in Paktika Province in east-central Afghanistan. There are varying accounts concerning the details of his disappearance. In a video made by his captors, Berghdal claimed that he had been taken prisoner after falling behind during a routine patrol mission. The Taliban asserted that he had been drunk and was ambushed after wandering off base. The U.S. Army and the Pentagon flatly denied the Taliban's claim. Berghdal's fellow soldiers, however, offered a third explanation—that he had purposefully walked away from his post after having repeatedly voiced his disillusionment with the Afghanistan War and U.S. tactics employed to wage it.

Since at least early 2013, U.S. military officials had been engaged in talks designed to reach a deal with the Taliban whereby up to five Taliban prisoners being held at the Guantánamo Bay Detainment Camp would be released. The purpose of the release was twofold. First, it was to be a gesture of goodwill intended to ease the way for a political settlement between the Afghan government under President Hamid Karzai and the Taliban and its allies. Second, it was intended to lead to Berghdal's release as a prisoner exchange. The negotiations broke down repeatedly over details of the deal, however, but when American officials became increasingly concerned about Berghdal's physical health, the Obama administration ultimately agreed to the exchange but under strict secrecy. The Guantánamo detainees were released to Qatar, which had helped broker the deal.

On May 31, 2014, Berghdal was released to members of the U.S. Army's Delta Force, a counterterrorism unit. When Berghdal's release was made public, the details of his imprisonment became widely known. He had been repeatedly tortured and beaten, and after he tried to escape, he was locked in a small metal cage—in complete darkness—for weeks at a time. In June 2014, the U.S. Army declared that there was no evidence that Berghdal had engaged in any inappropriate conduct during his imprisonment. Some of the men with whom he had served, however, alleged that Berghdal had willfully gone AWOL and had endangered his unit, which conducted a perilous search for him after his disappearance. In 2006, Berghdal had been given an "uncharacterized discharge" from the U.S. Coast Guard after 26 days of basic training. Such discharges are usually given to recruits suffering from psychological problems.

Berghdal's release created an immediate political firestorm. Under a law passed in the immediate aftermath of the September 11, 2001, attacks, the U.S. president is obligated to provide Congress with his intention—in writing—to release any prisoner from Guantánamo at least 30 days in advance of said release. The Obama administration did not do so and argued that the delicate nature of the negotiations, combined with concern about Berghdal's condition, made it impossible to follow the law to the letter. Many in Congress—especially

Republicans—were not entirely convinced, however. The Obama White House went on to assert that the U.S. Army, by tradition, does not leave any soldier behind, regardless of the circumstances of his or her imprisonment.

Others critical of the way in which the release was handled argued that the United States had abandoned its long-standing policy of not negotiating hostage ransoms with known terrorists. Congressman Mike Rogers, a Republican from Michigan and chairman of the House Intelligence Committee, fumed that Berghdal's release gave terrorists "around the world" a greater incentive to take American hostages. The White House shot back that Berghdal was not a civilian hostage but rather a U.S. Army soldier who became a prisoner of war in a recognized war zone. The Berghdal affair renewed America's angst and impatience with the long war in Afghanistan and provided much ammunition for Obama's detractors, who have taken issue with his conduct with the war on terror. Berghdal, meanwhile, was returned to active duty in July 2014. A thorough investigation into the circumstance of his capture was undertaken, and Berghdal was charged with desertion.

PAUL G. PIERPAOLI JR.

See also

Global War on Terror; Guantánamo Bay Detainment Camp; Karzai, Hamid; Obama, Barack Hussein, II; Qatar; Taliban

References

"Bowe Berghdal Fast Facts." CNN, July 21, 2014, http://www.cnn.com/2014/01/19/us/bowe-bergdahl-fast-facts.

Mendelsohn, Sarah E. *Closing Guantanamo: From Bumper Sticker to Blueprint.* Washington, DC: Center for Security and International Studies, 2008.

Biden, Joseph Robinette, Jr. (1941–)

Attorney, Democratic Party politician, U.S. senator representing Delaware (1973–2009), chairman of the powerful Senate Foreign Relations Committee (2001–2003, 2007–2009), and vice president of the United States (2009–present). Born in Scranton, Pennsylvania, on November 20, 1941, Joseph Robinette Biden Jr. was the first of four children born to Irish Catholic parents; his parents moved the family to Delaware during his childhood. Biden graduated from the University of Delaware in 1965 and earned a law degree at Syracuse University in 1968 before returning to Delaware to practice law in 1969.

In 1970 Biden was elected to a seat on the New Castle County Council in Delaware, and in 1972 he ran against Republican incumbent J. Caleb Boggs for the U.S. Senate from Delaware and won. Because Delaware is one of the few states small enough to have more senators than congressmen, Biden enjoyed an unusually rapid rise in his political career.

In the Senate Biden served on numerous committees, including the Judiciary Committee and the Foreign Relations Committee, and in time he would chair both on different occasions. He has adhered to a relatively moderate Democratic voting record, supporting industrial endeavors in Delaware as well as Amtrak and introducing legislation on antidrug, domestic violence, and college aid programs. In 1984, 1988, and 2008 he ran unsuccessfully to secure the Democratic nomination for president. Because Biden was a moderate and was well versed in national security issues, many considered him a serious contender who could reorient the party at the national level. In 1984 he quickly dropped out of the race, losing to the more liberal former vice president Walter Mondale. In the 1988 campaign Biden's reputation was seriously damaged by the Michael Dukakis campaign, which accused him of plagiarizing a speech by Neil Kinnock, a British Labour Party leader. The accusation had validity in that Biden had not always given attribution to Kinnock when using some phrases from his speeches, although on many occasions he did indeed cite Kinnock.

These failed White House bids in 1984 and 1988 nonetheless raised Biden's profile, and he continued to advance in seniority in the Senate. He chaired the Judiciary Committee from 1987 to 1995 and the Foreign Relations Committee from 2001 to 2003 and again from 2007 to 2009. During William J. Clinton's presidency, Biden, as the ranking Democrat on the Foreign Relations Committee, was a proponent of lifting arms embargoes in the Balkans and using force to stop ethnic cleansing in Bosnia and Kosovo. Later, Clinton adopted these positions and authorized the use of force by the North Atlantic Treaty Organization (NATO) against Serbia. Biden also supported the presence of U.S. troops in the Balkans who had been dispatched there by Clinton.

During the early George W. Bush presidency, Biden supported the administration's effort against Afghanistan in the aftermath of the terror attacks of September 11, 2001. On October 11, 2002, Biden, still the ranking Democrat and chairman of the Senate Foreign Relations Committee, voted, along with 28 other Democratic Party senators, to authorize the use of military force against Iraq to oust President Saddam Hussein. Although initially supportive of the war, Biden soon became critical of the administration's handling of it and repeatedly called for the use of more troops (including those from the international community) in the occupation.

He also urged the president to explain and reveal the full price of the commitment in Iraq to the American people.

In May 2006 Biden along with Leslie Gelb, a former president of the Council on Foreign Relations, outlined a plan for the future of Iraq in a *New York Times* op-ed piece prior to the release of the Iraq Study Group's Report. The op-ed called for a federalized Iraq that would allow for greater self-determination for the three largest ethnic groups in Iraq—the Shiites, Sunnis, and Kurds—while retaining a single state. Essentially, the central government would leave the three regions alone to determine their own affairs, restricting itself to foreign affairs, security, and the distribution of oil revenues. Such a plan, in the view of Biden and Gelb, would provide for stability while allowing for an American exit that would secure U.S. influence in the country. Critics of this plan, including Senator John McCain, have argued that in the long term this is little more than a three-state solution that would essentially destroy the nation of Iraq and lead to greater Iranian influence in the region, a claim that Biden hotly contests.

In 2004 Biden was a strong supporter of his friend Senator John Kerry's failed presidential campaign and was frequently mentioned as a potential running mate before Kerry's ultimate selection of Senator John Edwards. In 2007–2008 Biden once again was a contender for the Democratic presidential nomination, although he dropped out of the race in January 2008 after doing poorly in the Iowa primary. Biden subsequently was selected as Barrack Obama's vice presidential candidate, and after victory in the November 2008 presidential election Biden became the 47th U.S. vice president on January 20, 2009.

During Biden's first term, he supervised most of the spending allocation related to the economic stimulus package passed by Congress in 2009. He was also a major player in health care reform and had a key role in the passage of the Affordable Care Act (Obamacare), passed in 2010. Biden opposed the Obama administration's troop surge in Afghanistan (2010–2012) and traveled frequently to Iraq to ensure that the withdrawal of U.S. troops (accomplished in December 2011) proceeded according to plan. On occasion Biden's bluntness has resulted in spoken gaffes, but he has been uncommonly loyal to the president he serves. Although Biden campaigned hard for Democrats in the 2010 midterm elections, the Democrats lost control of the House to Republicans, an event that many blamed on Obamacare and the continuing sluggish economy. Using his many years of congressional experience, Biden was influential in reaching agreements with the Republicans on the Tax Relief, Unemployment Insurance Reauthorization, and Job Creation Act of 2010; the 2011 Budget Control Act, which temporarily resolved the debt ceiling controversy; and the American Taxpayer Relief Act of 2012.

Biden remained on the Obama ticket in the 2012 election, and both men won reelection by a comfortable margin. Biden played less of a role in brokering important fiscal deals with Republicans during 2013, however, a consequence of key Democratic congressional leaders having shut out both Biden and Obama from the negotiating process. Biden has been a champion of equal rights for gays and lesbians and strongly supported the Pentagon's ending of the "Don't Ask, Don't Tell" policy for U.S. service members. Biden's second term has been punctuated by many foreign trips, and during the Crimean Crisis of early 2014, he visited Europe and the Ukraine in an attempt to demonstrate American support for fellow NATO members as well as the Ukrainians.

Michael K. Beauchamp

See also
Iraq, History of, 1990–Present; Iraq Study Group; Obama, Barack Hussein, II; United States, National Elections of 2008; United States, National Elections of 2012; United States, National Elections of 2014; United States Congress and the Iraq War

References
Biden, Joseph Robinette, Jr. *Promises to Keep: On Life and Politics.* New York: Random House, 2007.
Danchev, Alex, and John Macmillan, eds. *The Iraq War and Democratic Politics.* New York: Routledge, 2003.
Woodward, Bob. *State of Denial: Bush at War, Part III.* New York: Simon and Schuster, 2006.

Bin Laden, Osama (1957–2011)

Islamic extremist and, as head of the Al Qaeda terrorist organization, the world's most notorious terrorist leader who Laden has been linked most notoriously to the September 11, 2001, terrorist attacks on the United States but also to numerous other acts of terrorism throughout the world. Born on March 10, 1957, in Riyadh, Saudi Arabia, Usamah bin Muhammad bin 'Awa bin Ladin is most usually known as Osama bin Laden. The Arabic meaning of the name Osama is "young lion." According to Arabic convention he should be referred to as bin Ladin, but in the West he is almost universally referred to as bin Laden.

Bin Laden's father, Muhammad bin Awdah bin Laden, was a highly successful and immensely wealthy construction manager from Yemen who prospered thanks to a close relationship with the Saudi royal family. His construction projects included first major highways and then also the reconstruction of the Muslim holy cities of Medina and Mecca. The elder bin Laden, who was also strongly opposed to Israel, reportedly had 21 wives and fathered 54 children. Osama was the 17th son but the only son of his father's 10th wife, Hamida al-Attas. The elder bin Laden died in a plane crash in 1967. He left an estate reported at $11 billion. Osama bin Laden's personal inheritance has been variously estimated at between $40 million and $50 million.

The family moved a number of times but settled in Jeddah, Saudi Arabia. There bin Laden attended al-Thagr, the city's top school. He had some exposure to the West through vacations in Sweden and a summer program in English at Oxford University. At age 17 bin Laden married a 14-year-old cousin of his mother. In 1977 he entered King Abdulaziz University (now King Abdul Aziz University) in Jeddah, where he majored in economics and business management. Bin Laden was an indifferent student, but this was at least in part because of time spent in the family construction business. He left school altogether in 1979, evidently planning to work in the family's Saudi Binladin Group that then employed 37,000 people and was valued at some $5 billion. This plan was apparently blocked by his older brothers.

As a boy bin Laden had received religious training in Sunni Islam, but around 1973 he began developing a fundamentalist religious bent. This was sufficiently strong to alarm other family members. Bin Laden also developed ties with the fundamentalist Muslim Brotherhood that same year. While in the university he was mentored in Islamic studies by Muhammad Qutb, brother of the martyred Sayyid Qutb, leader of the Muslim Brotherhood, and by Sheikh Abdullah Yussuf Azzam, a proponent of jihad (holy war). Both men had a profound influence on bin Laden.

Two events also exacted a profound influence. The first was the seizure of the Grand Mosque in Mecca by Islamists led by Juhaynan ibn-Muhammad-ibn Sayf al-Taibi and the subsequent martyrdom of the group. The second was the Soviet Union's invasion of Afghanistan in 1979. It is safe to say that the latter marked a major turning point in bin Laden's life.

In 1979 bin Laden traveled to Pakistan and there met with Afghan leaders Burhanuddin Rabbani and Abdul Rasool Sayyaf. Bin Laden then returned to Saudi Arabia to organize resistance to the Soviets in Afghanistan. There was considerable sentiment in Saudi Arabia for assisting the Afghans against the Soviets, and reportedly some 10,000 Saudis volunteered. Bin Laden returned to Pakistan with construction equipment, such as bulldozers, to aid the

Afghan mujahideen (freedom fighters, holy warriors) fighting the Soviet troops and allied Afghan government forces. This equipment was used to build roads, tunnels, shelters, and hospitals.

Bin Laden's organizational skills were more important than the equipment, however. He worked actively with Sheikh Abdullah Yussuf Azzau to recruit and train jihadists to fight in Afghanistan, much of the funding for which came from bin Laden's personal fortune. He also tapped his contacts in Saudi Arabia for additional funds. Azzam and bin Laden established the Mujahideen Services Bureau. Between 1985 and 1989, approximately 150,000 soldiers entered Afghanistan through training camps established in neighboring Pakistan by the Mujahideen Services Bureau.

In 1986 bin Laden, now having relocated to Peshawar, Pakistan, joined a mujahideen field unit and took part in actual combat. Notably, this included the 1987 Battle of the Lion's Den near Jaji. Such activity sharply increased bin Laden's prestige among the mujahideen.

The mysterious assassination of bin Laden's mentor Azzam on November 14, 1989, opened the way for bin Laden to assume a greater role in extremist Islamic politics. While he agreed with Azzam about the need for jihad against the enemies of Islam, bin Laden carried this philosophy a step further by insisting that it should be extended to a holy war on behalf of Islam around the world.

In the autumn of 1989 Azzam and bin Laden had founded the Al Qaeda (Arabic for "the base") organization. On its announcement, those present were required to sign a loyalty oath (*bayat*). With Azzam's death, bin Laden, at the age of 32, became the undisputed leader of Al Qaeda.

With the end of the Soviet-Afghan War, bin Laden returned to Saudi Arabia. He was now acclaimed as a hero by both the Saudi people and the government. Bin Laden soon approached Prince Turki al-Faisal, head of the kingdom's intelligence services, offering to lead a guerrilla effort to overthrow the Marxist government of South Yemen, but Turki rejected the suggestion. Bin Laden then settled in Jeddah and worked in the family construction business until Iraqi president Saddam Hussein sent his army into Kuwait in August 1990.

The Iraqi military takeover of Kuwait directly threatened Saudi Arabia, and bin Laden again approached the Saudi government, offering to recruit as many as 12,000 men to defend the kingdom. The Saudi government again rebuffed him. Instead, it allowed U.S. and other Western troops to be stationed in Saudi Arabia with the plan to drive the Iraqis from Kuwait by force if necessary. Incensed both at the

New Yorkers celebrate outside the ABC studio in New York's Times Square as news of Osama bin Laden's death is announced on the ticker, May 2, 2011. (AP Photo)

rejection of his services and the injection of hundreds of thousands of infidels into his homeland, bin Laden bitterly denounced the Saudi government. Indeed, he demanded that all foreign troops leave at once. His vocal opposition to Saudi government policy brought him a brief period of house arrest.

Bin Laden's opposition to Saudi government policies and the Persian Gulf War led him to leave the kingdom. He moved with his family first to Pakistan and then to Sudan, where he had earlier purchased property around Khartoum. He also moved his financial assets there and became involved in a series of business ventures including a road-building company, all of which added considerably to his personal fortune. From Sudan, bin Laden also mounted verbal attacks on the Saudi royal family and the kingdom's religious leadership, accusing them of being false Muslims. These attacks led the Saudi government to strip him of his citizenship in April 1994 and freeze his financial assets in the kingdom (his share of the family business was then estimated to be about $7 million). Bin Laden also roundly denounced Israel.

In Sudan, bin Laden also organized the terrorist activities of Al Qaeda, which were in place by 1989. Its goals were to incite all Muslims to join in a defensive jihad against the West and to help overthrow tyrannical secular governments. Bin Laden established an Al Qaeda training camp at Soba, north of Khartoum, and in 1992 he sent advisers and equipment to Somalia to aid the fight against the Western mission to restore order in that country. He also began terrorist activities directed against Americans in Saudi Arabia. On November 13, 1995, a car bomb in Riyadh killed 5 Americans and 1 Saudi and wounded 60 others. Other similar actions followed.

Mounting pressure by the Saudi and U.S. governments forced the Sudanese government to ask bin Laden to leave that country. In May 1996 bin Laden relocated to Afghanistan. He left Sudan with little money; the Sudanese government settled with him for only a small fraction of his reported, but no doubt overestimated, $300 million in assets.

Afghanistan was a natural location for bin Laden. The Islamic fundamentalist Taliban had come to power, and bin Laden had established a close relationship with its head, Mullah Mohammed Omar. Although there was some unease among the Taliban leadership about the possible consequences of hosting the now-acknowledged terrorist, their scruples were overcome by bin Laden's promises of financial assistance from his Arab contacts. In return, the

Taliban permitted bin Laden to establish a network of training camps and perpetrate worldwide terrorist activities. The alliance was firmly established when bin Laden directed Al Qaeda to join the fight against the Northern Alliance forces of General Ahmed Shah Massoud that were seeking to unseat the Taliban.

Now firmly established in Afghanistan, bin Laden began planning a series of attacks against the perceived worldwide enemies of Islam. His principal target was the United States, and on August 23, 1996, he issued a call for jihad against the Americans for their presence in Saudi Arabia. In February 1998 he broadened this to a global jihad against all enemies of Islam. Al Qaeda was in fact largely a holding organization with several dozen terrorist groups affiliated with it. Bin Laden's role was to coordinate, approve, and assist their various activities. Thus, when Khalid Sheikh Mohammed presented a plan to hijack large commercial airliners and crash them into prominent buildings in the United States, bin Laden approved the plan but left its implementation up to Mohammed.

Bin Laden expected that these attacks in the United States, if they were successful, would trigger a vigorous American response but that this, in turn, would produce an outpouring of support for his cause from within the Arab world. The first assumption proved correct. After the September 11, 2001, attacks on the World Trade Center in New York City and the Pentagon in Washington, D.C., the United States demanded that the Taliban turn over bin Laden and take action against Al Qaeda. When the leaders of the Taliban refused, U.S. forces, assisted by those of other Western nations, aided the Northern Alliance and attacked Afghanistan, driving the Taliban from power. The second assumption, that a forceful U.S. response would bring a Muslim backlash, proved false.

Bin Laden had also not expected the Taliban to be easily overthrown. When that occurred, he withdrew into his stronghold in Tora Bora, a cave complex in the White Mountains of eastern Afghanistan, where he remained until December 2001. U.S. efforts to capture him and his followers were botched, and he escaped, presumably into northwestern Pakistan. There Islamic fundamentalism and support for the Taliban and Al Qaeda is strong. Indeed, Western efforts to capture him made him something of a hero in the Muslim world, where a significant percentage of people profess admiration for him. There are indications that he was wounded in the arm in the U.S. bombing of Tora Bora in late 2001, and there was other speculation about the status of his health. Despite a reward of $50 million for his capture—dead or alive—Osama bin Laden continued to thwart efforts to bring him to justice for many years.

At about 1 a.m. on May 2, 2011 (Pakistan Standard Time), a group of Navy SEALs stormed bin Laden's compound, and he was subsequently killed in the resulting firefight. There were no U.S. casualties during the operation. The assault on bin Laden's compound did, however, cause problems in U.S.-Pakistani relations. The United States staged the mission without the knowledge or participation of the Pakistani government or military, which angered Pakistani leaders. This led to recriminations in Islamabad that the Americans had purposefully violated Pakistani sovereignty. The United States, in turn, implied that bin Laden could not have lived in Pakistan for so long without someone in the Pakistani government knowing of his whereabouts. After the bin Laden operation, U.S.-Pakistani relations remained difficult for quite some time. Nevertheless, bin Laden's death served as a powerful symbol in the Global War on Terror and temporarily boosted President Barack Obama's approval ratings.

HARRY RAYMOND HUESTON II AND SPENCER C. TUCKER

See also

Afghanistan; Al Qaeda; Global War on Terror; Jihad; Pakistan; September 11 Attacks; Taliban; Terrorism; Tora Bora

References

Atkins, Stephen E. *The 9/11 Encyclopedia.* 2nd ed. Santa Barbara, CA: ABC-CLIO, 2011.

Bergen, Peter L. *Holy War, Inc.: Inside the Secret World of Osama bin Laden.* New York: Touchstone, 2002.

Gunaratna, Rohan. *Inside Al Qaeda: Global Network of Terror.* New York: Berkley Publishing Group, 2003.

Randal, Jonathan. *Osama: The Making of a Terrorist.* New York: Knopf, 2004.

Biological Weapons and Warfare

Biological weapons are forms of natural organisms and modified versions of germs and toxins that are used as weapons to kill or harm people or animals. The first type of biological weapon includes diseases such as anthrax and smallpox, while the second category includes toxins or poisons such as ricin and aflatoxin. Along with nuclear and chemical arms, biological weapons are considered to be weapons of mass destruction (WMD).

Israel's advanced nuclear program prompted several Arab states to initiate biological weapons programs as a means to counter the Israeli nuclear arsenal. Indeed, the proliferation of WMD, including biological weapons, is one of the most serious security issues in the Middle East.

By the early 1970s, several Arab states had established biological weapons programs as a means to balance Israel's nuclear arsenal as they concurrently sought to develop their own nuclear and chemical weapons programs. Biological weapons were attractive to many states because they were perceived as being less expensive and easier to manufacture. Biological agents could also be developed far more quickly than nuclear or chemical programs.

The Middle Eastern country with the oldest biological weapons program is Israel. During the Israeli War of Independence (1948–1949), there were charges that Israeli units infected Arab wells with malaria and typhoid. Following independence, a biological weapons unit was created. Israel's program was designed to develop both offensive and defensive capabilities, and its successful nuclear program overshadowed its chemical and biological efforts. In the 2000s, Israel's biological and chemical weapons programs were increasingly focused on counterproliferation in the region and efforts to prevent bioterrorism.

Egypt began a wide-scale biological program in the 1960s and recruited European scientists to advance the program. By 1972, Egypt had an offensive biological weapons capability, a fact later confirmed by President Anwar Sadat in public addresses. In 1972 Egypt signed the Biological Weapons Convention (which bans the use of these arms) but did not ratify the convention. Among the Arab states, Egypt went on to develop one of the most comprehensive biological weapons programs, including anthrax, cholera, plague, botulism, and possibly smallpox. These agents were weaponized in such a fashion that they could be delivered in missile warheads. Beginning in the late 1990s, Egypt began working with the United States to develop more effective biological weapons defenses, ranging from decontamination plants to national contingency planning to stockpiles of personal gas masks.

Following the Yom Kippur (Ramadan) War of October 1973, evidence emerged from captured documents and equipment that Syria had a highly developed WMD program that included biological weapons such as anthrax, botulinum, and ricin. Syria's program proceeded with aid and products from Chinese and European firms. In the 1990s, Western intelligence agencies identified the town of Cerin as the center of Syria's biological weapons program. Toward the end of the decade, Syria also launched an effort to acquire missiles capable of delivering biological warheads into Israeli territory. Syria also developed a robust chemical weapons program. Syria's military planners hoped that its biological and chemical arsenals would deter Israel from using its nuclear weapons in the event of a conflict. In the fall of 2013, however, the Syrian government agreed to place all of its chemical weapons under international control. The last of Syria's chemical weapons were shipped out of the country by June 2014, but it is believed that the Syrian government still has an abundant supply of biological weapons. For Israel and the United States, Syria's biological weapons program continues to be troublesome because of the country's sponsorship of anti-Israeli groups such as Hezbollah and the fear that these weapons might fall into the hands of terrorists or rebel groups such as the Islamic State of Iraq and Syria (ISIS).

Libya attempted to develop a broad WMD program in the 1970s that included biological weapons. However, international sanctions prevented that nation from acquiring significant biological arms. Instead, its program remained primarily at the research level. In 2003 Libyan leader Muammar Qaddafi renounced WMD and pledged that his country would dismantle its WMD programs as part of a larger strategy to improve relations with the United States and Europe.

In 1974 the Iraqi government officially launched a biological weapons program, and within a year the country established facilities for research and development of biological agents. Through the 1970s and 1980s Iraq obtained cultures and biological agents from Western governments and firms through both legitimate and illicit means. Among the biological weapons that Iraq obtained were anthrax, salmonella, and botulinum. By 1983, Iraq began stockpiling biological warheads and accelerated its program, including efforts to develop new types of weapons.

During 1987–1988 Saddam Hussein's regime employed biological weapons against Iraq's Kurdish minority. There have been charges that this activity included rotavirus, a major killer of the young in developing countries. Iraq reportedly invested heavily in a rotavirus biological warfare program. Used either by itself or with other biological agents, rotavirus would produce major deaths and illness among children and infants.

Large-scale Iraqi production of anthrax and aflatoxin began in 1989, and that same year Iraqi scientists initiated field tests of biological weapons. In 1990 Iraq stockpiled some 200 bombs and 100 missiles capable of delivering biological agents.

Under the terms of the cease-fire that ended the 1991 Persian Gulf War, Iraq began destroying its biological weapons capability. Also in 1991, Iraq ratified the Biological Weapons Convention. United Nations (UN) weapons inspectors were granted limited access to biological weapons facilities and were able to verify the extent of the program and confirm that some materials had been destroyed. The belief by President George W. Bush's administration that Hussein's regime had not complied with UN resolutions to destroy its WMD programs was a major justification for the U.S.-led invasion in 2003. Following the occupation of Iraq, however, U.S. and international inspectors were unable to find any hidden WMD.

The Iranian military worked with the United States during the 1960s and 1970s to develop defensive strategies against biological weapons. Iran signed the Biological Weapons Convention in 1972 and ratified it a year later. Following the Iranian Revolution in 1979, however, the country began a secret biological weapons program. The Iraqi use of chemical weapons in the war between the two countries during 1980–1988 accelerated the Iranian program. Throughout the 1980s and 1990s, Iranian agents and representatives attempted to acquire biological agents both legally and illicitly. The country also hired large numbers of scientists and experts on WMD from the former Soviet Union. As a result, Iran has been able to develop small amounts of biological weapons. Iran has also developed the missile capabilities to deliver WMD to Israeli territory.

TOM LANSFORD

See also

Anthrax; Chemical Weapons and Warfare; Iran; IRAQI FREEDOM, Operation; Missiles, Intermediate-Range Ballistic; Persian Gulf War; Qaddafi, Muammar; Syria; Syrian Chemical Weapons Agreement

References

Cordesman, Anthony. *Iran's Developing Military Capabilities.* Washington, DC: CSIS, 2005.

Guillemin, Jeanne. *Biological Weapons: From the Invention of State-Sponsored Programs to Contemporary Bioterrorism.* New York: Columbia University Press, 2005.

Walker, William. *Weapons of Mass Destruction and International Order.* New York: Oxford University Press, 2004.

Zubay, Geoffrey, et al. *Agents of Bioterrorism: Pathogens and Their Weaponization.* New York: Columbia University Press, 2005.

Blackwater USA

Private U.S.-based security firm involved in military security operations in Afghanistan and Iraq. Blackwater USA (now known as Academi) was one of a number of private security firms hired by the U.S. government to aid in security operations in Afghanistan and Iraq. The company was founded in 1997 by Erik Prince, a former Navy SEAL, wealthy heir to an auto parts fortune, and staunch supporter of the Republican Party. He serves as the firm's chief executive officer (CEO). The firm was named for the brackish swampy waters surrounding its more than 6,000-acre headquarters and training facilities located in northeastern North Carolina's Dismal Swamp.

Details of the privately held company are shrouded in mystery, and the precise number of paid employees is not publicly known. A good number of its employees are not U.S. citizens. Blackwater also trained upwards of 40,000 people per year in military and security tactics, interdiction, and counterinsurgency operations. Many of its trainees were military, law enforcement, or civilian government employees, mostly American, but foreign government employees were also trained here. Blackwater claimed that its training facilities were the largest of their kind in the world. Nearly 90 percent of the company's revenues were derived from government contracts, two-thirds of which were no-bid contracts. It is estimated that between 2002 and 2009, Blackwater garnered U.S. government contracts in excess of $1 billion.

Following the successful ouster of the Taliban regime in Afghanistan in late 2001, Blackwater was among the first firms to be hired by the U.S. government to aid in security and law enforcement operations there. In 2003 after coalition forces ousted the regime of Iraqi president Saddam Hussein, Blackwater began extensive operations in the war-ravaged country. Its first major operation here included a $21 million no-bid contract to provide security services for the Coalition Provisional Authority and its chief, L. Paul Bremer. After that, Blackwater received contracts for several hundred million dollars more to provide a wide array of security and paramilitary services in Iraq. Some critics—including a number of congressional representatives and senators—took issue with the centrality of Blackwater in Iraq, arguing that its founder's connections to the Republican Party had helped it garner lucrative no-bid contracts.

Although such information was never positively verified by either Blackwater or the U.S. government, it is believed that at least 30,000 private security contractors operated in Iraq between 2003 and 2011; some estimates claim as many as 100,000. Of that number, a majority were employees or subcontractors of Blackwater. The U.S. State Department and the Pentagon, which both negotiated lucrative contracts with Blackwater, contended that neither one could function in Iraq without resorting to the use of private security firms. Indeed, the use of such contractors helped keep down the

Plainclothes members of Blackwater USA, the private security firm, participate in a firefight in Najaf, Iraq, on April 4, 2004. Iraqis loyal to Muqtada al-Sadr were attempting to advance on a facility defended by U.S. and Spanish soldiers. (AP Photo/Gervasio Sanchez)

need for even greater numbers of U.S. troops in Iraq and Afghanistan. After Hurricane Katrina smashed into the United States at the Gulf of Mexico in 2005, the U.S. government contracted with Blackwater to provide security, law enforcement, and humanitarian services in southern Louisiana and Mississippi.

In the course of the Iraqi insurgency that began in 2003, numerous Blackwater employees were injured or killed in ambushes, attacks, and suicide bombings. Because of the instability in Iraq and the oftentimes chaotic circumstances, some Blackwater personnel found themselves in situations in which they felt threatened and had to protect themselves by force. This led to numerous cases in which they were criticized, terminated, or worse for their actions. Because they were not members of the U.S. military they often fell into a gray area, which sometimes elicited demands for retribution either by the American government or Iraqi officials.

Loose oversight of Blackwater's operations led to several serious cases of alleged abuse on the part of Blackwater employees. One of the most infamous examples of this occurred in Baghdad on September 16, 2007. While escorting a diplomatic convoy through the streets of the city, a well-armed security detail consisting of Blackwater personnel and Iraqi police mistakenly opened fire on a civilian car that it claimed had not obeyed instructions to stop. Once the gunfire began, other forces in the area opened fired. When the shooting stopped, 17 Iraqi civilians lay dead, including all of the car's occupants. Included among the dead was a young couple with their infant child. At first there were wildly diverging accounts of what happened, and Blackwater contended that the car contained a suicide bomber who had detonated an explosive device, which was entirely untrue. The Iraqi government, however, faulted Blackwater for the incident, and U.S. Army officials backed up the Iraqi claims. Later reports stated that the Blackwater guards fired on the vehicle with no provocation.

The Baghdad shootings caused an uproar in both Iraq and the United States. The Iraqi government suspended Blackwater's Iraqi operations and demanded that Blackwater be banned from the country. It also sought to try the shooters in an Iraqi court. Because some of the guards involved were not Americans and the others were working for the U.S. State Department, they were not subject to criminal prosecution. In the U.S. Congress, angry lawmakers demanded a full accounting of the incident and sought more detailed information on Blackwater and its security operations.

To make matters worse, just a few days after the shootings federal prosecutors announced that they were investigating allegations that some Blackwater personnel had illegally imported weapons into Iraq that were then being supplied to the Kurdistan Workers' Party, which has been designated by the United States as a terrorist organization.

These incendiary allegations prompted a formal congressional inquiry, and in October 2007 Erik Prince, Blackwater's CEO, was compelled to testify in front of the House Committee on Oversight and Government Reform. Prince did neither himself nor his company much good when he stonewalled the committee, saying that Blackwater's financial information was beyond the purview of the government. He later retracted this statement, saying that such information would be provided upon a "written request." Blackwater then struggled under a pall of suspicion, and multiple investigations were soon under way involving the incident in Iraq, incidents in Afghanistan, and the allegations of illegal weapons smuggling by company employees. In the meantime, Congress considered legislation that would significantly tighten government control and oversight of private contractors, especially those involved in sensitive areas such as military security.

In February 2009 Blackwater officials announced that the company would now operate under the name Xe, noting that the new name reflected a "change in company focus away from the business of providing private security." There was no meaning in the new name, which was decided upon after a yearlong internal search. Prince abruptly announced his resignation as CEO and left the company in December 2010, at which time its ownership and management was taken over by an unnamed group of private investors. The investors substantially reorganized the company, changed its name to Academi in 2011, and drastically changed its mission. It largely divested itself of overseas private security programs and added a division that deals strictly with corporate governance and ethics issues.

In June 2009 the Central Intelligence Agency disclosed to Congress that in 2004 it had hired members of Blackwater as part of a secret effort to locate and assassinate top Al Qaeda operatives. Reportedly, Blackwater employees assisted with planning, training, and surveillance, but no members of Al Qaeda were captured or killed by them. By 2008, most Blackwater employees had left Iraq; U.S. troops were withdrawn from the country in December 2011. For a time, Blackwater/Xe continued to operate in Afghanistan but in much reduced numbers and with a much lower profile. By 2014, the company no longer operated in Afghanistan.

On October 21, 2014, four Blackwater employees who were involved in the September 16, 2007, shootings of 17 Iraqis in Baghdad were found guilty of manslaughter, murder, and weapons charges in a U.S. federal district court. The defendants were Paul A. Slough, Dustin L. Heard, Nicholas A. Slatten, and Evan S. Liberty, all of whom were Blackwater security guards at the time of the shootings. Only Slatten was convicted of murder; the other three defendants were found guilty of manslaughter and improperly using a weapon to commit a violent crime. A fifth defendant, Jeremy Ridgeway, had previously pleaded guilty to manslaughter and was a witness for the prosecution. The Blackwater personnel had argued that the shootings were inadvertent and an unfortunate example of collateral damage in an active war zone. U.S. prosecutors, however, portrayed the shootings as needless acts of recklessness that targeted innocent civilians who were not breaking the law. They also argued that the incident was not the result of an unintentional battlefield calamity but rather a criminal act. The case certainly highlights the potential problem of placing nonmilitary, private contractors into war zones when they do not technically fall under any U.S. military chain of command.

The trial was the culmination of a long, tortuous seven-year quest to bring the perpetrators of the massacre to justice. The trial was based chiefly on witness testimony, as there was little usable forensic evidence. The defendants claimed that the shootings had not been unprovoked and that they had genuinely feared for their lives and for the lives of the individuals they had been asked to protect. Lawyers for the defendants claimed that the verdicts were wrong and "incomprehensible." They also vowed to appeal the rulings. The U.S. government is empowered to prosecute crimes committed overseas by all government-employed contractors or other individuals who are acting at its behest. Some observers have lamented the fact that Blackwater founder Erik Prince, who is no longer involved with the company, was not in any way held legally accountable for the 2007 tragedy.

Paul G. Pierpaoli Jr.

See also

Afghanistan; Bremer, Lewis Paul; Iraq, History of, 1990–Present; Iraqi Freedom, Operation; Prince, Erik Dean; Private Security Firms

References

Buzzell, Colby. *My War: Killing Time in Iraq.* New York: Putnam, 2005.

Engbrecht, Shawn. *America's Covert Warriors: Inside the World of Private Military Contractors*. Dulles, VA: Potomac Books, 2010.

U.S. Congress. *Private Security Firms: Standards, Cooperation, and Coordination on the Battlefield; Congressional Hearing*. Darby, PA: Diane Publishing, 2007.

Blair, Tony (1953–)

British Labour Party politician and, as prime minister of the United Kingdom from May 2, 1997, to June 27, 2007, a major supporter of U.S. and coalition efforts in both Afghanistan and Iraq. Anthony (Tony) Charles Lynton Blair was born on May 6, 1953, in Edinburgh, Scotland. He graduated from Oxford with a second-class honors BA in jurisprudence in 1976. Shortly thereafter, Blair joined the Labour Party and became a member of Parliament for Sedgefield in 1983. He became leader of the Labour Party in Great Britain on July 21, 1994. When the Labour Party won the 1997 general election, Blair became the youngest person, at age 43, to become prime minister since Robert Jenkinson, Lord Liverpool, in 1812.

As prime minister, Blair lent strong support for the North Atlantic Treaty Organization (NATO) bombing campaign of Yugoslavia in 1999. He was among those urging NATO to take a strong line against Serbian strongman Slobodan Milosevic, the president of Yugoslavia, who was charged with violating human rights in his suppression of ethnic Albanians seeking secession from Yugoslavia, which precipitated the Kosovo War. Through his backing of the strong NATO response, Blair demonstrated that he would support the use of force in order to spread liberty and protect human rights. On April 22, 1999, in a speech in Chicago less than a

British Prime Minister Tony Blair (right) shakes hands with U.S. President George W. Bush following a news conference at Hillsborough Castle outside Belfast, Northern Ireland, on April 8, 2003. The two had met to discuss progress in the war with Iraq. (AP Photo/J. Scott Applewhite)

month after the bombing campaign against Yugoslavia had commenced, he put forth what became known as the Blair Doctrine. In it he argued that it was sometimes necessary to use force to prevent genocide and widespread harm to innocent peoples.

After the September 11, 2001, attacks against the United States that led to the deaths of nearly 3,000 people, Blair quickly aligned Britain with the United States. He was convinced that the perpetrators of the act should be dealt with quickly and decisively to prevent putting in motion a series of events that might set Muslims against the Western world. He thus helped form the international coalition that carried out the 2001 intervention in Afghanistan (Operation ENDURING FREEDOM) that toppled the extremist Taliban Islamist group that ruled Afghanistan at the time and was accused of supporting the terrorist group Al Qaeda. Al Qaeda, an organization whose objective was to bring down existing governments in the Middle East and impose radical Islamist rule on others around the world, became the top target in the Global War on Terror. Blair's government sent air, sea, and ground assets into Afghanistan during the initial thrust against the Taliban. The original deployment involved more than 5,700 British troops and then diminished to about 4,500.

In 2003 Blair enthusiastically supported President George W. Bush's call for an invasion of Iraq in order to overthrow the government of President Saddam Hussein. Blair argued that the Iraqi government, which had been ordered by the United Nations (UN) to dispose of its alleged weapons of mass destruction (WMD), had not cooperated with UN weapons inspectors and was therefore subject to attack. When the United States invaded Iraq on March 20, 2003, Blair's government sent 46,000 British troops to assist with the invasion. Britain was by far the largest non-U.S. contingent in the coalition that supported Operation IRAQI FREEDOM. British troops remained in Iraq throughout the rest of Blair's premiership, which ended on June 27, 2007. The number of British troops in Iraq decreased significantly since the initial invasion, however, and about 7,000 British troops remained in that country when Blair left office.

Blair faced much criticism in Great Britain, even from members of his own party, for his support of the U.S. war effort. Critics accused him of spinning questionable evidence to galvanize support for the invasion of Iraq. At the heart of this criticism is the Iraq Dossier, nicknamed the "Dodgy Dossier" by many. The dossier was a briefing document given to reporters in hopes of justifying the British role in the Iraq War. Critics attacked the dossier not only because much of it had been plagiarized from a PhD dissertation

available on the Internet but also because the claims that Iraq possessed WMD were never proven. Indeed, to date no WMD have been located in Iraq.

After resigning as prime minister on June 27, 2007, Blair was named an official Middle East envoy for the UN, the European Union, the United States, and Russia. He was succeeded as prime minister by his chancellor of the exchequer, Gordon Brown. Brown continued to support the United States in its reconstruction efforts in Iraq. He did, however, call for significant British troop reductions.

Domestically, Blair has been both credited and criticized for having moved the Labour Party to the center of the political spectrum. His promarket policies seemed to boost the British economy and kept the Conservatives from questioning his motives. Blair successfully pushed for more funds for education and health care, and he oversaw the implementation of a national minimum wage act. Despite his domestic success, however, foreign affairs greatly overshadowed his premiership, none more so than the divisive Iraq War.

Blair established the Tony Blair Faith Foundation, an interfaith philanthropy group, in 2008. In 2009 he followed this with the launch of the Faith and Globalization Initiative, which encourages university and graduate study in the fields of globalization and faith-based initiatives. Blair has also been a consultant for a number of companies and corporations. In 2010 he published his memoirs, *A Journey*.

GREGORY WAYNE MORGAN

See also

Brown, James Gordon; United Kingdom, Middle East Policy

References

Coughlin, Con. *American Ally: Tony Blair and the War on Terror.* New York: Ecco, 2006.

Naughtie, James. *The Accidental American: Tony Blair and the Presidency.* New York: PublicAffairs, 2004.

Short, Clare. *An Honourable Deception? New Labour, Iraq, and the Misuse of Power.* London: Free Press, 2004.

Blind Sheikh

See Abdel-Rahman, Omar

Blix, Hans (1928–)

Swedish diplomat, head of the United Nations (UN) International Atomic Energy Agency (IAEA) from 1981 to 1997, and head of the UN weapons inspection program in Iraq during the run-up to the Iraq War. Born in Uppsala, Sweden, on June 28, 1928, Hans Blix earned a degree in international law from the University of Stockholm in 1959 and also pursued studies at Trinity Hall, Cambridge University, from which he earned a doctorate in law. He was appointed associate professor of international law at the University of Stockholm in 1960.

Blix soon abandoned his academic career to pursue his passion for international politics. Between 1962 and 1978 he represented Sweden at the Disarmament Conference in Geneva, and from 1961 to 1981 he was a member of the Swedish delegation to the UN. During 1978–1979 he served as Swedish foreign minister in the government of the ruling Liberal Party.

In 1981 Blix was appointed to head the IAEA, a position he held until 1997. One of the major issues confronting the IAEA during his tenure was monitoring the nuclear weapons program of the Iraqi regime of Saddam Hussein. Although Blix made several inspection visits to the Iraqi nuclear reactor at Osiraq before it was destroyed by an Israeli air strike in June 1981, the IAEA failed to discover the Iraqi clandestine nuclear weapons program initiated during the 1970s. The full extent of the Iraqi nuclear program was discovered only during the 1991 Persian Gulf War, and Blix was forced to acknowledge that the Iraqis had misled the IAEA. Following the loss of credibility for the IAEA, Blix tendered his resignation.

Less than three years later in 2000, however, UN secretary-general Kofi Annan lured the veteran diplomat out of retirement to head the United Nations Monitoring, Verification and Inspection Commission (UNMOVIC), a body assigned the responsibility of monitoring Iraqi weapons program following the Persian Gulf War. Because of Blix's perceived failures as head of the IAEA, Washington opposed the appointment.

Blix now attempted to build a diplomatic consensus for avoiding war and assuring the world that Iraq was compliant with UN resolutions regarding weapons development. Be that as it may, he chastised Saddam Hussein for playing "cat and mouse" games with weapons inspectors and seemed to realize that his inspectors were not getting the full story from Iraq. Blix nevertheless believed that UNMOVIC's monitoring of Iraq's weapons program could be employed to foster Iraqi disarmament. Critics in the George W. Bush administration, who seemed anxious for any pretense to wage war against Iraq, asserted that Blix was not sufficiently aggressive in searching for weapons of mass destruction (WMD).

Following the invasion of Iraq by the United States and Great Britain in March 2003, Blix expressed considerable reservations regarding the war, asserting that the Bush administration had exaggerated the threat of WMD in order to bolster its case for regime change in Iraq. In June 2003 Blix left UNMOVIC to chair the Weapons of Mass Destruction Commission, an independent body based in Stockholm. Blix elaborated on his criticisms of the rush to war in Iraq and the spurious intelligence reports upon which it was based in his 2004 memoir *Disarming Iraq.*

RON BRILEY

See also

Bush, George Walker; Hussein, Saddam; Iraq, History of, 1990–Present; IRAQI FREEDOM, Operation; Nuclear Weapons, Iraq's Potential for Building; Persian Gulf War; United Nations; United Nations Monitoring, Verification and Inspection Commission; United Nations Weapons Inspectors; Weapons of Mass Destruction

References

Blix, Hans. *Disarming Iraq.* New York: Pantheon, 2004.

Williams, Ian. "Frustrated Neocons: Former U.N. Weapons Head Blix Assesses Year of War on Iraq." *Report on Middle East Affairs* 23 (May 1, 2004): 30–38.

Blount, Buford, III (1948–)

U.S. Army general who commanded the successful assault on Baghdad during the Iraq War (Operation IRAQI FREEDOM) and later became an outspoken critic of the U.S. war effort in Iraq. Buford "Buff" Blount III, born on September 15, 1948, in Travis County, Texas, was a career army officer who came from a family with a distinguished military background. In 1971 he graduated from the University of Southern Mississippi and was commissioned a second lieutenant in the U.S. Army. He later earned a master's degree in national security and strategic studies.

Throughout his career, Blount served primarily in armored and mechanized units. His command assignments included the 5th Infantry Division (Mechanized), Fort Polk, Louisiana; the 197th Infantry Brigade, Fort Benning, Georgia; commander, 3rd Battalion, 64th Armor, 3rd Infantry Division (Mechanized), U.S. Army Europe, and Seventh Army, Germany; and commander, 3rd Brigade, 4th Infantry Division (Mechanized), Fort Carson, Colorado. He also served as armor plans and operations officer, Office of the Program Manager, Saudi Arabian National Guard Modernization Program, Saudi Arabia.

On the eve of the Iraq War, Blount, now a major general, was in command of the 3rd Infantry (Mechanized) Division; he had held that assignment since 2001 and had worked diligently to prepare the division for combat operations after it had been engaged in humanitarian and peacekeeping operations in the Balkans. Blount, who was a strong advocate of maneuver warfare, argued strongly that the original invasion plans for Iraq should be changed to allow his division to move to the west of the Tigris and Euphrates Rivers and avoid the numerous river and stream crossings that would have delayed his advance. He was successful in convincing U.S. war planners of this more westerly advance toward Baghdad because the flat terrain was more conducive to armor.

When the war began on March 20, 2003, Blount's division of 19,000 troops and 8,000 vehicles was the lead unit of V Corps, the western column of the coalition's two-pronged advance on Baghdad. Blount's first major objective was capturing the airfield at Tallil, which allowed coalition forces to control several strategic bridges and two Iraqi highways. The ground attack began on March 21, and Blount's forces quickly took their main objectives and opened the main route to Baghdad.

Within three weeks Blount had moved his division 465 miles to the outskirts of the Iraqi capital in one of the most rapid armor advances in the history of modern warfare. During it, Blount coordinated his movements closely with air units to enforce close air support and concentrate maximum firepower against Iraqi forces, including elite Republican Guard units such as the Medina Division.

Blount rejected conventional military doctrine in laying siege to Baghdad, deciding instead to take the city in a succession of quick thrusts. Armored units usually do not perform well in urban combat because of the confines of streets and buildings and the potential for roadblocks and tank traps. Blount, however, believed that the rapid advance would not give the Iraqis time to establish substantial defenses and would demoralize the defenders. On April 5, 2003, he ordered a task force to conduct a reconnaissance of the Baghdad Airport in Operation THUNDER RUN. U.S. forces were able to capture the airport relatively quickly and also affirm weaknesses in the Iraqi defenses.

Blount was now convinced that the longer coalition forces waited to move on Baghdad, the more likely the Iraqis would be to reinforce the city and create a more robust defense. After a second thrust into Baghdad, Blount's division moved to capture government offices and presidential palaces. They met only minor and generally disorganized resistance. Meanwhile, elements of the I Marine Expeditionary Force, the eastern prong of the U.S. advance, had arrived on the outskirts of Baghdad. By April 12, U.S. forces had virtual control of the Iraqi capital.

Blount's effective leadership in the Battle for Baghdad earned him praise from both subordinates and superiors. He led his division from the front and was generally in the lead units during the advance. This provided the division commander with an intimate sense of the ebb and flow of the advance. He also had a reputation for being calm and collected under fire, and he generally allowed his subordinates wide latitude in conducting tactical operations. Blount would set the objectives and the parameters of the mission but left it to his subordinates to develop the course of action to achieve these. He also embraced the new technology utilized during the campaign, including the command and control system Force XXI Battle Command Brigade and Below/Blue Force Tracker (FBCB2/BFT). FBCB2/BFT provided soldiers with real-time awareness of coalition units and enhanced battlefield communications. Blount was able to accurately view the positions of his units at all times and make appropriate decisions based on that information.

After the capture of Baghdad, Blount found himself as the de facto mayor of the city, and he worked to maintain order with a limited number of troops. He opposed the decision to dismantle Iraqi security forces after their surrender, correctly forecasting that they would form the core of resistance to the U.S.-led occupation. He was also critical of the lack of planning to ensure the delivery of basic human services, food, and medicine in areas captured by the coalition. In October 2003 Blount was transferred to Washington, D.C., and became the U.S. Army's deputy chief of staff for operations and planning. He retired from active duty in 2004 as a major general. Since retirement he has publicly criticized the Iraq War effort, terming it "flawed" from the start. Observers have opined that his retirement was in part forced upon him because of his criticism of the war. Blount has steadfastly refused to comment on such observations, noting that he had generally supported the war plans in 2002 and 2003. Since 2004 he has taught at the university level and has given numerous speeches and interviews.

TOM LANSFORD

See also

Armored Warfare, Persian Gulf and Iraq Wars; Baghdad, Battle for; Baghdad, Iraq; IRAQI FREEDOM, Operation, Coalition Ground Forces; United States Army, Iraq War

References

Lacey, Jim. *Take Down: The 3rd Infantry's Twenty-one Day Assault on Baghdad.* Annapolis, MD: Naval Institute Press, 2007.

Zucchino, David. *Thunder Run: The Armored Strike to Capture Baghdad.* New York: Grove, 2004.

BMP-1 Series Infantry Fighting Vehicles

The BMP series of infantry fighting vehicles (IFVs) represented a revolutionary shift in doctrinal thinking not only for the Soviet military but also for other nations, including the United States. Prior to introduction of the BMP series in 1966, the predominant thinking about the use of mechanized infantry on the battlefield was that of the battlefield taxi, whereby the troops were moved to the combat area and then dismounted to fight on foot. The BMP dramatically changed this picture. While other nations such as the Federal Republic of Germany (West Germany) were working on their own IFVs, the BMP was the first to be fielded in any quantity.

Soviet doctrine in the 1950s was shifting to that of a nuclear battlefield, and to have infantry typically fighting on foot was a serious liability. The BMP was specifically designed with the nuclear battlefield in mind. The production model was armed with a 73-mm smoothbore gun that fired projectiles similar to those used in the handheld RPG-7 antitank launcher along with a rail to mount the new AT-3 Sagger 9M14M Malyutka wire-guided antitank missile (ATGM). The driver and vehicle commander were placed in tandem in the left front of the hull, while the gunner for the 73-mm gun and AT-3 was alone in the small turret basket. The infantry squad of eight men sat in the rear, four on each side back-to-back and each with a firing port and vision block to allow them to fight from within the vehicle.

BMPs saw combat service in the October 1973 Yom Kippur (Ramadan) War as well as action in southern Lebanon in 1982 and the Iran-Iraq War of the 1980s. In the latter, BMPs were used by both sides. Crews liked the BMP's speed and maneuverability but discovered that the Sagger ATGM was virtually useless when fired from within the vehicle, mostly due to the inability of inexperienced gunners to guide the missile onto the target. Infantry also found it difficult to engage targets with any effectiveness from inside the vehicle. As a consequence, tactics began to develop that appeared to be a return to the battlefield taxi role of previous carrier designs.

The lessons learned from the Yom Kippur War led to an overhaul of the BMP design, culminating in the BMP-2 and BMP-3. As the Soviets continued to improve and modify the design, remaining BMP-1s were shipped off to client states such as Iraq. Thus, it was the BMP-1, constantly upgraded and modified, that continued to see the lion's share of combat service in Middle East wars. The Iraqis also received an unknown quantity of BMP-2s equipped with a 23-mm autocannon and the AT-4 Fagot 9M111 ATGM. The Iraqi Army deployed hundreds of BMP-1s during the 1991 Persian Gulf War; U.S. and coalition forces damaged or destroyed many of them during the February 1991 ground campaign.

During the Iraq War (Operation IRAQI FREEDOM), U.S. Army tanks and helicopters engaged some BMPs, again in mixed combined-arms formations with tanks. Advancing elements of the 3rd Infantry Division encountered small combined-arms groups attached to larger formations of Iraqi infantry during their drive north to Baghdad. On April 4, 2003, just south of the city at a crossroads marked "Objective Saints" on battle maps, American forces destroyed several dozen BMP-1s and BMP-2s that were part of the Medina Armored Division. The Iraqi forces had bravely resisted, and at one point a platoon of BMP-2s had engaged the advancing Americans with accurate fire from their 30-mm cannon before they were destroyed by tankers of the 4-64 Armored Battalion. Later as American columns pushed into Baghdad, BMPs individually and in pairs attempted to ambush the Americans from the numerous narrow alleys of the city. As the Battle for Baghdad came to a close, there were numerous Iraqi tanks and BMPs littering the roadways. Unfortunately, precise loss statistics for the BMPs are not readily available for either the Persian Gulf War or the Iraq War. However, in the case of the former the losses may have been as high as 200.

Even though the BMP was outclassed by tanks and infantry vehicles of America and other Western nations, when used by smaller armies against comparable foes it proved itself an effective vehicle, as attested to by the Iraqi experience during the Iran-Iraq War. Therefore, BMPs of various configurations will likely be encountered on Middle Eastern battlefields into the foreseeable future.

Specifications of the BMP-1 are as follows:

Armament: 1 73-mm 2A28 smoothbore gun with a rate of fire of 7–8 rounds per minute; 1 coaxial 7.62-mm machine gun

Main gun ammunition: 40 rounds

Armor: 23-mm maximum

Crew/passengers: 3, with 8 infantry

Weight: 13.28 tons

Length: 22 feet 2 inches

Width: 9 feet 8 inches

Height: 7 feet 1 inch

Engine: V-6 diesel; 300 horsepower at 2,000 revolutions per minute

Speed: Road, 45 miles per hour

Range: 340 miles

RUSSELL G. RODGERS

See also
Baghdad, Battle for; IRAQI FREEDOM, Operation; Persian Gulf War;
T-62 Main Battle Tank; T-72 Main Battle Tank

References
Fontenot, Gregory, et al. *On Point: The United States Army in
Iraqi Freedom.* Annapolis, MD: Naval Institute Press, 2005.
Foss, Christopher, ed. *Jane's Armour and Artillery, 2007–2008.*
Coulsdon, Surrey, UK: Jane's Information Group, 2007.
Zaloga, Steven J. *BMP Infantry Combat Vehicle.* New Territories,
Hong Kong: Concord, 1990.

Bojinka Plot

The Bojinka Plot (also known as the Manila Air Plot) was a conspiracy engineered by Khalid Sheikh Mohammed and his nephew Ramzi Yousef. The plan was primarily aimed at blowing up 12 U.S. airliners as they crossed the Pacific Ocean but also included other goals, such as the assassinations of U.S. president Bill Clinton and Pope John Paul II during their respective visits to Manila in November 1994 and January 1995.

Mohammed and Yousef began planning Bojinka in 1994 when both men rented an apartment in the capital and started gathering the necessary chemicals and equipment for the plane bombs. They were later joined by a third man, Abdul Hakim Murad, who had undergone terrorist training in Pakistan; Murad's role was to help purchase explosives and timing devices in the Philippines.

The aviation part of the plan called for the targeting of U.S.-flagged airlines serving routes in East or Southeast Asia. Five individuals were to carry out the attacks. Each would board the plane on the first leg of its flight, then assemble and place the bomb and exit during its first layover. The bombs were timed to detonate as the airplane proceeded across the Pacific Ocean toward the United States. Most of the targeted flights were bound for Honolulu, Los Angeles, San Francisco, or New York. Four of the five bombers were to return to Karachi, Pakistan, while the fifth would go on to Doha, Qatar.

Mohammed left the Philippines for Pakistan in September 1994 and met Yousef in Karachi, where both men enlisted a fourth man, Wali Khan Amin Shah (also known as Usama Asmurai). Yousef and Shah returned to the Philippines to continue preparations for the operation. Yousef decided to conduct at least two trial runs for their improvised explosive device by detonating one in a Manila movie theater on December 1, 1994, and a second one 10 days later on an actual airline flight. For the airline test, Yousef chose a

Philippine Airlines 747 aircraft scheduled to fly from Manila to Tokyo, via Cebu. Yousef boarded the aircraft in Manila, during which time he positioned the explosive device under a passenger seat. Upon landing in Cebu, Yousef disembarked from the jet, which flew back to Manila before heading to Japan. While the Philippine Airlines aircraft was roughly 190 miles east of Okinawa the bomb exploded, killing a 24-year-old Japanese national and injuring eight others. The pilot was able to maintain control of the aircraft, however, landing it at Naha, Okinawa. Soon after, the Philippines-based Abu Sayyaf Group called an Associated Press office in Manila and claimed that it had conducted the attack. Authorities learned about (and hence disrupted) the Bojinka/Manila air plot on January 7, 1995, when volatile explosive compounds ignited a fire in the apartment rented by Yousef and Murad. Neighbors who witnessed smoke coming out of the unit quickly alerted security personnel, who after being denied entry called the police and fire department. Investigators subsequently discovered an assortment of items suggesting criminal behavior, including cartons of chemicals, Casio timers, and juice bottles with unknown substances inside. In addition, they found photographs of Pope John Paul II, Bibles, and confessional materials later linked to the assassination plot.

Yousef and Murad fled. Although the police quickly detained Murad (he was apprehended while attempting to retrieve a laptop computer that had been left in the apartment), Yousef escaped to Pakistan. Soon after he arrived in that country, however, U.S. embassy officials in Islamabad received a tip that Yousef was hiding somewhere in the city; he was subsequently discovered at a guest house and arrested on February 7, 1995.

In 1995 Yousef, Murad, and Shah (who had fled to Malaysia) were extradited to the United States. They were charged with various terrorism-related offenses related to the Bojinka Plot and prosecuted in a federal court in Manhattan. The trial lasted more than three months, and the jury heard from more than 50 witnesses and viewed over 1,000 exhibits. A critical part of the government's case involved the contents of the laptop that was seized in the Manila apartment in 1994; it contained airline schedules, photographs, evidence of money transfers, and a threat letter that warned of future attacks on American interests by the "Fifth Division of the Liberation Army." Ultimately, a federal jury in New York convicted the three men for their role in the Bojinka Plot. Yousef was also convicted on a separate count for his role in bombing the Philippine Airlines 747 jet. The Manila/Bojinka airline plot, however, provided a conceptual blueprint for subsequent aviation plots, including the September 11, 2001, terrorist attack in the United States and the August 2006 liquid-explosives airline plot that was disrupted in the United Kingdom. It has also been speculated that Bojinka may have provided the inspiration for other major attempted airline attacks, including those carried out by Richard Reid (the shoe bomber) and Umar Farouk Abdulmutallab (who attempted to detonate explosives hidden in his underwear on Christmas Day, 2009).

PAUL SMITH

See also

Abu Sayyaf; Yousef, Ramzi Ahmed

References

Bonner, Raymond. "Echoes of Early Design to Use Chemicals to Blow Up Airlines." *New York Times,* August 11, 2006.

"Disparate Pieces of Puzzle Fit Together." *Washington Post,* September 23, 2001.

Elegant, Simon. "Asia's Own Osama." *Time,* April 1, 2002.

"The Man Who Wasn't There." *Time,* February 20, 1995.

McDermott, Terry. "The Plot." *Los Angeles Times,* September 1, 2002.

McKinley, James. "Suspected Bombing Leader Indicted on Broader Charges." *New York Times,* April 1, 1995, http://www.nytimes.com/1995/04/14/nyregion/suspected-bombing-leader-indicted-on-broader-charges.html.

"Muslim Militants Threaten Ramos Vision of Summit Glory." *The Australian,* January 13, 1996.

"Plane Terror Suspects Convicted on All Counts." CNN, September 5, 1996, http://www.cnn.com/us/9609/05/terror.plot/index.html.

Ressa, Maria. "Philippines: U.S. Missed 9/11 Clues Years Ago." CNN, July 26, 2003, http://www.cnn.com/2003/WORLD/asiapcf/southeast/07/26/khalid.confession/index.html.

Spaeth, Anthony. "Rumbles in the Jungle." *Time,* March 4, 2002.

Boko Haram

Boko Haram is a militant Islamist terrorist organization based in northeastern Nigeria (as well as portions of Niger and Cameroon). The official name of the group is the Congregation of the People of Tradition for Proselytism and Jihad, but it is best known as Boko Haram in the Hausa language. Boko Haram is literally translated as "Western education is forbidden."

Mohammed Yasuf, who was killed in 2009, founded Boko Haram in 2002; since then, it has grown considerably in both membership and influence. The group hopes to rid society of all traces of Western influence and to create an Islamic state in Nigeria based strictly on sharia law (the traditional moral and religious codes of Islam). In recent years Boko Haram, which is a largely decentralized organization that lacks a strong chain of command, has been led by Abubakar Shekau and Momodu Bama. Estimates of its strength vary, but two studies completed in the summer of 2014 concluded that the organization had between 9,000 and 12,000 active members.

Boko Haram is uncompromising in its beliefs and goals and has frequently resorted to violence and intimidation in order to gain attention. Over the years it has bombed or attacked government facilities, Christian churches and organizations, schools, and police stations. It has also engaged in the abduction of Westerners and schoolchildren and has assassinated Islamic leaders believed to have been co-opted by the Nigerian government. The group has also employed child soldiers and suicide bombers. It should be noted that the vast majority of Nigeria's Muslim population does not support Boko Haram and is fiercely critical of its tactics.

The organization is strongest in Nigeria's northeastern states, where the government has declared a state of emergency. Unfortunately, the Nigerian government has had little success in suppressing Boko Haram or its activities, which became ever bolder in recent years. It is estimated that between 2002 and late 2014, more than 10,500 people died in violence perpetrated by Boko Haram; as many as 650,000 people have been internally displaced after fleeing their homes threatened by Boko Haram.

It remains somewhat unclear if Boko Haram has links to other terrorist organizations. Some observers have alleged that the group has ties to Al Qaeda in the Islamic Maghreb and may be receiving funding from that outfit, but this cannot be completely substantiated. Although the United States officially declared Boko Haram a terrorist organization in November 2013, thus far the group's attacks outside Nigeria have been few in number. Other observers believe that the group is motivated as much by interethnic tensions as it is by religious dogma. These individuals have claimed that Yusuf's initial goal was ethnic cleansing, which he disguised in religious overtones.

Whatever the group's ties might be and whatever its sources of funding, there is no doubt that Boko Haram has been a dangerous and destabilizing presence in Nigeria. In 2014, the organization was responsible for a series of stunning attacks and abductions. In February 2014 Boko Haram terrorists attacked a small village in Nigeria, resulting in 106 civilian deaths. Only days later terrorists attacked a government college preparatory school, which resulted in the deaths of 29 male students. On April 14, Boko Haram militants stormed a school and abducted 276 schoolgirls;

In this October 31, 2014, image from video footage shot by Nigeria's Boko Haram Islamic extremists, their leader Abubaker Shekaum announces that more than 200 kidnapped schoolgirls had all converted to Islam and been married off. (AP Photo)

their whereabouts are still unknown, but Abubakar Shekau claimed that he was going to sell them into slavery. Boko Haram has been targeting schools because it believes that the institutions are responsible for corrupting Islam and introducing Western ideas into society. On May 5, 2014, near the Nigerian-Cameroon border, Boko Haram launched an attack that left at least 310 innocent people dead. In the late summer of 2014, the group changed its strategy to one that deemphasized hit-and-run attacks and focused on seizing and holding territory within Nigeria.

Despite Nigerian government efforts to stem the mounting violence, Boko Haram has seemingly grown in strength. Its highly decentralized structure has certainly made it more difficult for government authorities to pursue and apprehend the militants. The government has also reportedly engaged in human rights abuses against suspected Boko Haram terrorists. In 2013, Amnesty International alleged that the Nigerian government presided over the deaths of some 950 Boko Haram suspects who had been detained in prisons.

On October 16, 2014, the Nigerian government announced amid much fanfare that it had reached a cease-fire agreement with Boko Haram. This would have ended the group's multiyear insurgency. At the time, Boko Haram's leadership reportedly assured the Nigerian government that the 276 schoolgirls abducted earlier in the year were "alive and well." However, on November 1 Abubakar Shekau flatly denied that his organization had agreed to a cease-fire and that the schoolgirls had been "married off." On November 10, press reports from Nigeria attributed a school explosion to Boko Haram that killed at least 46 students.

As further evidence that the October cease-fire agreement was either a shame or had been violated, on January 3, 2015, Boko Haram seized the town of Baga in northeastern Nigeria. The group also captured a key multinational military base located there. The troops stationed there reportedly turned and fled as Boko Haram approached and did not offer much resistance. On January 7, media reports indicated that Baga had been obliterated and that some 2,000 civilians (most of them women, children, and the elderly) had been massacred. On January 10, Boko Haram terrorists reportedly strapped explosives to a young girl (perhaps as young as 10), sent her into a crowded marketplace in Maidjguri, and remotely detonated them. The resulting explosion killed the girl as well at least 21 others. This was the fourth suicide bombing in Maidjguri since July 2014. These developments were viewed as significant setbacks in Nigeria's ongoing fight against Boko Haram.

PAUL G. PIERPAOLI JR.

See also

Ajuba, Nigeria, Mall Bombing; Terrorism

References

"Boko Haram: A Bloody Insurgency, a Growing Challenge." CNN, October 22, 2010, http://www.cnn.com/2014/04/17/world/africa/boko-haram-explainer/.

Pham, J. Peter. "Boko Haram's Evolving Threat." Africa Security Threat, April 2012, http://africacenter.org/wp-content/uploads/2012/04/AfricaBriefFinal_20.pdf.

"310 Killed in Latest Boko Haram Attack; Hundreds of Girls Remain Missing." CNN, May 8, 2014, http://www.cnn.com/2014/05/08/world/africa/nigeria-abducted-girls/.

Bolton, John Robert, II (1948–)

Attorney and U.S. representative to the United Nations (UN) during 2005–2006. John Robert Bolton II was born in Baltimore, Maryland, on November 20, 1948. He attended Yale University, graduating in 1970, and earned a law degree from Yale Law School in 1974, where he attended classes with future president Bill Clinton and future first lady Hillary Rodham Clinton. After graduating with his law degree, Bolton joined a Washington, D.C., law firm.

Bolton entered public service in 1981 as a counsel to the U.S. Agency for International Development (USAID), a post he held until 1982. From 1982 to 1983 he was assistant administrator of USAID. After several years back in private law practice, Bolton was assistant U.S. attorney general during 1985–1989 and then assistant secretary of state for international organization affairs from 1989 to 1993. From 1993 to 1999 he again practiced law; from 1997 to 2001 he was senior vice president for public policy research at the American Enterprise Institute.

By 2001 Bolton had firmly established his bona fides as a neoconservative, on record as disdaining the UN and America's participation in it. Following the contested 2000 presidential election, James Baker III, George W. Bush's chief strategist, dispatched Bolton to Florida as part of the administration's effort to halt the recount there. In 2001 President George W. Bush named Bolton undersecretary of state for arms control and international security affairs, a post he held until 2005. Bolton was reportedly closely allied with Secretary of Defense Donald Rumsfeld and other neoconservatives who pushed aggressively for war against Iraq in 2003.

Bolton confronted Iran over its nuclear program, and in 2002 he accused Cuba of harboring a clandestine biological weapons program. Reportedly, he tried to fire several State Department biological warfare experts when their intelligence did not support his own position, although Bolton denied this. Bolton also went on record as stating that the United States would disavow entirely the International Criminal Court.

In March 2005 Bush nominated Bolton as U.S. ambassador to the UN, a strange nomination considering Bolton's earlier harsh comments about that international body. The nomination caused a firestorm in Washington, and a Democratic filibuster in the Senate stopped it. During the bruising nomination process, testimony claimed that Bolton had mistreated and bullied subordinates and had tried to fire those who did not agree with him. Bolton denied the accusations in what became a thoroughly partisan debate.

Angered by the rebuff of his nomination, Bush instead appointed Bolton permanent U.S. representative to the UN in what is called a recess appointment on August 1, 2005. This essentially circumvented Congress in the appointment process. Although Bolton could not claim the title of ambassador, he was in essence fulfilling that role. Democrats especially excoriated the Bush White House over the appointment. In 2006 Bush twice resubmitted Bolton's nomination, and each time the move was rebuffed. In December 2006 with the handwriting on the wall, Bolton announced his desire to step down from his temporary appointment and withdraw his name from nomination.

Returning to private law practice, Bolton is involved with numerous national and international organizations as well as conservative think tanks. He became a vocal critic of President Barack Obama's foreign policies, terming them weak, vacillating, and indecisive. In December 2012, Bolton infamously accused Secretary of State Hillary Clinton of feigning an injury (for which she was hospitalized for nearly a week) to avoid testifying before Congress concerning the attack on the U.S. consulate in Benghazi, Libya, in September 2012.

Clinton later testified and took responsibility for the security failures in Benghazi.

PAUL G. PIERPAOLI JR.

See also
Benghazi, Attack on U.S. Consulate; Bush, George Walker; Neoconservatism; Rumsfeld, Donald

References
Draper, Robert. *Dead Certain: The Presidency of George W. Bush.* New York: Free Press, 2008.
Lugar, Richard G., ed. *Nomination of John R. Bolton: Reports from the Committee on Foreign Relations, U.S. Senate.* Darby, PA: Diane Publishing, 2006.

Bombs, Cluster

Small explosive submunitions, or bomblets, dropped from aircraft or fired by artillery that are designed to detonate prior to, on, or after impact. In the 1930s, munitions experts in the Soviet Union developed early versions of cluster bomb technology. However, it was the Germans who first used cluster bombs operationally in World War II during the Battle of Britain in 1940. Called "Butterfly Bombs" by the Germans, their usage was not widespread because they were difficult to produce and were very fragile aboard aircraft. Despite these limitations, both British firemen and civilians viewed bombs as extremely dangerous because they did not explode upon impact but instead detonated later under the slightest vibration.

Cluster bombs quickly grew in use and are now produced in many countries thanks to their versatility on the battlefield. The United States first used cluster bombs in the 1950–1953 Korean War as an antipersonnel weapon. Since then, the U.S. military has employed cluster munitions in Laos, Cambodia, Vietnam, Iraq, Kosovo, and Afghanistan. During the Persian Gulf War the U.S. Air Force used the weapon extensively, dropping a total of 34,000 cluster bombs. U.S. warplanes dropped an estimated 1,100 cluster bombs during the North Atlantic Treaty Organization's 1999 Operation ALLIED FORCE in Kosovo, deploying roughly 222,200 submunitions. Fighter pilots flying the A-10 Thunderbolt II attack aircraft in Kosovo preferred using cluster bombs because they enabled them to neutralize targets without using precision-guided ordnance.

Cluster bombs remain a primary weapon among world military arsenals because of their wide variety of battlefield applications. Relatively inexpensive to make, cluster munitions offer a wide array of options in combat. They can be fired from the ground or dropped from the sky and afford numerous methods for delivery and employment. Ground-based deployments include the firing of cluster munitions with artillery or rocket launchers. Aircraft, meanwhile, are able to drop cluster munitions in a bomb-shaped container, or cluster bomb unit, that breaks open at a predetermined height, scattering hundreds of bomblets over a wide area. Either delivery method results in a very effective weapon when used against personnel or armor. Cluster bombs are also frequently used against runways, electrical facilities, munitions dumps, and parked aircraft. Within the U.S. military, all four service branches use various forms of cluster munitions.

There are also many different types of cluster munitions. Some versions of cluster bombs are meant to be incendiary and ignite fires, while others are used as fragmentation bombs, designed to explode and scatter deadly pieces of metal in all directions.

Antitank versions of cluster munitions contain shaped-charge bomblets designed to penetrate armor more effectively. Sometimes the bomblets can be small mines, intended to function like regular land mines upon landing. Different types of submunitions may also be used together to increase lethality. These weapons, called combined-effects munitions, may implement incendiary, fragmentation, and armor-piercing bomblets in one dispenser to maximize the level of damage against different enemy targets located in the same vicinity.

The most controversial type of cluster bomb involves the air-dropped mines meant to immobilize enemy movements and act as an area denial weapon. These versions are designed to land softly and detonate only when the internal battery runs out, when the internal self-destruct timer runs out, or when they are disturbed in any way. Mine-laying cluster bombs proved relatively effective when used against Scud missile launchers during the Persian Gulf War in 1991. At the same time, these types of cluster bombs can cause many deaths and serious injuries to unsuspecting civilians who may run across them. A small percentage of the bomblets do not always explode or detonate as planned.

Mines deployed by cluster bombs pose a greater long-term threat to civilians living in a war zone. Roughly, up to 10 percent of cluster submunitions do not explode on impact, becoming deadly to any nonmilitary personnel who may stumble upon them. Thousands of such civilian casualties have been reported in Iraq, Kosovo, Afghanistan, Lebanon, and Israel.

In 1999 the U.S. Department of Defense estimated that there were 11,110 unexploded bomblets in Kosovo after

Operation ALLIED FORCE that caused an estimated 500 civilian deaths. Additionally, an estimated 1.2 million to 1.5 million unexploded submunitions still remained in Iraq after Operation DESERT STORM, claiming more than 4,000 civilian casualties.

While cluster munitions have caused controversy in many conflicts, their use in the summer of 2006 in the war between Israel and Hezbollah was especially controversial. After the brief conflict, an estimated 1 million unexploded cluster bomb submunitions littered southern Lebanon and northern Israel. Thousands of artillery rounds carrying cluster munitions were fired between the two combatants, according to the United Nations (UN) Mine Action Coordination Center. Human rights organizations have accused both belligerents of deliberately targeting civilians during the conflict, as many of the bomblets fell into villages and towns where civilians were living. Human rights organizations also reported more than 1,600 deaths in Kuwait and Iraq stemming from unexploded submunitions dropped during the 1991 Persian Gulf War. Examples such as these have given rise to increased efforts to outlaw cluster bombs internationally.

Following the Persian Gulf War, the U.S. Defense Department reviewed its use of cluster munitions in an attempt to minimize collateral damage and reduce the noncombatant casualty rate. Thanks to the inaccuracy of certain types of cluster munitions, such as the CBU-87 used during that war, the Defense Department established a goal of reducing the dud rate among cluster submunitions to less than 1 percent by 2001.

In the mid-1990s the U.S. Air Force began experimenting with Wind Corrected Munitions Dispensers (WCMDs) in a further effort to reduce the noncombatant death rate. WCMD features include directional aerodynamic fins and an internal navigation system that adjusts for wind variations after its release. Additionally, cluster bombs such as the CBU-105 have dispensers loaded with smart bomblets, designed to self-destruct if they do not hit their target. As an additional safety measure, these smart bomblets are designed to deactivate within minutes if they do not explode upon impact.

The U.S. military has also experimented with a new version of cluster munitions, substituting thousands of darts, or nails, for bomblets. When dropped from an aircraft or fired from the ground, these cluster munitions employ thousands of small nail-like pieces of metal that can destroy personnel and other soft targets. This method eliminates the possibility of duds, as there is no explosive submunition that could cause harm to an unsuspecting civilian.

During Operation IRAQI FREEDOM American forces made wide use of cluster bombs, much to the consternation of international human rights groups. It is estimated that in the opening weeks of the war some 13,000 cluster munitions were employed in Iraq, and despite their careful use, the bombs caused considerable civilian deaths and casualties. Some human rights watch groups have alleged that as many as 240,000 cluster bombs have been used in Iraq since March 2003, a number that cannot be verified because the Defense Department does not provide such figures. In Operation IRAQI FREEDOM the United States also used the CBU-105 smart-guided cluster bomb, which was dropped from B-52 bombers. Cluster bombs were also employed during Operation ENDURING FREEDOM in Afghanistan. The collateral damage caused by these munitions raised international concern and may have unwittingly precipitated a backlash against U.S. operations there among many Afghan citizens.

After successful efforts to ban antipersonnel mines, many countries initiated efforts to implement policies curbing the use of cluster bombs or advocating their complete elimination. In February 2007 Norway invited interested countries to Oslo and began to push for an international ban on cluster bombs. More than 45 countries participated in the discussions and agreed to meet again in February 2008. Once again led by Norway, more than 80 countries signed the Wellington Declaration at the Cluster Munitions Conference in New Zealand. This meeting committed the participating countries to solving the humanitarian problems created by cluster bombs and their unexploded ordnance.

Continuing on in the goal of banning cluster munitions altogether, 111 countries met in Dublin, Ireland, in May 2008 and agreed on a treaty banning certain types of cluster munitions. Furthermore, the signatories agreed to eliminate stockpiled cluster ordnance by 2016. Signatories also promised not to develop, produce, use, obtain, stockpile, or transfer additional cluster munitions. British prime minister Gordon Brown was among the many diplomats calling for a total ban on the use of cluster bombs. However, representatives from the world's largest producers of cluster bombs, which include the United States, Russia, and the People's Republic of China, did not attend. Diplomats from Israel, India, and Pakistan raised objections about a total ban. In June 2006, Belgium was the first country to issue a ban on the use, transportation, export, stockpiling, and production of cluster munitions. As of September 2014, the 2010 Convention on Cluster Munitions had been signed by 109 nations. The major military powers of the United States, Russia, China, and Israel are not among them.

In lieu of an outright ban on cluster bombs, the UN and human rights organizations have begun new efforts to minimize damage to noncombatants. Education emphasizing the dangers associated with unexploded cluster bomb submunitions is being distributed to civilians living in war-torn areas around the world. The United States has opposed the ban because of the extreme utility of these weapons, preferring instead to improve the safety measures in cluster bomb technology.

MATTHEW R. BASLER

See also

Antitank Weapons; Artillery; Brown, James Gordon; Mines, Sea, and Naval Mine Warfare, Iraq War; Mines, Sea, Clearing Operations, Iraq War; Mines and Mine Warfare, Land

References

Bailey, Jonathan B. A. *Field Artillery and Firepower.* Annapolis, MD: Naval Institute Press, 2004.

Conway, Simon. "Banning Bomblets." *World Today* 64(5) (May 2008): 13–15.

Hammick, Denise. "NZ Conference Paves Way for Cluster Munitions Treaty." *Jane's Defense Weekly* 45(10) (March 5, 2008): 7.

Lennox, Duncan, ed. *Jane's Air-Launched Weapons.* Alexandria, VA: Jane's Information Group–Sentinel House, 1999.

Bombs, Gravity

The terms "gravity bombs" and "dumb bombs" refer to bombs and other explosive ordnance that do not contain internal guidance systems. Before the days of cruise missiles, bombs were the primary weapons for aircraft attacking targets on the surface below, whether on water or land. Today, bombs lacking a guidance system are called dumb bombs because they fall dumbly to the target along a gravity-forced ballistic path, unable to adjust for poor aiming, weather, wind, or visibility conditions. Dumb bombs are simple in construction, consisting of an aerodynamically streamlined shape filled with high explosives. Up until Operation ENDURING FREEDOM in Afghanistan in 2001, "dumb" bombs constituted the vast majority of such weapons used in war, and they still remain the dominant bomb type in the arsenals of most Middle Eastern nations, including Israel.

On dumb bombs, stabilizing fins are attached at the back, and a detonating fuze is installed just before the bombs are loaded. The bombs come in four types: high explosive or general purpose, cluster, daisy cutter, and fuel air explosive. Of these, the first is the most commonly used and comes in

varying sizes based on weight, ranging from 220 to 2,200 pounds. U.S. and British bombs are designated by weight in pounds (250, 500, 1,000, 2,000), while most other countries use kilograms. For example, the former Soviet Union's bombs came in 100-, 200-, 500-, and 1,000-kilogram sizes. Fuzing is determined by the mission. Proximity or variable-timed fuzes, which detonate at various heights above the ground, are employed against dug-in infantry. "Quick fuzes" that detonate very quickly after impact are also used against surface targets to maximize blast effect. Delayed fuzes are placed in the bomb's tail to hold up detonation until the bomb has penetrated a predictable depth into the target to ensure destruction of armored targets such as bunkers.

As of September 2014, a 2010 convention banning cluster munitions had been signed by 109 nations. The major military powers of the United States, Russia, China, and Israel are not among them. Cluster munitions carry up to 100 smaller (50-kilogram) bombs within them that are released at a predetermined altitude above a target area about the size of a football field. They are employed against personnel and moving targets such as light-skinned vehicles and naval missile boats. They remain in the inventories of many Middle Eastern countries.

Daisy cutters refer to the 15,000-pound bomb dropped from Lockheed MC-130 Hercules aircraft to clear out a landing area for helicopters, collapse tunnels, or destroy troop concentrations. Fuel air explosives consist of an aerosol spray mist of fuel that, when ignited, creates an overpressure followed immediately by a series of alternating underpressures and overpressures to flatten objects such as vehicles and inflict maximum personnel casualties.

Dumb bombs constituted just 20 percent of the bombs dropped during Operations ENDURING FREEDOM in 2001, IRAQI FREEDOM in 2003, and UNIFIED PROTECTOR in 2011. Nevertheless, they still dominate the arsenals of the world's air forces. The United States and most Western nations have developed guidance kits to convert them into smart bombs. Increasingly, dumb bombs are used only on battlefields located some distance from civilian populations. This trend will likely continue in the years ahead as bombs become more deadly and the international community places increasingly stringent standards against inflicting innocent civilian casualties.

CARL OTIS SCHUSTER

See also

Bombs, Precision-Guided; ENDURING FREEDOM, Operation, U.S. Air Campaign; IRAQI FREEDOM, Operation, Air Campaign; Libyan Civil War

References

Frieden, David R. *Principles of Naval Weapons Systems.* Annapolis, MD: U.S. Naval Institute, 1989.

Werrell, Kenneth. *Chasing the Silver Bullet.* Washington, DC: Smithsonian Scholarly Press, 2003.

Yenne, Bill. *Secret Weapons of the Cold War.* New York: Berkley Publishing, 2005.

Bombs, Precision-Guided

Precision-guided munitions, commonly called smart bombs, refer to bombs that have integral guidance systems that compensate for environmental interference and poor aim and that ensure the bomb's accurate emplacement against the target. They differ from dumb or iron bombs in that they have an internal guidance system and a related power source. Typically, a modern smart bomb has a circular probable error of 20–94 feet. But even a highly trained pilot operating in an optimal environment can at best reliably place a dumb bomb within 300 feet of the aim point. Most modern smart bomb systems rely on a computer-based guidance system that accepts a target designated by the aircraft's pilot or weapons officer or a forward air or ground controller and guides the bomb onto it. The target's identification and designation are derived from electro-optical, infrared, or radar imaging. However, a growing number of guidance systems guide the bomb onto the target's geographic location using the target's and bomb's Global Positioning System (GPS) respective location. The bomb reverts to inertial guidance if the GPS link is lost. GPS-guided bombs are employed against fixed targets, while the others can be used against moving targets or those in which a specific entry point (e.g., ventilation shaft) is required.

The Germans employed the first guided bombs during World War II. The German Fritz bombs were radio-controlled bombs that the plane's bombardier glided into the target using a joy stick. He tracked the bomb's path via a flare in the bomb's rear. The Americans also employed a television-based guided bomb called the Azon bomb in 1945 and continued to pursue bomb-guidance systems after the war. The resulting AGM-62 Walleye relied on a TV camera installed in the bomb's nose that transmitted the target's image back to the aircraft's weapons officer. He steered the bomb to the target by keeping the aim in the TV crosshairs. The early Walleyes required so much operator attention, however, that they were primarily employed from crewed aircraft, such as the navy's A-6 Intruder.

In 1968 during the Vietnam War, the U.S. Air Force introduced the Bolt-117, the first laser-guided bomb. These early bombs guided onto the reflected beam of a laser designator that illuminated the target. The early versions had to be illuminated by a second aircraft in the target area. By 1972, this system had given way to an automatic laser-tracking illuminator that enabled the bombing aircraft to illuminate the target as it withdrew. However, these early laser-based systems were vulnerable to smoke and poor visibility, which interfered with the laser beam.

By the late 1970s, the United States introduced improved laser, infrared, and electro-optical target-designation systems. Israel acquired some of these weapons and used them in strike missions over Lebanon in the mid-1980s, but the first significant large-scale use of smart bombs came in 1991, when the United States led a United Nations coalition to drive Iraqi troops out of Kuwait in the Persian Gulf War. In that conflict, U.S. aircraft used precision weapons in approximately 20 percent of their strike missions over Iraq. They were employed primarily against high-priority targets located within population areas or in circumstances where the target's first-strike destruction had to be guaranteed (Scud surface-to-surface missile launchers, for example).

The lessons learned from that war drove the U.S. development of the Joint Direct Attack Munition (JDAM), the Joint Standoff Weapon (JSOW), and GPS-based bomb-guidance systems. During Operation ENDURING FREEDOM (2001), more than 80 percent of the bombs dropped were smart bombs, and a similar percentage marked the air missions over Iraq in Operation IRAQI FREEDOM (2003).

Precision weapons will continue to gain ground in the years ahead as the world takes an increasingly harsh view of collateral damage and casualties inflicted on civilians. The introduction of cost-effective retrofit guidance kits has enabled many countries to convert their dumb bombs into smart bombs at little expense. Israel and most of the Arab frontline states are now acquiring guidance kits for their bomb arsenals. However, blast effects remain a problem regardless of the weapon's precision. For example, the Palestinian terrorists' strategic placement of their facilities within apartment blocks and housing areas has driven Israel away from the use of bombs. Israel increasingly employs short-range tactical missiles with small warheads (less than 30 kilograms) against terrorist targets in the occupied territories and southern Lebanon. Still, smart bombs will figure prominently in any future Middle Eastern conflict.

CARL OTIS SCHUSTER

See also

Aircraft, Bombers; Bombs, Gravity; ENDURING FREEDOM, Operation, U.S. Air Campaign; IRAQI FREEDOM, Operation, Air Campaign; Persian Gulf War

References

Allen, Charles. *Thunder and Lightning: The RAF in the Gulf; Personal Experiences of War.* London: HMSO, 1991.

Drendei, Lou. *Air War Desert Storm.* London: Squadron Signal Publications, 1994.

Frieden, David R. *Principles of Naval Weapons Systems.* Annapolis, MD: Naval Institute Press, 1985.

Werrell, Kenneth P. *Chasing the Silver Bullet: U.S. Air Force Weapons Development from Vietnam to Desert Storm.* Washington, DC: Smithsonian Institution Scholarly Press, 2003.

Winnefeld, James A., Preston Niblack, and Dana J. Johnson. *A League of Airmen: U.S. Air Power in the Gulf War.* Santa Monica, CA: RAND Corporation, 1994.

Bonn Agreement (December 5, 2001)

Agreement reached among Afghan leaders in Bonn, Germany, on December, 5, 2001, to create a governing authority for Afghanistan in the aftermath of the toppling of the Taliban regime several weeks earlier. Sponsored by the United Nations (UN), the Bonn Agreement produced the Afghan Interim Authority (AIA), a temporary governmental entity. The AIA was inaugurated on December 22, 2001. The Bonn Agreement was designed to stabilize Afghanistan and bring an end to the 20-year civil war there. Afghanistan had been plunged into chaos in 1989, when the last Soviet troops were withdrawn from the country. Between 1989 and 2001, Afghanistan was a nation besieged by internal strife and without an effective government that could provide its people with basic needs and services. The U.S. government realized that before a permanent Afghan government could come to power, an interim governing body had to be established that could rally the Afghan people and work with the U.S. and allied forces. The Bonn Agreement was undertaken to accomplish these goals.

The AIA, which came into being on December 22, consisted of 30 Afghans, to be headed by a chairman. The AIA would have a six-month mandate, to be followed by a two-year period under a Transitional Authority. At the end of the two years, national elections were to be held and a permanent Afghan government established. Hamid Karzai was chosen to chair the AIA; he became interim president after the convening of the *loya jirga* (grand assembly) on June 22, 2002, and then president of Afghanistan in 2004. The Bonn Agreement also stipulated the creation of the Afghan Constitution Commission, charged with drafting a new Afghan Constitution that would be subjected to a future plebiscite. In the meantime, the AIA was asked to use the 1964 Afghan Constitution until the new one could be drawn up. The agreement also established a judiciary commission to help rebuild Afghanistan's judicial system and specifically called for the creation of a national supreme court.

Another important accomplishment of the Bonn Agreement was a mandate to create a development and security mission to be led by the North Atlantic Treaty Organization (NATO). Approved by the UN Security Council on December 20, 2001, this mission became the NATO-led International Security Assistance Force (ISAF), charged with pacifying and stabilizing Afghanistan and continuing the hunt for Taliban and Al Qaeda insurgents there. ISAF, which was the umbrella command organization for all allied military efforts and operations in Afghanistan, continued its work until December 31, 2014. At that time, its mandate ended. Beginning on January 1, 2015, the U.S.-Afghan status of forces agreement went into effect. Signed on September 30, 2014, by Afghanistan's newly installed president, Ashraf Ghani, the agreement left 9,800 American and 4,000 NATO troops in Afghanistan, at least until December 31, 2016.

PAUL G. PIERPAOLI JR.

See also

Afghanistan; International Security Assistance Force; Karzai, Hamid; *Loya Jirga,* Afghanistan; North Atlantic Treaty Organization

References

Abrams, Dennis. *Hamid Karzai.* Langhorne, PA: Chelsea House, 2007.

"Enduring Strategic Partnership Agreement between the Islamic Republic of Afghanistan and the United States of America." U.S. Department of State, May 1, 2012, http://photos.state.gov/libraries/afghanistan/231771/PDFs/2012-05-01-scan-of-spa-english.pdf.

Rashid, Ahmed. *Descent into Chaos: The United States and the Failure of Nation-Building in Pakistan, Afghanistan, and Central Asia.* New York: Viking, 2008.

Boston Marathon Bombing (April 15, 2013)

A terrorist attack perpetrated in Boston, Massachusetts, during the 117th running of the Boston Marathon on April 15, 2013. The marathon included 23,336 competitors from the United States and 92 foreign nations. The attack resulted in the deaths of 3 people: Krystle Campbell, Lu Lingzi, and

Emergency personnel carry a wounded person away from the scene of two explosions at the Boston Marathon in Boston, MA, on April 15, 2013. The explosions shattered the euphoria at the finish line, killing three people and injuring more than 260, some critically. (AP Photo/ Kenshin Okubo)

Martin Richard. More than 260 other people were injured, some critically.

At 2:49 p.m. on April 15, 2013, two bombs detonated near the marathon's finish line about 13 seconds and 180 yards apart. At that point, there were still some 5,500 marathoners who had yet to cross the finish line. The explosions occurred on Bolyston Street near Copley Square, on the edge of Boston's Back Bay. The area is in a densely populated commercial and residential part of the city. The bombings touched off a massive manhunt in Boston and its suburbs, which brought the city to a virtual halt for several days. The manhunt ended on April 19, with one suspect dead and the other captured but seriously wounded.

The blasts did not cause structural damage to nearby buildings, but they did blow out windows. Officials determined that the bombs were relatively crude devices, with low-yield explosives contained in enclosed pressure cookers and detonated remotely with a handheld device. They were packed with metal shards, perhaps ball bearings and nails,

to increase their lethality. The area had twice been swept for bombs by police and K-9 units, but the perpetrators had planted the bombs after the second sweep.

Police immediately sealed off the area and instructed hundreds of spectators to leave out of fear that more bombs might be set off. At the same time, city and state law enforcement authorities immediately contacted the Federal Bureau of Investigation (FBI), which termed the bombings an act of terror and mounted a massive search for evidence as well as the bombers themselves. Footage from nearby commercial surveillance cameras revealed two suspects carrying large backpacks but leaving the area without the packs. One of the backpacks could also be seen from media footage of the race; it had been placed near the edge of the sidewalk where many spectators were watching the event, and it seemed to match one of the backpacks seen in the surveillance footage.

Authorities quickly zeroed in on the two young men with the backpacks, releasing the surveillance images to the media, and received numerous calls from individuals who either knew the suspects personally or had seen them in the area of the explosions. Eventually the manhunt and investigation included local and state officials; the FBI; the Bureau of Alcohol, Tobacco, Firearms and Explosives; the Drug Enforcement Agency; the Central Intelligence Agency; and the National Counterterrorism Center.

Many Americans, especially Bostonians, remained on edge, not knowing if the bombings were part of a larger conspiracy. By April 18, officials had positively identified the two suspects: 26-year-old Tamerlan Tsarnaev and his 19-year-old brother Dzhokhar. Both were ethnic Chechens; Tamerlan was a legal alien, while Dzhokhar had become a U.S. citizen in 2012. Late on the evening of April 18, the suspects allegedly assaulted and killed security officer Sean Collier at the Massachusetts Institute of Technology in Cambridge. After that, they carjacked a Mercedes SUV, also in Cambridge. The man whose car was stolen told police that the two men had told him they were the bombers. Police were able to track the SUV because the owner's cell phone was left in the car.

In the very early morning hours of April 19, police in Watertown, Massachusetts, and law enforcement officials cornered the two suspects—one was in the SUV, and the other was in a Honda. Tamerlan was killed during an ensuing firefight and attempt to flee. His younger brother, however, escaped and sped from the scene in one of the stolen cars and then on foot. Authorities locked down Watertown and began a house-to-house search for the remaining suspect. Eventually, Dzhokhar was found hiding under a canvas covering a boat in the backyard of a Watertown home. He was taken into custody at 8:42 p.m. on April 18, seriously wounded and bleeding badly. Police believe that he had tried to kill himself in the boat. The suspect was taken to a hospital and remained in guarded condition as authorities interrogated him.

Dzhokhar was formally charged on April 22; one of the charges included employing a weapon of mass destruction. He was eventually indicted on 30 charges relating to terrorism, to which he pled not guilty. Several friends and acquaintances of the Tsarnaev brothers were subsequently detained and/or arrested by authorities. Three of them—Robel Phillipos, Dias Kadyrbayev, and Azamat Tazhayakov—were charged with conspiracy to obstruct justice after authorities discovered that they had tried to hide or destroy evidence linking Dzhokhar to the bombings and lied to police about their activities. In May 2014 another potential conspirator, Khairullozhon Matanov, was arrested on obstruction of justice charges. On July 20, 2014,

Tazhayakov was found guilty of conspiracy to obstruct justice; he is appealing the verdict. On August 20, 2014, Kadyrbayev's attorney announced that he would plead guilty to obstruction charges. On October 28, 2014, Phillipos was convicted on two counts of lying to investigators. Dzhokhar Tsarnaev's trial took place in Boston. He was found guilty and sentenced to death on June 24, 2015.

Paul G. Pierpaoli Jr.

See also

Terrorism

References

"Dzohkhar Tsarnaev Charged with Boston Marathon Bombings." *The Guardian,* April 22, 2013, http://www.guardian .com.uk/world/2013/apr/22/boston-bombings-one-week -suspect-dzohkhar-tsarnaev-live.

"Jurors Convict Friend of Tsarnaev." *Boston Globe,* July 21, 2014, http://www.bostonglobe.com/metro/2014/07/21 /jury-resumes-deliberations-trial-azamat-tazhayakov -friend-boston-marathon-bombing-suspect-dzhokhar -tsarnaev/6H1OxaskP38B3v15ryzvPJ/story.html.

"Terrorism Strikes Boston Marathon as Bombs Kill 3; Scores Wounded." CNN, April 16, 2013, http://www.cnn .com/2013/04/15/us/boston-marathon-explosions.

Bradley Fighting Vehicle

Lightly armored tracked infantry and cavalry fighting vehicle. In 1975 the U.S. Army requested proposals for an armored mechanized vehicle to carry infantry on the battlefield for combined-arms operations with the new M-1 Abrams tank. The new vehicle would gradually replace the M-113 armored personnel carrier, which the army did not believe could keep up with the new tank.

The Food Machinery Corporation, later United Defense and then BAE Systems, produced the XM-723 prototype in 1975, which differed slightly from the actual production models. It was an armored tracked vehicle with a 20-mm gun and a 7.62-mm machine gun in a turret. It had a crew of three and could carry eight infantrymen. A tracked vehicle with six road wheels, the original Bradley was 21.5 feet long, 11.75 feet wide, and 8 feet 5 inches tall. Its 22.58 tons were moved by a 500-horsepower Cummins V-8 diesel, and it had a top speed of 41 miles per hour with a range of 300 miles. It was capable of crossing water at a speed of 4 miles per hour. Aluminum and spaced-laminated armor protected the hull.

The Bradley program evolved into the development of two vehicles, which in 1981 were named Bradley Fighting Vehicles and are produced by BAE Systems Land and

A Bradley fighting vehicle provides security as soldiers of the U.S. Army's 3rd Infantry Division conduct a joint clearing operation with local Iraqi forces through a number of small villages south of Salman Pak, Iraq, on February 16, 2008. (U.S. Department of Defense)

Armaments. The M-2 is the infantry fighting vehicle, while the M-3 is designated as a cavalry fighting vehicle. The M-2 Bradley carries a crew of three—the commander, driver, and gunner—as well as six infantrymen. The M-3 transports two cavalry scouts and additional radios and ammunition. Crew size remained unchanged at three. The interiors of the two models differed, and the only exterior difference were gun ports to allow the infantry to fire shoulder weapons from inside the M2.

Some Bradley production models began an upgrade to the M-2 and M-3 A2 models, which had engines capable of producing 600 horsepower and a stronger drive wheel allowing a top speed of 45 miles per hour. Internal armor and improved ammunition storage were also added in production.

Both models differed from the XM-723, as their upgraded turrets mounted a 25-mm Bushmaster chain gun and a 7.62-mm machine gun. The main gun automatically fired armor-piercing or high-explosive rounds as selected by the gunner, who could also select single or multiple shots for each fire mission. The bushmaster has a range of 1.2 miles. The

vehicle could attack heavy armor with TOW (tube-launched, optically tracked, wire-guided) missile rounds, although it could not do so on the move but rather only after stopping for more than a minute and activating a collapsible launcher. Developers believed that the range of the TOW, 2.25 miles, and its ability to destroy any current armored vehicle with a missile that approached the speed of sound outweighed this drawback. The M-2 and M-3 also had smoke grenade launchers for concealment as well as the ability to generate their own smokescreen on the move. These models have a length of 21 feet 2 inches, a width of 10.5 feet, a height of 9.75 feet, and a weight of 25–33 tons, depending on the weight of additional armor for the A2 models.

The reduction in the number of infantrymen to six in the M-2 was controversial because of the impact on the force structure, but solid performance in the 1991 Persian Gulf War proved the viability of the reduced squad number. The U.S. Army's first order for the Bradley was in 1979, when 100 were to be produced, with subsequent orders for 600 yearly. By 1995, 6,375 vehicles had been delivered to the army, with 400 more produced for Saudi Arabia. About 2,200 Bradleys deployed for the Persian Gulf War, of which 1,619 were in maneuver units, with the rest at division level, in theater reserve, or declared excess. As of May 2000, a total of 6,724 Bradleys (4,641 M2s and 2,083 M3s) had been produced for the U.S. Army at a total cost of $5.7 billion, with the unit cost averaging $3.2 million.

Before the Persian Gulf War, work had already begun on upgrading the Bradleys, first to the A2 and then the A3 models. The A2 Bradleys had additional armor, which increased the weight to 30 tons and then an additional 3 tons with add-on tile armor. A 600-horsepower engine compensated for the additional weight.

Because of the threat of Iraqi tanks, the army rushed 692 A2s to the theater during Operation DESERT SHIELD in 1990, and by the time DESERT STORM began in early 1991, about half of the Bradleys involved were A2s. The Bradleys performed well during DESERT STORM. They had a reliability of 90 percent during the land war in spite of the fact that they traveled from 60 to 180 miles during the 100-hour land war. Twenty were destroyed, all but 3 from friendly fire, and only 12 were damaged, 4 of which were repaired quickly. The Bradleys kept pace with the Abrams tanks and accounted for more destroyed enemy armored vehicles than did the Abrams.

The conflict did reveal problems with the Bradleys, however. These led to further refinements, leading to the A3 model. Improvements included a position navigation system with GPS receiver. Coupled with sophisticated digital electronics and communications, the Bradley is now able to function in real time as an integral part of the combined-arms team of tanks, attack helicopters, and other weapons systems. Better sights and a laser range finder along with other digital upgrades allow for enhanced command and control as well as more lethal and reliable fire control. Upgrades to the identification of friend and foe (IFF) systems reduce the problem of friendly fire. Some crew functions were automated, and the vehicle's speed in reverse increased to match that of the tanks. The vehicle armor was also improved, with the requirement to resist rounds up to 30-mm and the introduction of reactive armor. The TOW missile system was changed to add a hydraulic lift for the launchers, and the range finder allowed the system to fire on the move. The wear and tear of operating in a desert environment also required changes to various components to reduce damage from sand and dust.

These changes were tested in Operation IRAQI FREEDOM, launched in March 2003 to topple Saddam Hussein. The Bradleys were an integral part of the mechanized infantry brigades in both the infantry and armored divisions deployed. The 100-hour ground war of DESERT STORM gave credence to the projection of a short conflict once the Iraqi capital was taken. That did not happen, however, and the conflict continued, thanks to the strong insurgency that began in earnest in 2004. Bradleys continued to be deployed, with units rotating to and from Iraq for 12- to 15-month deployments.

In the war, the Bradley proved somewhat vulnerable to the improvised explosive devices and rocket-propelled grenades employed by the insurgents, but personnel casualties were light. As of 2006, total losses included 55 Bradleys destroyed and some 700 others damaged. By 2007, the U.S. Army had stopped using the M2 Bradley in combat, in favor of more survivable mine-resistant ambush-protected vehicles. By the end of the war, some 150 Bradleys had been destroyed.

The army intended to replace the Bradley with the Future Combat Systems Manned Ground Vehicles program, initiated in 1999 but cancelled in 2009. In 2010, the army began the Ground Combat Vehicle (GCV) program to replace the Bradley with the GCV Infantry Fighting Vehicle, but this program was also cancelled in 2014. Discussions are ongoing about another infantry vehicle, known as the Future Fighting Vehicle, but it has not entered development.

As with the M-113 armored fighting vehicle, which is still in the inventory, the Bradley has been used as a platform for many functions. These include an air defense vehicle with Stinger rockets, an electronic fighting vehicle system, a fire-support team vehicle, an ambulance, and a platform for the stingray countermeasure system that detects enemy fire-control systems and destroys them with a laser transmitter. The multiple rocket launch system is based on the Bradley chassis.

DANIEL E. SPECTOR

See also

M1A1 and M1A2 Abrams Main Battle Tanks; Stryker Brigades

References

Cordesman, Anthony H., and Abraham R. Wagner. *The Lessons of Modern War*, Vol. 4, *The Gulf War*. Boulder, CO: Westview, 1996.

Hogg, Ian V. *The Greenhill Armoured Fighting Vehicles Data Book*. London: Greenhill Books, 2002.

Scales, Robert H. *United States Army in the Gulf War: Certain Victory*. Washington, DC: U.S. Army, 1993.

Thompson, Loren B., Lawrence J. Korb, and Caroline P. Wadhams. *Army Equipment after Iraq*. Arlington, VA: Lexington Institute, Center for American Progress, 2006.

Bradley Manning Trial

See Manning, Bradley, Trial of

Bremer, Lewis Paul (1941–)

U.S. diplomat, career U.S. State Department official, and administrator of the Coalition Provisional Authority in Iraq (2003–2004). Lewis Paul "Jerry" Bremer was born in Hartford, Connecticut, on September 30, 1941. He received a BA from Yale University in 1963 and an MBA from Harvard University in 1966. Later that same year, he joined the Foreign Service and began his lengthy career as a diplomat.

Bremer's tenure with the State Department featured posts as an assistant to National Security Advisor and then Secretary of State Henry Kissinger (1972–1976), ambassador to the Netherlands (1983), and ambassador-at-large for counterterrorism (1986). In 1981 Secretary of State Alexander Haig named Bremer executive secretary of the State Department, where he directed the country's round-the-clock crisis management and emergency response center.

In 2002 in the aftermath of the September 11, 2001, terrorist attacks, Bremer was appointed to the Homeland Security Advisory Council. Considered an expert on terrorism, he spent much of his career advocating a stronger U.S. position against states that sponsor or harbor terrorists.

On May 6, 2003, after Iraqi forces had been defeated in the first phase of the war, President George W. Bush named Bremer U.S. presidential envoy in Iraq. In this role, Bremer became the top executive authority in Iraq as the administrator of the Coalition Provisional Authority. He was tasked with overseeing the beginning of the transition from the U.S.-led military coalition governing Iraq to Iraqi self-governance. Bremer was brought in to replace retired U.S. Army general Jay Garner, who had been put in place only two weeks earlier. Bremer's job, which began just five days after Bush declared that major combat operations were completed, was to serve as the top civilian leader of

U.S. ambassador to Iraq L. Paul Bremer signs the Iraqi Sovereignty document transferring full governmental authority to the Iraqi Interim Government in Baghdad, June 28, 2004. (U.S. Department of Defense)

Iraq until such time that the nation was stable enough to govern itself.

Garner's leadership has been generally praised but was not without its problems. Under Garner's watch, looting of commercial and government buildings had been rampant, including the alleged theft of priceless archaeological treasures from Iraqi museums. Iraqi citizens also faced growing problems with failing infrastructure and burgeoning street violence.

Bremer's first move was to increase the number and visibility of U.S. military police in Baghdad while making the reconstruction of the Iraqi police force a high priority. Bremer also pushed to speed up the rebuilding of Iraq's infrastructure and to make certain that government workers were being paid. Despite his efforts, however, violence—both sectarian and by insurgents—continued to mount, and Iraqis were becoming increasingly frustrated with the U.S.-led coalition. Bremer was also forced to postpone establishing an Iraqi-led transitional government.

Bremer is given credit for making some critically important decisions in his role as envoy. Among these were the removal of all restrictions against freedom of assembly, the suspension of the death penalty, and the establishment of a central criminal court. However, many were critical of some of Bremer's decisions, particularly his decision to disband the Iraqi Army and to remove members of Saddam Hussein's Baath Party from critical government positions. Bremer responded to his critics that there was, in truth, no Iraqi Army left for him to dissolve, as that task had already been accomplished by the war. He also claimed that his Baath Party purge was directed at only the top 3 percent of the party leadership. During his tenure, Bremer was also the target of numerous failed assassination attempts. At one point, Al Qaeda leader Osama bin Laden placed a bounty of 10,000 grams of gold on the ambassador's head.

Despite the violence and the assassination attempts, Bremer was able to achieve many of his goals. On July 13, 2003, the Iraqi Interim Governing Council, chosen from prominent Iraqis, was approved. On March 8, 2004, the interim constitution was signed after being approved by the governing council. Then on June 28, 2004, the U.S.-led coalition formally transferred limited sovereignty to the interim government. In a move that surprised many, Bremer left Iraq the same day. After his departure, U.S. ambassador to Iraq John Negroponte became the highest-ranking U.S. civilian in Iraq.

After leaving Iraq, Bremer embarked on several speaking tours and coauthored a book, *My Year in Iraq*, published in 2006. He is currently serving as chairman of the advisory board for GlobalSecure Corporation, a firm that deals with homeland security issues. In late 2010, Bremer became president and CEO of World T.E.A.M. Sports, a nonprofit organization; he stepped down in March 2012.

KEITH MURPHY

See also

Baath Party; Bin Laden, Osama; Garner, Jay Montgomery; IRAQI FREEDOM, Operation; Terrorism

References

Bremer, L. Paul, ed. *Countering the Changing Threat of International Terrorism: Report from the National Commission on Terrorism.* Darby, PA: Diane Publishing, 2000.

Bremer, L. Paul, with Malcolm McConnell. *My Year in Iraq: The Struggle to Build a Future of Hope.* New York: Simon and Schuster, 2006.

Ricks, Thomas E. *Fiasco: The American Military Adventure in Iraq.* New York: Penguin, 2006.

Brooklyn Bridge Bombing Plot (2003)

On May 1, 2003, a Columbus, Ohio, trucker named Iyman Faris (alias Mohammad Rauf) pleaded guilty to plotting to destroy the Brooklyn Bridge and launch a simultaneous attack designed to derail trains near Washington, D.C. The plot was allegedly to have been carried out with direct Al Qaeda sanction and support.

Faris, born on June 4, 1969, in Pakistan-occupied Kashmir, entered the United States in 1994 on a student visa. He married in 1995 while he was working at an auto body shop in Columbus and obtained U.S. citizenship in 1999. He allegedly returned to Pakistan the following year.

According to court documents, Faris's first contact with Al Qaeda occurred in late 2000 when he traveled from Pakistan to Afghanistan with a longtime friend who was already an operative in the terror group. During a series of subsequent visits, Faris was apparently introduced to Al Qaeda kingpin Osama bin Laden and at least one senior operational leader (identified only as C-2 but thought to be the number three man in Al Qaeda), who allegedly instructed Faris to assess the feasibility of conducting attacks in New York and Washington, D.C., when he returned to the United States.

While continuing his job, now as an independent trucker, Faris conducted surveillance in New York City to ascertain the feasibility of destroying a major bridge by cutting the suspension cables with gas cutters. He also procured equipment to conduct a simultaneous attack aimed at derailing a train in the Washington, D.C., area. In communications with Al Qaeda, Faris referred to the gas cutters as "gas stations" and tools for the strike on the train as "mechanics shops."

In coded messages sent to his handlers in Afghanistan via an unnamed third party in the United States, Faris said that he was still trying to obtain "gas stations" and rent "mechanics shops" and was continuing to work on the project. After scouting the Brooklyn Bridge and deciding that its security and structure meant that the plot was unlikely to succeed, he passed along a message to Al Qaeda in early 2003 that said simply "The weather is too hot."

In addition to scouting for the New York and Washington, D.C., attacks, Faris also carried out several other tasks for Al Qaeda. These included acting as a cash courier, providing information about ultralight aircraft as potential getaway vehicles, ordering 2,000 sleeping bags for militants based along the Afghan-Pakistani border, obtaining extensions for six airline tickets for jihadists traveling to Yemen, and delivering cell phones to Khalid Sheikh Mohammed. It was the latter who, after he was captured in early 2003, provided information on Faris and his various activities.

On March 19, 2003, two agents from the Federal Bureau of Investigation (FBI) and one antiterror officer visited Faris and confronted him with Mohammed's testimony and voice recordings intercepted from telephone calls as part of the National Security Agency's secret eavesdropping program. Faced with overwhelming evidence, Faris agreed to work as a double agent, reporting to the FBI and cooperating with ongoing federal investigations into Al Qaeda. He was ordered to leave his home in Columbus and stay at a safe house in Virginia, from where he would continue to engage in discussions with his contacts and handlers. This cooperation continued until May 1, 2003, when Faris pleaded guilty to the New York and Washington, D.C., plots. He was eventually convicted on October 28, 2003, and sentenced to 20 years in prison for conspiracy to provide material support to terrorism.

DONNA BASSETT

See also

Al Qaeda; Mohammed, Khalid Sheikh; Terrorism

References

Emerson, Steven. *Jihad Incorporated: A Guide to Militant Islam in the U.S.* New York: Prometheus Books, 2006.

Fagin, James A. *When Terrorism Strikes Home: Defending the United States.* New York: Prentice Hall, 2005.

Brown, James Gordon (1951–)

British Labour Party politician and chancellor of the exchequer (1997–2007) who succeeded Tony Blair as prime minister on June 27, 2007, and remained in office until May 11, 2010. James Gordon Brown was born on February 20, 1951, in Glasgow, Scotland, but grew up in Kirkcaldy. His father was a minister in the Church of Scotland. The younger Brown attended an accelerated program at Kirkcaldy High School and entered the University of Edinburgh at the age of 16. He studied history, eventually earning a doctorate in 1982. While a student, Brown served as rector and chair of the University Court. He briefly worked as a lecturer at Edinburgh and then taught politics at Glasgow College of Technology. Brown subsequently worked as a journalist and editor for Scottish Television during 1980–1983.

Brown first ran for Parliament in 1979 but lost to Michael Ancram. In 1983 Brown ran again and was elected to represent Dunfermline East (boundary changes later renamed this constituency Kirkcaldy and Cowdenbeath). He was also named chair of the Labour Party's Scottish Council. In the House of Commons, Brown shared an office with fellow Labourite Tony Blair, who was elected that year to represent Sedgefield. The two young, energetic politicians became fast friends, and their careers would be closely linked during their rise through government.

Considered two leading modernizers, Brown and Blair set out to change the Labour Party. In 1987 Brown became the Labour Party's shadow chief secretary to the treasury, then controlled by the Conservative Party government. He served in that position until 1989, when he became shadow trade and industry secretary. He remained there until becoming opposition spokesperson on treasury and economic affairs (shadow chancellor) in 1992.

Brown reportedly wanted to run for the position of Labour Party leader in 1994, but he stood aside for Blair, who was elected that November. In 1997 the two achieved their goal of placing the Labour Party back in control after 18 years in the opposition. Rumors have since suggested that a deal between the two put Brown in charge of economic policy while Blair assumed the premiership, although that has never been confirmed. In May 1997 Brown was appointed chancellor of the exchequer, the equivalent of the U.S. treasury secretary. As chancellor, Brown presided over a long period of economic growth. He made the Bank of England independent and froze spending for two years. He controversially established five economic criteria that had to be met before allowing the public vote on joining the European

Monetary Union. His methods were often called ruthless, but no one could argue with his record of high employment and low inflation.

By 2007, Brown was the longest-serving chancellor of the exchequer in modern British history. As Blair's popularity declined because of his support of the U.S.-led Iraq War, Brown appeared poised to assume the premiership. Indeed, Brown was the leading contender when Blair announced in May 2007 that he would step down on June 27. Brown formally announced his bid for leadership of the Labour Party on May 11, facing no opposition. He became prime minister on June 27 with the approval of Queen Elizabeth II.

Observers at the time noted that Brown would not be a radical departure from Blair and the New Labour movement. However, Brown began to transfer several prime ministerial powers to Parliament and even some parliamentary powers to the general public. In the early days of his leadership, he faced an attempted terrorist attack on the airport in Glasgow and was praised for his handling of the incident. Although Brown pledged to address such issues as health care and housing during his leadership, he said that terrorism and the war in Iraq would remain at the forefront.

Although it was widely perceived that Brown was less enthusiastic about the Iraq War than Blair, Brown publicly remained staunchly loyal to the George W. Bush administration and the conflict in Iraq. At the same time, however, the prime minister began to draw down troops in Iraq, and he stated that he was becoming increasingly concerned about the flagging Afghanistan War. The close relationship between London and Washington was reiterated in the very early days of the Barack Obama administration, especially by Secretary of State Hillary Clinton. Beginning in the last quarter of 2008, the Brown government became enveloped in the global financial meltdown that began on Wall Street, and by early 2009 the British economy was mired in a deep recession. The poor economy prevented Brown from undertaking any meaningful reforms in the areas of housing or health care. In the summer of 2008, he survived an attempt by a group of Labour Party leaders to force his resignation, but the move nevertheless weakened him politically. That same year the Labour Party took a beating during local elections, which further eroded support for his leadership.

In April 2010 Brown called for new parliamentary elections, which ushered in the first full coalition government in Great Britain since 1945. Now badly weakened, on May 10 he announced that he would give up leadership of the Labour Party. The following day, he submitted his resignation as prime minister to Queen Elizabeth II. He was succeed by David Cameron, a Conservative. Brown remained in Parliament but has since been engaged in the private sector as well as several philanthropic endeavors. In 2012 he was named United Nations special envoy for global education.

MELISSA STALLINGS

See also
Blair, Tony; United Kingdom, Middle East Policy

References
Beckett, Francis. *Gordon Brown: Past, Present and Future.* London: Haus, 2007.
Bower, Tom. *Gordon Brown.* New York: Harper Perennial, 2005.
Routledge, Paul. *Gordon Brown: The Biography.* New York: Simon and Schuster, 1998.
Serfaty, Simon. *Architects of Delusion: Europe, America, and the Iraq War.* Philadelphia: University of Pennsylvania Press, 2008.

Brown, Monica Lin (1988–)

U.S. Army soldier who was awarded the Silver Star. Monica Lin Brown was born in Lake Jackson, Texas, on May 24, 1988. Joining the army, she was trained as a medic and assigned to the 4th Squadron, 73rd Cavalry Regiment, 4th Brigade Combat Team, in Afghanistan. On April 25, 2007, Specialist Brown was in a convoy of four Humvees in eastern Paktia Province when insurgents set off a roadside bomb, hitting one of the Humvees and wounding five of its occupants. Brown braved hostile small-arms fire and mortar rounds to run to the wounded and attend to them, shielding their bodies with her own. For her bravery under fire, Brown was awarded the Silver Star in March 2008, only the second American woman to be so recognized since World War II. Four army nurses were awarded the Silver Star in that conflict, and Sergeant Leigh Ann Hester received the Silver Star for bravery under fire during the Iraq War in 2005.

SPENCER C. TUCKER

See also
Hester, Leigh Ann

Reference
"Female Medic Earns Silver Star in Afghan War." NBC News, March 9, 2008, http://www.nbcnews.com/id/23547346/ns/us_news-military/t/female-medic-earns-silver-star-afghan-war/#.VGIRzDTF-Hg.

BTR Series Armored Personnel Carriers

The Soviet/Russian-designed BTR series of armored personnel carriers are some of the most ubiquitous armored transports on battlefields across the globe. The series includes several wheeled transports and one tracked version, as "BTR" is simply a designation given for any general infantry carrier. The BTRs followed the standard doctrinal practice of the battlefield taxi, in which a modestly armored transport would bring infantry to the fight, where they would then engage in combat dismounted. As a consequence, most BTR vehicles were lightly armed, primarily for protection against small-arms and artillery fire. Typical Soviet practice in the Cold War era (1945–1991) was to ship obsolescent vehicles to client states, and thus many of these became part of the inventories of a number of Middle Eastern countries. This practice would change after the collapse of the Soviet Union and the downsizing of the Russian military, for state-run factories would then seek customers for their unsold inventories of more modern equipment.

The earliest of these vehicles, the BTR-40, was a four-wheeled reconnaissance car based on the American White M-3 Scout Car that the Soviets had received via the Lend-Lease program during World War II. Numerous BTR-40s were exported to Soviet client states in the Middle East during the 1950s and 1960s, and they served mostly in reconnaissance roles and occasional infantry transport duties. However, this vehicle suffered from poor performance due largely to the inherent problems of cross-country mobility for a wheeled vehicle with just two axles.

A better cross-country armored transport was built in the early 1950s around the ZIL-157 chassis and was designated the BTR-152. It was an open-topped, six-wheeled vehicle that offered better mobility for a full infantry squad. The BTR-152 was a low-cost option that allowed the Soviets to motorize a large number of their units. These were shipped in large quantities to such countries as Egypt, Syria, Libya, and Iraq, and they saw extensive combat in the 1967 Six-Day War and 1973 Yom Kippur (Ramadan) War.

The BTR-152s were used not only as basic infantry carriers but also as self-propelled antiaircraft platforms and tractors for towed artillery and antitank guns. Nevertheless, even a six-wheeled chassis was deemed insufficient to

Iraqi security personnel position a Soviet BTR-80A armored personnel carrier in order to provide security for the Iraqi Democratic National Conference in Baghdad in 2004. (U.S. Department of Defense)

reduce the ground pressure on the tires and produce superlative cross-country performance. As a consequence, the Soviets embarked on an eight-wheeled transport program, which the Russians have maintained to this day.

The initial requirement for a new cross-country wheeled infantry carrier was initiated in 1959, and the resulting first vehicle, the BTR-60P, was delivered to Soviet forces by the end of 1960. By 1976, more than 25,000 BTR-60s had been produced by Soviet state factories, with many being exported to client states. Two primary models were produced—one with an open top and the other with an armored roof and a small turret armed with a 14.5-mm KPVT heavy machine gun. This version became the standard model, but both were shipped to Middle East nations in the 1960s and 1970s. Although the BTR-60 was an eight-wheeled vehicle that was fast and had some unique features, such as adjustable tire pressure and several firing ports for the troops within, it encountered significant performance problems, especially in a harsh desert environment.

The most critical problem involved the two 90-horsepower GAZ-49B engines used to drive the wheels on either side. It was extremely difficult to synchronize the two engines, and therefore many crews simply disengaged one of them, causing a subsequent loss in performance. This was a serious problem in loose terrain such as some of the sandy areas of the Sinai Peninsula, where Egyptian forces would operate in 1967 and 1973. Nevertheless, the BTR-60 was the infantry carrier of choice for many Middle Eastern countries that were cash-poor, as it was relatively inexpensive, easy to maintain, and easy for crews to operate. It continued to operate with Middle Eastern armies into the 1990s and was still being used by Iraq as late as the Iraq War (2003–2011). Its deficient cross-country ability and thin armor made it an easy target for coalition ground and air forces during the Persian Gulf War (1991) and the Iraq War. However, against more modestly armed opponents, it performed reasonably well.

The BTR-50 was the tracked equivalent of the BTR-60 and was based on the chassis of the PT-76 light tank. It was designed initially as a more expensive alternative for mechanized units, carrying infantry attached to Soviet tank forces. It still retained the battlefield taxi philosophy, and it was thus lightly armed with a 12.7-mm machine gun for self-defense. It was introduced in 1954 and, like the BTR-60, was exported in large numbers to Middle Eastern armies, forming the backbone of their mechanized units designed to escort tank forces into battle.

As a tracked vehicle, the BTR-50's cross-country performance was markedly superior to that of a wheeled vehicle, but this reduced its road speed compared to the BTR-60, and it was more complex to maintain and operate. The infantry exited the vehicle by climbing over the sides, and in later closed-topped versions this became difficult, as the men had to exit a series of large hatches. A similar version of this vehicle was built by Czechoslovakia and was known as the OT-62 Topaz. It too was exported to Middle Eastern nations.

The combat performance of these vehicles was unspectacular but sufficiently good to warrant continued use. They performed as designed, fulfilling their role as battlefield taxis. Many were destroyed in the host of wars in the Middle East in which they were used, including some lost during the coalition invasion of Iraq in 2003.

Unfortunately, there is little data as to the actual numbers lost in either the Persian Gulf War or the Iraq War. However, of the 6,000 BTRs available to Iraq during the Persian Gulf War, probably about 1,000 were destroyed or abandoned. Upgraded versions of the BTR-60, such as the BTR-80 and BTR-90, have seen limited export, with BTR-80s going to Turkey and BTR-90s specifically designed to meet the demands of the export markets of Middle East countries. However, they have seen little combat action. Thousands of BTR-50s and BTR-60s remain in the arsenals of nations ranging from China to Cuba to Bulgaria.

RUSSELL G. RODGERS

See also

IRAQI FREEDOM, Operation; Persian Gulf War

References

Fontenot, Gregory, et al. *On Point: The United States Army in Iraqi Freedom.* Annapolis, MD: Naval Institute Press, 2005.

Foss, Christopher. *Armoured Fighting Vehicles of the World.* London: Ian Allan, 1974.

Hull, Andrew W., David R. Markov, and Steven J. Zaloga. *Soviet/Russian Armor and Artillery Design Practices: 1945 to Present.* Darlington, MD: Darlington Publications, 1999.

Bush, George Walker (1946–)

Republican Party politician, governor of Texas (1995–2001), and president of the United States (2001–2009). George Walker Bush was born in New Haven, Connecticut, on July 6, 1946, and grew up in Midland and Houston, Texas. He is the son of George H. W. Bush, president of the United States during 1989–1993.

The younger Bush graduated from the exclusive Phillips Academy in Andover, Massachusetts, and from Yale University in 1968. He volunteered for the Texas Air National Guard after graduation and became a pilot, although questions later surfaced about his actual service. He earned an MBA from Harvard University in 1975 and returned to Texas, founding Arbusto Energy Company in 1977. He then served as a key staffer during his father's 1988 presidential campaign and later became one of the owners of the Texas Rangers baseball team.

In 1994, Bush was elected governor of Texas. As governor, he worked with the Democratic-dominated legislature to reduce state control and taxes. In 1996 he won reelection, by which time he had earned a reputation as an honest broker who could govern in a bipartisan manner.

In 2000, having set records for fund-raising and having campaigned as a "compassionate conservative," Bush easily won the 2000 Republican nomination for the presidency of the United States. His platform included tax cuts, improved schools, Social Security reform, and increased military spending. On foreign policy issues, he downplayed his obvious lack of experience but eschewed foreign intervention and nation building.

The U.S. presidential election of November 2000 was one of the most contentious in American history. The Democratic candidate, Vice President Al Gore, won a slim majority of the popular vote, but the electoral vote was in doubt. Confusion centered on Florida. Eventually after weeks of recounts and court injunctions, the issue reached the U.S. Supreme Court. On December 12, 2000, a deeply divided Court halted the recount in Florida, virtually declaring Bush the winner. For many Americans, Bush was an illegitimate and unelected president.

As president, Bush secured a large tax cut in hopes that this would spur the economy, and he pushed forward Social Security reform. He and the Republican-controlled Congress also enacted a tax rebate for millions of Americans in the late summer and early autumn of 2001. That same year, with prodding from the White House, Congress passed the No Child Left Behind Act, a standards-based reform measure designed to build more accountability into public education. Although the measure won broad bipartisan support, it later was criticized for being too narrowly conceived and incapable of accounting for differences in the way children learn. Many also came to believe that the mandate was not properly funded, especially in poorer school districts. In 2003 Bush was successful in passing a prescription drug act for U.S. citizens over the age of 65, but the measure ended up being far more expensive than originally forecast. Many also criticized the plan for being too complicated and offering too many options.

Bush sent many mixed messages about his commitment to environmental issues. Although he seemed to support the Kyoto Protocol dealing with climate change and global warming while campaigning in 2000, once in office he withdrew American support for the pact, citing conflicting scientific evidence on global warming. He also stated that the protocol could hurt the U.S. economy and American industry because neither India nor China had signed on to the agreement. His rejection of the Kyoto Protocol angered many environmentalists and other nations of the world that had already embraced the accord. This in fact was the first of many policy decisions that caused consternation in the international community. Throughout its first term, the Bush administration repeatedly downplayed the extent of global warming and the role that human activities play in it. In its second term, it seemed more accepting of the science on global warming but took few steps to mitigate it. In 2002, Bush did sign legislation mandating the cleanup of the Great Lakes, but he also supported limited drilling for oil in Alaska's Arctic National Wildlife Refuge, which is anathema to environmentalists and conservationists.

The course of Bush's presidency was forever changed on September 11, 2001, when 19 hijackers associated with the Al Qaeda terrorist organization seized commercial airliners and crashed them into the World Trade Center and the Pentagon. The attacks killed nearly 2,700 Americans and 316 foreign nationals. Over the next few days Bush visited the scenes of the attacks, reassuring the public and promising to bring those responsible to justice. The catastrophe of September 11 seemed to bring legitimacy and purpose to Bush's presidency, although it tilted the economy further into recession.

On September 20, 2001, Bush appeared before Congress and accused Al Qaeda of carrying out the attacks. He warned the American people that they faced a lengthy war against terrorism. He also demanded that the Taliban government of Afghanistan surrender members of Al Qaeda in their country or face retribution. When the Taliban failed to comply, U.S. and British forces began a bombing campaign on October 7. Initially, the United States enjoyed broad international support for the Global War on Terror and its campaign to oust the Taliban from Afghanistan. Indigenous Northern Alliance forces with heavy American support, chiefly in the form of air strikes, handily defeated the Taliban and by

November 2001 had captured the capital of Kabul. Taliban resistance continued thereafter, but the multinational coalition was nevertheless able to establish a new government in Afghanistan.

The Bush administration also sought to improve national security in the wake of September 11. A new Department of Homeland Security was created to coordinate all agencies that could track and defeat terrorists. In October 2001 at the behest of the Bush administration, Congress passed the so-called Patriot Act, giving the federal government sweeping powers to fight the war on terror. Many Americans were uncomfortable with this legislation and feared that it might undermine American freedom and civil liberties.

In 2002, the Bush administration turned its attentions toward Iraq. Intelligence reports suggested that Iraqi dictator Saddam Hussein was continuing to pursue weapons of mass destruction (WMD). When Bush demanded that he comply with United Nations (UN) resolutions seeking inspection of certain facilities, Hussein refused. Unfortunately, some of the intelligence dealing with Iraqi intentions and capabilities was faulty, and some have argued that the Bush White House pressured the Central Intelligence Agency and other intelligence services to interpret their findings in a way that would support armed conflict with Iraq. Still others claim that the White House and the Pentagon misled themselves and the public by reading into the intelligence reports more than what was actually there. By the end of 2002, the Bush administration had formulated a new policy of preemptive warfare (the Bush Doctrine) to destroy regimes that intended to harm the United States before they were able to do so.

In October 2002, Bush secured from Congress a bipartisan authorization to use military force against Iraq if necessary. Many in Congress had believed that all means of international diplomacy and economic sanctions would be exhausted before the United States undertook military action against the Iraqis. Such was not the case, however, for the White House seemed intent on war.

By the beginning of 2003, a military buildup against Iraq was already taking place. However, Bush's efforts to create a broad multinational coalition failed to achieve the success of the Persian Gulf War coalition against Iraq in 1991. Nearly all of the forces were American or British, and the UN failed to sanction military action against Iraq as it had done in 1990. The virtually unilateral U.S. approach to the situation in Iraq greatly angered much of the international community and even U.S. allies. Such longtime partners as

President George W. Bush stands, bull horn in hand, atop a burned-out fire truck with firefighter Bob Beck while rescue efforts continued at the site of New York City's World Trade Center, September 14, 2011, three days after the 9/11 attacks. (AP Photo/Doug Mills)

France and Germany refused to sanction American actions in Iraq, and relations with those nations suffered accordingly. To much of the world, the Bush Doctrine smacked of heavy-handed intimidation and hubris that simply circumvented international law whenever the Americans believed unilateral action to be necessary.

Military operations commenced on March 19, 2001, and Baghdad fell on April 9. At that point organized resistance was minimal, but manpower resources, while sufficient to topple Hussein, were clearly insufficient to maintain the peace. Rioting and looting soon broke out, and weapons stockpiles were pillaged by insurgents. Religious and ethnic tensions came to the fore between Sunnis, Shias, and Kurds. Far more American troops were killed trying to keep order in Iraq than had died in the overthrow of the regime.

Although Bush won reelection in November 2004 in large part because of his tough stance on the so-called Global War on Terror, support for the war in Iraq gradually waned, the consequence of mounting American military and Iraqi civilian dead, reports of American atrocities committed in Iraq, the war's vast expense, revelations that the White House trumped up or knowingly used questionable intelligence about Iraqi WMD, and general mismanagement of the war effort. Meanwhile, large budget deficits and trade imbalances piled up. Clearly, the failure to find WMD in Iraq undercut the stated reason for the attack, although Bush then claimed that the war was about overthrowing an evil dictatorship and bringing democracy to Iraq, a statement that was diametrically opposed to his insistence during the 2000 campaign that the United States should not undertake nation-building operations using the U.S. military.

The Bush administration was at first ambivalent toward the Arab-Israeli conflict, but with violence escalating, in August 2001 at the urging of Crown Prince Abdullah of Saudi Arabia, Bush issued a letter supporting the concept of a Palestinian state. September 11 and ensuing events in Iraq soon took precedence, however. Bush and his advisers realized that Arab support, or at least acquiescence, in his Iraq policies would be more likely if a peace process were under way.

On June 24, 2002, Bush publicly called for a two-state solution. He failed to outline specific steps but supported a process in which each side would meet certain criteria before moving to the next step. The result was called the Road Map to Peace. Bush agreed to work with the European Union, the UN, and Russia in developing it. This so-called Quartet developed a series of steps intended to provide assurances for each side but without involving the Israelis or Palestinians in its development.

The Road Map to Peace was unveiled in March 2003, just before the invasion of Iraq, but no details were announced. In June of that year, Bush arranged a summit conference at Aqaba, Jordan, involving Prime Minister Ariel Sharon of Israel and Prime Minister Mahmoud Abbas of the Palestinian National Authority. Progress on the plan stalled. The Bush administration's push for elections in the Palestinian-controlled West Bank backfired in January 2006 when these were won by the radical Hamas organization, which has called for the destruction of Israel and has continued to harass Israelis with random rocket attacks from Gaza and the West Bank. The peace process then ground to a halt. The Bush administration, faced with mounting American public dissatisfaction over the continuing American troop presence in Iraq, concentrated on that issue to the exclusion of virtually all other foreign developments.

Meanwhile, Bush suffered stunning setbacks at home. The White House was roundly denounced for its poor handling of relief efforts following Hurricane Katrina in the autumn of 2005 in which hundreds died in Louisiana and along the U.S. coast of the Gulf of Mexico. In the November 2006 midterm elections the Republicans lost both houses of Congress, and Bush was forced to fire Secretary of Defense Donald Rumsfeld, whose tenure had been rife with controversy. Many Americans placed the onus of blame for the Iraq debacle on his shoulders. The year before, Secretary of State Colin L. Powell had resigned because of sharp differences he had with the White House's foreign policy; he has since publicly regretted being taken in by faulty pre–Iraq War intelligence. By early 2007, Bush was besieged by bad news: plummeting approval ratings, a war gone bad in Iraq with no end in sight, and incipient signs that massive budget deficits fanned by Bush's spending and failure to veto appropriation bills were beginning to undermine the economy.

In January 2007 amid increasing calls for the United States to pull out of Iraq, Bush decided on just the opposite tack. His administration implemented a troop surge strategy that placed as many as 40,000 more U.S. soldiers on the ground in Iraq. Within six months the surge strategy seemed to be paying dividends, and violence in Iraq was down. At the same time, however, a growing Taliban insurgency in Afghanistan was threatening to undo many of the gains made there since 2001. Many critics, including a number of Republicans, argued that Bush's Iraq policies had needlessly diluted the U.S. effort in Afghanistan. But Bush was hard-pressed to send significantly more troops to Afghanistan because the military was already badly overstretched.

In the meantime, the White House's controversial policy of indefinitely detaining non-U.S. terror suspects, most of whom were being held at the Guantánamo Bay Detainment Camp in Cuba, drew the ire of many in the United States and the international community. Although most of the detainees were supposed to be tried in secret military tribunals, few were ever brought to trial. Some observers have alleged abuse and mistreatment at Guantánamo, which further eroded America's standing in the world. More recently, several U.S. courts have weighed in on the detainees' status and have ordered that they be tried or released. In June 2008, the U.S. Supreme Court ruled that terror detainees were subject to certain rights under the U.S. Constitution. Even more controversial has been the use of so-called coercive interrogation techniques on terror suspects and other enemy combatants. A euphemism for torture, this has included waterboarding, which goes against prescribed international norms for the treatment of prisoners of war. The Bush administration at first insisted that it had not authorized coercive interrogation, but when evidence to the contrary surfaced, the administration claimed that waterboarding had been used on some suspects. The White House, and especially Vice President Dick Cheney, however, attempted to assert that the technique did not constitute torture.

Not all the news on the international scene was bad, however. After the departure of such neoconservatives as Rumsfeld and Deputy Secretary of Defense Paul Wolfowitz, Bush's foreign policy became more pragmatic and less dogmatic. Secretary of State Condoleezza Rice worked diligently to try to repair America's standing in the world, and she met with some success by the end of the administration. President Bush's 2003 Emergency Plan for AIDS Relief, a multibillion-dollar aid package to African nations hit hard by the AIDS epidemic, drew much praise in the United States and abroad.

By 2008, Bush's approval ratings were as low as for any U.S. president in modern history. In the autumn the U.S. economy went into a virtual free fall, precipitated by a spectacular series of bank, insurance, and investment house failures and necessitating a massive government bailout worth more than $800 billion. Other corporate bailouts followed as more and more businesses teetered on the brink of insolvency. Unemployment began to rise dramatically in the fourth quarter of 2008, and consumer spending all but collapsed. The only bright note was a precipitous drop in the price of oil and gas, which had risen to dizzying heights in July 2008. Bush, a former oil man, and Vice President Cheney, who had also been in the petroleum-related business, had been excoriated for the run-up in energy prices, which certainly made the economic downturn even more severe. By the time Bush left office in January 2009, the nation was facing the worst economic downturn in at least 35 years.

The deep economic recession enabled the election of Democrat Barack Obama to the presidency in November 2008. He faced the daunting prospects of stabilizing the sinking economy, withdrawing all U.S. troops from Iraq, and reinvigorating the war in Afghanistan with an eye toward an American withdrawal from that country as quickly as possible.

Bush has kept an extraordinarily low profile since leaving office in January 2009. He has busied himself with building and organizing his presidential library, writing his memoirs, and participating in philanthropic work, including the Clinton-Bush Haiti Fund, which was created to help the residents of Haiti in the aftermath of a devastating earthquake in 2010. To his considerable credit, Bush has steadfastly refused to criticize his successor in public, stating that to do so would not be "good for the country."

TIM J. WATTS AND PAUL G. PIERPAOLI JR.

See also

Bush Doctrine; Cheney, Richard Bruce; Global War on Terror; Hussein, Saddam; IRAQI FREEDOM, Operation; Neoconservatism; Obama, Barack Hussein, II; Patriot Act; Powell, Colin Luther; Rice, Condoleezza; Rumsfeld, Donald; September 11 Attacks; September 11 Attacks, International Reactions to; Troop Surge, U.S., Iraq War; Wolfowitz, Paul

References

Baker, Peter. *Days of Fire: Bush and Cheney in the White House.* New York: Anchor Books, 2014.

Daalder, Ivo H., and James M. Lindsay. *America Unbound: The Bush Revolution in Foreign Policy.* Washington, DC: Brookings Institution, 2003.

Singer, Peter. *The President of Good & Evil: The Ethics of George W. Bush.* New York: Dutton, 2004.

Woodward, Bob. *Bush at War.* New York: Simon and Schuster, 2002.

Woodward, Bob. *Plan of Attack.* New York: Simon and Schuster, 2004.

Woodward, Bob. *State of Denial: Bush at War, Part III.* New York: Simon and Schuster, 2006.

Woodward, Bob. *The War Within: A Secret White House History, 2006–2008.* New York: Simon and Schuster, 2008.

Bush Doctrine

The Bush Doctrine is a foreign/national security policy articulated by President George W. Bush in a series of speeches following the September 11, 2001, terrorist attacks on the United States. The Bush Doctrine identified three threats against U.S. interests: terrorist organizations, weak states that harbor and assist such terrorist organizations, and so-called rogue states. The centerpiece of the Bush Doctrine was that the United States had the right to use preemptory military force against any state that is seen as hostile or that makes moves to acquire weapons of mass destruction, be they nuclear, biological, or chemical. In addition, the United States would "make no distinction between the terrorists who commit these acts and those who harbor them."

The Bush Doctrine represented a major shift in American foreign policy from the policies of deterrence and containment that characterized the Cold War and the brief period between the collapse of the Soviet Union in 1991 and 2001.

This new foreign policy and security strategy emphasized the strategic doctrine of preemption. The right of self-defense would be extended to use of preemptive attacks against potential enemies, attacking them before they were deemed capable of launching strikes against the United States. Under the doctrine, furthermore, the United States reserved the right to pursue unilateral military action if multilateral solutions cannot be found. The Bush Doctrine also represented the realities of international politics in the post–Cold War period, that is, that the United States was the sole superpower and aimed to ensure American hegemony.

A secondary goal of the Bush Doctrine was the promotion of freedom and democracy around the world, a precept that dates to at least the days of President Woodrow Wilson. In his speech to the graduating class at West Point on June 1, 2002, Bush declared that "America has no empire to extend or utopia to establish. We wish for others only what we wish for ourselves—safety from violence, the rewards of liberty, and the hope for a better life."

The immediate application of the Bush Doctrine was the invasion of Afghanistan in early October 2001 (Operation ENDURING FREEDOM). Although the Taliban-controlled government of Afghanistan offered to hand over Al Qaeda leader Osama bin Laden if it was shown tangible proof that he was responsible for the September 11 attacks and also offered to extradite bin Laden to Pakistan, where he would be tried under Islamic law, its refusal to extradite him to the United States with no preconditions was considered justification for the invasion.

The administration also applied the Bush Doctrine as justification for the Iraq War, beginning in March 2003 (Operation IRAQI FREEDOM). The Bush administration did not wish to wait for conclusive proof of Saddam Hussein's weapons of mass destruction (WMD), so in a series of speeches, administration officials laid out the argument for invading Iraq. To wait any longer was to run the risk of having Hussein employ or transfer the alleged WMD. Thus, despite the lack of any evidence of an operational relationship between Iraq and Al Qaeda, the United States, supported by Britain and a few other states, launched an invasion of Iraq. In the end, after months of exhaustive searching, no WMD were ever discovered in Iraq. Likewise, no direct connections between the Saddam Hussein regime and Al Qaeda have ever been firmly established.

The use of the Bush Doctrine as justification for the invasion of Iraq led to increasing friction between the United States and its allies, as the Bush Doctrine repudiated the core idea of the United Nations (UN) Charter. The charter prohibits any use of international force that is not undertaken in self-defense after the occurrence of an armed attack across an international boundary or pursuant to a decision by the UN Security Council. Even more vexing, the distinct limitations and pitfalls of the Bush Doctrine were abundantly evident in the U.S. inability to quell sectarian violence and political turmoil in Afghanistan or Iraq. The doctrine did not place parameters on the extent of American commitments, and it viewed the consequences of preemptory military strikes as a mere afterthought. This could be most clearly seen in Iraq, which in 2006 was teetering on a full-blown civil war more than three years after the initial invasion. And by 2011, an Islamist insurgency in Afghanistan was steadily gaining ground, despite a major troop surge in that country that began in early 2010 under the Barack Obama administration.

Not surprisingly, the Obama administration, which began in January 2009, has gone to great lengths to distance itself from the Bush Doctrine. Indeed, Obama has sought to mend fences with disgruntled international friends and allies and has emphasized the use of dialogue, diplomacy, and multilateral mechanisms to achieve foreign policy goals. Until the late summer of 2014, the administration in almost all situations had avoided the use of American military force abroad, with the exception of the ongoing war in Afghanistan. When the Arab Spring swept through the Middle East beginning in late 2010, Obama was reluctant to use any force in the region, with the exception of very limited air support (in concert with other nations) over the skies of Libya in 2011. Even amid irrefutable evidence that the Syrian government had employed chemical weapons to quash the civil war there in 2013, the Obama White House opted to engage the Syrian regime in an international plan to disarm it of such weapons rather than launch military strikes against it.

However, by the summer of 2014 the radical extremist group known as the Islamic State in Iraq and Syria (ISIS) was threatening the viability of the Iraqi government, and by then it had seized large swaths of northern and western Iraq and eastern Syria. In mid-August, Obama authorized air strikes against ISIS strongholds in Iraq; the campaign was extended into Syria the following month. Obama also authorized deployments of U.S. military advisers to Iraq, numbering some 3,000 by early November 2014. Obama's detractors have argued that he backtracked too far from the preemptory Bush Doctrine and that his hesitant actions toward the ISIS threat allowed the group to ensconce itself in Iraq and Syria. Nevertheless, the president's policies are certainly understandable in light of the calamities caused by Bush's military adventurism.

Keith A. Leitich

See also

Afghanistan; Al Qaeda; Bush, George Walker; IRAQI FREEDOM, Operation; Islamic State in Iraq and Syria; Libyan Civil War; Obama, Barack Hussein, II; September 11 Attacks; Syrian Civil War; Terrorism; Weapons of Mass Destruction

References

Baker, Peter. *Days of Fire: Bush and Cheney in the White House.* New York: Anchor Books, 2014.

Buckley, Mary E., and Robert Singh. *The Bush Doctrine and the War on Terrorism: Global Responses, Global Consequences.* London: Routledge, 2006.

Dolan, Chris J. *In War We Trust: The Bush Doctrine and the Pursuit of Just War.* Burlington, VA: Ashgate, 2005.

C

Cameron, David William Donald (1966–)

Conservative Party politician and prime minister of the United Kingdom since 2010. David William Donald Cameron was born on October 9, 1966, in London, England, to a wealthy family. A descendant of King William IV, Cameron spent his childhood in the town of Newbury, just west of London, where he attended private elementary schools before enrolling in the prestigious Eton College boarding school at age 13. After graduating in 1984, he took a year off from schooling, working briefly in Japan and traveling across Europe and the Soviet Union before attending the University of Oxford. He earned a degree in politics, philosophy, and economics there in 1988.

After obtaining his university degree, Cameron worked in the research department of the Conservative Party. In this role, he helped prepare Prime Minister John Major for interview questions and political meetings. In 1992 Cameron left the department to become special adviser to Chancellor of the Exchequer Norman Lamont. A year later Cameron moved on to work as special adviser to Home Secretary Michael Howard. In 1994, Cameron took a hiatus from politics and became director of corporate affairs for Carlton Communications, a private media company. He left that post in 2001, four years after making an unsuccessful attempt to win a seat in Parliament. In 2001 Cameron again ran for Parliament, this time winning a seat as a representative of the town of Witney.

Because the Conservative Party was not in power when Cameron became a member of Parliament, he held posts in the opposition shadow government, including deputy leader of the House of Commons and education secretary. From 2001 to 2003, he was part of the influential House of Commons Home Affairs Select Committee. In June 2003, Cameron became vice chairperson of the Conservative Party. Then when the Conservative Party lost to the Labour Party in 2005 elections, its chair, Michael Howard, resigned, leaving the party leadership open. Cameron announced his candidacy for chairperson in September. Although many questioned his inexperience and relative youth, Cameron won enough favor to be elected as Conservative Party chairperson in December 2005.

When the economy took a deep downward turn in 2007, the Labour Party began losing favor. The Conservative Party dominated local elections in 2008 and by the 2010 national elections was expected to win its first general election since 1992; however, when the votes were counted, the party wound up 20 seats shy of an overall majority. Having lost 91 seats in the May 6 elections, Labour Party leader Gordon Brown resigned as prime minister five days after the election. That same day, Cameron's distant relative, Queen Elizabeth, invited him to establish the country's new government. After forming a coalition with the Liberal Democratic Party, which held 57 seats in Parliament, Cameron took office as prime minister on May 11, 2010. A few months shy of 44 years old upon taking office in 2010, he became the youngest prime minister to lead the country since 1812.

As premier, Cameron faced large government deficits and pushed for austerity measures and changes to the welfare system, among others, to help resolve the nation's economic issues. He has also overseen the legalization of same-sex marriages in England and Wales. His eloquent plea for unity on the eve of the September 2014 referendum on Scottish independence, in which he warned that a "yes" vote would mean "the end of a country that people around the world respect and admire, the end of a country that all of us call home," is widely believed to have helped defeat the referendum.

During his tenure, Cameron has often been praised for his polished, media-savvy communication skills. On the other hand, he has been criticized for what appears to be an aloof, hands-off approach to leadership, and some church leaders have attacked his welfare reforms for leaving many to face hunger and greater poverty.

Although Cameron supported the Iraq War and his country's participation in it, he has been somewhat more circumspect in committing British military power abroad. In the fall of 2013 when his government requested that Parliament give its approval of a potential air campaign against Syrian government forces in the face of the chemical weapon attack at Ghouta, Parliament denied the request. This was the first time a British prime minister had lost a foreign policy vote in Parliament in more than 100 years. In the fall of 2014, Cameron somewhat reluctantly acceded to calls for Great Britain to participate in a coalition air campaign designed to break the back of the insurgency in Iraq and Syria being led by the Islamic State of Iraq and Syria (ISIS).

TAMAR BURRIS

See also

Islamic State in Iraq and Syria; Syrian Civil War

References

Heppell, Timothy, and David Seawright. *Cameron and the Conservatives: The Transition to Coalition Government.* London: Palgrave Macmillan, 2012.

Lee, Simon, and Matt Beech. *The Cameron-Clegg Government: Coalition Politics in an Age of Austerity.* London: Palgrave Macmillan, 2011.

Toynbee, Polly, and David Walker. *Dogma and Disarray: Cameron at Half-Time.* Wrotham, Kent, UK: Mount Caburn Publishing, 2012.

Campbell, John Francis (1957–)

U.S. Army officer and commander of the International Security Assistance Force (ISAF) since August 26, 2014. John Francis Campbell was born on April 11, 1957, in Maine, the son of a career U.S. Air Force noncommissioned officer. After living in various locations in the United States, Europe, and Asia, Campbell attended the U.S. Military Academy, West Point, graduating in 1979. He was commissioned a second lieutenant of infantry and moved steadily through the ranks, holding several command and staff positions with the 82nd Airborne Division. Subsequent to that, Campbell served as an assistant professor of military science at the University of California–Davis.

After attending the Command and General Staff College, Campbell again served with the 82nd Airborne Division before becoming aide-de-camp to the commander of the XVIII Airborne Corps, which was deployed to Haiti from 1994 to 1995 as part of Operation RESTORE DEMOCRACY. In 1996, he took command of the 2nd Battalion, 5th Infantry Regiment, 25th Infantry Division, at Schofield Barracks, Hawaii, before attending the U.S. Army War College at Carlisle, Pennsylvania. On June 1, 2000, Campbell was promoted to colonel. He was then given command of the 1st Brigade, 82nd Airborne Division, and the 504th Parachute Infantry Regiment. In late 2001, Campbell was deployed to Afghanistan during Operation ENDURING FREEDOM.

On October 1, 2005, Campbell was promoted to brigadier general and became deputy commanding general for maneuver for the 1st Cavalry Division, which was deployed to Iraq as part of Operation IRAQI FREEDOM. On November 7, 2008, he was promoted to major general and served as executive officer to the chief of staff of the army. In 2009, Campbell became commanding general, 101st Airborne Division, headquartered at Fort Campbell, Kentucky. He was then redeployed to Afghanistan, where he commanded Joint Task Force 101 from June 2010 until May 2011. On September 9, 2011, Campbell was promoted to lieutenant general and named army deputy chief of staff for operations, plans, and training.

Campbell was promoted to full general (four stars) on March 8, 2013, and named army vice chief of staff. On August 26, 2014, he assumed command of ISAF. His tenure in that post would witness major changes. After the Afghan government finalized the long-stalled status of forces agreement with the United States on September 30, 2014, Campbell supervised the steady drawdown of ISAF and North Atlantic Treaty Organization (NATO) forces from Afghanistan. By December 31, 2014, when the ISAF-NATO mission mandate was scheduled to end, about 14,000 foreign troops remained in Afghanistan. Of that number, all but some 4,000 troops would be American.

PAUL G. PIERPAOLI JR.

See also

Afghanistan War; International Security Assistance Force; IRAQI FREEDOM, Operation; Status of Forces Agreement, U.S.-Afghan

References

"Campbell Becomes Final ISAF Commander." Stars and Stripes, August 26, 2014, http://www.stripes.com/news/campbell-becomes-final-isaf-commander-1.300015.

"Campbell Takes Oath as Army's Vice Chief of Staff." U.S. Army, March 11, 2013, http://www.army.mil/article/98124/Campbell_takes_oath_as_Army_s_vice_chief_of_staff/.

Casey, George William, Jr. (1948–)

U.S. Army general, commander of U.S. forces in Iraq (Multi-National Force–Iraq) during 2004–2007, and army chief of staff from 2007 until 2011. George William Casey Jr. was born on July 22, 1948, in Sendai, Japan; his father, a career army officer, was serving with the army occupation forces there. (His father, Major General George William Casey Sr., died in Vietnam in 1970 in a helicopter crash.) Casey spent his early life on army posts throughout the United States and Europe and graduated from Georgetown University in 1970, where he was enrolled in the U.S. Army Reserve Officers' Training Corps.

In August 1970, Casey was commissioned a second lieutenant in the army. During the next decade he served in a variety of command and staff positions. In 1980, he earned an MA in international relations from the University of Denver. Casey continued his military education at the Armed Forces Staff College, completing his studies there in July 1981.

Shortly thereafter Casey was ordered to the Middle East, where he worked with the United Nations Truce Observer Supervision Organization. From February 1982 to July 1987 he was assigned to the 4th Infantry Division based at Fort Carson, Colorado. In December 1989, he became a special assistant to the army chief of staff. He was then assigned as chief of staff of the 1st Cavalry Division at Fort Hood, Texas, where he later commanded that division's 3rd Brigade. In July 1996 he was promoted to brigadier general and sent to Europe, where he served as assistant commander for the 1st Armored Division in Germany and participated in the peacekeeping missions to Bosnia and Herzegovina.

In 1999 following his advancement to major general, Casey commanded the 1st Armored until July 2001. At the end of October 2001 he was appointed lieutenant general and took control of strategic plans and policy for the Joint Chiefs of Staff. In January 2003 he became director, Joint Staff of the Joint Chiefs of Staff. That October, he became vice chief of staff of the army and was advanced to four-star rank.

Casey became a major figure in planning for the U.S. response to the terrorist attacks of September 11, 2001, and for the 2003 invasion of Iraq. As director of the Joint Staff, he had been directly involved in the allocation of units and personnel for the Iraq operation. One of his assignments was the allocation of military personnel for administration in the occupied areas. In December 2002 with planning for the invasion in full swing, Casey ordered the formation of a follow-on headquarters for the postwar occupation but gave it few resources. It was in his capacity as director of the Joint Staff that Casey first encountered conflict over troop levels for the impending invasion, which occurred between the field commanders and Secretary of Defense Donald Rumsfeld.

Conditions in Iraq in the wake of the March 2003 invasion became central to Casey's fortunes. For all of his success, Casey had attracted little notice outside military circles. This changed when he was assigned to head the commission to investigate the abuse of prisoners by American guards at Abu Ghraib prison in late 2003.

In the summer of 2004, Casey was appointed to command U.S. and coalition forces (Multi-National Force–Iraq). By the time he took command the Iraqi insurgency was in full swing, but the coalition response had been hampered by fundamental conflicts over strategy and tactics between the civilian commissioner in Iraq, L. Paul Bremer, and the military commander, General Ricardo Sanchez. Casey soon established a cordial working relationship with the new American ambassador to Iraq, John Negroponte.

Such a relationship was needed in the desperate situation the two men faced in 2004. Casey was shocked to discover that there was no counterinsurgency strategy. He and Negroponte thus worked to develop a coherent approach to combating the growing attacks on American forces and the threat of civil war. Casey's strategy involved securing transportation infrastructure, containing insurgent violence by aggressively attacking insurgent bases, reaching out to Iraq's Sunni Muslims, and building up Iraqi security forces. Under Casey's direction, U.S. counterinsurgency operations took on a clearer direction, but violence in Iraq continued to escalate, and the war grew profoundly unpopular in the United States.

In March 2007, Casey turned over his command to Lieutenant General David Petraeus and returned to the United States to assume the post of U.S. Army chief of staff. Casey was cautious but noncommittal in his support of the troop surge implemented by the George W. Bush administration in January 2007. Casey also warned that U.S. Army resources were being stretched dangerously thin by the concurrent wars in Iraq and Afghanistan.

As army chief of staff, Casey engaged in a successful modernization program that permitted the U.S. Army to become more efficient and responsive to 21st-century challenges. He presided over a modest growth of the force, introduced troop rotations that had been used successfully by the U.S. Marine Corps, and improved the readiness and training of both the Army Reserves and the Army National Guard. Casey left his post on April 11, 2011, at which time he retired from active duty. He subsequently moved to his boyhood hometown in Massachusetts.

WALTER F. BELL

See also

Abu Ghraib; Bremer, Lewis Paul; Bush, George Walker; Negroponte, John Dimitri; Petraeus, David Howell; Rumsfeld, Donald; Sanchez, Ricardo S.; Sunni Islam

References

Gordon, Michael R., and General Bernard E. Trainor. *Cobra II: The Inside Story of the Invasion and Occupation of Iraq*. New York: Pantheon Books, 2006.

Ricks, Thomas E. *Fiasco: The American Military Adventure in Iraq*. New York: Penguin, 2006.

Woodward, Bob. *State of Denial: Bush at War, Part III*. New York: Simon and Schuster, 2006.

Woodward, Bob. *The War Within: A Secret White House History, 2006–2008*. New York: Simon and Schuster, 2008.

Casualties, Operation ENDURING FREEDOM

Operation ENDURING FREEDOM and the attendant Global War on Terror began on October 7, 2001, in Afghanistan, a response to the terror attacks against the United States of September 11, 2001. Operation ENDURING FREEDOM ended officially on December 31, 2014, which marked the end of the longest war in American history. In terms of coalition casualties for North Atlantic Treaty Organization (NATO) and International Security Assistance Force (ISAF) personnel, as of the end of 2014 there were 3,485 U.S. and coalition military deaths in Afghanistan as part of Operation ENDURING FREEDOM. Americans sustained the largest number of deaths, which totaled 2,356. The U.S. total included Central Intelligence Agency personnel, most of whom died in the first few months of the war. Not included among the number of American casualties are the deaths of armed American private security company personnel.

Although American forces suffered the most coalition casualties, other nations experienced a spike in the numbers killed in action after 2008, especially in 2009 when the total killed was nearly double that of the previous year

(520 vs. 295). The peak year for coalition casualties was 2010 the same year the Barack Obama administration began implementing its troop surge, which endured until the late summer of 2012. In 2010, there were 711 coalition casualties; that same year also witnessed the largest number of deaths due to improvised explosive devices—603, accounting for 58.41 percent of all coalition casualties. Beginning in 2011 the number of casualties steadily decreased, and in 2014 there were just 75 casualties, the lowest figure since 2004.

After 2006, when ISAF expanded its jurisdiction to the southern regions of Afghanistan, which had previously been under U.S. military authority, the number of British and Canadian casualties increased. The highly volatile provinces of Helmand and Kandahar were particularly dangerous for coalition forces. As of the end of 2014, British forces had suffered 453 killed, the second-highest casualty rate of all coalition forces. The war in Afghanistan also resulted in the largest number of fatalities for any single Canadian military operation since the 1950–1953 Korean War. By the end of 2014, 158 Canadian troops had died.

Apart from the United States, the United Kingdom, and Canada, other coalition deaths by country as of December 31, 2014, were as follows: France, 86; Germany, 54; Italy, 48; Denmark, 43; Australia, 41; Poland, 40; Spain, 34; Georgia, 27; the Netherlands, 25; Romania, 21; Turkey, 14; New Zealand, 11; Norway, 10; Czech Republic, 10; Estonia, 9; Hungary, 7; Sweden, 5; Slovakia, 3; Latvia, 3; Jordan 2; Finland 2; Portugal, 2; Albania, 1; Belgium, 1; Lithuania, 1; and South Korea, 1. There were also 17 NATO deaths during the war, that is, NATO personnel representing the alliance and not attached to a particular nation's military.

After Operation ENDURING FREEDOM began, there were numerous incidents involving civilians killed during military operations against the Taliban and Al Qaeda. In the latter stages of the conflict, those same groups also staged attacks, including myriad suicide bombings, that frequently claimed civilian lives. U.S.-led coalition troops and NATO forces maintained that great efforts were made to avoid civilian casualties while trying to eliminate the insurgency. Nevertheless, they complained that insurgents often blended in with local populations when under attack, thus increasing the risk of more civilian casualties.

As to exact numbers of Afghan civilians killed, the debate continues, with numbers varying markedly. Estimates of dead range from 21,000 to as high as 50,000 during the initial invasion and subsequent war from all causes. The war also resulted in huge numbers of Afghan refugees who fled to neighboring countries (in 2013 that figure was estimated to be 2.2 million); in 2013, there were also at least 547,000 internally displaced persons.

Beginning in 2007, insurgents launched attacks that were both more aggressive and greater in number. That increased not only the number of collateral deaths but also the number of insurgent deaths. Casualties showed a dramatic increase in 2009. Afghan military and security casualty estimates remain fluid, but by the spring of 2014, an estimated 13,000 Afghan soldiers and police had died during the conflict. Insurgent losses were estimated at between 25,000 and 45,000, with some 26,500 taken prisoner.

CHARLES FRANCIS HOWLETT AND SPENCER C. TUCKER

See also

Afghanistan War; Afghanistan War, Consequences of; Al Qaeda; ENDURING FREEDOM, Operation, Initial Ground Campaign; International Security Assistance Force; North Atlantic Treaty Organization; Taliban; Troop Surge, U.S., Afghanistan War

References

Kunkel, Thomas. "Casualties of War." *American Journalism Review* 24 (January 1, 2002): 4.

"Operation ENDURING FREEDOM." Iraq Coalition Casualty Count, http://icasualties.org/ocf/.

"War Deaths Top 13,000 in Afghan Security Forces." *New York Times*, March 3, 2014, http://www.nytimes.com/2014/03/04/world/asia/afghan-cabinet-releases-data-on-deaths-of-security-personnel.html?partner=rss&emc=rss&smid=tw-nytimes&_r=0.

Casualties, Operation IRAQI FREEDOM

Casualties as a result of combat operations in Iraq during Operation IRAQI FREEDOM, which began on March 19, 2003, and ended on December 31, 2011, were a constant source of controversy, particularly in the United States. The quick and decisive victory won by the United States in the 1991 Persian Gulf War, which saw few American casualties, and the low initial American casualty count for the Afghanistan War, Operation ENDURING FREEDOM, had conditioned U.S. citizens and politicians to expect a speedy and relatively easy victory in Iraq. Although the initial combat phase (March 19–April 30, 2003) produced few U.S. and coalition combat deaths, the subsequent insurgency led to several thousand more. Many responded to the mounting IRAQI FREEDOM casualty numbers with incredulity and calls for a full or total withdrawal of American troops from Iraq. Other nations with large troop deployments in Iraq—particularly Great Britain—experienced similar developments.

Air Force officers oversee the transport of coffins containing the remains of 20 U.S. servicemen killed during Operation IRAQI FREEDOM. Pursuant to a Pentagon order of 2003, it was forbidden to disseminate to the public images such as this scene at Dover Air Force Base. Requests filed in 2004 under the Freedom of Information Act resulted in the successful release of more than 300 such photographs of flag-draped coffins and the honor guards charged with their transport. (U.S. Air Force)

The U.S. Department of Defense provided a continuously running tally of American casualties. Its figures included numbers of American personnel killed in action and wounded in action in both official Operation IRAQI FREEDOM combat operations (March 19, 2003–April, 30, 2003) and postcombat operations (May 1, 2003–present). In the first phase of the war, 139 American military personnel were killed, and 545 were wounded. Total U.S. military deaths from both phases of IRAQI FREEDOM were 4,488 through the end of 2011, while the total number of American military personnel wounded in action during the same period was about 34,000. Of those wounded, a majority returned to active duty within 72 hours, classified as wounded in action, returned to duty. Each fatality milestone occasioned an outcry of opposition to the war, and when the casualty count topped 4,000 in the spring of 2008 and coincided with a particularly heated presidential primary campaign, these numbers became a source of even greater political controversy.

In addition to the U.S. casualties, through December 15, 2011, a total of 318 coalition troops were killed, including 179 Britons. Also, the Iraq War claimed the lives of 139 journalists. More than 1,300 private contractors were also killed.

Although the Department of Defense makes information on U.S. casualties publicly available, precise figures documenting Iraqi casualties, both military and civilian, are more difficult to access, and nearly all figures come with caveats. Iraqi sources have reported that government agencies are not permitted to report the numbers of bodies buried daily. Credible sources indicate roughly 9,200 Iraqi combatant fatalities during the first phase of Operation IRAQI FREEDOM; estimates range from a low of 7,600 to a high of 10,800. According to the Iraq Coalition Casualty Count, by 2011 an estimated 8,825 members of the Iraqi Security Forces (ISF) had been killed in combat against Iraqi insurgents. The Iraq Coalition Casualty Count is one of the most thorough databases compiling this information, although the group does not provide numbers of wounded ISF personnel. Current and credible estimates of the number of insurgents killed are among the hardest statistics to obtain, because membership in those groups is both fluid and clandestine. According to calculations made in September 2007, the number of insurgents killed after the fall of Baghdad in April 2003 was 19,492; casualties continued to accumulate, although a reliably sourced updated estimate has not been released.

The number of Iraqi civilians killed during IRAQI FREEDOM has been widely disputed. The Lancet study of 2006, so-called for its publication in the British medical journal of that name, was carried out by Iraqi and American physicians and researchers from al-Mustansiriyya University and Johns Hopkins University through a cluster survey of households where respondents had to show death certificates. The study estimated a total of 426,369 to 793,663 Iraqi deaths to that date. A third study by experts from the Federal Ministry of Health in Baghdad, the Kurdistan Ministry of Planning, the Kurdistan Ministry of Health, the Central Organization for Statistics and Information Technology in Baghdad, and the World Health Organization was carried out the Iraq Family Health Survey (IFHS) Study Group (known as the WHO study in the media). The IFHS study estimated 151,000 Iraqi deaths from March 2003 to June 2006. The study actually presented a range of deaths from 104,000 to 223,000 for those years.

Other sources have estimated Iraqi civilian casualties from the war and sectarian violence as 600,000 to more than 1 million. The independent British-based Opinion Research Bureau estimated 1,220,580 Iraqis deaths by September 2007. Other than deliberate underreporting, some sources pointed to the suppression of statistics by the Iraqi government in the belief that to do so would compromise efforts to quell violence. In 2013, a study conducted by U.S. university researchers estimated the total number of civilian deaths (2003–2011) in Iraq to have been 461,000. This included deaths from all causes but related directly or indirectly to the ground war and subsequent insurgency.

Although there is great disagreement on the actual number of civilian deaths in Iraq, there is general agreement that the numbers were very high. Generally speaking, those who supported the war have denied the higher civilian casualty counts, while those who opposed the war held them to be valid.

The Iraq Coalition Casualty Count serves as a thorough clearinghouse for information on all coalition fatalities. During the period of official IRAQI FREEDOM combat (March 19–May 1, 2003), 33 soldiers from the United Kingdom were killed; no other coalition nation suffered any fatalities during this phase of operations. The Iraq Coalition Casualty Count cites the following fatality numbers for other coalition nations as of the end of 2011, when the operation officially ended: Australia, 2; Azerbaijan, 1; Bulgaria, 13; Czech Republic, 1; Denmark, 7; El Salvador, 5; Estonia, 2; Fiji, 1; Georgia, 5; Hungary, 1; Italy, 33; Kazakhstan, 1; Latvia, 3; Netherlands, 2; Poland, 23; Romania, 3; Slovakia, 4; South Korea, 1; Spain, 11; Thailand, 2; Ukraine, 18; and United Kingdom, 179. The group does not provide wounded in action casualty figures.

A high suicide rate among U.S. military and veterans has become a special matter of concern. Although no clear answers for this have emerged, it has been attributed to extended tours, too little time off between tours, the nature of the conflict, circumstances at home, and other factors.

Periodic lulls in violence and the achievement of certain strategic objectives resulted in temporary decreases in the rates of injury and death, but the nature of the guerrilla-style low-intensity conflict that characterized the Iraq War and the sectarian conflicts that continue to plague Iraq mean that Iraqi casualties will continue to accumulate.

REBECCA ADELMAN AND SHERIFA ZUHUR

See also

IRAQI FREEDOM, Operation

References

Baker, James A., III, and Lee Hamilton. *The Iraq Study Group: The Way Froward, a New Approach.* New York: Vintage Books, 2006.

Burnham, Gilbert, Riyadh Lafta, Shannon Doocy, et al. "Mortality after the 2003 Invasion of Iraq: A Cross-Sectional Cluster Sample Survey." *Lancet* 368(5945) (October 21, 2006): 1421–1429.

Capdevila, Luc, and Danièle Voldman. *War Dead: Western Society and Casualties of War.* Translated by Richard Veasey. Edinburgh, UK: Edinburgh University Press, 2006.

"Documented Civilian Deaths from Violence." Iraq Body Count, http://www.iraqbodycount.org/database.

Fischer, Hanna. "Iraqi Civilian Casualties Estimates." Washington DC: Congressional Research Service, January 12, 2009.

Iraq Family Health Survey Study Group. "Violence-Related Mortality in Iraq from 2002 to 2006." *New England Journal of Medicine* (January 31, 2008): 484–492.

Mueller, John. "The Iraq Syndrome." *Foreign Affairs* 84 (2005): 44–54.

"Operation IRAQI FREEDOM." Iraq Coalition Casualty Count, http://icasualties.org/Iraq/index.aspx.

"Operation Iraqi Freedom (OIF) U.S. Casualty Status." United States Department of Defense, http://www.defenselink.mil/news/casualty.pdf.

Roberts, Les, Riyadh Lafta, Richard Garfield, et al. "Mortality Before and After the 2003 Invasion of Iraq: Cluster Sample Survey." *Lancet* 364(9448) (October 29, 2004): 1857–1864.

Wood, Trish. *What Was Asked of Us: An Oral History of the Iraq War by the Soldiers Who Fought It.* New York: Little, Brown, 2006.

Central Intelligence Agency

Primary civilian government agency charged with carrying out intelligence and espionage activities for the United States. The Central Intelligence Agency (CIA), created by the National Security Act of 1947, exercised primary responsibility for intelligence collection and analysis but also for the conduct of covert actions.

The agency is the direct successor of the World War II Office of Strategic Services (OSS). In January 1946, President Harry S. Truman signed an executive order forming a Central Intelligence Group (CIG) patterned after the OSS, and on July 16, 1947, Truman signed the National Security Act, replacing the CIG with the new CIA as an independent agency within the executive branch. The CIA was to advise the National Security Council on intelligence matters and make recommendations regarding coordination of intelligence activities. Although the original intent was only to authorize espionage, broad interpretation of the act's provisions led to authorization of covert operations. The director of central intelligence was charged with reporting on intelligence activities to the president and Congress.

Known to insiders as "the Agency" or "the Company," the CIA played a key role in the overthrow of allegedly radical governments in Iran in 1953 and Guatemala in 1954. It was also active in assisting the Philippine government in crushing the Hukbalahap uprising; in Southeast Asia, especially in Laos, it operated Air America to funnel U.S. aid to anticommunist forces. Notable failures included the Bay of Pigs fiasco in Cuba in April 1961 and attempts to assassinate or discredit Cuban leader Fidel Castro. The CIA played an important role in the 1962 Cuban Missile Crisis, and its agents penetrated key governmental agencies in the Soviet Union. The CIA-sponsored Phoenix Program in Vietnam for the assassination of communist operatives engendered considerable controversy, as did its role in helping to oust Chilean president Salvador Allende in 1973. The CIA's involvement in assassination plots and domestic spying led to the creation of the President's Intelligence Oversight Board as well as an Intelligence Committee in each house of Congress. The CIA failed to predict the 1979 revolution overthrowing the shah of Iran, Mohammad Reza Shah Pahlavi. It provided important assistance to Afghan rebels following the Soviet invasion of that country. It also took part in the secret sale of arms to Iran arranged with the hostage release and funneling of the proceeds to Contra rebels fighting Nicaragua's leftist Sandinista government, the so-called Iran-Contra Affair. This activity led Congress in 1991 to pass a new oversight law to prevent a reoccurrence. The CIA did provide useful intelligence on the threat posed by Iraq to neighboring Kuwait, but it was caught off guard by the actual August 1990 invasion.

The sudden collapse of the Soviet Union beginning with the failed coup attempt against Mikhail Gorbachev in August 1991 came as a complete surprise to the agency. Although the CIA had warned that terrorists might attempt to seize control of civilian airliners and fly them into buildings, it failed to provide timely intelligence that might have prevented the September 11, 2001, terrorist attacks against the World Trade Center in New York City and the Pentagon in Washington, D.C.

In December 2004, President George W. Bush signed the Intelligence Reform and Terrorism Prevention Act. That legislation abolished the positions of director of central intelligence and deputy director of central intelligence and created the positions of director of the CIA and director of national intelligence, which took over some of the responsibilities that had been formerly handled by the CIA. These reforms were in response to the lapses of intelligence over the preceding years, including the September 11, 2001, attacks; bogus reports of weapons of mass destruction (WMD) in Iraq; and other incidents that called into question CIA credibility and effectiveness.

The CIA director is nominated by the president and approved by the U.S. Senate. Working with numerous staffs, the director is responsible for managing the operations, staff, and budget of the CIA. The director also oversees the National Human Source Intelligence division and interacts with the Department of Homeland Security to monitor terrorist and extremist activities within the United States. The CIA is organized into four primary directorates: the National Clandestine Service, the Directorate of Intelligence, the Directorate of Science and Technology, and the Directorate of Support. All four directorates are supposed to work together to collect, analyze, and distribute intelligence that is deemed necessary to protect national security.

In 1999 CIA director George Tenet had developed plans to deal with the Al Qaeda terrorist organization, which was headquartered in Afghanistan. The CIA was soon involved in sending flights over Afghanistan with drones to gather intelligence information on the terrorist training camps there. Following the terror attacks on September 11, 2001, the CIA came under great pressure regarding its previous efforts to combat terrorism, which in turn prompted the 2004 changes described above to America's intelligence-gathering apparatus.

The CIA has also received considerable criticism for its role in the Iraq War. Indeed, the agency was blamed, rightly or wrongly, for the assertion that Iraq possessed WMD, which was a key factor in the 2003 decision to invade the country. As it turned out no WMD were found, and public support for the war fell quickly after this was made public. Because the George W. Bush administration used the threat of WMD as a justification for the war, the CIA's reputation was badly tarnished. As the war in Iraq continued, more information regarding early CIA involvement was released. Since then, numerous people have come forward claiming that a large percentage of CIA officials did not support what the agency was claiming about WMD in Iraq. Many claim that the CIA was pressured by the Bush administration to produce reports with intelligence that the administration wanted the CIA to find, not necessarily the actual intelligence collected. More recently, the CIA has come under sharp criticism for its connection to the alleged torturing of terrorist suspects, especially the controversial technique of waterboarding. Coercive interrogation techniques were officially authorized by top CIA officials (and approved by Vice President Richard "Dick" Cheney and President Bush) in 2001.

On January 29, 2009, only days after he had assumed the presidency, Barack Obama signed an executive order mandating that the CIA use only 19 interrogation methods as outlined in the *Army Field Manual on Interrogation* unless it sought specific exemptions from the attorney general and provided sufficient cause to seek such exemptions. In May 2011, a secret operation that resulted in the apprehension and death of Osama bin Laden was launched from a forward CIA base located in Afghanistan; the agency played a major role in collecting and verifying intelligence concerning bin Laden's exact whereabouts. Although the Obama administration has attempted to distance itself from the more extreme measures associated with counterterrorism, it has acquiesced in the continuation of extraordinary renditions, which are typically conducted by the CIA.

Since 2009, leading congressional leaders, including former Speaker of the House Nancy Pelosi, charged the CIA with repeatedly lying to Congress or misrepresenting facts to Congress concerning the Global War on Terror and other matters relating to national security. These have included the use of waterboarding and an alleged program to assassinate suspected terrorists abroad, including leaders of foreign governments, which Congress had previously forbidden. In July 2014, the CIA was again embarrassed when it was forced to admit that it had spied on U.S. senators by hacking the computers of those senators who sat on the Intelligence Committee.

Arthur M. Holst

See also

Al Qaeda; Bin Laden, Osama; Bush, George Walker; Cheney, Richard Bruce; Coercive Interrogation; *Cole,* USS, Attack on; Counterterrorism Strategy; Dar es Salaam, Bombing of U.S. Embassy; Global War on Terror; Nairobi, Kenya, Bombing of U.S. Embassy; Obama, Barack Hussein, II; September 11 Attacks; Tenet, George John; Terrorism; Torture of Prisoners; Weapons of Mass Destruction

References

Jeffreys-Jones, Rhodri. *The CIA and American Democracy.* New Haven, CT: Yale University Press, 1998.
Jones, Ishmael. *The Human Factor: Inside the CIA's Dysfunctional Intelligence Culture.* New York: Encounter Books, 2010.
Kessler, Ronald. *Inside the CIA: Revealing the Secrets of the World's Most Powerful Spy Agency.* New York: Pocket Books, 1994.

Theoharis, Athan, ed. *The Central Intelligence Agency: Security under Scrutiny*. Westport, CT: Greenwood, 2006.

Central Intelligence Agency, Senate Report on (December 9, 2014)

A 6,000-page report released by the U.S. Senate Intelligence Committee on December 9, 2014, that exposed Central Intelligence Agency (CIA) activities since the September 11, 2001, terror attacks and during the Global War on Terror in general. Large portions of the report were heavily redacted for national security purposes, and some of the report's details merely repeated already-disclosed information. Nevertheless, the report proved highly controversial not only for its $40 million cost and five-year investigative duration but also because of its details on the CIA's use of coercive interrogation with terror suspects and the CIA's alleged activities intended to cover up such conduct.

The Senate report broadly concluded that the CIA's use of coercive interrogation, which many have termed as torture, has been generally ineffective as well as more widespread than had been previously acknowledged. The document also concluded that the CIA has routinely misled the American people, Congress, and even the president about its interrogation techniques. The report went on to assert that the CIA has repeatedly and purposely overstated the results of such techniques, including the thwarting of terror attacks and the location of Al Qaeda leader Osama bin Laden. Additionally, the document revealed the existence of a series of so-called black box sites located across the globe where the CIA has subjected terror detainees to various kinds of coercive interrogation, which may be easily interpreted as torture by another name.

The report claimed that the CIA resorted to waterboarding of detainees to the point of near death; depriving prisoners of sleep for as long as 180 continuous hours; beating and humiliating suspects; forcing detainees to remain in horribly uncomfortable "stress positions" for many hours, even when they had broken bones; and subjecting prisoners to "rectal feeding," or the forced administration of pureed food into the rectum. One vignette detailed the death of an internee from hypothermia after he had been shackled to a concrete floor with almost no clothes in temperatures as low as 25 degrees.

The Senate report, which described waterboarding as "near-drowning," went on to allege that many terror suspects were subjected to torture without being given the opportunity to answer interrogators' questions. Even worse, 26 of 119 detainees who were tortured had been wrongfully held. Two of the 26 were known CIA informants. An entire section of the report examined CIA director Michael Hayden's myriad and allegedly deliberate lies to cover up the fact that 26 prisoners had been detained and tortured by mistake. That same section blamed Hayden for the purposeful destruction of 98 videotapes depicting the waterboarding of prisoners.

President Barack Obama ended many of these practices after taking office in 2009, but when the report was unveiled he nevertheless defended U.S. intelligence officers as "patriots." At the same time, he stated clearly that the torture of prisoners—civilian or military—was "inconsistent with our values as a nation." Earlier in the Obama administration, U.S. attorney general Eric Holder had appointed a special prosecutor to investigate the CIA's activities, but he determined that there was no legal base with which to charge CIA interrogators or agency officers.

Not surprisingly, the CIA took exception to much of the Senate report, asserting that it had not misled Congress or government officials and insisting that while its interrogation program had "shortcomings," it had indeed helped prevent terror attacks. Former president George W. Bush patently denied that he had ever been misled by the CIA, and former vice president Dick Cheney lambasted the Senate committee's efforts as grossly partisan, wildly inaccurate, and harmful to America's image and national security. Republicans on the Senate Intelligence Committee promptly issued a 160-page dissent of the document. Indeed, only a few Republicans in Congress supported the release of the report—one of them was Senator John S. McCain, himself a victim of torture during the Vietnam War. He asserted that torture "actually damaged our security interests, as well as our reputation."

The release of the report also placed current CIA director John Brennan in the hot seat. Democratic senator Carl Levin planned to demand that Brennan fully declassify a March 2003 CIA cable that patently discounted any link between Iraqi leader Saddam Hussein and Al Qaeda prior to the September 11 attacks. The Bush administration cited this link—both before and after the 2003 invasion of Iraq—as one of the primary reasons for going to war against Hussein's regime. While many congressional Republicans decried the $40 million price tag for the report as excessive and wasteful, intelligence committee Democrats countered that the CIA itself was to blame for the massive cost overruns because it repeatedly tried to stymie the work of the committee and stonewalled on the release of "thousands" of allegedly incriminating documents. Democratic senator Mark Udall, a member of the intelligencer committee, took aim not only at the CIA but also the Obama administration, charging that the White House continued to obfuscate the truth and demanding that Obama terminate officials responsible for the CIA's activities.

PAUL G. PIERPAOLI JR.

See also

Al Qaeda; Bin Laden, Osama; Bush, George Walker; Central Intelligence Agency; Cheney, Richard Bruce; Global War on Terror; Intelligence, Iraq War; Obama, Barack Hussein, II

References

"Backing CIA, Cheney Revisits Torture Debate from Bush Era." *New York Times,* December 14, 2014, http://www.nytimes.com/2014/12/15/us/politics/cheney-senate-report-on-torture.html.

"The CIA's Grisly Torture Regime." *The Week,* December 19, 2014, 4.

"Torture Report: A Closer Look at When and What President Bush Knew." National Public Radio, December 16, 2014, http://www.npr.org/blogs/thetwo-way/2014/12/16/369876047/torture-report-a-closer-look-at-when-and-what-president-bush-knew.

Central Intelligency Agency in Afghanistan

Over the past 40 years or so, the United States Central Intelligence Agency (CIA) has focused much attention on and directed many resources toward Afghanistan. That nation has endured virtually 35 years of conflict and civil war, beginning in earnest with the Soviet invasion of Afghanistan in December 1979. After Muhammad Daud Khan overthrew the Afghan monarchy in 1973 and installed himself as president, the United States sought to strengthen ties with the new Afghan government, principally as a way to counter Soviet influence there. Thus, the U.S. government began funneling modest financial support to Daud's regime, nearly all of which was covert in nature. To ensure the secrecy of this aid, the CIA, together with the U.S. State Department, worked behind the scenes to direct financial resources to the Afghan government. After Daud was ousted by Afghan communists (who were loosely allied with the Soviets) in April 1978, the CIA began to focus more attention on Afghanistan in hopes of thwarting a complete Soviet takeover of that country.

During late 1978 and into 1979, the CIA conducted a broad overview of Afghanistan's internal affairs. The resulting report concluded that intertribal and interethnic turmoil was on the rise in Afghanistan, especially after the communist takeover; it also asserted that there was growing resistance to the pro-Soviet Democratic Republic of Afghanistan (DRA) on religious, tribal, and ethnic grounds.

When the Soviet Union invaded Afghanistan in late December 1979, ostensibly to prop up the fledgling communist government there and to ensure its pro-Soviet orientation, the CIA began organizing a major effort to help fund various antigovernment mujahideen groups. The plan was to destabilize the Afghan government and imperil the Soviets' occupation. This covert CIA program, known as Operation CYCLONE, would be among the CIA's longest and costliest covert operations in its history.

In 1980 during the Jimmy Carter administration, U.S. aid to Sunni mujahideen groups amounted to about $30 million per year. U.S. aid to Afghanistan increased dramatically during the Ronald Reagan administration. By 1987, the peak year of support, the Americans were providing nearly $630 million per year. It is estimated that between 1979 and 1992, the United States provided some $3 billion to the mujahideen. Much of the U.S. aid was funneled through Pakistani intelligence services, such as the Special Services Group (SSG) and Inter-Services Intelligence (ISI). The Pakistani government itself also provided millions of dollars of support to the Sunni mujahideen groups. Although the British extended only nominal monetary aid, their intelligence services worked closely with the Pakistanis and Americans to help distribute arms and other supplies. In addition to Pakistan, Great Britain, and the United States, several other nations also provided aid to the Sunni mujahideen. These included Saudi Arabia (which provided the greatest amount of financial support after the United States), Egypt, China, Kuwait, and Libya. These nations provided monetary support, training, and/or military equipment and hardware.

The United States was very careful not to send many of its own intelligence or military officers to the region for fear of being discovered by the Soviets or the Afghan government. At most, the CIA had perhaps only a dozen agents in the area at any one time. Nevertheless, various State Department and CIA officials visited Pakistani border areas to assess the progress of Operation CYCLONE. In 1986, the Americans began shipping large quantities of FIM-92 Stinger surface-to-air missiles to the mujahideen. The shoulder-fired missiles are credited with turning the tide of the war decisively against the Soviets and the DRA. Within a year, the Soviets were engaged in serious negotiations to extricate themselves from the conflict.

Between 1987 and 1993 another $4 billion of U.S. aid was allocated for Afghanistan, although the CIA's Operation CYCLONE was gradually phased out after the Soviets exited Afghanistan in 1989. It is estimated that American funding helped train at least 80,000 Afghan rebels between 1979 and 1993.

Despite legitimate claims that the foreign aid to the mujahideen tipped the Soviet-Afghan War in their favor and played a key role in forcing the Soviets from Afghanistan, there are a number of critics who have claimed that American aid may have done more harm than good, at least in the long term. Pakistan tended to support only particular insurgent commanders and rebel groups. The Pakistanis greatly favored Gulbuddin Hekmatyar and Jalaluddin Haqqani, for example, so much of the foreign aid that was funneled through Pakistan went to their forces exclusively. Hekmatyar was responsible for committing atrocities against Afghan civilians and was known to be an associate of a young Osama bin Laden, who later went on to form the terrorist group Al Qaeda. Haqqani also associated with bin Laden and other extremist foreign Islamists in Afghanistan and may well have protected him from other insurgent groups. Although the U.S. government has steadfastly denied that any of its support to the mujahideen ended up in the hands of bin Laden and other extremists, there is no way of knowing this for certain.

Operation CYCLONE was just a relatively small part of American strategy to roll back Soviet influence in Asia and the Middle East during the 1980s. However, the impact that it had on Afghanistan—over the long term—was certainly more pervasive. It helped fund and prolong the Afghan civil war, which raged from 1989 until 1996, and aided the rise of the Taliban to power in 1996. In short, the Soviet-Afghan War and the foreign support it engendered unleashed more than 35 years of bloodshed and war in Afghanistan, which continue to the present day. On the other hand, as some observers have suggested, U.S. support for the mujahideen may well have contributed to the thaw in U.S.-Soviet relations beginning in the mid-1980s and the dissolution of the Soviet Union in 1991.

After the September 11, 2001, terror attacks against the United States, which were perpetrated by Al Qaeda, the United States and other allies launched Operation ENDURING FREEDOM in October 2001, which was designed to topple the Taliban government and drive Al Qaeda from Afghanistan. The Taliban had given Al Qaeda aid and refuge between 1996 and 2001. It is worth nothing here that neither the CIA nor the Federal Bureau of Investigation had any reliable advance knowledge of the September 11 attacks and therefore had not taken any concrete measures to avert them or disrupt them.

Nevertheless, the CIA was at the forefront of Operation ENDURING FREEDOM, having largely devised the initial plan of attack and having provided CIA operatives to take part in some of the early combat. The agency's Special Activities Division was intricately involved in the early phases of the war; it mobilized, trained, and armed the Northern Alliance, which fought alongside U.S. and coalition forces, and worked closely with the U.S. Special Operations Command. Indeed, in late 2001, about 100 CIA operatives, most of them on horseback, served with several hundred U.S. Army Rangers and Special Forces soldiers, also on horseback, to flush out Taliban and Al Qaeda fighters in Afghanistan's rugged mountain areas. Among the most famous of these encounters was the December 2001 fighting at Tora Bora, in eastern Afghanistan adjacent to the Pakistani border. Ironically perhaps, the CIA had helped to heavily fortify and militarize that area during the 1980s as it aided the mujahideen.

The CIA has been credited for aiding in the prompt overthrow of the Taliban regime, with very few U.S. or coalition casualties. However, its subsequent activities relating to ENDURING FREEDOM and the Global War on Terror have been decidedly mixed. Reports about its use of so-called black box sites around the globe, where terror suspects—including Al Qaeda and Taliban prisoners from Afghanistan—have been subjected to torture and all manner of mistreatment have caused a firestorm of controversy in recent years. A number of prisoners captured in Afghanistan since 2001 have been housed at the Guantánamo Bay Detainment Camp in Cuba, where they have been denied basic humanitarian rights and where the use of coercive interrogation and mistreatment has also been reported. The CIA has also reportedly been involved in operations there too. In addition, the CIA has been criticized for having failed to predict or deter the Afghan insurgency, which has become increasingly problematic since 2007.

PAUL G. PIERPAOLI JR.

See also

Afghanistan; Afghanistan War; Al Qaeda; Bin Laden, Osama; Central Intelligence Agency; Central Intelligence Agency, Senate Report on; Coercive Interrogation; Global War on Terror; Guantánamo Bay Detainment Camp; Northern Alliance; Taliban

References

Braithwaite, Rodric. *Afgantsy: The Russians in Afghanistan, 1979–1989.* New York: Oxford University Press, 2011.

"The CIA's Grisly Torture Regime." *The Week,* December 19, 2014, 4.

Hopkins, B. D. *The Making of Modern Afghanistan.* New York: Palgrave Macmillan, 2008.

Johnson, Robert. *The Afghan Way of War: How and Why They Fight.* New York: Oxford University Press, 2011.

Lohbeck, Kurt. *Holy War, Unholy Victory: Eyewitness to the CIA's Secret War in Afghanistan.* Washington, DC: Regnery Gateway, 1993.

Chalabi, Ahmed Abd al-Hadi (1944–2015)

Prominent Iraqi dissident and founder and leader of the U.S.-funded Iraqi National Congress (INC) from 1992 to 1999. Born on October 30, 1944, in Baghdad, Iraq, Ahmed Abd al-Hadi Chalabi, a liberal Shiite Muslim, was a member of one of Iraq's wealthiest and most influential families. Prior to the 1958 revolution that overthrew the Iraqi monarchy, Chalabi's father, a prominent banker, was president of the Senate and an adviser to King Faisal II.

Although the entire royal family and many of its supporters were murdered by the revolutionaries, Chalabi's family managed to escape into exile, living primarily in England and the United States. Chalabi earned a BS degree in mathematics from the Massachusetts Institute of Technology in 1965. In 1969 he obtained a PhD in mathematics from the University of Chicago and subsequently taught mathematics at the American University in Beirut until 1977.

In 1977 Chalabi relocated to Jordan, where he established the Petra Bank. Within two years, Petra Bank had become the second-largest bank in Jordan. In 1989, Jordanian Central Bank governor Mohammad Said Nabulsi ordered the 20 banks operating in Jordan to deposit 30 percent of their foreign exchange holdings with the Central Bank. When Petra Bank refused to comply with the order, the Jordanian government launched an investigation of the bank's holdings, which revealed that most of the bank's stated assets in fact did not exist. Chalabi then fled to the United Kingdom. Although Chalabi later claimed that the entire situation was the result of Iraqi dictator Saddam Hussein's chicanery, the Jordanian government was forced to pay $200 million to depositors to avert the complete collapse of the Jordanian banking system. In 1992, the Jordanian government sentenced Chalabi in absentia to 22 years in prison for bank fraud. Chalabi continues to proclaim his innocence in the affair.

In 1991 immediately following the Persian Gulf War, Chalabi began lobbying influential members of the U.S. Congress, the Central Intelligence Agency (CIA), and the Pentagon for funding to sponsor a coup against Hussein's government. In 1992 Chalabi formed the INC. Between 1992 and 2004 he and the INC received more than $30 million from U.S. government sources.

Many within the CIA and the U.S. State Department eventually became suspicious of Chalabi's ability to deliver on promises made concerning the opposition and attacked his veracity. But his close ties with former defense secretary Vice President Dick Cheney and Deputy Secretary of Defense Paul Wolfowitz enabled Chalabi to continue to receive funding until the eve of the 2003 Anglo-American invasion of Iraq. In 1999 Chalabi broke with the INC and established the National Congress Coalition, a group that considered itself a less Islamist alternative to other Iraqi opposition groups. During the U.S. occupation of Iraq, Chalabi served as one of the deputy prime ministers in Ibrahim al-Jafari's cabinet.

When it had become patently clear that there were no weapons of mass destruction in Iraq, the existence of which had been a major pretext of the 2003 war, the George W. Bush administration became more concerned about its connections with Chalabi. The information that he had been giving the administration since at least mid-2001 was either falsified or unintentionally erroneous. Be that as it may, Chalabi steadfastly stood by the top-secret reports, much of which pointed to an illicit Iraqi program to build nuclear, chemical, and biological weapons. It is surprising that the Bush administration would have given so much credence to Chalabi's assertions, unless it was because they supported the administration's own conclusions.

On May 20, 2004, U.S. and Iraqi forces raided Chalabi's residence to determine the extent of his duplicity in his dealings with American officials. Charges were briefly drawn up against him, but these were later dropped. Nevertheless, in November 2005 Chalabi flew to Washington, D.C., to meet with high-level Bush administration officials.

From December 2005 to January 2006 Chalabi was Iraq's oil minister, and in April 2005 he was appointed deputy prime minister, a post he held from May 2005 to May 2006. In the December 15, 2005, elections, Chalabi suffered a humiliating defeat in his quest to become Iraqi prime minister. Allegations that he was bolstering his relations with Iranians and supposedly passed secret information to them in 2004 further tarnished his reputation in Washington. Paradoxically, his reputation in Iraq was troubled by his close relationship with the Americans.

In October 2007, Iraqi prime minister Nuri al-Maliki appointed Chalabi to head the Iraq Services Committee, a group that linked eight government service ministries and several Baghdad municipal agencies that were at the forefront of the recovery and modernization effort in postwar

Iraq. In 2012, the French government asserted that Chalabi was indeed an Iranian agent. Chalabi remains a divisive and distrusted figure in much of the West, and in recent years he has remained out of the Iraqi political scene. Chalabi died of a heart attack in Baghdad on November 3, 2015.

MICHAEL R. HALL

See also

Bush, George Walker; Cheney, Richard Bruce; Hussein, Saddam; Jafari, Ibrahim al-; Maliki, Nuri al-; Wolfowitz, Paul

References

Fox, Robert. *Peace and War in Iraq, 2003–2005*. Barnsley, UK: Leo Cooper, 2005.

Packer, George. *The Assassins' Gate: America in Iraq*. New York: Farrar, Straus and Giroux, 2005.

Ricks, Thomas E. *Fiasco: The American Military Adventure in Iraq*. New York: Penguin, 2006.

Chemical Ali

See Majid al Tikriti, Ali Hassan al-

Chemical Weapons and Warfare

Chemical weapons use the toxic effects from man-made substances to kill or incapacitate enemy forces. Chemical weapons range from such riot control agents as tear gas and pepper spray, which cause short-term incapacitation, to lethal nerve agents such as tabun and sarin, which can kill humans with only a miniscule exposure. The use of living organisms, such as bacteria, viruses, or spores, is classified not as chemical warfare but as biological warfare. However, certain chemical weapons such as ricin and botulinum toxins use products created by living organisms.

Chemical weapons are typically described by the effects they have on victims. The major classes of chemical weapons are nerve agents, blood agents, vesicants, pulmonary agents, cytotoxic proteins, lachrymatory agents, and incapacitating agents. Nerve agents quickly break down neuron-transmitting synapses, resulting in the paralysis of major organs and quick death. Blood agents cause massive internal bleeding or prevent cells from using oxygen, leading to anaerobic respiration, seizures, and death. Vesicants, also known as blistering agents, burn skin and respiratory systems, either of which can be fatal. Pulmonary agents suffocate victims by flooding the respiratory system. Cytotoxic agents prevent protein synthesis, leading to the failure of one or more organs. Lachrymatory agents cause immediate eye irritation or blindness, although the effects are deliberately temporary.

Incapacitating agents, also temporary, cause effects similar to drug intoxication.

The most important characteristics of an effective chemical weapon are its ability to be delivered accurately and to persist as a danger to enemy troops. Throughout history, delivery methods for chemical weapons have evolved from simple dispersion, often by releasing a gas into the wind, to artillery shells or missile warheads containing chemical agents and to aerodynamic dispersal from aircraft. Since World War II, binary chemical weapons have been developed that contain two substances that are harmless by themselves but when combined form a weapons-grade chemical agent.

By the 19th century, inventors in Britain and the United States proposed the development of artillery shells containing toxic gases. During World War I (1914–1918), more chemical weapons were used than during any other war in history. At the Second Battle of Ypres (April 22, 1915), German troops opened canisters of chlorine gas and waited for the wind to push the gas into Allied trenches. Soon both sides were using artillery shells to deliver chemical attacks, incorporating a wide variety of chemical agents.

Although they caused a great deal of panic and disruption on the battlefield and caused more than 1 million mostly nonlethal casualties in World War I, chemical weapons were never decisive by themselves. The chemical weapons of the period were relatively weak by modern standards, and no army of the time had developed nerve agents. Although early gas masks and other countermeasures were relatively primitive, they did neutralize the chemical effects to some degree. The Germans, under the artillery genius Colonel Georg Bruchmüller, came the closest to achieving decisive breakthroughs with chemical weapons during the 1918 offensives, but the German Army didn't have the operational mobility to exploit the tactical advantage.

During World War II (1939–1945), chemical weapons were used in a few isolated instances, although both the Axis and the Allies had developed large arsenals of extremely toxic agents. Both sides feared retaliation by the enemy, and neither chose to use its massive stockpiles of chemical weapons.

In the Middle East, the first modern large-scale use of lethal chemical agents occurred during the Iran-Iraq War (1980–1988). Early in the war, Iraq dropped bombs containing mustard agent and tabun on Iranian troops, causing 100,000 casualties including 20,000 deaths. Iraq accused Iran of having used chemical weapons first, but the allegations were never confirmed by United Nations investigators.

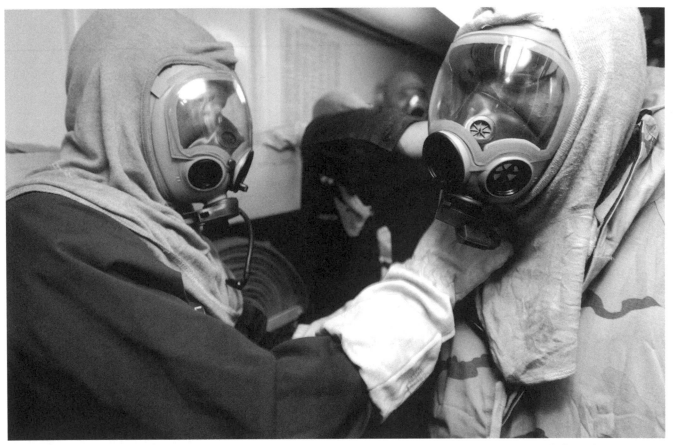

U.S. Navy sailors practice using their MCU-2P gas masks during a chemical, biological, and radiological exposure drill in February 2003. (U.S. Department of Defense)

Near the end of the war, the Iraqi government used chemical weapons against rebellious Kurdish Iraqi citizens, killing thousands of civilians.

During the 1991 Persian Gulf War, Iraq was accused of launching Scud missiles with chemical warheads against Israel, although no traces of chemical weapons were found. Iraq did not strike the attacking coalition forces with chemical weapons. One possibility is that the Iraqis feared that the coalition would retaliate with its own chemical weapons or perhaps even tactical nuclear weapons. A more likely possibility, however, is that the Iraqis never had the planning and coordination time necessary to employ chemical weapons. Virtually every successful use of chemical weapons in the 20th century was in an offensive operation, where the attacker had the initiative and necessary time to plan and tightly control the use of such weapons and their effects. Being on the defensive from the start, the Iraqis never had that flexibility.

Chemical weapons in the hands of terrorist groups pose a significant potential threat. On March 20, 1995, Aum Shinrikyo, a Japanese apocalyptic cult, released sarin gas on a Tokyo subway, killing 12 commuters and injuring more than 5,000. In 2002 the terrorist organization Al Qaeda released a videotape purportedly showing the deaths of dogs from a nerve agent. Al Qaeda has repeatedly announced its intention to obtain chemical, biological, and nuclear weapons.

There have been many attempts to prohibit the development and use of chemical weapons. In 1874 the Brussels Declaration outlawed the use of poison in warfare. The 1900 Hague Conference banned projectiles carrying poisonous gases, as did the Washington Arms Conference Treaty of 1922 and the Geneva Protocol of 1929. None of the prohibitions proved sufficient to eradicate chemical warfare, however. The most recent effort to eliminate chemical weapons was the multilateral Chemical Weapons Convention (CWC) of 1993. The CWC came into effect in 1997 and prohibited the production and use of chemical weapons. Numerous nations known to maintain or suspected of maintaining chemical weapons stockpiles refused to sign or abide by the treaty, including several in the Middle East. Egypt, Libya, and Syria, all known to possess chemical weapons, each refused to sign the CWC, although Libya acceded to the treaty in early 2004 and has reportedly dismantled its chemical weapons program.

In September 2013 during the ongoing Syrian Civil War, Russia and the United States brokered a deal with the Syrian government by which Syria would join the CWC and hand over all of its chemical weapons to international inspectors by June 2015. Efforts to do so began in late 2013, and by August 2014 all of the weapons had been shipped out of the country. Syrian president Bashar al-Assad agreed to the deal in order to prevent punitive air strikes by Western nations after evidence indicated that his government had employed chemical weapons against his own people.

Israel, long known to possess a sophisticated chemical weapons capability, signed the CWC but never ratified the agreement. Iran signed and ratified the CWC but refused to prove that it had destroyed known stockpiles of chemical weapons and does not allow international inspectors to examine its facilities.

In future Middle Eastern conflicts, chemical weapons are far less likely to be used in terrorist attacks than in large-scale military operations. Chemical weapons are not easy to use. They are difficult and awkward to store, transport, and handle; their use requires detailed and expensive planning and lead times; once they are released, their effects are difficult to predict and control; and one's own troops require specialized equipment and extensive training to operate in a chemical environment.

PAUL JOSEPH SPRINGER

See also

Al Qaeda; Biological Weapons and Warfare; Iraq, Army; Syrian Chemical Weapons Agreement; Terrorism; Weapons of Mass Destruction

References

Butler, Richard. *The Greatest Threat: Iraq, Weapons of Mass Destruction and the Growing Crisis in Global Security*. New York: PublicAffairs, 2000.

Solomon, Brian. *Chemical and Biological Warfare*. New York: H. W. Wilson, 1999.

Tucker, Jonathan B. *War of Nerves: Chemical Warfare from World War I to Al-Qaeda*. New York: Pantheon, 2006.

"U.S., Russia Agree on Framework on Syria's Chemical Weapons." CNN, September 15, 2013, http://www.cnn.com/2013/09/14/politics/us-syria/.

Cheney, Richard Bruce (1941–)

Politician, businessman, secretary of defense (1989–1993), and vice president (2001–2009). Richard Bruce "Dick" Cheney was born on January 30, 1941, in Lincoln, Nebraska. He grew up in Casper, Wyoming, and was educated at the University of Wyoming, earning a BA in 1965 and an MA in political science in 1966. He completed advanced graduate study there and was a PhD candidate in 1968.

Cheney acquired his first governmental position in 1969 when he became the special assistant to the director of the Office of Economic Opportunity. He served as a White House staff assistant in 1970 and 1971 and as assistant director of the Cost of Living Council from 1971 to 1973. He briefly worked in the private sector as the vice president of an investment advisory firm. In 1974, he returned to government service as President Gerald R. Ford's deputy assistant. In 1975, Ford appointed Cheney as White House chief of staff.

In 1978 Cheney was elected to the U.S. House of Representatives, serving six terms. He was elected House minority whip in December 1988. Cheney was known for his conservative votes: he opposed gun control, environmental laws, and funding for Head Start.

Cheney became secretary of defense on March 21, 1989, in the George H. W. Bush administration. In this position, Cheney significantly reduced U.S. military budgets and canceled several major weapons programs. In addition, in the

Richard "Dick" Cheney was vice president of the United States during 2003–2009. He was a major promoter of the U.S. invasion of Iraq in 2003 and has strongly defended the so-called "enhanced interrogation techniques" instituted during the War on Terror. (AP Photo)

wake of the Cold War he was deeply involved in the politically volatile task of reducing the size of the American military force throughout the world. Cheney also recommended closing or reducing in size many U.S. military installations, despite intense criticism from elected officials whose districts would be adversely impacted by the closures.

As secretary of defense, Cheney also provided strong leadership in several international military engagements, including the December 1989 Panama invasion and the humanitarian mission to Somalia in early 1992. It was Cheney who secured the appointment of General Colin Powell as chairman of the Joint Chiefs of Staff in 1989.

Cheney's most difficult military challenge came during the 1991 Persian Gulf War. He secured Saudi permission to begin a military buildup there that would include a United Nations (UN) international coalition of troops. The buildup proceeded in the autumn of 1990 as Operation DESERT SHIELD. When economic sanctions and other measures failed to remove the Iraqis from Kuwait, the Persian Gulf War commenced with Operation DESERT STORM on January 16, 1991. A five-week air offensive was followed by the movement of ground forces into Kuwait and Iraq on February 24, 1991. Within four days, the UN coalition had liberated Kuwait. Cheney continued as secretary of defense until January 20, 1993, when Democrat Bill Clinton took office.

Upon leaving the Pentagon, Cheney joined the American Enterprise Institute as a senior fellow. He also became president and chief executive officer of the Halliburton Company in October 1995 and chairman of its board in February 2000.

Only months later, Republican presidential candidate George W. Bush chose Cheney as his vice presidential running mate. After a hard-fought campaign, the Bush-Cheney ticket won the White House in December 2000, although only after a court fight and having lost the popular vote.

Arguably one of the more powerful vice presidents in U.S. history, Cheney endured much criticism for his hawkish views (he is believed to have strongly promoted the Iraq War) and his connections to the oil industry (Halliburton won several lucrative contracts for work in postwar Iraq). He also raised eyebrows by refusing to make public the records of the national energy task force he established to form the administration's energy initiatives.

Many people who knew Cheney personally have asserted that he became a changed man after the September 11, 2001, terrorist attacks. He became, they say, far more secretive, more hawkish than ever before, and, some say, even paranoid, seeing terrorists everywhere. As one of the principal promoters of the U.S. invasion of Iraq (Operation IRAQI FREEDOM), which began in March 2003, Cheney was well-placed to receive the burden of criticism when the war began to go badly in 2004. As the subsequent Iraqi insurgency increased in size, scope, and violence, Cheney's popularity plummeted. Following the 2006 midterm elections, which caused the Republicans to lose control of Congress principally because of the war in Iraq, Cheney took a far lower profile. When his fellow neoconservative Donald Rumsfeld, the secretary of defense, resigned in the election's aftermath, Cheney was increasingly perceived as a liability to the Bush White House, which was under intense pressure to change course in Iraq or quit it altogether.

Cheney did not help his approval ratings when he accidentally shot a friend during a hunting trip in February 2006 and the information was slow to be released. Even more damaging to Cheney was the indictment and conviction of his chief of staff, I. Lewis "Scooter" Libby, for his involvement in the case involving Joseph Wilson and his wife Valerie Plame Wilson, who's identity as a CIA operative was leaked. Some alleged that it was Cheney who first leaked the classified information to Libby and perhaps others, who in turn leaked it to the press. Cheney continued to keep a remarkably low profile. Beginning in 2007, a small group of Democrats in the House attempted to introduce impeachment proceedings against Cheney, but such efforts did not make it out of committee.

Since his retirement from politics in January 2009, Cheney has published a memoir and delivered a number of speeches, mainly to conservative groups. His precarious health has prevented him from taking on larger roles, but he has been a consistent and vocal critic of the Barack Obama administration, even suggesting at one point that Obama's policies were making the United States less safe during the Global War on Terror.

PAUL G. PIERPAOLI JR.

See also

Bush, George Walker; Global War on Terror; IRAQI FREEDOM, Operation; Libby, I. Lewis; Neoconservatism; Persian Gulf War; Rumsfeld, Donald; September 11 Attacks; Wilson, Joseph Carter, IV; Wilson, Valerie Plame

References

Baker, Peter. *Days of Fire: Bush and Cheney in the White House.* New York: Anchor Books, 2014.

Nichols, John. *The Rise and Rise of Richard B. Cheney: Unlocking the Mysteries of the Most Powerful Vice President in American History.* New York: New Press, 2005.

Woodward, Bob. *Bush at War.* New York: Simon and Schuster, 2002.

Woodward, Bon. *Plan of Attack*. New York: Simon and Schuster, 2004.

Woodward, Bob. *State of Denial: Bush at War, Part III*. New York: Simon and Schuster, 2006.

Woodward, Bob. *The War Within: A Secret White House History, 2006–2008*. New York: Simon and Schuster, 2008.

Chertoff, Michael (1953–)

Lawyer, judge, and secretary of homeland security from 2005 to 2009. Michael Chertoff was born on November 28, 1953, in Elizabeth, New Jersey. The son of a rabbi, he entered Harvard University in 1971 and graduated magna cum laude in 1975. He earned his law degree from Harvard in 1978. He then served as a clerk for appellate judge Murray Gurfein and then for U.S. Supreme Court justice William Brennan. Chertoff was admitted to the bar in the District of Columbia in 1980 and joined the law firm of Latham & Watkins.

In 1983, Chertoff began working in the U.S. attorney's office in New York City and was soon working on an organized crime investigation with U.S. attorney and future New York mayor Rudolph Giuliani. When Giuliani left that investigation to prosecute a case involving corruption in city government, Chertoff became lead prosecutor in the trials of several organized crime bosses. With successful convictions of the leaders of the Genovese, Colombo, and Lucchese crime families, Chertoff earned his bona fides as a talented trial lawyer.

Chertoff next became an assistant prosecutor for the State of New Jersey in 1987 and, after serving as interim U.S. attorney for the state, was named by President George H. W. Bush to the position permanently in 1990. Chertoff stayed at the post until 1994, when he returned to the firm of Latham & Watkins as a partner.

Beginning in 1994, Chertoff was special counsel to the committee investigating President Bill Clinton and First Lady Hillary Rodham Clinton in what became known as Whitewater. In 2000, Chertoff investigated racial profiling as special counsel to New Jersey's state Senate Judiciary Committee. During the presidential campaign that year, he advised candidate George W. Bush on criminal justice issues. Beginning in 2001, Chertoff served in the new Bush administration as assistant attorney general in the criminal division of the Justice Department. During his tenure, he led prosecutions against suspected terrorist Zacarias Moussaoui, the "American Taliban" John Walker Lindh, and the accounting firm of Arthur Andersen, which was convicted of destroying documents related to the collapse of the Enron Corporation.

While Chertoff was with the Justice Department, the United States was attacked by terrorists on September 11, 2001. He was one of the first law officials to advocate treating terrorist suspects as "material witnesses" and detaining them without charging them with a crime, a stance he justified by claiming that because the nation was at war, it had a right and obligation to do whatever was necessary to keep the United States secure.

In 2003, President Bush nominated Chertoff to the post of judge for the Third Circuit U.S. Court of Appeals. Chertoff served as an appellate judge until his confirmation as secretary of the Department of Homeland Security (DHS) on February 15, 2005.

Chertoff was often criticized for some of his hard-line positions. He was opposed to allowing judges discretion in the imposition of sentences and argued that there is no constitutional right for a defendant to be free of coercive questioning by police. His supporters, however, believed that he was well suited to serve in protecting the nation's homeland security. Indeed, they pointed out that he had been concerned with the threat of terrorism long before September 11, 2001. In 1996, he argued in "Tools against Terrorism," an article in the *New Jersey Law Journal,* that officials must have leeway in the prosecution of suspected terrorists, even if it means restricting some civil liberties.

In assuming leadership of DHS, Chertoff gave up a lifetime appointment as appellate judge on the Third Circuit. He faced the daunting task of overseeing some 22 separate agencies and over 170,000 employees. Chertoff's tenure became highly controversial after the government's bungled reaction to Hurricane Katrina, which struck the U.S. coast of the Gulf of Mexico—including New Orleans—in September 2005. Although the Federal Emergency Management Agency (FEMA) took the brunt of the criticism, Chertoff's sprawling agency included FEMA, and so blame was placed on his shoulders as well. Later President Bush tasked Chertoff with helping usher comprehensive immigration reform through Congress, but when that failed in the summer of 2007, Chertoff's image was further tarnished. DHS includes the Immigration and Naturalization Service. In 2008, Chertoff was criticized for having bypassed environmental protection laws during the hasty construction of a border fence between the United States and Mexico in the American Southwest. Those who believed that the Bush administration had not gone far enough to curb illegal immigration also cited Chertoff's weak and vacillating policies as part of the problem. In 2009,

Chertoff cofounded The Chertoff Group, a consulting and business development firm that specializes in mergers and acquisitions as well as risk management and private security.

PAUL G. PIERPAOLI JR.

See also

Patriot Act; Terrorism; United States Department of Homeland Security

References

McClellan, Scott. *What Happened: Inside the Bush White House and Washington's Culture of Deception.* New York: Public-Affairs, 2008.

Woodward, Bob. *The War Within: A Secret White House History, 2006–2008.* New York: Simon and Schuster, 2008.

Chirac, Jacques René (1932–)

French politician who served as mayor of Paris (1977–1995), premier (1974–1976, 1986–1988), and president (1995–2007). Jacques René Chirac was born on November 29, 1932, in Paris to a middle-class Roman Catholic family. He attended the Lycées Carnot and Louis le Grand and both the Institut d'Études Politiques de Paris and the École Nationale d'Administration. Upon graduation from the latter in 1959, Chirac embarked on a civil service career. In 1962 he became Premier Georges Pompidou's chief of staff. In 1967 Chirac was elected to the French National Assembly as a center-right Gaullist. He then held a series of important governmental posts, including state secretary of the economy (1968–1971), minister of agriculture and rural development (1972–1974), and minister of the interior in 1974.

Throughout this period, Chirac was more aligned with Pompidou than with the Gaullists but nevertheless was among the inner sanctum of Gaullist political circles. When Valéry Giscard d'Estaing was elected president in 1974, Chirac became premier, helping reconcile the Gaullist leadership to more social spending. In 1974–1975 Premier Chirac met with Iraqi leader Saddam Hussein to promote the interests of French businesses and oil companies in Iraq. Given the ties between the two nations, which were further advanced by Chirac, French companies sold the components necessary for the Iraqi nuclear reactor at Osiraq that was destroyed in an Israeli air strike in 1981. In the aftermath of the 1991 Persian Gulf War, documents seized suggested that the Iraqis had intended to use the facility as a means of constructing nuclear weapons.

Chirac resigned as premier in 1976, no longer able to bridge the gap between Giscard's policies and the more conservative Gaullists. In 1977 Chirac was elected mayor of Paris, a position he held until 1995 concurrently with the premiership. In 1981 he challenged d'Estaing for the conservative leadership, which may have contributed to socialist leader François Mitterrand's victory in the 1981 presidential election. As French patience with socialist economic prescriptions wore thin in 1986, the Right took control of the National Assembly, and Chirac again became premier.

In 1988 Chirac lost the presidential election to Mitterrand. This prompted Chirac to resign his post as premier, and some people began to write his political epitaph. Chirac was undeterred, however, and continued to set his sights on the presidency, announcing in 1993 that he had no desire to become premier in another government. He finally achieved the presidency in 1995, leading a center-right coalition that promised tax cuts and continued social spending. Chirac proved to be relatively popular, and he won reelection in 2002.

Domestically, Chirac's policies centered on job creation, tax cuts, and trimming government spending, certainly the hallmarks of modern conservative thinking. However, government-mandated austerity programs and the trimming of the very generous French welfare state created considerable friction with leftist and centrist parties and precipitated a series of major labor strikes. The Chirac government also endured its share of scandals, and in the president's second term challenges from the Far Right (such as Jean-Marie Le Pen's National Front party) and immigration issues that touched off nationwide rioting took up much of his administration's attention.

In foreign affairs, Chirac pursued a traditional Gaullist course by attempting to create a multipolar world capable of restraining American hegemony and maintaining French autonomy. However, he has differed from Gaullist foreign policy in his pursuit of greater European integration, generally along a French-German axis. In 1995 he created a national and international stir when he went forward with a nuclear test in French Polynesia, only to vow the next year that France would never again test a nuclear device. Chirac was a staunch proponent of the Constitution of the European Union (EU), and many viewed its defeat by referendum in France in 2005 as a personal failure for him.

Chirac was one of the first foreign leaders to condemn the September 11, 2001, terrorist attacks on the United States and offer French support. He also advocated invoking the North Atlantic Treaty Organization (NATO) Charter, which stipulates that an attack on one signatory is an attack on them all. Chirac supported the U.S.-led effort to topple the

Taliban regime in Afghanistan in 2001 and 2002, and France provided a small troop contingent as part of the NATO effort there. In January 2006 Chirac publicly warned would-be terrorists that France was able and willing to retaliate with tactical nuclear weapons for any large-scale terrorist attack on his country.

Yet for all his antiterrorist rhetoric and his early support of the George W. Bush administration, Chirac refused to support the preemptory attack on Iraq that began in March 2003. In this stance he was joined by the leaders of Germany, now France's closest ally. France, which had long maintained commercial ties to Iraq, and many other nations opposed the U.S. proposals to invade Iraq in 2003. Within the United Nations (UN), France favored a two-step process. One resolution would have required further inspections of Iraq's weapons program, while the second resolution would have been required to authorize the use of force in the case of a breach of trust. The Americans, meanwhile, worded the first resolution such that war would be a necessary means of restoring stability.

Chirac adamantly opposed the Iraqi invasion, believing that there was not yet adequate justification to go to war. He was, however, supportive of reconstruction efforts in Iraq. Chirac was also supportive of Saudi proposals to forestall the war by allowing Saddam Hussein to be exiled. Thus, Russia, the People's Republic of China, Germany, and France all issued statements calling for further inspections rather than war. Chirac also attempted to extend the weapons inspections for another 30 days, but the Americans chose to proceed.

Differences within Europe on Iraq disrupted one of the main pillars of the EU: a common foreign and security policy. This saw France and Germany heading a Europeanist bloc that acted with Russia and China on the UN Security Council to constrain the United States, while Great Britain, Italy, and many of the newer East European nations within the EU backed a more Atlanticist position that supported the United States in its war policy.

After deciding not to seek a third term as president, Chirac left office on May 16, 2007, and was succeeded as president by Nicolas Sarkozy. After leaving office Chirac established Fondation Chirac, which promotes world peace. In December 2011 he was tried and convicted of embezzling public funds while he was mayor of Paris. He was given a suspended sentence. Chirac has also published his memoirs, but increasingly frail health in recent years has kept him largely out of public view.

MICHAEL K. BEAUCHAMP AND PAUL G. PIERPAOLI JR.

See also

Bush, George Walker; France; Hussein, Saddam; Libya; Nuclear Weapons, Iraq's Potential for Building; September 11 Attacks, International Reactions to; United Nations; United Nations Weapons Inspectors

References

Madelin, Philippe. *Jacques Chirac: Une Biographie* [Jacques Chirac: A Biogrpahy]. Paris: Flammarion, 2002.

Sowerwine, Charles. *France since 1870: Culture, Society, and the Making of the Republic.* 2nd ed. London: Palgrave Macmillan, 2009.

Wright, Gordon. *France in Modern Times.* New York: Norton, 2002.

Christmas Day 2009 Airline Terror Plot

On December 25, 2009, Nigerian citizen Umar Farouk Abdulmutallab unsuccessfully attempted to bomb Northwest Airlines Flight 253 en route from Amsterdam to Detroit as it approached its final destination. The explosive device consisted of a six-inch packet of powdered PETN (which becomes a plastic explosive when mixed with triacetone triperoxide/TAPN) sewn into his underwear along with a syringe of liquid acid. The device ignited a small fire that was promptly put out by a passenger and flight crew members. After the incident, officials discovered that Abdulmutallab had been in regular communication with Anwar al-Awlaki, an American-born radical Islamist widely believed to be the chief ideologue of Al Qaeda in the Arabian Peninsula (AQAP) in Yemen.

American responses included a barrage of criticism aimed at the U.S. national security and intelligence organizations for not preventing the attempted bombing, especially given the billions of dollars that had been invested to improve aviation security since the September 11, 2001, terror attacks. The Transportation Security Administration was also pilloried for its failure to detect the assailant's explosive devices. Of particular concern was the fact that U.S. officials had received a warning from Abdulmutallab's father in November 2009, who was concerned about his son's increasingly extremist views. Although the 23-year-old Nigerian had been put on watch lists and was even denied a visa renewal by Great Britain in May 2009, his name was apparently lost among thousands of others and not flagged. Critics also pondered why X-ray checks had failed to detect the explosive materials he carried.

Three days after the attempted attack, President Barack Obama publicly addressed the incident while on vacation in Hawaii, receiving some criticism that he showed a lack of concern for Americans' fear for their safety. He mandated a thorough investigation of the event, which he officially blamed on AQAP a week later. A declassified report subsequently released to the public in January 2010 detailed the intelligence and defense agencies' failures to streamline their information and "connect the dots." The president ordered further reforms to fix these weak links and also instigated heightened security measures at airports, including the installation of whole-body scanners in airports and delaying the release of Yemeni prisoners at the Guantánamo Bay Detainment Camp in Cuba. He also announced that he would more than double the $70 million in security aid that Washington had sent to Yemen in 2009 and, along with the United Kingdom, would jointly finance a new counterterrorism unit in the country. Meanwhile, in the days immediately after the attempted bombing, Al Qaeda leader Osama bin Laden claimed that he had helped mastermind the plot.

Abdulmutallab was taken into custody on December 26, 2009, and charged with eight felonies, including the attempted use of a weapon of mass destruction and the attempted murder of 289 civilians. He was later found guilty of all eight counts and sentenced to life imprisonment without parole on February 16, 2012.

PETER CHALK

See also

Al Qaeda; Al Qaeda in the Arabian Peninsula; Bin Laden, Osama; Christmas Eve 2000 Bombings; Global War on Terror; Guantánamo Bay Detainment Camp; Obama, Barack Hussein, II; Transportation Security Administration

References

Baker, Peter. "Obama Says Al-Qaeda in Yemen Planned Bombing Plot, and He Vows Retribution." *New York Times,* January 2, 2010.

Borzou, Daragahi. "Bin Laden Takes Responsibility for Christmas Day Bombing Attempt." *New York Times,* January 24, 2010.

Savage, Charlie. "Nigerian Indicted in Terrorist Plot." *New York Times,* January 6, 2010.

"'Underwear' Bomber Pleads Guilty." BBC News, October 12, 2011, http://www.bbc.co.uk/news/world-us-canada-15278483.

Christmas Eve 2000 Bombings

On December 24, 2000, Islamic militants carried out a series of coordinated bombing attacks in Indonesia, targeting Christians and Christian-owned properties. They deployed 34 improvised explosive devices (IEDs), most left in cars parked outside selected venues, of which an estimated 19 detonated as planned. An additional 15 bombs were found before they detonated. Most but not all were successfully defused. In total, 10 cities in three provinces were hit: 6 in Java (Jakarta, Bekasi, Bandung, Sukabumi, Ciamis, and Mojokerto), 3 in Sumatra (Medan, Pematang and Sinatar), and 1 in Lombuk (Mataram). The combined attacks left 19 people dead and another 120 wounded and are thought to have cost around $47,000.

Because the bombings took place over such a large area and were highly coordinated, the press speculated that rogue elements of the Indonesian military might have been involved, accusing them of trying to manipulate religious conflict in an effort to shore up the army's influence, which had been abruptly curtailed following the fall of the Suharto regime in 1998. President Abdurrahman Wahid, who was under pressure to resign because of worsening political and economic conditions at the time of the explosions, accused his opponents of complicity, claiming they were trying to discredit him by creating fear and panic.

Several Islamist entities denied any responsibility for the attacks. The paramilitary organization Laskar Jihad issued a statement denouncing the bombings as "immoral and politically motivated." Gerakan Aceh Merdeka (Free Aceh Movement) similarly distanced itself from the incidents, with the group's spokesman, Teungku Amni bi Marzuki, affirming that "We have no connection with the bombings in several places in Indonesia because the conflict in Aceh is not a religious conflict."

On December 26, it was announced that two people had been arrested in connection with the attacks—one of whom (Dedi Mulyadi) later claimed to have received training in Afghanistan during the early 1990s. They were detained at a house in the Antapani area of Bandung after an IED detonated prematurely during the construction process. Both men were seriously injured in the blast, which killed 3 additional suspects and 10 civilians and injured at least 95 others. Authorities also announced that documents had been found in the course of the detentions implicating Jemaah Islamiyah (JI) field commander Nurjaman Riduan Isamuddin (Hambali) in the bombings. Abu Bakar Bashir (Abu Bakar Ba'asyir, also known as Abdus Samad), the spiritual leader of the group, was later tried for his alleged involvement but found not guilty. During the course of his trial, it was alleged that the attacks were part of a campaign of terror aimed at tilting the religious balance in Southeast Asia in order to create a pan-regional caliphate that was to include Indonesia, the southern Philippines, the Malay Muslim provinces of Thailand, and Brunei.

It is now known that the first planning meeting for the operation took place in Kuala Lumpur in October 2000. It was here that cities were selected for attack and arrangements were made for the procurement of explosives; the latter material was sourced out of Manila with the help of the JI's representative in Singapore, Faiz bin Abubakatheafana. At a subsequent gathering held on or around December 15, principal team members were identified, provided with money, and given basic instruction in bomb-making techniques. They were also told to place the IEDs in different churches and that if a suitable venue was not available, other "infidel" or Chinese-owned properties should be targeted.

On January 25, 2011, JI leader and explosives expert Umar Patek, also known as Pak Taek, Abu Syekh, and Zachy, was arrested in Pakistan. Like Al Qaeda leader Osama bin Laden, Patek had been hiding in Abbottabad, Pakistan. He was extradited to Indonesia the following August and under interrogation admitted his complicity in the Christmas Eve explosions as well as the 2002 attacks in Bali. Patek's capture was a major blow to the JI's so-called probombing faction and removed arguably the most dangerous terrorist in Southeast Asia from circulation. On June 21, 2012, an Indonesian court sentenced Patek to 20 years in prison for his role in terrorist plots.

Donna Bassett

See also

Al Qaeda; Al Qaeda in the Arabian Peninsula; Christmas Day 2009 Airline Terror Plot; Global War on Terror

References

Abuza, Zachary. *Militant Islam in Southeast Asia: Crucible of Terror.* Boulder, CO: Lynne Rienner, 2003.

Chalk, Peter, Angel Rabasa, William Rosenau, and Leanne Piggott. *The Evolving Terrorist Threat to Southeast Asia: A Net Assessment.* Santa Monica, CA: RAND, 2009.

Sidel, John T. *Riots, Pogroms, Jihad: Religious Violence in Indonesia.* Ithaca, NY: Cornell University Press, 2006.

Civil Reserve Air Fleet

U.S. civilian passenger and cargo aircraft that are contractually obligated by the Department of Defense to augment the U.S. military's airlift capabilities in times of war and other emergencies. The Civil Reserve Air Fleet (CRAF), formed in 1952 during the Korean War, is designed to be activated on short notice when airlift requirements exceed the military's airlift capacity. Currently, the CRAF consists of three components: international operations, national operations, and aeromedical evacuation operations. International operations are subdivided into long-haul and short-haul flights, while national operations are subdivided into domestic flights and Alaskan operations. Aeromedical operations may encompass both national and international flights.

Long-range international operations are made up of both civilian cargo and passenger aircraft capable of supplying transoceanic air-lift capacity. These are chiefly large wide-body commercial jets. For short-haul international or domestic operations, medium to small cargo and passenger jets are employed. The aeromedical evacuation operations are designed to employ civilian aircraft to transport wounded individuals from specific combat theaters to regional military hospitals or military hospitals within the continental United States. These same aircraft can also be used to fly supplies and medical personnel into theater hospitals. The preferred aircraft for this purpose is the Boeing 767, for which the military has special kits that can quickly convert the plane's interior into a flying ambulance.

The Department of Defense maintains contracts with numerous civilian airlines that participate in the CRAF, and as an incentive for taking part in the program, the government promises airlines a certain amount of peacetime airlift business. As of June 2014, the CRAF had enrolled 24 separate carriers and airlines, making available a total of 553 civilian aircraft. That number included 391 aircraft capable of long-haul international flights, 126 aircraft capable of short-haul international flights, and 36 aircraft capable of operating within the continental United States. These numbers are quite fluid and often change on a month-by-month basis.

To qualify as a CRAF contractor, an airline must guarantee that a minimum of 30 percent of its CRAF-eligible passenger aircraft and 15 percent of its CRAF-eligible cargo planes will be maintained in ready status at all times. Ready status means that the aircraft and its crew must be ready to fly within 24–48 hours, depending on the type of aircraft. Four complete crews for each CRAF-designated aircraft must also be maintained on standby status at all times.

CRAF has a three-stage call-up system for eligible aircraft: Stage 1 is reserved for regional emergencies, Stage 2 is reserved for major conflicts overseas, and Stage 3 is reserved for full-scale national mobilization. The Air Mobility Command (AMC), supervised by the U.S. Air Force and part of the U.S. Transportation Command, regulates most of CRAF's operations and decides which stage should be implemented in the event of a conflict or emergency requiring additional airlift capabilities.

The AMC requires that all of its CRAF contractors meet Federal Aviation Administration safety and operation guidelines and maintains its own team of airplane mechanics, engineers, and safety inspectors who conduct on-site inspections of airline equipment and facilities. Besides the aircraft themselves, AMC inspections scrutinize crew qualifications, training and instruction facilities, maintenance procedures, ground operations, and general quality-control procedures.

On August 17, 1990, the Department of Defense activated CRAF (Stage 1 and later Stage 2) for the first time in the history of the program. This was in response to the U.S. troop buildup in the Persian Gulf (Operation DESERT SHIELD), which began shortly after Iraq's invasion of Kuwait on August 2, 1990. Despite a few wrinkles early on, CRAF performed admirably well, helping to put in place more than 500,000 troops and many tons of supplies and military hardware. Between August 1990 and March 1991, CRAF aircraft flew two-thirds of all military personnel and one-quarter of all cargo to the Persian Gulf.

On February 8, 2003, in anticipation of the Anglo-American–led invasion of Iraq, CRAF was activated for the second time in its history, a Stage 1 mobilization. Stage 2 was implemented soon thereafter to augment the military's airlift capabilities. Once more, CRAF responded ably to the activation, using 51 commercial aircraft from 11 civilian airlines. CRAF flew some 1,625 missions during Operation IRAQI FREEDOM, transporting 254,143 troops to the front. Sixteen commercial air carriers also transported 11,050 short tons of cargo during the same period. CRAF was deactivated on June 18, 2003.

PAUL G. PIERPAOLI JR.

See also

Aircraft, Transport; IRAQI FREEDOM, Operation; Persian Gulf War; United States Transportation Command

References

Bickers, Richard Townshend. *Airlift: The Illustrated History of American Military Transport.* Botley, Oxford, UK: Osprey, 1998.

Wales, William S. "Civil Reserve Air Fleet Enhancement Program: A Study of Its Viability in Today's Environment." Master's thesis, Naval Postgraduate School, Monterey, CA, 1998.

Clark, William Ramsey (1927–)

Lawyer, U.S. attorney general of the United States under President Lyndon B. Johnson (1967–1969), and outspoken critic of U.S. wars in the Middle East since 1991. Born in Dallas, Texas, on December 18, 1927, William Ramsey Clark served in the U.S. Marine Corps from 1945 to 1946. He received his undergraduate degree from the University of Texas in 1949 and his MA in history and JD degrees from the University of Chicago in 1950. Clark then joined the Dallas law firm of Clark, Coon, Holt & Fisher, a firm founded by his grandfather, and worked there for 10 years, losing only one jury trial. Because his father Tom had become an associate justice of the U.S. Supreme Court in 1949, Ramsey avoided high court legislation except for one case in which his father recused himself.

Clark worked actively in Democratic Party politics, and in 1960 he campaigned for John F. Kennedy. In 1961 Kennedy appointed Clark assistant attorney general in charge of the Lands Division of the Justice Department (1961–1965). During his tenure, Clark instituted cost-cutting measures and reduced the backlog of cases. He also supervised other projects, mainly in the civil rights area. Clark headed federal civilian forces at the University of Mississippi after the 1962 riots there and served in Birmingham in 1963. He visited school officials throughout the South in 1963 to help them coordinate and implement desegregation plans. He also helped formulate the landmark 1964 Civil Rights Act.

As a consequence of his diligent work, Clark was appointed deputy attorney general in 1965. In this post he helped to draft the 1965 Voting Rights Act, and after the riots in the Watts section of Los Angeles in 1965 he headed federal forces sent to find solutions to the problems that led to the violence. When Attorney General Nicholas Katzenbach became undersecretary of state in 1966, President Lyndon B. Johnson appointed Clark acting attorney general. Five months later Johnson made the promotion permanent. Two hours after the official appointment, Justice Tom Clark announced his retirement from the Supreme Court to avoid any potential conflict of interest. On March 10, 1967, Ramsey Clark was sworn in as attorney general; his father administered the oath of office.

As attorney general from 1967 to 1969, Clark strongly supported civil rights for all Americans. He also opposed the death penalty, criticized police violence toward citizens and antiwar protesters, and steadfastly refused to use wiretaps except in cases of national security. These positions, in addition to his lenient stance on antiwar activities, attracted criticism from within the Johnson administration and from conservatives, who labeled Clark as soft on crime.

After leaving office in 1969, Clark actively opposed the Vietnam War, and in 1972 he visited North Vietnam to investigate American bombing of civilian targets. He also taught, first at Howard University (1969–1972) and then at Brooklyn Law School (1973–1981). Clark continued to practice law in New York City, and in 1974 he ran unsuccessfully for the U.S. Senate. In 1980 he led a group of private citizens to Tehran, Iran, during the hostage crisis there, and in 1982 he made a private fact-finding tour of Nicaragua. Clark also found time to write a book, *Crime in America* (1970), that examines the social and economic causes and potential solutions to crime.

In more recent years Clark has proven even more controversial, as he vigorously and publicly opposed the 1991 Persian Gulf War, the Global War on Terror, the Afghanistan War, and the Iraq War. In 1991 Clark accused the George H. W. Bush administration of crimes against humanity committed during the Persian Gulf War. Clark views the Global War on Terror as a war against Islam and believes that the conflict is eroding American's civil liberties. He has even gone so far as to propose that Al Qaeda was not behind the September 11, 2001, attacks; instead, he blames the U.S. government, which he believed planned and staged the event in order to wage war against the Taliban and Iraq. From 2003 to 2009, Clark was active in the drive to bring impeachment proceedings against President George W. Bush and Vice President Dick Cheney. After the 1999 North Atlantic Treaty Organization bombing campaign of Yugoslavia, Clark charged the organization with 19 counts of genocide.

Equally controversial have been the clients he has chosen to defend. They include Radovan Karadzic, Slobodan Milosevic, former Liberian strongman Charles Taylor, and former Iraqi president Saddam Hussein. Clark insisted that Hussein would be unable to receive a fair trial if it was held in Iraq. Nevertheless, Hussein was tried, convicted, and executed there. After Milosevic's death from a heart attack in 2006, Clark stated that both Hussein and Milosevic were the victims of a deeply flawed legal system. In 2009, Clark charged that Israel was guilty of genocide due to its policies toward the Palestinians, an allegation that earned him much enmity.

LAURA MATYSEK WOOD

See also

Antiwar Movement, Iraq War; Bush, George Walker; Cheney, Richard Bruce; Global War on Terror; Hussein, Saddam; IRAQI FREEDOM, Operation; Persian Gulf War; September 11 Attacks

References

Clark, William Ramsey. *Crime in America: Observations on Its Nature, Causes, Prevention and Control.* New York: Simon and Schuster, 1970.

Clark, William Ramsey. *The Fire This Time: U.S. War Crimes in the Gulf.* New York: Thunder's Mouth, 1994.

Who's Who in America, 1968–1969. New Providence, NJ: Marquis Who's Who, 1969.

Wohl, Alexander. *Father, Son, and Constitution: How Justice Tom Clark and Attorney General Ramsey Clark Shaped American Democracy.* Lawrence: University Press of Kansas, 2013.

Clarke, Richard Alan (1951–)

Longtime U.S. government employee, intelligence expert, and chief counterterrorism adviser on the U.S. National Security Council at the time of the September 11, 2001, terror attacks. Richard Alan Clarke was born in October 1951 in Boston, Massachusetts, to a working-class family. He earned an undergraduate degree from the University of Pennsylvania in 1972 and then attended the Massachusetts Institute of Technology, where he earned a degree in management. His first job, beginning in 1973, was with the U.S. Department of Defense as a defense analyst keeping tabs on the number of Soviet nuclear warheads. After a series of appointments, Clarke was promoted in 1985 to the post of assistant secretary of state for intelligence in the Ronald Reagan administration. By this time Clarke had earned a reputation as being blunt and on occasion abusive.

Clarke continued to work with the George H. W. Bush administration as an assistant secretary of state for politico-military affairs during 1989–1992, helping on security affairs during the 1991 Persian Gulf War. In 1992 Secretary of State James Baker fired Clarke for his apparent defense of Israel's transfer of U.S. technology to the People's Republic of China. Clarke then moved to the National Security Council, where he began to specialize in counterterrorism. Clarke was a holdover in the William J. (Bill) Clinton and George W. Bush administrations, continuing as a member of the National Security Council from 1992 to 2003.

Clarke's preoccupation was with counterintelligence. Among his contentions was that Osama bin Laden's Al Qaeda terrorist organization was a growing threat to the United States. President Clinton agreed with this assessment but was not, after all, able to deal effectively with the threat. Clarke lobbied for a Counterterrorism Security Group to be chaired by a new national security official, the national coordinator for infrastructure protection and counterterrorism. Clinton approved this office by signing Presidential Decision Directive 62 on May 22, 1998.

Clarke then presided over a working group that included the counterterrorism heads of the Central Intelligence

Agency (CIA), the Federal Bureau of Investigation, the Joint Chiefs of Staff, the Department of Defense, the Department of Justice, and the Department of State. But the national coordinator for infrastructure protection and counterterrorism had a limited staff of 12 and no budget; moreover, operational decision making could come only from the departments and agencies of the intelligence community. As Clarke has pointed out, he had the "appearance of responsibility for counterterrorism, but none of the tools or authority to get the job done."

Nevertheless, Clarke was in the middle of several counterterrorism operations. He was involved in decision making about the CIA's operation to apprehend Osama bin Laden in 1998. An Afghan team was to capture bin Laden at his residence at Tarnak Farms near Kandahar. This raid was called off because of a lack of confidence among CIA leadership, the White House, and Clarke that it would succeed.

Clarke continued his position on the National Security Council during the early years of the George W. Bush administration. Indeed, Clarke proposed a plan to combat Al Qaeda that included covert aid to the Afghan leader of the Northern Alliance, reconnaissance flights by the new unmanned aerial vehicle Predator, and ways to eliminate bin Laden as a threat to the United States, but there was little enthusiasm for this report within the Bush administration. In the meantime, the events of September 11, 2001, transpired, changing the American political and national security landscape dramatically.

On September 12, President Bush instructed Clarke to try to find evidence that Iraqi president Saddam Hussein was connected to September 11. Clarke sent a report to the White House stating categorically that Hussein had nothing to do with the terrorist attacks, but there is no evidence indicating that Bush read the report. It was sent back to be updated and resubmitted, but nothing came of it.

Clarke left government service in January 2003 and became an outspoken critic of the Bush administration and its policies prior to September 11. This led the White House to engage in a character assassination campaign against him. Clarke testified for 20 hours during the September 11 Commission hearings and made national headlines for his apology that the government had failed to prevent the September 11 attacks. In 2004 Clarke published his book *Against All Enemies: Inside America's War on Terror,* which gives his side of the controversy.

In his book, Clarke is especially critical of the Bush administration's 2003 invasion of Iraq. Most of Clarke's criticism stems from his belief that by redirecting attention away from bin Laden and Al Qaeda, the Bush administration allowed Al Qaeda to reconstitute itself into an ongoing threat to the United States. In Clarke's view, the invasion of Afghanistan was so halfhearted in its commitment of low numbers of American troops that bin Laden and nearly all of the Al Qaeda and Taliban leaders easily escaped. By not committing the necessary resources to rebuild Afghanistan, Clarke wrote, the Bush administration had allowed both Al Qaeda and the Taliban to threaten the pro-American Afghanistan state, all to depose Saddam Hussein.

Clarke has more recently been engaged in a wide array of consulting work; he has also taught, authored two works of fiction, and in 2010 published a book on cyberwarfare, which he believes is a growing threat to American security. In 2013 Clarke served as an adviser to the Barack Obama administration in the aftermath of revelations made by Edward Snowden that the National Security Agency had been engaged in a widespread and systematic snooping campaign against Americans. At that time, Obama had instructed a special advisory group to reform the agency's domestic spying programs with an eye toward bringing them in line with U.S. constitutional prerogatives.

STEPHEN E. ATKINS

See also
Al Qaeda; Bin Laden, Osama; Bush, George Walker; Clinton, William Jefferson; Global War on Terror; Hussein, Saddam; IRAQI FREEDOM, Operation; National Security Agency; September 11 Commission and Report; Snowden, Edward Joseph; Taliban

References
Benjamin, Daniel, and Steven Simon. *The Age of Sacred Terror.* New York: Random House, 2002.
Clarke, Richard A. *Against All Enemies: Inside America's War on Terror.* New York: Free Press, 2004.
Coll, Steve. *Ghost Wars: The Secret History of the CIA, Afghanistan, and Bin Laden, from the Soviet Invasion to September 10, 2001.* New York: Penguin, 2004.
Naftali, Timothy. *Blind Spot: The Secret History of American Counterterrorism.* New York: Basic Books, 2005.

Cleland, Joseph Maxwell (1942–)

U.S. Army officer, head of the Veterans Administration (1977–1981), Democratic Party politician, and U.S. senator (1997–2003). Born in Atlanta, Georgia, on August 24, 1942, Joseph Maxwell (Max) Cleland received a BA from Stetson University in Florida in 1964 and earned an MA in American history from Emory University the following year. Shortly thereafter he entered the U.S. Army, initially serving in the Signal Corps. After successfully completing Airborne School, in 1967 he volunteered for duty in Vietnam with the 1st Cavalry Division (Airmobile). The next year near Khe Sanh, Captain Cleland lost both legs and his right arm as a result of a grenade blast. He received numerous citations, including the Bronze Star Medal and the Silver Star.

Not released from the hospital until 1970, Cleland wasted little time in resuming a productive life. In 1971 he won a seat in the Georgia Senate and used his position to promote issues related to veterans and the handicapped. From 1975 to 1977 he served on the professional staff of the U.S. Senate Veterans Affairs Committee.

In February 1977 President Jimmy Carter nominated his fellow Georgian to head the Veterans Administration (VA). Speedy Senate confirmation followed, and Cleland became at age 34 the youngest person to ever head the VA and the first Vietnam veteran to hold the position. He launched a vigorous expansion of VA programs, including drug and alcohol treatment and counseling services. He also worked to improve the public image of the VA and Vietnam veterans. His tenure at the VA ended in 1981 with the election of President Ronald Reagan. Returning to Georgia, Cleland became secretary of state, holding that position from 1983 to 1997. In 1996 he received the Democratic nomination to fill the Senate seat vacated by Democrat Sam Nunn and won the election that November, joining such prominent Vietnam veterans as John Kerry (D-MA), Robert Kerrey (D-NE), and John McCain (R-AZ). In 2003 Cleland was among 29 Senate Democrats to vote for the authorization for war with Iraq. Later, he announced that he deeply regretted his decision and admitted that his vote was in part influenced by his upcoming reelection bid.

In 2002 Cleland experienced a bruising reelection campaign, running against Republican Saxby Chambliss. The election made national news after the Chambliss campaign ran incendiary television commercials implicitly questioning Cleland's patriotism because he had failed to support some of the George W. Bush administration's homeland security decisions. The ads featured likenesses of Saddam Hussein and Osama bin Laden. The ads were pulled amid much uproar, and Republican senators John McCain and Chuck Hagel chastised Chambliss for his tactless and mean-spirited campaign. Nevertheless, Cleland lost the election to Chambliss, who had no military experience at all.

The smear campaign against Cleland has been seen by some as a precursor of the later campaign that raised troubling questions about the Vietnam service of Senator John Kerry, who ran for president on the Democratic ticket in 2004. Cleland campaigned vigorously for Kerry, and when the anti-Kerry Swift Boat Veterans for Truth organization ran ads questioning Kerry's patriotism, war record, and troubling details regarding his award of the Silver Star and Purple Heart medals, Cleland paid a personal visit to President George W. Bush's Texas ranch to protest the ads. Cleland's appeal had little effect, however. Kerry lost the election to the incumbent Bush.

Cleland has written extensively on veterans' issues and the plight of Vietnam veterans. Since leaving the Senate, he served on the board of directors of the Export-Import Bank of the United States (2003–2007). In 2009, President Barack Obama appointed Cleland secretary of the American Battle Monuments Commission.

DAVID COFFEY

See also
Bush, George Walker; Hagel, Charles Timothy; IRAQI FREEDOM, Operation; Kerry, John Forbes; McCain, John Sidney, III; United States, National Elections of 2004

References
Cleland, Max. *Strong at the Broken Places.* Atlanta: Cherokee Publishing, 1989.

Cleland, Max, with Ben Raines. *Heart of a Patriot: How I Found the Courage to Survive Vietnam, Walter Reed, and Karl Rove.* New York: Simon and Schuster, 2009.

Who's Who in America, 1997. New Providence, NJ: Marquis Who's Who, 1996.

Cleveland, Charles T. (1956–)

U.S. Army general and longtime special operations officer with extensive experience in operations in Panama, El Salvador, and Bolivia in the decades before the Iraq War. Charles T. Cleveland was born in 1956 in Arizona and is the son of a U.S. Army career enlisted man. Cleveland graduated from the U.S. Military Academy, West Point, in 1978. He had attended secondary school in Panama and had a good understanding of Latin American culture. By 1989, he was a captain and company commander in the 3rd Battalion, 7th Special Forces Group, in Panama. He was also the battalion operations officer. Besides sending teams into El Salvador to help the government there with an ongoing guerrilla war, Cleveland developed plans to train an antidrug police force in Bolivia. While inspecting a police camp in the drug growing region of that nation, he helped defend it against an attack by guerrillas.

As relations between Panamanian president Manual Noriega and the U.S. government worsened during 1989,

Cleveland developed plans and lists of targets for his unit in the event of a U.S. military intervention. When the U.S. invasion (Operation JUST CAUSE) was launched on December 19, 1989, Cleveland's plans were the basis for special forces operations in the country. The operations were successful, and Noriega was taken into custody in January 1991 to stand trial for drug trafficking in the United States. Cleveland displayed a keen ability to improvise and work with local populations to carry out operations and achieve results. During the 1990s, he continued to showcase his abilities during peacekeeping operations in the Balkans.

By early 2003, Cleveland was commanding the 10th Special Forces Group. When planning got under way for Operation IRAQI FREEDOM, Cleveland's group was assigned to northern Iraq. They were expected to help the 4th Infantry Division drive from Turkey to capture the major cities of Mosul and Kirkuk as well as the northern oil fields. When the government of Turkey refused to allow American forces across its territory, Cleveland's men were ordered to carry on. Subsequently, on the night of March 24 the entire 173rd Airborne Brigade, staging out of Italy, dropped into northern Iraq. Meanwhile, the special forces teams were to cooperate with local Kurdish forces to keep regular army and Republican Guard units in the area from reinforcing Baghdad. They also worked to destroy terrorist camps in the region.

Colonel Cleveland's command was code-named Task Force Viking and consisted of his 2nd and 3rd Battalions of the 10th Special Forces Group, supplemented by the 3rd Battalion of the 3rd Special Forces Group. Cleveland's men worked with 65,000 lightly armed Kurdish militiamen from different groups. While Cleveland was to use the Kurds to help defeat Iraqi president Saddam Hussein's supporters in northern Iraq, he was not to allow the Kurds to become so strong or independent that the Turks would fear an independent Kurdistan movement.

Cleveland's first objective when war broke out was to eliminate the Ansar al-Islam terrorist training camps in northeastern Iraq. Aided by Kurdish militiamen, the 3rd Battalion attacked on March 27. Ansar al-Islam positions were taken out by laser-guided bombs dropped by navy fighters, with direction from the special forces. Lockheed AC-130 Spectre gunships blasted those who tried to run. The camps were completely eliminated, although a number of fighters managed to flee.

Cleveland then concentrated his efforts on the four Iraqi corps defending the Green Line that separated the Kurdish territory from the remainder of Iraq. Again, the special forces teams employed airpower and advanced antiarmor missiles to weaken the Iraqi defenders. They punched holes through the Iraqi defenses, forcing the defenders to withdraw. On April 11 Cleveland, a few special forces troops, and about 100 Kurdish militiamen drove into Mosul, virtually ending the campaign in northern Iraq in complete victory.

Cleveland's accomplishment was recognized in his appointment as chief of staff of the Army Special Forces Command. He was also promoted to brigadier general and became commander of Special Operations Command South (2005–2008). In April 2008 Cleveland was appointed commander of Special Operations Command Central; he was promoted to major general in September 2008, and on June 24, 2012, he was promoted to lieutenant general and became commander of the U.S. Army Special Operations Command, headquartered at Fort Bragg.

TIM J. WATTS

See also

Ansar al-Islam; IRAQI FREEDOM, Operation; United States Special Operations Command

References

Murray, Williamson, and Robert H. Scales Jr. *The Iraq War: A Military History.* Boston: Belknap, 2003.

Robinson, Linda. *Masters of Chaos: The Secret History of the Special Forces.* New York: PublicAffairs, 2004.

Clinton, Hillary Rodham (1947–)

Attorney, former first lady (1993–2001), U.S. senator (2001–2009), presidential candidate in 2008 and 2015, and secretary of state (2009–2013). Hillary Diane Rodham was born on October 26, 1947, in Chicago and was raised in Park Ridge, a prosperous Chicago suburb. Her family was staunchly Republican, and during the 1964 presidential campaign, while still a high school student, she actively campaigned for Republican nominee Barry Goldwater. She entered Wellesley College in 1965, and by 1968 she had become disenchanted with Republican politics and the Vietnam War. By 1968 she supported the Democratic antiwar presidential candidate Eugene McCarthy; the following year she graduated with a degree in political science.

Rodham enrolled at Yale Law School, where she met fellow student Bill Clinton, whom she would later marry. Graduating in 1973, she took a position with a child advocacy group. The next year she served as a staff attorney for the House Committee on the Judiciary during the Watergate Scandal that caused President Richard Nixon to resign in 1974. In 1975, she wed Bill Clinton.

U.S. Secretary of State Hillary Rodham Clinton testifies on January 23, 2013, before the House Foreign Affairs Committee hearing on the deadly September 11, 2012, attack on the U.S. diplomatic mission in Benghazi, Libya, that killed Ambassador Chris Stevens and three other Americans. (AP Photo/J. Scott Applewhite)

In 1976, Bill Clinton launched his political career when he was elected attorney general of Arkansas. The next year, Hillary Clinton joined the Rose Law Firm, the premier legal firm in Arkansas, where she specialized in intellectual property law and continued pro bono child advocacy legal work. Bill became governor of Arkansas in January 1979, the same year that Hillary Clinton became a full partner in the Rose Law Firm, the first woman to achieve such status. In 1981 Bill lost a reelection bid but was reelected in 1982; Hillary was again the first lady of Arkansas, an informal post that she would hold until her husband became president in January 1993. She continued her legal work and was active on several boards, including those of Arkansas-based Wal-Mart as well as Lafarge and TCBY.

Taking a leave of absence from the Rose Law Firm to help her husband campaign for the presidency in 1992, Clinton proved to be a formidable campaigner, repeatedly weathering allegations that her husband had engaged in extramarital affairs. After Bill Clinton upset incumbent president George H. W. Bush in the November 1992 elections, Hillary Clinton

became first lady in January 1993. She was an activist first lady, certainly more so than any of her immediate predecessors. Some pundits likened her to Eleanor Roosevelt, but it quickly became clear that Clinton would be a far more influential first lady than even Roosevelt.

Hillary Clinton's role in White House policy making was derided by the right wing of the Republican Party, and even some mainstream Democrats openly questioned her central role in decision making. In 1993 her husband named her chairperson of the Task Force on National Health Care Reform, a move that in retrospect was probably not a wise idea. Many questioned Hillary Clinton's motives, and the secrecy in which she conducted much of the task force's business only added to the public's skepticism. In the end, her health care plan was deemed too bureaucratic and too burdensome for business. The plan died in Congress and became a major campaign boon to the Republicans in the 1994 elections, which saw the Democrats lose their control of Congress. Despite the setback, Clinton actively promoted certain national legislation, including the State Children's

Health Insurance Program in 1997. She traveled widely, ultimately visiting 79 nations.

Clinton was at the epicenter of the fruitless Whitewater investigation, a Republican-inspired inquiry into a decade-old land deal in which the Clintons had been involved in Arkansas. As such, she became the only first lady to be subpoenaed by a federal grand jury. Although years of probing and $50 million of taxpayers' money went into the Whitewater inquiry, neither Clinton was found to have engaged in any illegal activity. Unfortunately, however, Whitewater revealed a sexual dalliance between Bill Clinton and a White House intern, Monica Lewinsky, which mortified Hillary Clinton and led to the president's impeachment in December 1998. While Mrs. Clinton's allegation that the persecution of her and her husband was the result of a "vast right-wing conspiracy" may have been hyperbole, there can be little doubt that the Clintons were subjected to endlessly harsh scrutiny and criticism, particularly by Republicans and other detractors.

In 2000 the Clintons purchased a home in New York, and Hillary Clinton ran for the state's senatorial seat being vacated by retiring U.S. senator Daniel Patrick Moynihan. Clinton was at first running against popular New York City mayor Rudolph Giuliani, and many believed that her chances of winning were not good. But after Giuliani dropped out of the race because of health problems, Clinton—now running against Rick Lazio, a relatively unknown congressman—was virtually assured a win. Clinton won the election by an impressive 12-point margin and took office in January 2001.

During her first term Clinton maintained a relatively low profile but garnered high marks for her intellect, excellent grasp of issues, and willingness to work in a bipartisan manner. Following the September 11, 2001, terror attacks on the United States, Clinton strongly backed the George W. Bush administration's response, including Operation ENDURING FREEDOM in Afghanistan and the 2001 Patriot Act. In October 2002 Clinton voted with the majority to grant the Bush administration authority to wage war in Iraq to enforce United Nations resolutions should diplomacy fail. She did not support an amendment that would have required another congressional resolution to invade Iraq. Meanwhile, Clinton visited both Afghanistan and Iraq to gauge the effectiveness of the U.S. war efforts there.

By 2005, already planning a run for the presidency in 2008, Clinton began to publicly criticize the Iraq War effort, noting the growing insurgency and the absence of firm plans to either extricate the United States from Iraq or quash the insurgents. She was careful to state, however, that a precipitous withdrawal was unwise if not dangerous, a position that chagrined many antiwar Democrats. Clinton did not back any of the Bush tax cuts, viewing them as economic grenades that would derail the economy, nor did she vote for Bush's two Supreme Court nominees, John Roberts and Samuel Alito.

In November 2006 Clinton, now quite popular with New York voters, won a landslide reelection. In early 2007 she began transferring leftover funds from her Senate race to her presidential campaign. On January 20, 2007, she announced her intention to form an exploratory committee for the 2008 presidential contest. That same year, she refused to support the Bush administration's troop surge in Iraq and backed unsuccessful legislation that would have forced the president to withdraw troops from Iraq based on a predetermined timeline. Forced to deal with her affirmative vote for the Iraq War, Clinton now had to explain that she probably would have voted against the 2002 resolution had she been privy to accurate and reliable intelligence. Her position change left many wondering why she had taken so long to come to such a conclusion.

By the autumn of 2007, Clinton seemed the person to beat amid a large Democratic presidential field. Following a mediocre performance in a debate in October, Clinton's momentum began to slip. After placing third in the January 2008 Iowa caucus, Clinton's campaign began to slowly unravel as Senator Barack Obama made significant inroads with Democratic voters. After waging a well-run and valiant campaign, Clinton finally dropped out of the race on June 7, 2008, and endorsed Obama's candidacy. President Obama subsequently nominated Clinton as secretary of state, and she was confirmed in that position by the Senate on January 21, 2009, by a vote of 94 to 2.

Clinton was sworn into office on January 21, making her the third female secretary of state. As the nation's top diplomat, Clinton attempted to repair relations with Europe, which had become tense during the George W. Bush administration, and sought to reset U.S.-Russian relations, which had also deteriorated under Bush. While her efforts to reengage U.S. partners in Europe paid dividends, her overtures to the Russians were decidedly less successful.

Clinton supported Obama's troop surge in Afghanistan in 2010 and tried to forge a pragmatic, largely nonideological foreign policy. She counseled caution during the Arab Spring movement, which began in early 2011 and witnessed major uprisings in Egypt, Libya, and Syria, among other nations. To her detractors, however, this initial caution appeared to be weakness. Nevertheless, as the Libyan Civil

War unfolded, Clinton came to favor limited U.S. military aid to the rebels in the way of air support in conjunction with other nations, which helped topple Libya's government under Muammar Qadaffi. In 2012, Clinton supported a plan by which the U.S. government would train and equip select rebel groups fighting in the Syrian Civil War, but the White House rejected the scheme. Clinton was also supportive of engaging in diplomacy and employing sanctions in order to convince Iran to abandon its suspected nuclear weapons program. Meanwhile, in late 2010 and early 2011, the secretary of state spearheaded the effort to limit the damage resulting from WikiLeaks documents that were critical of various foreign leaders and diplomats.

Perhaps Clinton's greatest test came after the September 11, 2012, terror attack against the U.S. consulate in Benghazi, Libya, in which three Americans, including the ambassador to Libya, were killed. She accepted full responsibility for the outcome of the debacle but flatly rejected Republicans' claims that she had been involved in a cover-up attempt after the attack.

Clinton left office on February 1, 2013, and was succeeded by John F. Kerry. Clinton maintained a fairly low profile, but in the early autumn of 2014 she criticized President Obama's approach to the Syrian Civil War, intimating that his overly cautious policies toward Syria had enabled the rise of the Islamic State of Iraq and Syria (ISIS). In the summer of 2014, Obama was compelled to take military action against ISIS in Iraq; in the fall, he expanded that effort to include air strikes against ISIS in Syria. In 2015, Clinton announced her intention to run for the presidency.

Paul G. Pierpaoli Jr.

See also

Arab Spring; Benghazi, Attack on U.S. Consulate; Clinton, William Jefferson; Iran; Islamic State in Iraq and Syria; Kerry, John Forbes; Libyan Civil War; Obama, Barack Hussein, II; Syrian Civil War; Troop Surge, U.S., Afghanistan War; WikiLeaks

References

Bernstein, Carl. *A Woman in Charge: The Life of Hillary Rodham Clinton.* New York: Knopf, 2007.

Clinton, Hillary Rodham. *Living History.* New York: Simon and Schuster, 2003.

Clinton, William Jefferson (1946–)

U.S. Democratic Party politician and president of the United States (1993–2001). William "Bill" Jefferson Clinton was born William Jefferson Blythe III in Hope, Arkansas, on August 19, 1946. His early life was characterized by hardships and struggles that formed his character and attitudes throughout his public life. His biological father, William Jefferson Blythe Jr., was killed in an automobile accident prior to Clinton's birth, and the young Blythe was raised by his mother, Virginia Kelley. His mother's marriage to Roger Clinton prompted William's adoption and the changing of his name to William Clinton just prior to starting secondary school. Roger Clinton, however, was physically abusive toward his wife, another development that profoundly affected Bill Clinton.

Clinton was a bright and astute student who hoped to pursue a medical career until he met President John F. Kennedy on a Boys' Nation trip to Washington, D.C. This experience led Clinton to focus his future career aspirations on public service and politics. He received an academic scholarship to attend Georgetown University, where he earned a bachelor's degree in international affairs. During his time at Georgetown, he spent a year assisting Arkansas senator J. William Fulbright. Clinton's credentials as a progressive Democrat and social liberal were further developed under the tutelage of this prominent senator. In 1968 as the United States was being transformed by social changes and wracked by protests against the Vietnam War, Clinton was selected as a Rhodes Scholar. He spent 1968 to 1970 studying at Oxford University. On his return to the United States, he enrolled in the Yale University School of Law.

While studying at Yale, Clinton met his future wife Hillary Rodham, who shared many of the liberal and progressive ideas that would become the hallmark of his political career. They were married in 1975.

Clinton's initial foray into national politics occurred shortly after receiving his law degree. In 1974 he was defeated in a congressional race for Arkansas's Third District. After a brief career as a professor at the University of Arkansas (1974–1976), he was named state attorney general and was elected governor in 1978 at age 32, the youngest governor in the nation. In 1980 he suffered a humiliating reelection defeat, caused by widespread opposition to an automobile licensing tax. Clinton's resiliency and commitment were apparent when he successfully regained the Arkansas governorship in 1982, a post he held until his election as president in 1992.

In the summer of 1992 Clinton secured the Democratic Party nomination to run against incumbent president George Herbert Walker Bush, a Republican. Clinton was bedeviled, however, by questions regarding marital infidelity and the emerging Whitewater real estate scandal in

Arkansas. In the race, he benefited from an economic downturn and businessman H. Ross Perot's Independent Party candidacy.

Clinton won the November 1992 election with a minority of the popular vote. During his first term he balanced domestic issues and foreign policy in a highly effective manner. At home, he lobbied unsuccessfully for major health care reform. Clinton was successful, however, in raising taxes and reducing expenditures to reduce and then eliminate the federal deficit and in pushing through major welfare reforms. In foreign affairs, he promoted free trade agreements, brokered peace efforts in the Middle East, removed U.S. military personnel from Somalia, and restored diplomatic relations with the Socialist Republic of Vietnam.

The congressional elections of 1994, however, brought Republican majorities in both the House and the Senate. The Republicans' "Contract with America," crafted chiefly by Republican congressman Newt Gingrich, called for reducing the role of government and continuing the conservative policies of Ronald Reagan and was a thorough repudiation of Clinton's presidency. A standoff between Clinton and congressional leaders led to a federal government shutdown in November and December 1995, which badly eroded public support for the Republicans.

In the 1996 presidential campaign Clinton promised a tough approach to crime, supported welfare reform, called for reducing the federal deficit, and insisted on the need to continue affirmative action programs. Robert Dole, a respected senator and World War II veteran, was the Republican Party candidate. The booming U.S. economy and continuing suspicions regarding the Republicans' agenda ensured a respectable Clinton victory. He was the first Democrat to secure a second presidential term since Franklin D. Roosevelt.

In 1997 Clinton submitted to Congress the first balanced budget in nearly three decades. The cooperation of congressional Republicans and major compromises by Clinton generated significant budget surpluses during the remainder of his presidency. By decade's end the American economy was more robust than at any time since the mid-1960s, unemployment stood at a historic low, and the stock market had reached new highs.

In addition to significant domestic accomplishments, Clinton responded effectively to a series of international crises. In 1998 in response to Iraqi president Saddam Hussein's noncompliance with United Nations weapons inspections, Clinton authorized air strikes in Iraq (Operation DESERT FOX) and sanctions to significantly hurt Iraq's economy. These,

however, failed to produce any significant change in the Iraqi dictator's behavior. In 1999 Clinton prodded the North Atlantic Treaty Organization to undertake military action in response to genocide conducted by Serbs against Albanians in Kosovo. He also worked mightily to secure a resolution to the Israeli-Palestinian conflict, a major Clinton administration goal.

Clinton urged all sides in the Arab-Israeli conflict to negotiate and come to an agreement, but his efforts were stymied by uncooperative leaders and events. The assassination of Israeli prime minister Yitzhak Rabin in November 1995 and the terrorist attacks by Islamic groups since 1994 were accompanied by a turn to the political Right in Israeli public opinion, which led to a right-wing cabinet under hard-line prime minister Benjamin Netanyahu. Netanyahu promised to bring peace and security but also pledged that he would not return any of the occupied territories. He delayed in carrying out troop withdrawals in accordance with the 1993 Oslo Accords, in which Israel had agreed to give up land for peace, while the Palestinian side failed to crack down on terrorism. Netanyahu also demanded that Yasser Arafat and the Palestinian National Authority (PNA) move directly against the Hamas terrorist organization.

With tensions dramatically increasing, Clinton intervened directly and applied pressure on both sides. In October 1998 he succeeded in bringing together Netanyahu and Arafat at the Wye River estate in Maryland. Following days of difficult negotiations and sometimes bitter wrangling, Clinton secured agreement in what became known as the Wye River Accords. Israel agreed to withdraw from an additional 13 percent of West Bank territory, and the PNA renounced the use of terrorism and agreed both to suppress it and to eliminate weapons that it had stockpiled. The PNA also agreed to halt the most virulent anti-Israeli propaganda.

Netanyahu returned to Israel, however, to find strong opposition from within his ruling Likud coalition to the additional territorial concession. He nonetheless carried out a partial withdrawal. Meanwhile, although the PNA did crack down on militants, it failed to implement most of the provisions in the Wye River Accords, whereupon a month later Netanyahu suspended withdrawals.

Forced to call new elections, Netanyahu curried favor with the Israeli religious Right, alienating many secular Israelis. In the ensuing May 1999 elections, Netanyahu was defeated by the Labor coalition known as One Israel, headed by former Israeli Army chief of staff Ehud Barak.

Clinton reached out to Barak, whose premiership began with much promise but ended after only 17 months. Barak

President Bill Clinton, center, Israeli Prime Minister Ehud Barak, left, and Palestinian leader Yasser Arafat at Camp David, Maryland, on July 11, 2000, at the start of the Mideast summit. (AP Photo/Ron Edmonds)

removed Israeli troops from southern Lebanon in May 2000, but negotiations with Arafat and the PNA ran afoul of right-wing charges that he was making too many concessions. Clinton again set up a meeting in the United States. During July 11–24, 2000, he hosted a summit at the presidential retreat of Camp David, Maryland. Despite generous concessions by Barak the parties were unable to secure agreement, and a new wave of violence, the Second (al-Aqsa) Intifada, erupted. Clinton made one last try, this time at the White House during December 19–23, 2000. Both his and Barak's terms were nearing their ends. The U.S. plan, apparently endorsed by Barak, would have ceded to the Palestinians a greater percentage of the West Bank and Palestinian control of the Gaza Strip, with a land link between the two. Barak also agreed that Arab neighborhoods of East Jerusalem might become the capital of the new Palestinian state. Certain Palestinian refugees would also have the right of return to the Palestinian state and compensation from a fund raised by international donors. These concessions were anathema to the Likud Party and other Israeli rightists, but in the end, despite heavy pressure from Clinton, it was Arafat who rejected and torpedoed the agreement. Barak, who

came under a storm of criticism for this process, was forced to step aside.

The Clinton White House also faced several foreign-inspired terrorist attacks on U.S. soil and on U.S. interests, the most serious of them being the 1993 World Trade Center bombing, the August 1998 truck bombing of two U.S. embassies in Kenya and Tanzania, and the bombing of USS *Cole* in Yemen in October 2000. The last two incidents were specifically linked to the Al Qaeda terrorist organization. In retaliation for the 1998 embassy attacks, Clinton ordered cruise missile strikes against suspected Al Qaeda headquarters and training camps in Khartoum, Sudan, and Afghanistan. The strikes were largely ineffective and engendered significant controversy in the United States and abroad.

Some observers have suggested that the Clinton administration did not focus adequate attention on the rising threat of Islamic terrorism because Clinton had routinely ignored or downplayed the role and importance of the Central Intelligence Agency (CIA) during his tenure in office. Indeed, some of his appointees who headed the agency tended to be controversial and ineffective. To a certain degree Clinton mistrusted the CIA, and that mistrust often manifested itself in an adversarial relationship between the White House and the agency. This was not, however, an indication that the Clinton administration entirely ignored the threat of terrorism.

In February 1995 the Clinton administration introduced the Omnibus Counter-terrorism Act of 1995, trying to bypass some of the limitations placed on intelligence operations in the fight against domestic and international terrorism. But even after the April 1995 Oklahoma City bombing, perpetrated by two domestic terrorists, the Republican-controlled House of Representatives refused to bring it to a vote. Disbelieving that a major terrorist threat was on the horizon, Republicans decided to sacrifice any efforts at counterterrorism and instead criticized the Clinton administration for its failures. In 1996 Congress did pass the Antiterrorism and Effective Death Penalty Act of 1996, but many of the original provisions involving firearms control were eliminated because of the objections of the gun lobby. Two important provisions were retained, however: chemical markers on high explosives and legal authority to bar terrorists from entering the United States (Alien Terrorist Removal Court).

During his second term in office, Clinton and his administration did become increasingly aware of the threat of both domestic and foreign terrorism. His appointment of George Tenet as CIA director helped stabilize the agency, but Clinton still had reservations about the reliability of intelligence coming from the CIA. The presence of Richard A. Clarke in the White House also brought counterterrorism to the forefront of the president's agenda.

On several occasions, the Clinton administration proposed special operations to be conducted by the military against terrorist targets. Each time, senior generals in the Pentagon were reluctant to undertake special operations against terrorism suspects. Yet Clarke later reported that these senior generals were eager to let the word spread down through the ranks that the politicians in the While House were reluctant to act. They also obliquely communicated this to members of Congress and the media.

Hostile criticism about the missile attacks against Al Qaeda targets in 1998 from Republicans certainly cooled the Clinton administration's ardor for further attempts to capture or kill Al Qaeda chief Osama bin Laden. Yet both the CIA and the Federal Bureau of Investigation (FBI) reported intelligence to the Clinton administration that Al Qaeda was planning terrorist activities within the United States. With these warnings still fresh, the Clinton administration slowly closed down any operations against bin Laden.

After the 1998 embassy attacks, the Clinton administration did attempt to disrupt Al Qaeda's financing. It took legal steps to freeze $240 million in Al Qaeda and Taliban assets in American bank accounts. Assets of Afghanistan's national airline, Ariana Afghan, were also frozen. These actions were inconvenient for Al Qaeda and made it shift its assets into commodities—diamonds and blue tanzanite—and led to the creation or use of Islamic charities to raise funds. Hindering the Clinton administration, however, was the weakness of international money-laundering laws. These laws were particularly weak in Kuwait, Dubai, the United Arab Emirates, Bahrain, and Lebanon. Also, the traditional Islamic banking system, the *hawala,* heavily used in Afghanistan and Pakistan, was cash based, leaving no written or electronic records. These factors brought limited success to the Clinton administration's efforts to restrict the flow of funds to Al Qaeda. Briefings about the urgency of terrorism and the bin Laden threat given by the outgoing Clinton administration to the incoming George W. Bush administration were virtually ignored. On September 11, 2001, less than nine months after Bush's inauguration, Al Qaeda struck the United States with great ferocity, resulting in nearly 3,000 civilian deaths.

After leaving office and after the 9/11 attacks by Al Qaeda, Clinton was insistent that his administration was fully aware of the danger that Al Qaeda posed to the United States but that it could not move quickly enough because neither the CIA nor the FBI was certain beyond all doubt as to Al Qaeda's complicity in the earlier attacks. He claimed that battle plans were already in place for an invasion of Afghanistan and a massive hunt for bin Laden, but the clock on his administration ran out before the plans could be put into motion.

Clinton's second term was also marked by personal scandal and legal problems. Kenneth Starr, the independent counsel investigating Whitewater, leveled against the president charges of sexual misconduct and lying to a federal grand jury. Starr did not, however, ever find evidence of wrongdoing in the Whitewater deal. The Whitewater investigation, which lasted for years, cost $39.2 million. The charges leveled against Clinton, which many suspected were politically motivated, stemmed from a brief dalliance Clinton had with a female White House intern in the mid-1990s and his attempt to conceal that relationship. In September 1998 the U.S. House of Representatives passed two articles of impeachment against the president, but in early 1999 the Senate acquitted Clinton on both counts along party lines. In order to end the Whitewater investigation, Clinton agreed to a five-year suspension of his law license and a $25,000 fine.

After leaving the presidency in January 2001, Clinton assisted his wife in her successful senatorial campaign in

New York and in her failed bid for the presidency in 2008, opened his own office in Harlem in New York City, and established a presidential library in Little Rock, Arkansas. He has also traveled extensively abroad and raised significant sums of money for charitable causes, including AIDS, and, with former president George H. W. Bush, relief for a devastating Asian tsunami. Clinton also helped form the William J. Clinton Foundation (now known simply as the Clinton Foundation), a global outreach enterprise that has helped millions of people around the world, and wrote his memoirs. Clinton continues to be a sought-after speaker and frequently appears on television news programs, voicing his analyses and opinions about both foreign and domestic developments. When Barack Obama won the 2008 Democratic presidential nomination, Clinton campaigned vigorously for him. Hillary Clinton served as Obama's secretary of state from 2009 until 2013, and Bill Clinton once again campaigned for Obama during his successful reelection bid in 2012. On several occasions, the Obama White House has tapped Clinton to give speeches or hold press conferences in support of legislation or other actions spearheaded by the Democrats.

James F. Carroll, Spencer C. Tucker, Stephen E. Atkins,
and Paul G. Pierpaoli Jr.

See also

Al Qaeda; Bin Laden, Osama; Bush, George Walker; Central Intelligence Agency; Clinton, Hillary Rodham; *Cole,* USS, Attack on; Dar es Salaam, Bombing of U.S. Embassy; Global War on Terror; Iraq, History of, 1990–Present; Israel; Nairobi, Kenya, Bombing of U.S. Embassy; Netanyahu, Benjamin; September 11 Attacks; Somalia, International Intervention in; Terrorism; World Trade Center Bombing

References

Benjamin, Daniel, and Steven Simon. *The Age of Sacred Terror.* New York: Random House, 2002.

Blumenthal, Sidney. *The Clinton Wars.* New York: Farrar, Straus and Giroux, 2003.

Clinton, Bill. *My Life.* New York: Knopf, 2004.

Coll, Steve. *Ghost Wars: The Secret History of the CIA, Afghanistan, and Bin Laden, from the Soviet Invasion to September 10, 2001.* New York: Penguin, 2004.

Maraniss, D. *First in His Class.* New York: Simon and Schuster, 1995.

Posner, R. A. *An Affair of State: The Investigation, Impeachment, and Trial of President Clinton.* Cambridge, MA: Harvard University Press, 1999.

Cluster Bombs

See Bombs, Cluster

Coalition Force Land Component Command–Afghanistan

The Coalition Force Land Component Command (CFLCC) was responsible for all land operations in Afghanistan from November 20, 2001, until May 21, 2002, at which time it was reorganized out of existence. Prior to September 11, 2001, the U.S. Third Army, commanded by Lieutenant General Paul T. Mikolashek, served as the Army Component (ARCENT) for U.S. Central Command (CENTCOM) and maintained a forward headquarters at Camp Doha, Kuwait. After the September 11, 2001, attacks on the World Trade Center and the Pentagon, CENTCOM—commanded by General Tommy Franks—responded to the new exigency.

Because ARCENT had already deployed to serve as the CFLCC for an exercise in Egypt, it did not assume control of land operations in the Afghanistan Joint Operational Area (JOA) as CFLCC-Afghanistan until November 20, 2001. Its mission as CFLCC was to direct land operations to destroy Al Qaeda and prevent the reemergence of international terrorist activities within JOA-Afghanistan and support humanitarian operations to create a peaceful and stable environment within Afghanistan. Mikolashek served as commander of CFLCC from November 20, 2001, until May 21, 2002, when command shifted to Lieutenant General Dan McNeil. At that point, CFLCC became a planning arm for the upcoming war in Iraq.

U.S. president George W. Bush ordered military action against the Taliban (Operation Enduring Freedom) on October 7, 2001. CENTCOM developed two ground approaches into Afghanistan. On the northern approach, elements of the 10th Mountain Division deployed to provide security, with other army units providing logistical support, for Joint Special Operation Task Force–North (JSOTF-N). JSOFT-N, with air force and army special operations elements, established a forward operating base at Karshi Kanabad (K2), Uzbekistan. Progress on the southern approach through two remote air bases in central Pakistan was secured initially by elements of the U.S. Marine Corps and later by elements of the 101st Air Assault Division. On November 20 the 10th Mountain Division established CFLCC-Forward headquarters at K2.

During November 25–26, 1,000 marines from the U.S. Fifth Fleet staged through Pakistan to a base near Kandahar to form the 1st Marine Expeditionary Brigade (MEB). Once it was firmly ashore, control over the 1st MEB shifted to the CFLCC. This permitted the CFLCC to expand its forces on the ground and, along with Southern Alliance and U.S. special operations units, to force the Taliban defenders of Kandahar to surrender the city on December 6.

In early December, ARCENT completed the CFLCC Operations Order for Land Operations in Afghanistan. Issued on December 11, 2001, this plan provided broad guidance for supervising the ongoing U.S. Army, U.S. Marine Corps, and special forces ground operations. Critical new tasks from CENTCOM, such as conduct detainee operations and sensitive site exploitation, created new unplanned requirements.

As many as 3,000 Taliban had surrendered to the Northern Alliance in November, and many had rioted as a result of their treatment. After processing, selected detainees would be held in temporary facilities constructed by the CFLCC at Kandahar and Bagram until they could be flown to the U.S. naval base at Guantánamo Bay for further interrogation or military tribunals. ARCENT deployed military police to augment the marines and army infantry units initially pressed into performing these missions and to conduct the detainee aerial escort mission. By August 2002, ARCENT had processed more than 4,500 detainees, transferred 377 to Cuba, repatriated 129 others, and held a further 167 in Afghanistan.

As operations continued around Kandahar, an estimated 1,200 Al Qaeda along with some Taliban, including Osama bin Laden, were detected in caves and tunnels along the Pakistani border in eastern Afghanistan. The offensive against Tora Bora began on December 1, 2001, with intense air strikes supporting Afghan forces advised by the JSOTF-N. Operations continued for several days, with an estimated 200 killed. The escape of large numbers of Al Qaeda indicated the risks of relying on Afghans to achieve U.S. operational goals and prompted General Franks to employ conventional ground forces as well.

Beginning in January 2002, the CFLCC replaced the 1st MEB with Task Force (TF) Rakkasans (3rd Brigade, 101st Airborne Division) and the 3rd Princess Patricia's Canadian Light Infantry Battalion. By the end of February, CFLCC forces had exploited 109 sensitive sites, inspected 59 suspected chemical sites, and delivered more than 1,000 tons of humanitarian assistance while also engaging numerous targets.

The CFLCC's next operation employed U.S. Army ground forces and Afghan allies against a buildup of Al Qaeda forces in the Shah-i-kot Valley. For better supervision, CFLCC-Forward, commanded by Major General Franklin L. Hagenbeck, relocated from Uzbekistan to Bagram on February 13 and became Coalition Joint Task Force (CJTF) Mountain.

Hagenbeck initiated Operation ANACONDA on March 2, 2002. Afghan forces maneuvered while two U.S. infantry battalions supported by army aviation established blocking positions on the slopes of the eastern ridge overlooking the valley. Because of the high altitude and weather, army helicopters would be operating at the outer limit of performance, and only Boeing CH-47 Chinooks would be used to lift the infantry. The assaulting troops suffered numerous wounded casualties on the first day in sharp firefights with Al Qaeda immediately after landing. U.S. infantry once again engaged the enemy in classic close combat, employing organic small arms and mortars. With Al Qaeda fighters so near that air support was often impossible, Hughes/McDonnell Douglas/Boeing AH-64 Apaches became the most effective fire support available to ground commanders, despite withering small-arms fire that damaged all seven of the helicopters.

After the initial engagement, CJTF Mountain obtained additional ground and air assets. The battle continued for several days as the allied air forces worked with Apaches to engage and destroy the determined Al Qaeda fighters. Marine helicopters, flown from ships in the Arabian Sea, and additional Apaches deployed directly from Fort Campbell provided reinforcements. The CFLCC committed the 2nd Brigade, 10th Mountain, with two additional army infantry battalions as well as the Canadians. By March 10, CENTCOM estimated that allied ground and air forces had killed more than 500 of the enemy.

After ANACONDA, the CFLCC shifted its conventional and special operations forces south of Gardez and elsewhere in eastern Afghanistan against remaining Al Qaeda and Taliban enclaves. In mid-April 2002, the CFLCC received additional multinational support from TF Jacana, with 1,700 British personnel drawn from the 3rd Commando Brigade.

At the end of April 2002, ARCENT conducted an assessment of its initial performance as CFLCC-Afghanistan. General Mikolashek observed that because of an imposed force cap of 7,000 personnel in country and unanticipated missions, the CFLCC had not been able to properly employ its units. However, the CFLCC had successfully and creatively integrated air, naval, marine, special operations, allied, and interagency forces in the conduct of a complex and unusual operation. In a move indicative of a long-term U.S. military commitment, XVIII Airborne Corps under Lieutenant General Dan McNeil deployed to Bagram on May 31, 2002, as Combined Joint Task Force 180 and assumed control of U.S. and coalition operations in JOA-Afghanistan. The total number of personnel under the CFLCC by the end of May 2002, at which time the command changed name and focus, was approximately 20,000. This change allowed ARCENT to refocus on the conduct of potential land operations against Iraq.

JOHN A. BONIN

See also

Al Qaeda; ANACONDA, Operation; Combined Joint Task Force 180; ENDURING FREEDOM, Operation, Initial Ground Campaign; Franks, Tommy; McNeill, Dan K.; United States Central Command

References

Bonin, John A. *U.S. Army Forces Central Command in Afghanistan and the Arabian Gulf during Operation Enduring Freedom, 11 September 2001–11 March 2003.* Carlisle, PA: Army Heritage Center Foundation, 2003.

Briscoe, Charles H., Richard L. Kiper, James A. Schroder, and Kalev I. Sepp. *Weapon of Choice: U.S. Army Special Operations Forces in Afghanistan.* Ft. Leavenworth, KS: Combat Studies Institute Press, 2003.

Mikolashek, Paul T. "'Patton's Own' Third U.S. Army: Always First, Versatile, Ready, Warfighting Command." *Army* (October 2002): 201–208.

Coalition Provisional Authority

Established on April 21, 2003, after Saddam Hussein's ouster, the Coalition Provisional Authority (CPA) was the head diplomatic and administrative office for the coalition occupation of Iraq. It was both an international body and an agency of the U.S. government. L. Paul Bremer, head of the CPA, would become associated with two of the most noteworthy actions of the early occupation: the de-Baathification policy and the decision to dissolve the Iraqi military. These two events ultimately spurred the insurgency in Iraq and affected the occupation throughout the remainder of the conflict. The CPA existed until June 28, 2004, when Iraq became a fully sovereign nation upon the authority's dissolution.

The CPA replaced the Office of Reconstruction and Humanitarian Assistance, headed by Jay Garner. The CPA had the approval of the United Nations (UN) Security Council through its resolutions 1483 and 1511, which recognized the occupation authority of both the United States and Britain. These resolutions made the CPA the official organization in charge of administering the occupation. Under U.S. law, the CPA derived its authority from the Emergency Supplemental Appropriations Act for Defense and for the Reconstruction of Iraq and Afghanistan, which was passed in 2003. This meant that the CPA had both international and U.S. authorization to create and implement policies to direct the actions of American and international forces in Iraq.

The CPA had direct oversight of many domestic departments, including the directors of oil policy, civil affairs policy, economic policy, regional operations, security affairs, and communications. In addition, the CPA had a general counsel consisting of a military staff, an operations support group, an executive secretariat, a strategic policy office, and a financial oversight group. It also had its own intelligence organization. Bremer had authority over the chair of the International Coordination Council, the body that organized humanitarian assistance from nongovernmental organizations and the UN.

One problem with the organization of the CPA was the lack of direct control over military forces in Iraq. Although Bremer was the senior U.S. civilian in the nation, he did not have any direct military authority. He could not order military forces to focus on any particular region or conduct any specific type of mission. He could coordinate or communicate his requirements, and although he was the head U.S. and international official in Iraq, he had no command authority. This meant that the CPA had difficulty achieving one of its major objectives, which was the provisioning of security, governance, economic, and essential services.

Iraqis did participate in the CPA, albeit in a limited fashion. The Iraqi Governing Council (IGC) acted as an advisory body to the CPA. The IGC could not veto legislation and initially functioned as more of a pro forma approval body. A point of concern was that Bremer's policies carried the full weight of law inside Iraq; this caused much frustration in the IGC. However, as the CPA's administration in Iraq continued, the IGC grew more confident and began to demand more input and authority over policies and laws considered by the CPA. This led to a deterioration of the CPA's efficiency but an increase in Iraqi sovereignty.

The first actions of the CPA included changes to the nation's currency, dissolution of the military, and elimination of Baath Party officials from most government posts. The two most problematic policies—the dissolution of the military and the de-Baathification policy—did not go through any Iraqi legislative process. The de-Baathification and dissolution of the military policies were the most far-reaching of the CPA policies and had serious second- and third-order effects on the future of the occupation mission in Iraq.

The decision to destroy the Baath Party came on May 16, 2003. This order was the first Bremer gave as head of the organization. The actual decision to remove party officials from government posts and destroy the Baath Party came from Washington. Douglas Fieth, head of the Department of Defense Office of Special Plans, drafted the policy.

Supporters of the policy included Iraqi exiles, Shia groups, and Kurds inside Iraq. For these groups, the Baath Party represented the worst of the Saddam Hussein regime and was inextricably linked to the horror of his rule.

When Bremer announced the policy, he included a caveat that his office could issue exemptions. Many Sunnis feared that de-Baathification would turn into a sectarian program to remove Sunnis from government posts and other positions of influence. The de-Baathification policy also overlooked the reality of life in Iraq and the power of the Baath Party. Many Iraqis under Hussein had to join the party in order to keep their jobs, earn promotions in government service, or get hired for certain government positions. Although Bremer's authority allowed him to offer exemptions, this would prove difficult. If he was too lenient, the policy would not have the desired effect. If he was too hard, he would alienate many of the Sunnis in the country and drive them away from participation in a new Iraq.

The dissolution of the Iraqi military was the second of Bremer's most influential decisions. This policy immediately left approximately 400,000 people unemployed. It also discounted the almost cultlike status that the Iraqi military had in the culture of Iraq. The military was the body that protected the nation from Iran and protected the Arab world from the threat of Persian invasion. Under Hussein, the military was a force that unified the people of Iraq. Dissolving this organization was a blow not only to the almost half a million soldiers employed by it but also to the identity of Iraq as a nation.

The CPA was short-lived; it ended its existence on June 28, 2004, with the resumption of full Iraqi sovereignty. It then turned over authority to the Iraqi Interim Government. However, the CPA did not leave the new government of Iraq a smooth path forward as it struggled to deal with the budding insurgency and growing sectarian strife.

GATES BROWN

See also

Baath Party; Bremer, Lewis Paul; Feith, Douglas; Garner, Jay Montgomery; Hussein, Saddam; Iraq, History of, 1990–Present; United Nations; United Nations Security Council Resolution 1483

References

Allawi, Ali. *The Occupation of Iraq: Winning the War.* New Haven, CT: Yale University Press, 2007.

Bensahel, Nora. *After Saddam: Prewar Planning and the Occupation of Iraq.* Santa Monica, CA: RAND Arroyo Center, 2008.

Sanchez, Ricardo, and Donald Philips. *Wiser in Battle: A Soldier's Story.* New York: HarperCollins, 2008.

Coercive Interrogation

Methods of interrogation meant to compel a person to behave in an involuntary way or reveal information by use of threat, intimidation, or physical force or abuse. In particular, coercive interrogation has been used during the U.S. Middle East wars to obtain information from prisoners, especially those being held as terrorists. Coercive interrogation has been labeled by numerous individuals and organizations as inhumane torture and war crimes that violate international law. In addition, coercive interrogation has been criticized by many for being ineffective; critics contend that it leads to false confessions.

There are various techniques of interrogation that can be described as coercive, including, but not limited to, sleep deprivation, food deprivation, ceaseless noise, sexual abuse, forced nakedness, cultural humiliation, exposure to extreme cold, prolonged isolation, painful postures, beating, and waterboarding. Waterboarding, a highly controversial interrogation method, involves positioning a victim on his back, with the head in a downward position, while pouring water over the face and head. As water enters the nasal passages and mouth, the victim believes that drowning is imminent. Waterboarding is a favored interrogation technique because it leaves no visible marks on the victim and can be very effective in extracting confessions.

During the 1991 Persian Gulf War, records indicate that the U.S. military generally abided by international law concerning treatment of civilian and military detainees. However, there is ample evidence that Iraqis tortured American prisoners of war by employing numerous coercive interrogation techniques. Coercive interrogation became a much larger issue during the George W. Bush administration after the Global War on Terror began in 2001. Although many international agreements signed by the United States forbid torture, President Bush, Vice President Richard Cheney, and his administration supported the use of coercive interrogation in the Global War on Terror, the Afghanistan War, and the Iraq War. After the September 11, 2001, terrorist attacks on the United States, the Bush administration acknowledged a need for new interrogation techniques.

Shortly after the September 11 attacks, the Bush administration worked to gain support for coercive interrogation techniques and began to change the definition of torture to better suit its needs. Numerous senior officials believed that the Central Intelligence Agency (CIA) had to employ coercive interrogation techniques to deal with Al Qaeda suspects and other terrorists. The administration now began to devise arguments for going against prevailing prescriptions vis-à-vis torture. First, Bush believed that as commander in chief he could use the inherent powers given to him in the U.S. Constitution to stretch U.S. policy to best protect the citizens of the United States. The administration argued repeatedly that terrorism is a major threat that cannot be fought with conventional means. Also, the White House repeatedly stated that coercive interrogation is not torture in the strict sense of the word. Most legal scholars on the subject disagree with this assessment.

Beginning in 2004, accounts surfaced of Iraqi prisoners being abused by U.S. soldiers in the Abu Ghraib prison in Iraq. Pictures showing U.S. military personnel abusing and violating prisoners by various means proved highly incendiary. Some methods used included urinating on prisoners, punching prisoners excessively, pouring phosphoric acid on prisoners, rape, forcing prisoners to strip nude and attaching electrodes to their genitals, or photographing prisoners in compromising positions to humiliate them. Eventually, 17 soldiers and officers were removed from duty because of the Abu Ghraib scandal; some eventually faced criminal charges and trial.

The situation was compounded when the CIA was accused of having destroyed evidence of the torture of civilian detainees in 2005. There were apparently two videotapes (subsequently destroyed) that contained images of Al Qaeda suspects being tortured. By 2007, the CIA admitted to some use of coercive interrogation. However, the agency admitted that this had happened rarely and that techniques such as waterboarding were used fewer than five times. In a television interview in December 2008, Vice President Cheney admitted that he has supported the use of waterboarding. More allegations of CIA-sponsored torture surfaced, but the Bush administration stuck to its support of coercive interrogation techniques, asserting that they were not cruel and unusual and therefore did not constitute torture. Nevertheless, under considerable pressure, Bush signed an executive order in July 2007 forbidding the use of torture against terror suspects; it did not, however, specifically ban waterboarding.

In early 2008, waterboarding was again a hot topic as Congress considered an antitorture bill designed largely to limit the CIA's use of coercive interrogation. The bill, which was passed in February 2008, would have forced the CIA to abide by the rules found in the *Army Field Manual on Interrogation* (FM 34-52). The manual forbids the use of physical force and includes a list of approved interrogation methods; waterboarding is not among them.

Arizona senator John McCain, who had been brutally tortured as a prisoner of war during the Vietnam War and had already engaged in a war of words with the Bush White House over the use of torture, voted against the bill. McCain, in defending his vote, argued that the CIA should have the ability to use techniques that are not listed in the *Army Field Manual of Interrogation*. He argued that there are other techniques available that are effective and not cruel and unusual. He continued to claim, however, that waterboarding is torture and illegal. Bush vetoed the February 2008 bill, and its proponents did not have the requisite votes to override it.

In 2009 after the Barack Obama administration began, President Obama stated his clear objection to most coercive interrogation techniques, including waterboarding. His attorney general, Eric Holder, told a Senate committee in January 2009 that he considered waterboarding a form of torture. However, several months later the Obama White House demurred on taking any prosecutorial or retributive actions against Bush administration officials—or other government personnel—who had authorized, condoned, or employed questionable interrogation methods. On January 29, 2009, Obama signed an executive order mandating that the CIA use only 19 interrogation methods as outlined in the *Army Field Manual on Interrogation* unless it sought specific exemptions from the attorney general. Although the justified flap over coercive interrogation has now faded into the background, there are those who continue to insist that the Obama administration's decision not to investigate or prosecute those responsible for such action is tantamount to culpability.

Arthur M. Holst

See also

Abu Ghraib; Al Qaeda; Bush, George Walker; Central Intelligence Agency; McCain, John Sidney, III; Obama, Barack Hussein, II; Torture of Prisoners

References

Bellamy, Alex J. "No Pain, No Gain? Torture and Ethics in the War on Terror." *International Affairs* 82 (2006): 121–148.

Dershowitz, Alan M. *Is There a Right to Remain Silent: Coercive Interrogation and the Fifth Amendment after 9/11*. Oxford: Oxford University Press, 2008.

Guiora, Amos N. *Constitutional Limits on Coercive Interrogation*. New York: Oxford University Press, 2008.

"Obama's Justice Department Grants Final Immunity to Bush's CIA Torture." *The Guardian*, August 31, 2012, http://www.theguardian.com/commentisfree/2012/aug/31/obama-justice-department-immunity-bush-cia-torturer.

Posner, Eric A., and Adrian Vermeule. *Terror in the Balance? Security, Liberty, and the Courts*. New York: Oxford University Press, 2007.

Cohen, William Sebastian (1940–)

Republican politician, U.S. senator, and secretary of defense (1997–2001). William Sebastian Cohen was born in Bangor, Maine, on August 28, 1940, to Russian immigrant parents. He attended Bowdoin College, graduating in 1962, and received a law degree from Boston University in 1965. After law school, he returned to Maine to practice law. Cohen subsequently became assistant county attorney for Penobscot and also served on the Bangor school board. In 1969 he was elected to the Bangor City Council, and during 1971–1972 he was mayor of Bangor.

In 1972 Cohen ran as a Republican to succeed Democratic congressman William Hathaway, who became a U.S. senator from Maine. Cohen won election to the U.S. House of Representatives and was reelected twice. In 1978 he ran against Hathaway for a Senate seat and won. During his three terms in the Senate (1979–1997) Cohen focused on national security issues, serving on the Senate Armed Services Committee and the Senate Intelligence Committee. He also served on the Governmental Affairs Committee. Cohen announced his retirement from the Senate in 1996 ostensibly to pursue other career objectives.

Later that year, however, after President Bill Clinton won reelection, Cohen was nominated to become secretary of defense. Although a Republican, Cohen was considered a moderate, and Clinton believed that his presence in the post would help to build a bipartisan consensus around his foreign policy. Cohen subsequently accepted the nomination, which sailed unanimously through the Republican-controlled Senate.

As defense secretary, Cohen focused on developing a lighter and more mobile and modernized fighting force and investing in new weapons systems. He did this while continuing to maintain the "two regional wars" template that had been part of Pentagon planning for many years. That is, U.S. forces were to be kept ready to wage two regional wars simultaneously. Cohen also drew increasing attention to the dangers posed by the proliferation of weapons of mass destruction (WMD), and he oversaw the expansion of the North Atlantic Treaty Organization (NATO) into Eastern Europe.

Cohen remained uneasy over troop commitments in the Balkans made during Clinton's first term, fearing that protracted humanitarian and peacekeeping missions might endanger U.S. forces. Cohen was also concerned that money expended on such endeavors might be better spent elsewhere. These monetary issues were real concerns for Cohen, given the budgetary constraints under which he had to work.

Indeed, because of the Clinton administration's determined plan to erase decades-long budget deficits and pay down some of the national debt, spending more on defense during a time of peace was not a viable option.

Cohen oversaw U.S. operations in the Balkans during his tenure in office. When Serbian forces began ethnic cleansing against Albanian Muslims from Kosovo, the United States, in concert with NATO, responded with a bombing campaign to force the Serbs to the peace table. This operation began on March 24, 1999, and ended on June 10, 1999, when the Yugoslav government agreed to return to the negotiating table. A number of naysayers believed that the bombing campaign was folly, but the relatively quick success of it silenced many of Clinton's critics who had derided his Balkans policy. Despite his reservations about troop deployments to the Balkans, Cohen nevertheless hoped to stop Serbian aggression. His public disagreement with General Wesley Clark, NATO's supreme allied commander who insisted that ground troops might be needed in Kosovo, led to the general's early retirement in 2000.

When Al Qaeda bombed U.S. embassies on August 7, 1998, in Dar es Salaam, Tanzania, and Nairobi, Kenya, Cohen oversaw the American response on August 20, 1998. Operation INFINITE REACH saw U.S. cruise missile attacks on sites in Afghanistan and Sudan. Much controversy surrounded the operation, however, as the Sudanese target in all likelihood was not a chemical weapons facility but rather a pharmaceutical plant. Some of President Clinton's detractors charged that the attacks were designed to take the public's attention off the Monica Lewinsky scandal, which was then being fully revealed.

Cohen also oversaw American military operations in Iraq. In 1998 after the consistent Iraqi failure to comply with United Nations (UN) weapons inspectors and UN Security Council resolutions, the United States and Great Britain authorized Operation DESERT FOX, which resulted in the bombing of Iraqi targets during December 16–19, 1998. Targets were chosen so as to disrupt the Iraqi regime but also to degrade the ability of the regime to produce WMD. Some Republicans attacked the timing of the largely ineffective operation as politically motivated, as it occurred at the same time as House impeachment hearings. In the aftermath of the September 11, 2001, terror attacks, many commentators criticized these responses as too tepid.

Since leaving office Cohen has been generally supportive of the Global War on Terror, although he has consistently argued that the nation should do more to gird itself for such an effort, including making shared sacrifices and instituting some form of compulsory national service. He currently presides over the Cohen Group, an international business consulting firm based in Washington, D.C., and has authored several books (including fiction) and many articles and essays.

MICHAEL K. BEAUCHAMP

See also

Al Qaeda; Clinton, William Jefferson; Global War on Terror; September 11 Attacks

References

Halberstam, David. *War in a Time of Peace: Bush, Clinton, and the Generals.* New York: Scribner, 2001.

Harris, John F. *The Survivor: Bill Clinton in the White House.* New York: Random House, 2005.

Cold War Peace Dividend, U.S. Troop/Force Structure Reductions

In the aftermath of the Cold War, the administrations of U.S. presidents George H. W. Bush and William J. Clinton sought to reduce military expenditures to secure a peace dividend whereby spending previously devoted to defense could be redirected to social programs, internal infrastructure improvements, etc. As early as the 1970s, U.S. officials had sought an elusive peace dividend from savings following the Vietnam War, which ended for the United States in January 1973.

In the late 1980s as Cold War tensions eased substantially, the Bush administration developed plans to reduce the nation's force structure while also cutting spending on advanced weaponry, including weapons of mass destruction (WMD). The administration pursued a three-track strategy that included reductions in standing troops and the redeployment of forces, consolidation of military bases and facilities, and arms control and disarmament efforts. All three tracks were interrelated. As arms control measures such as the 1990 Treaty on Conventional Forces in Europe mandated significant cuts in standing military forces in Europe, the United States was able to redeploy and reduce troop strength and eliminate both foreign and domestic bases. The United States was also able to decommission sizable numbers of nuclear missile forces, a result of historic arms-reduction efforts begun under Bush's predecessor, President Ronald Reagan.

Under the Bush administration, the number of active-duty U.S. military personnel was reduced from 2.24 million in 1989 to 1.92 million by 1992. The number of U.S.

forces deployed overseas was also reduced significantly. For example, U.S. forces in Europe declined from 300,000 in 1989 to 150,000 by 1993. U.S. military expenditures fell from 5.5 percent of gross domestic product (GDP) to 4.8 percent from 1989. Overall, defense spending fell from $303.4 billion in 1989 to $273.3 billion in 1991 before rising again to $298.4 billion in 1992 with the costs associated with the 1991 Persian Gulf War. Bush reoriented U.S. defense policy so that the nation's military was no longer mandated to be prepared to fight two major military campaigns simultaneously (for instance, a World War II–style campaign in Europe and a similar effort in Asia). Instead, the Pentagon was required to be ready to fight simultaneously two regional conflicts of the size and scale of the 1991 Persian Gulf War. The administration also initiated a series of military facility closures and consolidations under the Base Realignment and Closure Commission (BRAC). Throughout the 1990s there were four rounds of cuts under BRAC, including the closure of 97 major domestic bases and 55 realignments. Overseas, more than 960 facilities were closed. BRAC produced $16 billion in savings during the 1990s, with annual savings thereafter of at least $6 billion.

In 1993 the Clinton administration launched the Bottom-Up Review (BUR) of U.S. defense needs and capabilities. BUR kept the requirement to fight two simultaneous regional conflicts but suggested a new approach, the win-hold-win strategy in which the country would maintain the capability to win one regional war while preventing defeat in the second (the hold strategy). After victory in the first conflict, forces would be redeployed to the second to gain victory. BUR also recommended $105 billion in defense cuts through 1999. These recommendations became the basis for the Clinton administration's defense policy.

By 2000, U.S. forces had been reduced to 1.49 million, while defense expenditures had been cut to 3 percent of GDP. Defense spending declined from 1993 through 1998, falling from $291.1 billion in 1993 to $268.5 billion in 1998; however, spending did increase in 1999 and 2000, rising to $294.5 billion the last full year Clinton was in office (2000).

A range of problems emerged with the Cold War peace dividend. The first was that the reduction in defense expenditures contributed to the 1992–1993 recession, as defense firms cut research and production and laid off approximately one-third of all their civilian workers by the late 1990s. Especially hard hit were California, Massachusetts, and Texas, which were home to significant numbers of high-tech and defense-related firms. There was also a wave of mergers and consolidations among military contractors, resulting in an industry dominated by several large firms including Boeing, General Dynamics, Halliburton, Northrop Grumman, and Lockheed Martin. By 1998, more than 500 smaller defense firms had gone out of business or been acquired by larger competitors.

In addition, the BRAC closings had a significant impact on many communities that had come to depend on military facilities to power the local economy. While some localities were able to recover quickly by using the former military facilities in new and often innovative ways, other towns and cities were hard-pressed to replace the impact of federal outlays. One result was increased political opposition to BRAC's recommendations. The cuts in military personnel were not accompanied by significant alterations in force structures in that the U.S. military continued to emphasize conventional forces designed to counter Cold War–style threats instead of transitioning to lighter, more mobile forces. Troop reductions also created future problems by increasing the reliance on military reserve units and National Guard forces. This became a major problem after 2003, when the George W. Bush administration attempted to wage two wars simultaneously without making any arrangements for a larger standing force.

By 2007–2008 amid the troop surge in Iraq, America's armed forces were being stretch to the limit, with military personnel enduring multiple deployments to Iraq and Afghanistan and with more and more reservists and National Guardsmen being pressed into active duty. By 2012 after U.S. troops had been withdrawn from Iraq, the situation had stabilized, however.

TOM LANSFORD

See also
Bush, George Walker; Clinton, William Jefferson

References
Braddon, Derek. *Exploding the Myth? The Peace Dividend, Regions and Market Adjustment.* Amsterdam: Oversees Publishers Association, 2000.

Hogan, Michael J., ed. *The End of the Cold War: Its Meaning and Implications.* New York: Cambridge University Press, 1992.

Markusen, Ann, Peter Hall, Scott Campbell, and Sabrina Deitrick. *The Rise of the Gunbelt: The Military Remapping of Industrial America.* New York: Oxford University Press, 1991.

Cole, USS, Attack on (October 12, 2000)

The attack on USS *Cole* in Yemen on October 12, 2000, marked the first time a modern U.S. Navy warship was successfully targeted by terrorists. On October 12, 2000, the 8,600-ton displacement (full load), 506-foot-long U.S. Navy destroyer *Cole* (DDG-67) was docked in the Yemeni port of Aden for a refueling stop. At 11:18 a.m. local time, 2 suicide bombers in a small harbor skiff pulled alongside the anchored ship and detonated explosives. The blast killed both bombers and 17 members of the *Cole*'s crew; another 39 were injured.

The explosives blew a gaping hole in the ship's hull that measured 35 feet high and 36 feet long. Crew members aboard the *Cole* clearly recollect having seen the two men as they approached the ship. The bombers, however, made no untoward moves and indeed appeared friendly. Several aboard the *Cole* believed that the men were workers for the harbor services, collecting trash or performing some other kind of routine task. When the skiff neared the ship, there was no warning of trouble until the explosion.

Three days later, the stricken destroyer was taken aboard the Norwegian ship *Blue Marlin* off Yemen and transported to the United States. It reached its home port of Norfolk, Virginia, in December and continued on to Pascagoula, Mississippi, for extensive renovations. Repairs took approximately one year and cost more than $240 million. While still undergoing repair, the ship was towed a short distance to a mooring at Ingalls Shipbuilding in southern Mississippi on September 16, 2001, in a symbolic message of the nation's resolve following the September 11, 2001, World Trade Center and Pentagon attacks.

U.S. and Yemeni officials stated on the day after the bombing that key suspects in the affair had fled to safety in Afghanistan. There was no immediate credible claim of responsibility, but American officials made Al Qaeda and Osama bin Laden the focus of their investigation. Still, however, some military and national security officials faulted the Bill Clinton and George W. Bush administrations for failing to take appropriate retaliatory measures after the bombing.

The *Cole* bombing prompted an investigation into the ease with which the attackers were able to approach the ship. An initial Pentagon inquiry found that the commanding officer had acted reasonably and that the facts did not warrant any punitive action against him or any other member of the *Cole*'s crew.

Coordination between U.S. and Yemeni officials investigating the incident was aided by a counterterrorism agreement signed by Yemen and the United States in 1998, and the trial of 12 suspects formally commenced in June 2004. In late September 2004, Abd al-Rahim al-Nashiri and Jamal

Port side view showing the damage sustained by the U.S. Navy Arleigh Burke-class destroyer *Cole* on October 12, 2000, after a terrorist bomb exploded during a refueling stop in the port of Aden, Yemen. Seventeen U.S. sailors died in the attack. (U.S. Department of Defense)

Mohammed al-Badawi both received the death penalty for their participation in the terrorist act. Four other participants were sentenced to 5–10 years in jail.

PAUL G. PIERPAOLI JR.

See also

Al Qaeda; Bin Laden, Osama; Global War on Terror; Terrorism; Yemen

References

Williams, Paul. *The Al Qaeda Connection: International Terrorism, Organized Crime, and the Coming Apocalypse.* Amherst, NY: Prometheus Books, 2005.

Wright, Lawrence. *The Looming Tower: Al-Qaeda and the Road to 9/11.* New York: Vintage Books, 2007.

Combat Applications Group

See Delta Force

Combined Forces Command, Afghanistan

The highest-level U.S. military command in Afghanistan for Operation ENDURING FREEDOM from November 2003 to February 2007. By the spring of 2003, combat operations in Afghanistan had scaled down. As a result of the relatively stable environment in the country and to conserve manpower, which was now crucial with the beginning of Operation IRAQI FREEDOM in March 2003, the headquarters in Afghanistan shifted from a three-star corps-level command down to that of a two-star division level, designated Combined Joint Task Force 180 (CJTF-180). Overwhelmed with too many tasks, however, CJTF-180 focused on issues relating directly to military operations rather than on larger political and strategic concerns.

In the summer of 2003 the commanding general of U.S. Central Command, General John Abizaid, decided that

Afghanistan required a different and more effective head-quarters organization that could focus on political-military efforts. In September 2003 Abizaid ordered the creation of a new three-star–level coalition headquarters in Afghanistan to take over high-level political, military, and strategic planning, which would permit the divisional headquarters to focus on combat operations. Newly promoted lieutenant general David W. Barno took command in October 2003.

Barno moved the new headquarters out of Bagram Air Base, which was the headquarters for CJTF-180, into the Afghan capital of Kabul. He began with a staff of six and had to borrow facilities and personnel from CJTF-180 to operate. Staff also came from active-duty personnel from all U.S. military services and from the U.S. reserve forces as individual ready reservists and individual mobilization augmentees, service members serving separately from rather than with a unit. Coalition partners also contributed personnel. Great Britain, for example, filled the deputy commander position. In early 2004 the new headquarters was designated Combined Forces Command–Afghanistan (CFC-A). By 2005, the CFC-A had grown to a staff of more than 400 personnel, about 10 percent of whom were from coalition nations including France, South Korea, and Turkey. The CFC-A provided needed continuity because rotations of the staff were staggered to keep some personnel with knowledge and experience in the command at all times; meanwhile, combat units rotating through Afghanistan stayed for a year or less and were replaced with units often unfamiliar with conditions on the ground.

The CFC-A was responsible for Afghanistan as well as southern Uzbekistan, southern Tajikistan, and Pakistan, with the exception of Jammu and Kashmir. CFC-A commanders regularly traveled and coordinated with senior leadership in these countries. During the command's duration, Afghan and Pakistani leaders met with the CFC-A commander for a quarterly conference to coordinate border security and other issues. Under Barno's command, the CFC-A also had a close working relationship with the U.S. embassy in Kabul, headed by Ambassador Zalmay Khalilzad. Taking a few staff members with him, Barno moved into an office in the embassy and lived in a trailer complex within the embassy compound. Barno and Khalilzad coordinated and integrated military and civilian efforts throughout Afghanistan.

In early 2004 Barno established regional commands, designated Regional Command East, Regional Command South, and Regional Command West. The regional commanders assumed responsibility for all military forces in their areas of operation. Before this change military units stayed on large bases, went out into the countryside to conduct an operation for a week or two, and then returned to their bases. The new organization allowed commanders to become more familiar with their areas of operation, work in them for the duration of their tours of duty in Afghanistan, and build relationships with local Afghans as part of a counterinsurgency campaign to prevent the reemergence of the Taliban and other insurgent groups.

One of the first tasks of the CFC-A was to create a campaign plan for Afghanistan to address security, stability, and reconstruction issues. Begun by the British director of planning, this campaign plan evolved into a counterinsurgency approach supported by the U.S. embassy, the Afghan government, and the international community. It required keeping the Afghan people the central focus of the campaign rather than killing the enemy. The strategy included a broad range of activities meant to defeat terrorism and deny the enemy safe sanctuary, enable the Afghans to provide their own security, promote good local and provincial governments, and encourage reconstruction.

During his tenure, Barno had to respond to accusations that American military personnel acted too aggressively and used firepower too heavily when conducting military operations. As a result, the CFC-A created a list of guidelines for American military personnel to follow during operations in order to reduce tensions with the Afghan people. One guideline, for example, required service members to ask locals to open locked doors whenever possible instead of forcing entry.

Lieutenant General Karl W. Eikenberry took over command of the CFC-A in May 2005, shifting the emphasis of operations back to fighting enemy forces. He also moved back into the military compound located at Bagram Air Base. Eikenberry oversaw the transition of Operation ENDURING FREEDOM from an American-led operation to an effort led by the international community. In mid-2005 the North Atlantic Treaty Organization (NATO) began to take responsibility for military operations in Afghanistan, beginning in the north and moving into the west and south. In late 2006 NATO assumed command of all operations throughout Afghanistan except for an area along the Pakistani border, which U.S. forces still controlled.

With this shift in responsibility to NATO, Eikenberry supervised the closure of the CFC-A, which was deactivated in February 2007. Combined Joint Task Force 76, a division-level command based on the U.S. Army's Southern European Task Force and 173rd Airborne Brigade, both deployed from Italy, assumed responsibility for all U.S.

forces in Afghanistan, while the Combined Security Transition Command–Afghanistan, another division-level command, retained the mission to train the Afghan National Army and police forces. Before the dissolution of the CFC-A, General John Abizaid presented the command with three Joint Meritorious Unit Awards.

LISA MARIE MUNDEY

See also

Abizaid, John Philip; Afghanistan; Barno, David William; Combined Joint Task Force 180; Combined Security Transition Command–Afghanistan; Eikenberry, Karl W.; North Atlantic Treaty Organization; United States Central Command

References

Barno, David W. "Fighting 'The Other War': Counterinsurgency Strategy in Afghanistan, 2003–2005." *Military Review* (September–October 2007): 32–44.

Combat Studies Institute, Contemporary Operations Study Group. *A Different Kind of War: The United States Army Operation Enduring Freedom (OEF), September 2001–September 2005.* Fort Leavenworth, KS: Combat Studies Institute Press, 2009.

Rasanayagam, Angelo. *Afghanistan: A Modern History.* London: I. B. Tauris, 2005.

Stewart, Richard W. *The United States Army in Afghanistan: Operation Enduring Freedom, October 2001–March 2002.* Washington, DC: U.S. Government Printing Office, 2003.

Combined Joint Task Force 180

The highest-level U.S. military organization in Afghanistan during Operation ENDURING FREEDOM from May 2002 to November 2003. The Combined Joint Task Force (CJTF) included the two-star divisional command from November 2003 to February 2007 and one of the two division-level U.S. military headquarters from February 2007 onward.

In December 2001 Major General Franklin L. Hagenbeck established a military headquarters to command U.S. Army forces operating in Afghanistan. In accordance with standard operations, it was designated Coalition Forces Land Component Command Forward, or CFLCC-Forward. Located in Karshi Kandabad, Uzbekistan, CFLCC-Forward oversaw combat operations and logistics during the early phases of Operation ENDURING FREEDOM, which had begun in October 2001. While CFLCC-Forward commanded U.S. Army forces, other military units, such as air assets, special operations forces, and coalition troops, all reported through separate chains of command and to different commanders.

A new three-star corps-level headquarters was created to bring U.S. military forces in Afghanistan under one senior commander, who reported directly to U.S. Central Command (CENTCOM), the organization that has overall authority for U.S. military operations in the Middle East. In May 2002 Lieutenant General Daniel K. McNeill took command of the new headquarters, designated Combined Joint Task Force 180 (CJTF-180). It was established at Bagram Air Base, close to Afghanistan's capital, Kabul. Personnel for CJTF-180 came from the XVIII Airborne Corps Headquarters as well as from the U.S. Marine Corps, the U.S. Air Force, and coalition forces. A brigadier general from the U.S. Air Force acted as both the deputy commander for CJTF-180 and the commander for the air component. Aviation, logistics, special forces, and civil-military operations all reported to CJTF-180.

Hagenbeck's command, now renamed Coalition Task Force Mountain, became subordinate to CJTF-180. Coalition Task Force Mountain served as the tactical headquarters directing ground forces. The CJTF-180's mission focused on hunting down the remnants of the Taliban and Al Qaeda. Combat operations centered on the Afghan-Pakistani border and included air assaults into areas of suspected enemy activity, the use of aerial bombardment against enemy compounds, the capture of Al Qaeda and Taliban fighters and leaders, and the interception of enemy forces along the border. In 2002 the 82nd Airborne took over responsibility for CJTF-180, and the 10th Mountain Division returned for another rotation leading CJTF-180 in 2003.

American and coalition military operations successfully disrupted Al Qaeda and Taliban forces. By the spring of 2003 the military scaled back combat operations to focus on stability and reconstruction efforts. With this shift in focus and to save on manpower with a new war beginning in Iraq in March 2003, CJTF-180 was downsized to a two-star division. The smaller CJTF-180 continued to have responsibility for tasks usually given to three-star commands as well as the duties assigned to two-star headquarters. Overwhelmed with too many missions, CJTF-180 focused on issues relating directly to combat operations rather than the larger strategic concerns of a corps-level headquarters. To address this issue, CENTCOM ordered the creation of a new three-star headquarters in October 2003, designated Combined Forces Command–Afghanistan (CFC-A). While CFC-A took over strategic and political efforts, CJTF-180 served as the two-star division-level command for combat operations. CJTF-180 then initiated a series of campaigns to fight the growing Taliban insurgency and clear the Afghan-Pakistani border of enemy forces. In December 2003 CJTF-180 forces also provided security for the Afghan *loya jirga* (grand assembly) that established a new constitution.

When the 25th Infantry Division rotated into Afghanistan in April 2004, it took over responsibility for CJTF-180, which was renamed CJTF-76. CJTF-76 conducted combat and presence patrols in villages, air assault operations into suspected enemy strongholds, and cordon and search operations to cut off and surround suspected enemy compounds. It also provided security for national elections, supporting reconstruction efforts and tightening border security. By 2004 the Taliban had changed tactics from fighting coalition forces in large numbers to targeting soft nonmilitary targets, such as civilian aid agencies. As a response, the coalition adopted a counterinsurgency strategy to develop relationships with the Afghan people rather than focusing exclusively on combat operations to kill and capture enemy forces. In May 2005 the Southern European Task Force replaced the 25th Infantry Division as the CJTF-76.

In mid-2005 the North Atlantic Treaty Organization (NATO) began to take over responsibility for combat operations in Afghanistan, assuming full control in late 2006. With this change in command authority, the CFC-A was inactivated in February 2007, elevating CJTF-76 to the highest U.S. combat command in Afghanistan. The Combined Security Transition Command is the other divisional command and had the responsibility for training Afghan security forces. The CJTF controlled Regional Command East, which encompassed 14 provinces along the Afghan-Pakistani border. Its mission was to provide security along the border, support the Afghan Army and police forces, remove corrupt or ineffective provincial leaders, and continue to seek out and destroy Al Qaeda and Taliban forces.

The designation for the CJTF changed with each new rotation. During 2006–2007 the 82nd Airborne named it CJTF-82, and the 101st Airborne named it CJTF-101 during the next rotation. Although the CJTF continued to search for suspected insurgents and conducted combat operations to deny sanctuary to enemy forces, the Taliban regained strength and numbers beginning in 2007. As a result, the CJTF refocused it efforts on killing enemy forces and an aggressive use of airpower. The CJTF underwent several subsequent permutations, with the final command designated CJTF-10. The mission ended on November 4, 2014, as the NATO mandate in Afghanistan transitioned to a support role, Resolution Support Mission. At the beginning of 2015, approximately 7,000 regular U.S. Army troops remained in the country.

LISA MARIE MUNDEY

See also

Afghanistan; Afghanistan War; Coalition Force Land Component Command–Afghanistan; Combined Forces Command, Afghanistan; Combined Security Transition Command–Afghanistan; Hagenbeck, Franklin L.; North Atlantic Treaty Organization; Status of Forces Agreement, U.S.-Afghan; United States Central Command

References

Barno, David W. "Fighting 'The Other War': Counterinsurgency Strategy in Afghanistan, 2003–2005." *Military Review* (September–October 2007): 32–44.

Combat Studies Institute Contemporary Operations Study Group, *A Different Kind of War: The United States Army Operation Enduring Freedom (OEF), September 2001–September 2005.* Fort Leavenworth, KS: Combat Studies Institute Press, 2009.

"New Afghanistan Pact Means America's Longest War Will Last At Least Until 2024." *The Guardian,* September 30, 2014, http://www.theguardian.com/world/2014/sep/30/us-troops-afghanistan-2024-obama-bilateral-security-agreement.

Rasanayagam, Angelo. *Afghanistan: A Modern History.* London: I. B. Tauris, 2005.

Stewart, Richard W. *The United States Army in Afghanistan: Operation Enduring Freedom, October 2001–March 2002.* Washington, DC: U.S. Government Printing Office, 2003.

Combined Security Transition Command–Afghanistan

The mission of the Combined Security Transition Command–Afghanistan (CSTC-A) is to assist in the development of a stable Afghanistan, strengthen the rule of law, and combat terrorism by working in partnership with the government of the Islamic Republic of Afghanistan and other elements of the international community that are engaged in coordinated activities. As a primary component of this mission, the CSTC-A provides plans and programs and implements reforms for the Afghan National Security Forces (ANSF), which consists of the Afghan National Army and the Afghan National Police (ANP). On April 4, 2006, the Office of Security Cooperation–Afghanistan (OSC-A) was redesignated the CSTC-A and headquartered at Camp Eggers in Kabul. The CSTC-A, which is under the organizational control of the U.S. Central Command, is a joint military services organization that draws military personnel from several coalition partners and employs thousands of civilian contract personnel.

The CSTC-A provides military and civilian personnel to help both the Afghan Ministry of Defense and the Ministry of the Interior organize, train, equip, employ, and support the ANSF in its war against the Taliban and Al Qaeda insurgency and its allied functions of providing internal security, fostering conditions for economic development, and gaining the support of Afghanistan's populace. The goal is to create an ANSF that is professional, literate, representative of the ethnic diversity of the country, and competent to perform its security functions.

Examples of specific tasks include recruiting soldiers and policemen; providing training both for the personnel and the recruiters; organizing the Ministry of Defense and Ministry of the Interior; mentoring the military general staff and civilian political leaders; acquiring weapons, uniforms, and equipment; and developing policies and processes required by a modern army and police force. The CSTC-A also assists the ANSF in establishing matériel acquisition systems, personnel systems, and other internal infrastructure needed for effective security forces and operations.

The CSTC-A also had operational control over the Combined Joint Task Force–Phoenix (CJTF-Phoenix), which had a military strength of more than 6,000 personnel. CJTF-Phoenix concentrated directly on training, mentoring, and advising the Afghan National Army and the ANP. CJTF-Phoenix was gradually phased out after 2009, however. The CSTC-A also coordinates with other international groups that are engaged in similar tasks, such as the European Police Mission in Afghanistan, which was scheduled to be phased out at the end of 2014.

The CSTC-A is a prime example of the evolving and changing administrative structures dedicated to developing and assisting Afghanistan in assuming responsibility for its own destiny. Although the North Atlantic Treaty Organization mission mandate ended on December 31, 2014, the CSTC-A endured, as U.S. and coalition forces took up a mainly support role that will focus on continued training for Afghan security and military forces, with counterterrorism also a major mission for coalition forces in Afghanistan.

JOE P. DUNN

See also

Afghanistan; Combined Forces Command, Afghanistan; International Security Assistance Force; Taliban; Task Force Phoenix; United States Central Command

References

Barno, David W. "Fighting 'The Other War': Counterinsurgency Strategy in Afghanistan, 2003–2005." *Military Review* (September October 2007): 32 44.

Combat Studies Institute, Contemporary Operations Study Group. *A Different Kind of War: The United States Army Operation Enduring Freedom (OEF), September 2001–September 2005.* Fort Leavenworth, KS: Combat Studies Institute Press, 2009.

Jalali, Ali A. "The Future of Afghanistan." *Parameters* (Spring 2006): 4–19.

Maloney, Sean M. *Enduring the Freedom: A Rogue Historian in Afghanistan.* Washington, DC: Potomac Books, 2007.

Sundquist, Leah R. *NATO in Afghanistan: A Progress Report.* Carlisle Barracks, PA: U.S. Army War College, 2008.

Cone, Robert (1957–)

U.S. Army officer who commanded the Combined Security Transition Command–Afghanistan (CSTC-A) from July 16, 2007, until December 15, 2008. The CSTC-A employs military personnel from a number of coalition nations and civilian contract agents in a wide range of activities to assist in the development of a stable Afghanistan. At the heart of this development is the building, training, mentoring, and professionalization of the Afghanistan National Security Forces, which consists of the Afghan National Army (ANA) and the Afghan National Police (ANP). The CSTC-A reports to the U.S. Central Command.

Cone was born on March 19, 1957, in Manchester, New Hampshire, and was commissioned as a second lieutenant in the armor branch upon graduation from the United States Military Academy, West Point, in 1979. He earned a master of arts degree in sociology from the University of Texas at Austin in 1987 and a master of arts degree in national security and strategic studies from the Naval War College in 1988. He was promoted to brigadier general on May 1, 2004, and to major general on August 8, 2007.

Cone's previous command assignments included 1st Squadron, 3rd Armored Cavalry Regiment, III Corps, at Fort Bliss, Texas, and later at Fort Carson, Colorado, and 2nd Brigade, 4th Infantry Division (Mechanized), at Fort Hood, Texas. His staff positions included executive officer, 11th Armored Cavalry Regiment, Fulda, Germany; operations officer, 4th Infantry Division, Fort Hood, Texas; director, Joint Advanced Warfighting Program, Institute for Defense Analysis, Alexandria, Virginia; and director, Joint Center for Operation Analysis, U.S. Joint Forces Command, Operation IRAQI FREEDOM. Cone has also served as an instructor and an assistant professor at the U.S. Military Academy. His immediate previous assignment before becoming commanding general of CSTC A was commanding general, U.S. Army National Training Center and Fort Irwin in California.

At an October 2008 ceremony to celebrate the inauguration of a sleeve insignia patch for the CSTC-A, Major General Cone reflected that over the last year during his command, the ANA had fielded 2 brigade headquarters and 24 battalions; 26 units had received a military competency rating to operate on their own; ANA units had led 62 percent of operations, which constituted a 14 percent increase over the previous year; the Afghanistan Army Air Corps was flying 90 percent of the missions to support the ANA; and 20,000 new ANP soldiers were in the field in 24 districts under reform. Cone left Afghanistan on December 15, 2008.

On September 23, 2009, Cone was given command of III Corps, based at Fort Hood, Texas. Promoted to lieutenant general, in March 2010 he deployed to Iraq, still commanding III Corps, and was named deputy commanding general for operations; Cone remained in Iraq until February 8, 2011. On April 29, 2011, Cone was promoted to full general (four stars) and named commanding general of the U.S. Army Training and Doctrine Command (TRADOC), which post he held until March 17, 2014. Cone retired from the army that same day.

JOE P. DUNN

See also

Afghanistan; Combined Security Transition Command–Afghanistan; United States Central Command

References

Lambeth, Benjamin S. *Air Power against Terror: America's Conduct of Operation Enduring Freedom.* Santa Monica, CA: RAND Corporation, 2005.

Rashid, Ahmed. *Descent into Chaos: The United States and the Failure of Nation-Building in Pakistan, Afghanistan, and Central Asia.* New York: Viking, 2008.

Congregation of the People of Tradition for Proselytism and Jihad

See Boko Haram

Conscientious Objection and Dissent in the U.S. Military

Conscientious objection—the refusal to wage war because of religious, ethical, moral, philosophical, or humanitarian convictions—is a basic human right confirmed by the Universal Declaration of Human Rights (1948) and other United Nations (UN) conventions, including the nonbinding 1998 General Assembly resolution that explicitly asserts the right for soldiers already performing military service to claim conscientious objector status. In international law, conscientious objection is complemented by Article 4 of the Nuremberg Principles established after World War II, which

mandates that following orders does not relieve one from responsibility for war crimes. Although bona fide conscientious objector status has been a part of the American identity since the Revolutionary War, conscientious objection by members of the U.S. armed forces since 2001 has frequently proven controversial, with many conscientious objectors imprisoned or driven into exile. Issues surrounding conscientious objector status and dissent during the 1991 Persian Gulf War were extremely limited in scope because of the very short duration of that conflict.

U.S. Department of Defense Directive 1300.6 (revised 2007) provides a narrowed definition of conscientious objection. Conscientious objectors may be officially recognized if claimants establish "sincere objection to participation in war in any form, or the bearing of arms, by reason of religious training and/or belief." While the Defense Department guidelines do encompass "moral and ethical beliefs" outside traditional religion, they exclude "selective" conscientious objection to specific conflicts or modes of warfare. Each armed service has regulations codifying the processing of conscientious objector claimants (e.g., chaplain and psychiatrist interviews, a hearing before an investigating officer, Defense Department review board, etc). In accordance with inactive Selective Service guidelines for conscription, bona fide conscientious objectors are to be discharged from the military or reassigned to noncombatant duties.

Between 2002 and 2006, the Pentagon reported 425 requests for conscientious objector status, with 224 (53 percent) approved, covering both the Afghanistan War and the Iraq War. However, in September 2007 the U.S. Government Accountability Office acknowledged a potential underreporting of applicants. Meanwhile, a consortium of churches, veterans, and peace groups networked in the GI Rights Hotline has reported counseling thousands of soldiers who have experienced a crisis of conscience. Alleging that many conscientious objection claims are not represented in official figures because they never reach the Pentagon, the Center for Conscience and War has lobbied Congress for new legislation that would streamline conscientious objector processing and recognize the "selective" objection encompassed by UN guidelines and many religious doctrines. At the same time, dissenting soldiers continued to manifest objection to the wars in Afghanistan and Iraq in other ways.

Echoing similar actions by the GI Movement against the Vietnam War, these demonstrations of opposition to U.S. war policies are rooted in isolated acts of individual conscience. However, the current all-volunteer U.S. armed forces means that today's conscientious objectors are in an entirely different situation than those in the Vietnam War–era, when the draft brought hundreds of thousands into the armed forces involuntarily. Since today's conscientious objectors volunteered to join the armed forces, implying their willingness at least at the time of enlistment to engage in combat, the Defense Department understandably carefully examines each petition for conscientious objector status today.

The first soldier to publicly oppose Operation IRAQI FREEDOM was U.S. Marine Corps Reserve lance corporal Stephen Funk, who learned of the possibility of claiming conscientious objector status just before his unit was activated in February 2003, a month before the war began. After missing deployment to prepare his conscientious objection claim, Funk turned himself in and explained that he went public with his claim to allow others to realize that conscientious objector status was an option. Because of his unauthorized absence, Funk's conscientious objection claim was not processed, and he was sentenced to six months' imprisonment and a bad conduct discharge.

In the months that followed as public criticism of the George W. Bush administration's justifications for the Iraq War intensified and American occupation policies drew international censure, more U.S. service members became disillusioned. By the beginning of 2006, according to a Zogby Poll, almost 30 percent of American troops in Iraq wanted the United States to withdraw immediately, and 72 percent believed that American forces should leave the country within a year. An *Army Times* poll conducted later that same year revealed that only 41 percent of soldiers believed that the war should have occurred. Press reports have noted increased alcohol and drug abuse, and one out of three combat veterans has sought psychological counseling. Also, between 2002 and 2008, the U.S. Army suicide rate nearly doubled, and it has remained high even after the end of the Iraq War in December 2011. Although other factors related to military service, such as more frequent overseas deployments, multiple combat tours, the pressures of family separations, etc., are more likely contributing factors in the rise in the negative statistics, opposition to the war should not be ruled out.

Meanwhile, more than 150 members of the U.S. military publicly refused to fight in Iraq, resulting in criminal charges, imprisonment, and bad conduct discharges. Some of them were declared prisoners of conscience by the human rights organization Amnesty International. The more highly publicized cases include Staff Sergeant Camilo Mejia, an army squad leader who refused to return to Iraq from leave in 2003 and was sentenced to 12 months in prison; Kevin Benderman, an army sergeant and Iraq War veteran who resisted redeployment in 2005 and was sentenced to 15 months in prison; U.S. Navy petty officer third class Pablo Paredes, who abandoned ship in 2004 and was sentenced to 3 months' hard labor without confinement; and Texas Army National Guard specialist Katherine Jashinski, who after her conscientious objector claim was denied following 18 months of processing was court-martialed in 2006 for refusing weapons training in preparation for deployment to Afghanistan and was sentenced to 120 days of confinement. These cases unfolded amid the climate of a threefold increase, between 2002 and 2006, in the number of army soldiers court-martialed for desertion, defined by the military as being absent without leave (AWOL) for more than 30 days. Most deserters were to be serving in Iraq; desertion rates for those serving in Afghanistan were considerably lower.

While tens of thousands of service members have gone AWOL since 2001, such absences range from as short as a few hours to as long as weeks and months. It is impossible to know for certain service members' individual reasons for being AWOL; however, some 200 have sought sanctuary in Canada, where more than three dozen have formally applied for political asylum. Refusing to consider the legality of the Iraq War, the Conservative government refused to grant any of the AWOL Americans official refugee status. However, on June 3, 2008, the Canadian Parliament passed a nonbinding resolution asking the prime minister to allow conscientious objectors from wars not sanctioned by the UN to become Canadian residents. Canadian courts have stayed a number of threatened deportations.

Questions concerning the Iraq War's legality as well as the limited Defense Department definition of conscientious objection were also highlighted in the prosecution of First Lieutenant Ehren Watada, a U.S. Army infantry officer who asserted in June 2006 that it was his "command responsibility" to refuse participation in "war crimes." In February 2007 a court-martial judge declared a mistrial, ruling that the legality of Watada's deployment orders was a "nonjusticiable political question." That October, the army's attempt at another court-martial was declared unconstitutional double jeopardy by a U.S. district court, which ruled that Watada could not be tried on three of the five counts with which he was charged.

By the end of 2008 Watada remained on active duty at Fort Lewis, Washington, as the Defense Department decided whether to appeal the case further or try him on the two remaining counts of conduct unbecoming an officer. When the Barack Obama administration took office in January 2009, the U.S. Justice Department asked that the appeal brought to the U.S. 9th Circuit Court of Appeals be dismissed. It was indeed dismissed on May 6, 2009. Watada was formally discharged from the army on October 2, 2009, and no other charges—military or civilian—were brought against him.

The contested nature of active service members' First Amendment right to free speech provided the context for another high-profile development in military dissent. Knowing that soldiers are explicitly permitted by law to contact their congressional representatives, in late 2006 U.S. Navy seaman Jonathan Hutto instigated an "Appeal for Redress," an Internet statement and organizing tool that by the end of 2008 had mobilized more than 2,200 service members, including some 100 field officers, to publicly declare that "As a patriotic American proud to serve the nation in uniform, I respectfully urge my political leaders in Congress to support the prompt withdrawal of all American military forces and bases from Iraq. Staying in Iraq will not work and is not worth the price. It is time for U.S. troops to come home."

Hutto sought assistance from and was supported by David Cortright, a Vietnam War veteran and author of *Soldiers in Revolt,* an account of military dissent during that war; Courage to Resist, a San Francisco–based coalition of activists that originated in community support mobilized during Lance Corporal Funk's court-martial in 2003; and Iraq Veterans against the War (IVAW).

Modeled after the influential Vietnam Veterans Against the War group established in 1967, the IVAW was founded in 2004 at the annual convention of Veterans for Peace, a national peace group encompassing all veterans who have embraced nonviolence. As with the "Appeal for Redress," these organizations capitalized on the credibility gained by their members having served their country in uniform to legitimate their antiwar message.

Conscientious objection during the Obama administration became less of an issue, chiefly because Obama ended the war in Iraq and withdrew the last U.S. troops from that country in December 2011. Still, however, a very small number of U.S. soldiers continue to claim conscientious objection toward the war in Afghanistan. In 2013, U.S. Army private Chris Munoz refused to deploy to Afghanistan because he believed that he would be unable to carry out the full responsibilities of a soldier if called upon to do so. U.S. government officials suggest that the total number of legitimate conscientious objectors in 2013 amounted to no more than 100 or so individuals out of some 1.35 million active-duty personnel and 850,000 reservists. The Obama administration has not substantially changed the requirements for conscientious objection.

The point needs to be emphasized that the vast majority of the members of the all-volunteer U.S. armed forces, regardless of how they might personally have felt about the Afghanistan War and the Iraq War, continued to perform their duties as they signed on to do. Despite several high-profile instances of war resistance and of military personnel claiming conscientious objector status, the impact of such actions has apparently not had an appreciable effect on armed forces recruiting or on reenlistment rates, both of which remain high.

JEFF RICHARD SCHUTTS

See also

Abu Ghraib; IRAQI FREEDOM, Operation; Weapons of Mass Destruction

References

Hutto, Jonathan W., Sr. *Antiwar Soldier: How to Dissent within the Ranks of the Military.* New York: Nation Books, 2008.

Iraq Veterans against the War and Aaron Glantz. *Winter Soldier Iraq and Afghanistan: Eyewitness Accounts of the Occupations.* Chicago: Haymarket Books, 2008.

Lauffer, Peter. *Mission Rejected: U.S. Soldiers Who Say No to Iraq.* White River Junction, VT: Chelsea Green, 2006.

Conway, James Terry (1947–)

U.S. Marine Corps officer, veteran of Operations DESERT STORM and IRAQI FREEDOM, and the 34th commandant of the U.S. Marine Corps from November 2006 to October 2010. James Terry Conway was born in Walnut Ridge, Arkansas, on December 26, 1947. His family moved back and forth between St. Louis, Missouri, and Walnut Ridge before finally settling in St. Louis in 1958. Conway graduated from Southeast Missouri State University in 1969 and was commissioned a second lieutenant in the U.S. Marine Corps in 1970. His first duty station was Camp Pendleton, California. He then served aboard the aircraft carrier *Kitty Hawk.* Conway next served in the 2nd Marine Regiment and as operations officer for the 31st Marine Amphibious Unit with sea duty in the western Pacific and in operations off the coast of Beirut, Lebanon, in 1983. Returning to the United States, he was for two years senior aide to the chairman of the Joint Chiefs of Staff. After completing further U.S. Marine Corps schooling in 1990, Conway took command of the 3rd Battalion, 2nd Marines. The next year he commanded the

Battalion Landing Team during its eight-month deployment to Southwest Asia as a diversionary unit during Operation DESERT STORM.

In 1993 Conway assumed command of the Marine Basic School at Quantico, Virginia. He was promoted to brigadier general in December 1995. Conway's next assignment was to the Joint Chiefs of Staff. In 1998 he served as president of the Marine Corps University at Quantico. Advanced to major general in 2000, he served as commander of the 1st Marine Division and was deputy commanding general of Marine Forces Central. In 2002 he was promoted to lieutenant general and assumed command of the I Marine Expeditionary Force, serving two combat tours in Operation IRAQI FREEDOM. In Iraq, Conway's 60,000 men included not only U.S. marines but also U.S. Army troops, U.S. Navy personnel, and British special forces. His I Marine Expeditionary Force was among the first U.S. forces to enter Baghdad in March 2003 and also formed a key component in Operation VIGILANT RESOLVE in the Battle of Fallujah in Iraq during April 4–May 1, 2004.

Conway was advanced to the rank of full general and assumed the post of commandant of the U.S. Marine Corps on November 13, 2006. Upon assuming his post, he stated that he hoped to provide the nation with a U.S. Marine Corps fully prepared to meet any contingency in keeping with his motto, "Be most ready when the nation is least ready." He also set out to improve the quality of life for marines and their families and to reinstill the core values and warrior ethics that have served the U.S. Marine Corps so well in past conflicts. Conway stepped down as commandant on October 22, 2010, and was succeeded by General James F. Amos. Conway retired from the U.S. Marine Corps on November 1, 2010. Just prior to his stepping down, he caused a stir when he publicly stated that President Barack Obama's schedule to begin drawing down troops from Afghanistan might give encouragement to America's enemies and was based on political calculations rather than sound military policy. Postretirement, Conway has become a sought-after speaker.

RANDY JACK TAYLOR

See also

IRAQI FREEDOM, Operation; Persian Gulf War; United States Marine Corps, Iraq War

References

Anderson, Jon Lee. *The Fall of Baghdad.* New York: Penguin, 2004.

Brady, James. *Why Marines Fight.* New York: Thomas Dunne Books/St. Martin's, 2007.

Franks, Tommy, with Malcolm McConnell. *American Soldier.* New York: Regan Books, 2004.

Keegan, John. *The Iraq War: The Military Offensive, from Victory in 21 Days to the Insurgent Aftermath.* New York: Vintage, 2005.

Reynolds, Nicholas E. *Basrah, Baghdad, and Beyond: The U.S. Marine Corps in the Second Iraq War.* Annapolis, MD: Naval Institute Press, 2005.

West, Bing, and Ray L. Smith. *The March Up: Taking Baghdad with the 1st Marine Division.* New York: Bantam, 2003.

Cook, Robin (1946–2006)

British Labour Party politician, secretary of state for foreign and commonwealth affairs (1997–2001), and leader of the House of Commons (2001–2003) who refused to support British prime minister Tony Blair's decision to go to war with Iraq in March 2003 and resigned his post as a result. Robin Cook was born on February 28, 1946, in Bellshill, Scotland, to a lower middle-class family. Cook studied at the University of Edinburgh, ultimately earning a master's degree in English there in 1968. Following in his father's footsteps, he taught school for a brief time before entering politics in 1971, at which time he became a councilman (councilor) in Edinburgh on the Labour Party ticket. In February 1974 he was elected to the British House of Commons, representing Edinburgh's central district. In 1983 his district changed to Livingston. Cook remained in Parliament until his untimely death in 2006.

Cook was in the left wing of the Labour Party and was especially critical of Britain's Conservative governments during the 1980s and into the 1990s. He only tepidly backed Labour leader Blair's attempt to modernize the Labour Party in the 1990s, believing it to be too rightist leaning. Cook soon earned a reputation for his formidable debating skills and fiery oratory. He was also an excellent parliamentarian, effectively using the rules of the House of Commons to his own and his party's benefit. By the late 1980s Cook had risen through the ranks of the leadership, and in 1987 he began holding shadow cabinet posts (unofficial parliamentary posts that shadow official government posts held by the opposition party, in this case the Conservative Party). He was the shadow social services secretary (1887–1989), shadow health secretary (1989–1992), shadow trade secretary (1992–1994), and shadow foreign secretary (1994–1997).

In 1997 after many years in Britain's political wilderness, an invigorated Labour Party came to power, with Blair as prime minister. Cook was not entirely enamored with Blair, whom he found too conservative for his own taste, but Cook nevertheless welcomed Labour's ascendancy and sought out the highly coveted cabinet post of chancellor of the exchequer. Blair had apparently already promised that position to another Labourite, however, so Cook was offered the post of secretary of state for foreign and commonwealth affairs, which he readily accepted. Upon assuming office, he promised to return an "ethical dimension" to the United Kingdom's foreign policy, a statement that was viewed with considerable skepticism by many Britons.

Cook's tenure was marked chiefly by the British intervention—along with the North Atlantic Treaty Organization—in the Kosovo War in 1999, which witnessed an air campaign that lasted for more than two months. The Kosovo intervention brought considerable criticism to both Blair and Cook because many Britons were uncomfortable with a military action that had not been officially blessed by the United Nations.

After the June 2001 general elections, Blair and other Labour leaders implored Cook to return to the House of Commons, where they believed that his leadership was now sorely needed. Cook reluctantly gave up his cabinet post and began serving as leader of the House of Commons and lord president of the council later that month. Cook immediately set about reorganizing Parliament, taking particular pains to bring about reform in the House of Lords. After the September 11, 2001, terror attacks against the United States, when the Blair government began to move in unison with the George W. Bush administration, Cook found himself in the uneasy position of defending Britain's pro-American foreign policy initiatives. This became more and more difficult, however, as the United States and Great Britain moved closer and closer to a preemptive war against Iraq.

By early 2003, Cook was on record publicly and privately for his opposition to war against Iraq. He reportedly had numerous meetings with Blair and prepared several memoranda in which he implored the Labour government not to follow the United States in lockstep fashion toward war. When war looked inevitable, Cook resigned his position as leader of Parliament on March 17, 2003, just three days before the war began. His speech announcing his resignation made clear his opposition to a war in Iraq. Reportedly, Cook's speech was the first to receive a standing ovation in the House of Commons.

Cook remained in Parliament working quietly behind the scenes, but there can be no doubt that his dramatic resignation demonstrated how split the British electorate was on the subject of the Iraq War. Cook died suddenly from a massive heart attack while hiking near Sutherland, Scotland, on August 6, 2006.

PAUL G. PIERPAOLI JR.

See also

Blair, Tony; United Kingdom, Middle East Policy

References

Cook, Robin. *The Point of Departure.* New York: Simon and Schuster, 2004.

Stephens, Phillip. *Tony Blair: The Making of a World Leader.* New York: Viking Books, 2004.

Counterinsurgency

A warfare strategy employed to defeat an organized rebellion or revolutionary movement aimed at bringing down and replacing established governmental authority. Among the more confusing terms relating to the practice of warfare, the term "counterinsurgency" implies both the purpose of military operations and the methods selected. U.S. interest in counterinsurgency soared in 2005 as it became increasingly apparent that an insurgency was gravely undermining the efforts of the United States and its allies to establish a new regime in Iraq after the 2003 Anglo-American–led invasion and occupation. To a lesser degree, a revived Taliban movement has also hindered U.S. progress in nation building in Afghanistan, and counterinsurgency tactics are being employed there as well.

Understanding the term "counterinsurgency" requires an appreciation of its logical opposite: insurgency. Counterinsurgency originated as a conceptual response to the spread of insurgencies, particularly as carried out by anticolonialist or communist movements during the Cold War from the late 1940s to the 1980s. Insurgents typically lacked key sources of power, such as financial wealth, a professional military, or advanced weaponry, that were available to established regimes or governments. Consequently, insurgents adopted asymmetric tactics and strategies that focused on avoidance of direct combat until such time as governmental power had been gravely weakened. Instead, skillful insurgents blended an array of methods including propaganda, attacks on public institutions and infrastructure, the creation of secret support networks, and use of unconventional or guerrilla combat tactics. By these means, insurgents could whittle away at the strength of existing regimes or occupying powers while slowly increasing their own capabilities.

U.S. interest in counterinsurgency, sometimes referred to as counterrevolutionary warfare, grew during the Vietnam War. Efforts to defeat the Viet Cong guerrillas in South Vietnam were considered important but more often than not took a backseat to the conduct of conventional

U.S. soldiers from the 2nd Infantry Division distribute newspapers to villagers in Pir Zadeh, Afghanistan, on December 3, 2009, while conducting counterinsurgency operations in support of Operation ENDURING FREEDOM. (U.S. Department of Defense)

military operations against the People's Army of Vietnam (North Vietnamese Army). With the American withdrawal from Vietnam in 1973, however, the U.S. military resumed focusing on conventional war, and the study of counterinsurgency by the U.S. Army waned. Even with the end of the Cold War in 1991, the U.S. military did not regard the study of counterinsurgency as equally important to the mastery of conventional combat.

To many, Operation DESERT STORM in Iraq in 1991 justified the American focus on conventional combat. The Persian Gulf War provided an awesome demonstration of U.S. military proficiency and technology. Indeed, American dominance was so compelling that it may have dissuaded future potential opponents from attempting to challenge American might on any conventional battlefield. One result of this was perhaps to encourage adversaries to attack U.S. interests by asymmetric means, such as guerrilla insurgency tactics or terror. There was also a growing perception among enemies of the United States that American politicians and military leaders were extremely uncomfortable in situations in which

they could not bring superior conventional military power to bear. The deaths of 18 U.S. Army soldiers on October 3–4, 1993, during a raid against a renegade warlord in Somalia may have been the exception that proved the rule. Largely a product of events in Somalia, Bill Clinton's casualty-averse posture of U.S. forces in subsequent peacekeeping missions in Haiti, Bosnia, and Kosovo during the 1990s tended to reinforce the view that Americans were reluctant to suffer any casualties in scenarios short of unconstrained conventional combat.

The startling terror attacks on U.S. soil on September 11, 2001, led to a swift reorientation in American military thinking. The immediate American response was to strike against the Taliban regime in Afghanistan that had provided refuge for Al Qaeda terrorists claiming responsibility for the attacks. Informed by its own support for the mujahideen guerrilla resistance to the Soviet occupation of Afghanistan during the 1980s, the United States decided to rely as much as possible on small teams of special operations forces, which would support allied indigenous forces with cutting-edge technologies, rather than on massed conventional forces. The fall of the Taliban regime within three months now placed American forces in the position of stabilizing a fledgling regime under Hamid Karzai.

Very soon the tools of counterinsurgency would prove most relevant in Afghanistan against surviving remnants of the Taliban that found sanctuary along the Pakistani frontier. One important measure taken was the creation and deployment of Provincial Reconstruction Teams beginning in 2003. These combined a small number of military specialists with representatives of various U.S. or other foreign governmental agencies possessing expertise in diplomacy, policing, agriculture, and other fields relevant to the process of fostering security and development. Found to be effective in Afghanistan in extending governmental reach to remote areas, the concept soon found application in Iraq as well.

In the meantime, the invasion of Iraq in March 2003, while initially marking another triumph of conventional operations, did not result in a smooth transition to a stable civilian government. Indeed, coalition forces in Iraq soon faced a formidable counterinsurgency challenge for which neither military nor civilian officials had fully prepared. In fact, many critics maintain that the early failure to establish public order, restore services, and identify local partners provided the insurgency, which Iraqis term "the resistance," with an interval of chaos that enabled it to organize and grow. Since Iraqi politics had consistently shown wave after wave of resistance, purges, and new coups, such a challenge could reasonably have been expected. Sectarian leaders and their militias began to assert influence, and Al Qaeda fighters infiltrated key provinces in anticipation of a new struggle to come.

By 2005, spreading ethnic and religious violence in Iraq resulted in the deaths of many civilians as well as local governmental and security personnel. Suicide bombings as well as the remote detonation of improvised explosive devices became signature tactics of the Iraqi insurgency. Furthermore, repeated attacks on United Nations personnel and foreign relief workers caused a virtual suspension of outside aid to the Iraqi people.

Recognition of the need to focus on counterinsurgency methods led to a vitally significant effort to publish a military doctrinal manual on the subject. An initial indicator of the official shift in U.S. military thinking was the release of Department of Defense Directive 3000-05 on November 28, 2005, which specifically acknowledged responsibility for planning and carrying out so-called support and stability operations essential to any counterinsurgency campaign.

Under the leadership of Lieutenant General David Petraeus during his tenure as commander, Combined Arms Center, and commandant of the U.S. Army Command and General Staff College at Fort Leavenworth, Kansas, in 2006–2007, a team of writers and practitioners with experience in Iraq and Afghanistan undertook a crash project to draft, revise, and publish the new manual.

In his opening address to the Combat Studies Institute Military History Symposium on August 8, 2006, Petraeus set forth several points of emphasis of the soon-to-be-published U.S. Army Field Manual 3-24 (also known as U.S. Marine Warfighting Publication No. 3-33.5), titled *Counterinsurgency*. Asserting that T. E. Lawrence (of Arabia) had figured out the essentials of counterinsurgency during World War I, Petraeus contended that any prospect of success depended upon identifying capable local leaders, providing them necessary assistance without doing the hard work for them, fostering the development of public institutions, forming a partnership with existing security forces, and maintaining a flexible and patient outlook. In other words, counterinsurgency would require far more of military leaders than the performance of traditional and familiar combat tasks. Petraeus himself had practiced these principles in Iraq, where in late 2004 he served as the first commander of the Multi-National Security Transition Command–Iraq, which focused on the training of local personnel to become civilian and military leaders in Iraq.

Officially released in December 2006, *Counterinsurgency* attracted great attention in the press and conveyed the impression that the military was not stuck in an outmoded mind-set. Rather, U.S. Army and U.S. Marine Corps leaders on the ground in Afghanistan and Iraq became increasingly adaptive and creative in the search for improved solutions to the problem of combating insurgency where nation building was still very much in progress. *Counterinsurgency* devoted a majority of its eight chapters and five appendices to tasks other than war fighting. Lengthy sections also related to ethics, civilian and military cooperation, cultural analysis, linguistic support, the law of war, and ethical considerations.

Of course, the U.S. Army and the U.S. Marine Corps had not ignored the principles of counterinsurgency before the new doctrine was published. However, publication signaled to the American public and the U.S. Congress that the military was wholly committed to the implementation of counterinsurgency principles. Implementation of this new counterinsurgency doctrine began to bear fruit but could not overcome the political decisions of the Iraqi government headed by Prime Minister Nuri al-Maliki (in power from May

2006 to September 2014), which took a decidedly sectarian approach that favored the Shiite majority at the expense of the Sunni and Kurdish minorities. The insurgency therefore continued well after the withdrawal of U.S. forces at the end of 2011, although it is now sometimes referred to as the Iraq Crisis.

ROBERT F. BAUMANN

See also

Al Qaeda; Al Qaeda in Iraq; Improvised Explosive Devices; IRAQI FREEDOM, Operation; Karzai, Hamid; Petraeus, David Howell; Somalia, International Intervention in; Taliban

References

Keegan, John. *The Iraq War: The Military Offensive, from Victory in 21 Days to the Insurgent Aftermath.* New York: Vintage, 2005.

Kitson, Frank. *Low Intensity Operations: Subversion, Insurgency and Peacekeeping.* London: Faber and Faber, 1971.

Nagl, John A. *Learning to Eat Soup with a Knife: Counterinsurgency Lessons from Malaya and Vietnam.* Chicago: University of Chicago Press, 2005.

Counterterrorism Center

U.S. government agency designed to combat terrorism. In 1985, the Central Intelligence Agency (CIA) decided to create a new section to fight international terrorism. This decision came shortly after intelligence failures in Lebanon had led to the deaths in October 1982 of 241 U.S. marines when their barracks was bombed and the kidnapping and killing of CIA section chief William Buckley in 1982. President Ronald Reagan pressed CIA director William J. Casey to do something about terrorism.

Casey soon approached Duane R. "Dewey" Clarridge, a respected veteran field officer, to make a recommendation as to how the CIA could most effectively fight terrorism. Clarridge recommended an interdisciplinary center in the CIA that had an international reach and could utilize all the capabilities of the agency. Part of its mission was to launch covert action against known terrorists, so the Special Operations Group was transferred to the Counterterrorism Center. It was to be a section staffed by 100 persons with representation from the Federal Bureau of Investigation (FBI). Casey accepted Clarridge's recommendation and appointed him as its head. Instead of the original plan for a staff of 100, however, Casey authorized it at a staffing of 250. The Counterterrorism Center became operational in February 1986.

Clarridge's first target as head of the Counterterrorism Center was the Abu Nidal Organization (ANO). In the 1970s and 1980s the ANO, named after its leader, was the most violent terrorist group in operation and had become the number one terrorist threat. The CIA was able to recruit a source within the ANO, and this individual provided inside information. Much of it appeared in a State Department publication, *The Abu Nidal Handbook.* After this information became public, Abu Nidal became so concerned about penetration of his organization that he ordered the execution of a large number of his followers in Libya. This purge ended the effectiveness of the ANO.

The next target was Hezbollah (Party of God) in Lebanon. Hezbollah, which the United States considers a Shia terrorist organization, was blamed for complicity in the bombing of the U.S. Marine Corps barracks in Beirut, and factions that became a part of Hezbollah had taken hostage a number of Westerners. Among these was William Buckley, the CIA agent in Lebanon, who had died from harsh treatment. The campaign against Hezbollah was less successful, although it involved attempted assassinations of the leadership. Efforts to launch covert operations were also hampered by the Lebanese position that the organization was no more terrorist than any other during the Lebanese Civil War period and was the only effective force in battling the Israeli and Israeli-proxy occupation of southern Lebanon.

Clarridge soon became frustrated by the lack of support for the Counterterrorism Center. His role in the Iran-Contra Affair also led his superiors in the CIA to question his judgment. He maintained that Lieutenant Colonel Oliver North had misled him in the exchange of hostages from Iran for weapons to be used by the opposition Contras to fight against the Sandinista government in Nicaragua. Clarridge's goal had been to make the center a proactive force against terrorism. Instead, he found that his new boss, CIA director William Webster, who had assumed control of the CIA on May 26, 1987, was averse to risk. This lack of support led Clarridge to leave the Counterterrorism Center later in 1987.

Clarridge's successor, Fred Turco, picked the next major target for the Counterterrorism Center as the Peruvian Shining Path organization. Abimael Guzman, a philosophy professor, had founded the Maoist terrorist group in 1970, and it had opened a war against the Peruvian government. The Counterterrorism Center provided the Peruvian police with sophisticated electronic surveillance equipment and training that enabled them to capture Guzman in a Lima suburb in September 1992.

The Counterterrorism Center's activities assumed more importance in 1993. By this time the new head of the Counterterrorism Center was Winston Wiley, who had assumed the position in November 1992. Two events mobilized this activity. First was the murder of two CIA employees in Langley, Virginia, by Mir Amal Kasi on January 25, 1993. Believing the CIA responsible for countless Muslim deaths, Kasi opened fire with an AK-47 assault rifle just outside of CIA headquarters, killing the CIA employees in their automobiles. Kasi was from Baluchistan, and he managed to escape back to Pakistan, where he promptly disappeared. A special CIA unit was set up to locate and capture him; he was finally apprehended on June 15, 1997.

An even bigger task was investigation of the conspiracy behind the February 23, 1993, World Trade Center bombing. While the domestic investigation was left up to the FBI, the Counterterrorism Center established a subunit to gather intelligence about the bombing. Information was slow to surface, and at first the Counterterrorism Center suspected that it had been a state-sponsored terrorist operation, with Iraq, Libya, and Iran as the prime suspects. Over time, the intelligence analysts came to realize that it was an independent operation led by Ramzi Yousef. In a combined CIA-FBI operation, Yousef was captured in Islamabad, Pakistan, on February 7, 1995.

The Counterterrorism Center continued to target terrorist groups. First under Geoff O'Connell and then under J. Cofer Black, the center planned counterterrorist operations. Black's target was Osama bin Laden and Al Qaeda. Black was also able to count on an expanded Counterterrorism Center. The center had grown from only 20 analysts in 1986 to 340 people, of whom more than a dozen were FBI agents, by early 2001. Despite the additions, the staffing of the Counterterrorism Center was too low to handle the volume of information flowing into it. Not surprisingly, the leaders and the staff of the Counterterrorism Center were caught unawares on September 11, 2001.

American pressure on Sudan had led bin Laden to move from Sudan to Afghanistan in 1996. Bin Laden, his family, and retainers traveled to Afghanistan by aircraft on May 18, 1996. The staff of the Counterterrorism Center thought that this presented a golden opportunity to capture bin Laden in transit. A proposal to do so was given to President William J. Clinton but never received presidential approval. Members of the Counterterrorism Center were furious over this lost opportunity.

Throughout the late 1990s, analysts in the Counterterrorism Center monitored bin Laden's activities from sources within Afghanistan. The problem was that bin Laden was constantly moving, so tracking him was almost impossible. There was also an ongoing and unresolved debate in the Clinton administration about whether it was legal to assassinate bin Laden. Attorney General Janet Reno made it plain to George Tenet, head of the CIA, and Geoff O'Connell, head of the Counterterrorism Center, that any attempt to kill bin Laden was illegal. All schemes thus involved capturing bin Laden first and killing him only in self-defense.

Another problem was the issue of collateral damage in an attack on bin Laden. Isolating bin Laden from civilians was almost impossible. Members of the Counterterrorism Center wanted to proceed with covert action regardless of the likelihood of collateral civilian losses.

In the middle of the debate over bin Laden, the U.S. Navy destroyer *Cole* was attacked while anchored in the harbor in Aden, Yemen, on October 12, 2000. The attack killed 17 American sailors and wounded scores more. This incident caught the Counterterrorism Center by surprise. It thus took a while for the analysts to find the evidence connecting this attack with Al Qaeda, but the evidence was indeed found. Counterterrorism Center staffers sought retaliation, but the American military was reluctant to undertake any such operations and so advised the White House. To the leadership of the Counterterrorism Center, the only option was to support the Afghan leader General Ahmad Shah Massoud and his war against the Taliban. But the Clinton administration was reluctant to do this and forbade the Counterterrorism Center from increasing aid to him. The Clinton administration left office in 2001 with the problem of bin Laden and Al Qaeda unresolved.

Counterterrorism analysts continued to be frustrated by the inaction of the George W. Bush administration toward terrorism. Reports indicated increased activity by Al Qaeda, but the problem was that there was no evidence of what kind of operation it might undertake or where. A series of warnings came out of the Counterterrorism Center that Tenet took to President Bush and other prominent administration figures. These warnings coincided with similar warnings from the FBI. Some of them even made the case that Al Qaeda operatives might carry out an operation in the United States. What weakened these frequent warnings was the lack of specific details. The Bush administration listened to the warnings, noted the lack of specifics, and took no action. Bush wanted more specific intelligence before he would authorize any action.

Tenet now ordered the CIA to round up suspected Al Qaeda members to gather information on what Al Qaeda was planning. This tactic had two purposes: to gather intelligence and to delay Al Qaeda missions. Several Al Qaeda plots were uncovered, and a massive amount of intelligence material arrived at the Counterterrorism Center. The problem was that there were not enough translators and analysts to handle the mass of material. Frustration was high among the intelligence analysts because they were fearful that important information was being overlooked. In mid-July 2001 Tenet ordered the Counterterrorism Center analysts to search back in its files and its current information on bin Laden's major plots. Tenet was suspicious that bin Laden might be targeting the United States for a terrorism mission. Tenet took what information the Counterterrorism Center had uncovered and presented the report, titled "Bin Laden Determined to Strike in United Statesm" to President Bush at his Crawford, Texas, ranch on August 6, 2001. In early September the Bush administration began to consider a plan to attack terrorism, especially bin Laden and Al Qaeda, but there was no sense of haste.

Following the September 11, 2001, terrorist attacks, resources poured into the Counterterrorism Center. By the summer of 2002, Tenet had expanded its staff to 1,500. This number of workers was able to handle 2,500 classified electronic communications a day and could produce 500 terrorist reports a month.

The Counterterrorism Center was also given the responsibility for the interrogations of important Al Qaeda prisoners. A series of secret interrogation centers was established in friendly countries. Meanwhile, top Al Qaeda prisoners were kept at an interrogation center, Bright Lights, the location of which was not known even to analysts in the Counterterrorism Center. These interrogations are ongoing, with some of the information making it back to intelligence circles.

There have also been reports of CIA interrogators using questionable interrogation techniques and torture, including the controversial waterboarding process. The FBI refuses to have anything to do with these interrogations. Several news reports have confirmed this information, and CIA agents have become increasingly uncomfortable about their legal position over these interrogations. This nervousness about interrogation techniques led to controversy in December 2007 when news surfaced that the secret tapes of CIA interrogations had been destroyed in 2005. This action was defended by the then head of the CIA, Michael V. Hayden, but there have been congressional efforts to hold hearings on whether this action was illegal.

Although Bush and his successor, President Barack Obama, have denied allegations that the CIA employs torture during its interrogations, many believe that the practice continues. In January 2009, U.S. attorney general Eric Holder issued an order forbidding the CIA from conducting "coercive interrogations," but it is impossible to tell if such techniques have since been employed. The Counterterrorism Center continues its work in Afghanistan, the Middle East, and other areas of the world in which terroristic activity is a concern, but due to the extreme clandestine nature of its operations, it rarely becomes a subject of media reporting. Indeed, since 2006, the head of the Counterterrorism Center has remained anonymous for security reasons; he is usually referred to simply as "Roger" when he is referenced in public documents.

STEPHEN E. ATKINS

See also

Alec Station; Al Qaeda; Bin Laden, Osama; Bush, George Walker; Central Intelligence Agency; Clinton, William Jefferson; Coercive Interrogation; Counterterrorism Strategy; Nidal, Abu; Tenet, George John; Terrorism

References

"At CIA, a Convert from Islam Leads the Terrorism Hunt." *Washington Post,* March 24, 2012, http://www.washingtonpost.com/world/national-security/at cia a convert to islam-leads-the-terrorism-hunt/2012/03/23/gIQA2mSqYS_print.html.

Coll, Steve. *Ghost Wars: The Secret History of the CIA, Afghanistan, and Bin Laden, from the Soviet Invasion to September 10, 2001.* New York: Penguin, 2004.

Kessler, Ronald. *The CIA at War: Inside the Secret Campaign against Terror.* New York: St. Martin's Griffin, 2003.

Miller, John, Michael Stone, and Chris Mitchell. *The Cell: Inside the 9/11 Plot, and Why the FBI and CIA Failed to Stop It.* New York: Hyperion, 2002.

Naftali, Timothy. *Blind Spot: The Secret History of American Counterterrorism.* New York: Basic Books, 2005.

Risen, James. *State of War: The Secret History of the CIA and the Bush Administration.* New York: Free Press, 2006.

Tenet, George. *At the Center of the Storm: My Years at the CIA.* New York: HarperCollins, 2007.

Counterterrorism Strategy

A general approach toward the struggle against terrorism that involves the selection, distribution, and application of all resources and means available to achieve the desired aims (i.e., the prevention and/or eradication of terrorism). A successful counterterrorism strategy must target the vital dimensions of terrorism, address its current and prospective trends, reflect its rapidly changing nature, complexity, and flexibility; and employ a wide array of military, political, economic, social, ideological, cultural, law enforcement, and other means in often intermingled offensive and defensive efforts.

Terrorist activity, especially from Islamic extremists based in the Middle East, has in recent years demonstrated significantly increasing diversity and complexity. There is a wide range of participants with a diverse set of motivations, goals, structures, and strategies. Despite the destruction of the Al Qaeda sanctuaries in Afghanistan after the September 11, 2001, terrorist attacks, this global terrorist clearinghouse network continues to operate and, utilizing global information technology, continues to recruit and train supporters, share experiences, coordinate activities of various widely dispersed terrorist cells, and advance its ideological and strategic goals. These include the eradication of Western influence and presence in the region and the overthrow of existing regimes that accommodate the Western powers. In very recent years, Islamic extremist groups such as Boko Haram (Africa) and the Islamic State of Iraq and Syria (ISIS) have provided new challenges to counterterrorism strategies.

Hezbollah, more structured than Al Qaeda, is headquartered in Lebanon and retains some potential for regional and even overseas terrorist activity. However, Hezbollah currently is concentrating its efforts on securing additional political influence within Lebanon and is not engaging in violence within Lebanon against Lebanese. The Palestinian terrorist organization Islamic Jihad has continued sporadic terrorist activities, mainly within the framework of the Israeli-Palestinian confrontation. Syria and Iran view support for organizations such as Hamas and Hezbollah as a means to promote their own national interests and ambitions in the region.

The successful expansion of transnational terrorism, according to American analysis under President George W. Bush, owes much to the emergence of so-called failed states such as Afghanistan, where such terrorism was able to prosper, virtually unchecked, due to the combination of political and social disintegration, fierce civil strife, and a lack of interest and support from the international community. The concept of a failed state is, however, disputed in the region, where underdevelopment and incomplete political control are commonplace. According to the Western ideas about transnational terrorists, the latter use the paramount anarchy in the failed states as well as weak governmental control over some portions of territory to obtain safe haven and to set up their training camps and communication centers, exploiting the remains of local infrastructure. In the late 1990s Al Qaeda managed to secure a close alliance with the Taliban in Afghanistan. The Taliban, after being driven from power in Afghanistan in 2001, has managed to reestablish itself in certain areas, including the remote Afghan-Pakistani border, and the long-term prospects of a stable, insurgent-free Afghanistan faded considerably after 2012.

Meanwhile in Iraq, radical Islamists, including ISIS, have gained a significant foothold in that country, a development that has been abetted by a chaotic political system and weak and ineffectual leadership under President Nuri al-Maliki, who finally resigned in September 2014. Would-be terrorists, including Al Qaeda cells and their allies, initiated a major insurgency in Iraq, which began soon after the last U.S. troops exited the country in December 2011. By January 2014 most of Iraq's Anbar Province had been taken over by insurgents, including members of Al Qaeda and ISIS. This led the Barack Obama administration to worry that terrorists might use Iraq as a base of operations from which they could launch strikes against the United States or other Western interests. By early 2014, the Obama administration had begun sending costly arms shipments to Iraq to help the Maliki government fend off the growing insurgency. By the fall of 2014, the Obama administration had dispatched some 3,000 military advisers to Iraq and was engaged in a bombing campaign against ISIS in both Iraq and Syria.

Any effective counterterrorism strategy must take into account new developments in strategy and tactics of the terrorist actors. The terrorists have constantly tried to acquire more lethal weapons. This is particularly true with respect to weapons of mass destruction. Until 2001 Al Qaeda, using sanctuaries in Afghanistan, planned to launch chemical or biological attacks on U.S. and European targets. In addition to the continuous pursuit of more deadly weapons, the terrorists persistently employ suicide bombings to increase the lethality of their attacks.

Terrorist leaders have also demonstrated their ability to adjust to changing conditions. The decentralized, loose organizational structure of Al Qaeda allowed it to continue to operate even after the loss of Afghanistan in 2001. This has been amply demonstrated in its terrorist attacks in Yemen, Tunisia, Saudi Arabia, Jordan, and Kuwait as well as in Istanbul, Madrid, and London. The U.S. government had argued that Al Qaeda operated a network that recruited and operated in the Muslim communities of Britain, Spain, France, Germany, Italy, Spain, the Netherlands, and Belgium. Current thinking, however, sees Al Qaeda more as an inspiration to and clearinghouse for local groups who are autonomous of it. By active participation in the Iraqi insurgency since 2003, the terrorist networks have also acquired experience in urban warfare and enhanced their skills in ambush tactics, assassinations, and kidnappings.

The profound transformation, both in the scale and the complexity of operations that terrorists could undertake, allowed powerful, well-organized, and devoted groups and associations as well as smaller ones to evade state powers and to obtain global-reach capability. These terrorists are able to endanger the international security profoundly. Because the terrorist challenge amounts to a new form of warfare, successful counterterrorism strategy must constantly realign itself with the developments of the threats. Conventional military force has played a strong role in the struggle against alleged terrorism, as the long history of Israeli military campaigns against the Palestine Liberation Organization, the Israeli-Hezbollah War of 2006, the Gaza War of 2009, and the coalition campaign against ISIS beginning in 2014 demonstrate. Israel's strategy of heavy punishment of a neighboring state for permitting and/or abetting terrorism while inflicting disproportionate loss of life and property damage does not seem to have ended terrorist activity, however, which its proponents regard as rightful and necessary resistance, and has led to serious criticism of the Jewish state, even from its traditional allies.

Special operations forces play an important role in the struggle against terrorism. While capable of a global reach, military operations against terrorists need to be pinpointed and limited in scale to avoid civilian and collateral damage. This is particularly important because of the inability or reluctance of particular governments to attack the terrorist leadership and cells directly. Special operations transcend national boundaries and reflect the transnational character of the struggle against terrorism. The Israeli experience of deep-penetration commando raids and targeted assassinations of terrorist leaders reveals the ability of special operations to undermine the morale and disrupt activities of terrorist organizations and to violate state sovereignty as well as the terms of truces concluded with the enemy, although there are limits to what special operations can accomplish. Primarily, these special operations have angered the local population, making the resistance, or terrorism, that much more difficult to uproot.

Conventional military approaches retain their importance in dealing with state-sponsored terrorism, namely to wage wars against nations and achieve regime change, surely denying safe haven for the terrorists. At the same time, as the U.S.-led campaigns in Afghanistan in 2001 and Iraq in 2003 demonstrated, even victorious conventional campaigns can be complicated by ensuing insurgencies, which demand much greater flexibility on the part of the military. Here again, special operations come into play.

While the achievement of a decisive military victory remains elusive because of the dispersed and decentralized organizational structure of modern terrorism and while the use of military means resembles an endless war of attrition, the readiness to apply overwhelming and destructive military force can work to some extent. As recent changes in the policies of the Palestinian National Authority and Libya suggest, providing government bodies with enticements to stop terrorist activities can also work to curb terrorist activity. These include economic, territorial, and governing incentives.

Diplomacy is another essential tool in fighting terrorism. International cooperation is vital in collecting information on terrorist cells, which includes the tracking and disrupting of financial transactions, recruitment, and propaganda activities of the terrorists. It is also of paramount importance in seeking to isolate regimes that sponsor terrorism.

Intelligence gathering is essential in any successful counterterrorist strategy. Simply gathering the information is not sufficient; it must be properly disseminated and coordinated within government agencies. The failure of the U.S. intelligence community to provide early warning about the September 11 terrorist attacks demonstrates this all too clearly.

Defensive efforts within the framework of counterterrorism strategy focus predominantly on homeland security and encompass enhanced border security. This includes monitoring and protecting likely terrorist targets (transportation, communication systems, and other elements of infrastructure as well as high-profile objects and places of significant concentration of populations) using intelligence, law enforcement, and military means. While Israel over the years has dealt with existential threats by developing comprehensive, integrated, and highly effective systems of territorial defense, the United States and European countries remain vulnerable to terrorist attacks because of porous borders and/or the ability of the Islamic terrorists to strike from inside, mobilizing militants from the Muslim diaspora, particularly in Western Europe. While the Western democracies' domestic counterterrorism strategies have improved vastly since September 11, 2001, they still remain deficient compared to those of Israel.

Comprehensive and multifaceted counterterrorism strategies must also involve political efforts to mobilize domestic support, social and cultural efforts to resist extremist propaganda efforts, and a determination to resolve problems and issues that terrorists often use for their own advantage. This is perhaps the most challenging aspect of any successful counterterrorism strategy. Political activities should include the resolution of the regional disputes, especially the Israeli-Palestinian issue; the advancement of economic development; addressing economic inequality and poverty; the promotion of democracy; high-quality governance; and the rule of law.

PETER J. RAINOW

See also

Al Qaeda; Boko Haram; Bush, George Walker; Central Intelligence Agency; Democratization and the Global War on Terror; Failed States and the Global War on Terror; Global War on Terror; Islamic State in Iraq and Syria; Martyrdom; Narcoterrorism; Taliban; Terrorism; Weapons of Mass Destruction

References

Berntsen, Garry. *Human Intelligence, Counterterrorism, and National Leadership: A Practical Guide.* Washington, DC: Potomac Books, 2008.

Forrest, James J. F. *Countering Terrorism and Insurgency in the 21st Century.* 3 vols. Westport, CT: Praeger Security International, 2007.

Freedman, George. *America's Secret War: Inside the Worldwide Struggle between America and Its Enemies.* New York: Broadway Books, 2004.

Guiora, Amos N. *Global Perspectives on Counterterrorism.* New York: Aspen Publishers, 2007.

Crocker, Ryan Clark (1949–)

Career U.S. diplomat. Ryan Clark Cocker was born on June 19, 1949, in Spokane, Washington. He attended University College Dublin and Whitman College in Walla Walla, Washington, from which he received his bachelor's degree in 1971. That same year he entered the U.S. Foreign Service. Crocker became a specialist in Middle East affairs, learning Persian and holding a wide variety of posts in the region. During 1984–1985 he studied at Princeton University, concentrating on Near East studies. Articulate, intelligent, and effective, Crocker moved quickly up the State Department's career ladder.

Crocker held diplomatic posts in Iran, Iraq, Egypt, Qatar, and Lebanon, among other nations, in addition to stints in Washington, D.C. He served as the U.S. ambassador to Lebanon (1990–1993), Kuwait (1994–1997), Syria (1998–2001), and Pakistan (2004–2007). From August 2001 to May 2003 he held the position of deputy assistant secretary of Near East affairs in the George W. Bush administration. In January 2002 after the defeat of the Taliban regime in Afghanistan, the Bush administration sent Crocker to Kabul as interim U.S. envoy to Afghanistan. Crocker was charged with reopening the U.S. embassy there.

After the major fighting was declared over in the 2003 invasion of Iraq, Crocker went to Baghdad in May 2003, where he served as the director of governance for the new Coalition Provisional Authority. He stayed in Iraq until August 2003. In September 2004 President Bush granted Crocker the rank of career ambassador, the highest-ranking ambassadorial position in the U.S. State Department. After being nominated for the position of U.S. ambassador to Iraq, Crocker was confirmed and assumed his new duties in Baghdad on March 29, 2007.

According to Karen De Young's biography of Colin L. Powell, in the autumn of 2002 Secretary of State Powell tasked Crocker and another official with drafting a memorandum outlining the potential risks of launching a war against Iraq. The result was a six-page report that stated unambiguously that ousting Saddam Hussein from power would likely lead to sectarian and ethnic turmoil. It also posited that the United States would face a long and expensive reconstruction effort in a postwar Iraq. The memorandum proved quite prescient.

In September 2007 Crocker was called upon to testify—along with General David H. Petraeus, commander of the Multi-National Force in Iraq—before the U.S. House and Senate on the progress of the war in Iraq. While carefully avoiding any politically charged rhetoric, Crocker reported that Iraq remained a troubled and traumatized nation. He also stated that he believed that Iraqi officials would eventually take control of their own affairs but that this would likely take longer than anyone had envisioned or desired. Crocker continued in his role as ambassador to Iraq until February 13, 2009, having expressed his pleasure with the progress made in Iraq since between 2007 and 2009. On January 15, 2009, Crocker was awarded the Presidential Medal of Freedom for his service to the United States.

In January 2010, Crocker became dean of the Bush School of Government and Public Service at Texas A&M University. In April 2011, President Barack Obama nominated Crocker to the ambassadorship of Afghanistan. Crocker assumed the post on July 25, 2011, and remained in Afghanistan until July 13, 2012. In 2013, Crocker began serving on the Broadcasting Board of Governors. In December 2013, Crocker wrote an op-ed piece for the *New York Times* in which he argued that accommodation with Syrian president Bashar al-Assad might be the best way to temper advances being made by the Islamic State of Iraq and Syria (ISIS) and other extremist groups that threatened the stability of Iraq and Syria.

PAUL G. PIERPAOLI JR.

See also
Afghanistan; Afghanistan War; Assad, Bashar al-; Iraq, History of, 1990–Present; Islamic State in Iraq and Syria; Petraeus, David Howell; Powell, Colin Luther; Syrian Civil War

References
De Young, Karen. *Soldier: The Life of Colin Powell.* New York: Knopf, 2006.

Keegan, John. *The Iraq War: The Military Offensive, from Victory in 21 Days to the Insurgent Aftermath.* New York: Vintage, 2005.

Cruise Missiles

See Missiles, Cruise

Cruisers, U.S.

Cruisers are warships that possess moderate armament and yet are capable of high speed. The ancestor of the cruiser is the 18th-century frigate, which was detached from a battle fleet to "cruise" in search of enemy forces. Ticonderoga-class cruisers constitute the backbone of the U.S. Navy's post–Cold War cruiser force. Designed for versatility at the height of the Cold War, these warships have performed a wide range of missions within carrier battle groups and amphibious assault groups as well as in independent operations.

Incorporating the hull design of the Spruance-class destroyer, the Ticonderoga class was initially conceptualized as a guided missile destroyer until its redesignation in 1980. The *Ticonderoga* (CG-47) was commissioned in January 2983 and decommissioned in September 2004. The last ship in the class, the *Port Royal* (CG-73), was commissioned in 1994.

Displacing 9,600 tons and powered by four General Electric LM-2500 gas turbine engines, these cruisers can exceed 30 knots, with a range of 6,000 nautical miles at 20 knots. Normal crew complement is 24 officers and 334 sailors, although berthing is available for several dozen more. The Ticonderga class is also equipped with the command, control, communications, computer, and intelligence (C4I) systems to support an embarked staff. From an equipment perspective, that is the primary difference between today's cruisers and destroyers in U.S. naval service.

The Ticonderoga class inaugurated the use of the Aegis weapons system, giving it the most integrated and automated war-fighting capability on any surface warship worldwide. A central advantage to Aegis is the AN/SPY-1 phased-array radar that allows for continuous detection and tracking functions in all directions from sea level up to 85 degrees of elevation.

Through Aegis, Ticonderoga-class cruisers, like the subsequent Arleigh Burke–class destroyers, enjoy an unparalleled degree of efficiency in managing a multithreat combat environment. Twenty-two of the cruisers are equipped with a vertical launching system (VLS) for a more rapid employment of the Tomahawk land-attack missile with a range of at least 700 nautical miles, the standard missile for air targets, and the antisubmarine rocket. The five pre-VLS cruisers relied on two twin Mk 26 Mod 5 launcher systems. Two Mk 45 5-inch/54-caliber gun mounts provide naval gunfire support, antiship capabilities, and a limited antiair option. All Ticonderoga-class cruisers sport two launchers with a total of eight Harpoon antiship missiles with a range of more than 60 nautical miles. The combination of the SQS-53 hull-mounted and SQR-19 passive towed-array sonars give this class the ability to hunt submarines more effectively than any previous cruiser. Two Mk 32 Mod 14 torpedo launchers provide short-range protection against submarines. Two Mk 15 Mod 2 Falcon Phalanx close-in weapons system Gatling guns utilize depleted uranium or tungsten shells to deal with attacking aircraft and missiles at close quarters. All but the first two of the cruisers built have an embarked crew and maintenance team for the Sikorksy SH-60B Seahawk helicopter.

In 1996, the *Yorktown* (CG-48) was selected as the pilot vessel for the U.S. Navy's Smart Ship Project to enhance automation in order to reduce manning requirements. Innovations such as fiber-optic technology and wireless communications helped reduce the ship's crew by 4 officers and 44 sailors. The normal watch standing team on the bridge dropped from 13 to 3, with only 4 personnel necessary to monitor the entire engineering plant. As an outgrowth of the Smart Ship initiative, most of the Ticonderoga-class ships have participated in the Integrated Ship Controls program to cut costs through modernization without compromising mission readiness. In 2005, the *Cape St. George* (CG-71) initiated the practice of using digital navigation charts in place of roughly 12,000 paper charts.

Operation ENDURING FREEDOM (October 2001) included an entirely Aegis-equipped cruiser contingent of 15 warships. Since the 1991 Persian Gulf War, their Tomahawk targeting cycle had dropped from 101 minutes to 19 minutes. Operation IRAQI FREEDOM (March–April 2003) saw 11 Ticonderoga-class cruisers in action, playing a major role in the firing of more than 800 Tomahawk cruise missiles. In February 2008, the *Lake Erie* (CG-70) used an SM-3 missile to down a U.S. satellite in orbital decay at a range of 133 miles. Speculation ensued that the operation served as a de facto experiment in reviving the Strategic Defense Initiative of space-based weapons that stalled during the 1990s.

The 5 pre-VLS cruisers (CG-47 through CG-51) have been retired; the remaining 22 are still in service. The navy plans a gradual phase-out of the rest of the class between 2018 and 2045. The Cruiser Conversion Program has been implemented to provide nearly all of these assets with the upgrades necessary to remain competitive. Among other things, missile defense capabilities will be enhanced, lasers may replace the Phalanx close-in weapons system, and the electromagnetic rail gun will replace the 5-inch cannon if it proves operationally successful. There is no cruiser replacement program, but work on a new cruiser design probably will begin after 2020.

JEFFREY D. BASS AND CARL OTIS SCHUSTER

See also

Tomahawk BGM-109 Land-Attack Missile; United States Navy, Afghanistan War; United States Navy, Iraq War

References

Murray, Williamson and Scales, Robert. *The Iraq War: A Military History.* Cambridge, MA: Harvard University Press, 2003.

Silverstone, Paul. *The Navy of the Nuclear Age, 1947–2007.* New York: Routledge, 2008.

Wertheim, Eric. *Naval Institute Guide to Combat Fleets of the World, 16th Edition.* Annapolis, MD: Naval Institute Press, 2013.

Cultural Imperialism

The term "cultural imperialism" refers to the process of imposing cultural values on another culture or entity, often for the purposes of assimilation and political domination or long-term economic ties. It is also seen in policies that assume that the cultural values of the dominant country are the norm, while those of another culture are deviant, traditional, or less desirable. The ambiguity in defining this term in relation to the Middle East stems from the highly politicized attitudes of the West toward the Middle East coupled with an almost total ignorance of the region's cultures. A similar Middle Eastern lack of sustained contact with and knowledge of the United States and distrust of its political motives in the region exists, as does as a long-standing embrace and defense of traditionalism.

Imperialism implies the extension of power over another entity for exploitative purposes. Typically, this term is used in reference to empires, colonies, nations, and states. Culture generally refers to patterns of human activities and symbolic expressions. So, while imperialism takes the forms of military hostilities, political dominance, or economic leverage, cultural imperialism is a more subtle process achieved mainly through symbolism, language, education, and meaning via consumer products, civil institutions, and the media.

Since at least the turn of the 20th century, some have labeled the United States a cultural hegemon that practices the transmittal of cultural imperialism through both government-sponsored means and private enterprise. Indeed, the concept of American exceptionalism, the idea that the U.S. democratic political system represents not only the best of all systems but should stand as an example, a "shining city on a hill" for other countries to emulate, dates back to the founding of the republic. Much of this American attitude was embodied in President Woodrow Wilson's Fourteen Points, his plan to remake the post–World War I world by calling for self-determination of peoples and representative institutions. Nationalists throughout the Middle East embraced Wilson's program. At the same time, they saw no need to give up their own cultures.

Most Middle Eastern populations, while they had had little contact with Americans, had experienced extensive cultural imperialism accompanied by political manipulation at the hands of French, British, Italian, and other European nations. Thus, in the case of Egypt everything that was native Egyptian, or *baladi,* was degraded, whereas that which was foreign, of Turko-Circassion origin or Levantine, French, or British, was prized. Those who embraced the occupying foreigners and their cultures secured special legal and economic privileges through the capitulatory treaties.

The impact of Western cultural influences in the Middle East accelerated rapidly after World War II with the advent of modern communication and transportation technologies that figuratively shrunk the world. The sheer size and dominance of the U.S. economy in the decades after World War II ensured that American cultural values would spill into all corners of the globe, mainly through the media and consumerism. In the Middle East as in other parts of the Third World, this influence mostly impacted the upper elites but also coincided with new governmental policies and national pride in indigenous language, customs, traditions, and the arts. Many countries in the region sought to overcome disadvantageous balances of trade, which accompanied colonial suppression of native industries. Many people saw and wanted American products and tried to buy them whenever possible. However, these came with heavy tariffs, as certain governments, such as Egypt until 1974 and Syria, applied protective policies so as to bolster indigenous industries and agricultural products. Western foods and customs of eating more protein foods, such as red meat and chicken, often displaced local consumption patterns as Western-style one-stop supermarkets replaced traditional markets.

As far as social culture was concerned, the worlds of the Middle East and the United States and other Western nations were at polar opposites. Many in the Middle East did not understand or wish to replicate American individualism and societal independence, in which people live at great distances from their relatives, may marry or not as they choose, have relationships outside of marriage without censure, and are not expected to care for their parents in old age.

Many young people in the Middle East, however, embraced American popular culture, products, and business methods. In a number of countries, the U.S. Information Service offered English classes and general programs about the United States and American culture, which were very popular. At the same time, however, Arab populations in general were critical of U.S. Middle East foreign policy that appeared to offer unconditional support to Israel or that, even though principally intended to counter Soviet influence in the region during the Cold War, seemed intended to secure American dominance in the region.

In the 1970s the rise of more militant Islamist movements and groups coincided with economic changes that saw a greater influx of imported consumer goods, such as cars and electronic items from the West, that not all could afford. Conservative and new Islamist groups were specifically critical of the way their nations' elites and youths aped Western styles and overspent to acquire the latest products. Many were highly suspicious of U.S. motives and saw American culture as antithetical to their own basic values.

This theme was the subject of a book in prerevolutionary Iran by Jalal-e Ahmad that identified *gharbzadeghi,* or Westoxification, as a primary problem. Islamists elsewhere complained of women dressing in Western styles, and Islamic businesses and banks responded to consumers' desire to spend where they would not be contributing to usury.

U.S. cultural imperialism in the Middle East has been most evident in political campaigns and efforts to influence Islamic beliefs and societies since both the September 11, 2001, terrorist attacks against America and the commencement of the Iraq War in 2003. It has manifested itself in a battle to win the hearts and minds of the Muslim world, specifically in Iraq and Afghanistan, but also to pressure the broader Islamic world to refrain from and reject militant Islamic policies. In this, the so-called Global War on Terror has been used as a vehicle for promoting American culture in the region that had given birth to the 9/11 terrorists. The basic logic of U.S. cultural imperialism followed that if American values could be brought to bear in radical Islamic societies, then potential terrorists would not hate America.

The official campaigns that involved winning hearts and minds claimed that the United States invaded Iraq in 2003 to overthrow an evil dictator and establish democracy there. However, it was clear to most people in the Middle East that this was a war of choice, waged for other reasons, and many believed that securing Iraq's oil industry was a primary reason.

Americans had promoted democracy, although not its attendant cultural aspects, in a region historically dominated by authoritarian rulers and repressive regimes. However, in the case of key allies, U.S. foreign policy in the region had often downplayed democratization in favor of stability. Thus, the United States had not promoted democracy in Saudi Arabia, nor did it insist that the shah of Iran democratize or that the Egyptian and Syrian governments do so.

The Middle East was bombarded in the years following 2001 with Western critiques of its culture and deeply held religious beliefs. Such messages of cultural superiority were ill-timed, coming as they did after decades of programs aimed to build pride in national and religious identity.

Various U.S. organizations engaged in information warfare, information campaigns, or information operations and understood that such programs could be the strongest weapons in the Global War on Terror. The processes of this cultural imperialism are manifested primarily through media outlets, with the basic goal of the United States being to expunge the enemy's civil and governmental media and replace it with its own. For example, Iraqi radio and television stations were among the first U.S. targets at the beginning of the March 2003 invasion. Iraqis laughed at many of these programs because they had extensive experience with official propaganda under Hussein's regime. The bright side was a mushrooming of many smaller news publications, even though many have been censored.

There were various tangible applications of what results in cultural imperialism by several branches of the U.S. government. The Public Diplomacy and Public Affairs Office conceived of promoting positive images of the United States to the Arab/Muslim world after 9/11. The Office of Global Communications was also created immediately after 9/11 by the White House to synchronize official opinion among various organizations such as the Central Intelligence

Agency, the Department of Defense, and the State Department. The Advertising Council of America, a World War II creation, formulated positive television advertisements for the White House. As per military operations, press agencies called Coalition Information Centers were created in November 2001 by the U.S. government to ensure that official opinions were aired during Operation ENDURING FREEDOM in Afghanistan.

During the Iraq War, coalition air forces dropped leaflets with the intention of warning civilians of upcoming military dangers or to threaten Iraqi military forces of the dire consequences of resisting. The U.S. Department of Defense converted all Iraqi television stations into the al-Iraqiyya Network, while the State Department created a satellite and cable network, known as 911, for promoting American-friendly programming. Many other organizations also performed information operations funded annually by the federal government.

A more extensive example of an American information operation concerns Radio Sawa (sawa meaning "together"). This station broadcasts in FM and medium-wave frequencies, day and night, to Middle Eastern and North African countries. Radio Sawa replaced Voice of America in the region, which was never as popular as the BBC radio service. Radio Sawa took advantage of new rules that permitted establishment of private FM radio stations; in the past, all were state controlled. Syria and Saudi Arabia have not yet liberalized their radio station practices, however.

Listeners can also tune in to Radio Sawa via the Internet. Its stations are located in Washington, D.C., and Dubai, United Arab Emirates. In addition, Radio Sawa has several news centers in the region. The broadcast language is Arabic, and the content consists of information and entertainment programs friendly to American culture. The station broadcasts a strange mix of Arabic, American, and Spanish music. It is a service of U.S. International Broadcasting, which is organized, managed, and funded by the Broadcasting Board of Governors, an agency of the State Department under supervision of the U.S. Congress. The station is meant to counterbalance the frequently anti-American Arabic news organizations. However, its impact is minimal in much of the region where, like the decidedly unpopular American-created Alhurra (al-Hurra) television satellite channel, it is regarded as a propaganda outlet. Actually, far more popular than Radio Sawa are many smaller radio stations, some of which focus on Arabic musical heritage and now broadcast hard-to-find recordings, more popular types of music, or controversial news programs.

Despite American efforts, positive Arab sentiments toward the United States decreased with exposure to information warfare. Prior to 9/11, the Arab world was already resentful of American financial and moral support of Israel. However, immediately after 9/11, most moderate Arabs expressed genuine sympathy for American suffering and support for the Global War on Terror. This did not last long, however, as antipathy toward the United States skyrocketed in the wake of the Iraq War and the occupation and pacification campaign there. In the absence of a United Nations resolution calling for armed intervention in Iraq, many in the Arab world viewed the U.S.-led war as illegal, and the mere existence of Iraq's large oil reserves created skepticism toward the motives behind the American-led invasion amid U.S. calls for democracy and freedom. When no weapons of mass destruction were discovered in Iraq, many Muslims became even more cynical of U.S. motives. In Iraq and Afghanistan, impatience with the continuing presence of American troops also served to disillusion many who initially welcomed the action.

Many Arabs feared that the U.S. attempt to shape Iraq into a democracy would merely be the opening step in a U.S. effort to transform the entire region. Indeed, some U.S. officials, such as Paul Wolfowitz, had long asserted this to be a U.S. objective. People in the region do not object to democracy but do object to a pseudodemocracy set up by a foreign government by military means that imposes a particular set of foreign policies on the new government.

Many of the new political leaders in Iraq support the imposition of Islamic law rather than the Iraqi civil code. Indeed, the Iraqi Constitution sets out the role of Islamic law in Iraq. With the intensely Islamist atmosphere in Afghanistan and Pakistan, many American programs, products, and movies are highly controversial and are banned by Islamist conservatives throughout the region. Tying the creation of markets to democratization tends to confuse the issue of cultural imperialism in the Middle East. The recent upsurge in extremist Islamist groups such as Boko Haram (literally translated as "Western education is forbidden") and the Islamic State of Iraq and Syria (ISIS), which specifically target Western cultural manifestations and Westerners in general, is a good indication that U.S. efforts to export its cultural influence abroad can be quite problematic.

Many Americans believe in the universality of their goods, ideas, and culture and that deep within every Iraqi or Afghan there is an American waiting to leap out. This is not the case.

DYLAN A. CYR AND SHERIFA ZUHUR

See also

Boko Haram; Bush Doctrine; IRAQI FREEDOM, Operation; Islamic State in Iraq and Syria; Radio Baghdad

References

Eckes, Alfred, and Thomas Zeiler. *Globalization and the American Century.* Cambridge: Cambridge University Press, 2003.

Harding, Jim. *After Iraq: War, Imperialism and Democracy.* Black Point, Nova Scotia: Fernwood, 2004.

Said, Edward. *Culture and Imperialism.* New York: Knopf, 1999.

Schiller, Herbert. *Communication and Cultural Domination.* New York: M. E. Sharpe, 1976.

Tatham, Steve. *Losing Arab Hearts and Minds: The Coalition, Al-Jazeera and Muslim Public Opinion.* London: Hurst, 2006.

D

Dadullah, Mullah (1966–2007)

A leading figure in the Taliban movement in Afghanistan from 1995 until his death in 2007. Mullah Dadullah (aka Mullah Dadullah Akhund), born probably in 1966, was a member of the Kakar tribe from Uruzgan Province. He fought in the Soviet-Afghan War and reportedly lost a leg in that war in the 1980s. Little is known of his activities prior to the late 1990s.

Dadullah emerged as a key figure in Taliban leadership circles beginning in the late 1990s. He was reportedly responsible for the brutal repression of the religious minority Shia population throughout Afghanistan and the ethnic minority Hazara population near Bamyan in 2000. In 2001 he was engaged in fighting against the Northern Alliance in northern Afghanistan. A leading military commander on the northern front, he escaped encirclement in the city of Kunduz, returning to Kandahar on foot and becoming a local hero to Taliban sympathizers in the Pashtun-controlled southern provinces of Afghanistan.

Following the U.S.-assisted ouster of the Taliban government, Dadullah became one of the early leaders of the Taliban insurgency. In 2002–2003 he was engaged in recruiting fresh Pashtun volunteers from madrasas in Baluchistan and Karachi. In 2004 he traveled to Pakistan's Federally Administered Tribal Areas to coordinate activity with Taliban fighters in that region. Taliban leader Mullah Mohammed Omar selected Dadullah as 1 of the original 10 members of the 2003 Rahbari Shura (leadership council), and Dadullah was retained as 1 of the 12 members when the Rahbari Shura expanded in 2004. Dadullah was initially appointed 1 of 3 military leaders of the Taliban southern front in 2003, sharing command with Abd al-Razzaq Akhund and Akhtar Osmani.

Although Dadullah was a powerful and innovative leader, many of his cohorts considered him an extremist. He reportedly had significant disagreements, including a physical confrontation, with fellow Rahbari Shura member Akhtar Osmani, a conflict that ended with Osmani's death in late 2006. Some Taliban sources claim that Osmani's death resulted from a Dadullah tip-off to North Atlantic Treaty Organization (NATO) forces in Afghanistan.

By 2004 Dadullah had full command of the Taliban southern front, and his influence in the movement expanded as he began innovative new practices. Dadullah initiated the tactic of launching repeated attacks, regardless of casualties, against the same targets in remote districts. This demonstrated Taliban commitment to success whatever the cost encouraged local officials to either leave their posts or cooperate with local Taliban cadres. In early 2006 Dadullah announced the creation of Taliban political representatives in all districts, facilitating the establishment of a Taliban shadow government throughout southern and southeastern Afghanistan in particular. By the end of that year he was negotiating to win tribal loyalties in the countryside, promising to share power and resources with tribal leaders in return for their support.

These efforts were all aimed at sustaining the Taliban's so-called final offensive in 2006. It began in the first week of February, with attacks in Helmand. By early summer, thousands of Taliban forces were engaged throughout the south and southeast, sometimes operating in battalion-sized units of up to 400 men each. The offensive surprised many analysts but eventually proved too difficult to sustain, and Dadullah called an end to the campaign in November 2006.

Dadullah was a great innovator, at least in the context of the very conservative Taliban movement. He deliberately chose a flamboyant lifestyle, which became a useful propaganda tool. His extended family lived openly just outside Quetta, and in September 2003 he held a spectacular family wedding that was attended by local Pakistani political leaders and military officers. He encouraged the creation and distribution of a series of brutal videos depicting the execution of prisoners, and he advocated Taliban atrocities against Westerners and humanitarian aid workers. He was also one of the few leaders willing to be photographed and even agreed to interviews with the Al Jazeera news network.

In 2005 Dadullah announced that he was accepting assistance from Al Qaeda in Iraq, which may account for the increased emphasis on and effectiveness of suicide bombings. This shift reflected not only access to expertise from the international extremist community but also an interest in generating greater publicity for the upcoming final offensive. Suicide bombings increased from just 6 in 2004 to an average of more than 10 per month in 2006 and 2007. These bombings were carried out primarily by foreign volunteers; through 2007, most suicide bombers came from Afghan refugee camps or madrasas in Pakistan. Dadullah was involved in recruitment efforts in Pakistan, and he took credit for having "hundreds" of suicide bombers ready by mid-2006.

On May 13, 2007, Dadullah was killed in a firefight with NATO and Afghan government forces outside the town of Garmser in Helmand Province. Reportedly, he had traveled there from Quetta and had been tracked by units of the British Special Boat Service, which had spearheaded the effort to track him down.

TIMOTHY D. HOYT

See also

Afghanistan War; Al Qaeda in Iraq; Madrasas; Omar, Mohammed; Taliban

References

Giustozzi, Antonio. *Koran, Kalashnikov, and Laptop: The Neo-Taliban Insurgency in Afghanistan.* New York: Columbia University Press, 2008.

Rashid, Ahmed. *Descent into Chaos: The United States and the Failure of Nation-Building in Pakistan, Afghanistan, and Central Asia.* New York: Viking, 2008.

Dallas Skyscraper Plot

On September 24, 2009, Hosam Maher Husein Smadi, a 19-year-old Jordanian, was arrested and charged with attempting to bomb the Wells Fargo Bank office tower, a 60-story skyscraper near Fountain Place in downtown Dallas, Texas. The Federal Bureau of Investigation (FBI) had been monitoring his movements and activities ever since he had been discovered communicating with an online group of extremists. Between March and September, undercover agents interacted more than 60 times with the Jordanian, during which times he made clear his intention to act as a "soldier" for Osama bin Laden and conduct violent jihad.

According to sworn testimony presented in court, Smadi initially wanted to target the Dallas/Fort Worth International Airport but had abandoned this plan because the facility was too strong and well protected. On July 16 he allegedly contacted one of the undercover FBI agents and said he was going to bomb the building containing the bank in order to further disrupt the economy, which was already weak, in Texas and the United States.

Eventually Smadi and the undercover agent had a meeting where it was decided that a vehicle-borne improvised explosive device (IED) would be used for the attack. Federal agents then built a dummy bomb and placed it in a 2001 Ford Explorer Sport Trac. According to documents filed on September 24, 2009, Smadi knowingly took possession of the vehicle believing that it contained an active weapon of mass destruction. The indictment went on to say that he drove the Ford to Dallas, parked it at 1445 Ross Avenue (the address of the Wells Fargo Bank office tower), and activated a timer device connected to the bomb. He apparently then left the truck and departed from the scene in a car with an undercover law enforcement agent.

Smadi pleaded guilty on May 26, 2010, to one count of attempted use of a weapon of mass destruction. On October 19, 2010, U.S. District Court judge Barbara M. G. Lynn sentenced him to 24 years in prison.

DONNA BASSETT

See also

Al Qaeda; Brooklyn Bridge Bombing Plot; Millennium Plots; Sears Tower Bomb Plot; Times Square Bomb Plot

References

Emerson, Steven. *Jihad Incorporated: A Guide to Militant Islam in the US.* Foreword by Peter Hoekstra. Amherst, NY: Prometheus Books, 2006.

"Jordanian Man Pleads Guilty in Dallas Bomb Plot." CBS News, May 6, 2010. http://www.cbsnews.com/stories/2010/05/26 /national/main6522078.shtml, accessed May 2, 2011.

Morrow, Stacy, and Elvira Sakmari. "FBI Arrests Man in Dallas Skyscraper Bomb Plot." NBC News, September 25, 2009, http://www.nbcdfw.com/news/local-beat/FBI-Arrests-Man -Accused-in-Skyscraper-Bomb-Plot—61272512.html.

"Terror Plot Foiled: Inside the Smadi Case." Federal Bureau of Investigation, November 5, 2010, http://www.fbi.gov/news /stories/2010/november/terror-plot-foiled/terror-plot-foiled.

Damluji, Maysoon Salem al- (1962–)

Liberal Iraqi politician and women's rights activist. Maysoon (Maysun) Salem al-Damluji was born in Baghdad in 1962 to a prominent family of doctors and political figures. Damluji moved to London in 1962 when she and her family were forced to leave Iraq because they would not join the Baath Party. Settling in Britain, she graduated from the Architectural Association in London in 1985 and began a successful practice as an architect in West London. Despite residing in Britain, Damluji retained a keen interest in her homeland, at first promoting the arts among Iraqi exiles in Britain and, after 1990, becoming involved in active political opposition to the Saddam Hussein regime.

Within a few weeks of the end of the Hussein regime in 2003, Damluji returned to Baghdad. Soon she was active in women's rights there, forming the Iraqi Independent Women's Group. She became president of that organization and also edited its magazine, *Noon.* In late 2003 she accepted the post of deputy minister of culture in the new Iraqi administration and continued in that position with the transfer of Iraqi sovereignty. Damluji worked to save art produced during the period of Baath rule because these are considered to be the best art of the period, and often the artists had no connection with Hussein's regime. Many Shiite religious groups have opposed this approach, preferring to start afresh with purely Islamic art.

In February 2006 Damluji gave up her government post to become a member of the Iraqi parliament representing the city of Mosul. In the parliament, she has spoken out in favor of preserving human rights in the face of sharia (Islamic law). Her stance on these issues has produced frequent threats on her life. In 2010, Damluji became the official spokesperson for the secular Iraqi National List (Iraqiya), a coalition of secular Iraqi political figures and groupings.

SPENCER C. TUCKER

See also

Hussein, Saddam; Iraq War; Sharia

References

Al-Ali, Nadje, and Nicola Pratt. *What Kind of Liberation: Women and the Occupation of Iraq.* Berkeley: University of California Press, 2009.

Al-Jawaheri, Yasmin Husein. *Women in Iraq: The Gender Impact of International Sanctions.* Boulder, CO: Lynne Rienner, 2008.

Dar es Salaam, Bombing of U.S. Embassy (August 7, 1998)

Bombing of the U.S. embassy in Dar es Salaam, Tanzania, by Al Qaeda terrorists. Early on the morning of August 7, 1998, Al Qaeda operatives, using a truck bomb, attacked the U.S. embassy, killing 12 people and injuring 86 others. U.S. Federal Bureau of Investigation (FBI) agents concluded that the bomb was most likely planted in a refrigeration truck. The building suffered major damage and was deemed unusable. A year prior to the attack there had been a warning of a possible terrorist attack on the embassy, but it had been ignored because the source could not be verified.

The attack on the embassy in Dar es Salaam caused far fewer casualties than the nearly simultaneous attack on the U.S. embassy in Nairobi, Kenya, also targeted by Al Qaeda. In fact, none of the Dar es Salaam personnel inside the building were killed in the attack. The Tanzanian embassy was located farther from the city center, which helped to minimize civilian casualties. According to reports, the truck bomber was unable to penetrate the outer wall of the embassy because a water tanker had blocked its path. When the bomb detonated, the tanker absorbed much of the blast that otherwise would undoubtedly have caused greater damage to the chancery building.

The investigators concluded that Osama bin Laden, leader of Al Qaeda, had masterminded the embassy attacks. As a result, the U.S. government issued indictments against him and offered a $5 million reward for his capture. In 2001, four men were convicted in U.S. federal courts and sentenced to life in prison for their role in the bombings of the U.S. embassies in Kenya and Tanzania. Bin Laden was killed by U.S. special forces in Abbotabad, Pakistan, on May 1, 2011.

In response to the attacks on the U.S. embassies, President Bill Clinton pledged to wage a war against international terrorism. In retaliation for the bombings, on August 20, 1998, the United States launched cruise missiles against three terrorist camps in Afghanistan and a suspected chemical weapons plant in Sudan. The operation was code-named INFINITE REACH. The attacks on the camps in Afghanistan killed 24 people but failed to kill bin Laden. The attack on the plant in Sudan came under great criticism because there was no corroborating evidence to justify the attack, and many believe that the plant produced pharmaceuticals rather than chemical weapons. That attack killed the night watchmen at the plant.

In the United States, some cynics accused President Clinton of mounting the retaliatory attacks to distract the public's attention from the still-unfolding Monica Lewinsky scandal. The cruise missile attacks precipitated massive protests around the world, mostly in Muslim countries. In addition, bin Laden pledged to strike the United States again, a threat that he made good on with the devastating attacks in New York and Washington, D.C., on September 11, 2001.

DANIEL W. KUTHY

See also

Al Qaeda; Bin Laden, Osama; Nairobi, Kenya, Bombing of U.S. Embassy; Terrorism

References

Ferguson, Amanda. *The Attack against the U.S. Embassies in Kenya and Tanzania.* New York: Rosen Publication Group, 2003.

Labéviere, Richard. *Dollars for Terror: The United States and Islam.* New York: Algora Publishing, 2000.

Obwogo, Subiri. *The Bombs That Shook Nairobi & Dar es Salaam: A Story of Pain and Betrayal.* Nairobi: Obwogo and Family, 1999.

Dawa Party

See Islamic Dawa Party

Debecka Pass, Battle of (April 6, 2003)

Engagement that unfolded in northern Iraq on April 6, 2003, during Operation IRAQI FREEDOM, the Iraq War. U.S. strategy for the Iraq War called for the major thrust against Iraq to come from the south. A secondary offensive featuring the 4th Infantry Division would move through Turkey and invade northern Iraq. When Turkey refused permission

for the 4th Division to transit across its territory, however, strategists revised the plan for a northern thrust. The new plan called for a joint force consisting of the 173rd Airborne Brigade, the 26th Marine Expeditionary Unit, and U.S. Army Special Forces operating in cooperation with Kurdish fighters known as Peshmerga ("those who face death").

The 10th Special Forces Group, commanded by Colonel Charlie Cleveland, opened the second front in northern Iraq. Its mission was to destroy training camps used by Ansar al-Islam terrorists and to prevent Iraqi forces in northern Iraq from reinforcing the units defending Baghdad. The particular objectives of the 10th Special Forces Group were the cities of Mosul and Kirkuk and the northern oil fields near these cities.

The basic unit of the special forces was the Operational Detachment-A, or A-Team. A captain commanded the 12-man A-Team with a warrant officer serving as second-in-command. Noncommissioned officers composed the balance of the team, with two each possessing specialty training in one of the five special forces functional areas: weapons, engineering, medical, communications, and operations and intelligence.

For the push into northern Iraq, the special forces utilized specially modified Humvees (high-mobility multipurpose wheeled vehicles). The Humvees served as a mobile headquarters and fighting platform, and they had sophisticated communications equipment to enable the men to call in air strikes. Each vehicle carried several machine guns, Mark 19 grenade launchers, sniper rifles, side arms, Stinger shoulder-fired antiaircraft missiles, and the new Javelin fire-and-forget antitank missile. The Stinger launcher and missile weighed about 50 pounds. Consequently, a single soldier could carry and operate it. The Javelin had a range of about 2,750 yards. The missile used an internal guidance system to fly to the target and then dive down to strike the top of an armored vehicle, its most vulnerable spot because top armor was thinner than front or side armor. The Javelins figured prominently in the April 6, 2003, Battle of Debecka Pass.

Two special forces A-Teams and forward air controllers (26 personnel in all) were given the task of securing a key intersection on Highway 2 near the town of Debecka in northern Iraq between the cities of Irbil to the north and Kirkuk to the south. Accompanied by as many as 80 Peshmerga fighters, the team deployed to block Iraqi troop movements along Highway 2 in either direction. However, a surprise Iraqi counterattack featuring some 150 infantry, eight armored personnel carriers, and four T-55 tanks with

100-mm main guns struck the special forces, forcing them to withdraw to a nearby ridgeline.

From their new position the Americans engaged the approaching Iraqi armored forces with Javelin antitank missiles, .50-caliber machine guns, and Mark 19 40-mm grenade launchers. One Javelin destroyed an armored personnel carrier from a distance of 2,950 yards, 200 yards beyond the rated maximum engagement range. During this phase of the battle, of eight Javelins fired by the special forces, seven struck their intended targets, destroying five armored personnel carriers and two trucks. The Javelin strikes stopped the momentum of the Iraqi attack. The Iraqis then moved the tanks behind an earthen berm, where they could not be targeted by the Javelins because the Javelins required the operator to have a clear line of sight to the target. The Iraqis did not know that the Americans had only three Javelins remaining.

Meanwhile, a request for air support brought U.S. Navy Grumman F-14 Tomcat fighters. U.S. Air Force forward air controllers operating with the special forces directed the Tomcats to attack the Iraqi armor at the intersection. In a case of mistaken identify, an F-14 Tomcat bombed friendly Kurdish fighters operating behind the special forces, killing 16 Kurds and wounding another 45. A British Broadcasting Corporation (BBC) film crew was present and broadcast a description of this incident as it occurred.

The special forces were holding their position until an Iraqi battery of D-20 towed 152-mm howitzers opened fire. The special forces had no answer to this fire and were again compelled to relocate. In their new position they received a resupply of Javelin missiles. The Americans were also able to see more clearly the Iraqi T-55 tanks as well as the surviving armored personnel carriers. The special forces again opened fire with the Javelins. When an Iraqi tank tried to change positions it emerged into the open, where it was promptly destroyed by a Javelin. This event broke the morale of the Iraqi forces.

At 12:45 p.m. local time, about 15 Iraqi soldiers appeared from a ravine indicating that they wished to surrender. Suddenly, two white Toyota Land Cruisers appeared and disgorged Iraqi security personnel, who began shooting down the surrendering Iraqi soldiers. A laser-guided bomb dropped from an American airplane then destroyed the Land Cruisers. During the final phase of the combat, another Javelin missile destroyed another Iraqi T-55 tank. The remaining Iraqi soldiers abandoned their vehicles and fled.

In a telephone interview in the autumn of 2003, one of the special forces sergeants in the battle attributed the American victory to the Javelin missiles. Without them, the special forces would not have been able to hold off the Iraqi tanks. The Americans suffered no casualties, but the Peshmerga sustained 16 dead and 45 wounded from the friendly fire incident; 1 civilian was also killed. Iraqi killed and wounded are unknown, but 20 were taken prisoner. The Iraqis also lost at least two T-55 tanks, eight armored personnel carriers, and four trucks. The Battle of Debecka Pass was an example of how small, highly trained, well-led units with sophisticated weaponry can defeat larger conventional units.

JAMES ARNOLD

See also

Antitank Weapons; High-Mobility Multipurpose Wheeled Vehicle; IRAQI FREEDOM, Operation; Peshmerga; T-54/55 Series Main Battle Tank

References

Antenori, Frank, and Hans Halberstadt. *Roughneck Nine-One: The Extraordinary Story of a Special Forces A-Team at War.* New York: St. Martin's, 2006.

Gordon, Michael R., and General Bernard E. Trainor. *Cobra II: The Inside Story of the Invasion and Occupation of Iraq.* New York: Pantheon Books, 2006.

Murray, Williamson, and Robert H. Scales Jr. *The Iraq War: A Military History.* Cambridge, MA: Belknap, 2005.

Stilwell, Alexander. *Special Forces Today: Afghanistan, Africa, Balkans, Iraq, South America.* Dulles, VA: Potomac Books, 2007.

Defense Intelligence Agency

Formally established at the direction of Secretary of Defense Robert McNamara on October 1, 1961, the Defense Intelligence Agency (DIA) is the leading intelligence agency for the Department of Defense (DOD). The DIA is directly responsible for meeting the intelligence requirements of the secretary of defense, the Joint Chiefs of Staff, and each of the Combatant Commands. Prior to the agency's establishment, each of the military services collected, analyzed, and disseminated their own intelligence separately to their own service chiefs, components, and the Unified and Specific Commands (now called Combatant Commands).

The Defense Reorganization Act of 1958, which gave birth to the DIA, sought to reduce the duplication and uncoordinated efforts that derived from those separate efforts. It also hoped to provide integrated intelligence analysis and support to the Joint Chiefs of Staff and the secretary of defense. The DIA acquired the mandate for all aspects and phases of the Defense Department's intelligence production except those intelligence-collection platforms and activities specifically assigned to the individual military services.

The 1962 Cuban Missile Crisis was the first major test for the DIA and was followed almost immediately by the Berlin Crisis. For a new agency, the DIA performed surprisingly well in both instances.

The Vietnam War saw the DIA become the primary authority and coordinating agency for military intelligence related to facilities and infrastructure. In the late 1970s, it also became the coordinating agency for any DOD relationships with foreign military intelligence organizations. By the 1980s, the DIA became the DOD's coordinating agency for national collection assets as well as its spokesperson before Congress on budgeting and national intelligence production priorities.

Driven by the lessons learned from the 1991 Persian Gulf War (Operation DESERT STORM), the DIA's authority and mission expanded in consonance with the increasing integration of U.S. military forces into a joint structure and operations. Combatant Command intelligence centers now report their production requirements to and acquire their operating funds from the DIA. Although dissenting intelligence analysis is included in the DIA's coordinated national intelligence assessments, the DIA's assessment has become the dominant one.

The September 11, 2001, terror attacks on the United States perpetrated by Al Qaeda and the sequelae from these have placed a spotlight on the DIA and its activities. The September 11 Commission, charged with evaluating the U.S. response to the 9/11 attacks, was critical of the DIA's inability to thwart them and called into question its ability to effectively compile and disseminate intelligence information to prevent another September 11.

Similarly, the DIA has been criticized by the Weapons of Mass Destruction (WMD) Commission for its role in the faulty intelligence surrounding Iraq's alleged WMD program prior to the Anglo-American invasion of Iraq in March 2003. The George W. Bush administration was later embarrassed when no WMD were found in Iraq. Their presence had been one of the key reasons for the invasion. Indeed, both commissions cited the DIA's failure to use open and human intelligence sources effectively. In all fairness, however, other intelligence agencies were criticized in similar fashion.

The intelligence-gathering reforms based on the commissions' recommendations began in 2005 but were not fully implemented until the end of the decade. In 2005 a new cabinet-level intelligence position was created: director of national intelligence. The director serves as the president's chief intelligence adviser and also serves as principal adviser to the National Security Council and the Department of Homeland Security. As such, the post calls upon the director to coordinate information from the DIA and other intelligence-gathering agencies.

CARL OTIS SCHUSTER

See also

Bush, George Walker; IRAQI FREEDOM, Operation; Nuclear Weapons, Iraq's Potential for Building; September 11 Attacks; September 11 Commission and Report; Terrorism; Weapons of Mass Destruction

References

Richelson, Jeffrey T. *The U.S. Intelligence Community.* 4th ed. Boulder, CO: Westview, 1999.
Roberts, Pat, ed. *Report on U.S. Intelligence Community's Prewar Intelligence Assessments on Iraq: Conclusions.* Washington, DC: Diane Publishing, 2004.
United States. *21st Century Complete Guide to American Intelligence Agencies.* Washington, DC: U.S. Government Printing Office, 2002.

Defense Meteorological Satellite Program

A satellite program developed by the U.S. Department of Defense to provide worldwide meteorological, oceanographic, and solar-geophysical data and imagery to the U.S. military for use in planning and executing military operations. The U.S. Air Force Space and Missile Systems Center (SMC), Los Angeles Air Force Base, California, designed, built, and launched the Defense Meteorological Satellite Program (DMSP) satellites. Since the launch of the first DMSP satellite in 1965, the air force has launched 34 more. In December 1972 the Department of Defense made DMSP data available to civil and scientific communities. In June 1998 the air force transferred the control of the satellites to the National Oceanographic and Atmospheric Administration, but the SMC retained responsibility for the development and acquisition of future DMSP satellites.

DMSP satellites send images and data to tracking stations in New Hampshire, Greenland, Alaska, and Hawaii. These sites in turn send the images to the U.S. Air Force Weather Agency (AFWA), Offutt Air Force Base, Nebraska; the 55th Space Weather Squadron, Falcon Air Force Base, Colorado; and the U.S. Navy's Fleet Numerical Meteorology and Oceanography Center (FNMOC), Monterey, California.

The AFWA and the FNMOC process the images and data into a product that is then sent to military installations, where meteorologists develop up-to-date weather observations and forecasts for use by unit commanders in scheduling and planning military operations.

During the Vietnam War, early DMSP satellites supplied cloud-cover information to military headquarters in Saigon and to aircraft carriers in the Gulf of Tonkin for more precise planning of tactical air missions. DMSP imagery provided highly accurate weather forecasting that operational commanders used to plan air strikes over the Democratic Republic of Vietnam (North Vietnam) and close air support over the Republic of Vietnam (South Vietnam), determine air-to-air refueling tracks, and plan rescue operations. The DMSP weather data eliminated the need for weather reconnaissance aircraft in Southeast Asia.

For Operations DESERT SHIELD/DESERT STORM from August 1990 to February 1991, the SMC procured the Rapid Deployment Imagery Terminal, which, supplemented by older weather terminals, provided DMSP data and images directly to the commanders of fielded forces in the Persian Gulf region. The terminals provided commanders with high-resolution nearly real-time weather information that allowed them to select targets and munitions, especially laser-guided weapons that required clear weather for accurate targeting, during the air campaign.

Commanders also used weather data and images to plan and redirect aerial and ground missions and optimize night-vision equipment and night-capable targeting systems. DMSP satellites also provided information to alert troops to sandstorms and to predict the possible use and spread of chemical agents.

In December 1990 the U.S. Air Force launched a third DMSP satellite to augment coverage in the Persian Gulf area. With the additional capability of detecting areas of moisture and standing water, DMSP imagery helped coalition ground forces plan movement routes into Kuwait during Operation DESERT STORM. DMSP and other weather satellites also provided extensive imagery and data of the oil fires ignited by the Iraqi Army as it fled Kuwait in February 1991. The fires produced large smoke plumes, causing significant environmental effects on the Persian Gulf region.

There have been some problems with the terminals and dissemination networks, however. For example, the incompatibility of the four different types of terminals delayed the receipt of timely weather data. With rapidly changing weather conditions, field units often did not have the latest target-area weather data, and high-quality satellite imagery

did not get to the flyers. Some navy ships could not receive DMSP data at all. These problems emphasized the need for more compatible and user-friendly systems. During Operations ENDURING FREEDOM and IRAQI FREEDOM a number of these problems had been eliminated, and DMSP provided badly needed weather data to troops in both theaters of war.

ROBERT B. KANE

See also

IRAQI FREEDOM, Operation; Persian Gulf War

References

Hall, R. Cargill. *A History of the Military Polar Orbiting Meteorological Satellite Program.* Chantilly, VA: National Reconnaissance Office History Office, 2001.

History Office, Space and Missile Systems Center, Los Angeles Air Force Base. *Historical Overview of the Space and Missile Systems Center, 1954–2003.* Los Angeles: Missile Systems Center, 2003.

Peeples, Curtis. *High Frontier: The United States Air Force and the Military Space Program.* Washington, DC: Air Force History and Museum Program, 1997.

Spires, David N. *Beyond Horizons: A Half Century of Air Force Space Leadership.* 2nd ed. Maxwell Air Force Base, AL: Air Force Space Command and Air University Press, 2007.

Defense Satellite Communications System

A constellation of nine satellites in geosynchronous orbit 22,300 miles above Earth that provides high-volume secure voice and data communications among the White House, senior U.S. defense officials, and U.S. military forces in the field worldwide. The U.S. Air Force launched the first Defense Satellite Communications System (DSCS) satellite in 1966. In 1967 DSCS I satellites transmitted reconnaissance photographs and other data from military headquarters in the Republic of Vietnam (South Vietnam) to Hawaii and from Hawaii to Washington, D.C. In 1968 the air force declared the satellite system, along with 2 fixed and 34 mobile ground terminals, to be operational and changed the system's name to the Initial Defense Satellite Communication System (IDCS).

After having launched 26 IDCS satellites, the U.S. Air Force renamed the program the Defense Satellite Communications System. In 1971 the air force began launching a more sophisticated satellite, DSCS Phase II (DSCS II). DSCS II, the first operational military communications satellite system to occupy a geosynchronous orbit, became fully operational in early 1979. By 1989 the air force had launched 16 DSCS II satellites.

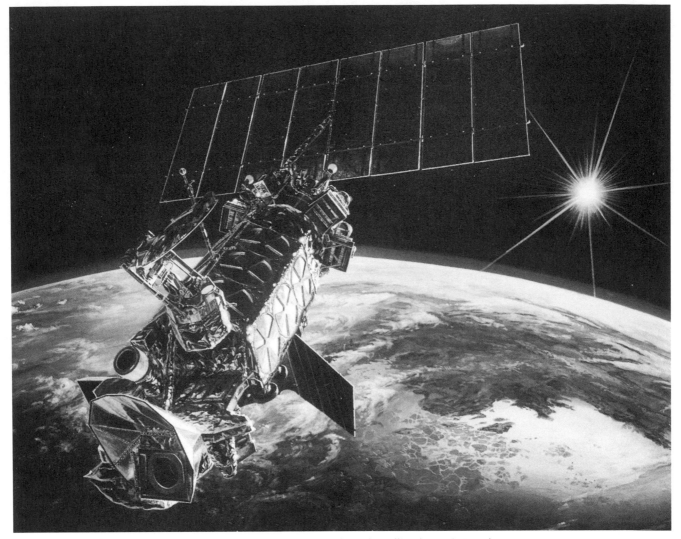

An illustration showing a Defense Satellite Communications System (DSCS) satellite. (U.S. Air Force)

In 1982 the U.S. Air Force launched the first DSCS III, the only current model of the DSCS family still operational, and achieved a full constellation of five satellites in 1993. The DSCS III satellites carry multiple beam antennas that provide flexible coverage over six communication channels and resistance to jamming.

The U.S. Air Force Space Command's Space and Missile Systems Center, Los Angeles Air Force Base, California, contracted with Martin Marietta to build the DSCS III satellites and ground segment. The Electronics Systems Center, Hanscom Air Force Base, Massachusetts, developed the air force portion of the terminal segment. The 3rd Space Operations Squadron, 50th Space Wing, Schriever Air Force Base, Colorado, provides command and control of the DSCS satellites.

During Operations DESERT SHIELD and DESERT STORM (August 1990–February 1991), satellite communications provided essential command and control of deployed coalition forces. Although military communications were very tenuous at the start of DESERT SHIELD, U.S. military forces within the first 90 days established more military communications connectivity to the Persian Gulf than they had achieved in Europe over the previous 40 years.

Operation DESERT SHIELD forces communicated through a U.S. Navy Fleet Satellite Communications satellite (FLT-SATCOM), a Leased Satellite (LEASAT) program satellite, and two DSCS satellites over the Indian Ocean. In addition, the U.S. Department of Defense used FLTSATCOM satellites over the Atlantic Ocean and DSCS satellites over the eastern Atlantic to facilitate communications between the U.S. Central Command headquarters in the Persian Gulf and various headquarters in the United States.

DSCS III satellites also provided long-haul communications for U.S. military forces during Operation DENY FLIGHT (1993–1995) and Operation ALLIED FORCE (1999) in the Balkans and during Operations ENDURING FREEDOM and IRAQI FREEDOM in the Middle East beginning in 2001. Throughout these operations, communications requirements steadily grew, reaching the capacity of the DSCS satellites to provide for the increasing needs. For Operation ENDURING FREEDOM, the U.S. Air Force reconfigured the DSCS satellites to provide added bandwidth. The introduction of unmanned aerial vehicles (drones) and increased use of digital imagery and data in Middle Eastern combat operations contributed to the growing demand for large communications networks.

Since 2000 the U.S. Air Force, through the DSCS Service Life Enhancement Program, has upgraded the last four DSCS III satellites prior to launch to extend the usable lifetime of the satellites. In addition, the air force has incorporated several technology upgrades to increase the capabilities of the DSCS satellites prior to launch into orbit.

ROBERT B. KANE

See also

IRAQI FREEDOM, Operation; Satellites, Use of by Coalition Forces; United States Central Command; Unmanned Aerial Vehicles

References

History Office, Space and Missile Systems Center, Los Angeles Air Force Base. *Historical Overview of the Space and Missile Systems Center, 1954–2003*. Los Angeles: Missile Systems Center, 2003.

Levis, Alexander H., John C. Bedford (Colonel, USAF), and Sandra Davis (Captain, USAF), eds. *The Limitless Sky: Air Force Science and Technology Contributions to the Nation*. Washington, DC: Air Force History and Museums Program, 2004.

Peeples, Curtis. *High Frontier: The United States Air Force and the Military Space Program*. Washington, DC: Air Force History and Museum Program, 1997.

Spires, David N. *Beyond Horizons: A Half Century of Air Force Space Leadership*. 2nd ed. Maxwell Air Force Base, AL: Air Force Space Command and Air University Press, 2007.

Delta Force

The 1st Special Forces Operational Detachment–Delta Airborne, officially known as the Combat Applications Group and known commonly to the general public as Delta Force, is a special operations force of the United States Army Special Operations Command.

Although the force had diverse capabilities, Delta Force's main task is counterterrorism. Delta Force is widely known for its activities during Operation RESTORE HOPE (1993) in Somalia, Operations DESERT SHIELD (1990) and DESERT STORM during the Persian Gulf War (1991), and the U.S.-led Iraqi invasion in March 2003 (Operation IRAQI FREEDOM). It is modeled on other elite counterterrorism forces worldwide, such as the British Special Air Service (SAS), the Australian Special Air Service Regiment, the Israeli Sayeret Matkal, and Germany's GSG-9 and KSK.

Delta Force was created in 1977 by U.S. Army colonel Charles Beckwith in response to numerous terrorist incidents that had occurred in the 1970s. From its inception, Delta Force was heavily influenced by the British SAS, a result of Colonel Beckwith's one-year exchange tour with that unit.

The force is organized into three operating squadrons (A, B, and C), which are subdivided into small groups known as troops. Each troop specializes in either high-altitude low-opening skydiving, high-altitude high-opening skydiving, or scuba diving. The troops can be further divided into smaller units as needed. Delta Force maintains support units that handle selection and training, logistics, finance, and the unit's medical requirements. Within these units is a vital technical unit responsible for maintaining covert eavesdropping equipment.

The Department of Defense doggedly protects detailed information about Delta Force and publicly refuses to comment on specifics about the unit. The unit is able to deploy anywhere in the world with 18 hours' notice. Delta Force specializes in airborne operations; direct action operations; raids; infiltrating and ex-filtrating by sea, air, or land; intelligence; recovery of personnel and special equipment; and support of general-purpose forces.

Delta Force recruits its members solely from the U.S. Army, usually from the U.S. Army Special Forces, specifically the Green Berets and Rangers. Headquartered in a remote facility at Fort Bragg, North Carolina, Delta Force's compound holds numerous shooting facilities, both for close-range and longer-range sniping; a dive tank; an Olympic-size swimming pool; a climbing wall; and a model of an airliner.

Delta Force operatives are granted an enormous amount of flexibility and autonomy. They do not maintain a general uniformed presence and usually wear civilian clothing while on or off duty at Fort Bragg in order to conceal their identity. Hairstyles and facial hair are also allowed to grow to civilian standards to allow for greater anonymity. In addition, Delta Force soldiers carry highly customized weapons. While the unit's weapon of choice is the M4 carbine, operatives often carry foreign weapon systems that are used by the enemy in the area of operation. This allows them to remain inconspicuous and to employ the ammunition from slain enemy fighters if necessary.

While Delta Force specializes in counterterrorism operations, it also engages in hostage rescue. For example, the unit took part in Operation EAGLE CLAW, the failed attempt to rescue the American hostages from the U.S. embassy in Iran in April 1980. The mission failed when a severe sandstorm clogged engine intakes on U.S. helicopters and reduced visibility, forcing two helicopters to collide in midair. After the failure of EAGLE CLAW, the U.S. Army created the 160th Special Operations Aviation Regiment to transport special forces personnel anywhere in the world.

At the beginning of Operation DESERT SHIELD in 1990, Delta Force was deployed to the Persian Gulf to serve as bodyguards for senior army officials. They then worked with British SAS units to search for and destroy mobile Scud missile launchers in Iraq's northern deserts. The primary mission for both the SAS and Delta Force, however, was to locate and designate targets for destruction by coalition warplanes. This contributed immensely to the quick and relatively painless victory of coalition forces in the Persian Gulf War.

Delta Force was also involved in Operation GOTHIC SERPENT in Somalia. That operation led to the Battle of Mogadishu and was later detailed in Mark Bowden's *Black Hawk Down: A Story of Modern War* (2000). In 2001, the unit also played an important role in overthrowing the Taliban regime in Afghanistan in Operation ENDURING FREEDOM. Two years later, Delta Force personnel played a vital role in Operation IRAQI FREEDOM, the Anglo-American operation to oust Iraqi dictator Saddam Hussein from power. Accompanied by Navy SEALS from DEVGRU (the U.S. Navy Special Warfare Development Group), the unit entered Baghdad in advance of the attack to build networks of informants while eavesdropping on and sabotaging Iraqi communication lines.

Delta Force has been involved in many other missions, but most of these remain classified and are thus not publicly known.

CHARLENE T. OVERTURF

See also
Persian Gulf War

References
Beckwith, Charlie A., and Donald Knox. *Delta Force: The Army's Elite Counterterrorist Unit*. New York: Avon, 2000.
Bowden, Mark. *Black Hawk Down: A Story of Modern War*. New York: Penguin, 2000.
Haney, Eric. *Inside Delta Force: The Story of America's Elite Counterterrorist Unit*. New York: Dell, 2003.

Democratization and the Global War on Terror

The link between democratization and the Global War on Terror has been one of the most controversial elements of post–September 11, 2001, U.S. foreign policy. However, democratization has also been a consistent plank of U.S. foreign policy especially in the Middle East, although more often stated than fully supported. Democratization is the complex process whereby a democracy replaces a nondemocratic political regime or pluralism is increased. Free elections for government control, the participation of a legal opposition or multiple parties, the application of equal rights, and the extension of liberal rules of citizenship and laws are typically considered minimum requirements of democratization. In turn, the term "Global War on Terror" may take either of two meanings. First, it may refer to a general state of conflict against violent radicalism, broadly defined. In this sense, the George W. Bush administration contended that democratization was the key to winning the Global War on Terror, especially in the Middle East. Second, the term "Global War on Terror" may refer to a bundle of unilateralist and often forceful security strategies initiated by the United States after the September 11 terror attacks. This interpretation of the Global War on Terror is also closely associated with an assertive promotion of democracy, including by military imposition, as seen in the U.S.-led invasions of Afghanistan (2001) and Iraq (2003). This entry focuses on the second meaning of the term "Global War on Terror."

The notion that democratization enhances national and global security is deeply rooted in the study of international relations as well as U.S. foreign policy. The liberal (sometimes called idealist) approach to international relations views nondemocratic governments as a primary cause of war. Eighteenth-century German philosopher Immanuel Kant proposed that perpetual peace requires an alliance of liberal states. Such governments, he reasoned, need the consent of citizens who are averse to the risks of war. In 1917 President Woodrow Wilson justified the U.S. intervention in World War I by condemning traditional balance-of-power politics as the undemocratic "old and evil order" that pushed nations toward war. Future world peace, Wilson asserted, must be founded upon political liberty. When he spelled out U.S. war aims in his Fourteen Points speech of January 8, 1918, Wilson made an international organization of nations one of them. The representatives at the Paris Peace Conference of 1919 set up the League of Nations called for by Wilson, and its covenant was very much along the lines he proposed. While the U.S. Senate failed to ratify the treaty that would have brought U.S. membership in the League of Nations—and indeed the United States never joined that organization—liberal Wilsonian internationalism continues to influence U.S. foreign policy. President Franklin

Roosevelt was a firm believer in Wilsonian principles and continued this approach. Roosevelt was an ardent champion of the successor to the League of Nations, the United Nations (UN), which came into being after World War II.

In recent years, scholars have turned to historical evidence to test whether or not democracies are indeed more pacific than undemocratic regimes. Proponents of the democratic peace theory argue that similar liberal institutions, cultures, laws, and linked economies make democracies especially unwilling to fight each other. Consequently, Michael Doyle argues that liberal democracies have reached a separate peace among themselves, although they remain insecure and conflict-prone toward nations that are not democratic.

Liberal theorists therefore expect that an increase in the number of democracies will expand existing zones of the democratic peace. Not all agree, however, on the full implications to the world system. For example, John Owen argues that a peaceful union of liberal countries would still need nondemocratic states against which to define themselves.

Many notable scholars, particularly those working in the dominant realist tradition of international relations, vigorously dispute the premises of democratic peace theory. They maintain, for example, that the theory neglects how peace among Western democracies during the Cold War was induced by a shared Soviet threat. Moreover, Edward Mansfield and Jack Snyder conclude that emerging democracies are historically more, not less, war-prone than other states.

Such criticisms aside, democratic peace theory's impact on U.S. policy makers since the 1980s is hard to exaggerate. Proponents, including both Republican and Democratic presidents, presented the 1989 fall of the Berlin Wall, the 1991 collapse of the Soviet Union, and a roughly concurrent rise in the global number of democracies as bellwethers of a freer, more secure international order. Political theorist Francis Fukuyama's famous thesis on the emergence of Western liberal democracy (*The End of History and the Last Man*) as "the final form of government" captured liberalism's optimistic, even triumphal spirit at the start of the post–Cold War era.

Complicating the picture, however, was the distinctive neoconservative political philosophy that also gained influence in the 1980s, especially within the Republican Party. With the Soviet collapse, neoconservatives contend that the proper role of the United States as the sole remaining superpower is to forge and maintain a benevolent world order. Neoconservatives share liberals' confidence that democracies do not fight each other, but they depart from traditional liberalism by arguing that the United States should shun reliance on international organizations—including the UN, toward which they have much antipathy—in promoting democracy overseas. Rather, the United States should be willing to use unilateral force if necessary to bring democracy to steadfastly nondemocratic states and regions.

Significantly, a public letter from associates of the neoconservative think tank Project for the New American Century urged President William J. Clinton to consider removing Iraqi dictator Saddam Hussein militarily more than three years before the 2001 terror attacks. The 1998 letter was signed by numerous individuals who would go on to occupy top foreign and national security policy posts in the first and second George W. Bush administrations, including Secretary of Defense Donald Rumsfeld, Deputy Secretary of Defense Paul Wolfowitz, Undersecretary of Defense for Policy Douglas Feith, and U.S. representative to the UN John Bolton.

Neoconservative influence became most pronounced after September 11, which the Bush administration framed as an attack on liberal democracy around the world. Shortly after the invasion of Afghanistan, neoconservative speechwriter David J. Frum coined the phrase "axis of evil" to describe undemocratic Iran, Iraq, and North Korea for the president's January 2002 State of the Union address. This address was widely seen as setting the stage for further U.S. military action overseas. Other aspects of the Global War on Terror strategy reflect neoconservative precepts, including the Bush Doctrine of preemptive war, the decision to invade Iraq despite strong international and UN opposition, the belief that a lack of democracy in the Middle East fosters terrorism, and the argument that democratization justifies military action.

The ideas of Israeli politician and former Soviet dissident Natan Sharansky also align with neoconservative priorities. In 2005 President Bush praised Sharansky's recent work, which argues that the United States must lead the drive for democratization, as "a great book" that validated his own policies. However, observers note a decline in the more forceful aspects of the administration's prodemocracy rhetoric after Egyptian Islamists made notable gains in 2005 parliamentary elections and the armed Hamas movement won the Palestinian parliamentary elections of January 2006.

Policy makers continue to debate both the desirability of an alliance of democracies and the U.S. role in promoting democracy abroad. Critics of the current strategy linking democratization to national security and the Global War on Terror reflect a number of ideological and theoretical approaches and include former Bush administration officials. They can be divided into three major camps, with frequent overlap. One camp emphasizes pragmatism and feasibility. These critics see efforts to propel democracy via military invasion and occupation as unworkable, fed by false analogies to post–World War II Germany and Japan. They may also judge the strategy counterproductive, arguing that it heightens anti-Americanism and hurts the legitimacy of local prodemocracy groups in target countries. A second camp is rooted in ethical or nationalistic concerns. While some critics label the democratization strategy hypocritical in light of close American ties to Saudi Arabia and other undemocratic states, others assert that neoconservatives in the Bush administration have crafted a Global War on Terror strategy that privileges Israel over U.S. security concerns. A third camp argues that the Global War on Terror is a veiled and fundamentally anti-democratic attempt to enhance U.S. power in regions rich in important natural resources, such as oil.

The difficulty of installing stable, workable, and effective governments in Afghanistan and Iraq offers a prime example of the problems associated with linking democratization to the Global War on Terror. In nations that have no history of democratic organizations, imposing democracy—even by use of force—is rife with difficulties and contradictions. Furthermore, in nations in which the economic system was either nonexistent (such as Afghanistan) or badly damaged (such as Iraq), the cultivation of democracy is not as important as survival for the great majority of the citizenry. Democracy and widespread poverty and economic and social inequalities do not often go together very well.

RANJIT SINGH

See also
"Axis of Evil"; Bolton, John Robert, II; Bush, George Walker; Bush Doctrine; Failed States and the Global War on Terror; Feith, Douglas; Global War on Terror; Neoconservatism; Rice, Condoleezza; Rumsfeld, Donald; Terrorism; Wolfowitz, Paul

References
Doyle, Michael W. "Liberalism and World Politics." *American Political Science Review* 80 (December 1986): 1151–1169.

Fukuyama, Francis. *The End of History and the Last Man.* New York: Free Press, 1992.

Kant, Immanuel. *Perpetual Peace, and Other Essays on Politics, History, and Morals.* Translated by Ted Humphrey. Indianapolis: Hackett, 1983.

Mansfield, Edward D., and Jack Snyder. *Electing to Fight: Why Emerging Democracies Go to War.* Cambridge, MA: MIT Press, 2005.

Owen, John M., IV. *Liberal Peace, Liberal War: American Politics and International Security.* Ithaca, NY: Cornell University Press, 1997.

Sharansky, Natan, and Ron Dermer. *The Case for Democracy: The Power of Freedom to Overcome Tyranny and Terror.* New York: PublicAffairs, 2004.

Woodward, Bob. *State of Denial: Bush at War, Part III.* New York: Simon and Schuster, 2006.

Dempsey, Martin E. (1954–)

U.S. Army general and acting commander of the U.S. Central Command (CENTCOM) during March–December 2008. Born in 1954, Martin E. Dempsey began his army career when he was commissioned a second lieutenant upon graduation from the United States Military Academy, West Point, in June 1974. His first posting, from June 1975 to June 1978, was as a scout and platoon leader in the 2nd Armored Cavalry Regiment. In August 1982 Dempsey earned an MA degree in English from Duke University, and in 1984 he returned to West Point to teach English. After earning a master's degree in military art and science in 1988 from the Command and General Staff College (Fort Leavenworth, Kansas), Dempsey served as a battalion executive officer in the 3rd Armored Division in Friedburg, Germany. As operations officer and then executive officer for the 3rd Brigade, he deployed with the 3rd Armored Division to Saudi Arabia in Operation DESERT SHIELD and Operation DESERT STORM (1990–1991).

In 1993 Dempsey was assigned as chief of the Armor Branch at the U.S. Total Army Personnel Command in Arlington, Virginia. He then earned another master's degree, in national security and strategic studies, at the National War College in Washington, D.C., in 1995, the same year he was promoted to colonel. The next year Dempsey took command of the 3rd Armored Cavalry Regiment at Fort Carson, Colorado. He has served in numerous leadership positions at all levels, including assistant deputy director for Politico-Military Affairs Europe and Africa J5. From July 1998 to September 2001 he was a special assistant to the chairman of the Joint Chiefs of Staff in Washington, D.C.

In 2001 Dempsey was promoted to brigadier general, and from September 2001 to June 2003 he served in Riyadh, Saudi Arabia, as a program manager and headed a U.S. effort to modernize the elite Saudi force assigned to protect the kingdom's royal family. From June 2003 to July 2005 Dempsey commanded the 1st Armored Division, and from June 2003 to July 2004 he served in Iraq in support of Operation IRAQI FREEDOM. During his time in Iraq he had charge of the Task Force Iron command, consisting not only of the 1st Armored Division but also, attached to it, the 2nd Armored

Cavalry Regiment and a brigade of the 82nd Airborne Division. It was one of the larger divisional-level commands in the history of the U.S. Army. Dempsey's command tour coincided with the dramatic growth of the Sunni insurgency. He had charge of the Baghdad Area of Operations and received high marks for his handling of a difficult situation.

Dempsey redeployed his division to Germany and completed his command tour in July 2005. From August 2005 until the spring of 2007, he commanded the Multi-National Security Transition Command–Iraq with responsibility for recruitment, training, and equipment of the Iraqi Security Forces. Promoted to lieutenant general on March 27, 2007, Dempsey became deputy commander of CENTCOM at Mac-Dill Air Force Base, Florida. He served in that post until March 28, 2008, when he was named acting commander of CENTCOM, temporarily replacing General David Petraeus. On December 8, 2008, Dempsey was promoted to full (four-star) general and assumed command of the U.S. Army Training and Doctrine Command. On April 11, 2011, he succeeded General George Casey as chief of staff of the U.S. Army. On May 30, 2011, however, President Barack Obama nominated Dempsey to take over as chairman of the Joint Chiefs of Staff upon the retirement of Admiral Michael Mullen on September 30, 2011. Dempsey assumed the post on October 1, 2011, and remained chairman in late 2014.

On November 13, 2014, in testimony before the Senate Armed Services Committee, Dempsey declared that he would consider deploying a limited number of U.S. forces to accompany Iraqi troops in the field in complex offensive operations to retake Mosul and other key Iraqi areas now controlled by the Islamic State of Iraq and Syria (ISIS).

GARY LEE KERLEY

See also

Fallujah; Iraq War; Islamic State in Iraq and Syria; Mullen, Michael Glenn; Petraeus, David Howell; United States Central Command

References

Ricks, Thomas E. *Fiasco: The American Military Adventure in Iraq.* New York: Penguin, 2006.

Schwartz, Anthony J. "Iraq's Militias: The True Threat to Coalition Success in Iraq." *Parameters* 37(1) (2007): 55–58.

Zelnick, Robert. "Iraq: Last Chance." *Policy Review* 140 (2006): 3–6.

Department of Defense Reform Act of 1986

See Goldwater-Nichols Defense Reorganization Act

DESERT CROSSING, **Operation Plan**

A plan developed in June 1999 to stabilize Iraq in the event of the death or overthrow of Iraqi president Saddam Hussein. Following the liberation of Kuwait in 1991 during Operation DESERT STORM, the United States adopted a Middle East policy based in part on dual containment. Dual containment sought to restrain both further adventurism by Iraq and Iran's exportation of its Islamic fundamentalist revolution. With respect to Iraq, Hussein's actions and threats in the years immediately after the Persian Gulf War prompted the United States and its allies to react at least annually with several options—from low-end shows of force to the four-day intensive bombing campaign of December 1998 known as Operation DESERT FOX. For seven years, the Iraqi part of dual containment consisted of a cycle of provocation and response.

Late in 1998, U.S. national security adviser Samuel R. "Sandy" Berger stated in a speech that the United States would eventually remove Hussein from power and would do so with force if necessary. That speech effectively replaced dual containment with a policy of containing Iran while preparing for Iraqi regime change at a time and place of U.S. choosing. Following the speech, commentators and pundits focused on what it meant and how regime change might be accomplished.

The impact on the U.S. Central Command (CENTCOM) was somewhat different. One of the U.S. regional combatant commands, CENTCOM was responsible for U.S. military peacetime operations as well as combat operations in a geographic area that encompasses most of the Middle East, including Iraq.

In CENTCOM'S daily planning directorate staff meeting following the Berger speech, an epiphany of sorts occurred. The question that the planners believed should have been considered long before was what would happen to Iraq absent Hussein (for any number of reasons, including a coup, an accident, or regime-replacement operations) and consequently what would be the command's responsibilities in a potentially unstable situation. Key concerns were how unstable would Iraq be after two decades of centralized repression and what kind of response would be required to reestablish stability and prevent the potential crisis from spreading beyond Iraq's borders. Thus began a planning effort that resulted in a planning document or operation plan (OPLAN). An OPLAN provides broad concepts of operations versus operational detail. CENTCOM's effort in this regard came to be code-named DESERT CROSSING.

As DESERT CROSSING was developed over the next few months, it became evident that a true interagency response would be required. Intelligence estimates indicated that a post-Hussein Iraq would indeed be highly and dangerously unstable. Probable scenarios included ethnic strife fueled by the emergence of the majority Shia population and dis-enfranchisement of the ruling but minority Sunnis, retribution against the Sunni Baath Party, and efforts to secure autonomy or even independence by the Kurds in the north. Other possibilities included the emergence of one or more Hussein-like strongmen, interference by outside entities, fierce competition among players within each of the three major Iraqi groups, and the expansion of a separate Kurdish state into Turkey and Iran. Stabilization would require not only military and police forces to provide security but also the application of numerous instruments of international power, including diplomacy; humanitarian, financial, and technical assistance; facilitation of a rational Iraqi political process; and coordination of the contributions that could be made by nongovernmental organizations (NGOs).

While CENTCOM planners could lay down broad concepts, the best product would result from an interagency effort. CENTCOM leaders believed that the most efficient approach would be a two- to three-day tabletop simulation to test the planners' assumptions and concepts. The resulting DESERT CROSSING seminar, held during June 28–30, 1999, brought together senior officials from the State Department, the Defense Department, the National Security Council, the Central Intelligence Agency, and senior officers from the Joint Staff, the CENTCOM staff, and the army, navy, air force, and marine commands subordinate to CENTCOM.

The seminar participants were organized into four groups: two replicated the U.S. interagency process, one represented Iraq, and one represented the international community. The two U.S. groups acted as the principals' committee (cabinet-level officials providing direct advice to the president) and deputies' committee (principals' deputies charged with considering alternative courses of action and making recommendations to the principals). Each of the four groups was presented with information that they would be likely to have in a real-world scenario and was asked to evaluate their options given the ideas contained in the draft OPLAN.

The simulation proved highly successful in developing valuable insights that helped to refine the plan. The key points considered included triggering events that would require U.S. and international intervention; reactions by neighboring states and what should be done about them; the assembling and maintenance of a military coalition; humanitarian concerns involved in an invasion of Iraq; the

disposition of the Iraqi military postinvasion; the avoidance of a fragmented Iraq; the synchronization of humanitarian, military, and civilian activities in a postwar environment; and the development of an exit strategy.

The seminar exercise reached the following goals: the end result should be a stable unified Iraq with effective governance in place and a military capable of defending Iraq's borders but not threatening to Iraq's neighbors; Turkish and Iranian interests must be understood, addressed, and managed, primarily through effective diplomacy; an international coalition would best be built around humanitarian considerations and a stable outcome; NGOs must be included; military and police forces would be required in large numbers to achieve and maintain the long-term broad-based security; and the actual interagency process, in accordance with standing presidential directives, should commence immediately to plan for the eventuality of regime change in Iraq.

OPLAN DESERT CROSSING was modified and refined as a result of the seminar. A planned follow-on seminar did not occur, however, and the revised plan was shelved to be used as a starting point should real-world events dictate an Iraqi invasion or regime change. When Operation IRAQI FREEDOM commenced in March 2003, DESERT CROSSING was largely ignored and was not utilized in the George W. Bush administration's planning.

JOHN F. SIGLER

See also

Hussein, Saddam; IRAQI FREEDOM, Operation; IRAQI FREEDOM, Operation, Planning for; United States Central Command

References

Byman, Daniel, and Matthew C. Waxman. *Confronting Iraq: U.S. Policy and the Use of Force since the Gulf War.* Santa Monica, CA: RAND Corporation, 2002.

Clancy, Tom, with Anthony Zinni and Tony Kolz. *Battle Ready.* New York: Putnam, 2004.

Ricks, Thomas E. *Fiasco: The American Military Adventure in Iraq.* New York: Penguin, 2006.

Destroyers, U.S.

Originally known as torpedo boat destroyers and designed to protect the battle fleet against torpedoes, destroyers were utilized in hunting submarines, escorting convoys, and providing gunfire support in amphibious landings. Modern destroyers have grown more versatile to meet the demands of a smaller navy. In the 21st century, destroyers have routinely delivered long-range missiles while guarding against air, surface, and subsurface threats. They are also the major naval units in the U.S. antipiracy effort in the Western Indian Ocean.

The Spruance class constituted the backbone of the U.S. destroyer fleet after 1990, but the navy retired the last of them in 2005. They played only a small role in the Afghanistan War; nine participated in Operation ENDURING FREEDOM, launching Tomahawk cruise missiles against Taliban and Al Qaeda targets at the beginning of the war in October 2001. Seven joined Operation IRAQI FREEDOM during March–April 2003 for Tomahawk strikes and other missions.

The Arleigh Burke–class destroyer (DDG-51) has been regarded as the navy's most capable and survivable surface combatant since its introduction to the fleet in 1991. This class displaces 8,300 tons, is capable of a peak speed of more than 30 knots, and has a cruising range of 4,400 nautical miles at 20 knots. A new hull design allows for better sea keeping at high speeds and in rough conditions. These warships are visually distinctive thanks to their "V" shape at the waterline and a tilted mast for reduced radar cross-section. The Arleigh Burke–class destroyer has a crew of some 30 officers and 302 sailors. Since 1994, the destroyers have been constructed with a hangar to house two LAMPS Mk III (SH-60) helicopters. Flight I of this class contained only a flight deck without permanently housed helicopters.

All Arleigh Burke–class ships are equipped with the Aegis air defense system, featuring the AN/SPY-1D phased array radar. Older rotating radars are only capable of registering a target once during each 360-degree cycle of their antenna. A separate tracking radar must then engage each contact. Aegis combines these functions with beams of electromagnetic energy transmitted simultaneously in all directions. Moreover, Aegis integrates the various weapons and sensor suites more effectively than other system currently found in the world's navies. The latest upgrade to the Aegis system enables the ship to engage ballistic missiles, expanding the destroyer's mission to include theater missile defense. The Aegis fire-control system also works in tandem with the Harpoon antiship cruise missile launcher and the 5-inch/54 gun. Engagement parameters can be preset such that Aegis can strike targets without further operator interface. The Block 1 upgrade to the Phalanx close-in weapons system supplies the last line of defense against air threats by firing depleted uranium or tungsten shells through its electrically driven Gatling gun (3,000 rounds a minute). To ensure target destruction even if the target maneuvers, the Phalanx tracks both its rounds and the target, making corrections to bring the two together.

The Arleigh Burke class employs a 90-cell vertical launching system for missile launches (either Standard, Tomahawk, or ASROC) against surface, air, and land targets. Antisubmarine warfare is facilitated through both hull-mounted (AN/SQS-53C) towed array (AN/SQR-19) sonars. The latter is particularly effective, as its depth can be altered to place a sensor in the same temperature and acoustic conditions as a submarine to increase the likelihood of detection and tracking. The ships' antisubmarine warfare helicopters can drop sonobuoys to help pinpoint target location before torpedoes or the ASROC are brought to bear.

The engineering plant features the latest in gas turbine engine technology with a high degree of plant automation through an interconnected system of control consoles. Four General Electric LM2500 gas turbine engines supply propulsion with three gas turbine generator sets providing 450 VAC, three-phase, 60-hertz power.

Survivability was a prime consideration in the planning for this class. The destroyer's internal spaces can be sealed off from the weather decks and further compartmentalized into several zones using the Collective Protective System in the event of a chemical, biological, or nuclear attack. Dedicated facilities are available to decontaminate personnel exposed to harmful agents. The ships' all-steel construction with additional armor around vital systems offers enhanced protection against fragments from weapon detonations. The class is also equipped to withstand electromagnetic pulse damage. Sound isolators in machinery spaces have reduced noise output substantially. Halon firefighting systems that can be locally or remotely activated protect the engineering plant.

Fifteen Arleigh Burke–class destroyers participated in Operation ENDURING FREEDOM. Eleven joined the carrier battle groups engaged in the Iraq War (Operation IRAQI FREEDOM). During the latter conflict, they supported ground operation with Tomahawk launches. Today, they and the Aegis-equipped Ticonderoga-class guided missile cruisers increasingly operate independently in lieu of aircraft carriers. Both ship types can be integrated into a theater missile defense network, conduct antismuggling and antipiracy patrols, or support ground force and antiterrorism operations with cruise missile or long-range artillery strikes.

Current plans call for the Arleigh Burke–class ships to remain in service through 2043, although the first eight units are expected to be decommissioned by 2029. The others will undergo significant upgrades in the next decade. In addition to new combat sensor and command and control systems, the ships will receive new weapons systems that once were limited to science fiction. The navy is deploying a prototype laser weapon in 2015 and a 120 nautical mile-range electromagnetic rail gun in 2016. These new weapons will replace the Phalanx close-in weapons system and the Mark 45 5-inch/62 cannon, respectively. The new weapons offer several advantages over their predecessors. There is no ammunition attendant to the laser, and the rail gun's use of electromagnetic propulsion for its shells effectively doubles the ship's onboard ordnance capacity. The rail gun inflicts damage by sheer speed, employing electromagnetic force to blast a missile 125 miles at 7.5 times the speed of sound. Given the modular construction and extensive electrical generating capacity of the Arleigh Burke class, the upgrades will be considerably cheaper than initiating new construction. It remains to be seen if the controversial and expensive Zumwalt-class destroyers will the replacement for the Arleigh Burke class.

The new U.S. Navy destroyer *Zumwalt* (DDG-1000), launched in 2013 and costing $3 billion, is the largest destroyer in the modern navy by some 65 percent. At 610 feet in length and with a beam of 80 feet, it is about 100 feet longer and 20 feet wider than the Arleigh Burke–class destroyers. But while about 300 sailors man the similar warships, the *Zumwalt*'s minimum compliment is only 130, made possible by advanced automated systems.

The ship is also stealthy, with much of it built on angles that help make it 50 times harder to spot on radar than an ordinary destroyer. The *Zumwalt* will be armed with two Advanced Gun Systems (AGS) that can fire rocket-powered computer-guided shells capable of destroying targets 63 miles away, three times farther than ordinary destroyer guns can fire. It is also anticipated that it will be armed with the laser weapon and electromagnetic rail gun. The *Zumwalt* is undergoing trials in 2015 and is expected to join the fleet in 2016.

JEFFREY D. BASS AND CARL OTIS SCHUSTER

See also

Afghanistan War; Cruisers, U.S.; Tomahawk BGM-109 Land-Attack Missile; United States Navy, Afghanistan War; United States Navy, Iraq War

References

Crawford, Steve. *Twenty-First Century Warships: Surface Combatants of Today's Navies.* St. Paul, MN: MBI Publishing, 2002.

Sanders, Michael. *The Yard: Building a Destroyer at Bath Iron Works.* New York: Harper Perennial, 2001.

Tomajczyk, Steve. *Modern U.S. Navy Destroyers.* St. Paul, MN: MBI Publishing, 2001.

Wertheim, Eric. *Naval Institute Guide to Combat Fleets of the World, 16th Edition.* Annapolis, MD: Naval Institute Press, 2013.

Diego Garcia

British-held atoll in the Indian Ocean and site of a jointly controlled American and British naval air base. Diego Garcia is located in the southern Indian Ocean about 1,000 miles south of the Indian coast and 7 degrees north of the equator. The atoll is part of the Chagos Archipelago and is the largest of the Chagos chain, which stretches from 4 degrees to 7 degrees north latitude. Because of its location, Diego Garcia has a tropical climate characterized by hot humid summers and warm wet winters. It receives upwards of 100 inches of rain per year. The island is also subject to tropical cyclones but only infrequently, and it has not been hit by a serious tropical storm in more than 40 years. Diego Garcia, which is relatively flat, comprises 66 square miles, only 12 of which are landmass; the remainder is coral reef and a huge lagoon, which is approximately 48 square miles in area. The land area almost completely surrounds the lagoon except for an opening in the north that leads to open ocean. Because of this, it is quite easy to limit marine access. Discovered by Portuguese mariners in the early 1500s. The atoll then passed under French control. The British took possession in 1814.

In the late 1960s the British and U.S. governments began to make plans to turn Garcia Diego into a naval and air force base. Beginning in 1967, the British began relocating the small native population on the island to the Seychelles and Mauritius. By 1971 the last of the copra plantations was phased out, and the atoll had been depopulated. Per previous agreements, London leased the use of Diego Garcia to the U.S. government, which began to construct a joint naval and air force base there. Although Great Britain retains sovereignty over the island, the U.S. government controls the military base. By the 1990s Diego Garcia was home to 16 different sea- and air-based commands, including the important U.S. Navy Support Facility. The Support Facility's function is to provide forward-deployed logistical support to operational forces in the Persian Gulf and the Indian Ocean. The Military Sealift Command located on Diego Garcia is also an important forward-based command.

Access to the atoll is limited, and it is not open to the general public. Because of its great isolation and restricted access, it is believed that the U.S. government is using the island as a small detention facility for captured members of Al Qaeda. The U.S. government has declined to verify this.

Outfitted with facilities and runways to accommodate the largest military aircraft, Diego Garcia was used during the 1991 Persian Gulf War as a staging area for Boeing B-52 Stratofortress bombers. During Operation DESERT FOX (December

1998), B-52s based at Diego Garcia launched nearly 100 cruise missiles at Iraqi targets. In 2001 during Operation ENDURING FREEDOM in Afghanistan, the island served as a forward base for B-52 and Rockwell B-1 Lancer bombers.

Diego Garcia also played a key role in Operation IRAQI FREEDOM, beginning in March 2003, as a base for B-1, Northrop Grumman B-2 Spirit, and B-52 bombers, which were among the first to assault Baghdad in the opening hours of the campaign. Because Turkey forbade the United States from using its territory to attack Iraq in 2003, Diego Garcia played an even larger role than it had in the 1991 Persian Gulf War.

Diego Garcia's great strategic importance is expected to last well into the 21st century as long as American priorities in the Middle East and the Persian Gulf region remain high. The National Aeronautics and Space Administration also claims the atoll as an alternate landing area for the space shuttle; in fact, it is the only designated landing facility in the Indian Ocean.

PAUL G. PIERPAOLI JR.

See also

Afghanistan War; Aircraft, Bombers; IRAQI FREEDOM, Operation; Iraq War; Persian Gulf War

References

Bandjunis, Vytautas. *Diego Garcia: Creation of the Indian Ocean Base.* Chestnut Hill, MA: Writer's Showcase, 2001.

Gerson, Joseph, and Bruce Birchard. *The Sun Never Sets: Confronting the Network of Foreign U.S. Military Bases.* Cambridge, MA: South End Press, 1991.

Donkey Island, Battle of (June 30– July 1, 2007)

Military engagement between U.S. forces and Al Qaeda in Iraq insurgents during June 30–July 1, 2007. The Battle of Donkey Island occurred on the banks of a canal leading from Ramadi to Lake Habbaniyah near the city of Tash, south of the city of Ramadi, in Anbar Province, Iraq. The island is named for the wild donkeys native to the region. This skirmish pitted elements of the U.S. Army Task Force 1–77 Armor Regiment and the 2nd Battalion, 5th Marines, against a force of Al Qaeda in Iraq insurgents, who outnumbered the Americans.

The insurgent force had gathered in the area to launch a planned assault on Ramadi, employing daytime suicide attacks to break the shaky peace that had been recently established in the city. American forces discovered the company-sized insurgent force while conducting a routine

patrol in Humvee vehicles on the evening of June 30. The insurgents had opened fire on the convoy. Despite being outnumbered, a U.S. platoon-sized element, along with the original patrol group, counterattacked with superior firepower a short while later and defeated the insurgent group after what turned out to be a 23-hour on-again, off-again gun battle. Although a clear military victory for the American forces, the engagement demonstrated that Al Qaeda in Iraq, along with other insurgent groups, still had the ability to organize forces effectively in an attempt to destabilize the Anbar region.

American forces suffered 2 dead and 11 wounded, while an estimated 32 insurgents were killed out of an estimated force of 40–70 fighters. U.S. forces also managed to destroy two trucks operated by the insurgents that had carried considerable numbers of arms and ammunition.

RICHARD B. VERRONE

See also

Al Qaeda in Iraq

References

Cockburn, Patrick. *Muqtada: Muqtada al-Sadr, the Shia Revival, and the Struggle for Iraq.* New York: Scribner, 2008.

Ricks, Thomas E. *The Gamble: General David Petraeus and the American Military Adventure in Iraq, 2006–2008.* New York: Penguin, 2009.

Dostum, Abd al-Rashid (1954–)

Uzbek warlord, chief of staff to the commander in chief of the Afghan Army (2003–2008), and leader of the National Islamic Movement of Afghanistan. Born in Khwaja Dukoh in Jowzjan Province, Afghanistan, in 1954, Abd al-Rashid Dostum completed his national service as a paratrooper before commencing work in a state-owned gas refinery in 1970. During his employment he engaged in union politics and emerged as a communist union boss, a position he retained until 1978 when he joined the Afghan military in the fight against the Soviet Union's 1979 invasion.

In the early 1980s, however, Dostum began a six-year battle against the Afghan mujahideen as a regional commander of his own militia. By the mid-1980s his aptitude for rallying Uzbek and Turkmen mujahideen soldiers to both government and personal causes enjoyed considerable success. With some 20,000 men under his command, he pacified the northern provinces and established control there. While his force recruited throughout his native Jowzjan Province and had a relatively broad base, the majority of his initial troops and commanders originated from Dostum's home village, Khwaja Dukoh, and represented the core of the force both during the civil war and upon the force's reconstitution in 2001. Despite his military prowess, Dostum's predilection for meting out merciless punishments on the enemy as well as his own men cemented his reputation as a skilled military tactician and a ferocious, uncompromising leader.

Initially allied with the government of President Mohammed Najibullah, in 1992 Dostum switched allegiance as the Soviet-backed government crumbled amid economic woes and internal strife. Despite his communist past, Dostum joined the moderate Tajik leader of the Northern Alliance, Ahmad Shah Massoud, in toppling the Afghan communist government and fought in a coalition against Gulbuddin al-Hurra Hekmatyar, the Kharuti Pashtun leader of the Islamic Party of Afghanistan (Hezb-e-Islami Afghanistan) in 1992.

Between 1992 and 1997 Dostum ran a secular fiefdom based in Mazar-e Sharif and the surrounding provinces. Under his watch, women enjoyed the freedom to attend school, ventured outside without burqas, and were permitted to wear high-heeled shoes; Mazar-e Sharif's university had 1,800 female students. Boasting the last academic institution in Afghanistan, Mazar-e Sharif was the final bastion untouched by the oppression exercised by the Taliban regime.

As the Taliban forces of Mullah Mohammed Omar approached his stronghold, Dostum assumed a defensive stance and led his Turkmen and Uzbek forces into an ill-fated battle. In May 1997 Dostum's Uzbek commander in Faryab, Abd al-Malik, switched allegiance to the Taliban midway through a skirmish as the Pashtun leader of Balkh and Mazar-e Sharif, Juma Khan Hamdard, attacked from the east and obliterated Dostum's forces. By 1998 with the gates to Mazar-e Sharif now open, Hamdard flowed into the secularized city with his Pashtun Taliban brothers, and sharia law was enforced. Dostum went into self-imposed exile in Turkey, where he remained until April 2001. In 2000 he suffered an additional blow to his reputation upon the publication of Ahmed Rashid's book, *Taliban: Militant Islam, Oil, and Fundamentalism in Central Asia,* in which the author related the gruesome tale of a soldier being punished by Dostum for stealing.

In the aftermath of the September 11, 2001, terror attacks, Dostum moved to redeem his reputation as a leader, and he offered his services to the United States in its quest to defeat the Taliban. With a small company comprising 2,000 horse-mounted rangers, Dostum and U.S. special forces secured a pivotal victory over the Taliban in the Hindu Kush Mountains in November 2001, thereby liberating much of northern Afghanistan.

Serving first as deputy defense minister to Afghan president Hamid Karzai, in 2003 Dostum also assumed the position of chief of staff to the commander in chief of the Afghan Army. In 2004 he entered the presidential race but captured only 10 percent of the vote. In response to this loss, Dostum resurrected the Uzbek militia force, much to the chagrin of President Karzai. In a bid to thwart his political endeavors, Karzai urged the commander who had defied Dostum, Abdul Malik, to return to the north and there establish a rival political party, Hezb-e Azadi-ye Afghanistan (Afghan Liberation Party). Karzai also placed a governor in Faryab who called for Dostum's indictment for war crimes. The measures were neatly countered, however, when pro-Dostum supporters rioted and drove the appointed governor out of Faryab later that year.

Because the north is one of the few areas of Afghanistan in which relative stability has been maintained, government opposition to Dostum has been more recently muted, and his authority prevails for the time being. Holding the northern provinces of Jowzjan, Saripul, Balkh, Faryab, Baghlan, and Kunduz, Dostum also assisted in the establishment of the Islamic National Party (Jumbesh-e-Milli Islami Afghanistan). In February 2008 Dostum reportedly ordered the kidnapping of a political rival, Akbar Bai. In the process, Bai's son and several associates were beaten and injured. Government forces subsequently surrounded Dostum's home, demanding that he be held accountable for the Bai incident. Dostum claimed that he had not ordered the kidnapping and refused to cooperate with a government investigation. As a result, he was stripped of his army position.

Dostum then settled in Turkey, where some say he was exiled. In August 2009 he returned from Turkey to support Karzai for reelection, flying to his stronghold of Sheberghan, where he was greeted by thousands of supporters. In the April 2014 Afghanistan national election, Dostum was elected vice president.

K. Luisa Gandolfo

See also

Afghanistan; Afghanistan Warlords; Karzai, Hamid; Taliban

References

Ewans, Martin. *Afghanistan: A Short History of Its History and Politics.* New York: Harper Perennial, 2002.

Rashid, Ahmed. *Taliban: Militant Islam, Oil, and Fundamentalism in Central Asia.* New Haven, CT: Yale University Press, 2001.

Saikal, Amin. *Modern Afghanistan: A History of Struggle and Survival.* London: I. B. Tauris, 2004.

Tanner, Stephen. *Afghanistan: A Military History from Alexander the Great to the Fall of the Taliban.* New York: Da Capo, 2003.

Drones

See Unmanned Aerial Vehicles

Dumb Bombs

See Bombs, Gravity

E

Eagleburger, Lawrence Sidney (1930–2011)

Diplomat, influential adviser to several U.S. presidents, and U.S. secretary of state (1992–1993). Lawrence Sidney Eagleburger was born in Milwaukee, Wisconsin, on August 1, 1930. He graduated from the University of Wisconsin–Madison with a BS in 1952 and immediately enlisted in the U.S. Army, serving during the Korean War (1950–1953) and attaining the rank of first lieutenant. Eagleburger returned to Madison to receive his MA in 1957. That same year he entered the U.S. Foreign Service, where he worked in Honduras and as a desk officer for Cuban affairs in the Department of State's Bureau of Intelligence and Research. Eagleburger served in Belgrade, Yugoslavia, from 1961 to 1965 and returned to Washington in 1965 to serve as the special assistant on North Atlantic Treaty Organization (NATO) affairs to presidential adviser Dean G. Acheson.

In 1969 Henry Kissinger, President Richard M. Nixon's national security adviser, appointed Eagleburger as his assistant. In September 1969 Eagleburger left the National Security Council to assume successive appointments in the Nixon administration to the U.S. mission to NATO, the Department of Defense, and the Department of State. Eagleburger served as the ambassador to Yugoslavia in the James (Jimmy) Carter administration from 1977 to 1980 before President Ronald Reagan appointed Eagleburger undersecretary of state for political affairs in 1982.

Retiring from the State Department, Eagleburger became the president of Kissinger Associates, Inc., a New York–based international consulting firm founded by Henry Kissinger, from 1984 to 1989. In 1989 President George H. W. Bush appointed Eagleburger deputy secretary of state, a position in which he served as Bush's chief adviser on Yugoslavia that, at the time, was descending into chaos as a result of the end of communist rule there. Controversy often marked Eagleburger's role as adviser on Yugoslavia. When he refuted reports that the Yugoslavian National Army and Serbian paramilitary forces had perpetrated war crimes, media outlets in both the United States and Europe labeled him a Serbian enthusiast.

In 1992 when Secretary of State James Baker resigned to manage Bush's unsuccessful reelection campaign, Eagleburger replaced him as acting secretary in August 1992. Eagleburger became secretary of state on December 8, 1992. When Bush left office in January 1993, Eagleburger joined the law firm of Baker, Donelson, Bearrnan and Caldwell as the senior foreign policy adviser. In 1998 he became the chairman of the International Commission on Holocaust-Era Insurance Claims, which offered $16 million to Holocaust victims and their heirs in 2005.

In 2002 Eagleburger publicly questioned the timing of a likely invasion of Iraq and stated that the evidence linking Saddam Hussein to weapons of mass destruction was not altogether conclusive. In 2003 after the Bush administration sharply reprimanded Syria and Iran, Eagleburger again openly warned that military action in either country could be disastrous. In 2006 he replaced Robert Gates in the Iraq Study Group, also known as the Baker-Hamilton Commission, charged by Congress with assessing the situation of the Iraq War.

Eagleburger was also chairman of the board of trustees for the Forum for International Policy and served on the Board of Advisors of the Washington Institute for Near East Policy. Eagleburger died on July 4, 2011, in Charlottesville, Virginia.

CHRISTOPHER R. W. DIETRICH

See also

Bush, George Walker; Iraq Study Group; IRAQI FREEDOM, Operation; Weapons of Mass Destruction

References

Barilleaux, Ryan J., and Mark J. Rozell. *Power and Prudence: The Presidency of George H. W. Bush.* College Station: Texas A&M University Press, 2004.

Hess, Stephen, and Marvin Kalb, eds. *The Media and the War on Terrorism.* Washington, DC: Brookings Institution Press, 2003.

Langholtz, Harvey J. *The Psychology of Peacekeeping.* Westport, CT: Praeger, 1998.

Eikenberry, Karl W. (1952–)

U.S. Army general; commander of the Combined Forces Command, Afghanistan; and U.S. ambassador to Afghanistan. Born in 1952 and raised in Indiana, Karl W. Eikenberry graduated from the U.S. Military Academy, West Point, in 1973 and was commissioned as a second lieutenant in the U.S. Army. His education includes master's degrees in East Asian studies from Harvard University and political science from Stanford University. He also studied at the British Ministry of Defence Chinese Language School in Hong Kong and at Nanjing University in China. Eikenberry was a national security fellow at the John F. Kennedy School of Government, Harvard University.

During his military career, Eikenberry has served as a commander and staff officer with mechanized, light, airborne, and ranger infantry units in both the continental United States and overseas in Hawaii, Korea, Italy, China, and Afghanistan. In 2001 he was promoted to major general and began direct support of Operation ENDURING FREEDOM. He served two tours of duty in Afghanistan. During his first Afghanistan assignment (2002–2003), he was instrumental in building up the Afghan Army following the displacement of the Taliban government.

During Operation IRAQI FREEDOM, under the direction of Secretary of Defense Donald Rumsfeld, Eikenberry led a survey team in Iraq during late 2003. The mission of the team was to determine the facts on the ground. Eikenberry reviewed the training of the Iraqi military and police and concluded that Iraqi security forces were not growing at a rate that could keep up with the burgeoning insurgency. At the time, Iraqi security training was controlled by the Coalition Provisional Authority. In the interest of centralized control over Iraqi security efforts, Eikenberry recommended that responsibility for the training and control of Iraqi security forces be given to the U.S. military instead. His recommendation was accepted by Rumsfeld and implemented by the U.S. commander in Iraq, Lieutenant General David Petraeus.

In 2005 Eikenberry was promoted to lieutenant general. During his second tour in Afghanistan, he served as commander of all North Atlantic Treaty Organization (NATO) troops in the nation (Combined Forces Command, Afghanistan) from May 2005 to February 2006. He has testified before Congress multiple times regarding the progress and challenges of coalition forces in that country.

Eikenberry is the former president of the Foreign Area Officers Association and is a member of the Council on Foreign Relations. He is widely published on national security subjects. His works include *Explaining and Influencing Chinese Arms Transfers* (1995) and *China's Challenge to Asia-Pacific Regional Stability* (2005). In January 2007 Eikenberry was assigned as deputy chairman of the NATO Military Committee in Brussels, Belgium.

In a highly unusual appointment of a military man to a diplomatic post, Eikenberry was nominated as U.S. ambassador to Afghanistan, serving in that position from April 29, 2009, to July 25, 2011. On his confirmation, he retired from the army as a lieutenant general on July 28, 2009. On leaving his diplomatic post, Eikenberry became Payne Distinguished Lecturer at the Freeman Spogli Institute for International Studies at Stanford University.

BENJAMIN D. FOREST

See also

Combined Forces Command, Afghanistan; North Atlantic Treaty Organization; Petraeus, David Howell; Rumsfeld, Donald

References

Eikenberry, Karl W. *Explaining and Influencing Chinese Arms Transfers.* Washington, DC: National Defense University, 1995.

Ricks, Thomas E. *Fiasco: The American Military Adventure in Iraq.* New York: Penguin, 2006.

Woodward, Bob. *State of Denial: Bush at War, Part III.* New York: Simon and Schuster, 2006.

ElBaradei, Mohamed Mustafa (1942–)

Egyptian diplomat, United Nations (UN) official, and director general of the International Atomic Energy Agency (IAEA) since 1997. Mohamed Mustafa ElBaradei (al-Baradei) was born in Cairo, Egypt, on June 17, 1942. His father was Mostafa ElBaradei, a lawyer and former president of the Egyptian Bar Association. The younger ElBaradei earned a bachelor's degree in law from the University of Cairo and a master's degree (1971) and doctorate (1974) in international law from the New York University School of Law.

ElBaradei joined the Egyptian Ministry of Foreign Affairs in 1964. He was twice in the Egyptian permanent missions to the UN in New York and Geneva with responsibilities for political, legal, and arms control issues. In between these postings, during 1974–1978 he was a special assistant to the Egypt foreign minister. ElBaradei became the senior fellow in charge of the International Law Program at the United Nations Institute for Training and Research in 1980, and in 1984 he became a senior staff member of the IAEA Secretariat, where he served as its legal adviser (1984–1993).

During 1984–1987 ElBaradei was also the representative of the IAEA director general to the UN in New York. During 1981–1987 he also taught as an adjunct professor of international law at the New York University School of Law. ElBaradei served as the assistant director general for external relations for the UN during 1993–1997. In January 1997 he accepted the position of director general of the IAEA, which position he held until December 2009.

Prior to the beginning of the Iraq war, ElBaradei and Hans Blix, the Swedish diplomat who headed the United Nations Monitoring, Verification and Inspection Commission from January 2000 to June 2003, led the UN inspection team in Iraq. ElBaradei and Blix asserted that Iraq had no weapons of mass destruction (WMD).

ElBaradei has since publicly questioned the WMD rationale used by the George W. Bush administration to initiate the Iraq War (2003). ElBaradei has also served as the point man for the UN in the ongoing controversy over Iran's alleged drive to develop nuclear weapons. In September 2005 despite U.S. opposition, ElBaradei was appointed to his third term as director of the IAEA. The Bush administration contended that ElBaradei had been reluctant to confront Iran on its ability to turn nuclear material into weapons-grade fissionable material. Nevertheless, in October 2005 ElBaradei and the IAEA were jointly awarded the Nobel Peace Prize for efforts "to prevent nuclear energy from being used for military purposes and to ensure that nuclear energy for peaceful purposes is used in the safest possible way."

ElBaradei favored a diplomatic solution to Iran's developing nuclear weapons capability and worked diligently through European and Russian diplomats along with the UN Security Council to limit Iran's nuclear capability. ElBaradei favored the imposition of diplomatic and economic sanctions on Iran sufficient to bring it into compliance with the Nuclear Non-Proliferation Pact and the IAEA mission Atoms for Peace. Despite criticism from Israel and the United States that his stance toward Iran was too lenient, in June 2008 ElBaradei issued a statement proclaiming that while the IAEA had been conducting exhaustive inspections there, it had not as yet been able to conclude with certainty that Iran had abandoned all plans for an atomic weapon. He urged Iran to be more forthcoming so that the verification process could be concluded. Not surprisingly, ElBaradei's comments were met with much derision in Washington and Tel Aviv. ElBaradei has also repeatedly dismissed any talk of the use of force against Iran, claiming that to do so would be counterproductive and would invite a similar scenario that ensued after the 2003 invasion of Iraq.

After leaving his UN position, ElBaradei became an important figure in Egyptian politics, particularly the 2011 revolution that ousted President Hosni Mubarak and in the 2013 protests and military coup that toppled President Mohamed Morsi. During July–August 2013 ElBaradei was acting vice president of Egypt. He resigned on August 14 following a violent crackdown by Egyptian security forces.

RICHARD M. EDWARDS

See also

Blix, Hans; International Atomic Energy Agency; Iran; United Nations Monitoring, Verification and Inspection Commission; Weapons of Mass Destruction

References

Kile, Shannon N., ed. *Europe and Iran: Perspectives on Non-Proliferation.* SIPRI Research Reports. Oxford: Oxford University Press, 2006.

Timmerman, Kenneth R. *Countdown to Crisis: The Coming Nuclear Showdown with Iran.* New York: Three Rivers, 2006.

United Nations, ed. *Basic Facts about the United Nations.* New York: United Nations, 2003.

ENDURING FREEDOM, Operation

See Afghanistan War

ENDURING FREEDOM, Operation, Initial Ground Campaign (October 7– December 17, 2001)

Operation ENDURING FREEDOM opened on October 7, 2001, less than a month after the September 11, 2001, terror attacks perpetrated by Al Qaeda. The invasion of Afghanistan occurred when the Taliban government ruling the country refused to hand over Al Qaeda terrorist organization leader Osama bin Laden or cooperate with American efforts to bring those responsible for the attacks to justice. The stated goals of the operation were the capture of bin Laden and other Al Qaeda leaders, the destruction of terrorist training camps and infrastructure within Afghanistan, and an end to all terrorist activities there.

In the invasion the United States and its allies opted for an asymmetric strategy, which on the ground relied heavily on indigenous warlords who were opposed to the Taliban and Al Qaeda, especially the Northern Alliance, consisting mainly of Tajik, Uzbek, and Hazara forces.

Having first severely reduced the Taliban war machine in cruise missile attacks and air strikes, the U.S. Air Force then provided close ground support for the Northern Alliance. From the beginning of the war the U.S. Air Force, supported by coalition tanker, cargo, and surveillance aircraft, enjoyed complete command of the air. With this and the fact that the fighting forces involved were relatively few in number, the country was vast, and the front lines were porous, the ground situation changed very quickly.

The general strategy was to cut off the Taliban lines of communications between the northern part of the country and their stronghold in the south, liberate those areas, and then eliminate the remnants of resistance in remote mountain areas. The ground fighting was left largely to the Northern Alliance, with U.S. and non-Afghan coalition military involvement during the initial phase of the ground war limited mainly to special operations and focusing on assisting the Northern Alliance's advance and coordinating it with the air strikes.

To oversee the allied land campaign, the U.S. Central Command established the Combined Forces Land Component Command, led by Lieutenant General Paul T. Mikolashek, that moved to Camp Doha (Kuwait) on November 20, 2001. In order to provide direct assistance to Northern Alliance forces and to conduct special operations, the Joint Special Operation Task Force Dagger, under Colonel John Mulholland, was deployed to Karshi Kandabad air base in Uzbekistan. It included the 5th Special Forces Group (Airborne); elements of the 160th Special Operations Aviation Regiment; Special Tactics personnel from Air Force Special

Operations Command; the 1st Battalion, 87th Infantry; and the 10th Mountain Division (Light). The British furnished unspecified numbers of special forces, including units of the Special Air Service (SAS) and Special Boat Service (SBS).

U.S. special forces began their operations on October 19, 2001, when they joined the 6,000-strong Northern Alliance force under General Abd al-Rashid Dostum in its attack on the strategic city of Mazar-e Sharif along with some 10,000 troops under Fahim Khan and Bissmullah Khan advancing through Panjsher Valley to Kabul. The special forces teams called and coordinated close air support provided by Rockwell/Boeing B-1 Lancer and Boeing B-52 Stratofortress bombers, Grumman F-14 Tomcat, McDonnell Douglas/Boeing F-15 Eagle and McDonnell Douglas/Boeing/Northrop F-18 Hornet fighter-bombers, and Fairchild Republic A-10 Thunderbolt II combat support aircraft. These attacked key Taliban command posts, tanks and armored vehicles, artillery pieces, troop concentrations, bunkers, and ammunition storage areas. The heavy application of airpower had a huge and demoralizing psychological effect on the Taliban fighters and allowed Northern Alliance forces to soon seize key strategic targets. On November 9, 2001, the anti-Taliban forces secured Mazar-e Sharif.

From the north coalition forces carried out a rapid advance, surprising and outflanking the Taliban defenders. Boosted by large-scale defections among the local Taliban commanders, Northern Alliance forces were able to retake many towns and villages without firing a shot. On November 14, 2001, Northern Alliance troops took the capital city of Kabul.

After that in just a few days of quick and fierce fighting and negotiated surrenders, all central and western Afghan provinces including the key city of Herat were liberated from Taliban control. To assist command and control functions in providing assistance to the Afghan forces, supplies and humanitarian aid via Task Force Bagram were organized at Bagram Air Base under the command of Colonel Robert Kissel. At the same time, a number of U.S. Delta Force commandos, Central Intelligence Agency (CIA) agents, and British SAS and SBS and French intelligence agents were deployed in central Afghanistan to conduct strategic reconnaissance of targets linked to Al Qaeda.

On November 16, 2001, the siege of Kunduz, the remaining Taliban stronghold in the north, began with heavy air strikes over a nine-day period. During the siege the U.S. Green Berets along with British SAS and SBS forces assisted Northern Alliance troops under General Mullah Daud in the destruction of Taliban tanks, cargo trucks, bunker complexes, and personnel. On November 23, 2001, remaining

Taliban forces in the Kunduz area surrendered. Some 3,500 prisoners of war were transported to the fortress-prison in Mazar-e Sharif, where they subsequently rebelled and were only suppressed after several days of heavy fighting in which coalition airpower and U.S. and British special forces took part. This last battle of Mazar-e Sharif saw the first introduction of coalition conventional ground troops in Afghanistan: the 1st Battalion, 87th Infantry, of the 10th Mountain Division (Light) from Uzbekistan, which helped to secure the perimeter around the fortress and secured the local airfield.

The next phase in the ground campaign was aimed at defeating the Taliban in its political and spiritual birthplace, the Pashtun heartland around the city of Kandahar. There as early as October 19–20, 2001, a detachment of the U.S. Army Rangers who had flown in from bases in southern Pakistan and Oman conducted swift assaults in Kandahar and secured a deserted airstrip, known as Camp Rhino, as a future forward operational base for hit-and-run raids. Following the scheme already tested in the north, the U.S. special forces established contacts with and supplied ammunition, weapons, and close air support to some 3,000 anti-Taliban Pashtun forces under Hamid Karzai and Gul Afha Sherzai, effectively establishing a new front by November 19, 2001.

On November 25 nearly 1,000 U.S. marines of Task Force 58 were ferried in from a carrier group in the Arabian Sea. Establishing a forward operational base at Camp Rhino, they joined the fight by cutting off the Taliban supply lines. In early December U.S. Army special operations troops, U.S. Navy SEALs, Navy Seabee construction teams, and Australian special forces reinforced the marines at Camp Rhino. Taliban forces surrendered Kandahar on December 6, and the marines secured its airport by December 13.

By mid-December, the remnants of the Taliban and Al Qaeda forces (about 2,000 militants) were besieged in pockets of resistance in the mountainous area of Tora Bora, with its extensive fortifications and stockpiles of weapons and ammunition, in the eastern part of Afghanistan. The operation in the Tora Bora area involved U.S. and British special forces, CIA paramilitaries, and about 2,000 Afghan tribesmen under Hazrat Ali. The U.S.-led coalition also employed Lockheed/Boeing AC-130 Spectre gunships for close air support and intense bombing of the underground tunnels with bunker-busting bombs. By December 17, 2001, the last cave complex in Tora Bora was cleared of enemy fighters.

From the point of view of its immediate and purely military aims, the ground component of Operation ENDURING FREEDOM was a highly successful effort that toppled the Taliban and inflicted severe damage to Al Qaeda and its Afghan

allies. The joint application of air and ground assaults as well as intelligence operations and psychological warfare, frequently called synergetic warfare, strengthened the coalition's abilities to challenge the Taliban forces asymmetrically. The combination of familiar strategic and tactical approaches, including the application of overwhelming airpower assets, stealthy commando raids, and active and multifaceted support of proxy ground forces, allowed the United States and its allies to avoid committing a large number of their own troops in combat and prevented significant American losses (12 U.S. servicemen were killed in action in 2001) while creating necessary conditions for the swift and decisive destruction of the Al Qaeda sanctuary in Afghanistan.

At the same time, as the continued and even spreading Taliban-led insurgency has demonstrated since 2002, the broader task of stabilizing the country, even militarily, would be much more difficult, complicated by the fact that key Al Qaeda leaders, including Osama bin Laden, were allowed to escape.

PETER J. RAINOW

See also

Al Qaeda; ANACONDA, Operation; Casualties, Operation ENDURING FREEDOM; Coalition Force Land Component Command–Afghanistan; Dostum, Abd al-Rashid; ENDURING FREEDOM, Operation, Planning for; ENDURING FREEDOM, Operation, U.S. Air Campaign; Hekmatyar, Gulbuddin al-Hurra; Karzai, Hamid; McKiernan, David Deglan; Taliban

References

Biddle, Stephen. *Afghanistan and the Future of Warfare: Implications for Army and Defense Policy.* Carlisle, PA: Strategic Studies Institute, 2002.

Boaz, John, ed. *The U.S. Attack on Afghanistan.* Detroit: Thompson/Gale, 2005.

DeLong, Michael, with Noah Lukeman. *Inside CENTCOM: The Unvarnished Truth about the Wars in Afghanistan and Iraq.* Washington, DC: Regnery, 2004.

Franks, Tommy, with Malcolm McConnell. *American Soldier.* New York: Regan Books, 2004.

Stewart, Richard W. *Operation Enduring Freedom: The United States Army in Afghanistan, October 2001–March 2002.* Washington, DC: U.S. Army Center of Military History, 2003.

ENDURING FREEDOM, **Operation, Planning for**

Planning for Operation ENDURING FREEDOM, the U.S.-led invasion of Afghanistan, began immediately after the connection had been established between the terrorist network Al Qaeda, which struck the United States on September 11,

2001, and the Taliban regime that had harbored Al Qaeda in Afghanistan. The initial name of the operation—Operation INFINITE JUSTICE—was dropped in deference to Muslim belief that only Allah can provide people with infinitive justice.

There were several relatively low-risk retaliatory options discussed at the U.S. Central Command (CENTCOM), which has primary responsibility for the region militarily. These included cruise missile strikes from ships, submarines, and aircraft; attacking Taliban and Al Qaeda training camps, barracks, command and control facilities, communications centers, and support complexes; and a combination of cruise missile assaults and a bombing campaign of 3–10 days to take out specific targets. At the same time, the declared strategic goals of the operation—to topple the Taliban regime, disrupt Al Qaeda's base of operations, and bring Al Qaeda's leader Osama bin Laden and his associates to justice—unavoidably determined the planning for the operation as a combination of air war with some sort of ground invasion.

From the very beginning, the strategic conditions in the Afghan theater presented serious challenges to the planners at CENTCOM, which was led by U.S. Army general Tommy R. Franks. Indeed, there were a number of daunting peculiarities and complexities. Afghanistan was already in the midst of the civil war. This conflict pitted Taliban forces (25,000–45,000 troops, 650 tanks and armored vehicles, 15 combat planes, 40 cargo planes, 10 transport helicopters, and some 20 missiles, old Soviet SA-7 and American-made Stingers), supported by some 3,000 Al Qaeda militants, who controlled about 80 percent of the country's territory, against their opponents of the Northern Alliance, a loose confederation of warlords and factions (12,000–15,000 troops, 60–70 tanks and armored vehicles, 3 cargo planes, 8 transport helicopters, and some 25 surface-to-surface and short-range ballistic missiles), concentrated in the remote northern parts of Afghanistan.

The difficult mountainous terrain and harsh climate of Afghanistan and its archaic infrastructure, shattered by more than 20 years of war, enormously limited maneuverability and complicated the logistics of any modern military force. At the same time, these very conditions led light and mobile Taliban forces to believe that they could engage and exhaust any invader in sudden ambushes and attacks. Afghans had a history of successfully repelling invaders, particularly the British in the 19th century and, more recently, the Soviets in the 1980s.

Bearing in mind the harsh conditions of the theater and the fanatical character of the enemy, some military observers and analysts foresaw a long and bloody campaign in Afghanistan. According to some estimates, it would take as many as 100,000 U.S. troops to occupy and control the country. Such a large-scale operation would be put under additional risk by approaching winter, which limited the time available. The Taliban, for its part, expected that the United States would follow the Soviet example of a massive ground invasion. The Taliban therefore prepared to lure the Americans in and outmaneuver them, employing its key tactic of using highly mobile strike squads mounted on pickup trucks.

The general strategic scheme of the U.S. operation in Afghanistan was designed to avoid a Vietnam War–style gradual escalation and involvement in a long and bloody ground war. Thus, instead of committing a large number of U.S. ground troops, the Americans sought to execute the operation with a combination of air strikes and special operations, which would be closely coordinated with the U.S.-backed ground assault by the anti-Taliban Northern Alliance forces.

The American war plan for Afghanistan had important new elements, which reflected distinctive local realities and the intention of the U.S. command to engage the enemy asymmetrically, exploiting its vulnerabilities and outmaneuvering its strengths. The plan envisaged the use of the most advanced military and communications technology in the world on one of the world's most primitive battlefields. The dispersed nature of warfare in the Afghan deserts, high plateaus, and foreboding mountains as well as the decentralized structure of the Taliban and Al Qaeda forces demanded a major emphasis on special operations to take the fight to the enemy, keeping it off balance as well as seizing and maintaining the initiative on the battlefield. In coordination with an intense bombing campaign and military pressure from the Northern Alliance, this, it was hoped, would swiftly reshape the situation on the ground.

The political dimension of the war was of much importance also. The United States actively exploited the unpopularity and vulnerability of the Taliban regime inside and outside Afghanistan as a result of its violent character and extreme interpretation of Islamic law. To isolate the Taliban further, the United States publicly emphasized the just and defensive character of its war on terror and stressed the puppet role of the Taliban under Al Qaeda. U.S. representatives established contacts with the exiled Afghan king Zahir Shah, then living in Rome, who had some influence in the country, particularly among the Pashtuns, Afghanistan's largest ethnic group. Additionally, the military campaign would be paralleled by a large-scale humanitarian effort, with U.S. cargo planes conducting massive food drops for starving Afghans.

The United States would also work on managing the tremendous logistics problems of waging a war over such a long distance and in a landlocked country. The measures to undertake this would include access to bases and facilities in Bahrain, Oman, Pakistan, and Uzbekistan; flight rights over these and other countries; and efforts to achieve understanding with major regional players—India, China, and Russia—about American motives, aims, and actions. U.S. airlift capability using its midair refueling abilities (employing the McDonnell Douglas KC-10 Extender and Boeing KC-135 Stratotanker) was to play a critical role during the 2001 Afghan campaign. The logistical challenges of ENDURING FREEDOM also prompted the seizure of airfields inside Afghanistan at earlier stages of the campaign, and that was an important and integral part of the plan.

In planning and preparing for ENDURING FREEDOM and the Global War on Terror, the United States received active support from the North Atlantic Treaty Organization (NATO) and other allied countries, including intelligence cooperation and offers to put troops on the ground. The allied naval presence in the Arabian Sea was instrumental in creating additional pressure on Pakistan to join the coalition. Nevertheless, the Pentagon tried to avoid the multilateral bureaucratic wrangling it had experienced during the 1999 NATO bombing of Yugoslavia and carefully crafted the operation as a primarily American effort. The only exceptions were with the British and, to a lesser extent, the Australians. The British role in ENDURING FREEDOM (code-named Operation VERITAS by the British), while modest by comparison, had aims virtually identical with those of the Americans. The United States also placed much value on British contributions thanks to the professionalism and experience of the British military, particularly special operations forces.

The completed plan was to occur in four consecutive phases while simultaneously executing multiple lines of operation. In Phase One, the United States planned to set conditions for the operation, including interservice coordination; buildup of forces; coalition building, basing, and staging arrangements; and providing support for the Northern Alliance. The coalition had assembled a formidable U.S. force (three aircraft carrier battle groups with cruisers, destroyers, attack submarines, frigates, and support ships; more than 400 aircraft; and some 50,000 sailors, airmen, marines, and soldiers including special forces, about 4,000 of them deployed inside Afghanistan by the beginning of

2002); a British force (3 Royal Navy attack submarines, 1 support aircraft carrier, a naval task group, and 4,200 military personnel, including sailors, marines, and special forces), and a small detachment of the Australian Special Operations Forces.

The actual war (Phase Two) would begin with 3–5 days of a U.S.-British bombing campaign across Afghanistan using cruise missiles, jets from aircraft carriers, and strategic bombers (Northrop Grumman B-2 Spirit and Boeing B-52 Stratofortress aircraft) flying concurrently from the United States and Diego Garcia. Then the Northern Alliance forces would begin their attack on Taliban strongholds in the northern part of the country, securing the area for further movements. The special operations forces, drawn from the Central Intelligence Agency Special Activities Division, U.S. Army Green Berets, and U.S. Navy SEALs, were to execute reconnaissance and direct-action line of operation, making contact with the Northern Alliance troops on the ground and providing training and tactical support for them. The U.S. Air Force combat air controllers would also infiltrate the area to pinpoint enemy targets for the coalition strike aircraft (operational fires line of operation).

During Phase Three, a limited number of coalition conventional troops would move in to eliminate the remaining pockets of enemy resistance. Even the conventional forces were to be employed unconventionally, by flexible and rapid-reaction airborne and helicopter-borne night assaults. The concluding Phase Four would concentrate on stabilization and rebuilding efforts in Afghanistan.

While the planning of Operation ENDURING FREEDOM did demonstrate creative and innovative approaches in addressing numerous challenges in Afghanistan and succeeded in eliminating Al Qaeda sanctuaries in the country, the continuing guerrilla war there, which followed the fall of the Taliban, has stimulated critical evaluations of the plan and the operation. Critics maintain that by putting so much effort in the quick and impressive toppling of the Taliban regime, the United States underestimated the complexity and urgency of the stabilization efforts needed in Afghanistan to consolidate the coalition's initial victory and bring Al Qaeda and Taliban top commanders to justice. Some critical assessments also blame the initial American plan for its failure to capitalize on the interim disagreements between Al Qaeda and the Taliban and within the Taliban structure itself. There have also been critical overviews of U.S. coalition-building efforts. Some have argued that the Pentagon's determination to carry out the operation largely alone set the stage for the rift between the United States and Europe on the critically important issue of burden sharing that was to deepen the longer the war progressed.

PETER J. RAINOW

See also

Afghanistan; Al Qaeda; Bin Laden, Osama; Central Intelligence Agency; Franks, Tommy; Global War on Terror

References

DeLong, Michael, with Noah Lukeman. *Inside CENTCOM: The Unvarnished Truth about the Wars in Afghanistan and Iraq.* Washington, DC: Regnery, 2004.

Franks, Tommy, with Malcolm McConnell. *American Soldier.* New York: Regan Books, 2004.

Woodward, Bob. *Bush at War.* New York: Simon and Shuster, 2002.

ENDURING FREEDOM, Operation, U.S. Air Campaign (October 2001)

Following the September 11, 2001, attacks on the World Trade Center and the Pentagon, the United States requested that the Taliban-controlled government of Afghanistan hand over leaders of Al Qaeda, the terror organization responsible for the attacks. Among these was Al Qaeda leader Osama bin Laden. The administration of President George W. Bush considered the Taliban's failure to extradite bin Laden and his compatriots to the United States with no preconditions as sufficient justification for invading Afghanistan.

Prior to the ground assault led by the Northern Alliance, the U.S.-led alliance began an aerial bombing campaign of Afghanistan in October 2001. The targets selected during the first wave of bombings in the initial phase of Operation ENDURING FREEDOM provide insights into the political bargaining by the United States to enlist support from Afghanistan's neighbors, Uzbekistan and Pakistan, into the antiterror coalition. In order to gain access to Uzbekistan's military facilities, the United States agreed to destroy the bases of the Islamic Movement of Uzbekistan (IMU), located in Taliban-controlled Afghanistan. Several IMU bases in the Balkh and Kunduz Provinces near the Uzbek border were among the first targets hit in Afghanistan. To secure the cooperation of Pakistan, the U.S.-led alliance agreed not to target key Taliban defensive positions in and around Kabul.

Afghan civilians examine damage caused by a U.S. air strike in the capital of Kabul, October 11, 2001. (AP Photo)

On October 7, 2001, American and British forces began the aerial bombing of Al Qaeda training camps as well as the Taliban air defenses. Initial strikes focused on the heavily populated cities of Kabul, Kandahar, and Herat. Within a few days most of the Al Qaeda training camps had been destroyed, and the Taliban air defenses had been neutralized. The bombing campaign then shifted toward communications and the command and control structure of the Taliban government. Two weeks into the bombing campaign America's Afghan ally, the Northern Alliance, sought and received aerial support in its efforts to attack Taliban frontline positions. The bombing of population centers caused a refugee problem, however, as large numbers of Afghans fled to avoid the strikes.

In the next phase of the aerial campaign, Taliban frontline positions were bombed with 1,500-pound daisy cutter bombs and cluster bombs that caused extensive casualties. By early November, Taliban frontline positions had been wiped out. In the last remaining Taliban stronghold, Mazar-e Sharif, the United States carpet-bombed the Taliban defenders, enabling the Northern Alliance to take the city after several days of fierce fighting.

The early success of the bombing campaign in destroying Taliban positions was not without controversy. The relentless aerial bombing of Afghanistan led to a high number of civilian casualties, estimated at between 3,700 and 5,000. In fact, the civilian death toll surpassed those incurred during the 1999 North Atlantic Treaty Organization bombing campaign of Kosovo and Serbia. When credible reports of bombing mishaps and accidental civilian casualties emerged, U.S. policy makers and military spokespersons consistently denied these claims. Nevertheless, the U.S. willingness to bomb heavily populated areas in Afghanistan using heavy ordnance bombs stoked fierce criticism of U.S. foreign policy. Allied and Muslim nations alike complained that the bombing victimized the innocent, exacerbated the humanitarian disaster in Afghanistan, and created widespread resentment across the Muslim world. Worse still, reports that U.S. troops participated in a massacre of Taliban prisoners of war in Mazar-e Sharif in late November 2001 further inflamed world opinion. In spite of the apparent success of the air campaign, however, Al Qaeda mastermind Osama bin Laden was not captured or killed and remained at large.

KEITH A. LEITICH

See also

Afghanistan; Al Qaeda; Bin Laden, Osama; ENDURING FREEDOM, Operation, Initial Ground Campaign; Global War on Terror; September 11 Attacks; Taliban

References

Docherty, Bonnie L. *United States/Afghanistan: Fatally Flawed; Cluster Bombs and Their Use by the United States in Afghanistan.* New York: Human Rights Watch, 2002.

Dudley, William, ed. *The Attack on America, September 11, 2001.* San Diego: Greenhaven, 2002.

Fiscus, James W. *America's War in Afghanistan.* New York: Rosen, 2004.

Miller, Raymond H. *The War on Terrorism: The War in Afghanistan.* Chicago: Lucent Books, 2003.

Schroen, Gary. *First In: An Insider Account of How the CIA Spearheaded the War on Terror in Afghanistan.* Novato, CA: Presidio, 2005.

Erdoğan, Recep Tayyip (1954–)

Turkish politician, prime minister (2003–2014), and president (2014–) of Turkey. Recep Tayyip Erdoğan was born on February 26, 1954, in Istanbul, the son of a coast guard worker. He spent his early years in Rize, but in 1967 his father moved the family back to Istanbul in search of a better life. As a teenager, Erdoğan sold food on the streets of Istanbul to earn money and attended a local Islamic school. He became interested in politics at a relatively young age, joining the youth group of the Welfare Party, an Islamic fundamentalist group, at age 15.

After graduating from Istanbul's Marmara University with a business degree, Erdoğan became a professional soccer player. Although he enjoyed the sport, his involvement with the Welfare Party grew deeper, and after a few years his political career began to take shape.

In 1994, Erdoğan was elected mayor of Istanbul. Often thought of as one of Turkey's most charismatic politicians, he earned praise even from some opponents. Despite their dissatisfaction with his ban on alcohol in Istanbul's cafés, many of Erdoğan's secular critics admitted that he had done an excellent job of cleaning up the city. He was also widely viewed as fair and honest and had not been corrupted by power.

Erdoğan's pro-Islamist leanings made him popular with devout Muslims who felt slighted by Turkey's secular government; however, these same leanings also brought controversy and legal trouble. In 1998 just as he left office as mayor, Erdoğan was convicted for inciting religious hatred after reading a bellicose Islamic poem aloud at a public function. The recitation earned him a 10-month jail sentence, although he was released after having served just 4 months. That same year the government banned the Welfare Party because officials believed that it was undermining the government's secular policies.

After Erdoğan was released from jail, he joined the reformist wing of the Virtue Party, the pro-Islamic political grouping founded on the ashes of the banned Welfare Party. Alongside friend and fellow Virtue Party member Abdullah Gul, Erdoğan worked to disavow the hard-line religious views of his past. When the Virtue Party was banned in 2001, Erdoğan and Gul formed the Justice and Development Party (AKP).

With promises that the AKP would eschew the Turkish Islamic movement's radical past, Erdoğan's new party attracted press attention and many followers. In November 2002 legislative elections the AKP won a surprise landslide victory, placing Erdoğan at the forefront of national politics. However, his previous conviction barred him from taking office as prime minister. Gul took office instead, promising to step down once the law was changed to allow Erdoğan to become premier. In February 2003, the Turkish national electoral board ruled that Erdoğan was able to participate in by-elections, and on March 9 it was announced that he had secured sufficient votes to become a member of the National Assembly. Two days later Gul tendered his resignation, paving the way for Erdoğan to take office on March 14, 2003.

While there were concerns about the AKP's Islamic-based ideology, Erdoğan focused on economic reform and securing Turkey's entrance into the European Union. Throughout Erdoğan's tenure as premier, Turkey's economy not only weathered the global recession but continued to grow, contributing to the AKP's (and Erdoğan's) reelection in 2007 and 2011. In 2011, Erdoğan became the country's first premier to win a third term. Despite protests in 2013 over the AKP's Islamist influence in the government, Erdoğan was elected president by popular vote in 2014, taking office on August 28. Nevertheless, there have been sporadic and large demonstrations against his agenda, which some moderates and leftists view as an Islamic brand of authoritarianism.

Erdoğan's long tenure has proven controversial in terms of Turkey's foreign affairs. His government has frequently acted bellicosely toward the minority Kurds, and in 2007 he asserted that Turkey had every reason to invade and occupy Iraqi Kurdistan, given numerous attacks by the Kurdistan Workers' Party (PKK) on Turkish soldiers and civilians. Erdoğan has labeled the PKK a terrorist group. While the Turkish government has been battling PKK fighters, it has also attempted to engage moderate Kurds in dialogue that would eventually lead to a broad rapprochement between Kurds and Turks.

Turkish-Israeli relations plummeted as Erdoğan's government sharply condemned Israel's deadly May 2010 raid against a flotilla of ships carrying arms and supplies to Hamas in Gaza while in international waters of the Mediterranean. Until that time, Turkish-Israeli relations had been quite cordial. Relations between the two countries improved after Israel apologized for the deaths of Turkish activists in the raid, but the 2014 Israel-Gaza conflict resulted in another diplomatic donnybrook after Erdoğan asserted that Israeli policies were more "barbaric" than those of Adolf Hitler.

Much to the chagrin of the North Atlantic Treaty Organization, which includes Turkey, Erdoğan has engaged the Russians in a series of bilateral commercial and energy agreements in recent years to include a pipeline deal in December 2014 and has been largely silent regarding the Russian seizure of Crimea and intervention in eastern Ukraine.

Not surprisingly, Turkish relations with Washington have been tense and sometimes confrontational. Erdoğan's decision in 2003 not to permit the United States to use Turkey as a base of operations for the Iraq War alienated the Americans for years thereafter. Although U.S.-Turkish relations appeared to be on the upswing after Barack Obama became president in 2009, they have plummeted in more recent years. Erdoğan's decision to aid antigovernment rebels in the Syrian Civil War before properly vetting them irked Washington, as has his noncommittal approach to stopping the Islamic State of Iraq and Syria (ISIS). Indeed, some have claimed that the Turkish government is providing covert support to ISIS. In the early fall of 2014 when the United States asked permission to use Turkey's Incirlik Air Base as a staging area for air strikes against ISIS in Iraq and Syria, Erdoğan replied that he would accede to the request only after Syrian president Bashar al-Assad had been removed from power. This outraged Washington and may have cost Turkey a seat on the United Nations Security Council.

Tamar Burris and Paul G. Pierpaoli Jr.

See also

Assad, Bashar al-; Islamic State in Iraq and Syria; Kurdistan Workers' Party; Kurds; Syrian Civil War; Turkey

References

Carkoglu, Ali, and William Hale, eds. *The Politics of Modern Turkey.* London: Taylor and Francis, 2008.

Lashnits, Tom. *Recep Tayyup Erdoğan.* New York: Chelsea House, 2005.

"U.S. and Turkey's Push-and-Shove Diplomacy Has Kurds in the Middle." *The Guardian,* October 7, 2014, http://www.the guardian.com/us-news/2014/oct/07/us-turkey-diplomacy -isis-kurds-kobani.

Euphrates Valley

See Tigris and Euphrates Valley

Europe and the Afghanistan and Iraq Wars

In the first decade of the 21st century, the United States, with significant assistance from Great Britain, launched wars in Afghanistan in October 2001 and then against Iraq in March 2003 to overthrow governments that those powers considered intolerable threats to their own interests and replace them with more amenable regimes. In the first conflict, the administration of President George W. Bush initially received almost unanimous support from European governments as it sought to deprive the radical Islamist Al Qaeda forces of the safe haven they had found in Afghanistan under the sympathetic Taliban regime. Al Qaeda had been responsible for the September 11, 2001, terrorist attacks on the United States. The second war, designed to overthrow President Saddam Hussein of Iraq, proved more problematic, dividing European nations and provoking serious internal dissent and criticism in even those European countries whose governments supported American policies against Iraq.

By the time Bush had completed his second term in January 2009, even the British government, once Bush's strongest backer, had grown weary of involvement in what seemed to be one—if not two—almost interminable wars that produced a low-level but constant toll of casualties among British troops.

The immediate reaction of Europeans to the terrorist attacks of September 11, 2001, upon the United States was one of near unalloyed sympathy for the American people and their government. For the first time in its more than 50-year history, the North Atlantic Treaty Organization (NATO) invoked the provision in its charter whereby an attack upon one member state constituted war against all. The source of the suicidal air raids upon the World Trade Center towers in New York and the Pentagon building in Washington, D.C., was soon identified as Al Qaeda, headed by Osama bin Laden. The Taliban leaders refused to repudiate Al Qaeda and surrender bin Laden and his followers to the United States.

With strong support from other NATO members, in October 2001 a coalition of American, British, Australian, and anti-Taliban Afghan Northern Alliance forces launched an invasion of Afghanistan. By the end of the year they had taken Kabul, the capital, and driven Taliban and Al Qaeda forces into the mountainous areas of Afghanistan bordering on Pakistan. In December 2001 the United Nations (UN) established the International Security Assistance Force (ISAF) to help restore order in Afghanistan, first in the area around Kabul and eventually throughout the country. In the following years, many other European nations outside the original coalition contributed troop contingents to ISAF.

Much has been made of America's failure to enthusiastically embrace NATO's early offers of support. In largely going it alone at first, the United States lost a lot of goodwill. Undoubtedly, this was a major political error that only reinforced many of the world's deeply held prejudices about American arrogance and unilateralism. On the operational level, however, there were reasons for this approach. The command and control of NATO's war against Serbia over Kosovo was a nightmare of command decision by committee. After that experience, U.S. military and political leaders vowed not to repeat it. The second reason is that with the exceptions of Britain and France, the rest of NATO's armies, navies, and air forces have sharply declined since the end of the Cold War. Although still impressive on paper, those armies—especially the German Bundeswehr—have been starved of funds and resources for almost two decades since the end of the Cold War. Much of their equipment is obsolete; their soldiers are untrained, unskilled, and unmotivated; and their communications systems are completely incompatible with modern systems. They have almost no logistics capability and no strategic lift.

While the invasion of Afghanistan attracted massive international support and while almost every European country subsequently participated in some manner in ISAF, the invasion of Iraq slightly less than 18 months later failed to win comparable backing. Before September 11, 2001, the Bush administration had focused primarily on the possibility of overthrowing President Saddam Hussein of Iraq, whose regime still remained in power a decade after his country's defeat in the 1991 Persian Gulf War. Once apparent victory had been attained in Afghanistan, American officials quickly returned to their preoccupation with Iraq, erroneously arguing that close links existed between Hussein and Al Qaeda and that Iraq already possessed large quantities of weapons of mass destruction (WMD) and was well on the way to producing many more, which would enable Hussein to destabilize and dominate the Middle East.

Bush's national security team sought to persuade the UN to pass resolutions demanding that Iraq allow inspection teams full access to all its potential weapons facilities and surrender or destroy all WMD and authorizing the use of military force should Iraq refuse to comply. Bush argued that even if Iraq did not at that time pose a real military threat to the United States and its allies, it might do so in the future, and preemptive action to overthrow Hussein's rule was therefore justified.

The Bush administration's efforts were energetically seconded by Tony Blair, the Labour prime minister of Britain, who had established a very close relationship with Bush. The two men shared what appeared to be an almost visceral hatred of Hussein and a passionate desire to overthrow his regime. Blair faced strong opposition from within his own Labour Party, many of whom rejected his rationale for war, including former foreign secretary Robin Cook, who resigned in protest as leader of the House of Commons. In March 2003 Blair won a parliamentary majority in favor of war, including most of the opposition Conservative Party, while some 135 Labour members voted against him. Broader public support for the war in Britain was at best lukewarm, with massive public demonstrations against an invasion of Iraq organized shortly before Britain and the United States launched their invasion. As the Iraq War dragged on and a major insurgency plunged Iraq into virtual chaos, Blair's approval ratings plummeted, as did Britons' support for the conflict. Blair left office in 2007, and by the end of 2009 all British troops had been withdrawn from Iraq.

Similar demonstrations took place across most of Western Europe, as Bush and Blair signally failed to convince the people and often the leaders of many other European countries that war against Iraq was either desirable or justified. In early 2003 they were unable to win a resolution from the UN fully endorsing military action against Iraq to enforce the existing ban on its possession or development of WMD. Germany, France, and Russia (the latter two countries holding permanent UN Security Council seats with veto power) all strongly opposed the passage of such a resolution and were entirely unwilling to contribute troops to any invasion force. This stance attracted fierce verbal criticism from U.S. secretary of defense Donald Rumsfeld, who derisively condemned the nations of "Old Europe"—meaning such long-established noncommunist West European nations as France and Germany—as being effete, spineless, and decadent, corrupted by too many years of comfortable prosperity, and contrasted them unfavorably with those of "New Europe"—such as postcommunist states including Albania, Azerbaijan, Bosnia, Bulgaria, the Czech Republic, Georgia, Hungary, Latvia, Lithuania, Macedonia, Poland, Romania, and Ukraine—that were prepared to join in the "coalition of

the willing," led by the United States and Britain, that went to war against Iraq in late March 2003.

The invasion itself was undertaken by U.S., British, and Australian military forces, but numerous other countries subsequently dispatched modest contingents of troops to assist in postinvasion efforts to restore order. Since Denmark, Italy, the Netherlands, Norway, Portugal, and Spain had all done so by the end of 2003, the correlation between Old Europe and nonparticipation was by no means precise. Rumsfeld's words, and such American actions as informal suggestions that patriotic Americans should refuse to eat French wine or cheese and should speak of "freedom fries" rather than "French fries," generated great resentment as well as ridicule in France and much of Europe.

At this juncture Robert Kagan, a well-known American political commentator and former diplomat, stirred up further controversy with a provocative article arguing that whereas Americans possessed, respected, and were willing to deploy muscular military power to maintain global order, Europeans had a totally different mind-set, being relatively weak in terms of defense and thus placing a higher value on diplomacy, conciliation, cooperation, and tolerance. Kagan feared that unless the United States abandoned its growing unilateralism and displayed greater regard for European sensitivities, the ranks of the world's liberal democratic powers would be divided and ineffective on the international stage.

The apparently rapid coalition victory in Iraq and the overthrow of Hussein's government initially seemed to vindicate the invasion, somewhat moderating European governmental and popular opposition to it. Widely publicized revelations of the deposed regime's use of terror and brutality to maintain itself in power and crush antagonists gave some credibility to American and British claims that the dictator's removal was a victory for human rights. The failure to locate any substantial stores of WMD in Iraq did, however, prove to be a continuing basis for controversy over the purpose of the war. At best it cast doubt on the reliability of the intelligence data they had been citing to support their case for military intervention in Iraq, and at worst it cast doubt on the good faith of top American and British political leaders. Official discomfiture in both countries was compounded by public revelations in May 2003 that Blair and his advisers, like the Bush administration, had massaged intelligence data so as to greatly exaggerate the strategic threat from Iraq to its neighbors and others. The suicide in July 2003 of David Kelly, a scientist in the British Ministry of Defense suspected of leaking this information to the media, added further bitterness to this controversy, which the January 2004 report of a public inquiry headed by Lord Hutton failed to resolve.

These revelations were only one reason why popular disillusionment with the conflict in Iraq became steadily more pronounced throughout much of Europe. The tactics that the United States used to prosecute suspects in both Iraq and the Global War on Terror aroused widespread public revulsion and destroyed much of the credibility of American claims that the invading forces were defending liberal democracy and human rights. In 2004 photographs and videotapes of the abuse, torture, and humiliation of Iraqi political detainees by American troops at Abu Ghraib prison were widely circulated in the international media and proved particularly embarrassing to the United States. So too did the Bush administration's sanction of so-called enhanced interrogation techniques, considered torture and disreputable by many, in disregard of the Geneva Conventions; the detention without trial or legal redress at the U.S. overseas military facility at Guantánamo, Cuba, of hundreds of alleged terrorists; and the rendition, or kidnapping, in foreign jurisdictions of individuals suspected for some reason of involvement in terrorist activities and their physical transfer to countries where harsh interrogation methods were employed. Most European governments, even those such as Germany that declined to sanction the invasion of Iraq, permitted American intelligence and security operatives to undertake such renditions within their countries. Anti-American sentiment mounted almost across the board in Europe, and condemnation of American disregard for liberal values and human rights and the insensitive unilateralism of the United States in international affairs was widespread.

Most European nations, including France and Germany, which had opposed the war in Iraq, nonetheless contributed funding and sometimes personnel to aid and training programs intended to assist both Iraq and Afghanistan. While refraining from any military involvement in Iraq, in October 2003 the German Bundestag did vote to send German forces to Afghanistan, and by February 2009 Germany had the third-largest national contingent of troops in ISAF, although these were restricted to reconstruction rather than combat operations.

In most European nations, war weariness with what seemed unwinnable conflicts also steadily intensified. Although Bush declared an end to major combat operations in Iraq early in May 2003, for several years the situation in Iraq remained extremely unstable, with the country deeply divided among majority Shiite, Sunni, and Kurdish political groupings. The new coalition-backed Iraqi government initially failed to win military or political control of large swaths of territory. Violence and insurgency, sometimes involving Al Qaeda operatives from outside Iraq, had escalated by 2006 to a point where a state of virtual civil war existed in much of the country. Casualties among the foreign occupation forces as well as deaths among Iraqi government personnel and civilians mounted steadily, and significantly more coalition troops died in action after the supposed end of major hostilities than before. Foreigners of all nationalities, including journalists, civilian security personnel, businesspeople, and others, also became repeated targets of kidnappings and murder by a variety of Iraqi insurgent elements, as increasingly were Iraqis themselves, causing a huge number to flee the country. Anglo-American preoccupation with the war in Iraq meant that fewer resources of every kind, personnel, economic assistance, or attention were devoted to Afghanistan. By 2005 Taliban and other insurgent forces in Afghanistan had regrouped, posing a major military threat to that country's stability and undermining the authority of the Afghan government in substantial areas of its own territory.

In many European nations, radical Islamic elements of the population deeply resented their governments' involvement in hostilities in Iraq and Afghanistan and, more broadly, what they perceived as disrespect for their own religious faith and values. The emergence of Muslim extremists ready to resort to violence aroused growing concern across Western Europe. One consequence was increased official security surveillance of the Muslim communities in each nation, generally undertaken in conjunction with government-sponsored efforts to reach out to and enter into dialogues with the less radicalized portions of their substantial Muslim populations. In March 2004 extremist Spanish Muslims exploded several bombs on commuter trains at the Madrid railway station, killing 191 people and injuring 1,800. In July 2005 British Muslims launched similar suicide bombing attacks on the London transport system, leaving 56 dead and around 700 injured. Further terrorist attempts took place in Britain in the summer of 2007 shortly after Gordon Brown replaced Blair as Labour prime minister. Violence against individuals who were seen as unfriendly to Islam also occurred. In May 2002 the independent Dutch politician Pim Fortuyn, who had condemned Islam as intolerant and called for an end to further Muslim immigration into the Netherlands, was assassinated. Two years later in November 2004, the Dutch filmmaker Theo van Gogh, another well-known personality who had strongly criticized

Islam, was likewise assassinated by a Muslim extremist. In 2005 a Danish newspaper published uncomplimentary cartoons of the Prophet Muhammad, provoking massive demonstrations from Muslims within Denmark and outside Danish embassies across the Middle East on the grounds that these were racist. Most European governments found the emergence of indigenous Muslim terrorism among their own populations an ominous development.

As the wars in Afghanistan and Iraq continued with little apparent prospect of any conclusive resolution, European governments bent to popular pressure and became less willing to contemplate indefinite military involvements in those countries. Three days after the Madrid bombings, a new government won power in Spanish elections and shortly afterward withdrew the remaining Spanish troops from the occupation of Iraq. Hungary, the Netherlands, and Portugal likewise withdrew their forces from Iraq in 2005; Italy and Norway followed suit in 2006. Early in 2007 the United States adopted a new policy of a surge of temporary troop increases in Iraq combined with intensive efforts to strengthen the Iraqi government, eradicate hard-line opponents, win over potentially friendly elements, and train Iraqi security and other personnel in the hope of stabilizing the country. The withdrawals of European forces continued, with Lithuania and Slovakia removing their troop contingents in 2007. In 2008 the Iraqi government itself requested the gradual removal of coalition forces, and all remaining military personnel from Albania, Armenia, Azerbaijan, Bosnia, Bulgaria, the Czech Republic, Denmark, Estonia, Georgia, Latvia, Macedonia, Moldova, Poland, and Ukraine were gone by December of that year. Of the European powers, by early 2009 only Britain and Romania still had troops in Iraq.

Brown, the new British premier, was widely believed to be a far less enthusiastic supporter than Blair of both wars. To the dismay of American officials, in late 2007 Brown withdrew British forces from Basra Province and the city of Basra in Iraq and restricted their mission to training the Iraqi military. Brown also reduced the number of British troops in Afghanistan.

In November 2008 the election as president of the United States of Barack Obama, a Democrat who had not voted for intervention in Iraq and planned a phased withdrawal of virtually all American forces in that country, brought at least temporarily a new warmth, even euphoria, to U.S. relations with Europe. European officials and the public generally welcomed Obama's decisions to end the use of so-called enhanced interrogation techniques against terrorist suspects and to close the detention center at Guantánamo

Bay, Cuba. They also applauded his efforts to reach out to Islamic leaders and populations around the world and his emphasis on multilateral rather than unilateral solutions to international problems. Less popular with European governments and their people was Obama's belief that while the situation in Iraq was under control, mounting military and political problems in Afghanistan and across the border in neighboring Pakistan warranted a major boost in American and allied forces deployed in Afghanistan as a preliminary to stabilizing those countries. In the spring of 2009, Obama announced his intention of temporarily increasing American deployments in Afghanistan from 32,000 to between 50,000 and 60,000 personnel, and he called upon other countries that belonged to the NATO alliance to send additional troops to ISAF.

In February 2009, 34 European countries still had more than 30,000 military personnel in Afghanistan, with the largest contingent, 8,300, coming from Britain. Their response to Obama's request for greater manpower was decidedly unenthusiastic. Belgium promised an additional 150 men and four jet fighters; France pledged to send a few hundred troops, with additional personnel for the European Gendarmerie Force, to help train the new Afghan police, plus some Eurocopter Tiger attack helicopters; Italy contributed an additional 800 support troops to assist with police training and economic development; Poland offered 320 additional combat troops to help with the security of forthcoming Afghan elections; Spain offered a further 450 for the same purpose; Slovakia promised up to 176 more troops; Georgia promised as many as 500 troops; and Sweden pledged between 100 and 125 troops. In early 2009 British prime minister Brown increased British troops levels from 8,000 to 8,300, a number he pledged to increase temporarily to 9,000 until after the August 2009 elections in Afghanistan. Overall, these new forces amounted to perhaps 4,000 additional personnel altogether, well below the major boost that Obama had hoped for.

It was clear, moreover, that some European nations, including the Netherlands, intended to bring all their troops home within two years, and several, including Britain, Poland, and Spain, planned to reduce their Afghan commitments once the summer 2009 elections were over. Across Europe, governments and the public alike had been worn down by a steady trickle of casualties and believed that almost a decade of inconclusive war in Afghanistan was long enough. As Taliban and Al Qaeda forces enjoyed a resurgence in Afghanistan and even more in neighboring Pakistan, it was clear that while most European governments wished the Obama administration well, the United States itself would have to find the great bulk of whatever resources were needed to bring the war in Afghanistan to a conclusion that American officials considered acceptable.

On December 31, 2014, ISAF's mandate in Afghanistan expired. As of April 1, 2014, there were 51,178 foreign troops still deployed as part of ISAF. This number had shrunk to 34,512 by October 6. Among these, 24,050 U.S. troops made up 70 percent of the total. Major European troop deployments as of October 6, 2014, included 2,839 from Britain, 1,707 from Germany, and 1,400 from Italy. ISAF was disbanded at the end of 2014. Some troops remained in Afghanistan in an advisory role as part of the 12,500-man allied Resolute Support Mission.

PRISCILLA ROBERTS

See also

Abu Ghraib; Afghanistan War; Blair, Tony; Brown, James Gordon; Guantánamo Bay Detainment Camp; International Security Assistance Force; IRAQI FREEDOM, Operation; Taliban; United Kingdom, Middle East Policy

References

Andrews, David M., ed. *The Atlantic Alliance under Stress: US-European Relations after Iraq.* Cambridge: Cambridge University Press, 2005.

Baylis, John, and Jon Roper, eds. *The United States and Europe: Beyond the Neo-Conservative Divide?* London: Routledge, 2006.

Campbell, Alastair, and Richard Stott, eds. *The Blair Years: Extracts from the Alastair Campbell Diaries.* London: Hutchinson, 2007.

Cook, Robin. *The Point of Departure.* New York: Simon and Schuster, 2003.

Joffe, Josef. *Überpower: The Imperial Temptation of America.* New York: Norton, 2006.

Judt, Tony, and Denis Lacorne, eds. *With Us or against Us: Studies in Global Anti-Americanism.* New York: Palgrave Macmillan, 2005.

Lindberg, Tod, ed. *Beyond Paradise and Power: Europe, America and the Future of a Troubled Partnership.* New York: Routledge, 2005.

Merkl, Peter H. *The Rift between America and Old Europe: The Distracted Eagle.* London: Routledge, 2005.

Serfaty, Simon. *Architects of Delusion: Europe, America, and the Iraq War.* Philadelphia: University of Pennsylvania Press, 2008.

Explosive Reactive Armor

Explosive reactive armor (ERA) is a common form of add-on armor employed in many armored fighting vehicles (AFVs), such as tanks. AFVs utilize an armor casing to protect the crew and the machinery against strikes from enemy antitank weapons. The antitank weapons, in turn, work by piercing the armor and killing the crew or damaging hardware and software. ERA is only effective against chemical energy anti-armor weapons, such as high-explosive antitank (HEAT) rounds. ERA is not effective against kinetic energy weapons, such as sabot rounds.

In the late 1970s the Israel Defense Forces developed the new ERA technology to protect AFVs. The concept underlying ERA was accidently discovered in 1967–1968 by a German researcher, Manfred Held, who was then working in Israel. Held and his team conducted tests by firing shells at wrecked tanks left over from the 1967 Six-Day War. They noticed that tanks that still contained live ordnance exploded and that this explosion could disrupt the penetration of a shaped charge. This insight led to the manufacture of ERA.

ERA utilizes add-on protection modules, called tiles, made from thin metal plates layered around a sloped explosive sheath. The sheath explodes when it senses the impact of an explosive charge, such as a HEAT projectile. By creating its own explosion the HEAT warhead detonates prematurely, which prevents the plasma jet of molten metal from the shell penetrating into the crew compartment of the AFV. ERA is most effective against HEAT rounds. Once used, an ERA tile has to be replaced.

The early ERA models effectively defended tanks and other AFVs from single strikes. However, after they performed their task, the explosive sheath was spent, leaving the AFV vulnerable to another shell in the same location. More recent ERA uses a combination of energetic and passive materials to withstand multiple strikes. These modern designs employ smaller tiles and more complex shapes to offer optimal plate slopes to counter potential threats including missile warheads, exploding shells, and rocket-propelled grenades (RPGs).

In early 1991, technicians installed ERA on the nose and glacis plate of Challenger 1, the main battle tank of the British Army. Likewise, the U.S. Army Materiel Command applied reactive armor plates to the U.S. Marine Corps M60-series tanks. Since that time, modern AFVs such as the Abrams M-1A2, the British Challenger 1 and 2, and a variety of Russian tanks have all demonstrated excellent protection by using ERA.

New generations of antitank guided missiles continue to pose a threat. In addition, in urban combat such as that which occurred in the Iraq War after 2003, enemy infantry armed with RPGs fired from multiple directions at close range have the potential to overwhelm the target's ERA. One downside to the use of ERA is the potential to harm nearby friendly troops. In times past, infantry soldiers commonly used tanks as a means of transport. They would even ride on the tanks as they entered combat. ERA-equipped tanks made this practice too dangerous.

During the 1991 Persian Gulf War, the Iraqi military fielded almost 6,000 main battle tanks ranging from the obsolete T-55 to the modern T-72. Iraqi tanks lacked ERA. The main Iraqi battle tank, the T-72, had reactive armor but not ERA.

Development of ERA technology has continued. Advanced versions of ERA were based on better understanding of the science associated with ERA systems, and they utilized lower masses of explosives. These considerations have had significant implications on the logistics, storage, and handling of AFVs and protection systems without a reduction in the protection levels. Future ERA models are likely to employ so-called smart armor concepts that will integrate sensors and microprocessors embedded into the armor. These devices will sense the location, type, velocity, and diameter of the projectile or jet and trigger smaller explosive elements precisely tailored to defeat a specific penetrator.

JAMES ARNOLD

See also

M1A1 and M1A2 Abrams Main Battle Tanks; T-54/55 Series Main Battle Tank; T-62 Main Battle Tank; T-72 Main Battle Tank

References

Dunnigan, James F., and Austin Bay. *From Shield to Storm: High-Tech Weapons, Military Strategy, and Coalition Warfare in the Persian Gulf.* New York: William Morrow, 1992.

Hutchison, Kevin Don. *Operation Desert Shield/Desert Storm: Chronology and Fact Book.* Westport, CT: Greenwood, 1995.

Jane's Armour and Artillery, 2001–2002. London: Jane's Information Group, 2001.

F

Fahrenheit 9/11

Documentary film released on June 25, 2004, by Michael Moore that sharply criticized the George W. Bush administration's handling of the Global War on Terror and the rationale for the March 2003 invasion of Iraq. *Fahrenheit 9/11* earned record box office receipts for a documentary but did not achieve the filmmaker's goal of preventing Bush's reelection.

Moore is an iconoclastic author, filmmaker, and liberal activist whose controversial work enjoys considerable commercial success. His best-selling books—*Stupid White Men* (2002) and *Dude, Where's My Country* (2003)—both satirized and challenged the nation's political establishment. Moore's excellent documentary *Roger & Me* (1989) focused on the director's efforts to secure a meeting with General Motors chief executive officer Roger Smith. Moore had accused Smith of abandoning the filmmaker's hometown of Flint, Michigan. In *Bowling for Columbine* (2002), Moore addressed the subject of guns and violence in U.S. society. At the 2003 Oscar Awards, Moore received an Academy Award for *Columbine* as best documentary feature. The filmmaker used the occasion to make a brief speech criticizing the U.S. invasion of Iraq.

Moore's controversial Oscar appearance was the beginning of a political firestorm that engulfed his next feature, *Fahrenheit 9/11*. On May 22, 2004, *Fahrenheit 9/11* was awarded the prestigious Palme d'Or at the 57th Cannes Film Festival. Moore's detractors sneered that the award was another example of French anti-Americanism; however,

there was only one French citizen on the nine-person jury. Prerelease publicity for the film was also ensured when executives of the Disney Corporation blocked their subsidiary Miramax from distributing the film. Lion's Gate, however, was willing to replace Disney. Moore asserted that Disney was bowing to political pressure from the Bush administration.

Fahrenheit 9/11 earned $23.9 million on its first weekend of release in Canada and the United States, making it the number one box office hit of the weekend. This was all the more remarkable because the film was in limited release. In fact, those weekend receipts alone exceeded the total amount earned by Moore's *Bowling for Columbine*, which was the largest grossing documentary film before *Fahrenheit 9/11*. By the weekend of July 24, 2004, the film was in European release and had grossed over $100 million.

In *Fahrenheit 9/11*, Moore indicts the Bush administration for manipulating the outcome of the 2000 presidential election as well as mishandling the war on terror and the occupation of Iraq. Employing information from Craig Unger's *House of Bush, House of Saud* (2004), Moore critiques the close relationship between the Bush family and Saudi officials, observing that most of the 9/11 hijackers were Saudis rather than Iraqis. Moore also chastises the U.S. military for targeting the poor and minorities in recruitment campaigns for the Iraq War.

Fahrenheit 9/11 focuses on the story of Lila Lipscomb from Flint, Michigan. Lipscomb was initially a strong

In this advertisement for his controversial documentary *Fahrenheit 9/11*, director Michael Moore and President George W. Bush appear in a computer-altered image under the title "Controversy . . . What controversy?" Moore's film is highly critical of the Bush administration's handling of the War on Terror. (Lions Gate Entertainment)

supporter of the Iraq War, but she began questioning the war after her son was killed in the conflict. A grieving Lipscomb asks Moore why her son had to die in a needless conflict. Moore concludes the film by asserting that the nation must never again send its brave young men and women unnecessarily into harm's way. This theme was reiterated by Moore in his book *Will They Ever Trust Us Again?* (2004).

Critics on the political Right labeled the film as in-your-face propaganda, attacking Moore and the accuracy of his arguments. Moore responded that his critics failed to understand that documentaries were not objective and that *Fahrenheit 9/11* might be best described as an "op-ed piece." Although acknowledging that his film was indeed opinionated, Moore defended the accuracy of his case.

Perhaps Moore's condemnation of corporate media's support for the war accounted for the growing criticism of the film in the mainstream press and media. Historian Robert Brent Toplin asserts that Moore's detractors were successful in casting doubt upon the veracity of the film. Accordingly, many Americans who were undecided on the war refused to see the film, and its impact on the 2004 presidential election was minimal. The negative political reaction to the film was also apparent in its failure to garner any Academy Award nominations. Moore did not submit his film for consideration as a documentary, hoping to attain a Best Picture nomination.

Those who shared Moore's political perspective flocked to the film. By January 2005, the film had grossed $220 million in world distribution. And more than 2 million copies, record sales for a documentary, were purchased upon its DVD release on October 5, 2004. Although a target of the political Right, Moore remains politically active and later produced *Sicko*, a 2007 documentary film that indicted America's health care system. In 2009, Moore's film titled *Capitalism: A Love Story* documented the financial and economic crisis that began in late 2008 and the Bush and Barack Obama administrations' reactions to it.

RON BRILEY

See also

Antiwar Movement, Iraq War; Bush, George Walker; Iraq War

References

Moore, Michael. *Will They Ever Trust Us Again?* New York: Simon and Schuster, 2004.

Topllin, Robert Brent. *Michael Moore's Fahrenheit 9/11: How One Film Divided a Nation.* Lawrence: University Press of Kansas, 2006.

Unger, Craig. *House of Bush, House of Saud: The Secret Relationship between the World's Two Most Powerful Dynasties.* New York: Scribner, 2004.

Failed States and the Global War on Terror

A failed state is characterized as a nation whose governing institutions do not provide minimum services to its population, especially in terms of security. Although still not accepted by many political experts, the concept of failed states gained currency during the George W. Bush presidency as a way of rationalizing interventionism in the Global War on Terror or explaining how 9/11 could have arisen. The concept of failed states was discussed in a volume edited by Robert Rotberg and then became part of an index in the influential journal *Foreign Policy* to measure certain facts in a number of countries.

In the popularized concept of failed or collapsed states, they may be paralyzed by corruption, may be unable to initiate or maintain economic or development programs, and may have ineffective judicial systems and little democracy. The novel factor now of interest as supposedly the true test of failure is the presence of large-scale endemic violence. The concept of failed states was specifically crafted to explain the rise of Osama bin Laden, so it was employed to identify ungoverned or poorly governed areas that harbor those who are violent.

A primary function of the state is to provide security for its citizens by means of what German sociologist Max Weber referred to as a monopoly on the legitimate use of violence. Failure to maintain this monopoly, by permitting or being unable to prevent nonstate groups to exercise violence on a large scale within the borders of the state, calls into question the existence of the state as a system of governance.

Those who employ the label "failed states" may point to such countries as Afghanistan, Lebanon, and even Pakistan. Failed states became an issue in the years following World War II as new nation-states were established in the European powers' former colonial empires and as former colonies rebelled and abruptly gained their independence. Some of these new states lacked strong central-governing bureaucratic institutions or well-trained government officials and civil servants. They were unable to govern their territories and populations in an efficient manner, leaving many of their citizens to search for other sources of basic services and security.

Many of the new states' borders were not aligned with ethnic or tribal boundaries, which had been in place for decades and in some cases centuries, creating new territorial conflicts or making old ones worse. This resulted in groups within the states attempting to take on some of the powers normally held by the state, either as a means to provide security for themselves and their constituents or simply to attain autonomous power within the state's boundaries.

One supposed central characteristic of a failed state is the breakdown of law and order. This is often the result of the increased power of criminal organizations such as drug cartels, militias, insurgents, and terrorist organizations arrayed against the poor-quality military and security forces of the state.

With the weakening and failure of the state, areas of these nations may come under the control of these organizations, especially as they become more capable of imposing their will on the security forces and leadership of the state. The concept of failed states has been particularly important in the U.S. approach to the Global War on Terror because most terrorist organizations seek areas of weak governmental control, which they take advantage of for the purposes of training, organization, and staging attacks.

Terrorist organizations may take advantage of state weakness in a number of ways. Terrorists often seek to operate from regions that are difficult to reach due to geographical distances from the country's center or because of difficult terrain, typically mountainous, or both. In some cases, such as in Afghanistan under the Taliban, the central government may welcome a terrorist organization such as Al Qaeda as an ideological ally. Sometimes the terrorists will come to an informal agreement of live and let live with the government, promising not to challenge government authority or get involved in domestic politics in return for a free hand to operate in their sanctuaries. Attacks in Pakistan by a rebuilt Taliban in 2008 have led to attempts by the Pakistani government to arrange such an agreement with the terrorists. Because failed states are still considered sovereign by their citizens and governments, military action by other states against terrorist organizations in their territory involve issues of international law and politics that relate to interstate conflict and war.

While the American-led invasion of Afghanistan in 2001 was aimed at Al Qaeda, it was premised on the overthrow of the Taliban regime and reconstructing Afghanistan so that it would no longer serve as a haven for terrorist organizations. However, the Taliban remains active in Afghanistan, and the insurgency that followed the quick 2001 American victory over the Taliban and Al Qaeda illustrates how difficult it can be to establish a strong state until adequate leadership and institutions can be established, positioned, and strengthened.

Among states considered in 2014 by many experts as falling in the category of "failed" are Somalia, the Democratic Republic of Congo, Sudan, South Sudan, Chad, and Yemen.

ELLIOT PAUL CHODOFF

See also

Afghanistan; Al Qaeda; Democratization and the Global War on Terror; Global War on Terror; Pakistan; Somalia, Federal Republic of; Taliban; Terrorism; Yemen

References

Fearon, James D., and David D. Laitin. "Ethnicity, Insurgency, and Civil War." *American Political Science Review* 97 (2003): 75–76.

Hironaka, Ann. *Neverending Wars: The International Community, Weak States, and the Perpetuation of Civil War.* Cambridge, MA: Harvard University Press, 2005.

Jones, Seth G. "The Rise of Afghanistan's Insurgency: State Failure and Jihad." *International Security* 32 (2008): 7–40.

Levitt, S. *Why Nations Fail: The Origins of Power, Prosperity and Poverty.* London: Profile Books, 2012.

Rotberg, Robert I., ed. *When States Fail: Causes and Consequences.* Princeton, NJ: Princeton University Press, 2003.

Taylor, A. *State Failure. Global Issues.* London: Palgrave MacMillan, 2013.

Fallon, William Joseph (1944–)

U.S. Navy officer and commander of U.S. Central Command (CENTCOM) during 2007–2008. William Joseph "Fox" Fallon was born in East Orange, New Jersey, on December 30, 1944, and grew up in Merchantville, New Jersey. He was commissioned in the U.S. Navy through the navy's Reserve Officers' Training Corps program after graduating from Villanova University in 1967. He then completed flight training and became a naval aviator. Fallon later graduated from the Naval War College, Newport, Rhode Island, and the National War College, Washington, D.C. He also earned an MA degree in international studies from Old Dominion University in 1982.

Fallon's career as a naval aviator spanned 24 years with service in attack squadrons and carrier air wings, during which he logged more than 1,300 carrier-arrested landings and 4,800 flight hours. It included combat during the Vietnam War and service in the Mediterranean, Atlantic, Pacific, and Indian Oceans in a number of different carriers.

Fallon's commands included Carrier Air Wing 8 aboard the *Theodore Roosevelt* deployed in the Persian Gulf during Operations DESERT SHIELD and DESERT STORM, during which he led 80 air strike missions into Iraq and Kuwait between August 1990 and February 1991; Carrier Group Eight (1995); and Battle Force Sixth Fleet as part of the *Theodore Roosevelt* Battle Group during the North Atlantic Treaty Organization combat Operation DELIBERATE FORCE (August 29–September 14, 1995) in Bosnia.

Fallon held numerous staff assignments. He also served as deputy director for operations, Joint Task Force, Southwest Asia, in Riyadh, Saudi Arabia; deputy director, aviation plans and requirements on the staff of the chief of naval operations in Washington, D.C.; assistant chief of staff, plans, and policy for Supreme Allied Command, Atlantic (his first flag officer position); deputy and chief of staff, U.S. Atlantic Fleet; and deputy commander in chief and chief of staff, U.S. Atlantic Command.

Fallon was promoted to full (four-star) admiral and became the 31st vice chief of naval operations, a post he held from October 2000 to August 2003. While serving in that capacity, he publicly apologized to the president of Japan following a collision between the U.S. submarine *Greeneville* and the Japanese fishing training ship *Ehime Maru* off the coast of Hawaii in February 2001. In 2002 Fallon asserted before the U.S. Senate Committee on Environment and Public Works that the ability to conduct military operations superseded obedience to environmental laws. He commanded the U.S. Fleet Forces Command (October 2003–February 2005) and the U.S. Pacific Command (February 2005–March 2007), where his approach to the People's Republic of China was less confrontational than previous commanders and was not well received by some American policy makers who favored a tougher stance toward China.

In March 2007 Fallon replaced U.S. Army general John P. Abizaid as the first naval officer to command CENTCOM. Fallon's tenure lasted only one year, from March 16, 2007, to March 28, 2008. Although the impetus for his abrupt retirement as CENTCOM commander is not disputed, its voluntariness is. Despite the fact that Fallon was publicly lauded by President George W. Bush and Secretary of Defense Robert Gates, Gates noted that Fallon's resignation was due in part to controversy surrounding an article by Thomas P. M. Barnett titled "The Man between War and Peace," published in *Esquire* magazine on March 11, 2008. In it, Fallon was quoted as having disagreements with the Bush administration on the prosecution of the war in Iraq and a potential conflict with Iran regarding its nuclear weapons program. The article portrayed Fallon as resisting pressure from the Bush administration for war with Iran over the latter's pursuit of nuclear weapons. Besides Fallon's rather open opposition to Bush's war policies, the admiral purportedly disagreed with General David Petraeus regarding Iranian covert exportation of weapons to Iraqi insurgents and the pace of future American troop reductions in Iraq. Many believed that Fallon was forced out principally because his superiors blamed him for the failure to halt Iranian weapons from entering Iraq.

RICHARD M. EDWARDS

See also

Abizaid, John Philip; Bush, George Walker; Gates, Robert Michael; Petraeus, David Howell

References

Barnett, Thomas P. M. "The Man between War and Peace." *Esquire,* March 11, 2008, 1–4.

Dorsey, Jack. "Navy Taps 2nd Fleet's Adm. William J. Fallon for 4-Star Pentagon Post." *Virginian Pilot*, September 7, 2000, 1.

Lambeth, Benjamin S. *American Carrier Air Power at the Dawn of a New Century*. Santa Monica, CA: RAND Corporation, 2005.

Fallujah

City located in central Iraq within the so-called Sunni Triangle and a center of insurgency activity after the March 2003 Anglo-American–led invasion of Iraq. On the eve of the Iraq War, Fallujah had a population of approximately 440,000 people, the great majority of whom were Sunni Muslims. The city is located along the Euphrates River about 42 miles to the west of the capital city of Baghdad. The city consisted of more than 2,000 city blocks laid out in regular grid fashion. A typical block grid featured tenements and two-story concrete houses surrounded by courtyard walls and divided by narrow alleyways. Highway 10, a two-lane road that runs through the city, becomes a four-lane throughway in the city's center.

The area encompassing Fallujah has been inhabited for many centuries, and its history can be traced back at least as far as the reign of the Babylonian king Hammurabai, during 1780–1750 BCE. After the Babylonian captivity of the Jews and beginning in circa 219 CE, the area now encompassed by Fallujah became a center of Jewish learning and scholarship that included many Jewish academies. This lasted until circa 1050. The city was a crossroads during the many centuries of Ottoman rule.

Following World War I, the British established a mandate over the area of Iraq. With a rise of Iraqi nationalism, in April 1941 during World War II there was a coup that brought Rashid Ali al-Gaylani to power. He formed a cabinet that contained a number of individuals with Axis connections. Encouraged by hints of Axis aid, Gaylani refused to honor a 1930 treaty that allowed the transportation of British troops from Basra across Iraq. The Iraqi government also positioned troops and artillery around British bases in Iraq. In the ensuing fighting, British troops defeated the Iraqi Army near Fallujah.

In 1947 the city had just 10,000 inhabitants, but it grew exponentially in the decades to follow because of Iraq's growing oil wealth, Fallujah's strategic position along the Euphrates, and Iraqi dictator Saddam Hussein's program designed to make it a centerpiece of his power base beyond Baghdad. Many Sunnis from the city held positions within the government, and the ruling Baath Party claimed many important ties to Fallujah. The city came to be highly industrialized under Hussein's rule, although westward-running Highway 1, a four-lane divided superhighway, bypassed the city and caused it to decline in strategic importance by the early 2000s. Fallujah retained its political importance thanks to the many senior Baath Party members from the area.

During the 1991 Persian Gulf War, bridges spanning the Euphrates River in Fallujah were targeted by coalition aircraft. In the process several markets were hit, resulting in substantial civilian casualties. As many as 200 Iraqi civilians may have been killed in these bombing raids.

During the initial stages of Operation IRAQI FREEDOM Fallujah remained largely unaffected by the fighting because Iraqi troops who had garrisoned the city fled, leaving considerable military equipment behind. However, as the war progressed and Hussein's regime was toppled, Fallujah was struck by a spasm of violence and looting, with individuals sacking military storage areas, stores, hospitals, and restaurants. To make matters worse, Hussein had released all political prisoners held in the nearby Abu Ghraib prison, which flooded the area with an assortment of bitter political exiles and criminals who delighted in the anarchy of Fallujah in the spring and summer of 2003. Inhabitants fled the city by the thousands, leaving behind the remnants of their lives and livelihoods. A large percentage of the male population of Fallujah was unemployed, and they proved to be a major source of recruits for the Iraqi insurgency movement. The Iraqis of Fallujah perceived themselves as having lost the status they had enjoyed under Hussein and believed that they had little to gain in a new governmental system dominated by his former enemies.

In April 2003 U.S. occupation forces finally attempted to exert control over the city, but by then the major damage had already been done, and the city was increasingly anti-American. Sunni rebels had soon taken root in Fallujah, as had foreign insurgents allied with Al Qaeda. Operation VIGILANT RESOLVE (the First Battle of Fallujah), launched in April 2004 by U.S. forces, failed to wrest the city away from the insurgents. During November–December 2004 U.S. and Iraqi security forces launched Operation PHANTOM FURY (the Second Battle of Fallujah), a large and bloody affair that caused the insurgents to flee the city. However, the coalition and Iraqi forces had to conduct yet another operation in Fallujah in June 2007.

Fallujah's population trickled back into the city, but they returned to a disaster zone. Half of the city's housing was destroyed, much of its infrastructure lay in ruins or disrepair, and city services were absent. Reconstruction proceeded slowly, with almost 150,000 refugees residing in massive tent cities on the outskirts of Fallujah. In 2009 the Iraqi government estimated the population of the city at 350,000, but Fallujah struggled to return to normalcy.

Early in 2014 several different sources reported that at least parts of the city were controlled either by Al Qaeda or its affiliated Islamic State of Iraq and Syria (ISIS, also known as the Islamic State of Iraq and the Levant, or ISIL), while the Anbar Military Council controlled the rest.

PAUL G. PIERPAOLI JR.

See also

Al Qaeda in Iraq; Baath Party; Fallujah, First Battle of; Fallujah, Second Battle of; Hussein, Saddam; Sunni Triangle

References

Buzzell, Colby. *My War: Killing Time in Iraq*. New York: Putnam, 2005.

Keegan, John. *The Iraq War: The Military Offensive, from Victory in 21 Days to the Insurgent Aftermath*. New York: Vintage, 2005.

Ricks, Thomas E. *Fiasco: The American Military Adventure in Iraq*. New York: Penguin, 2006.

Fallujah, First Battle of (April 4–May 1, 2004)

A U.S. military operation, the principal goal of which was to retake the Iraqi city of Fallujah after insurgents had seized control. Code-named VIGILANT RESOLVE, it occurred during April 4–May 1, 2004. Sunni insurgents, including Al Qaeda fighters, had steadily destabilized Anbar Province in Iraq in the aftermath of the 2003 U.S.-led invasion. Fallujah, located some 42 miles west of Baghdad in the so-called Sunni Triangle, emerged as a focal point for anticoalition attacks. The town was dominated by Salafist groups who were extremely suspicious of all outsiders, particularly foreigners; family and clan ties dominated personal relationships. The collapse of Iraqi president Saddam Hussein's regime had left some 70,000 male inhabitants in the city unemployed, providing a major source of recruits for the Iraqi insurgency movement.

Growing violence in Fallujah in March 2004 led the U.S. military to withdraw forces from the city and conduct only armed patrols. On March 31 insurgents ambushed four contractors working for Blackwater USA, a private contracting company that provided security personnel to the Coalition Provisional Authority (CPA). The insurgents dragged the bodies through the streets and then hanged them from a bridge. Television cameras transmitted the grisly images around the world, prompting a strong response to offset the perception that coalition forces had lost control of the area.

In an effort to regain control of the city and the surrounding province, the U.S. military launched a series of operations against suspected insurgent groups and their bases. The lead unit was the I Marine Expeditionary Force, which had been deployed to Anbar in March. The ground forces were supported by coalition aircraft and helicopter units. U.S. lieutenant general James Conway had overall command of the operation. On April 4 some 2,200 marines surrounded Fallujah. They blockaded the main roads in and out of the city in an effort to allow only civilians to escape the fighting. The commanders on the ground believed that the marines should remain outside of the city because they lacked the troops to effectively control the area and the population; nevertheless, they were ordered to seize the city.

In the opening days of the operation, U.S. forces conducted air strikes on suspected targets and undertook limited incursions into Fallujah, including a strike to take control of its main radio station. At least one-quarter of the civilian population fled the city as insurgents used homes, schools, and mosques to attack the marines, who responded with devastating firepower that often produced high collateral damage and civilian casualties.

Within the city there were an estimated 15,000–20,000 insurgent fighters divided among more than a dozen insurgent groups of various origins. Some were former members of Hussein's security forces. They were armed with a variety of weapons, including light arms, rocket-propelled grenades, mortars, and improvised explosive devices (IEDs). The insurgents used guerrilla tactics against the marines, including ambushes, mortar attacks, and mines and IEDs. Sniper fire was common throughout the operation. U.S. forces responded with artillery and air strikes, including the use of heavily armed Lockheed AC-130 gunships. Support from Bell AH-1W Super Cobra attack helicopters, however, was limited because of significant ground fire. Meanwhile, the marines attempted to secure neighborhoods one or two blocks at a time using air support and tanks.

There were problems coordinating movements in the dense urban environment, especially because maps were not standardized between the various units. Meanwhile, many of the remaining Iraqi security forces within the city either joined the insurgents or simply fled their posts. After three days of intense fighting, the marines had secured only about one-quarter of Fallujah.

In response to the escalating violence, the failure of the marines to make significant progress in the city, growing pressure from Iraqi political leaders, and increasing domestic pressure on the George W. Bush administration that was largely the result of media coverage, the U.S.-led CPA ordered a unilateral cease-fire on April 9 and initiated negotiations with the insurgent groups. The marines allowed humanitarian aid into the city; however, in spite of the cease-fire, sporadic fighting continued. Throughout the negotiations, it was decided that the United States would turn over security for the city to a newly formed ad hoc Iraqi militia force, the Fallujah Brigade. The United States agreed to provide arms and equipment for the brigade, which included former soldiers and police officers of the Hussein regime.

On May 1 U.S. forces completely withdrew from Fallujah, but they maintained a presence outside of the city at an observation base. More than 700 Iraqis had been killed in the fighting (the majority of these, perhaps as many as 600, were civilians), while 27 U.S. marines were killed and 90 were wounded.

The Fallujah Brigade failed to maintain security and began to disintegrate during the summer of 2004. Many of its members joined or rejoined the insurgency, and the military announced that Abu Musab al-Zarqawi, the leader of Al Qaeda in Iraq, was headquartered in Fallujah. The coalition undertook a second campaign in Fallujah in the autumn of 2004, code-named Operation PHANTOM FURY.

TOM LANSFORD

See also

Fallujah; Fallujah, Second Battle of; United States Marine Corps, Iraq War

References

Afong, Milo. *Hogs in the Shadows: Combat Stories from Marine Snipers in Iraq*. New York: Berkley, 2007.

Cockburn, Patrick. *The Occupation: War and Resistance in Iraq*. New York: Verso, 2007.

O'Donnell, Patrick K. *We Were One: Shoulder to Shoulder with the Marines Who Took Fallujah*. New York: Da Capo, 2007.

West, Bing. *No True Glory: A Frontline Account of the Battle for Fallujah*. New York: Bantam, 2006.

Fallujah, Second Battle of (November 7–December 23, 2004)

Major battle fought in and around the city of Fallujah, some 42 miles west of Baghdad, between U.S., Iraqi, and British forces and Iraqi insurgents (chiefly Al Qaeda in Iraq but also other militias). Following the decision to halt the coalition assault on Fallujah in Operation VIGILANT RESOLVE (First Battle of Fallujah, April 4–May 1, 2004), the U.S. marines

had withdrawn from the city and turned over security to the so-called Fallujah Brigade, an ad hoc force of local men who had formerly served in the Iraqi Army. The Fallujah Brigade failed dismally in this task, giving the insurgents another chance to claim victory and attract additional recruits. During the summer and autumn months, the Fallujah police turned a blind eye as the insurgents fortified positions inside Fallujah and stockpiled supplies. The Iraqi Interim Government, formed on June 28, 2004, then requested new efforts to capture and secure Fallujah.

In preparation for the ground assault, coalition artillery and aircraft began selective strikes on the city on October 30, 2004. Coalition ground forces (American, Iraqi, and British) cut off electric power to the city on November 5 and distributed leaflets warning people to stay in their homes and not use their cars. This was a response to insurgent suicide bombers who had been detonating cars packed with explosives. On November 7 the Iraqi government announced a 60-day state of emergency throughout most of Iraq. Because of all these warnings, between 75 and 90 percent of Fallujah's civilian population abandoned the city before the coalition ground offensive began. Many of them fled to Syria, where they remain as refugees.

The Americans initially labeled the assault Operation PHANTOM FURY. Iraqi prime minister Ayad Allawi, however, renamed it AL-FAJR (NEW DAWN). The operation's main objective was to demonstrate the ability of the Iraqi government to control its own territory, thereby bolstering its prestige. The American military focused on the important secondary objective of killing as many insurgents as possible while keeping coalition casualties low. About 10,000 American soldiers and marines and 2,000 Iraqi troops participated in Operation AL-FAJR. Some Royal Marines also took part. The American forces involved had considerable experience in urban combat.

The assault plan called for a concentration of forces north of Fallujah. Spearheaded by the army's heavy armor, army and marine units would attack due south along precisely defined sectors. The infantry would methodically clear buildings, leaving the trailing Iraqi forces to search for insurgents and assault the city's 200 mosques, which coalition tacticians suspected would be used as defensive insurgent strongpoints. Intelligence estimates suggested that some 3,000 insurgents defended the city, one fifth of whom were foreign jihadists. Intelligence estimates also predicted fanatical resistance.

Ground operations associated with the Second Battle of Fallujah commenced on November 7, 2004, when an

Insurgents, employing small arms and a mortar, prepare to launch an attack on U.S. forces in Fallujah, Iraq, on November 8, 2004. (AP Photo/Bilal Hussein)

Iraqi commando unit and the U.S. Marine Corps 3rd Light Armored Reconnaissance Battalion conducted a preliminary assault. The objective was to secure the Fallujah General Hospital to the west of the city and capture two bridges over the Euphrates River, thereby isolating the insurgent forces inside the city. This preliminary assault was successful, allowing the main assault to commence after dark the following evening. The American military chose this time because it knew that its various night-vision devices would provide it a tactical advantage over the insurgents. Four marine infantry and two army mechanized battalions attacked in the first wave. M-1A2 Abrams tanks and M-2A3 Bradley infantry fighting vehicles provided mobile firepower for which the insurgents had no answer. The M-1A2 Abrams tanks exhibited the ability to absorb enormous punishment and keep operating. The speed and shock of the massed armor overwhelmed the insurgents, enabling the American soldiers to drive deep into Fallujah. Iraqi forces also performed surprisingly well. After four days of operations, coalition forces had secured about half the city.

By November 11, the methodical American advance had driven most of the insurgents into the southern part of

Fallujah. Three days of intense street fighting ensued, during which time the Americans reached the southern limits of the city. On November 15 the Americans reversed direction and attacked north to eliminate any insurgents who had been missed in the first pass and to search more thoroughly for insurgent weapons and supplies. For this part of the operation, the ground forces broke down into squad-sized elements to conduct their searches. By November 16 American commanders judged Fallujah secured, although the operation would not end officially until December 23, by which time many residents had been allowed to return to their homes.

U.S. casualties in the Second Battle of Fallujah were 95 killed and 560 wounded; Iraqi Army losses were 11 killed and 43 wounded. Insurgent losses were estimated at between 1,200 and 2,000 killed, with another 1,000 to 1,500 captured. The disparity in the casualties indicated the extent of the coalition's tactical advantage. Indeed, postbattle army and marine assessments lauded the tremendous tactical skill in urban warfare displayed by American forces. However, the intense house-to-house fighting had caused the destruction of an estimated 20 percent of the city's buildings, while another 60 percent of the city's structures were damaged. The tremendous damage, including that to 60 mosques, enraged Iraq's Sunni minority. Widespread civilian demonstrations and increased insurgent attacks followed the Second Battle of Fallujah. Although the 2005 Iraqi elections were held on schedule, Sunni participation was very low partially because of the Sunnis' sense of grievance over the destruction in Fallujah.

JAMES ARNOLD

See also

Al Qaeda in Iraq; Allawi, Ayad; Fallujah; Fallujah, First Battle of; Sunni Islam; Sunni Triangle

References

Ballard, John R. *Fighting for Fallujah: A New Dawn for Iraq.* Westport, CT: Praeger Security International, 2006.

Bellavia, David. *House to House: An Epic Memoir of War.* New York: Free Press, 2007.

Gott, Kendall D., ed. *Eyewitness to War: The U.S. Army in Operation Al Fajr; An Oral History.* 2 vols. Fort Leavenworth, KS: Combat Studies Institute Press, 2006.

Fatwa

A fatwa (*responsa*) is a question and answer process referred to in the Koran (4:127, 176) that began in early Islam as a means to impart knowledge about theology, philosophy, hadith, legal theory, religious duties, and, later and more specifically, sharia (Islamic law). Fatwas may deal with a much broader series of subjects than did the Islamic courts, and a fatwa, unlike a court ruling, is not binding. The reason it is not binding is that in a court, a *qadi* (judge) is concerned with evidentiary matters and may actually investigate these and hear two sides to an argument, but a cleric or authority issuing a fatwa is responding instead to just one party, should the question involve a dispute, and as the question might be formulated in a particular way.

In modern times, a fatwa is usually defined as a legal opinion given by someone with expertise in Islamic law. However, so long as a person mentions the sources he uses in a legal opinion, other Muslim authorities or figures may issue fatwas. A modern fatwa usually responds to a question about an action, form of behavior, or practice that classifies it as being obligatory, forbidden, permitted, recommended, or reprehensible. Traditionally, a fatwa could be issued by a Muslim scholar knowledgeable of both the subject and the theories of jurisprudence. These persons might be part of or independent from the court systems. However, other persons might issue fatwas as well. Muslim governments typically designated a chief mufti, who was in the role of the sheikh of Islam in the Ottoman Empire.

In the colonial period the Islamic madrasas (*madaris* is the Arabic plural), which can mean either simply a school or a higher institute of Islamic education, began in some cases to include a fatwa-issuing office, a *dar al-ifta*. Muslim governments continued efforts to control and limit the issuing of fatwas, as in the Higher Council of Ulama or the Permanent Council for Scientific Research and Legal Opinions in Saudi Arabia or the Council of Islamic Ideology in Pakistan. However, many Muslim authorities—from lesser-trained sheikhs to political figures to legal specialists classified as *fuqaha* (specialists in jurisprudence), mujtahids, and muftis—issue fatwas. Some are no more than a short response to the inquiry, whereas others are recorded, published, or circulated along with explanations.

For many reasons, including the development of differing legal schools within Islam and the history of opinions concerning religious requirements as opposed to mere duties, fatwas may conflict with each other. For example, the legal opinions concerning women's inheritance under Jafari, or Twelver Shia law, and that given by a Hanafi Sunni jurist would differ. At times, even councils of jurists from a single sect may issue a complex opinion with, for instance, each indicating their agreement with or reservations about different implications or subquestions of a fatwa.

Muslim countries today may govern with civil laws that are partially dependent on principles of Islamic law or are derived in part from Ottoman law. When matters of civil legal reform are discussed, then the opinions of religious authorities might be consulted. A fatwa may also be issued by popular figures outside of the venue of civil authorities. Other countries, however, operate on the basis of uncodified Islamic law. At the supranational level, there is no single authoritative person or body that can settle conflicting issues or declare binding fatwas in Islamic law (as the pope and the Vatican issue religious decrees for Roman Catholicism).

In 1933 clerics in Iraq issued a fatwa that called for a boycott of all Zionist-made products. In 2004 the very popular Egyptian Sunni Muslim cleric and scholar Yusuf al-Qaradawi declared a fatwa similarly calling for a boycott of goods manufactured in Israel or the United States.

Other much-disputed questions have concerned the necessary resistance of Palestinians to Israeli rule or the actual status of Palestine and the status of Iraqi resistance to coalition forces. Many fatwas were issued earlier to confront foreign occupation in Muslim lands, in Morocco, Egypt, Syria, Iraq, Iran, and elsewhere. Modern responses that affect the right to wage jihad (holy war) concern the land's status (*dar al-Islam*) as an Islamic territory. That is the generally agreed status of Iraq and of Palestine because of the presence of the holy sites at the al-Aqsa Mosque complex, from which the Prophet Muhammad experienced the Miraj and the Isra (the Night Journey and the Ascent to Heaven, respectively), as well as other holy sites in Palestine. Because the country is an Islamic land and yet many Palestinian Muslims cannot visit their holy sites or practice their religion and have had their lands and properties seized, some fatwas assert that jihad in this context is an individual duty, incumbent on Muslims. Divergent fatwas identify the country, now Israel, as *dar al-kufr,* a land of unbelief (somewhat like India under British rule) from which Muslims should flee, as in a highly disputed fatwa by Sheikh Muhammad Nasir al-Din al-Albani. While Palestinian Islamic Jihad issued a lengthy fatwa in 1989 that legitimated suicide attacks by Palestinians in the context of jihad, no leading clerics actually signed this document. It could be countered by a statement by the grand mufti of Saudi Arabia, made on April 21, 2001, that Islam forbids suicide attacks and is referred to as if it were a formal fatwa. On the other hand, Sheikh Qaradawi issued a fatwa in 2002 that said women could engage in martyrdom operations in conditions when jihad is an individual duty.

PAUL G. PIERPAOLI JR. AND SHERIFA ZUHUR

See also

Jihad; Sharia

References

Coulson, Noel J. *A History of Islamic Law.* Edinburgh, UK: Edinburgh University Press, 1994.

Esposito, John L. *Islam: The Straight Path.* New York: Oxford University Press, 1991.

Messick, Brinkley. *The Calligraphic State: Textual Domination and History in a Muslim Society.* Berkeley: University of California Press, 1993.

Peters, Rudolph. *Islam and Colonialism: The Doctrine of Jihad in Modern History.* The Hague: Brill, 1979.

Faw Peninsula

Strategically important peninsula located in southeastern Iraq adjacent to the Persian Gulf. The Faw (Fao) Peninsula lies to the south and east of Basra, Iraq's principal port and second-largest metropolis, and west of the Iranian city of Abadan. The peninsula separates Iraq from Iran and lies to the immediate west of the critical Shatt al-Arab waterway, which is Iraq's only access to the sea and only seagoing route

to the port at Basra. Control of the Faw Peninsula has thus been strategically essential to Iraq, as loss of control there likely means being cut off from access to the Persian Gulf.

The Faw Peninsula is also important because it has been home to some of Iraq's largest oil installations, including refineries. The country's two principal terminals for oil tankers—Khor al-Amayya and Mina al-Bakr—are also located here. The only significant population center on the peninsula is Umm Qasr, the base of former Iraqi dictator Saddam Hussein's navy.

The Faw Peninsula was a center of attention during the 1980–1988 Iran-Iraq War and was the site of several pitched battles, as both nations struggled to control the Shatt al-Arab waterway. In February 1986 Iranian forces were able to overwhelm the poorly trained Iraqi forces charged with guarding the peninsula. Despite desperate fighting the Iraqis were unable to dislodge the Iranians from the area, even in the face of numerous offensives. The Iranians were then able to threaten Basra and Umm Qasr and use the Faw Peninsula as a base from which to launch missiles into Iraq, into naval and merchant assets in the Persian Gulf, and into Kuwait, which was backing Iraq in the war. In April 1988 the Iraqis launched a new and determined effort to dislodge the Iranians from the peninsula. With almost 100,000 troops, heavy artillery, and aerial bombing that included chemical weapons, the Iraqis finally drove the Iranians out after a 35-hour offensive.

In the lead-up to the 1991 Persian Gulf War, the Faw Peninsula and Shatt al-Arab waterway became a bone of contention between Iraq and Kuwait, as both nations jockeyed to control access to Umm Qasr as well as two small adjacent islands. Hussein used the dispute as part of his justification for the August 1990 Iraqi invasion of Kuwait. When Operation DESERT STORM began in January 1991, coalition air forces heavily bombed the Faw Peninsula, wiping out much of Iraq's naval assets and oil facilities. Although no significant ground actions occurred there, Iraqi shipping was closed down by the bombardment, meaning that Iraq was cut off from any seaborne trade or resupply efforts.

During Operation IRAQI FREEDOM, which began in March 2003, American and British plans called for the immediate seizure and occupation of the Faw Peninsula to deny Iraq access to the Persian Gulf and to open Umm Qasr and Basra to humanitarian and military resupply missions. Military planners also hoped to secure the peninsula before Iraqi troops could damage or destroy its oil facilities.

The coalition attack on Umm Qasr, led by U.S. and British marines and Polish special land forces, began on March 21 but ran into unexpectedly heavy Iraqi resistance. After four days of sporadically heavy fighting, however, Umm Qasr and the Faw Peninsula had been largely secured, and the adjacent waterway had been cleared of Iraqi mines. Pockets of Iraqi resistance endured in the old city of Umm Qasr until March 29, when the entire peninsula had essentially been occupied and secured. Almost immediately coalition forces opened the port at Umm Qasr, which then became the primary entrepôt for humanitarian and civilian aid to Iraq.

PAUL G. PIERPAOLI JR.

See also

Basra, Battle of; IRAQI FREEDOM, Operation; Persian Gulf; Shatt al-Arab Waterway; Umm Qasr, Battle of

References

Keegan, John. *The Iraq War: The Military Offensive, from Victory in 21 Days to the Insurgent Aftermath.* New York: Vintage, 2005.

Tripp, Charles. *A History of Iraq.* Cambridge: Cambridge University Press, 2007.

Fayyad, Muhammad Ishaq al- (1930–)

One of the five grand ayatollahs who make up the *marjaiyya* (the highest level of Shiite clerics), the informal council of Iraq's senior resident Twelver Shia religious scholars, of Najaf. He has frequently served as the council's representative public voice in the post-2003 invasion of Iraq. Born in 1930 in a small village in the Afghan province of Ghazni to a family of farmers, Muhammad Ishaq al-Fayyad is an ethnic Hazara, a Dari-speaking people who reside in Afghanistan and parts of Iran and northwestern Pakistan. Despite this the grand ayatollah is fluent in Arabic, although Western reporters and scholars who have met him say that he speaks it with a distinct Dari Afghan accent. He is widely considered to be one of the most influential members of the *marjaiyya* (meaning those who can be emulated, or followed, as spiritual guides) and is also one of the most publicly engaged, arguably even more so than Grand Ayatollah Ali al-Husayni al-Sistani, Iraq's most senior Shia scholar.

As with many young Muslims from religious families, Fayyad began his informal religious studies early, at the age of 5, learning the Koran from the village mullah, the local religious scholar. According to some reports, Fayyad and his family moved to Najaf when he was 10 years old. As he grew older he began studying other subjects, including the Arabic language and grammar, rhetoric, logic, Islamic philosophy, *ahadith* (traditions of the Prophet Muhammad and the 12 Shiite imams), and Islamic jurisprudence. He ultimately pursued his studies under the supervision of Grand Ayatollah Abu al-Qasim al-Khoi, one of Iraq's senior resident Shia scholars during the 1970s and the most senior during the 1980s until his death in 1992.

According to accounts from individuals close to both Fayyad and Khoi, the former excelled at his studies and is widely acknowledged to have been one of the latter's best students. Some reports hold that Fayyad was, in fact, Khoi's best student and now is the most senior member of the *marjaiyya*, but he did not seek to chair the council because scholars who are not Iraqi or Iranian have little chance of gaining followers among Arabs and Iranians, who make up the majority of the world's Shias. In 1992 when the *marjaiyya* was left without a chair after Khoi's death, Fayyad, along with the council's other members, supported Sistani for the position.

Following the March 2003 invasion and subsequent occupation of Iraq by the United States and Great Britain, aided by a relatively small coalition of other countries, Fayyad proved to be the most willing to engage with the Americans and British. Unlike Sistani, he has met occasionally with U.S. and British officials, both diplomatic and military, in order to relay the position of the *marjaiyya*. Fayyad has stated that Iraqi law must take into account Islamic religious law, particularly with regard to social and family issues. He has spoken out strongly against forced secularization of Iraqi society and has argued that there can be no absolute separation of the state from religion. However, like Sistani, Fayyad has also rejected the implementation of an Iranian-style governmental model for Iraq, one based on Grand Ayatollah Ruhollah Khomeini's concept of *wilayat al-faqih*, the governance of the supreme religious jurist in the absence of the Twelfth Imam, Muhammad al-Mahdi, whom Twelver Shias believe went into a mystical hiding, or occultation, in the 10th century and will return at a time appointed by God.

Thus, Fayyad has gone on record as being opposed to clerical rule in Iraq, although he does believe that the *ulama* (Muslim religious scholars) should exercise some influence over Iraqi society, specifically ensuring the protection of Muslim moral and social values. According to a December 2007 report from the Associated Press, Fayyad was supervising the seminary studies of Muqtada al-Sadr, the populist Iraqi Shia leader and head of the Sadr Movement, although Fayyad and the *marjaiyya* do not approve of Sadr's approach toward politics and have pressured him to clamp down on his more militant followers.

The *marjaiyya* backed the United Iraqi Alliance (UIA), a loose coalition of mainly Shiite Arab political parties that includes the Supreme Islamic Iraqi Council (SIIC) and the Party of Islamic Call (Hizb al-Da'wa al-Islamiyya), in the January 2005 interim elections and the December 2005 formal elections. Despite their early support, Fayyad and his council colleagues reportedly became increasingly critical of the UIA's performance, particularly the combative political sectarianism of the SIIC (then known as the Supreme Council for the Islamic Revolution in Iraq) and the Islamic Dawa Party. The *marjaiyya,* through senior spokespeople for the various members, let it be known in the latter half of 2008 that it would not back any slate of candidates and would instead urge its followers to vote for the party or parties that had the best plan for improving the situation in Iraq.

CHRISTOPHER PAUL ANZALONE

See also

Iraq, History of, 1990–Present; Islamic Dawa Party; Sadr, Muqtada al-; Shia Islam; Supreme Iraqi Islamic Council; United Iraqi Alliance

References

Cole, Juan R. I. *The Ayatollahs and Democracy in Iraq.* ISIM Paper 7. Leiden, Netherlands: Amsterdam University Press and the International Institute for the Study of Islam in the Modern World, 2006.

Hendawi, Hamza, and Qassim Abdul-Zahra. "Iraq's Maverick Cleric Hits the Books." *USA Today,* December 13, 2007.

Khalaji, Mehdi. *Religious Authority in Iraq and the Election.* Policy Watch #1063. Washington, DC: Washington Institute for Near East Policy, 2005.

Nasr, Seyyed Vali Reza. "Iraq: The First Arab Shia State." *Missouri Review* 29(2) (2006): 132–153.

Visser, Reidar. *Shi'i Separatism in Iraq: Internet Reverie or Real Constitutional Challenge?* Oslo, Norway: Norwegian Institute of International Affairs, 2005.

Fedayeen

Term used to refer to various groups or civilians (usually Muslim) who have engaged in either armed struggle or guerrilla tactics against foreign armies. The term "fedayeen" is the English transliteration of the term *fida'iyuna,* which is the plural of the Arabic word meaning "one who is ready to sacrifice his life" (*fida'i*) and referred historically to different types of Muslim fighters, including Muslim forces waging war on the borders; freedom fighters; Egyptians who fought against the British in the Suez Canal Zone, culminating in a popular uprising in October 1951; Palestinians who waged attacks against Israelis from the 1950s until the present

(including fighters of Christian background); Iranian guerrillas opposed to Mohammad Reza Shah Pahlavi's regime in the 1970s; Armenian fighters in Nagarno-Karabakh (also Christian); and a force loyal to Iraqi dictator Saddam Hussein (the Fedayeen Saddam) during the Iraq War that began in 2003.

Following the rejection by Jewish and Arab leaders of the 1947 United Nations partition plan that would have created a Palestinian state in the West Bank and the Gaza Strip and the resulting declaration of the State of Israel the following year, Palestinian refugees were driven from their homes and flooded into the areas surrounding the new Jewish state. Anti-Israel activity became prevalent, particularly in the West Bank and Gaza Strip areas. Supported by money and arms from a number of Arab states, Palestinians carried out attacks against Israeli military forces and also Israeli settlers, and in 1951 the raids became more organized. These fighters were referred to as fedayeen since they were an irregular rather than a government force. The fighters created bases in Egypt, Jordan, and Lebanon, with Egyptian intelligence training and arming many of them. Between 1951 and 1956 the fedayeen orchestrated hundreds of raids along the Israeli border, killing an estimated 400 Israelis and injuring 900 others.

The fedayeen operated primarily out of Jordan and Lebanon, causing these countries to bear the brunt of the retaliation campaigns carried out by the Israel Defense Forces and paramilitary groups. Fedayeen attacks and subsequent retaliations were significant factors in the outbreak of hostilities during the 1956 Suez Crisis. The fedayeen also launched attacks into Israel from the Jordanian-controlled territory of the West Bank. The fighters included those associated with the Palestine Liberation Organization (PLO), the Popular Front for the Liberation of Palestine, and various other militant groups.

King Hussein of Jordan was initially supportive of the groups, but by 1970 he deemed their presence detrimental to Jordan and a threat to his own political power. Although based in refugee camps, the fedayeen were able to obtain arms and financial support from other Arab countries and therefore clashed with Jordanian government troops who attempted to disarm them beginning in 1968. The civil war that erupted in 1970 during what has been called Black September saw the eventual defeat and removal of the fedayeen from Jordanian soil.

The fedayeen were forced to recognize Jordanian sovereignty via an October 13, 1970, agreement between PLO leader Yasser Arafat and King Hussein. Although PLO members often participated in commando raids, the PLO denied playing a role in several terrorist attacks. After being ousted from Jordan, the PLO and the fedayeen relocated to Lebanon, where they continued to stage attacks on Israel. At present, the terms *fida'iyuna* and *fida'iyin* are still used by many Arabs for Palestinian militants, and the Arabs see the militants as freedom fighters who struggle for the return (*awda*) of their lands and property in Palestine.

Fidayan-e Islam (in Farsi there is an "e," while in Arabic there is none) was the name taken by a radical Islamist group opposed to the reign of Mohammad Reza Shah Pahlavi of Iran beginning in the 1940s. Between 1971 and 1983 these Iranian fedayeen carried out numerous attacks, including political assassinations, against people supportive of the Pahlavi regime. The same name was adopted by a radical group in Islamabad, Pakistan.

The freedom fighter term was also given to a group created by ousted Iraqi leader Saddam Hussein. The Fedayeen Saddam was so-named to associate the force with patriotic self-sacrifice and anti-imperialism. Initially led by Hussein's son Uday in 1995, the group's leadership was handed over to his other son, Qusay, when it was discovered that Uday was diverting Iranian weaponry to the group. Many of them became part of the Iraqi resistance, or *muqawamah,* who following the March 2003 U.S.- and British-led invasion used rocket-propelled grenades, machine guns, and mortars to attack coalition forces, forces of the new Iraqi government, and Sadrists. In January 2007 the group recognized Izzat Ibrahim al-Duri as the rightful leader of Iraq and secretary-general of the Iraqi Baath Party following the execution of Saddam Hussein.

JESSICA BRITT AND SHERIFA ZUHUR

See also

Hussein, Qusay; Hussein, Saddam; Hussein, Uday; Iraq, History of, 1990–Present; Terrorism

References

Abdullah, Daud. *A History of Palestinian Resistance.* Leicester, UK: Al-Aqsa Publishers, 2005.

Khoury, Elias. *Gate of the Sun.* Translated by Humphrey Davies from *Bab al-Shams.* New York: St. Martin's, 2006.

Laqueur, Walter, and Barry Rubin, eds. *The Israel-Arab Reader: A Documentary History of the Middle East Conflict.* London: Penguin, 2001.

Nafez, Nazzal, and Laila A. Nafez. *Historical Dictionary of Palestine.* Lanham, MD: Scarecrow, 1997.

O'Neill, Bard E. *Revolutionary Warfare in the Middle East: The Israelis vs. the Fedayeen.* Boulder, CO: Paladin, 1974.

Rubin, Barry. *Revolution until Victory? The Politics and History of the PLO.* Cambridge, MA: Harvard University Press, 1996.

Federal Emergency Management Agency and Response to the September 11 Attacks

The Federal Emergency Management Agency (FEMA) is part of the U.S. Department of Homeland Security. It was created by Presidential Reorganization Plan No. 3 of 1978. FEMA's primary purpose is to coordinate and provide direct assistance in response to a natural or man-made disaster within the United States that is too great for the resources of local or state authorities.

FEMA had a mixed record in dealing with the aftermath of September 11, 2001. In September 2001 it was a large agency, with 2,600 employees and nearly 4,000 standby reservists. On September 11, 2001, Joe M. Allbaugh was the director of FEMA. Allbaugh was a Texan with close ties to President George W. Bush.

Where FEMA excelled was in its prompt response to the disaster. Emergency services personnel from 18 states responded almost immediately to the sites of the attacks. FEMA sent 28 urban search-and-rescue task forces to the sites of the disasters. Each task force had 62 members. The urban search-and-rescue task forces sent to the World Trade Center complex site to locate survivors worked 24-hour days, with the personnel working two 12-hour shifts. Conditions were horrible, and the dust from the debris made the task extremely difficult for the searchers. They employed portable cameras to spot survivors, sniffer dogs to smell for survivors, and sensitive life-detector sensors to look for signs of life. Despite these heroic efforts, few survivors were found because of the horrendous impact of the collapse of the Twin Towers. As it became apparent that there would be no more survivors, FEMA started pulling out its search-and-rescue teams. The last to leave was an Oakland, California, unit, which left on October 6, 2001. A spokesperson for FEMA stated that the site had been turned over to the Fire Department City of New York (FDNY) and the Army Corps of Engineers.

FEMA also sent in Critical Incident Stress Management (CISM) teams to assist workers at the site of the attacks. These teams had psychologists, psychiatrists, social workers, and professional counselors whose mission was the prevention and mitigation of disabling stress among the personnel working at the World Trade Center site. There were nearly as many members of these CISM teams as there were workers at the site. This caused some difficulty, because members of these teams were so eager to help that they became intrusive. They soon earned the nickname "therapy dogs" from workers at the site. Members of these teams undoubtedly helped some of those working at the site, but others resented their constant interference with the urgent job at hand.

FEMA's greatest failure was in its handling of the September 11 disaster relief funds. September 11 had caused the loss of 75,000 jobs and $4.5 billion in lost income. Despite promises of quick financial relief for those who had lost their jobs, FEMA's administrators changed the rules in the aftermath of September 11, making it more difficult for people to qualify for financial relief. Thousands of people were denied housing aid after FEMA decided to limit benefits to those who could prove that their lost income was a "direct result" of the attacks rather than merely the "result" of the attacks, which had been the previous standard. This seemingly minor change in language led to FEMA's rejection of the claims of 70 percent of the people applying for relief under the mortgage and rental program after losing their jobs. Between September 11, 2001, and April 2002, less than $65 million was paid out by FEMA to help families in the disaster area pay their bills, avoid eviction, and buy food.

Decisions on accepting or rejecting claims were made by FEMA agency evaluators (two-thirds of whom were temporary workers) at processing centers in Texas, Maryland, and Virginia. These evaluators had little or no knowledge of New York City or its culture, institutions, or geography. Moreover, the application form had not been changed to make it possible for evaluators to determine whether job losses were directly related to the disaster, and all the forms were printed exclusively in English. It was only on November 14, 2001, that the application form was revised and issued in six languages, but even the new forms did not explain how FEMA defined "direct result."

FEMA evaluators also made a number of odd decisions. One applicant provided the name of the restaurant where he had worked in the World Trade Center and his supervisor's telephone number, as required by the application. His application was denied because the evaluator was unable to make contact by telephone with the restaurant, which had of course been destroyed on September 11.

As bad as the situation was in New York City, it was even worse in Virginia. Thousands of workers had lost jobs by the closing of Reagan National Airport in Washington, D.C., in September, but the evaluators were slow to recognize this fact. Only a handful of applications from those workers had been approved by April 2002.

Criticisms of FEMA reached the halls of Congress. Under pressure from politicians, FEMA reevaluated its program in late June 2002 and eased its eligibility criteria. But the negative feelings were hard to overcome.

The immediate result of the change in direction was that FEMA approved more applications. Between September 2001 and June 2002, FEMA sent $20.6 million to 3,585 households. After June 2002, FEMA dispersed $25.3 million to 3,053 households in less than two months. This relaxation of eligibility rules helped the financial situation for people in New York and Virginia, but widespread distrust of FEMA remained.

STEPHEN E. ATKINS

See also

Bush, George Walker; September 11 Attacks; United States Department of Homeland Security

References

Chen, David W. "More Get 9/11 Aid, but Distrust of U.S. Effort Lingers." *New York Times,* August 27, 2002, B1.

Henriques, Diana B., and David Barstow. "Change in Rules Barred Many from September 11 Disaster Relief." *New York Times,* April 26, 2002, A1.

Keegan, William, Jr., with Bart Davis. *Closure: The Untold Story of the Ground Zero Recovery Mission.* New York: Touchstone Books, 2006.

Mitchell, Kirsten B. "Government Trying to Decide FEMA's Fate." *Tampa Tribune,* August 7, 2002, 1.

Feith, Douglas (1953–)

Attorney, foreign and military policy expert, neoconservative, and undersecretary of defense for policy (2001–2005). Born on July 16, 1953, in Philadelphia, Douglas Feith attended Harvard University, earning a BA degree in 1975. In 1978 he earned a law degree from Georgetown University. While in law school, Feith interned at the Arms Control and Disarmament Agency, where he met Fred Iklé, John Lehman, and Paul Wolfowitz. After graduation Feith practiced law in Washington, D.C., and wrote articles on foreign policy. As Feith grew older, he developed positions on foreign policy that would eventually identify him as a neoconservative who believed in the use of force as a vital instrument of national policy.

Feith entered government service in 1981 during the Ronald Reagan administration, working on Middle East issues for the National Security Council. Feith then transferred to the Department of Defense as special counsel for Assistant Secretary of Defense Richard Perle and later served as deputy assistant secretary of defense for negotiations from March 1984 to September 1986. After that Feith left government to form a law firm, Feith & Zell, P.C., which he managed until 2001, although he continued to write and speak on international affairs.

In April 2001 President George W. Bush nominated Feith as undersecretary of defense for policy. Confirmed in July 2001, Feith held that position until August 2005. His tenure would prove to be highly controversial. At the Pentagon, Feith's position was advisory; he was not within the military chain of command, yet his office held approval authority over numerous procedures. He was the number three civilian in the Pentagon, next to Secretary of Defense Donald Rumsfeld and Deputy Secretary of Defense Paul Wolfowitz.

As undersecretary, Feith became associated with three projects that, although well known, did not bear fruit. First, he hoped to engage America's opponents in the Global War on Terror in a battle of ideas. In the late autumn of 2001 Feith supported the development of the Office of Strategic Influence (OSI), a division of the Department of Defense that would seek to counter propaganda sympathetic to terrorist groups such as Al Qaeda through psychological campaigns. The clandestine nature of the OSI and a lack of oversight forced Rumsfeld to close it down in February 2002.

Second, Feith advocated the arming of a force of Iraqi exiles to accompany the U.S. invasion of Iraq in 2003. According to Feith, the idea was not well received in the Pentagon, the State Department, or the Central Intelligence Agency (CIA). Third, before Operation IRAQI FREEDOM began, Feith and his staff developed a plan for the creation of an Iraqi Interim Authority, which would have allowed for joint American-Iraqi control of Iraq after the defeat of Saddam Hussein's regime, as a prelude to a new Iraqi government. This plan was nixed by U.S. administrator in Iraq Paul Bremer in the autumn of 2003.

During his time at the Pentagon, Feith became a lightning rod for criticism of the Bush administration's conduct of the Global War on Terror and the Iraq War. Feith has been blamed for a myriad of policy miscues in Afghanistan and Iraq, and some have accused him of pursuing policies that led to the highly damaging Abu Ghraib prison scandal in 2004. Former vice president Al Gore called for Feith's resignation in a speech at New York University on May 26, 2004.

In various press accounts, Feith has been accused of setting up a secret intelligence cell designed to manipulate the prewar intelligence on Iraq to build a case for war. Feith's account of events in his memoirs differs considerably, however. He presented the Policy Counter Terrorism Evaluation Group, which evaluated prewar intelligence, as a small group of staffers tasked with summarizing the vast amounts of intelligence that had crossed his desk. Far from being a cadre of Republican political operatives, he argued, the small staff included Chris Carney, a naval officer and university professor who won a seat in Congress in 2006 as a Democrat.

In addition, Feith was accused of attempting to politicize intelligence and to find and publish evidence of links between Iraq and Al Qaeda that did not exist. In his memoirs, Feith states that he tasked career intelligence analyst Christina Shelton with reviewing intelligence on Iraqi–Al Qaeda connections and that she developed a view that was critical of the methods by which CIA analysts examined that intelligence. A subsequent Senate Intelligence Committee investigation concluded that staffers of the Office of the Undersecretary of Defense for Policy did not, in fact, pressure intelligence analysts into changing their product. However, intelligence and military analysts as well as other policy experts and media were either concerned by the scrutiny of or influenced by Rumsfeld's and Feith's office, and this did in fact affect their products.

In August 2005, with both Rumsfeld and Wolfowitz gone and discredited and the Bush administration's war and national security policy under attack from both Democrats and Republicans, Feith tendered his resignation and left government service. In 2006 he took a position at Georgetown University as visiting professor and distinguished practitioner in national security policy. His contract at Georgetown was not renewed in 2008. Also in 2006, Feith published his memoirs, *War and Decision: Inside the Pentagon at the Dawn of the War on Terrorism*, which offered a sustained defense of his reputation and an explanation of the decisions that he made while serving in government. The book hardly appeased his legion of critics and detractors, however, and Feith now operates on the margins of policy, but his ideas still retain influence. He is currently director of the Center of National Security Strategies and a senior fellow at the Hudson Institute, a conservative think tank.

MITCHELL MCNAYLOR

See also

Abu Ghraib; Bush, George Walker; Global War on Terror; Neoconservatism; Rumsfeld, Donald; Wolfowitz, Paul

References

Feith, Douglas. *War and Decision: Inside the Pentagon at the Dawn of the War on Terrorism.* New York: Harper, 2008.

U.S. Senate. *Report of the Select Committee on Intelligence on the U.S. Intelligence Community's Prewar Assessments on Iraq.* Washington, DC: U.S. Government Printing Office, 2004.

Woodward, Bob. *State of Denial: Bush at War, Part III.* New York: Simon and Schuster, 2006.

Film and U.S. Wars of the 21st Century

While the 1991 Persian Gulf War superseded the Vietnam War as America's great televised war, the Global War on Terror launched against perceived radical Islamist threats in the wake of the September 11, 2001, terrorist attacks against the United States and subsequent military campaigns in Afghanistan and Iraq may well become known as the first of the multimedia wars. With a plethora of online data available, the public has available to it a wide range of sources for images and analyses of the conflicts. Consequently, movies based on contemporary conflicts face a difficult task, that of competing with a flood of documentaries and Internet-based information. The documentary film has risen to unprecedented prominence in recent years, while many fictional movies have met with either failure or little more than modest success. Whether this failure is due to the success of documentaries, mounting criticism of the conflicts in Afghanistan and Iraq, public rejection of the theatrical films' general antimilitary themes, or other factors is a difficult question to answer.

In the post–World War II era, earlier filmmakers certainly faced problems in trying to sell the Korean War (1950–1953) to an indifferent public, and the one Korean War blockbuster, *M*A*S*H* (1970), did not emerge until well after the armistice, when America was engaged in the even more controversial war in Vietnam. In fact, the film's director, Robert Altman, admitted later that *M*A*S*H* is actually a film about the Vietnam War but that he had to disguise it by setting it ostensibly during the less controversial Korean War or would not have been allowed to make the film at all. Also, apart from John Wayne's prowar *Green Berets* (1968), the major Vietnam War movie successes—such as *Coming Home* (1978), *The Deerhunter* (1978), *Apocalypse Now* (1979), *Platoon* (1986), and *Full Metal Jacket* (1987)—also emerged well after the conflict. Current filmmakers dealing with continuing wars in the Middle East lack the benefits of hindsight and are, in essence, forced to write a script of ongoing conflicts with unknown outcomes. Other limitations may well also influence the success of movies focusing on modern Middle Eastern wars: bleak desert and urban settings limit visual appeal, the heavily armored gear-laden soldiers of today are hard to distinguish as individual characters, and Middle Eastern combatants and civilians often function as little more than type characters. Moreover, it may well be that movies about ongoing or more recent conflicts have yet to find their voice.

Afghanistan War

Cinematically, the conflict in Afghanistan, launched 10 years after the Persian Gulf War, could, like the Korean War, be termed the "forgotten war," for it has inspired relatively few movies to date. As with the Persian Gulf War, documentaries predominate. Released soon after September 11, 2001, the National Geographic documentary *Afghanistan Revealed* (2001) includes interviews with Afghan resistance leader Ahmad Shah Massoud, killed two days before the 9/11 attacks; Taliban prisoners with the Northern Alliance; and refugees from the Taliban. In support of the U.S. counterattack against Al Qaeda leader Osama bin Laden, Mullah Mohammed Omar, and the Al Qaeda network held responsible for 9/11, *Operation Enduring Freedom: America Fights Back* was released in 2002, supported by the U.S. Department of Defense and introduced by Secretary of Defense Donald Rumsfeld.

Soon, however, dissident voices sounded, as with Irish filmmaker Jamie Doran's *Massacre in Afghanistan: Did the Americans Look On?* (2002), amid protests and denials from the U.S. State Department. The documentary focuses on the alleged torture and slaughter of some 3,000 prisoners of war who had surrendered to U.S. and allied Afghan forces after the fall of Konduz. Some years later, the PBS Frontline documentary *Return of the Taliban* (2006) reported the resurgence of the Taliban on the Afghan-Pakistani border.

Focusing on international journalists covering the conflict, *Dateline Afghanistan: Reporting the Forgotten War* (2007) highlights the dangers and frustrations of war reporting. More controversially, Alex Gibney's *Taxi to the Dark Side* (2007) deals with a young Afghan taxi driver allegedly beaten to death at Bagram Air Base. In an attempt to counter mounting criticism of the U.S.-led engagement in Afghanistan, there is the 2008 episode "The Battle for Afghanistan" of the series *War Stories,* narrated by Oliver North. This episode follows a U.S. Marine Corps battalion deployed in Helmand Province. Concurrently, other documentaries from allied forces in the International Security Assistance Force in Afghanistan reflect growing disquiet about mounting casualties, as in *Waging Peace: Canada in Afghanistan* (2009).

One of the earliest movies dealing with Afghanistan is perhaps the most powerful, Michael Winterbottom's *In This World* (2002) that begins in the Shamshatoo refugee camp in Peshawar in Pakistan's North-West Frontier Province, where some 50,000 Afghan refugees, displaced either by the Soviet invasion of Afghanistan in 1979 or the post-9/11 U.S. bombing, lead a miserable existence. Two teenagers set out on the ancient Silk Road in an attempt to reach London. The film was first shown at the Berlinale Film Fest, and the premiere of the film preceded a massive antiwar demonstration at the Brandenburg Gate.

September Tapes (2004) follows a filmmaker and his team in an attempt to find Al Qaeda leader Osama bin Laden. Using a combination of real and spurious documentary footage to chronicle their way, the group eventually disappears as it approaches Taliban fighters. While the 2004 Danish movie *Brodre* (*Brothers*) powerfully probes sibling rivalry and post-traumatic stress disorder (PTSD) psychoses, little of this film actually deals with the Afghanistan War. Captured by Afghan rebel fighters after surviving a helicopter crash, the central character is manipulated into killing his feckless fellow prisoner to save his own life. Upon his return to Denmark after rescue, he is severely traumatized.

On a different tack, the American movie *Lions for Lambs* (2007) suggests dissent about the war by tracing three stories involving a warmongering Republican senator, a skeptical journalist, and a California university professor, two of whose students have been trapped behind enemy lies in Afghanistan and a third student who needs convincing to do something with his life. In a bizarre twist, the hero of *Iron Man* (2008), a successful arms trader captured by Afghan insurgents, escapes, only to return to America as a pacifist. He no longer wants weapons that he has designed to be deployed against American forces. *Lone Survivor* (2009) is based on the memoir of U.S. Navy Seal Marcus Luttrell, the lone survivor from his unit during Operation REDWING on the Afghan-Pakistani border. Yet another little-known movie release, *The Objective* (2008), is concerned with special operations reservists who go missing on a mission in Afghanistan. Although dealing with covert arms supplies to the mujahideen after the Soviet invasion of Afghanistan in 1979, *Charlie Wilson's War* (2007) is still relevant in the current context, as it suggests that by arming its anti-Soviet allies of the past, many of whom later joined the Taliban, the United States had been in essence aiding its present-day foes.

In 2010 a docudrama, *The Taking of Prince Harry*, was released to British television audiences; it chronicles the fictional capture of Prince Harry, the son of Charles, Prince of Wales. The young prince had been secretly deployed to Afghanistan during 2007–2008. *Dear John* (2010), an American film based on a Nicholas Sparks novel, chronicles the tale of a young couple in love whose lives are turned upside down when the young male protagonist serves in the Afghanistan War. He returns home to find that he has lost his love to another man. In the 2011 techno-thriller *Source Code,* the protagonist finds himself in a nightmare world in which he straddles two worlds: one in which he is a Chicago schoolteacher and the other in which he is a special agent in Afghanistan. *Le Militaire* (2013), a Canadian drama, deals with an ex-French soldier who served in Afghanistan and leads a cloistered existence in Montreal. Traumatized during the war, he enters into a series of poisonous relationships with women, only to finally meet a woman who makes him realize that his failed relationships are manifestations of unresolved war trauma. In the 2013 Hollywood film *Lone Survivor,* audiences are treated to a thrilling tale, based on actual events, about a U.S. Navy SEAL team's hunt for a major Taliban leader in Afghanistan.

A number of Middle Eastern movies have also addressed the conflict. Set shortly before 9/11, Iranian producer Mohsen Makhmalbaf's 2001 film *Kandahar* (originally titled *Safar-e Ghandehar*) follows an Afghan Canadian woman who sets forth on a disturbing journey to find her sister and displays the Taliban's savagery. Afghans also produced their own movie, *The White Rock* (2009), about a massacre of refugees by the Iranians in 1998. In a dark comedy, Afghan writer-director Siddiq Barmaq's *Opium War* (2008) is about two American airmen who crash into a remote poppy field and attack an old Soviet tank, which they assume shelters Taliban or Al Qaeda fighters. It turns out that this is the home of a family forced to grow opium poppies to survive.

Iraq War

The conflict in Iraq, which began in March 2003 and ended in December 2011, inspired the bulk of documentaries and movies to date. Accompanying the intense debate about the presence of weapons of mass destruction (WMD) in Iraq, United Nations weapons inspector Scott Ritter released a documentary, *In Shifting Sands: The Truth about UNSCOM and the Disarming of Iraq* (2001), for distribution in 2003. *Uncovered: The Whole Truth about the Iraq War* (2003) deals with media treatment of the developing push to invade Iraq; an expanded version appeared in 2004. One of the most controversial documentaries came from Al Jazeera, the Arab news network. *Control Room* (2004) follows the Iraqi war from the American military information station in Qatar to the streets of Baghdad during Operation IRAQI FREEDOM, showing Iraqi civilian casualties, dead American soldiers, and U.S. assaults that kill a number of journalists, including an Al Jazeera cameraman when the network's

Baghdad office is attacked. Other documentaries, such as *Alpha Company: Iraq Diary* (2005), shot by Gordon Forbes as a journalist embedded with a reconnaissance battalion, and *The War Tapes* (2006), shot by soldiers themselves, deal with the everyday lives of U.S. forces in Iraq. An Emmy Award–winning documentary, *Baghdad ER* (2006), moves the perspective to a military hospital, while *Gunner Palace* (2005) consists of firsthand accounts of servicemen faced with a dangerous and chaotic military situation. A Veterans' Day special, *Last Letters Home: Voices of American Troops from the Battlefields of Iraq* (2005), features the families of eight men and two women killed in Iraq. Also with a personal focus, *The Ground Truth: After the Killing Ends* (2006) addresses the effects of the war, including PTSD, on veterans, family members, and friends.

As the conflict lengthened, criticism of the war's handling became more intense. In *Iraq for Sale: The War Profiteers* (2006), four major U.S. government contractors came under attack for profiteering and doing shoddy work. In a series of 35 interviews with former government officials alongside journalists and former servicemen, *No End in Sight* (2007) focuses on the major mistakes of the Iraqi occupation, which include disbanding the Iraqi Army and dismissing experienced bureaucrats. With *Ghosts of Abu Ghraib* (2007) yet another Iraq War scandal reached the screen, this time examining the events of the 2004 Abu Ghraib torture and prisoner abuse scandal, a theme also taken up in Errol Morris's *Standard Operating Procedure* (2008). In a further condemnation of the foreign policies of the George W. Bush administration, *Finding Our Voices* (2008) weaves together the voices of eight people, including former government officials and soldiers who refused to return to Iraq. The 2012 film *The Prosecution of an American President* traces President George W. Bush's alleged attempts to invade Iraq in 2003 under false pretenses.

Other documentaries focus on the effects of the conflicts on the people of Iraq. In *About Baghdad* (2004), exiled Iraqi writer Sinan Antoon returns to his city to probe recent developments in a collage of walking tours through war-ravaged streets, interviews with political prisoners tortured under the Hussein regime, conversations with intellectuals, and commentaries by the outspoken Antoon. Similarly, *In the Shadow of the Palms* (2005), shot by Australian filmmaker Wayne Coles-Janess, offers footage of the lives of Iraqis before Hussein's deposition, during the fall of the government, and throughout the U.S. occupation. An Iraqi-made documentary, *Dreams of Sparrows* (2005), follows director Haydar Daffar's team in encounters with Iraqi citizens, a

project that results in a crew member's death. Two documentaries from 2006, *My Country, My Country* and *The Blood of My Brother*, focus on individual Iraqis caught up in the bloodshed of the growing Shia insurgency.

Predictably, studies of Saddam Hussein have accompanied the Iraqi conflict. Among these, *Our Friend Saddam* (2003) examines the dictator's earlier relationship with Western countries that supplied him with weapons, a theme also taken up in the 2004 French television documentary *Saddam Hussein: Le procès que vous ne verrez pas* (*Saddan Hussein: The Trial You Will Not See*). *Saddam Hussein: Weapon of Mass Destruction* (2005) chronicles the rise and fall of the dictator, while *America at a Crossroads: The Trial of Saddam Hussein* (2008) raises questions on procedural aspects of the trial and the ethno-religious differences within Iraq that it mirrors.

One of the earliest Iraqi War–based movies, *Saving Jessica Lynch* (2003), evoked accusations of media manipulation when it was revealed that the "rescue" of Private Lynch, supposedly captured in an ambush, did not take place; rather, the Iraqi hospital in which she was under treatment willingly handed her over to military forces. *Over There* (2005), a television series about a U.S. Army unit on its first tour of duty, met with little success in spite of explosions, amputations, and grisly footage. An Italian movie, *La tigre e la neve* (*The Tiger and the Snow,* 2005), is a love story about a man who attempts to court a woman writing the biography of an Iraqi poet in Baghdad. Unsuccessful in his attempt, he is finally mistaken as an Iraqi insurgent and arrested. *American Soldiers* (2005) deals with an American patrol's struggle against fedayeen fighters; eventually they release mistreated prisoners, running afoul of the Central Intelligence Agency (CIA).

Also a combat movie, *A Line in the Sand* (2006) deals with two soldiers with different views of the war who survive an ambush and struggle to reach safety. Based on an incident of November 19, 2005, *The Battle for Haditha* (2007) investigates the alleged murder of 24 Iraqi civilians by marine forces in retaliation for a roadside bombing. Using creative nonfictional filming techniques that combine a soldier's home movies, documentaries, newscasts, and Internet postings, *Redacted* (2007) is based on a real event wherein a squad persecutes an innocent Iraqi family and rapes a young girl.

Other recent movie releases focus on a chaotic battlefront, as in the seven-part television series *Generation Kill* (2008), where members of the U.S. Marine Corps 1st Reconnaissance Battalion face unclear conditions and military ineptitude.

The Hurt Locker (2008) deals with the sergeant of a bomb disposal team who recklessly exposes his subordinates to urban combat, while *Green Zone* (2009) is a fictional treatment of a U.S. Army inspection squad hunting for WMD, misled by covert and faulty intelligence. *No True Glory: Battle for Fallujah* (2009) takes up the familiar theme of the confusion and frustration of the Iraqi insurgency in its account of the fighting in Fallujah in 2004 between insurgents and U.S. forces. The heart-wrenching 2009 film *Taking Chance* chronicles the real-life story of a U.S. Army officer who is tasked with escorting back to the United States the body of Chance Phelps, a young soldier killed in the Iraq War. In the 2010 film *Green Zone,* starring Matt Damon, audiences are treated to a depiction of life within Baghdad's Green Zone, an area secured by coalition forces and one of the only truly safe havens in Iraq after the 2003 Anglo-American invasion.

Increasingly, however, Iraq War movies turned to the home front. After harrowing experiences in Iraq, for instance, four soldiers in *Home of the Brave* (2006) must deal with their physical and psychological trauma upon their return home. Similarly, *Four Horsemen* (2007) focuses on four high school friends: one is killed in action, another is permanently maimed, and the remaining two return to Iraq after leave. The main character in *Stop Loss* (2008), however, refuses to return when, as a decorated hero, he experiences PTSD following his first tour of duty. With a different twist, *In the Valley of Elah* (2007) is about a father's search to discover what has happened to his soldier son Mike, who has gone absent without leave (AWOL) after his return from Iraq. A complex investigation leads to shocking discoveries: first that Mike had been guilty of prisoner abuse in Iraq and second that his fellow soldiers have stabbed him and dismembered his body. Similarly, the British television movie *The Mark of Cain* (2007) follows three young men who suffer the effects of what they have seen and done after their tour of duty. Dealing with family bereavement, *Grace Is Gone* (2007) concerns a father's difficulty in breaking the news of his wife's death in Iraq to his two daughters. The 2011 film *Return* depicts the return home from combat of a female reservist who saw action in the Middle East wars; she is haunted by her wartime experiences and has a difficult time readjusting to civilian life in the American Midwest.

Among Iraqi-made movies, *Ahlaam* (2005), directed by Mohamed Al-Daradji, an exile during Hussein's reign, was inspired by the sight of psychiatric patients let loose in the streets of Baghdad in the wake of Operation IRAQI FREEDOM. The movie focuses on a mental institution and interweaves the narratives of three characters. Filming in 2004 proved dangerous, for Al-Daradji and three crew members were once kidnapped twice in the same day. *Valley of the Wolves* (2006), based on a popular Turkish television series, is set in northern Iraq and begins with U.S. forces capturing 11 Turkish special forces soldiers.

An Egyptian black comedy, *The Night Baghdad Fell* (2006), was extremely popular. It lampooned American officials, and the story line dealt with preparations to prevent the United States from continuing its invasion into Egypt. Condoleezza Rice and U.S. marines figure in the repressed fantasies of the film characters. An earlier comedy, *No Problem, We're Getting Messed Over,* featured an Egyptian who sends his son to Iraq to deliver mangoes and then must rescue him from a U.S. prison. He falls into Hussein's hiding place and is fired on by insurgents, arrested by Americans, and taken to President Bush, who forces him to wear a beard and confess to bombing the U.S. embassy.

Global War on Terror

While films dealing with the ongoing conflicts in Afghanistan and Iraq are virtually inseparable from the Global War on Terror, other documentaries and movies address the conflict in a more general Middle Eastern context. Arabic films have portrayed this topic for several decades. A classic piece portraying a conventional view of Islamist terrorists was *Irhabi* (*The Terrorist*) of 1993, starring Adel Imam. John Pilger's documentary *Breaking the Silence: Truth and Lies in the War on Terror* (2003) criticizes American and British involvement in the Middle East since 9/11, questioning the real motives for the Global War on Terror, as does Noam Chomsky's *Distorted Morality* (2003), which claims that America is the world's biggest endorser of state-sponsored terrorism. Most notably, Michael Moore's *Fahrenheit 9/11* (2004), which holds the current box office record for a political documentary, attacks the Global War on Terror agenda of the Bush government, alleging connections with Saudi royalty and the bin Laden family. The film provoked rebuttals, such as *Fahrenhype 11* (2004). Produced by the BBC in 2004, the documentary series *The Power of Nightmares: The Rise of the Politics of Fear* parallels the American neoconservative movement with radical Islamism, arguing as well that the threat of Islamism is a myth perpetuated to unite the public through fear. Subsequent documentaries include *The Oil Factor: Behind the War on Terror* (2005), which examines the link between U.S. oil interests and current conflicts, and *The Road to Guantánamo* (2006), a docudrama on four Pakistani brothers who, in Pakistan for a wedding, venture into Afghanistan. Captured, they spend three years at Guantánamo Bay. *War on Terror,* a

2011 Austrian film, is a documentary about the war on terror that began in 2001 and its effects throughout the world; it also features interviews with two former detainees at the Guantánamo Bay Detainment Camp.

American movies have addressed the theme of rampant Muslim terrorism for decades, and recent films carry on the tradition. The global oil industry is the focus of *Syriana* (2005), a political thriller in which a CIA operative is caught up in a plot involving a Persian Gulf prince. Inspired by terrorist bombings in Saudi Arabia in 1996 and 2003, *The Kingdom* (2007) follows a Federal Bureau of Investigation inquiry into the bombing of a foreign-worker complex. In *Rendition* (2007), a terrorist bomb kills an American envoy, and the investigation leads to an Egyptian American who, after arrest, is sent overseas for torture and interrogation. Touching upon all recent Middle Eastern conflicts, Oliver Stone's *W.* (2008) is not only a mildly entertaining biopic of President George W. Bush but also a withering representation of the decision making that preceded the declaration of a Global War on Terror and military deployments in Afghanistan and Iraq. The film includes a flashback to President George H. W. Bush's decision to stop the Persian Gulf War early and pull out U.S. troops at the end of the conflict.

Zero Dark Thirty (2012), a major motion picture directed by Kathryn Bigelow, chronicles the search for Al Qaeda leader Osama bin Laden and his eventual apprehension and murder in a Pakistani compound in May 2011. The film was critically acclaimed and nominated for five Academy Awards, but some of its content—including the depiction of American employment of coerced interrogation—precipitated controversy. *Seal Team Six: The Raid on Osama Bin Laden* (2013), a made-for-television docudrama, takes up the same subject but has received mixed reviews.

ANNA M. WITTMANN

See also

Abu Ghraib; Afghanistan War; Al Jazeera; Al Qaeda; Bin Laden, Osama; Bush, George Walker; Coercive Interrogation; *Fahrenheit 9/11;* Global War on Terror; Green Zone in Iraq; Guantánamo Bay Detainment Camp; IRAQI FREEDOM, Operation; Persian Gulf War; Post-Traumatic Stress Disorder; September 11 Attacks; Terrorism

References

Rollins, Peter C., and John E. O'Connor, eds. *Why We Fought: America's Wars in Film and History.* Lexington: University of Kentucky Press, 2008.

Slocum, J. David, ed. *Hollywood and War: The Film Reader.* New York: Routledge, 2006.

Westwell, Guy. *War Cinema: Hollywood on the Front Line.* London: Wallflower, 2006.

1st Special Forces Operational Detachment–Delta Airborne

See Delta Force

Foreign Intelligence Surveillance Act of 1978

The Foreign Intelligence Surveillance Act (FISA) of 1978 was passed as a result of the abuses of the Federal Bureau of Investigation (FBI) in conducting warrantless surveillance of American citizens in the 1960s and early 1970s. Recommendations came out of the 1975 Church Committee on ways to prevent the warrantless surveillance of U.S. citizens by the FBI. Committee members also wanted to end decades of presidentially approved electronic surveillance for national security purposes without a judicial warrant and thus prevent irregularities in surveillance activities. This committee also believed that the U.S. judiciary lacked the expertise to rule on matters concerning foreign intelligence surveillance.

Provisions of the FISA allowed for a special court to be established that would issue warrants after receiving requests from law enforcement agencies. This court was given the name Foreign Intelligence Surveillance Court (FISC). A search warrant or a wire tap could be issued by the FISC if the subject was an agent of a foreign power, which was defined as either a foreign country or an international terrorist group, or if the subject was engaged in international terrorism or activities in preparation for terrorism on behalf of a foreign power. FISC orders are classified and kept secret. In the history of FISC only a few warrants have ever been turned down, because FISA permits search warrants to be issued based on a lower standard than the standard of probable cause used for criminal search warrants.

Despite the reputation of FISC for almost never turning down a request from a law enforcement agency, the FBI had been reluctant to apply for warrants from the court before September 11, 2001. An elaborate and time-consuming procedure had to be followed to apply for a warrant from FISC. Once the agents at a field office had determined that there was probable cause for a FISA warrant, an electronic communication with supporting documents would be sent to the FBI headquarters unit overseeing the investigation. That unit would add any supporting documents and send the package to the National Security Law Unit (NSLU). This unit consists of lawyers with expertise in national security law. Lawyers in the NSLU would review the case on its merits. If these lawyers agreed that the case met the threshold of probable cause, then the dossier would be forwarded to the Department of Justice. If not, the case would end at the NSLU. At the Department of Justice, the case would be examined anew by its Office of Intelligence Policy Review, where lawyers would once again examine the case for a FISA warrant. Only if the case could pass all of these roadblocks could it be forwarded to the FISA court in the form of a declaration and be signed off by a FISA court judge.

Part of the problem was that the FBI's lawyers interpreted the FISA law in a more restrictive manner than the legislation had intended. This strict interpretation of the law was the case with the FISA request from the Minneapolis field office for a warrant concerning Zacarias Moussaoui, the so-called 20th hijacker on September 11, 2001. FBI agents had requested authority for a warrant several times for Moussaoui, including one from FISC, but each time their request was turned down by FBI headquarters. Moussaoui had been in Chechnya assisting the Chechen rebels fighting against Russia. The head of the Radical Fundamental Unit at FBI headquarters refused to classify the Chechen rebels as part of a so-called recognized foreign power.

The final interpretation of FBI headquarters in the Moussaoui case was that he was not associated with a foreign power, nor was the Chechen rebel group a recognized terrorist group. This decision was made despite the warning from French security agents that Moussaoui had been associating with Muslim extremists and even though it was well known in intelligence circles that the Chechen rebels had extensive contacts with Al Qaeda.

Everything changed after the events of September 11, and the FBI had no trouble obtaining a criminal warrant against Moussaoui in the aftermath of the attacks. An examination of his computer after September 11 revealed his contacts with the Hamburg Cell, which had carried out the 9/11 attacks, and Al Qaeda. The FBI's strict adherence to its interpretation of FISA has been blamed as part of the wall that hindered the flow of information and thwarted the effectiveness of the FBI's efforts against terrorism.

Since September 11, 2001, the controversy over FISC has intensified. The George W. Bush administration made its view known that the onerous requirements of FISA stood in the way of intelligence gathering. In a secret court proceeding before the FISA Appeals Court on September 9, 2002, with only government lawyers present, the Bush administration presented its case that FISC had hindered the flow of information and had obstructed the president's authority to conduct warrantless searches to obtain foreign intelligence information. The court accepted the government's position, and the U.S. Supreme Court refused to hear any appeals. This judgment was the legal grounds for subsequent warrantless searches, which were conducted by the National Security Agency in secret and under presidential authority. After news of the warrantless searches became public in December 2005, however, Bush instructed the various intelligence organizations that the FISC system be used for all intelligence-gathering activities. Since taking office in January 2009, President Barack Obama and other members of his administration have reiterated Bush's view that it is the president's executive prerogative to circumvent FISA.

Several acts have amended FISA in recent years. In 2004 a "lone wolf" provision was added, allowing FISA courts to grant warrants for the surveillance of non-U.S. citizens believed to be engaging in international terrorism but not linked to a particular government or organization. The Protect America Act of 2007, signed into law on August 5, 2007, officially allowed for the warrantless surveillance of international communications by the U.S. government without FISA oversight. The act, however, expired on February 17, 2008.

The Foreign Intelligence Surveillance Act of 1978 Amendments Act of 2008, enacted on July 10, 2008, prevents telecommunications companies from being prosecuted for their complicity in the government's warrantless wiretapping programs. It extends the period of time the government may conduct surveillance on an individual without a warrant from two days to seven days. It also permits the government to not keep records of its searches and surveillance and allows it to destroy existing records after 10 years.

Despite the efforts of the Bush and Obama administrations to bypass the FISC system, FISA courts still exist, and the number of warrant requests coming before them has increased significantly in recent years. The use of FISA and its courts does protect the government from accusations that it violates the Fourth Amendment rights of U.S. citizens. The debate over FISA and its courts is ongoing, with many critics believing that both the law and its implementation are hindering the war on terrorism.

STEPHEN E. ATKINS

See also
Moussaoui, Zacarias

References
Graham, Bob. *Intelligence Matters: The CIA, the FBI, Saudi Arabia, and the Failure of America's War on Terror*. New York: Random House, 2004.
Meason, James E. "The Foreign Intelligence Surveillance Act: Time for Reappraisal." *International Lawyer* 24 (Winter 1990): 1043.

Schmitt, Gary. "Constitutional Spying: The Solution to the FISA Problem." *Weekly Standard* 11(16) (January 2–January 9, 2006): 1–2.

Yoo, John. *War by Other Means: An Insider's Account of the War on Terror.* New York: Atlantic Monthly Press, 2006.

Fort Dix Plot

On May 7, 2007, agents from the Federal Bureau of Investigation (FBI) arrested six Muslim extremists, originally from the Middle East, after two tried to buy automatic weapons from an undercover officer in a plot to attack the Fort Dix military base in New Jersey. They were charged and convicted for trying to kill military personnel and, although not connected to Al Qaeda, were alleged to have been inspired by Osama bin Laden and his concept of jihad in the defense of Islam.

The group included three brothers: Dritan Duka, 28; Shain Duka, 26; and Eljvir Duka, 23. The trio were ethnic Albanians from Debar in the Republic of Macedonia and had first entered the United States illegally in 1984. Between 1996 and 2006, police had charged Dritan and Shain with a number of traffic citations and minor offenses, including marijuana possession. They had been fined amounts varying from $20 to $830.

The other three individuals were Agron Abdullahu, 24, an Albanian from Kosovo who was living legally in New Jersey and who gave the group weapons training; Mohamad Ibrahim Shnewer, 22, Dritan's brother-in-law and a Palestinian cab driver from Jordan who became a naturalized U.S. citizen; and Serdar Tatar, 23, born in Turkey, a legal resident of Philadelphia who had worked at a Super Mario Pizza owned by his family.

The six men trained on firing semiautomatic weapons at a Gouldsboro, Pennsylvania, shooting range and used cell phones to video-record their sessions while shouting in Arabic "God is great." On January 31, 2006, the group went to a Circuit City store in Mount Laurel, New Jersey, to convert the electronic images into a DVD. However, they failed to effectively screen the cell phone from outside purview, and after store employee Brian Morgenstern saw the content, he contacted authorities.

The FBI then began a 16-month investigation and infiltrated the group with two paid informants who recorded the members planning their attacks. Additional incriminating evidence was extracted from their cell phones, which clearly indicated that they wanted to kill as many Americans as possible at Fort Dix.

The 26-page indictment showed that the group had no formal military training, no apparent connection to Al Qaeda or other foreign terrorist organizations, no clear ringleader (although some reports cited Shnewer as the main commander), and very little chance of actually succeeding in their plans. Court records said that the cell had first considered attacking Fort Monmouth in New Jersey, Delaware's Dover Air Force Base, and the U.S. Coast Guard Building in Philadelphia. However, the six had settled on Fort Dix because Tatar had delivered pizzas there from his family's Super Mario Pizza and had a map of the installation. To carry out their plans, the men had attempted to purchase weapons from an undercover FBI agent, including AK-47s, M16s, M60s, and rocket-propelled grenades.

On May 11, 2007, all six were ordered held without bail in Philadelphia. Their trial opened the following October and lasted a month. All were convicted. The Duka brothers and Shnewer all received life sentences, Tatar received a sentence of 23 years, and Abdullahu accepted a plea bargain deal for a 5-year sentence.

DONNA BASSETT

See also

Al Qaeda

References

Emerson, Steven. *Jihad Incorporated: A Guide to Militant Islam in the US.* Foreword by Peter Hoekstra. Amherst, NY: Prometheus Books, 2006.

Lawrence, Bruce. *Messages to the World: The Statements of Osama bin Laden.* London: Verso, 2005.

Temple-Raston, Dina. *The Jihad Next Door: The Lackawanna Six and Rough Justice in the Age of Terror.* New York: Perseus Books, 2007.

France

Since the inauguration of the Fifth Republic in 1958, France has had a bicameral parliamentary system in which much executive power is vested in a popularly elected president, who is head of state. The prime minister, who is elected by parliament, serves as the head of government. The French president wields considerable clout, especially in foreign and military affairs and national security. Since 2000, France has had three presidents: Jacques Chirac (1995–2007), Nicolas Sarkozy (2007–2012), and François Hollande (2012–present).

Following Iraq's invasion of Kuwait in August 1990, French president François Mitterrand, who held office during 1981–1995, committed French army, naval, and air force

In a chilling video, two masked Islamic terrorists fire their weapons outside the offices of the French satirical newspaper *Charlie Hebdo*, in Paris on January 7, 2015. The attackers killed 11 people and wounded another 11 before they themselves were hunted down and killed. (AP Photo)

units to the allied coalition forming to drive Iraqi forces from Kuwait. Indeed, France contributed 14,500 ground troops to the Persian Gulf War in 1991, making it, after Great Britain, the second-largest non-U.S. contributor of ground forces.

Since early 2002 France also contributed troops to Afghanistan as part of the some 50,000-strong North Atlantic Treaty Organization (NATO) International Security Assistance Force–Afghanistan (ISAF). By early 2009 some 2,500 French troops were deployed in the country, mostly in the capital of Kabul but also in the southern city of Kandahar, where French fighter aircraft were based and provided air support for NATO allied troops. France also trained thousands of Afghan military officers as well as Afghan special forces units.

With mounting violence in Afghanistan and a rise in attacks by the Taliban, on March 26, 2008, French president Nicolas Sarkozy announced the deployment of an additional battalion of troops to eastern Afghanistan close to the Pakistan border, raising the number of French troops to about 3,300 men. Despite the death of 10 French troops and the wounding of 21 in a Taliban ambush 30 miles east of Kabul on August 18, 2008, and polls showing strong public opinion against the French mission in Afghanistan, Sarkozy announced that his "determination remained intact" to continue France's mission in that country. A month later, the

French parliament voted to continue that mission over the objections of the opposition Socialist Party. Foreign Minister François Fillon informed the National Assembly that withdrawing French troops from Afghanistan would mean that Paris was indifferent to Afghanistan's fate, no longer assumed its responsibilities, and abandoned its allies.

In the wake of the August 18, 2008, attack, France sent to Afghanistan transport and attack helicopters, drones, surveillance equipment, mortars, and 100 additional troops. By year's end it had drawn down some of its troops, which then numbered about 2,700 men. These numbers were subsequently drawn down, however, and on October 6, 2014, there were only 90 French military personnel in ISAF.

The French government headed by Jacques Chirac opposed the 2003 Anglo-American–led invasion of Iraq. As a result, France did not participate in that endeavor and has steadfastly refused to send troops, even for postwar reconstruction and humanitarian efforts. The attitude of the French government toward the Iraq War severely strained relations with the United States for several years. Making matters even worse was persistent public criticism of the war effort emanating from Paris. After President Sarkozy assumed office in 2007, there were efforts by both sides to heal the rift, and U.S.-French relations steadily improved.

France also played a key role in the NATO intervention in the 2011 Libyan Civil War. France was the first nation to recognize the National Transitional Council as the legitimate government of Libya, and French aircraft conducted the first military strike on the forces loyal to Libyan strongman Muammar Qaddafi.

Given its long-standing historical involvement in Africa, France has played a key role in the Global War on Terror, intervening in such nations as Gabon and Mali. In a divergence from a noninterventionist position advanced by President Hollande, in January 2013 in Operation SERVAL Hollande ordered troops to Mali. Radical Islamists had conquered the north and were then threatening the strategic city of Bamako. The French military intervention, which was supported by the great majority of the Muslim Mali population, turned back the insurgents and probably prevented them from seizing control of the entire country. France still has forces there, as does the United States, which has a drone base at Niamey.

In mid-2013 Hollande supported Western military intervention in the ongoing Syrian Civil War (2011–present), following charges that the Syrian government had employed chemical weapons against its own people.

During early January 2015, France fell victim to terrorist attacks that occurred in Paris. These were carried out by 3 Islamic extremists, 2 of whom were purportedly acting on orders from Al Qaeda in the Arabian Peninsula and the other having pledged allegiance to the Islamic State of Iraq and Syria. The first attack was on the office of French satirical magazine *Charlie Hebdo,* which has often printed cartoons of the Prophet Muhammad, and a kosher market in Paris. The two attacks killed 17 innocent French civilians. French authorities apprehended and shot to death the 3 perpetrators in two separate firefights. The French public was shocked and outraged, but there are a great many Muslims in France, many living on the economic fringe, and anti-Semitism has been on the rise. On January 11, some 3.7 million Frenchmen took to the streets in rallies intended to demonstrate French solidarity with the victims and their families and support freedom of expression and religion. At least 1.5 million people crowded the streets of Paris that day, where dozens of heads of state marched arm in arm, including Israeli prime minister Benjamin Netanyahu and Palestinian National Authority president Mahmoud Abbas. At the same time, President Hollande announced the deployment of at least 10,000 troops to major French cities to deter further terrorist attacks; his government also vowed to step up security around Jewish schools, places of worship,

and Jewish-owned businesses. Meanwhile, U.S. president Barack Obama announced that the U.S. government would soon be convening a major international conference in Washington, D.C., to coordinate international responses to global terrorism.

STEFAN BROOKS AND SPENCER C. TUCKER

See also

Chirac, Jacques René; International Security Assistance Force; North Atlantic Treaty Organization; Persian Gulf War; Syrian Chemical Weapons Agreement; Syrian Civil War

References

Atkinson, Rick. *Crusade: The Untold Story of the Persian Gulf War.* New York: Mariner Books, 1994.
Crocker, H. W., III. *Don't Tread on Me.* New York: Crown Forum, 2006.
Ryan, Mike. *Battlefield Afghanistan.* London: Spellmount, 2007.

Franks, Tommy (1945–)

U.S. Army general. Tommy Ray Franks was born in Wynnewood, Oklahoma, on June 17, 1945, and grew up in Oklahoma and Midland, Texas. After studying briefly at the University of Texas, Franks joined the U.S. Army in 1965 and went into the artillery. He served in Vietnam, where he was wounded three times. He attended the University of Texas but dropped out and joined the army after being placed on academic probation.

Franks later earned his master's degree in public administration at Shippinsburg University (1985), then graduated from the Armed Forces Staff College (1967). He also attended the University of Texas, Arlington (1970–1972), and in 1972 attended the USA Field Artillery Center at Fort Sill, Oklahoma. From 1976 to 1977, he attended the Armed Force Staff College, Norfolk, Virginia, and in 1984–1985 he attended the U.S. Army War College at Carlisle Barracks, Pennsylvania.

After advancing through the ranks, in the 1991 Persian Gulf War Franks was an assistant division commander of the 1st Calvary Division. He was promoted to brigadier general in July 1991 and to major general in April 1994. From 1994 to 1995 he was the assistant chief of staff for combined forces in Korea. Franks was promoted to lieutenant general in May 1997 and to general in July 2006. After the September 11, 2001, terrorist attacks on the United States, he was named U.S. commander in chief for the successful Operation ENDURING FREEDOM in Afghanistan. In 2003, he was the commander in chief of Central Command (CENTCOM) for Operation IRAQI FREEDOM, the invasion of Iraq.

Franks was a principal author of the plans for the ground element of the invasion of Iraq and was an advocate of the lighter, more rapid mechanized forces that performed so well during it. He designed a plan for the 150,000 American troops and for the few thousand coalition troops who would be under his command. His plan involved five ground prongs into Iraq, with two main thrusts: one by the 1st Marine Expeditionary Force up the Tigris River and one through the western desert and up the Euphrates by the army's 3rd Armored Division. The plan allowed for great flexibility, and even though CENTCOM advertised a "shock and awe" bombing campaign, in fact there was never any such intention, as Franks's plans called for a near-simultaneous ground and air assault.

When missiles struck Saddam Hussein's compound on March 19, 2003, ground forces moved into Iraq. Franks emphasized speed and bypassing cities and Iraqi strongpoints. Contrary to media reports that coalition forces were "bogged down" and had not occupied many cities, Franks maintained that this was by design: CENTCOM did not want the Iraqis to see demonstrated in Basra or Najaf the method and tactics by which coalition forces planned to take Baghdad.

The campaign was an unprecedented success, going further and faster with fewer casualties, than any other comparable military campaign in history. This reflected what Franks called "full-spectrum" war, in which not only were the enemy's military forces engaged, but there were simultaneous attacks on computer and information facilities, the banking/monetary structure, and public opinion. Franks expanded the concept of command, control, communications, and intelligence (C3I) to include computers in C4I. For the first time, American forces operated in true joint operations, wherein different service branches could speak directly to units in other service branches, and featured true combined-arms operations, in which air, sea, and land assets were all simultaneously employed by commanders in the field to defeat the enemy.

Although many sources suggest that Franks was offered a position on the Joint Chiefs of Staff, he wanted to retire to be with his family and build his personal fortune. He therefore retired from the army on July 7, 2003, at the rank of full general and subsequently wrote his memoirs, *American Soldier* (2004). In 2003 Franks also established his own consulting firm, which specializes in disaster recovery. He has also sat on a member of corporate and nonprofit boards of directors, including those of Bank of America and the National Park Foundation.

LARRY SCHWEIKART

See also

Hussein, Saddam; IRAQI FREEDOM, Operation; Rumsfeld, Donald; September 11 Attacks; United States Central Command

References

Cordesman, Anthony. *The Iraq War: Strategy, Tactics, and Military Lessons.* London: Center for Strategic and International Studies, 2003.

Fontenot, Gregory, et al. *On Point: The United States Army in Operation Iraqi Freedom.* Washington, DC: Office of the Chief of Staff, 2004.

Friendly Fire

Friendly fire, fratricide, or blue-on-blue are attacks involving troops firing on their own units, usually unknowingly, in which they wound or kill members of their own force. Although military establishments work hard to prevent such incidents, they are inevitable in the fog of war. Of the 613 American casualties in the 1990–1991 Operations DESERT SHIELD and DESERT STORM, 146 were killed in action, and 35 died in so-called friendly fire incidents. Of 467 wounded, 78 were a result of friendly fire. Nine British soldiers were killed in such incidents, and 11 others were wounded during DESERT SHIELD/DESERT STORM. Remarkably, with thousands of coalition aircraft flying missions in the Kuwaiti theater of operations, no coalition aircraft were lost in the conflict to friendly fire.

A total of 28 separate incidents of friendly fire were recorded during the Persian Gulf War, 16 of which were in ground-to-ground engagements in which coalition ground forces mistakenly fired on other coalition ground forces. In these incidents, 24 coalition troops were killed and 27 were wounded. Nine died in friendly fire incidents involving aircraft striking ground targets. In all, 11 servicemen were killed and 27 were wounded by air-to-ground friendly fire incidents. The majority of the friendly fire incidents during the war involved armored units and personnel.

Friendly fire incidents have also occurred in the Afghanistan War and the Iraq Wars. In the Afghanistan War, four Canadian soldiers were killed and eight others wounded on the night of April 18, 2002, when a U.S. Air Force Lockheed Martin F-16 Fighting Falcon dropped a bomb on their unit during a night-firing exercise near Kandahar. Subsequently court-martialed, Air National Guard pilot Major Harry Schmidt blamed the accident on drugs ("go pills," which he said the pilots were encouraged to take during missions) and the fog of war. Found guilty of dereliction of duty, he was fined and reprimanded.

The best-known friendly fire incident in Afghanistan was the killing of Corporal Pat Tillman, who left a promising and lucrative National Football League career to serve in the army following the September 11, 2001, terrorist attacks on the United States. Tillman was serving with the 2nd Ranger Battalion when he was shot and killed at close range by three shots to the forehead on April 22, 2004, in what was initially reported as an ambush on a road outside the village of Sperah, about 25 miles southwest of Khost near the Pakistani border. An Afghan militiaman was also killed, and two other rangers were wounded. The subsequent cover-up regarding the circumstances of Tillman's death ultimately caused great outrage in the United States. The first investigation held that the deaths were the result of friendly fire brought on by the intensity of the firefight, but a second and more thorough investigation held that no hostile forces were involved in the firefight and that two allied groups had fired on each other in confusion following the detonation of an explosive device. The incident continues to be the subject of considerable speculation.

Among numerous other friendly fire incidents in Afghanistan, a U.S. Air Force F-15 called in to support British ground forces dropped a bomb into the same British unit, killing two British soldiers and wounding two others. Two Dutch soldiers were also shot and killed by men from their same unit, and British Javelin antitank missiles killed two Danish soldiers during an operation in Helmand Province. On July 9, 2008, nine British soldiers were wounded during patrol when a British helicopter fired on them.

The so-called Black Hawk Incident was the most costly single incident of friendly fire during U.S. and coalition operations in Iraq. It occurred during Operation PROVIDE COMFORT—the effort to protect the Kurds of northern Iraq from Iraqi military attack. On April 14, 1994, two U.S. Air Force F-15s mistakenly identified two U.S. Army UH-60 Black Hawk helicopters flying over the northern part of the country as Iraqi Mil Mi-24 Hind helicopters and shot them down. The attack killed all 26 U.S., British, French, Turkish, and Kurdish military personnel and civilians aboard.

During the Iraq War (Operation IRAQI FREEDOM), U.S. aircraft attacked Kurdish and U.S. special forces, killing 15 people, including a British Broadcasting Corporation reporter. As the result of a design flaw, which rendered missile operators unable to identify friendly aircraft, a Patriot missile downed a Lockheed F-18 Hornet aircraft near Karbala, killing the pilot. Another Patriot shot down a British Panavia Tornado, killing its 2-man crew.

In fighting at Nasiriyah on March 23, 2003, an A-10 Warthog supporting the ground effort there attacked marines on the north side of a bridge after mistaking them for Iraqis, killing six. Among other incidents, an American air strike killed eight Kurdish soldiers, and a British Challenger II tank came under fire from another British tank during a nighttime battle; the Challenger's turret was blown off, and two crew members were killed.

The incidents related above demonstrate only friendly forces firing against their own side and do not include the numerous casualties inflicted by mistake on noncombatants.

STEVEN FRED MARIN AND SPENCER C. TUCKER

See also

Casualties, Operation ENDURING FREEDOM; Casualties, Operation IRAQI FREEDOM; Tillman, Patrick Daniel

References

Friedman, Norman. *Desert Victory: The War for Kuwait.* Annapolis, MD: Naval Institute Press, 1991.

Kirke, Charles M., ed. *Fratricide in Battle: (Un)Friendly Fire.* New York: Continuum International Publishing Group, 2012.

Regan, Geoffrey. *Blue on Blue: A History of Friendly Fire.* New York: Avon Books, 1995.

Regan, Geoffrey. *More Military Blunders.* London: Carlton, 2004.

Fuchs M93A1 NBC Vehicle

Military reconnaissance armored personnel vehicle designed to detect and protect its crew against nuclear, biological, or chemical (NBC) materials on a battlefield and other areas of military activity. Until 1989 or so, the U.S. military focused on countering the Soviet threat, especially in Central and Western Europe. Soviet use of chemical and biological weapons was never discounted, but following the 1973 Yom Kippur (Ramadan) War, that threat was reassessed. During the Yom Kippur War, Israel captured many Soviet armored vehicles that had the capacity of operating in a chemical environment without the crew being encumbered by unwieldy protection suits and filtering masks. Because these same weapons were designed for use in a war in Europe, the conclusion was that Soviet military doctrine included use of offensive chemical agents, requiring protection for Soviet forces passing through already contaminated areas.

The result of these findings was a program begun in the 1980s to develop a reconnaissance vehicle that would detect, identify, and provide warning to friendly forces of chemical contamination as well as the hazards of biological agents and radiological contamination. The U.S. Chemical Corps had responsibility for this program.

The Fuchs (Fox) M93 NBC Vehicle. Built in Germany, both the United States and Great Britain purchased the Fuchs, which is employed to detect nuclear, biological, and chemical contamination on the battlefield. (U.S. Department of Defense)

In 1979 the Federal Republic of Germany fielded a new armored personnel carrier (APC), the Tpzl (Transportpanzer1) Fuchs. This vehicle was a successor to the 1960s-era American M-113 tracked APC. The Fuchs, known in the United States as the Fox, was a wheeled vehicle manufactured by Thyssen-Henschel. The original Fox had a crew of 2 and could carry 10 soldiers, the same capacity of the tracked M-113. Like the M-113, the Fox could serve as a platform for a wide range of military needs. West Germany had already configured the Fox as an NBC reconnaissance vehicle.

The U.S. Army, as the lead agency for NBC defense, decided to explore the use of the M-113 or the Fox as a platform upon which to build an NBC reconnaissance vehicle to identify and mark hazards from weapons of mass destruction (WMD). In September 1986 the army began a program to lease 48 German Fox vehicles and in October cancelled the M-113 program. Negotiations with the Germans led to an agreement in March 1990 for General Dynamics to manufacture the Fox in the United States. Until it could be

type classified, the Fox was identified as the XM-93 Fox NBC Reconnaissance Vehicle.

The XM-93 required a four-man crew. It was a 6-by-6 wheeled vehicle with sloped armor and featured six-wheel drive, with the forward four wheels providing steering. It weighed 37,400 pounds and measured 22.2 feet long, 9.74 feet wide, and 8 feet high. It had an overpressure system that allowed the crew to operate in a contaminated area without being encumbered by bulky NBC protective suits and masks. The Mercedes-Benz–built eight-cylinder diesel engine provided 320 horsepower to propel the vehicle at speeds of up to 65.2 miles per hour and up a 60 percent slope. It had armor to protect against small-arms fire of up to 14.5 millimeters as well as mine protection. It was amphibious at a speed of 6.2 miles per hour and had a maximum range of 497 miles.

The Fox featured a chemical mass spectrometer programmed to identify a wide range of chemical hazards and a remote marking device that could mark the hazards. Radiological detection equipment allowed the crew to identify and mark radiological hazards. There was no capability to identify biological hazards, but the overpressure system provided crew protection.

After August 1990 when Iraq invaded Kuwait, the XM-93 moved from the regular pace of research, development, testing, and fielding to a high-priority item for immediate use. It became evident that the United States would deploy forces to the Persian Gulf to contain the Iraqis and potentially expel them from Kuwait. Iraq had used chemical weapons in its war with Iran from 1980 to 1988 and had also employed them against its own Kurdish population.

The XN-93 first entered service in Operation DESERT SHIELD when the 24th Infantry Division received 2 of them. Eventually the Germans provided 60 of these vehicles. All were "Americanized" and equipped with air-conditioning for operation in the heat of the Persian Gulf. The German NBC School at Sondhofen also translated operating manuals and trained eight U.S. Army and U.S. Marine Corps platoons. By the start of Operation DESERT STORM in January 1991, there were about 40 Fox vehicles in the theater, a number that increased to 61 by the end of hostilities in February.

The XM-93 performed reasonably well, but the rapid deployment did lead to problems. Among these were a lack of a doctrine regarding its use; overestimation of its capabilities to detect chemical vapors while the vehicle moved faster than five miles per hour, a lack of time to train operators fully and to test their performance before deployment, a Vehicle Orientation System that was not useful in off-road operations over long distances, problems with the sampling wheel in off-road conditions, and false alarms caused by diesel fuel, smoke from burning oil fields, and vehicle exhaust.

These shortcomings were addressed in the development of the NBC Reconnaissance Vehicle, which in 1998 entered into service as the M-93A1 Fox. The M-93A1, of which there are currently more than 120 in the U.S.

military, features more automated chemical and radiological equipment that reduces the crew requirement to three. The M-21 remote sensing chemical alarm allows 180-degree rotation, and there is a monitor for the vehicle commander that provides either the screen from the MM-1 mass spectrometer or the M-21's aiming camera. A separate screen is provided to the crew member operating the MM-1 in the rear of the vehicle. There is a Global Positioning System (GPS) that more accurately locates the vehicle and allows precise marking of hazards. This, along with the communications system in the new vehicle, provides automatic production and broadcast of NBC warning reports. The M-93A1 is manufactured in both the United States, by General Dynamics, and Germany, by Thyssen Henschel. Other North Atlantic Treaty Organization countries as well as several nations in the Middle East have acquired the M-93A1. Research is ongoing to add a credible biological weapons detection capability.

DANIEL E. SPECTOR

See also

Biological Weapons and Warfare; Chemical Weapons and Warfare; Weapons of Mass Destruction

References

Cordesman, Anthony H., and Abraham R. Wagner. *The Lessons of Modern War,* Vol. 4, *The Gulf War.* Boulder, CO: Westview, 1996.

Hogg, Ian V. *The Greenhill Armoured Fighting Vehicles Data Book.* London: Greenhill Books, 2002.

Spector, Daniel E. *U.S. Army Chemical School Annual Historical Review: 1 January through 31 December 1990.* Fort McClellan, AL: U.S. Army Chemical School, 1991.

Spector, Daniel E. *U.S. Army Chemical School Annual Historical Review: 1 January through 31 December 1991.* Fort McClellan, AL: U.S. Army Chemical School, 1992.

Spector, Daniel E. *U.S. Army Chemical School Annual Historical Review: 1 January through 31 December 1992.* Fort McClellan, AL: U.S. Army Chemical School, 1993.

G

Gadahn, Adam Yahya (1978–)

American citizen indicted in absentia in October 2006 by a U.S. federal court for treason, providing material support to the Al Qaeda terrorist organization, and aiding and abetting terrorists because of his ties to Al Qaeda. Gadahn reportedly has worked as a translator and a media adviser for Al Qaeda, possibly attended an Al Qaeda training camp, and acted as a spokesman and propagandist for the organization.

Adam Yahya Gadahn—also known as or referred to as Abu Suhayb al-Amriki, Abu Suhayl al-Amriki, Abu Suhayb, and Azzam al-Amriki (meaning "Azzam the American")—was born Adam Pearlman in Oregon on September 1, 1978. His father, born Jewish, had become a Christian before his son's birth and changed his last name to Gadahn. Adam spent his early life on a goat farm in rural Winchester, California. Home-schooled by his parents, he moved in with his grandparents as an adolescent in Santa Ana, California, and became a Muslim during a period of involvement with the Islamic Society of Orange County. In the late 1990s he left the United States for Pakistan, maintaining intermittent contact with his family until 2001.

By early 2004 Gadahn was wanted by the Federal Bureau of Investigation (FBI) for questioning. He appeared in his first Al Qaeda video that October. He is believed to have remained in Pakistan until at least 2010.

The 2006 indictment in *U.S. v. Gadahn* cites excerpts from Gadahn's videos as evidence of his crimes, including his declaration of membership in Al Qaeda, which he describes as "a movement waging war on America and killing large numbers of Americans," on October 27, 2004; his warning of attacks on Los Angeles and Melbourne, on September 11, 2005; his admonition to Muslims on July 7, 2006, that they should not "shed" any "tears" over attacks on Western targets; his lament on September 2, 2006, about the state of America's "war machine"; and his reflection on September 11, 2006, about the September 11, 2001, terror attacks, in which he refers to the United States as "enemy soil." After the indictment, Gadahn continued to appear in more videos. On May 29, 2007, he referenced the shooting massacre at Virginia Tech, which occurred on April 16, 2007, and intimated that Al Qaeda had even grislier plans. On January 7, 2008, he urged attacks on President George W. Bush during the president's visit to the Middle East. In August 2013, Gadahn released a video calling for attacks against U.S. embassies around the world; that exhortation prompted the Barack Obama administration to temporarily close a number of American embassies. Gadahn released an audio tape in late December 2013, at which time he denounced the capture of Al Qaeda operative Anas al-Libi.

In early 2008 Internet rumors began to circulate that Gadahn had died in the Central Intelligence Agency Predator strike that killed Abu Laith al-Libi. The FBI was unable to confirm or deny these reports and intensified its efforts to gather intelligence on Gadahn's whereabouts. Suspicions of Gadahn's death were reinvigorated in September 2008, when he failed to release a video marking the anniversary of 9/11; however, in early October he appeared in a message focusing on the U.S. relationship with Pakistan and the American economic crisis. Through 2014 there had been several other reports of Gadahn's death or capture, but none had been confirmed.

Gadahn's primary service to Al Qaeda has been as a propagandist, whether by conveying Al Qaeda's official messages in English; providing Arabic-to-English translations for others' messages, including perhaps those of Al Qaeda leader Osama bin Laden; or capitalizing on his status as an American convert to their cause. He remains high on the FBI's list of most wanted terrorists. Gadahn is the first American to be charged with treason since World War II, and he remains the only person currently charged with this capital crime. Even John Walker Lindh, an American captured in Afghanistan during the 2001 invasion of that nation, was charged with less serious crimes.

Despite the gravity of the charges against Gadahn, most observers contend that they are largely symbolic, citing significant obstacles to capturing and prosecuting him. Although Gadahn has not been implicated in any violence against Americans, his actions underscore the importance of media in the Global War on Terror and the difficulty in controlling it.

REBECCA ADELMAN

See also

Al Qaeda; Bin Laden, Osama; Global War on Terror; Terrorism

References

"Adam Gadahn Calls for Attacks on U.S. Diplomats." CNN, August 19, 2013, http://www.cnn.com/2013/08/19/politics/adam-gadahn-ambassador-attack-video/.

Greenberg, Karen J., ed. *Al Qaeda Now: Understanding Today's Terrorists.* Cambridge: Cambridge University Press, 2005.

Stern, Jessica. "Al Qaeda, American Style." *New York Times,* July 15, 2006, A:15.

Garner, Jay Montgomery (1938–)

U.S. Army general who, after retirement from active duty, in 2003 served as the first civilian director of the Office for Reconstruction and Humanitarian Assistance (ORHA) for Iraq. Jay Montgomery Garner was born on April 15, 1938, in Arcadia, Florida. After service in the U.S. Marine Corps, he earned a degree in history from Florida State University and secured a commission in the army. He later earned a master's degree from Shippensburg University in Pennsylvania.

Garner rose steadily through the ranks, holding a series of commands in the United States and in Germany and

Retired U.S. Army general Jay Garner, named by U.S. president George W. Bush as director of the Office of Reconstruction and Humanitarian Assistance in Iraq following the overthrow of Iraqi president Saddam Hussein. (U.S. Department of Defense)

rising to major general by the time of the Persian Gulf War (Operation DESERT STORM) in 1991. Garner helped develop the Patriot antimissile system and oversaw the deployment of Patriot batteries in Saudi Arabia and Israel during the Persian Gulf War. Garner subsequently managed efforts to improve the Patriot systems and to finalize and deploy the joint U.S.-Israeli Arrow theater antiballistic missile systems. He also worked with Israel, Kuwait, and Saudi Arabia on the sale of the Patriot system. Garner next commanded Operation PROVIDE COMFORT, the coalition effort to provide humanitarian assistance to Kurds in northern Iraq. He directed international forces that included U.S., British, French, and Italian troops in the delivery of food, medicine, and other supplies and in efforts to prevent reprisals by Iraqi government forces. Garner was subsequently named to command the U.S. Space and Strategic Defense Command.

Garner retired in 1997 as a lieutenant general and assistant vice chief of staff of the army. In September 1997 he was named president of SY Technology, a defense contractor, and he served on a variety of advisory boards on security issues, including the Commission to Assess United States National Security Space Management and Organization.

In March 2003 Garner was named head of ORHA for the Coalition Provisional Authority of Iraq, to coincide with Operation IRAQI FREEDOM and the allied postwar occupation. In this post, Garner was the senior civilian official during the initial period after the overthrow of Saddam Hussein in April 2003. Garner reported directly to the U.S. military commander in Iraq, General Tommy Franks. Garner's previous service in the region and work during Operation PROVIDE COMFORT made him an attractive candidate for the position, and the George W. Bush administration hoped that he would be able to integrate civilian and military occupation efforts in Iraq.

Garner's occupation strategy emphasized a quick turnover of appropriate authority to the Iraqis and a withdrawal of U.S. and coalition forces to protected bases outside of major urban areas. He also advocated early elections to create an interim Iraqi government with widespread popular legitimacy. Senior defense officials opposed his plans, however, and argued that too rapid a withdrawal of coalition forces would create a power vacuum and might lead to increased sectarian strife. U.S. officials also sought to ensure that former political and military officials linked to Hussein's Baath Party would be purged from their positions (a policy known as de-Baathification). Meanwhile, Garner's status as a former general and his close ties to Secretary of Defense Donald Rumsfeld undermined his ability to work with nongovernmental organizations and non-U.S. officials. Both groups saw him as an indication that the United States was not committed to democratic reform in Iraq.

Garner was confronted with a range of challenges. There was a growing insurgency being waged by Hussein loyalists and foreign fighters, and the country's infrastructure was in worse condition than anticipated as a result of the international sanctions of the 1990s, coalition military action, and a scorched-earth policy carried out by the former regime to deny assets to the invading forces. As a result, Garner was unable to restore basic services in a timely manner.

After initially dismissing the nation's security forces, Garner recalled policemen and initiated a new recruitment and screening process to expedite both the return of former police officers without close ties to the regime and the hiring of new officers. This was part of a broader effort to counter growing lawlessness in major cities, such as Baghdad. Garner also made the initial Iraqi appointments to various ministries as part of the foundation of a transitional government.

Garner was critical of the failure of the United Nations to immediately end sanctions on Iraq, and he called for the world body to act quickly to facilitate economic redevelopment and the rebuilding of the country's oil-producing infrastructure. Nevertheless, the blunt and plainspoken Garner faced increasing criticism for the deteriorating conditions in Iraq. He was replaced on May 11, 2003, by career diplomat L. Paul Bremer, who reported directly to Rumsfeld instead of to the coalition's military commander. Most members of Garner's senior staff were also replaced. Garner returned to the United States to work in the defense industry. He has remained largely silent on his short and tumultuous tenure in Iraq.

TOM LANSFORD

See also

Bremer, Lewis Paul; Iraq, History of, 1990–Present; IRAQI FREEDOM, Operation; Patriot Missile System; Rumsfeld, Donald

References

Allawi, Ali A. *The Occupation of Iraq: Winning the War, Losing the Peace.* New Haven, CT: Yale University Press, 2007.

Bremer, L. Paul, with Malcolm McConnell. *My Year in Iraq: The Struggle to Build a Future of Hope.* New York: Simon and Schuster, 2006.

Gates, Robert Michael (1943–)

U.S. Air Force officer, president of Texas A&M University, director of the Central Intelligence Agency (CIA), and secretary of defense from December 18, 2006, until July 1, 2011. Robert Michael Gates was born in Wichita, Kansas, on September 25, 1943. He graduated in 1965 from the College of William and Mary with a bachelor's degree in history, then earned a master's degree in history from Indiana University in 1966 and a PhD in Russian and Soviet history from Georgetown University in 1974.

Gates served as an officer in the U.S. Air Force's Strategic Air Command (1967–1969) before joining the CIA in 1969 as an intelligence analyst, a post he held until 1974. He was on the staff of the National Security Council from 1974 to 1979, before returning to the CIA as director of the Strategic Evaluation Center in 1979. Gates rose through the ranks to become the director of central intelligence/deputy director of central intelligence executive staff (1981), deputy director for intelligence (1982), and deputy director of central intelligence (1986–1989).

U.S. Secretary of Defense Robert Gates. President George W. Bush appointed Republican and former Central Intelligence Agency director Gates to replace the controversial Donald Rumsfeld as secretary of defense in 2006. New President Barack Obama continued Gates in the post, and he served until 2011. (U.S. Department of Defense)

Nominated to become director of the CIA in 1987, Gates withdrew his nomination when it appeared that his connection with the Iran Contra Affair might hamper his Senate confirmation. He then served as deputy assistant to the president for national security affairs (March–August 1989) and as assistant to the president and deputy national security adviser from August 1989 to November 1991.

The Iran Contra Affair erupted in 1987 when it was revealed that members of President Ronald Reagan's administration had sold weapons to Iran and illegally diverted the funds to the Nicaraguan Contras, the rightist anti-Sandinista rebels. Gates's political enemies assumed that he was guilty because of his senior status at the CIA, but an exhaustive investigation by an independent counsel determined that Gates had done nothing illegal, and on September 3, 1991, the investigating committee stated that Gates's involvement in the scandal did not warrant prosecution. The independent counsel's final 1993 report came to the same conclusion. In May 1991 President George H. W. Bush renominated Gates to head the CIA, and the Senate confirmed Gates on November 5, 1991.

Gates retired from the CIA in 1993 and entered academia. He also served as a member of the Board of Visitors of the University of Oklahoma International Programs Center, and as an endowment fund trustee for the College of William and Mary. In 1999 he became the interim dean of the George Bush School of Government and Public Service at Texas A&M University, and in 2002 he became president of Texas A&M University, a post he held until 2006.

Gates remained active in public service during his presidency, cochairing in January 2004 a Council on Foreign Relations task force on U.S.-Iran relations, which suggested that the United States engage Iran diplomatically concerning that nation's pursuit of nuclear weapons. Gates was a member of the Iraq Study Group (March 15, 2006–December 6, 2006), also known as the Baker-Hamilton Commission, a bipartisan commission charged with studying the Iraq War, when he was nominated to succeed the controversial and discredited Donald Rumsfeld as defense secretary. Gates assumed the post on December 18, 2006.

In addition to the challenges of the Iraq War, Gates was faced in February 2007 with a scandal concerning inadequate and neglectful care of returning veterans by Walter Reed Army Medical Center. In response, he removed both Secretary of the Army Francis J. Harvey and U.S. Army surgeon general Kevin C. Kiley from their posts. Gates further tightened his control of the Pentagon when he did not recommend the renomination of U.S. Marine Corps general Peter Pace as chairman of the Joint Chiefs of Staff that June. Pace would have certainly faced tough questioning by Congress. It was also Gates's job to implement the so-called troop surge initiated by Bush in January 2007.

In March 2008 Gates accepted the resignation of Admiral William Joseph "Fox" Fallon, commander of the U.S. Central Command, a departure that was due in part to the controversy surrounding an article by Thomas P. M. Barnett titled "The Man between War and Peace," published in *Esquire* magazine on March 11, 2008. The article asserted policy disagreements between Fallon and the Bush administration on the prosecution of the war in Iraq and potential conflict with Iran over that nation's nuclear arms program. Gates rejected any suggestion that Fallon's resignation indicated a U.S. willingness to attack Iran in order to stop its nuclear weapons development.

Unlike his abrasive predecessor, Gates brought an era of calm and focus to the Pentagon and was far more willing to engage in discussion and compromise over matters of defense and military policy. In April 2009 Gates proposed a major reorientation in the U.S. defense budget, which would entail deep cuts in more traditional programs that provide for conventional warfare with such major military powers as Russia and China, and shift assets to those programs that would aid in fighting the insurgencies in both Iraq and Afghanistan. Among his proposed cuts were missile defense, the army's Future Combat Systems, navy shipbuilding, new presidential helicopters, and a new communications satellite system. Gates would delay development of a new air force bomber and order only 4 additional F-22 fighters, for a total of 197, while purchasing as many as 513 of the less expensive F-35 strike fighters over the next five years. Purchases of large navy ships would be delayed. At the same time, the new budget would provide for a sharp increase in funding for surveillance and intelligence-gathering equipment, to include the Predator-class unmanned aerial vehicles, and increase manpower in the army to include special forces and the U.S. Marine Corps. These decisions triggered major debate in Congress over defense spending and priorities.

Although Gates had been looking forward to leaving the Pentagon at the end of Bush's administration (he kept a countdown timer in his briefcase), he agreed to stay on as defense secretary in the new Barack Obama administration, which took office in January 2009. Some questioned the choice because Obama had been a vocal critic of the Iraq War during his 2008 presidential campaign, but others saw the choice as a smart bipartisan move, as Gates had support on both sides of the aisle in Congress. Gates also agreed with Obama on key matters, including the need to reduce the number of U.S. troops in Iraq as soon as practical. Obama advisers also noted that with the country fighting two wars, keeping Gates on was a way of maintaining stability during a time of significant transition in the executive branch. Because he already held the position, Gates did not have to be confirmed by the Senate. In December 2009 Gates was the first senior U.S. official to visit Afghanistan after President Obama announced his intention to deploy 30,000 additional military personnel to that country.

On July 1, 2011, Secretary of Defense Gates voluntarily stepped down and was replaced by Leon Panetta. At his retirement ceremony President Obama presented Gates with the Presidential Medal of Freedom for his 40-year career in the intelligence services and the Pentagon.

On February 3, 2012, Gates became the chancellor of the College of William and Mary in Williamsburg, Virginia. He has also served on the board of directors of several companies, including Starbucks. In January 2014 Gates's memoir, *Duty: Memoirs of a Secretary at War,* created controversy because in it he criticized President Obama's approach to the war in Afghanistan. Gates suggested that Obama was not entirely sold on the troop surge strategy his administration implemented in Afghanistan during 2010–2012, writing that "I never doubted [his] support for the troops, only his support for their mission."

RICHARD M. EDWARDS

See also

Afghanistan War; Bush, George Walker; Central Intelligence Agency; Fallon, William Joseph; IRAQI FREEDOM, Operation; Iraq Study Group; National Security Council; Obama, Barack Hussein, II; Pace, Peter; Rumsfeld, Donald

References

Barnett, Thomas P. M. "The Man between War and Peace." *Esquire,* March 11, 2008, 1–4.

Gates, Robert M. *Duty: Memoirs of a Secretary at War.* New York: Knopf, 2014.

Gates, Robert M. *From the Shadows: The Ultimate Insider's Story of Five Presidents and How They Won the Cold War.* New York: Simon and Schuster, 1996.

Gates, Robert M. *Understanding the New U.S. Defense Policy through the Speeches of Robert M. Gates, Secretary of Defense.* Rockville, MD: Arc Manor, 2008.

Oliphant, Thomas. *Utter Incompetents: Ego and Ideology in the Age of Bush.* New York: Thomas Dunne Books, 2007.

Gays in the U.S. Military

From the early 1990s until 2011, the issue of whether or not gays and lesbians should be permitted to serve as members of the American military establishment remained a thorny and contentious issue. The matter was not definitely settled until September 20, 2011, at which time the ban on openly gays and lesbians from serving in the military was finally lifted. During that nearly two-decade period, there was a sea change in Americans' tolerance of and support for gay rights in general, which has now come to include increasing support for same-sex marriages. When the ban was lifted in 2011, the United States joined a host of other mainly Western, industrialized nations that had already permitted gays to serve in their militaries. Israel, South Africa, Brazil, and South Korea also maintained similar policies prior to 2011.

Homosexuals were not specifically singled out in the U.S. military establishment until 1942, when U.S. Army regulations were revised for World War II. The other service branches adopted virtually the same guidelines, which forbade homosexuals from serving in the military and made homosexual acts committed by service personnel punishable offenses. Upon discovery, most gays at that time were quietly discharged. New regulations adopted in 1944 and

1947 further solidified the ban on gays and lesbians, and thereafter homosexuals were routinely and summarily discharged from the armed services regardless of whether or not they had engaged in any homosexual activity. These regulations remained in place until the early 1990s.

Meanwhile, changing social mores and the rise of the gay rights movement beginning in the late 1960s led some Americans to question the continuation of an apartheid-like system based on sexual orientation. Nevertheless, in the early 1980s the U.S. Department of Defense reconfirmed the ban on gays and lesbians in the military, asserting that homosexuality was "incompatible" with military service. This stance prevailed until the 1992 presidential election, when the issue first became a major item.

During the 1992 election, all of the Democratic presidential candidates vying for their party's nomination supported lifting the ban on military service by gays and lesbians. The Republican candidates demurred and did not choose to state a precise position on the ban. While campaigning, Democratic presidential candidate Bill Clinton pledged to lift the ban on gays and lesbians if elected, thus garnering considerable support from the lesbian, gay, bisexual, and transgender (LGBT) community. Once Clinton took office in 1993, however, he was stymied by considerable opposition to such a move within the military establishment and from among the majority of Americans.

After a bruising political battle, the best the Clinton administration could do was to institute the so-called "Don't Ask, Don't Tell" (DADT) policy, which became official via a Defense Department directive on December 21, 1993. DADT took full effect on February 28, 1994. The directive disappointed many of Clinton's LGBT supporters and was far from popular within the armed services. In sum, DADT prohibited homosexuals or bisexuals serving in the military from disclosing their sexual orientation to any member of the armed services. If there was such a disclosure or if homosexual activities were made known, discharge from the military would ensue. DADT prohibited military superiors from asking military personnel about their sexual orientation or activities and prohibited superiors from investigating personnel unless disallowed behavior had been personally witnessed. DADT was far from ideal and was flawed in any number of ways, but it at least provided a way in which gays and lesbians could serve honorably without being summarily dismissed simply because of their sexual orientation.

The issue remained largely off the radar until the summer of 1999, when U.S. Army private first class Barry Winchell was murdered by a fellow soldier while on active duty because of Winchell's alleged sexual orientation. The murder was precipitated by rampant antigay discrimination in some military outfits and promptly became headline news. Shortly thereafter, President Clinton signed an executive order permitting evidence of a hate crime to be admitted to the record during the sentencing phase of military trials. Winchell's death reinvigorated the debate to gays in the military.

In 2001, 1,273 military personnel were given discharges under the DADT guidelines. This represented the peak of such discharges. During the next decade as the United States became embroiled in major wars in Afghanistan and Iraq, the number of discharges dwindled steadily. There were several reasons for this. First, the wars placed a great strain on America's military resources, and efforts were taken to strengthen recruitment and retention efforts in order to maintain the desired number of active-duty personnel. Second, antigay bias within the military began to wane, and military commanders stepped up their efforts to discourage such biases. Third, Americans became increasingly more supportive of LGBT issues and rights.

The election of Barack Obama as president in November 2008 provided the impetus for a major change in military policy vis-à-vis gays and lesbians. Like Clinton before him, President Obama vowed to open up military service to all Americans, regardless of sexual orientation. In early 2010, the White House and congressional leaders began to formulate a repeal of the gay and lesbian ban, which would be part of the 2011 defense authorization bill. On January 27, Obama announced in his State of the Union address that he would work with the Pentagon and Congress to craft new legislation and set a timetable for the repeal of DADT.

During 2010, the Defense Department and the Joint Chiefs of Staff undertook a major effort designed to establish a blueprint for a postrepeal military establishment. That report was completed on November 30, 2010, and detailed a specific timetable for the repeal of DADT. The report was quickly embraced by Secretary of Defense Robert M. Gates, who urged its prompt implementation. Following congressional hearings, the Senate voted to repeal DADT on December 18. President Obama signed the measure into law on December 22; it became effective on September 20, 2011.

There have been virtually no negative ramifications of the repeal of DADT, and on September 30, 2011, the Pentagon announced that military chaplains would be permitted to perform same-sex marriages of active-duty service members wherever local laws allowed. In July 2012, the Pentagon allowed military personnel to wear their uniforms while participating in a Gay Pride parade in San Diego. That marked the first time uniforms were permitted at such a venue. Although some Republican presidential candidates called for the reinstatement of DADT during the 2012 election, the new regulations now in place are unlikely to be overturned, and all indications suggest that the military establishment has continued to work well under them.

PAUL G. PIERPAOLI JR.

See also

Bush, George Walker; Clinton, William Jefferson; Gates, Robert Michael; Obama, Barack Hussein, II

References

Frank, Nathaniel. "The President's Pleasant Surprise: How LGBT Advocates Ended Don't Ask, Don't Tell." *Journal of Homosexuality* 60(2–3) (2013): 159–213.

Miller, Debra A., ed. *Gays in the Military*. Detroit: Greenhaven, 2012.

Rimmerman, Craig A. *Gay Rights, Military Wrongs Political Perspectives on Lesbians and Gays in the Military*. Hoboken, NJ: Taylor and Francis, 2013.

Ghani, Ashraf (1949–)

Afghan academic, diplomat, and politician who assumed office as president of Afghanistan on September 29, 2014. Ghani Ashraf was born in Logar Province, Afghanistan, on February 12, 1949. An ethnic Pastun, he is from the Ahmadzai tribe. After earning a bachelor's degree from the American University in Beirut in 1973, Ghani taught anthropology at Kabul University until 1977. He then went to the United States to pursue graduate studies in cultural anthropology at Columbia University. He subsequently taught at the University of California, Berkeley (1983), and Johns Hopkins University (1983–1991).

In 1991 Ghani took a position with the World Bank, where he built a reputation as an expert on economic development projects and institutional reform in East and South Asia as well as Russia. After the September 11, 2001, terror attacks on the United States, he left the World Bank and became a regular fixture on U.S. and Western news channels, including CNN, PBS, NPR, and the BBC. In early December 2001 after the fall of the Taliban regime, Ghani returned to Afghanistan for the first time in 24 years. He promptly agreed to serve as an adviser to Hamid Karzai, then interim president. Later, Ghani helped convene *loya jirgas* (grand assemblies) to pave the way for the drafting of the new Afghan Constitution, which was approved in 2004.

From June 2, 2002, until December 14, 2004, Ghani served as Afghanistan's finance minister. He also served as a special adviser to the United Nations mission in Afghanistan. As minister of finance, Ghani faced the daunting task of rebuilding his war-torn country and improving its moribund economy. In December 2004, he informed President Karzai that he would prefer to serve as chancellor of Kabul University, a position that better suited his temperament and academic background. Ghani remained in that post until December 21, 2008.

A political independent and a quintessential centrist, Ghani soon became involved in electoral politics. Frustrated with Karzai's inability to quash the renewed insurgency in Afghanistan or to bring unity to the country, Ghani decided to run for the presidency in the 2009 elections. He placed fourth in the polling, however, and Karzai was reelected.

Ghani subsequently refocused his attention on the Institute for State Effectiveness, an organization he cofounded in 2005 that focuses on helping nations better serve their citizens and advises governments that are in danger of becoming failed states.

Ghani again ran for the Afghan presidency in 2014. By then Karzai, who was constitutionally barred from seeking another term, was unpopular at home and abroad. And he had a particularly contentious relationship with the United States. It was clear that Afghanistan needed a fresh start with a president who could bring some semblance of unity to the country. In the first round of voting held on April 5, Ghani captured 31.5 percent of the vote; his main challenger, Abdullah Abdullah, took 45 percent. Because neither candidate received 50 or more percent of the vote, a run-off election was scheduled for June 14. In that balloting, it was announced that Ghani received slightly more than 56 percent of the vote, but there were persistent allegations of massive voting irregularities and electoral fraud. This plunged Afghanistan into a constitutional crisis as both Ghani's and Abdullah's supporters jockeyed for influence.

The electoral stalemate threatened to plunge Afghanistan into considerable turmoil, but in August 2014 U.S. secretary of state John F. Kerry brokered a deal that resulted in a detailed recount of some 8 million votes. The agreement also created the post of chief executive, which would function as Afghanistan's premiership. By mid-September the recount was complete, and Ghani maintained a comfortable edge over Abdullah. Ghani then agreed to form a unity government in which he would serve as president and Abdullah would serve as prime minister.

Ghani took office on September 29, 2014. He has pledged to bring unity to Afghanistan, promote economic development, strengthen the military, and defend his nation from Islamic extremists. On September 30 Ghani signed a status of forces agreement with the United States, which Karzai had steadfastly refused to do even after he had negotiated it and the Afghan parliament had approved it. The agreement guarantees the continued presence of about 14,000 troops (9,800 of them American) in Afghanistan after December 31, 2014, for at least an additional year if not longer.

PAUL G. PIERPAOLI JR.

See also

Abdullah, Abdullah; Afghanistan War; Karzai, Hamid; Kerry, John Forbes; *Loya Jirga,* Afghanistan; Status of Forces Agreement, U.S.-Afghan

References

Barfield, Thomas. *Afghanistan: A Cultural and Political History.* Princeton, NJ: Princeton University Press, 2012.

"Ghani Is Sworn in as Afghan President." *Wall Street Journal,* September 29, 2014, http://online.wsj.com/articles/ghani -sworn-in-as-afghan-president-1411974821.

Ghilzai Tribe

The largest and best-known Afghan tribe, a subset of the predominant Pashtun tribe. Also known as Khiljis or Ghaljis, the Ghilzais are located mainly in the southeastern portion of Afghanistan, roughly between Ghazni and Kandahar. There are also large numbers to be found in western Pakistan and the Suleiman Mountains. In the last several decades, they have staunchly opposed Durrani-led Afghan governments and supported the Taliban regime before it was toppled by U.S.-led forces in late 2001.

Although the Ghilzais' precise origins are uncertain, some ethnologists believe that they are descended from Turkish bloodlines and can trace that relationship to at least the 10th century CE. Most Ghilzais speak Pashto and/or Dari, a form of Persian. By the early 18th century, the group had become ascendant in what is now Afghanistan, and Mirways Khan Hotak, a Ghilzai, ruled the region from 1709 to 1738. By the late 1800s, however, many Ghilzais had been driven into northern and eastern Afghanistan by the Durranis, which explains the continuing Ghilzai antipathy toward that group. In 1978 the Ghilzais were the major instigators of the revolt against Mohammad Daoud Khan's government, which triggered the Soviet intervention and occupation of Afghanistan that began the following year. Although the succeeding three rulers of Afghanistan, all backed by the

Kremlin, were Ghilzais, a large number of the mujahideen fighting the Soviet occupation were themselves Ghilzais. Historically the group has been nomadic, in opposition to its chief rival tribe, the Durranis, who tend to be sedentary.

During the 1990s while Afghanistan was convulsed by civil war after the Soviet withdrawal in 1989, the Ghilzais dominated the rising Taliban movement, which sought to institute an Islamic theocracy over Afghanistan. Indeed, Taliban leader and head of state Mullah Mohammed Omar was a member of the Ghilzai tribe. Today, the Ghilzai population in Afghanistan is thought to number about 9 million, with an additional 1 million located in western Pakistan. They thus make up as much as one-quarter of the total Afghan population. Almost all Ghilzais adhere to Sunni Islam (of the Hanafi School), and most are devoutly religious. In present-day Afghanistan, the Ghilzais oppose the government of President Hamid Karzai, who is Durrani, and many are part of the resurgent insurgency movement attempting to topple the Afghan national government, rid the nation of Western (chiefly U.S.) influences, and reinstall a Taliban regime.

PAUL G. PIERPAOLI JR.

See also

Afghanistan; Karzai, Hamid; Omar, Mohammed; Taliban

References

Ewans, Martin. *Afghanistan: A Short History of Its History and Politics.* New York: Harper Perennial, 2002.

Tanner, Stephen. *Afghanistan: A Military History from Alexander the Great to the Fall of the Taliban.* New York: Da Capo, 2003.

Giuliani, Rudolph William Louis, III (1944–)

Attorney, Republican politician, and mayor of New York City (1994–2001) who achieved worldwide fame for his actions in the immediate aftermath of the September 11, 2001, terror attacks. Rudolph William Louis "Rudy" Giuliani III was born on May 28, 1944, in Brooklyn, New York, to a working-class family. His collegiate years were spent at Manhattan College in the Bronx, from which he graduated in 1965. Next, Giuliani earned a law degree from New York University Law School in 1968. His first job was clerking for a U.S. district judge for the Southern District of New York.

The majority of Giuliani's career was spent in government service. His first position was with the Office of the U.S. Attorney in 1970. After stints as the chief of the narcotics unit and as executive U.S. attorney, he left for Washington, D.C., in 1975 to become the associate deputy attorney

New York City Mayor Rudolph W. L. "Rudy" Giuliani, right, shows the World Trade Center attack site to UN Secretary General Kofi Annan, center, and New York Governor George Pataki, left, on September 18, 2001, one week after the terrorist attack that destroyed the landmark Twin Towers. (AP Photo)

general and chief of staff to the deputy attorney general. Giuliani briefly left government service in 1977 to practice law privately. Then in 1981 the Ronald Reagan administration recruited Giuliani to the office of associate attorney general. Giuliani was subsequently appointed the U.S. attorney for the Southern District of New York and earned a reputation for tackling tough high-profile cases.

Giuliani's law-and-order reputation ultimately led to his candidacy for mayor of New York. His first attempt as the Republican candidate was unsuccessful; he lost to David Dinkins in 1989 in a close race. Giuliani's second attempt in 1993, which featured a campaign that attacked crime and high taxes, was successful. He won reelection in 1997 by a large margin, and his administration ushered in a sizable reduction in crime. New York City's two-term limit for mayors meant that Giuliani could not run for a third term, but he remained mayor in September 2001.

Giuliani's political career received a major boost because of his role in the management of New York City in the aftermath of the September 11, 2001, attacks on the World Trade Center. His response immediately after the assault on the Twin Towers was to coordinate the response of various city departments, and he made quick contact with state and federal authorities. Giuliani made contact with President George W. Bush and received prompt assurances of federal aid. In the next new few weeks, Giuliani held meetings several times a day to coordinate aid and relief. He also worked closely with the fire commissioner, Thomas Von Essen, and the police commissioner, Bernard Kerik, on the activities at the World Trade Center site. Von Essen described the mayor's style as barking, pleading, commiserating, and questioning. At every meeting Giuliani demanded measurable progress on the situation from his subordinates. He was also present and often talked at ceremonies honoring the dead. Giuliani did run into some difficulty when he attempted to reduce the number of firefighters at the World Trade Center site, and he had to back down during a confrontation with fire officials that took place in early November 2001. This conflict made him furious, but he realized that he faced a growing public relations problem unless he compromised.

Because the scheduled date of the mayoral primary was September 11, that primary had to be rescheduled. Few people could make it to the polls on September 11 because the city had been all but closed down. Giuliani first sought an emergency override of the term-limit law, but this attempt ran into political opposition, as did his effort to have his term of office extended four months. He left the mayoral office on December 31, 2001.

Giuliani left office with a national reputation, and *Time* magazine named him its Person of the Year for 2001. Shortly after leaving office Giuliani founded a security consulting business, and he purchased the accounting firm Ernst & Young's investment banking unit, which he named Giuliani Capital Advisors LLC. He also traveled around the country making speeches. Giuliani campaigned vigorously for the reelection of President George W. Bush in 2004. Bush responded by inviting Giuliani to replace Tom Ridge as secretary of homeland security, but Giuliani turned down the offer. Then in March 2005 Giuliani joined the firm of Bracewell & Patterson LLP, which was promptly renamed Bracewell & Giuliani LLP. Giuliani has maintained his political contacts in the Republican Party, and he has constantly been advanced as a candidate for national office. In the meantime, he was appointed to Congress's Iraq Study Group. This group had the mission of assessing the military situation in Iraq.

Giuliani's role as a hero of September 11 has been challenged in more recent years. Much of the criticism has come from family members of the victims of September 11. The most vocal have been the families of firefighters. They have criticized Giuliani for separating the police and firefighter command posts on the morning of September 11 and for not holding emergency drills to check on communication equipment prior to the attacks.

Giuliani has continued to pursue a political career. In 2007 he announced his intention to seek the 2008 Republican presidential nomination. After low vote totals in the primaries, he dropped out of the presidential race on January 31, 2008. Giuliani has since remained in the business world and continues to give speeches and appear on television news programs.

STEPHEN E. ATKINS

See also

Iraq Study Group; September 11 Attacks; Terrorism

References

Barrett, Wayne, and Dan Collins. "The Real Rudy: The Image of Rudy Giuliani as the Hero of September 11 Has Never Been Seriously Challenged. That Changes Now." *American Prospect* 17 (September 1, 2006).

Newfield, Jack. *The Full Rudy: The Man, the Myth, the Mania.* New York: Thunder's Mouth, 2003.

Polner, Robert. *America's Mayor: The Hidden History of Rudy Giuliani's New York.* New York: Soft Skull, 2005.

Von Essen, Thomas, with Matt Murray. *Strong of Heart: Life and Death in the Fire Department of New York.* New York: Regan Books, 2002.

Global War on Terror

"Global War on Terror" is the term used to describe the military, political, diplomatic, and economic measures employed by the United States and other allied governments against individuals, organizations, and countries that are committing terrorist acts, might be inclined to engage in terrorism, or support those who do commit such acts. The Global War on Terror is an amorphous concept and a somewhat indistinct term, yet its use emphasizes the difficulty in classifying the type of nontraditional warfare being waged against U.S. and Western interests by various terrorist groups that do not represent any nation. The term was coined by President George W. Bush in a September 20, 2001, televised address to a joint session of the U.S. Congress and has been presented in official White House pronouncements, fact sheets, State of the Union messages, and such National Security Council position papers as the *National Security Strategy* (March 2006) and the *National Strategy for Combating Terrorism* (February 2003 and September 2006 editions).

Bush administration objectives in what became formally known as the Global War on Terror included the destruction of terrorist organizations such as Al Qaeda, denying state sponsorship of terrorist activities, working with other nations to create an antiterrorist network, and seeking to diminish conditions in states that terrorists are able to exploit. Although the war on terror was truly global and included operations as far flung as the Philippines, its centerpiece was the U.S.-led military intervention in Afghanistan.

Since 2001, the Global War on Terror has been directed primarily at Islamic terrorist groups but has also been expanded to include actions against all types of terrorism. During the Bush administration, Secretary of Defense Robert Gates also called it the "Long War." As with the Cold War, the Global War on Terror is being waged on numerous fronts against many individuals and nations and involves both military and nonmilitary tactics.

President Bush's announcement of the Global War on Terror was in response to the September 11, 2001, terror attacks against the United States, which led to the deaths of nearly 3,000 civilians, mostly Americans but representing civilians of 90 different countries.

Although the fight against terrorism constitutes a global effort, stretching into Asia, Africa, Europe, and the Americas, the Middle East remains a focal point. The ongoing conflict and the manner in which it has been waged has been the source of much debate. There is no widely agreed-upon estimate regarding the number of casualties during the Global War on Terror, because it includes the invasion of Afghanistan in 2001 and the war in Iraq as well as many acts of terrorism around the world. Some estimates, which include the U.S.-led coalition invasion of Afghanistan in 2001 and the invasion of Iraq in March 2003, claim that well over 2 million people have died in the struggle.

Following the September 11, 2001, terror attacks, the United States responded quickly and with overwhelming force against the organizations and governments that supported the terrorists. Evidence gathered by the U.S. government pointed to the Al Qaeda terrorist organization. Al Qaeda at the time was being given aid and shelter by the Taliban regime in Afghanistan. On September 20, 2001, President George W. Bush announced to a joint session of Congress that the Global War on Terror would not end simply with the defeat of Al Qaeda or the overthrow of the Taliban. "Our 'war on terror,'" he said, "begins with Al Qaeda, but it does not end there. It will not end until every terrorist group of global reach has been found, stopped, and defeated." These broad aims implied attacks on countries known to support terrorism, such as Iran and Syria. Bush further assured the American people that every means of intelligence, tool of diplomacy, financial pressure, and weapon of war would be used to defeat terrorism. He told the American people to expect a lengthy campaign. Bush also put down an ultimatum to every other nation, stating that each had to choose whether it was with or against the United States. There would be no middle ground. Clearly Bush's pronouncements were far-reaching, yet the enemies were difficult to identify and find.

Less than 24 hours after the September 11 attacks, the North Atlantic Treaty Organization (NATO) declared them to be against all member nations, the first time the organization had made such a pronouncement since its inception in 1949. Within a few weeks France, Great Britain, and other NATO members—including Turkey, Canada, New Zealand, and Australia—become part of an American-led antiterrorist coalition.

On October 7, 2001, U.S. and coalition forces (chiefly British) invaded Afghanistan to capture Osama bin Laden, the head of Al Qaeda, to destroy his organization and to overthrow the Taliban government that supported him. Eventually Canada, Australia, France, and Germany, among other nations, joined that effort. However, when a U.S.-led coalition invaded Iraq in March 2003, there was considerable international opposition to this campaign being included under the rubric of the Global War on Terror. One problem for national leaders who supported President Bush's policies was that many of their citizens did not believe that the overthrow of Iraqi dictator Saddam Hussein was really part of the Global War on Terror and questioned other reasons stated by the Bush administration to justify the U.S.-led invasion. International opinion polls have shown that support for the war on terror has consistently declined since 2003, likely the result of opposition to the Bush administration's preemptive invasion of Iraq in 2003 and later revelations that Iraq possessed neither ties to Al Qaeda nor weapons of mass destruction.

The Global War on Terror has also been a sporadic and clandestine effort since its inception in September 2001. U.S. forces were sent to Yemen and the Horn of Africa to disrupt terrorist activities, while Operation ACTIVE ENDEAVOR is a naval operation intended to prevent terror attacks and limit the movement of terrorists in the Mediterranean. Terrorist attacks in Pakistan, Indonesia, and the Philippines led to the insertion of coalition forces into these countries as well and concerns about the situation in other Southeast Asian countries. In the United States, Congress has also passed legislation intended to help increase the effectiveness of law enforcement agencies in their search for terrorist activities. In the process, however, critics claim that Americans' civil liberties have been steadily eroded, and government admissions that the Federal Bureau of Investigation and other agencies have engaged in wiretapping of international phone calls without requisite court orders and probable cause have caused a storm of controversy, as have the methods used to question foreign nationals.

The Bush administration also greatly increased the role of the federal government in the attempt to fight terrorism at home and abroad. Among the many new government bureaucracies formed was the Department of Homeland Security, a cabinet-level agency that counts at least 210,000 employees. The increase in the size of the government combined with huge military expenditures, most going to the Iraq War, added to the massive U.S. budget deficit.

Proponents of the Global War on Terror believe that proactive measures must be taken against terrorist organizations to effectively defeat global terrorism. They believe that in order to meet the diverse security challenges of the 21st century, a larger global military presence is needed. Without such a force, they argue, terrorist organizations will continue to launch strikes against innocent civilians. Many believe that the United States, Great Britain, Spain, and other countries, which have been the victims of large-scale attacks, must go on the offensive against such rogue groups and that not doing so will only embolden the attackers and invite more attacks. Allowing such organizations to gain more strength may allow them to achieve their goal of imposing militant Islamist rule.

Critics of the Global War on Terror claim that there is no tangible enemy to defeat, as there is no single group whose defeat will bring about an end to the conflict. Thus, it is virtually impossible to know if progress is being made. They also argue that terrorism, a tactic whose goal is to instill fear into people through violent actions, can never be truly defeated. There are also those who argue against the justification for preemptive strikes, because such action invites counterresponses and brings about the deaths of many innocent people. Many believe that the Iraqi military posed no imminent threat to the United States when coalition forces entered Iraq in 2003, but the resultant war has been disastrous for both the Iraqi and American people. Civil rights activists contend that measures meant to crack down on terrorist activities have infringed on the rights of American citizens as well as the rights of foreign detainees. Furthermore, critics argue that the war and the amount of spending apportioned to military endeavors negatively affects the national and world economies. Others argue that the United States should be spending time and resources on resolving the Arab-Israeli problem and trying to eradicate the desperate conditions that feed terrorism.

As support for the Global War on Terror effort has diminished, the debate over its effectiveness has grown. Terrorist attacks have continued, and the deliberation over the best way to ensure the safety of civilian populations around the world continues.

Barack Obama was sworn in as president in January 2009. His administration eschewed the terms "Global War on Terror" and "Long War" in defense fact sheets. Rather, U.S. government agencies were instructed to use the term "overseas contingency operations." Former White House press secretary Robert Gibbs explained that Obama was "using different words and phrases in order to denote a reaching out to many moderate parts of the world that we believe can be important in a battle against extremists."

However, the term "Global War on Terror" continued to be used, particularly in the media.

On May 1, 2011, the Global War on Terror reached a milestone of sorts with the killing of Osama bin Laden. After intelligence information suggested that bin Laden was in Abbottabad, Pakistan, Central Intelligence Agency (CIA) operatives and American military forces raided a compound at which he was staying. According to reports, bin Laden was killed in an ensuing firefight. President Obama addressed the nation to announce bin Laden's death, declaring that "justice has been done" but admonishing Americans to "remain vigilant at home and abroad."

In a much-anticipated speech at the National Defense University on May 23, 2013, President Obama said that it was time to narrow the scope of the grinding battle against terrorists and begin the transition to a day when the country would no longer be on a war footing. Declaring that "America is at a crossroads," the president called for redefining what had been a global war into a more targeted assault on terrorist groups threatening the United States. As part of a realignment of counterterrorism policy, he said that he would diminish the use of drone strikes, which have taken out a number of terrorist leaders but also killed many innocent civilians; recommit to closing the prison for terror suspects at Guantánamo Bay, Cuba; and seek new limits on presidential war powers, including for himself. The president suggested that the United States return to the state of affairs that existed before Al Qaeda toppled the World Trade Center, when terrorism was a persistent but not existential danger. With Al Qaeda's core now "on the path to defeat," he argued, the nation must adapt to new realities.

Nearly simultaneous with Obama's far-ranging speech were revelations by U.S. whistle-blower and former CIA and National Security Agency (NSA) employee Edward Snowden about the extent to which these agencies engaged in snooping on American citizens as well as friendly and adversarial governments abroad. Snowden's information suggested that the NSA had been keeping data logs of phone calls as well as Internet activity of millions of innocent U.S. citizens, all in the name of the Global War on Terror. These revelations seemed to undergird Obama's point that the conventional war on terror was becoming too costly and unwieldy.

GREGORY WAYNE MORGAN

See also

Al Qaeda; Bin Laden, Osama; Counterterrorism Strategy; Guantánamo Bay Detainment Camp; IRAQI FREEDOM, Operation; Obama, Barack Hussein, II; September 11 Attacks; Snowden,

Edward Joseph; Terrorism; United States Department of Homeland Security; Unmanned Aerial Vehicles; Yemen

References

Bacevich, Andrew J. *The New American Militarism: How Americans Are Seduced by War.* New York: Oxford University Press, 2005.

Mahajan, Rahul. *The New Crusade: America's War on Terrorism.* New York: Monthly Review, 2002.

Woodward, Bob. *Bush at War.* New York: Simon and Schuster, 2002.

Golden Mosque Bombing (February 22, 2006)

The Askariya shrine, also known as that Golden Dome Mosque, in Samarra, Iraq, is one of Shia Islam's most holy sites. The mosque holds the tombs of two ninth-century Shia imams, Hassan al-Askari and Muhammad al-Mahdi. On February 22, 2006, terrorists tied to Al Qaeda in Iraq bombed the mosque, destroying the golden dome as well the imams' tombs. This event unleashed a series of reprisal attacks on Sunnis in the Samarra area. The bombing of the mosque was the beginning of a sharp escalation in sectarian clashes in Iraq, which ultimately precipitated the U.S. military's troop surge strategy in 2007.

There were no fatalities in the actual attack; however, the day of the bombing, Shia and Sunni groups fought in Samarra. That sectarian fighting killed 20 people. The violence then spread throughout Iraq. The following day more than 100 people died in clashes, including several Sunni clerics. This began the most violent period of sectarian violence during the Iraq War. The terrorists who destroyed the dome disguised themselves in Iraqi military uniforms. They entered the shrine, subdued the guards, and then placed explosives in the dome.

In addition to housing the tombs of the two imams, the mosque was also the place where the Hidden Imam, a messianic figure in the Shia branch, left his followers in the ninth century. The golden dome, built in 1905, contained some 70,000 golden tiles. Many faithful believe that the Hidden Imam will return to the mosque and emerge from the crypt underneath the blue mosque that is next to the shrine. These religious figures and their association with the shrine and its adjacent mosque make this site key to Shia faith and identity. It has long been a place of pilgrimage and a vital part of Iraqi Shia culture.

The eight Al Qaeda in Iraq terrorists who executed the attack succeeded in their goal of instigating sectarian strife throughout Iraq. Although the violence began in Samarra with the burning of Sunni businesses, it soon engulfed the entire nation. By the end of 2006, more than 10,000 Iraqis had died as a result of the sectarian violence that began in Samarra. This violence was part of the reason for President George W. Bush's decision to increase the number of American troops in Iraq.

This bombing demonstrated the fragile nature of the relative peace that was in place by early 2006, as the attack struck a key aspect of Shia identity. The Shias retaliated with attacks on Sunnis. These clashes drove the two groups further apart, resulting in mass violence and complicating hopes of a relatively quick American withdrawal from Iraq. In June 2007, Al Qaeda in Iraq insurgents bombed the mosque again, destroying its two 10-story minarets. After extensive repairs, the mosque was reopened in 2009.

GATES BROWN

See also

Al Qaeda in Iraq; Iraq, History of, 1990–Present; Shia Islam; Sunni Islam; Troop Surge, U.S., Iraq War

References

Hammer, Joshua. "Samarra Rises." *Smithsonian* 39(10) (January 2009): 28–37.

Worth, Robert. "Blast Destroys Shrine in Iraq, Setting Off Sectarian Fury." *New York Times,* February 22, 2006, http://www.nytimes.com/2006/02/22/international/middleeast/22cnd-iraq.html.

Goldwater-Nichols Defense Reorganization Act (1986)

Congressional act, formally known as the Department of Defense Reform Act of 1986, designed to enhance the ability of the U.S. Armed Services to operate more effectively in joint operations. This act, named for its lead sponsors Senator Barry M. Goldwater (R-AZ) and Congressman William "Bill" Nichols (D-AL), was designed to address lingering problems associated with the compromises made in the crafting of the National Security Act of 1947, which established the Department of Defense structure. Congressional sponsors and defense reform advocates had pushed for the changes to address problem areas generated by bureaucratic inefficiencies and interservice competition as well as issues that had been identified in prior combat operations, ranging from the Korean War to Operation URGENT FURY (the U.S. invasion of Grenada in 1983).

The primary objectives of the Goldwater-Nichols act were to strengthen civilian authority, improve the military advice provided to senior civilian leaders, reduce the effects of service parochialism and interservice rivalry, enhance the role of the chairman of the Joint Chiefs of Staff (JCS) and the Joint Staff, and improve the operational authority of the commanders in chief (CINCs) of the unified combatant commands.

The Goldwater-Nichols act strengthened the authority of the secretary of defense and made the chairman of the JCS the "principal military adviser" to the president, secretary of defense, and the National Security Council. Previously, under a system requiring unanimity, the JCS had provided collective recommendations, which were often watered-down compromises made among the service chiefs. Prior to the passage of Goldwater-Nichols, any service chief, to protect the parochial interests of his own service, could block a Joint Staff action. The new act established the chairman as the final approval authority for all Joint Staff actions, allowing the chairman to override any service objections. Although the chairman and the individual service chiefs remained outside the formal operational chain of command (which flows from the president through the secretary of defense directly to the combatant commanders in the field), the reforms allowed the president and the defense secretary to pass operational orders to the combatant commanders, including both the geographic theater joint commanders and the functional joint command commanders through the JCS chairman.

The act also established a vice chairman position for the JCS and revised the Joint Staff responsibilities to clarify and enhance the staff's role in the planning and decision-making process. Goldwater-Nichols also adjusted the defense personnel system to encourage service in joint organizations and to require that senior officers have career experiences and professional education that provide a joint perspective in their leadership roles. Additionally, the act clarified and enhanced the roles of the CINCs. At the time the act was passed the JCS chairman was Admiral William J. Crowe Jr., although the first chairman to be appointed under the new structure was General Colin L. Powell.

The effects of Goldwater-Nichols were clearly evident in the conduct of the 199i Persian Gulf War, in response to the Iraqi invasion of Kuwait. During the conflict, General Powell played a key role in the national leadership as the principal military adviser. Additionally, President George H. W. Bush and Secretary of Defense Dick Cheney used Powell as the primary conduit for orders flowing to the theater CINC, General H. Norman Schwarzkopf. Schwarzkopf also found it useful to pass information back through the JCS chairman as well as to report directly to the defense secretary and the president.

Within the theater itself, Schwarzkopf fully exploited the Goldwater-Nichols authority and the emphasis on joint efforts to create a highly effective joint and coalition force structure and to conduct a well-coordinated joint campaign for the liberation of Kuwait. The Persian Gulf War was viewed by many analysts as a validation of the wisdom of the reforms implemented by the Goldwater-Nichols act. In October 2002 Secretary of Defense Donald Rumsfeld directed that the functional and regional CINCs be referred to as "combat commanders" or "commanders," arguing that there can be but one commander in chief—namely, the president of the United States. During U.S. military operations in Afghanistan (Operation ENDURING FREEDOM) in 2001 and Iraq (Operation IRAQI FREEDOM) in 2003, the wisdom of Goldwater-Nichols was once again clearly evident, as both operations were conducted with a great deal of efficiency and joint effort.

JEROME V. MARTIN

See also

Afghanistan War; Cheney, Richard Bruce; IRAQI FREEDOM, Operation; Powell, Colin Luther; Rumsfeld, Donald

References

Lederman, Gordon Nathaniel. *Reorganizing the Joint Chiefs of Staff: The Goldwater-Nichols Act of 1986.* College Station: Texas A&M University Press, 2002.

Locher, James R. *Victory on the Potomac: The Goldwater-Nichols Act Unifies the Pentagon.* College Station: Texas A&M University Press, 2002.

Goss, Porter Johnston (1938–)

Republican politician, intelligence operative, U.S. congressman (1989–2004), and director of the Central Intelligence Agency (CIA) from 2004 to 2006. Porter Johnston Goss was born on November 26, 1938, in Waterbury, Connecticut, to a well-to-do family. His early education was at the exclusive Fessenden School in West Newton, Massachusetts, and the equally elite Hotchkiss High School in Lakeville, Connecticut. He attended Yale University, graduating in 1960.

Most of Goss's early career was with the CIA, specifically with the Directorate of Operations (DO), which carries out the clandestine operations of the agency. Goss worked as a CIA agent in the DO from 1960 to 1971. Most of his activities in the CIA are still classified, but it is known that his area of operations included Latin America, the Caribbean, and Europe. In 1970, while he was stationed in London, health problems led him to resign his post.

Goss began his political career in 1975, serving as mayor of Sanibel City, Florida, from 1975 to 1977 and again during 1981–1982. In 1988 he ran for the U.S. House seat in Florida's 13th congressional district and retained it until 1993. In 1993 he became the congressional representative from Florida's 14th congressional district, and he held this seat until September 23, 2004, when he resigned it to head the CIA. During his 16 years in Congress, Goss served on specialized committees that had oversight on intelligence. Although Goss had always been supportive of the CIA, he endorsed legislation in 1995 that would have cut intelligence personnel by 20 percent over a five-year period as a budget-cutting measure. Goss served as chair of the House Permanent Committee on Intelligence from 1997 to 2004, and he helped to establish and then served on the Homeland Security Committee. Throughout his political career, Goss defended the CIA and generally supported budget increases for it. He also was a strong supporter of CIA director George Tenet.

The September 11, 2001, attacks brought Goss to the political forefront. He, along with his colleague and friend U.S. Senator Bob Graham (D-FL), began to call for a bipartisan investigation into the events surrounding September 11. Both in the Senate and in the House of Representatives there was reluctance to proceed, however. Opposition was even stronger in the George W. Bush administration against such an investigation. Most feared that an investigation would invite finger pointing and be tainted by politics. This fear on both the Republican and the Democratic sides slowed down the creation of the Senate-House Joint Inquiry on Intelligence, and the length of time provided to produce a report was unrealistically short. Despite the short time span—and reluctance or refusal to cooperate on the parts of the CIA, the Federal Bureau of Investigation, and the White House—a valuable report was finally issued, albeit with sections of it censored.

Goss ultimately opposed the creation of the September 11 Commission and many of its recommendations. Like many of his fellow Republicans, he was fearful that the commission would become a witch hunt against the Bush administration. Even after it was apparent that the commission was bipartisan, Goss opposed its recommendations on intelligence matters. His biggest concern was the report's recommendation to create the position of national intelligence director, whose job would be to oversee all intelligence agencies. As a conservative Republican, Goss defended the Bush administration in its Global War on Terror and was a severe critic of what he called the failures of the Bill Clinton administration.

The Bush administration noted Goss's loyalty. When George Tenet resigned as director of the CIA on June 3, 2004, Goss was nominated to become director. Despite opposition from some Democratic senators, Goss won confirmation on September 22, 2004. During his confirmation hearings, Goss promised that he would bring change and reform to the CIA.

Goss's tenure as head of the CIA provided to be a mixed record. He began on September 24, 2004, with a mandate for change, but the top leadership of the CIA showed reluctance to accept him. These leaders were already distressed by how the CIA had been made a scapegoat for past mistakes by both the Clinton and Bush administrations. Several of Goss's top subordinates, particularly his chief adviser Patrick Murray, clashed with senior CIA management, leading three of the CIA's top officials to resign. An attempt by Goss to make the CIA more loyal to the Bush administration also brought criticism. His memo to CIA staff that it was their job "to support the administration and its policies" became a cause of resentment. Finally, Goss's promotion of his friend Kyle Dustin "Dusty" Foggo from the ranks to a high CIA position and his links to former congressman Randy "Duke" Cunningham, who was convicted of accepting bribes, lowered morale in the CIA.

Eventually Goss lost out in a power struggle with his nominal boss, John Negroponte. One of the reforms called for in the final report of the September 11 Commission was coordination of intelligence efforts. This recommendation led to the creation of the position of director of national intelligence and the appointment of Negroponte, a career diplomat, to that post. Goss and Negroponte had disagreements about how to reform intelligence gathering. Goss was reluctant to transfer personnel and resources from the CIA to the National Counterterrorism Center and the National Counter Proliferation Center. These disagreements led to Goss's surprising resignation on May 5, 2006, after only a 19-month tenure. His replacement was Negroponte's principal deputy director for national intelligence, U.S. Air Force general Michael Hayden.

Goss has maintained a very low profile since leaving government. For a time he was active in the lecture circuit, but more recently he has taken up organic farming in Virginia.

STEPHEN E. ATKINS

See also

Bush, George Walker; Central Intelligence Agency; Clinton, William Jefferson; Counterterrorism Center; Global War on Terror; Negroponte, John Dimitri; September 11 Commission and Report; Tenet, George John

References

Graham, Bob. *Intelligence Matters: The CIA, the FBI, Saudi Arabia, and the Failure of America's War on Terror.* New York: Random House, 2004.

Risen, James. "Rifts Plentiful as 9/11 Inquiry Begins Today." *New York Times,* June 4, 2002, A1.

Rizzo, John. *Company Man: Thirty Years of Controversy and Crisis in the CIA.* New York: Scribner, 2014.

Grand Council, Afghanistan

See Loya Jirga, Afghanistan

Green Zone in Iraq

Highly fortified walled-off section of central Baghdad (Iraq), also know as the International Zone, that is the location of many of Iraq's government buildings. The Green Zone was established soon after the March 2003 invasion of Iraq by U.S. and coalition forces and became the area in which most U.S. and coalition occupation authorities worked and lived. The Green Zone is approximately four square miles in land area.

The Green Zone is entirely surrounded by reinforced concrete walls capable of absorbing explosions from car and truck bombs, improvised explosive devices (IEDs), and suicide bombers. The walls are topped by barbed and concertina wire to foil anyone attempting to scale them. In areas where the likelihood of insurgent infiltration is high, the blast walls are supplemented by thick earthen berms. There are fewer than a half dozen entry and exit points into and out of the zone, all of which are manned around the clock by well-trained and well-armed civilian guards and military police.

After 2006, Iraqis began to bear the largest burden of protecting the Green Zone. They are aided in their mission by American-supplied M1-Abrams tanks, Humvees, and armored personnel carriers equipped with .50-caliber machine guns.

The Green Zone is home to many of Iraq's most important government buildings and ministries, including the Military Industry Ministry, as well as numerous foreign embassies. The Green Zone encompasses several presidential palaces and villas used by former president Saddam Hussein, his sons Uday and Qusay, and other Baath Party loyalists. The Republican Palace, the largest of Hussein's residences, is located there. Considered Hussein's principal base of power,

Construction proceeds on the new U.S. embassy compound in Baghdad's fortified Green Zone on August 31, 2006. The compound includes 21 buildings on 104 acres (only six acres less than the entire Vatican City). It is the world's largest, most fortified, and expensive diplomatic compound. (Getty Images)

it was akin to the White House for the U.S. president. For that reason, it was a key target for coalition forces as they moved into Iraq in 2003.

The zone includes several large markets, stores, shops, restaurants, and large hotels and a convention center. Also found in the Green Zone are the former Baath Party headquarters, a military museum, and the Tomb of the Unknown Soldier. There is also an elaborate underground bunker constructed to shield key government officials during time of war.

Since the coalition invasion of Iraq in 2003, the Green Zone housed all the occupation officials' offices and residences. It is also currently home to the Iraqi government. The vast majority of civilian contractors and independent security firm personnel are also located there. The American, British, Australian, and other international embassies and legations as well as most media reporters are located within the Green Zone.

Despite the elaborate security measures within the Green Zone, the area has been targeted on numerous occasions for attacks by truck bombs, suicide bombers with explosives-laden backpacks, and rockets and mortars. After measures were taken to further limit egress into the Green Zone such incidents declined, although they were not entirely eliminated. Nevertheless, rebels and insurgents continue to attack the Green Zone, employing rocket-propelled grenades, IEDs, and even Katuysha rockets.

Some Iraqis and those in the international community have criticized the existence of the Green Zone because it has entirely isolated occupation officials and Iraqi government officials from the grim and perilous realities of life in Iraq. Outside the Green Zone lies what has come to be called the Red Zone, an area into which occupation authorities rarely venture and lawlessness and chaos abound. On January 1, 2009, the entire Green Zone came under the control of Iraqi security forces. Although occupation forces were criticized for having established an artificial oasis in a worn-torn nation, the Green Zone will likely remain in place for some time, walled off from the remainder of Iraq unless or until violence perpetrated by insurgents and terrorists comes to an end. Indeed, with the emergence of the insurgency perpetrated by the Islamic State of Iraq and Syria (ISIS) during 2013–2014, the Green Zone has taken on renewed importance.

PAUL G. PIERPAOLI JR.

See also

Baghdad, Iraq; Improvised Explosive Devices; IRAQI FREEDOM, Operation; Rocket-Propelled Grenades

References

Bayati, Latif al-. *180 Days in the Green Zone.* London: AuthorHouseUK, 2014.

Chandrasekaran, Rajiv. *Imperial Life in the Emerald City: Inside Iraq's Green Zone.* New York: Viking Books, 2007.

Mowle, Thomas S., ed. *Hope Is Not a Plan: The War in Iraq from Inside the Green Zone.* Westport, CT: Praeger, 2007.

Ground Zero Mosque Controversy

Commonly referred to as the "Ground Zero Mosque," Park51 is an Islamic community center under development in New York City. Although often identified in the media as a mosque, the 13-story building would feature many facilities, including a 500-seat auditorium, a performing arts center, a swimming pool, a fitness center, a bookstore, a culinary school, an art studio, and a September 11 memorial, in addition to a prayer space that could accommodate up to 2,000 people. Although the community center would not actually be located at Ground Zero, the project has sparked significant debate because of its proximity to the site of the September 11 attacks.

The community center would occupy 45–51 Park Place, about two blocks north of the World Trade Center site. In July 2009, Soho Properties bought half of the lot (45–47 Park Place), which was occupied at the time by a three-story building that had been heavily damaged during the September 11 attacks. The other half of the lot (49–51 Park Place) is owned by the utility Con Edison and leased to Soho Properties. Although Soho Properties chief executive officer Sharif El-Gamal initially intended to turn the site into a condominium complex, he was convinced by Imam Feisal Abdul Rauf, a well-known Muslim religious leader in New York City, to construct a community center instead. The project's chief investors—the American Society for Muslim Advancement and the Cordoba Initiative—are both nonprofit organizations founded by Rauf.

Plans to build the community center were first made public in the *New York Times* on December 9, 2009, although they attracted little notice. On May 25, 2010, Lower Manhattan Community Board 1 backed the secular aspects of the project through a nonbinding vote of 29 to 1, although the religious component of the planned community center caused some anxiety among board members. By mid-2010, Pamela Geller and Robert Spencer, founders of the group Stop Islamization of America, had brought national attention to the project, which they vocally criticized and dubbed the Ground Zero Mosque.

Most Park51 opponents assert that this is not an issue of religious freedom or racism and that they object only to the location of the community center. They argue that building Park51 only a few blocks from Ground Zero is insensitive to the memory of 9/11 victims, who lost their lives at the hands of Islamic terrorists, and their families. More extreme opponents, however, have labeled the construction project a blatant Islamic threat. Others have speculated about Park51's funding sources, voicing concerns that the project's investors might take money from Hamas, Iran, or other entities hostile to the United States. Those opposed to Park51 include a number of families of 9/11 victims, the American Center for Law & Justice, the Zionist Organization of America, and the Center for Islamic Pluralism. Prominent politicians who have spoken out against the project include Republican senator John McCain, former Alaska governor Sarah Palin, former Speaker of the House Newt Gingrich, and former New York City mayor Rudy Giuliani.

Supporters counter that opponents are motivated by intolerance and baseless fear and hatred. They assert that it is important to distinguish between mainstream Islam and the radical brand of Islam practiced by those who committed the September 11 attacks. Concerns have also arisen that the controversy over Park51 will fuel anti-Americanism around the world and serve as a powerful recruiting tool for Islamic extremist groups. Supporters of the project include the September 11th Families for Peaceful Tomorrows, the Council on American-Islamic Relations, the Muslim Public Affairs Council, and the American Civil Liberties Union. Many New York City officials have backed Park51, including former mayor Michael Bloomberg and Manhattan Borough president Scott Stringer. Former president Bill Clinton, Texas representative Ron Paul, and other well-known politicians have also given their support.

Polls have revealed that the majority of Americans as well as the majority of residents living in New York state and the larger New York City metropolitan area oppose the building of Park51 near the World Trade Center, although a majority of respondents also agree that the developers have a legal and constitutional right to build the community center at that site. A majority of Manhattan residents, however, support the building of Park51 at its planned location.

In addition to the issue of location, even the community center's name has proven controversial. The development's original name—Cordoba House—was inspired by Cordoba, Spain, where, according to Rauf, Muslims, Jews, and Christians lived harmoniously and cooperatively during the 8th through 11th centuries. Detractors contend that the

name was a clear and hostile reference to the Muslim conquest of the Iberian Peninsula. To minimize objections, the community center's name was changed to Park51, referring to its address on Park Place. Supporters of the project argue that the popular nickname "Ground Zero Mosque" is inaccurate and misused by the media in order to increase public anxiety about the development.

In late September 2011, the developer of Park51 opened a small 4,000-square foot Islamic center at the site. In August 2014, it was announced that the temporary structure would be razed and replaced by a larger building featuring a three-story museum, a prayer center, and condominiums. It remains unclear, however, if the developer has the necessary funds to move forward with the latest plan.

SPENCER C. TUCKER

See also

Global War on Terror; September 11 Attacks; Terrorism; World Trade Center

References

Barret, Devlin. "Mosque Debate Isn't Going Away." *Wall Street Journal*, August 3, 2010.

"Con Ed Sells Building Near Ground Zero Where Plans for Mosque Caused Uproar." New York Times, August 20, 2014, http://www.nytimes.com/2014/08/21/nyregion/con-edison-sells-lot-near-ground-zero-where-plans-for-mosque-caused-uproar.html?partner=rss&emc=rss&_r=3.

Ghosh, Bobby. "Mosque Controversy: Does America Have a Muslim Problem?" *Time*, August 19, 2010.

Guantánamo Bay Detainment Camp

Detention camp operated by the U.S. government to hold enemy combatants taken prisoner during the Global War on Terror, which began in late 2001 following the September 11, 2001, terror attacks against the United States. The Guantánamo Bay Detainment Camp is situated on the Guantánamo Bay Naval Base, operated by the United States in southeastern Cuba. The base covers approximately 45 square miles. In one of the most controversial aspects of the Global War on Terror, prisoners held at the camp have been stripped of legal protections afforded to citizens of any nationality under U.S. and international law. Legally classified as "enemy combatants," prisoners may be detained indefinitely, without formal charges brought against them and without access to legal counsel. Hundreds of such detainees from more than 35 nations have been kept prisoner at the camp since 2002 without formal charges and beyond the legal protection of the Geneva Conventions.

The Camp Justice compound, the military prison facility on the U.S. naval base at Guantánamo Bay, Cuba. (AP Photo/Brennan Linsley)

The U.S. military acquired Guantánamo Bay as a naval base as a consequence of the Spanish-American War of 1898. It has maintained the facility since 1903, despite tensions with the communist regime in Cuba led by Fidel Castro and his brother Raul Castro. Until the terrorist attacks of September 11, 2001, the U.S. military had used the base primarily as a gathering place for Cuban and Haitian refugees. Although the facility is only 45 square miles in size, more than 9,000 U.S. personnel are permanently stationed there.

Guantánamo has come under intense international scrutiny since 2002. The U.S. military moved its first detainees of the war on terrorism in Afghanistan there on January 11, 2002, and by late 2014, 779 individuals from more than 35 nations had been held there (some were later released or transferred) without formal charges and with no access to lawyers or contact with their families, diplomats, or national government officials. The Guantánamo Bay detainees have also been denied the rights accorded to prisoners of war under the Geneva Conventions. In short, detention of these prisoners at Guantánamo Bay violates the rights accorded prisoners of war as understood by most scholars of international law.

The administration of President George W. Bush refused to change its policies regarding the detainees, however. The Bush administration contended that detainees at Guantánamo Bay fell into a new legal category of "enemy combatants" and as such must be assumed to be guilty until proven innocent, although precisely what evidentiary or legal avenues remained open to detainees is unclear. Bush's successor, President Barack Obama, vowed to close the facility when he took office in 2009, but as of mid-2015, the facility was still open.

Human rights organizations such as Amnesty International and the International Committee of the Red Cross as well as former military officials working at Guantánamo Bay have described the conditions of prison life there, and they are far from pleasant. Prisoners are alleged to have been kept in isolation cells for many days at a time; beaten and otherwise physically harmed; exposed to aggressive dogs, loud music, and strobe lights; and kept caged but exposed in outdoor cells during violent tropical weather. Prisoners are also alleged to have been subjected to extremely hot and cold temperatures, chained in uncomfortable or strenuous positions, and denied food and water and have been forced to defecate and urinate upon themselves. Other allegations claim that prisoners have been sexually harassed and abused and have had their religious beliefs ridiculed. The U.S. government refuses to grant the International Committee of the Red Cross access to prisoners.

One of the most controversial allegations is that foreign nationals have in recent years been abducted by U.S. forces (a process termed extraordinary rendition); tortured in their native countries with U.S. assistance and instruction, chiefly by the Central Intelligence Agency (CIA); and then sent to Guantánamo Bay for indefinite detention. Evidence has been presented to Amnesty International, the Red Cross, and the British government that nationals of Pakistani, Chinese, Afghan, Egyptian, Syrian, Canadian, and Iraqi descent, among others, have been detained in this way. A handful of missing people throughout the world have become "ghost detainees"; that is, they are believed by many to have been abducted in such fashion and then completely disappeared.

Those known to be held at Guantánamo Bay have been routinely denied access to lawyers, and non-U.S. detainees are not given the rights to have any levied charges tried in courts where appeals are possible. A variety of legal rulings by U.S. courts, including the Supreme Court, have asserted that Guantánamo Bay detainees have the right to military tribunals as prisoners of war, and even to U.S. military or criminal courts in some cases. Nevertheless, the Bush administration unilaterally declared that any trials of camp detainees would be conducted by a new body formed in June 2004 and known as the Combatant Status Review Board (CSRB). That board was directly responsible only to the executive branch of the government, and there was no appeals process. Moreover, its tribunals accept coerced testimony or admissions as evidence. Defense lawyers, if they are consulted at all, are not given access to any evidence presented by the government. Because of this, the CSRB violated both international law and generally accepted human rights law.

On January 22, 2009, two days after taking office, President Barack Obama signed an executive order that mandated a suspension of criminal proceedings at Guantánamo Bay and the closure of the facility by year's end. This drew the immediate ire and suspicion of a number of Americans, who believed that such a move would imperil national security. In May 2009, the U.S. Senate voted to deny funds that might be used for the transfer or release of Guantánamo Bay detainees. Nevertheless, in December 2009 Obama signed another executive order that would have transferred all prisoners to an Illinois prison. That move caused outrage in Illinois, Obama's adoptive home state. Early the next year, the Guantánamo Review Task Force concluded that 126 detainees were eligible for transfer but that 40 others were deemed too dangerous to move. Meanwhile, many U.S. states flatly refused to take any of the prisoners, so Guantánamo Bay remained open.

Realizing that he was losing the battle to close the facility, in 2011 Obama signed an order forbidding the transfer of certain prisoners to the U.S. mainland, effectively ensuring that Guantánamo Bay would remain open. Attempts to try some of the suspects held there in U.S. civilian courts have likewise been stymied. Guantánamo Bay was the subject of renewed scrutiny in late May 2014, when the Obama administration secured the release of U.S. Army soldier Bowe Berghdal, who had been held by the Taliban in Afghanistan since 2009. In return for Berghdal's release, the Obama White House agreed to release five detainees from the Guantánamo Bay facility.

Berghdal's release created an immediate political firestorm. Under a law passed in the immediate aftermath of the September 11, 2001, attacks, the U.S. president is obligated to provide Congress with his intention—in writing—to release any prisoner from Guantánamo at least 30 days in advance of said release. The Obama administration did not do so and argued that the delicate nature of the negotiations, combined with concern about Berghdal's condition, made it impossible to follow the law to the letter. Many in Congress—especially Republicans—were not entirely convinced, however. The Obama White House went on to assert that the U.S. Army, by tradition, does not leave any soldier behind, regardless of the circumstances of his or her imprisonment.

As of late 2014, about 127 detainees were still incarcerated at Guantánamo Bay. In 2013 after his November 2012 reelection, Obama had vowed to renew his push to close the prison completely, but there is little support for this in Congress, and the likelihood of such an event remains remote. On December 20, 2014, the Obama administration announced the release of 4 Guantánamo detainees; they were transported to their home country of Afghanistan. On December 30, the U.S. government reported the release of 5 more Guantánamo detainees, who had been held without being charged since 2002. Three were Tunisians and 2 were Yemenis, but they were not permitted to return to their native countries; instead, they were transported to Kazakhstan for resettlement there. Over the course of 2014, some 29 prisoners at the facility had been released or transferred to other nations.

Nancy L. Stockdale and Paul G. Pierpaoli Jr.

See also

Berghdal, Bowe, Release of; Bush, George Walker; Coercive Interrogation; Global War on Terror; Obama, Barack Hussein, II; September 11 Attacks; Taliban

References

"Bowe Berghdal Fast Facts." CNN, July 21, 2014, http://www.cnn.com/2014/01/19/us/bowe-bergdahl-fast-facts.

Epstein, Edward. "Guantanamo Is a Miniature America." *San Francisco Chronicle,* January 20, 2002, A6.

Hansen, Jonathan M. "Making the Law in Cuba." *New York Times,* April 20, 2004, A19.

Mendelsohn, Sarah E. *Closing Guantanamo: From Bumper Sticker to Blueprint.* Washington, DC: Center for Security and International Studies, 2008.

"Obama Calls on Congress to Do More on Guantánamo Bay." Reuters, December 26, 2013, http://www.reuters.com/article/2013/12/26/us-usa-obama-defense-idUSBRE9BP0H620131226.

Saar, Erik, and Viveca Novak. *Inside the Wire: A Military Intelligence Soldier's Eyewitness Account of Life at Guantanamo.* New York: Penguin, 2005.

Yee, John. *War by Other Means: An Insider's Account of the War on Terror.* New York: Atlantic Monthly, 2006.

Gulf Cooperation Council

The Gulf Cooperation Council (GCC) was formed by Arab states on May 25, 1981, mainly as a counter to the threat posed from the Islamic Republic of Iran. At the time, Iran was in the early stages of its fundamentalist Islamic revolution and was involved in fighting Iraq in the Iran-Iraq War of 1980–1988. In general, the region's Arab nations eyed Iran with great suspicion and hoped to contain Islamic fundamentalism to that state.

The GCC is currently made up of six member states: Bahrain, Kuwait, Oman, Qatar, Saudi Arabia, and the United Arab Emirates (UAE). Among these countries, the political systems, socioeconomic forces, and overall culture are quite similar, making cooperation among them relatively easy to achieve. Led by Saudi Arabia, together these states possess roughly half of the world's known oil reserves. The GCC's power is therefore principally economic, and its main goal is to boost the economic might of its members.

On the military side, the GCC established a collective defense force in 1984 (effective since 1986), sometimes called the Peninsula Shield, based in Saudi Arabia near King Khalid Military City at Hafar al Batin and commanded by a Saudi military officer. Even before the mutual security pact was established, joint military maneuvers had been carried out since 1983. The Peninsula Shield consists of one infantry brigade and is currently estimated to be maintained at 7,000 troops. Oman's proposal to extend the force to 100,000 troops in 1991 was turned down. The force did not participate in the 1991 Persian Gulf War as a distinct unit. Through the GCC, military assistance has been extended to Bahrain and Oman, funded mostly by Kuwait and Saudi Arabia. Plans to integrate naval and ground radar systems and to create a combined air control and warning system based on Saudi AWACS aircraft have been repeatedly delayed until just recently.

While all GCC members agree in their desire to become more independent from U.S. security arrangements, they have yet to find consensus as to how this could best be achieved. This became a contentious issue during the conflict with Iraq in 1991, with some states, foremost Kuwait and Saudi Arabia, forming parts of the international coalition against Iraq, while others remained opposed the action. Notably, in March 1991 just weeks after the Persian Gulf War ended, the GCC agreed—together with Egypt and Syria—to form a security alliance to protect Kuwait against renewed aggression.

Deep divisions also exist as to whether or how Iran, Iraq, and Yemen could be brought into the GCC. The same is true on the issue of political reforms. Militant Islam is seen as a significant threat by Saudi Arabia, while some other members would like to speed up liberalization of the political process, including the admittance of Islamic parties. Since 2004, the GCC countries also share intelligence in the fight against terror but to a limited extent. In November 2006, Saudi Arabia proposed expanding the GCC's military force, and by 2011 its military arm numbered about 40,000 troops.

The GCC's structure includes a Supreme Council, the highest decision-making body, composed of the heads of the six member states. Meetings are held annually; the presidency of the council rotates in alphabetical order. Decisions by the Supreme Council on substantive issues require unanimous approval. The Supreme Council also appoints a secretary-general for a three-year term, renewable once. The secretary-general supervises the day-to-day affairs of the GCC. Since April 1, 2011, Abdullatif bin Rashid Al Zayani, from Bahrain, has served as secretary-general. The Ministerial Council convenes every three months, proposes policies, and manages the implementation of GCC decisions. It is usually made up of the member states' foreign ministers. Should problems among member states arise, the Commission for the Settlement of Disputes meets on an ad hoc basis to seek a peaceful solution to disagreements. A Defense Planning Council also advises the GCC on military matters relating to its joint armed forces.

In 2011 the GCC began the process of admitting Jordan and Morocco and in 2013 also began to contemplate the admission of Yemen. In early 2014, Saudi Arabia, Bahrain, and the UAE all protested Qatar's support for the Muslim Brotherhood, and all three countries withdrew their ambassadors from Qatar in protest. In September 2014, the GCC agreed to participate in a U.S.-led coalition designed to eradicate the Islamic State of Iraq and Syria (ISIS), which was threatening both of those nations. The GCC began air strikes that same month and pledged to aid anti-ISIS rebels within Syria. The GCC also agreed to permit the use of members' air bases by foreign air assets.

THOMAS J. WEILER

See also

Bahrain; Iraq, History of, 1990–Present; Islamic State in Iraq and Syria; Muslim Brotherhood; Qatar; Saudi Arabia; United Arab Emirates

References

Dietl, Gulshan. *Through Two Wars and Beyond: A Study of the Gulf Cooperation Council.* New Delhi: Lancer Books, 1991.

Ramazani, Rouhollah K. *The Gulf Cooperation Council: Record and Analysis.* Charlottesville: University Press of Virginia, 1988.

"Saudi Arabia, UAE, Bahrain Withdraw Envoys from Qatar." CNN, March 5, 2014, http://edition.cnn.com/2014/03/05/world/meast/gulf-qatar-ambassadors/.

H

Haass, Richard Nathan (1951–)

Foreign policy expert, prolific author, and national security/foreign policy official in the George H. W. Bush and George W. Bush administrations. Richard Nathan Haass was born in Brooklyn, New York, on July 28, 1951. He received his BA degree from Oberlin College (Ohio) in 1973. Selected as a Rhodes Scholar, Haass continued his education at Oxford University, from which he ultimately earned both a master's and a doctoral degree. Haass subsequently held a series of academic posts at Hamilton College and the John F. Kennedy School of Government at Harvard University. He also served as vice president and director of foreign policy studies at the Brookings Institute and held posts with the prestigious Carnegie Endowment for International Peace and the International Institute for Strategic Studies. Although Haass's interests and research are wide reaching, most of it deals with foreign policy and national security issues. By the end of the 1980s, he had become especially interested in the Middle East.

Haass began his government service in 1979 as an analyst for the Department of Defense, a post he held until 1980. Concomitantly, he was a legislative aide for the U.S. Senate. In 1981 he began serving in the U.S. State Department, where he remained until 1985. By 1989 Haass had earned a reputation as a thoughtful yet cautious foreign policy adviser. That year he began serving as a special assistant to President George H. W. Bush as senior director for Near East and East Asian affairs on the National Security Council. As such, Haass was deeply involved in the policy decisions surrounding Operations DESERT SHIELD and DESERT STORM. Indeed, he helped facilitate the Bush administration's success in cobbling together an impressive international coalition that ultimately defeated Iraq in 1991 and reversed that nation's occupation of Kuwait. In 1991 Haass was given the Presidential Citizens Medal for his work before and during the Persian Gulf War. He resigned his post in 1993 at the end of Bush's term in office.

When President George W. Bush took office in January 2001, Haass was appointed the State Department's director of policy planning, arguably the most influential foreign policy post next to that of secretary of state. His main role during this time was to act as Secretary of State Colin L. Powell's chief adviser. Remaining in this post until June 2003, Haass had a significant role in the U.S. reaction to the September 11 terror attacks, the subsequent war in Afghanistan (Operation ENDURING FREEDOM), and the lead-up to war with Iraq in March 2003. Perhaps reflecting Powell's caution and skepticism toward the implementation of a second war with Iraq, Haass was not seen as a war hawk, at least not in the same league as neoconservatives such as Deputy Secretary of Defense Paul Wolfowitz, Secretary of Defense Donald Rumsfeld, and Vice President Richard (Dick) Cheney. While Powell's more cautious stance was cast aside in the months leading up to the war, Haass nevertheless remained publicly loyal to Bush's foreign policy.

For a brief time Haass served as policy coordinator for U.S. policy in Afghanistan after the fall of the Taliban regime there. He also served as special U.S. envoy to the Northern Ireland peace process, succeeding Senator George Mitchell. In late 2003 Haass chose to step down from government service and was awarded the Distinguished Honor Award from the U.S. Department of State.

In July 2003 Haass accepted the post of president of the Council on Foreign Relations (CFR), and upon his departure from government he dedicated all of his efforts to the CFR. The CFR is a nonpartisan independent think tank and publisher dedicated to studying and articulating the foreign policies of the United States and other nations of the world. The author of a dozen books, Haass lives in New York City.

PAUL G. PIERPAOLI JR.

See also

Bush, George Walker; Cheney, Richard Bruce; IRAQI FREEDOM, Operation; Neoconservatism; Powell, Colin Luther; Rumsfeld, Donald; Wolfowitz, Paul

References

DeYoung, Karen. *Soldier: The Life of Colin Powell.* New York: Knopf, 2006.

Haass, Richard. *The Opportunity: America's Moment to Alter History's Course.* New York: PublicAffairs, 2006.

Haass, Richard. *War of Necessity, War of Choice: A Memoir of Two Iraq Wars.* New York: Simon and Schuster, 2009.

Haditha, Battle of (August 1–4, 2005)

Military engagement during August 1–4, 2005, between U.S. marines and Iraqi insurgents belonging to Ansar al-Sunna, a militant Salafi group operating in and around Haditha, Iraq. Haditha is a city of some 100,000 people located in Anbar Province in western Iraq about 150 miles to the northwest of Baghdad. The city's population is mainly Sunni Muslim.

The battle was precipitated when a large force of insurgents ambushed a 6-man marine sniper unit on August 1; all 6 marines died in the ensuing fight. The rebels videotaped part of the attack, which included footage allegedly showing a badly injured marine being killed. On August 3 the marines, along with a small contingent of Iraqi security forces, decided to launch a retaliatory strike against Ansar al-Sunna, dubbed Operation QUICK STRIKE. Those involved included about 1,000 personnel from Regimental Combat Team 2.

The operation commenced with a ground assault against insurgent positions southwest of Haditha; this was augmented by four Bell AH-1 Super Cobra attack helicopters. U.S. officials reported at least 40 insurgents killed during this engagement. The next day, August 4, insurgents destroyed

a marine amphibious vehicle using a large roadside bomb; 15 of the 16 marines inside it were killed, along with a civilian interpreter. Meanwhile, the marines had conducted a raid on a house suspected of harboring insurgents outside Haditha. In so doing, they discovered a large weapons cache containing small arms and improvised explosive devices and detained seven insurgents for questioning. Later, six of the men admitted to having ambushed and killed the six marines on August 1.

After the roadside bombing, coalition forces decided to regroup for a more concerted attack on Haditha itself, which would come in early September. In total, the marines suffered 21 killed; insurgent losses were estimated at 400.

On September 5, 2005, the 3rd Battalion, 1st Marines, launched a full-scale assault against Haditha, expecting heavy resistance. The resistance did not materialize, however, and the marines took the entire city in four days with very minimal insurgent activity. The operation uncovered more than 1,000 weapons caches and resulted in the detention of an additional 400 militants. Four marines were casualties. In early 2006 eight Iraqis suspected of involvement in the initial attack on the marine snipers were tried by an Iraqi court, found guilty, and executed.

PAUL G. PIERPAOLI JR.

See also

United States Marine Corps, Iraq War

References

Hashim, Ammed S. *Insurgency and Counter-Insurgency in Iraq.* Ithaca, NY: Cornell University Press, 2006.

Tracy, Patrick. *Street Fight in Iraq: What It's Really Like Over There.* Tucson: University of Arizona Press, 2006.

Haditha Incident (November 19, 2005)

The alleged murder of 24 Iraqi civilians in Haditha, in Anbar Province, on November 19, 2005, by U.S. marines of the 1st Squad, 3rd Platoon, K Company, 3rd Battalion, 1st Marine Regiment, 1st Marine Division. The incident gained international notoriety when it eventually became public knowledge, fueling critics' attacks on the conduct of the U.S.-led coalition's counterinsurgency operations in Iraq and raising charges that the U.S. Marine Corps had initially attempted to cover up the killings before reporters broke the story.

Domestic and international pressure to investigate the incident fully and to prosecute those involved gained increasing momentum, as public knowledge of the Haditha Incident in early 2006 coincided with other allegations of unnecessary violence against Iraqi civilians by U.S. military personnel during military operations elsewhere in the country. Strong criticism of the incident and the handling by the U.S. Marine Corps of its aftermath by congressional opponents of the George W. Bush administration was led by U.S. congressman John Murtha (D-PA). Murtha's status as a former marine combat veteran of the Vietnam War has frequently made him the Democrats' point man in attacks on the Bush administration's handling of the Global War on Terror. Murtha was subsequently sued by one of the alleged marine participants in the Haditha Incident. Although several marine participants were eventually brought up on criminal charges for their roles in the incident, as of 2009 only one of them still faced prosecution and court-martial for the killings.

In November 2005 Anbar Province was one of the most dangerous places in Iraq, the heart of the Iraqi insurgency. The murders are alleged to have been in retaliation for the death of U.S. Marine Corps lance corporal Miguel Terrazas and the wounding of two other marines on November 19 after a four-vehicle U.S. convoy triggered the detonation of an improvised explosive device (IED) and came under attack by small-arms fire.

The U.S. Marine Corps initially reported that 15 civilians had been killed by the bomb's blast and that 8 or 9 insurgents had also been killed in the ensuing firefight. However, reports by Iraqi eyewitnesses to the incident, statements by local Iraqi officials, and video shots of the dead civilians in the city morgue and at the houses where the killings occurred contradicted the initial U.S. military version of events. Some of the Iraqi eyewitness reports were particularly compelling, such as testimony by a young girl who said that she saw marines shoot her father while he was praying. The vividness and detail of Iraqi eyewitness reports gave substantial credibility to their claims, making it virtually impossible for U.S. military authorities to ignore them. The Iraqi claims contradicting the official military report prompted *Time* magazine to publish a story alleging that the marines deliberately killed 24 Iraqi civilians, including women and 6 children.

Although *Newsmax* questioned *Time*'s sources for the story, claiming that the dead were known insurgent propagandists and insurgent-friendly Haditha residents, based on the *Time* report and the international outcry it generated, on February 24, 2006, the U.S. military initiated an investigation. Led by U.S. Army major general Eldon Bargewell, the investigation was charged with determining how the incident was reported through the chain of command. On March 9 a criminal investigation was also launched, led by the Naval Criminal Investigative Services to determine if the marines deliberately targeted and killed Iraqi civilians. As *Newsweek* stated in a report on the Haditha Incident dated October 9, 2007, "the sinister reality of insurgents' hiding among civilians in Iraq has complicated the case" and was one of the main obstacles military investigators have faced in trying to determine if any Iraqi civilians were deliberately killed.

Marines on patrol in Haditha initially reported that 1 marine and 15 Iraqi civilians had been killed by an IED, whereupon insurgents opened fire on the marines, who proceeded to kill the 8 or 9 alleged insurgents. The U.S. Marine Corps then subsequently reported that the 15 Iraqi civilians had instead been accidentally killed as marines cleared four nearby houses in front of the road where the IED had exploded and in which they believed the insurgents were firing from and/or hiding in. According to Iraqi accounts, however, after the IED explosion, the incensed marines went on a rampage, set up a roadblock, and first killed 4 Iraqi students and a taxi driver who were all unarmed and surrendering to the marines at the time. The marines then stormed the four nearby houses and killed numerous people (accounts vary as to the exact number), including perhaps as many as 5 women and 6 children. Details beyond that remain sketchy and changeable.

On April 9, 2007, one marine, Sergeant Sanick De La Cruz, was granted immunity from prosecution for unpremeditated murder in exchange for his testimony. He testified on May 9, 2007, that he and others, including his squad leader, Staff Sergeant Frank Wuterich, killed the four Iraqi students and the driver of a white taxi who were attempting to surrender. De La Cruz further testified that Wuterich then told the men under his command, including De La Cruz, to lie about the killings. According to De La Cruz, the five Iraqis, including the driver, had been ordered out of a taxi by Wuterich and himself after the marines had put up a roadblock following the ambush of the convoy.

Other marines, however, reported that shortly after the explosion of the IED they noticed a white unmarked car full of "military-aged men" arrive and then stop near the bombing site. Suspecting the men of being insurgents or having remotely detonated the IED, Wutterich and De La Cruz ordered the five men to stop and surrender, but instead they ran; they were all shot and killed. As reinforcements arrived, the marines began taking small-arms fire from several locations on either side of their convoy, and while taking cover they identified at least one shooter in the vicinity of a nearby house. Lieutenant William Kallop ordered Wuterich and an ad hoc team to treat the buildings as hostile and to clear them. They forced entry and shot a man on a flight of stairs and then shot another when he made a movement toward a closet. The marines say that they heard the sound of an AK-47 bolt slamming, so they threw grenades into a nearby room and fired; they killed five occupants, with two others wounded by grenade fragments and bullets. Wuterich and his men pursued what they suspected were insurgents running into an adjacent house. They led the assault with grenades and gunfire, in the process killing another man. Unknown to the marines, two women and six children were in a back room. Seven were killed. It was a chaotic and fast-moving action conducted in the dark in close-range quarters, causing accounts to diverge on the precise chronology and exact sequence of events.

After the firefight ended around 9:30 p.m., the marines noted men suspected of scouting for another attack peering behind the wall of a third house. A marine team, including Wuterich and Lance Corporal Justin Sharratt, stormed the house and found women and children inside (who were not harmed). They moved to a fourth house off a courtyard and killed two men inside wielding AK-47s, along with two others.

Thirty minutes after the house clearing, an intelligence unit arrived to question the marines involved in the operation. Shortly after the IED explosion, an unmanned aerial vehicle (UAV) flew over the blast area and for the rest of the day transmitted views of the scene to the company command headquarters and also the to battalion, regimental, and divisional headquarters. *Newsmax* reported that the UAV recorded marines sweeping the four houses for suspected insurgents and also showed four insurgents fleeing the neighborhood in a car and joining up with other insurgents. Based on Staff Sergeant Wuterich's account that in the first house he cleared he observed a back door ajar and believed that the insurgents had fled to another nearby house, it is possible that the four fleeing insurgents seen by the UAV were probably the same ones who left through the back door of the first house that Wuterich and other marines were clearing. The UAV followed both groups of insurgents as they returned to their safe house, which was bombed around 6:00 p.m. and then stormed by a squad from K Company.

On December 21, 2006, in accordance with U.S. Marine Corps legal procedures, criminal charges were brought against eight marines for war crimes in the Haditha killings. Four enlisted marines (including Wuterich) were accused of 13 counts of unpremeditated murder, and four officers were charged with covering up their subordinates' alleged misdeeds by failing to report and investigate properly the deaths of the Iraqis. In 2007 the charges against three of the four enlisted marines were dismissed, and by the summer of 2008 the charges against three of the officers were dismissed; the other was found not guilty by court-martial. Kallop was never charged with a crime.

On June 17, 2008, military judge Colonel Steve Folsom dismissed all charges against Lieutenant Colonel Jeffrey R. Chessani, the most senior officer to face charges, because the officer overseeing the Haditha investigation, Lieutenant General James Mattis, had been improperly influenced by legal investigator Colonel John Ewers, who was a witness to the case and later became a legal adviser to Mattis. The judge ruled that Ewers should not have been allowed to attend meetings and discussions with Mattis because Ewers's participation prejudiced and tainted the decision to charge and prosecute Chessani, who was accused of failing to report the incident and investigate the alleged killing of civilians by marines under his command. The U.S. Marine Corps has appealed the ruling to the Navy and Marine Court of Criminal Appeals, postponing indefinitely Chessani's case.

By June 17 the cases of six defendants had been dropped, and a seventh defendant was found not guilty. The sole exception was Staff Sergeant Frank Wuterich, the platoon sergeant implicated in the Haditha killings. On January 24, 2012, Wuterich was convicted of a single count of negligent dereliction of duty. He received a rank reduction and pay cut but avoided jail time. Many Iraqis expressed disbelief and voiced outrage that six years had passed and that no marines had been sentenced to prison, and there were threats to bring the case to international courts.

Wuterich insists that his unit followed the rules of engagement and did not purposefully attack civilians and that his squad entered the houses to suppress insurgent fire and pursue gunmen who had opened fire on them. He further asserts that the civilian deaths occurred during the sweep of nearby homes in which fragmentation grenades and clearing fire were used before entering the houses. Wuterich also said that his unit never attempted to cover up the incident and immediately reported that civilians had been killed in Haditha.

The Department of Defense has said that the rules of engagement in effect at Haditha prohibited unprovoked attacks on civilians, but this of course assumes that the marines knew that the homes were populated by civilians. In addition, marines are trained as a matter of combat survival to suppress enemy fire with overwhelming force, including the tossing of grenades into a room before entering. The lead investigator of the Haditha incident has confirmed that some training the marines received conflicted with their rules of engagement and led them to believe that if fired upon from a house, they could clear it with grenades and gunfire without determining whether civilians were inside.

The Haditha Incident stands as a classic example of the profound difficulties and the immense potential for human tragedy encountered by conventional military forces engaged in combating an insurgency in which the insurgents' very survival depends upon blending in with—and often becoming indistinguishable from—the local civilian population. Indeed, even when conventional forces win a tactical battle against insurgents, they risk incurring a more important strategic loss when they kill civilians (intentionally or accidentally) in the process. Inevitably, conventional forces conducting counterinsurgency operations are confronted by an unavoidable double standard: while being held strictly accountable for observing all of the internationally accepted laws of war, they must fight an enemy whose tactics principally rely on terror and indiscriminate killing of civilians and combatants alike. The very thought that Al Qaeda or other terrorist group leadership would conduct war crimes investigations for atrocities committed by its members as the U.S. Marine Corps has done in the wake of the Haditha Incident seems absurd; atrocities are the insurgents' main tactic, not aberrations occurring during the heat of battle.

The Haditha Incident also emphasizes that a conventional counterinsurgency force's major actions and policies must be in place in order to prevent or at least limit civilian deaths: effective training, strict discipline, individual accountability, rigidly enforced rules of engagement, and competent leaders at every level of command who remain totally involved in the conduct of all combat operations. Not even one of these critical elements can be lacking or ignored, as that raises the risk of a repeat of such incidents as that which occurred at Haditha. When an atrocity occurs or is even suspected to have taken place, it must be rigorously investigated and, whenever warranted, vigorously prosecuted. A cover-up (or even the appearance of one) not only denies justice to the victims but, in a practical military sense, is also ultimately counterproductive.

STEFAN BROOKS

See also

Improvised Explosive Devices; United States Marine Corps, Iraq War

References

Brennan, Phil. "New Evidence Emerges in Haditha Case." *Newsmax,* June 26, 2006.

Ephron, Dan. "Haditha Unraveled." *Newsweek,* October 29, 2007.

McGirk, Tim. "Collateral Damage or Civilian Massacre at Haditha." *Time,* March 19, 2006.

"What Happened at Haditha." Editorial. *Wall Street Journal,* October 19, 2007.

White, Josh. "Marine Says Rules Were Followed." *Washington Post,* June 11, 2006.

Hadley, Stephen John (1947–)

Attorney, national security and defense expert, and national security adviser to President George W. Bush (2005–2009). Stephen John Hadley was born in Toledo, Ohio, on February 13, 1947. He earned a BA degree from Cornell University in 1969 and a law degree from Yale University in 1972. From 1972 to 1975 he served in the U.S. Navy. Hadley ultimately became a senior partner in the law firm of Shea & Gardner in Washington, D.C., but also became involved in defense and national security work for Republican administrations, including those of Richard Nixon, Gerald Ford, Ronald Reagan, and George H. W. Bush. Between 1995 and 2001 Hadley was also a principal in the Scowcroft Group, an international advisory company specializing in international business development and consultation. Brent Scowcroft, founder of the concern, had been national security adviser to Presidents Ford and George H. W. Bush and was a mentor to Hadley.

From 1989 to 1993 Hadley worked under Paul Wolfowitz as assistant secretary of defense for international security policy. In this post Hadley was involved with numerous arms-control agreements, including START I and START II, and he worked closely with Secretary of Defense Dick Cheney and Secretary of State James Baker. From 1986 to 1987 Hadley served as counsel to the Special Review Board created by President Reagan to investigate the Iran-Contra Affair (popularly known as the Tower Commission).

In 2000 Hadley served as a foreign policy and national security adviser to George W. Bush's presidential campaign. When Bush won, Hadley also served on the president-elect's transition team. In 2001 Bush named Hadley deputy national security adviser, meaning that he reported to National Security Advisor Condoleezza Rice. Just prior to his taking office, Hadley had served on a prominent conservative think tank panel that had urged the United States to make small tactical nuclear weapons a centerpiece of its nuclear arsenal. The group advocated the use of such weapons against nations that harbored illicit weapons of mass destruction. Having worked for Cheney, Wolfowitz, and other neoconservatives, Hadley generally shared their get-tough approach to U.S. defense and national security policy, although he tended to be somewhat less rigid and dogmatic than they, probably the result of his relationship with Scowcroft, who believed in a more measured approach to defense policy.

Hadley reportedly was a member of the White House Iraq Group in 2002; the group's primary aim was to shape public opinion for a possible war with Iraq. In July 2003 some four months after the invasion of Iraq, Hadley offered his resignation to President Bush, claiming that he had allowed Bush to use in his January 2003 State of the Union address the now-discounted document showing that Iraq had tried to buy yellowcake uranium from Niger. The document had been used as proof of Iraq's alleged nuclear weapons program. The president refused to accept the resignation. Later on Hadley was mentioned as the possible source of the leak that precipitated the Valerie Plame Wilson controversy, but he was cleared of any wrongdoing in that scandal. Nevertheless, Hadley has been blamed for a number of botched intelligence reports that were used to justify the Iraq War.

In 2005 Hadley became national security adviser when Rice was tapped to become secretary of state. Hadley kept a relatively low profile during Bush's second term, especially given the departure of two hard-core neoconservatives: Secretary of Defense Donald Rumsfeld and Deputy Secretary of Defense Paul Wolfowitz. Hadley is believed to have supported a change in strategy in the Iraq War that resulted in the 2007 troop surge, and he worked quietly behind the scenes to mend political fences with some of the disgruntled U.S. allies.

After leaving government service, Hadley has served on the board of directors of Raytheon, a major U.S. defense contractor. He has also served as senior adviser for international affairs at the United States Institute of Peace, based in Washington, D.C.

PAUL G. PIERPAOLI JR.

See also

Bush, George Walker; Cheney, Richard Bruce; Global War on Terror; IRAQI FREEDOM, Operation; Neoconservatism; Niger, Role in Origins of the Iraq War; Rice, Condoleezza; Rumsfeld, Donald; Troop Surge, U.S., Iraq War; Wilson, Valerie Plame

References

Mann, James. *Rise of the Vulcans: The History of Bush's War Cabinet.* New York: Viking, 2004.

Woodward, Bob. *State of Denial: Bush at War, Part III.* New York: Simon and Schuster, 2006.

Woodward, Bob. *The War Within: A Secret White House History, 2006–2008.* New York Simon and Schuster, 2008.

Hagel, Charles Timothy (1946–)

Broadcaster, business executive, Republican U.S. senator from Nebraska (1997–2009), and U.S. secretary of defense (2013–2014). Charles (Chuck) Timothy Hagel was born on October 4, 1946, in North Platte, Nebraska. After attending the local public school system, he attended the Brown Institute for Radio and Television in Minneapolis, Minnesota, until 1966, when he joined the U.S. Army. From 1967 to 1968 Hagel served in Vietnam as an infantry squad leader, where he was awarded two Purple Hearts. Leaving the military, he earned a bachelor of science degree from the University of Nebraska, Omaha, in 1971.

In 1971 Hagel became an administrative assistant to U.S. representative John McCollister (R-NE), a position Hagel held until 1977. During 1977–1980 he worked in the private sector as the manager of government affairs for Firestone Tire and Rubber Company. During 1981–1982 he was deputy director of the Veterans Administration. He then established his own firm, Collins, Hagel & Clarke, and served as its president during 1982–1985. He left the firm to help found Vanguard Cellular Systems and served as its chairman from 1985 to 1987.

In 1990 Hagel became deputy director and chief operating officer of the Economic Summit of Industrialized Nations. He also served as chief executive officer of the United Service Organizations. Hagel was also president and chief executive officer of the Private Sector Council in Washington, D.C. During the mid-1990s he joined McCarthy & Company, an Omaha investment banking firm, as president.

In 1996, Hagel won election to the U.S. Senate from Nebraska. In 1997 he was named Republican majority deputy whip. Hagel was reelected in 2002.

Although Hagel had initially supported the Iraq War, he became a vocal critic of the conflict, believing that it had been waged under questionable premises. He also criticized the George W. Bush administration's prosecution of the war and came to believe that it had diluted America's more legitimate war effort in Afghanistan. Hagel did not seek reelection in 2008. On leaving office, he publicly urged the incoming Barack Obama administration to end the conflict in Iraq as soon as possible. Two years later, Hagel issued a similar exhortation about the Afghanistan War.

Following his retirement from the Senate, Hagel taught at the Edmund A. Walsh School of Foreign Service at Georgetown University in Washington, D.C. He also served as cochair of the President's Intelligence Advisory Board and was a member of the Defense Policy Board Advisory Committee. Hagel was a member of numerous boards in the private sector as well, including the Chevron Corporation and Deutsche Bank's Americas Advisory Board.

In early January 2013 after Secretary of Defense Leon Panetta decided to retire, President Obama named Hagel as his replacement. Senate Republicans, including former ally John McCain, strongly opposed the nomination, concerned about Hagel's apparent willingness to negotiate with Iran as well as his opposition to select sanctions against that nation. He also came in for criticism for comments he made in 2006 that the "Jewish lobby intimidates a lot of people," for which he later apologized.

On February 14, 2013, Republicans used a filibuster to block a vote on Hagel's nomination, the first time the Senate had ever filibustered a vote to confirm a secretary of defense. The filibuster was overridden, with 71 senators voting to end it. On February 26 Hagel was confirmed as secretary of defense in a vote of 58 to 41 vote and was sworn in the next day.

In November 2013, Hagel announced a new defense strategy emphasizing renewed focus on the Arctic region, a clear warning to an increasingly bellicose Russia. In late August, he announced the Pentagon's readiness to launch air strikes against Syria should they become necessary. When the Ukraine Crisis commenced in early 2014, Hagel warned both the Russian and Ukrainian governments not to engage in a conflict that would result in civilian casualties. In the spring of 2014, he announced strong support for the North Atlantic Treaty Organization in light of the Russian government's menacing moves in Eastern Europe. Hagel also supported the Obama administration's decision in August 2014 to assemble an international coalition designed to eradicate the Islamic State of Iraq and Syria (ISIS). U.S. air strikes in Iraq began that same month and were extended into Syria the following month.

On November 25, 2014, in something of a surprise, President Obama announced Hagel's resignation. The decision was apparently reached by mutual agreement. While Hagel carried out the administration's goals of cutting the defense budget and winding down the Afghanistan War, there was a growing sentiment in the administration that Hagel was not up to the challenges posed by ISIS and the aggressive Russian moves in Ukraine.

CHRISTINA GIROD

See also

Afghanistan War; Iran; IRAQI FREEDOM, Operation; Islamic State in Iraq and Syria; Obama, Barack Hussein, II; Panetta, Leon Edward

References

"Biographical Directory of the United States Congress." U.S. Congress, http://bioguide.congress.gov.

"The Heartland Dissident." *New York Times*, February 12, 2006, http://www.nytimes.com/2006/02/12/magazine/12hagel.html?pagewanted=all&_r=0.

Hagenbeck, Franklin L. (1949–)

U.S. Army general and commander of coalition Joint Task Force Mountain during Operation ENDURING FREEDOM in Afghanistan. Born in Morocco on November 25, 1949, the son of a U.S. Navy officer, Franklin L. Hagenbeck attended high school in Jacksonville, Florida, and went on to graduate from the United States Military Academy, West Point, in 1971, when he was commissioned a second lieutenant. His subsequent military education included courses at the U.S. Army Command and General Staff College and the Army War College. Hagenbeck also earned a master's degree in exercise physiology from Florida State University and a master's degree in business administration from Long Island University.

Among Hagenbeck's earlier staff assignments were tours as director of the Officer Personnel Management Directorate and assistant division commander of the 101st Airborne Division. He also served abroad as an instructor in tactics at the Royal Australian Infantry Center. Having previously commanded at company, battalion, and brigade levels, Hagenbeck assumed command as a major general of the 10th Mountain Division at Fort Drum in New York in the autumn of 2001. He entered the public spotlight in the aftermath of the September 11, 2001, terrorist attacks on the United States. With the commencement of Operation ENDURING FREEDOM in Afghanistan in October 2001, the 10th Mountain Division received a warning that it would provide the first conventional forces to support ongoing special operations against the Taliban regime. After initially sending a small security element, the 10th Mountain contributed a portion of the 1,200 infantrymen who took part in Operation ANACONDA in March 2002 under Hagenbeck's immediate command.

Although a tactical success, ANACONDA was not without its problems in intelligence and fire-support coordination. Thus, a debate over the operation and the responsibility for its shortcomings occurred in which Hagenbeck would play a prominent role. In particular, in an interview published in *Field Artillery* magazine in 2002 he called into question the effectiveness of fire support provided solely by the U.S. Air Force, the problem being that the 10th Mountain Division was not allowed to deploy to Afghanistan with its organic artillery, and thus tactical air support was the division's sole source of fire support. His analysis drew a sharp rejoinder from U.S. Air Force spokespersons. Whatever the problems, they almost certainly stemmed in part from a hasty planning process as well as a long-standing history of imperfect interservice coordination.

Hagenbeck next assumed the post of U.S. Army deputy chief of staff, personnel (G-1). In this position he testified several times before Congress on the challenges facing the army in recruitment and retention resulting from waging concurrent wars in Iraq and Afghanistan. In June 2006 Lieutenant General Hagenbeck became the superintendent of the United States Military Academy, West Point; he served in that post until July 2010, at which time he retired from the U.S. Army. Hagenbeck thereafter served on several institutional and corporate boards, has been a speaker and consultant, and became director of the Engineering Leadership Institute at the University of Florida in October 2013.

ROBERT F. BAUMANN

See also

ANACONDA, Operation

References

"Afghanistan: Fire Support for Operation Anaconda; An Interview with MG Franklin L. Hagenbeck." *Field Artillery* (September–October 2002): 5–9.

Andres, Richard, and Jeffrey Hukill. "Anaconda: A Flawed Joint Planning Process." *Joint Forces Quarterly* 47 (4th quarter, 2007): 135–140.

Lambeth, Benjamin S. *Air Power against Terror: America's Conduct of Operation Enduring Freedom.* Santa Monica, CA: RAND Corporation, 2005.

Naylor, Sean. *Not a Good Day to Die: The Untold Story of Operation Anaconda.* New York: Berkley Trade, 2006.

Haifa Street, Battle of (January 6–9, 2007)

A two-staged combined-arms action by American and Iraqi troops against Sunni insurgents in central Baghdad during January 6–9, 2007. In the Battle of Haifa Street, U.S. Army infantry and cavalry units fought alongside Iraqi soldiers to successfully dislodge enemy insurgents from key urban areas.

The engagement pitted about 1,000 U.S. and Iraqi troops against an undetermined number of insurgent fighters.

Haifa Street, a broad boulevard located in central Baghdad, runs northwest from the Green Zone, the home of the Coalition Provisional Authority, for two miles along the west bank of the Tigris River. Many of the buildings along the street, including the former residences of wealthy Sunni government officials, are 20-story high-rise apartments. Amid increasing sectarian violence in 2006, Sunni and Al Qaeda in Iraq insurgents had taken control of the street and its surrounding neighborhood. They also made use of the high-rise apartment buildings from which they were able to fire down into the streets, posing a serious hazard to civilians and coalition troops. Throughout 2006 insurgents sporadically engaged American and Iraqi forces by sniper fire and grenades lobbed from the residential and office buildings.

The catalyst for the Battle of Haifa Street occurred on January 6, 2007, when Iraqi troops killed 30 Sunni insurgents after discovering a fake checkpoint manned by insurgents. In retaliation, the insurgents executed 27 Shias and distributed leaflets threatening to kill anyone who entered the area. Following an unsuccessful attempt by Iraqi soldiers to clear the neighborhood on January 8, American troops prepared a full-scale offensive to assist the Iraqis.

The first stage of the battle involved approximately 1,000 American and Iraqi troops. On January 9 a reinforced U.S. Army battalion from the 2nd Infantry Division joined the Iraqi 6th Infantry Division to engage in pitched street-by-street combat to clear buildings from north to south along Haifa Street. During the intense one-day operation, the Americans employed snipers and Stryker combat vehicles to methodically clear insurgent strongholds. Ground troops were supported by Boeing/McDonnell Douglas AH-64 Apache attack helicopters and precision-guided munitions. The U.S. and Iraqi forces mounted a successful retaliation effort against the strong insurgent resistance that included machine-gun fire, rocket-propelled grenades, and coordinated mortar fire. In the course of the battle approximately 70 insurgents were killed or captured, including several foreign fighters. Some 25 others were captured.

U.S. troops subsequently withdrew, leaving Iraqi forces to patrol the area. However, insurgents reinfiltrated the area over the next two weeks. Before dawn on January 24, 2007, Iraqi troops joined a larger American force consisting of two reinforced battalions from the 2nd Infantry and 1st Cavalry Divisions to clear the street again. This second stage of the battle, named Operation TOMAHAWK STRIKE 11, lasted less than one day. U.S. Army units used both Bradley and Stryker combat vehicles to control the street, supported by Iraqi and American troops who cleared apartments while taking sniper and mortar fire. By evening the street and surrounding buildings had been cleared, and a large weapons cache had been seized. Approximately 65 insurgents, including numerous foreign fighters, were killed or captured on January 24. Iraqi forces suffered 20 killed during both engagements. Although a substantial American presence remained for several days following the second battle, control and responsibility for the sector had been relinquished to the Iraqi Army by February 1, 2007.

WILLIAM E. FORK

See also

Al Qaeda in Iraq; Baghdad, Iraq; Green Zone in Iraq

References

Cave, Damien, and James Glanz. "In a New Joint U.S.-Iraqi Patrol, the Americans Go First." *New York Times,* January 25, 2007.

Kagan, Kimberly. "The Iraq Report; From 'New Way Forward' to New Commander." *Weekly Standard,* January 10, 2007–February 10, 2007, 7–10.

Zavis, Alexandra. "The Conflict in Iraq: Military Offensive in Baghdad; U.S.-Iraqi Forces Strike 'Sniper Alley.'" *Los Angeles Times,* January 25, 2007.

Hakim, Abdul Aziz al- (1950–2009)

Iraqi Shia cleric, leader of the Supreme Islamic Iraqi Council, and sayyid (descendant of the Prophet Muhammad). Abdul Aziz al-Hakim was born sometime in 1950 in the southern Iraqi city of Najaf, a descendant of the Prophet Muhammad and the fourth caliph, Ali ibn Abi Talib. Hakim is a *hujjat al-Islam* (literally "proof of Islam") with the lower-level ranking of cleric, not a *mujtahid*. More important, he is the current leader of the Supreme Islamic Iraqi Council (SIIC), one of the two largest Iraqi Shia political parties, a position he inherited upon the assassination of his brother, Ayatollah Muhammad Baqir al-Hakim, who was killed by a massive car bomb in Najaf in August 2003.

Abdul Aziz al-Hakim's father was Grand Ayatollah Sayyid Muhsin al-Hakim (1889–1970), the preeminent Shia religious scholar and authority in Iraq from 1955 until his death. The family has deep roots in Iraq as one of the premier Arab Shia scholarly families based in Najaf, where Imam Ali's shrine is located, although the family originally came from the Jabal Amil in southern Lebanon. Abdul Aziz al-Hakim's brother, Sayyid Muhammad Mahdi (1940?–1988), another activist, was also assassinated in Khartoum,

Sudan, most likely on the orders of Iraqi president Saddam Hussein. All three of the Hakim brothers studied religious subjects under both their father and then Ayatollah Sayyid Muhammad Baqir al-Sadr (1935–1980), one of their father's leading students and an activist scholar who was one of the intellectual founders of the Islamic Dawa Party (Hizb al-Da'wa al-Islamiyya), Iraq's other large Shia political party.

Abdul Aziz al-Hakim's earliest social and political activism occurred in tandem with his father and older brothers, all of whom were actively opposed to the growing influence of the Iraqi Communist Party (ICP) among segments of Shia youths during the 1950s and 1960s. Grand Ayatollah Hakim was an outspoken critic of communism, and he passed a juridical opinion (fatwa) against membership in the ICP in February 1960. He was also instrumental in the formation and support of the Jamaat al-Ulama (Society of Religious Scholars), a coalition of religious scholars (*ulama*) opposed to the growing influence of the ICP and other Iraqi secular political parties. Due to his age, Hakim was not actively involved in the Jamaat al-Ulama and the earlier stages of the Islamic Dawa Party, although his brothers were.

Following the Iraqi invasion of Iran in September 1980 and the outbreak of the Iran-Iraq War (1980–1988), when Hussein issued orders calling for the execution of members of the Dawa Party, Abdul Aziz al-Hakim and his brother Muhammad Baqir left Iraq for Iran along with thousands of other Iraqi Shias, many of them political activists. The Iraqi government claimed that it might face traitorous actions by Iraq's long-disenfranchised Shia Arab majority. Ayatollah Baqir al-Sadr had been executed along with his sister, Amina bint Haydar al-Sadr (also known as Bint al-Huda), in April 1980.

In November 1982 Baqir al-Hakim announced the formation of the Supreme Council for the Islamic Revolution in Iraq (SCIRI), which initially was an umbrella organization that brought together officials from the various Iraqi exiled opposition movements, although it eventually became its own political party as other groups broke away over policy and ideological disputes. SCIRI's leadership was based in Tehran and was more heavily influenced by Iranian individuals and political competition than the Dawa Party. In 1982–1983 SCIRI's paramilitary wing, the Badr Organization, was founded under Hakim's leadership. Badr was made up of recruits from among the Iraqi exile community living in Iran as well as Iraqi Shia prisoners of war, who received training and equipment from the Iranian Revolutionary Guard Corps on the instructions of Grand Ayatollah

Abdul Aziz al-Hakim, leader of the Supreme Council for the Islamic Revolution in Iraq, votes in Baghdad on January 30, 2005. (U.S. Department of Defense)

Ruhollah Khomeini, Iran's revolutionary leader. On the eve of the U.S.- and British-led invasion of Iraq of March 2003, Badr reportedly fielded 10,000–15,000 fighters, with a core elite group of several thousand fighters.

Abdul Aziz al-Hakim and Muhammad Baqir returned to Iraq on May 12, 2003, making their way to the southern Iraqi port city of Basra, where the ayatollah gave a rousing speech in front of an estimated 100,000 Iraqi supporters in the main soccer stadium, rejecting U.S. postwar domination of the country. The Hakims were soon joined by thousands of SCIRI members and Badr fighters who flooded into southern Iraq. Following his brother's assassination on August 29, 2003, Abdul Aziz al-Hakim assumed control of SCIRI, which several years later was renamed the Supreme Iraqi Islamic Council. He maintained a close relationship with the U.S. government. In fact, he was the favorite of various American figures to succeed Ibrahim al-Jafari, perhaps due to his English skills and demeanor, but was not as popular with Iraqis, as was demonstrated at the polls. During Hakim's tenure as party chief, SCIRI achieved a key electoral victory in December 2005 as part of the United Iraqi

Alliance, a loose coalition of primarily Shia political parties that, together with the Kurdish political list, dominated Iraqi politics. In the past, he supported attempts to create a decentralized federal system. He vocally supported the creation of an autonomous Shia region in southern and central Iraq, a move that has been repeatedly opposed by other Shiite parties such as Fadhila and by Sunni Arab politicians and Tayyar al-Sadr (Sadr Movement), the sociopolitical faction led by Muqtada al-Sadr.

Badr officials and fighters are heavily represented in the Iraqi state security forces and important ministries, including the Ministry of the Interior. They were blamed for summarily arresting, kidnapping, torturing, and murdering Sunni Arabs, often political rivals and random civilians, in the streets, particularly in mixed Sunni-Shia neighborhoods, which they sought to cleanse of Sunni Arabs. The SIIC leadership denies involvement in such attacks despite strong evidence to the contrary.

Beginning in 2004 and reaching its apogee in the spring of 2008, Badr fighters, many of them while in their capacity as Iraqi state security, engaged in running street battles with the Sadrists over political power, reportedly seeking to weaken them before the 2009 municipal elections. Heavy fighting under the direction of the official Iraqi state, backed by Prime Minister Nuri al-Maliki and the U.S. military, took place between SIIC-dominated Iraqi security forces and Sadrist fighters in Baghdad in 2007 and in Basra during the spring and early summer of 2008.

Hakim was aided by his two sons, Muhsin (1974–) and Ammar (1972–), who both head various offices and departments within the SIIC. Ammar was the secretary-general of the al-Mihrab Martyr Foundation, an SIIC affiliate organization that has built mosques, Islamic centers, and schools throughout southern Iraq and Shia areas of Baghdad, the Iraqi capital; he was also the second-in-command of the SIIC.

The SIIC publicly recognizes Grand Ayatollah Sayyid Ali al-Sistani, Iraq's senior resident Shia religious authority, as its official religious guide and scholar, although the degree to which it actually follows his religious edicts is unclear because the SIIC and Sistani have their own networks of mosques, which reinstituted Friday sermons after the fall of Hussein. SIIC and Badr fighters have notably ignored Sistani's calls for intercommunal harmony and a cessation of sectarian/intercommunal killings by both Sunnis and Shias. Hakim and other SIIC leaders have also publicly denied that they seek to establish a religious state in Iraq, as this was the original goal of the SIIC. The party has insisted on a prominent role for Islamic morals, sharia, and institutions, particularly Shia ones, in the present and future Iraqi state.

Stricken with lung cancer, Abdul Aziz al-Hakim flew to Houston, Texas, in May 2007 for treatment and then on to Tehran, Iran, for chemotherapy. He died in Tehran on August 26, 2009.

Christopher Paul Anzalone

See also

Baath Party; Badr Organization; Hakim, Muhammad Baqir al-; Hussein, Saddam; Islamic Dawa Party; Maliki, Nuri al-; Shia Islam; Sistani, Sayyid Ali Husayn al-; Sunni Islam; Supreme Iraqi Islamic Council; United Iraqi Alliance

References

Dagher, Sam. "Rising Player with a Vision for Shiite Iraq." *Christian Science Monitor,* November 20, 2007.

Jabar, Faleh A. *The Shi'ite Movement in Iraq.* London: Saqi Books, 2003.

Samii, A. William. "Shia Political Alternatives in Postwar Iraq." *Middle East Policy* 10 (May 2003): 93–101.

Visser, Reidar. *Shi'a Separatism in Iraq: Internet Reverie or Real Constitutional Challenge?* Oslo: Norwegian Institute of International Affairs, 2005.

Hakim, Muhammad Baqir al- (ca. 1939–2003)

Iraqi ayatollah and founding leader of the Supreme Council for Islamic Revolution in Iraq (SCIRI), since renamed the Supreme Islamic Iraqi Council (SIIC), one of the two largest Iraqi Shia political parties. Muhammad al-Hakim Baqir was born in Najaf, Iraq, either in 1939 or 1944. His father was Grand Ayatollah Sayyid Muhsin al-Hakim (1889–1970), the preeminent Shia religious scholar and authority in Iraq from 1955 until his death in 1970. The Hakim family is one of Iraq's preeminent Shia scholarly families, with deep roots in the southern Iraqi shrine city of Najaf, where the first Shia imam and fourth Muslim caliph, Ali ibn Abi Talib, is buried. The family originally came from the Jabal Amil region of historical Syria in present-day southern Lebanon.

Muhammad Baqir was one of three sons, the others being his younger brother Abdul Aziz (1950–2009), future SIIC leader, and Muhammad Mahdi (1940?–1988), commonly known simply as Mahdi, who was assassinated in Khartoum, Sudan, probably at the behest of the ruling Iraqi Baath Party under President Saddam Hussein. All three of the Hakim brothers were born in Najaf and studied under both their father and Ayatollah Sayyid Muhammad Baqir al-Sadr (1935–1980), one of their father's premier students and an activist scholar who was one of the intellectual founders of the Islamic Dawa Party (Hizb al-Da'wa al-Islamiyya), Iraq's other large Shia political party. Both Muhammad Baqir and his brother Mahdi were involved in the formation of the Dawa Party, and the latter was also active in the Jamaat al-Ulama, a clerical association formed in Najaf during the 1950s to combat the rising popularity of communism among Iraqi Shiite youths.

Muhammad Baqir was a well-known Shiite activist throughout the 1960s and 1970s. He was arrested, tortured, and imprisoned in 1972 and again from February 1977 to July 1979. He left Iraq for Iran with his brother Abd al-Aziz and thousands of other Iraqi Shias, mainly political activists, in the autumn of 1980 following the execution of Ayatollah Muhammad Baqir al-Sadr and his sister, Amina bint Haydar al-Sadr (also known as Bint al-Huda), in April and the outbreak of the Iran-Iraq War that September. In November 1982 Muhammad Baqir al-Hakim announced the formation of SCIRI, which initially was envisioned as an umbrella organization that would bring together the various exiled Iraqi opposition movements, topple Hussein, and bring about an Islamic state.

SCIRI eventually was transformed into its own political party as other parties broke away over policy and ideological disputes. Grand Ayatollah Ruhollah Khomeini, Iran's revolutionary leader, was actively supportive of the new group, seeing it as a tool to harass the Saddam Hussein regime. In 1982–1983 the Badr Organization was founded under the leadership of Abdul Aziz al-Hakim, forming the paramilitary wing of the SIIC. Officers from the Iranian Revolutionary Guard Corps provided military training and equipment for the several thousand Iraqi Arab exiles and prisoners of war who filled Badr's ranks.

During his 23 years in exile, Muhammad Baqir built up SCIRI networks among the tens of thousands of Iraqi exiles living in Iran. On the eve of the U.S.- and British-led invasion of Iraq in March 2003, SCIRI officials claimed to have 10,000 armed fighters in the Badr Corps. The organization's networks inside Iraq were not as developed as SCIRI propaganda claimed, however, because Baath Party security forces had been largely successful in limiting their growth inside the country. Prior to 2003, Badr agents carried out attacks on Iraqi government targets both inside and outside of Iraq, and Badr fighters were active participants in northern Iraq (Iraqi Kurdistan) during the Iran-Iraq War. Muhammad Baqir and SCIRI were criticized by segments of the Iraqi Shia community for siding with Iran against Iraq during the war; unlike Dawa Party members, some in SCIRI fought Iraq, and many Iraqi Sunnis have therefore alleged that the organization is controlled by the Iranians.

Muhammad Baqir and his brother, together with other SCIRI leaders and members, returned to southern Iraq on May 12, 2003. Muhammad Baqir delivered a rousing speech in front of an estimated 100,000 Iraqis in the main soccer stadium in the southern Iraqi port city of Basra, publicly thanking Iran for its longtime support in resisting Saddam Hussein and rejecting U.S. postwar domination of the country. The Hakims were soon joined by thousands of SCIRI members and Badr fighters who flooded into southern and central Iraq's cities, towns, and villages.

In his public pronouncements and interviews, Muhammad Baqir was supportive of the role of the *marjaiyya,* the informal council of Iraq's five senior grand ayatollahs based in Najaf. He also did not call for his followers to fight the U.S. and British forces in the country, although he remained opposed to their long-term presence in the country. He called for the establishment of an Islamic state in Iraq but did not call for any immediate implementation of such a state. He acknowledged that the *marjaiyya* (whose religious leadership is senior to any other in Iraq) should occupy a major advisory role for the government.

On August 29, 2003, Muhammad Baqir was assassinated by a massive car comb following Friday prayers, before which he delivered the requisite sermon, at the Imam Ali Shrine in Najaf. Between 84 and 125 other people were also killed, and scores more were wounded in the bombing. This attack is believed to have been carried out by the Tawhid wa al-Jihad organization, later renamed Al Qaeda in the Land of the Two Rivers (al-Qa'ida fi Bilad al-Rafhidayn), led by the Jordanian Abu Musab al-Zarqawi (1966–2006). Muhammad Baqir's brother Abduk Aziz al-Hakim then took up the leadership of SCIRI.

CHRISTOPHER PAUL ANZALONE

See also

Baath Party; Hakim, Abdul Aziz al-; Islamic Dawa Party; Supreme Iraqi Islamic Council

References

Hijazi, Ihsan A. "Iraqi's Death in Sudan Linked to Iran Faction." *New York Times,* January 24, 1988.

Jabar, Faleh A. *The Shi'ite Movement in Iraq.* London: Saqi Books, 2003.

Joffe, Lawrence. "Ayatollah Mohammad Baqir al-Hakim." *The Guardian,* August 30, 2003.

Samii, A. William. "Shia Political Alternatives in Postwar Iraq." *Middle East Policy* 10 (May 2003): 93–101.

Halliburton

A multinational corporation based in Houston, Texas, Halliburton provides specialty products and services to the oil and gas industries and also constructs oil fields, refineries, pipelines, and chemical plants through its main subsidiary KBR (Kellogg, Brown, and Root). Although the company conducts operations in more than 120 countries, controversy regarding Halliburton Energy Services has focused on U.S. government contracts awarded to the company following the Iraq War and allegations of conflict of interest involving former vice president Dick Cheney, who had been Halliburton's chief executive officer (CEO).

In 1919 during the midst of the oil boom in Texas and Oklahoma, Mr. and Mrs. Erle P. Halliburton began cementing oil wells in Burkburnett, Texas. That same year, the Halliburtons established their business in Dallas, Texas. They then moved the business to Ardmore, Oklahoma. In 1924, the Halliburton Oil Well Cementing Company was incorporated. A significant expansion of the company occurred in 1962 with the acquisition of Brown & Root, a construction and engineering firm that became a wholly owned subsidiary of Halliburton. Brown & Root had been established in

Civilian contractors employed by Halliburton fight a fire within the Green Zone in Baghdad when someone apparently tried to steal electricity from a power line. Halliburton, a Houston-based multinational corporation once headed by U.S. vice president Dick Cheney, provided substantial support for U.S. government operations in Iraq. (U.S. Department of Defense)

1919 by brothers George and Herman Brown along with their brother-in-law Dan Root. Employing political patronage with influential figures such as Lyndon B. Johnson, Brown & Root grew from fulfilling small road-paving projects to garnering military contracts constructing military bases and naval warships. Brown & Root was part of a consortium responsible for providing approximately 85 percent of the infrastructure required by the U.S. military during the Vietnam War.

The relationship between Halliburton and the U.S. military establishment was enhanced in 1992 when the Pentagon, under the direction of Secretary of Defense Dick Cheney, offered the company a contract for the bulk of support services for U.S. military operations abroad. Three years later Cheney was elected chairman and CEO of Halliburton. One of Cheney's first initiatives at Halliburton was the acquisition of rival Dresser Industries for $7.7 billion. Halliburton, however, also inherited the legal liabilities of Dresser for asbestos poisoning claims. The asbestos settlement caused Halliburton's stock price to plummet 80 percent in 1999. Nevertheless, during Cheney's five-year

tenure at Halliburton (1995–2000), government contracts awarded to the company rose to $1.5 billion. This contrasts with just $100 million in government contracts from 1990 to 1995.

Upon assuming the vice presidency in the George W. Bush administration in 2001, Cheney declared that he would be severing all ties with the company. He continued, however, to earn deferred compensation worth approximately $150,000 annually, along with stock options worth more than $18 million. Cheney assured critics that he would donate proceeds from the stock options to charity.

Even if Cheney did not personally profit, Halliburton secured several lucrative government contracts to rebuild Iraq and support the U.S. military presence in that nation following the U.S.-led invasion of Iraq in March 2003. By 2006, it was estimated that Halliburton's Iraq contracts alone were worth as much as $18 billion. Although the company enjoys relatively low profit margins from its military contracts, Halliburton stock hit a record high in August 2008 of $43.94 per share. In February 2003 one month before the invasion of Iraq, Halliburton stocks were selling for just $10.13 per share. By March 2010 as the Iraq War was winding down, the company's stock had retreated to $30.15 per share.

These profits, however, were subject to charges of corruption. For example, in 2003 a division of Halliburton overcharged the government by some $61 million for buying and transporting fuel from Kuwait into Iraq. Halliburton insisted that the high costs were the fault of a Kuwaiti subcontractor. Halliburton also received criticism for a $7 billion no-bid contract to rebuild Iraqi oil fields. Defenders of Halliburton insist that few companies have the resources and capital necessary to carry out the large-scale assignments given to Halliburton. Company executives also point out that if Halliburton had not provided support operations, far more combat troops would have been needed in Iraq. The controversies surrounding Halliburton's role in the Iraq War continue to raise questions as to the rationale for the initial March 2003 invasion.

More recently, Halliburton again came under fire for its involvement in the 2010 Deepwater Horizon oil spill in the Gulf of Mexico that released some 4.9 million barrels of crude oil into gulf waters. The oil well was owned by BP, but Halliburton had been a prime subcontractor on the project. In July 2013, Halliburton pleaded guilty to having deliberately destroyed evidence that BP had demanded once the leak was sealed. The company was forced to pay a $200,000 statutory fine for this action and continues to face other legal problems related to the spill.

RON BRILEY

See also

Bush, George Walker; Cheney, Richard Bruce; Iraq, History of, 1990–Present; IRAQI FREEDOM, Operation

References

Briody, Dan. The *Halliburton Agenda: The Politics of Oil and Money*. Hoboken, NJ: Wiley, 2004.

Purdum, Todd S., and Will Shortz. *A Time of Our Choosing: America's War in Iraq*. New York: Times Books, 2003.

Hamburg Cell

Terrorist cell formed by a group of radical Islamists affiliated with Al Qaeda in Hamburg, Germany. The Hamburg Cell, which played an important role in the September 11, 2001, terror attacks on the United States, began when Muhammad Atta, Ramzi ibn al-Shibh, and Marwan al-Shehhi took up lodgings together on November 1, 1998, in an apartment on 54 Marienstrasse in Hamburg. They were members of a study group at the al-Quds Mosque run by Mohammad Belfas, a middle-aged postal employee in Hamburg who was originally from Indonesia. Both in the study group and at the apartment, the men began talking about ways to advance the Islamist cause. Soon the original three attracted others of a like mind. The nine members of this group were Muhammad Atta, Said Bahaji, Mohammad Belfas, Ramzi ibn al-Shibh, Zakariya Essabor, Marwan al-Shehhi, Ziad Jarrah, Mounir al-Motassadez, and Abd al-Ghani Mzoudi.

At first Belfas was the leader of the group, but he was soon replaced by Atta and left the cell. Although Atta became the formal leader, Shibh was its most influential member because he was more popular within the Muslim community than Atta.

Initially the members of the Hamburg group wanted to join the Chechen rebels in Chechnya in their fight against the Russians. Before this move could take place, the leaders of the cell met with Mohamedou Ould Slahi, an Al Qaeda operative in Duisburg, Germany, who advised that they first undertake military and terrorist training in Afghanistan. Atta, Shibh, Jarrah, and Shehhi traveled to Kandahar, Afghanistan, where they underwent extensive training in terrorist techniques. They also met with Al Qaeda leader Osama bin Laden, at which time Atta, Jarrah, and Shehhi were recruited for a special martyrdom mission in the United States. Shibh was to have been a part of this mission, but he was never able to obtain a visa to travel to the United States. Instead, Shibh stayed in Hamburg, serving as the contact person between the Hamburg Cell and Al Qaeda. He also served as the banker for the hijackers in the September 11 plot.

What made those in the Hamburg Cell so important was that the individuals in it were fluent in English, well educated, and apparently accustomed to a Western lifestyle, so they were more likely to be able to live in a Western country without raising any suspicions. They also had the capability to learn with some training how to pilot a large aircraft.

Shibh ended communication with the Hamburg Cell as soon as he learned the date of the attacks. He made certain that all those connected with it were forewarned so that they could protect themselves. Shibh destroyed as much material as possible before leaving for Pakistan. Only later did German and American authorities learn of the full extent of the operations of the Hamburg Cell.

German authorities had been aware of the existence of the Hamburg Cell, but German law prevented action against its members unless a German law was violated. This restriction did not prevent Thomas Volz, a veteran U.S. Central Intelligence Agency officer attached to the American consulate in Hamburg, from attempting to persuade German authorities to take action against the Islamist extremists who were allegedly part of the cell and known to be at the Hamburg mosque. Volz had become suspicious of several members of the group and their connections with other Muslim terrorists. He hounded the German authorities to do something until his actions alienated them to the point that they almost had him deported from Germany.

After the September 11 attacks, German authorities began a serious investigation of the Hamburg Cell and its surviving members. By that time there was little to examine or do except to arrest whoever had been affiliated with it. The German authorities finally learned the extent to which Al Qaeda had been able to establish contacts in Germany and elsewhere in Europe.

STEPHEN E. ATKINS

See also

Al Qaeda; Atta, Muhammad; Bin Laden, Osama; September 11 Attacks; Shibh, Ramzi Muhammad Abdallah ibn al-

References

Bernstein, Richard. *Out of the Blue: The Story of September 11, 2001, from Jihad to Ground Zero.* New York: Times Books, 2002.

McDermott, Terry. *Perfect Soldiers: The 9/11 Hijackers; Who They Were, Why They Did It.* New York: HarperCollins, 2005.

Posner, Gerald. *Why America Slept: The Failure to Prevent 9/11.* New York: Ballantine Books, 2003.

Sageman, Marc. *Understanding Terror Networks.* Philadelphia: University of Pennsylvania Press, 2004.

Hanjour, Hani (1972–2001)

The leader and probable pilot of the terrorist group that seized American Airlines Flight 77 and crashed it into the Pentagon on September 11, 2001; he was a last-minute recruit because the September 11 conspirators needed one additional pilot. Hani Saleh Husan Hanjour was born on August 30, 1972, in Taif, Saudi Arabia. His father was a successful food-supply businessman. Hanjour was a devout Muslim, and this colored virtually all of his conduct.

Because he was an indifferent student, Hanjour was only persuaded to stay in school by his older brother. This older brother, who was living in Tucson, Arizona, encouraged him to go to the United States. Hanjour arrived in the United States on October 3, 1991, and stayed in Tucson, where he studied English at the University of Arizona.

After completing the English program in three months, Hanjour returned to Taif. He spent the next five years working at his family's food-supply business. In 1996 he briefly visited Afghanistan. Following this visit, he decided to move back to the United States. He stayed for a time with an Arab American family in Hollywood, Florida. Then in April 1996, Hanjour moved in with a family in Oakland, California. This time he attended Holy Names College and took an intensive course in English. He then decided to become a pilot and fly for Saudi Airlines. Hanjour also enrolled in a class at the Sierra Academy of Aeronautics, but he withdrew because of the cost.

Leaving Oakland in April 1996, Hanjour moved to Phoenix, Arizona. This time he paid for flight lessons at CRM Flight Cockpit Resource Management in Scottsdale, Arizona, but his academic performance there was disappointing. His instructors found him to be a terrible pilot, and it took him a long time to master the essentials of flying.

While in Phoenix, Hanjour roomed with Bandar al-Hazmi. In January 1998 Hanjour took flying lessons at Arizona Aviation, and after a three-year struggle he finally earned his commercial pilot rating in April 1999 but was unable to find a job as a pilot. His Federal Aviation Administration (FAA) license expired in 1999 when he failed to take a mandatory medical test.

Frustrated in his job hunting, Hanjour traveled to Afghanistan. He arrived there just as Khalid Sheikh Mohammed's men were looking for another pilot for the September 11, 2001, terror plot. Hanjour seemed made to order. After his recruitment by Al Qaeda, he returned to the United States. In September 2000 when he moved to San Diego, California, Hanjour met up with Nawaf al-Hazmi. Hanjour returned to Phoenix to continue his pilot training at the Jet Tech Flight School. He was so inept as a flyer and his English was so poor that the instructors contacted the FAA to check on whether his commercial license was valid. The FAA confirmed this. Hanjour spent most of his time at Jet Tech on the Boeing 737 simulator. In the early spring of 2001 he moved to Paterson, New Jersey. There he met several times with other members of the September 11 conspiracy.

On September 11, 2001, Hanjour is believed to have served as the hijackers' pilot of American Airlines Flight 77. Despite his lack of flying ability, after the crew had been subdued he managed to fly that aircraft into the Pentagon. Hanjour put the Boeing 757 into a steep nose dive and slammed the jet into the building at 9:37 a.m. All 58 passengers aboard the plane perished, as did Hanjour and 4 other hijackers. An additional 125 people died on the ground upon and after impact.

STEPHEN E. ATKINS

See also
Mohammed, Khalid Sheikh; September 11 Attacks

References
Graham, Bob. *Intelligence Matters: The CIA, the FBI, Saudi Arabia, and the Failure of America's War on Terror.* New York: Random House, 2004.
McDermott, Terry. *Perfect Soldiers: The 9/11 Hijackers: Who They Were, Why They Did It.* New York: HarperCollins, 2005.

Harakat ul-Jihad al-Islami

Harakat ul-Jihad al-Islami (Islamic Struggle Movement, HuJI) is a Pakistan-based terrorist group that adheres to the Deobandi sect of Islam and espouses a virulent anti-Indian, anti–United States, and anti-Pakistani government agenda. Conflicting reports exist regarding the precise date of HuJI's founding and its creators; however, most sources agree that the organization was established during the Afghan jihad to fight against occupying Soviet forces and that Qari Saifullah Akhtar and Maulana Irshad Ahmed were prominent early members. Following Moscow's withdrawal from Kabul in 1989, HuJI refocused its efforts toward fighting Indian rule in the predominantly Muslim state of Jammu and Kashmir with the prominent support and backing of Pakistan's InterServices Intelligence (ISI) Directorate.

HuJI suffered an early setback when a ranking member named Fazlur Rehman Khalil broke away from the group to establish his own militant organization, the Harakat-ul-Mujahideen (Holy Warriors' Movement, HuM). At the behest of militant Deobandi clerics and the ISI, the two agreed to reunite in 1993 under the banner of Harakat-ul-Ansar (Helpers' Movement, HuA). Three years later the new entity staged a series of international kidnappings that resulted in the deaths of five Western tourists. The abductions led the United States to proscribe the HuA as a foreign terrorist organization, which subsequently prompted HuM and HuJI to terminate their merger and revert to their own independent existence.

HuJI developed strong ties with the Taliban government in Afghanistan during the late 1990s, and several sources suggest that by this time Akhtar was serving as a political adviser to Mullah Omar. HuJI relocated much of its training infrastructure to Afghanistan, establishing a major training camp in Rishkot, and assisted the Taliban in combat operations against the Northern Alliance—eliciting perhaps the first known use of the term "Punjabi Taliban." HuJI's

leadership was also reportedly close to Al Qaeda and is believed to have been a principal force in helping to solidify links between Osama bin Laden and Mullah Omar.

Following the fall of the Taliban in late 2001, much of the group's membership relocated to Pakistan, establishing a strong presence in the Federally Administered Tribal Areas and the Northwest Frontier Province (now known as Khyber-Pakhtunkwha). The group also set up various smaller branches in other parts of the country. Akhtar reportedly fled from Afghanistan first to South Waziristan, then to Saudi Arabia, and finally to Dubai. He was deported to Pakistan in 2004 following suspicions of his involvement in two foiled plots to assassinate President Pervez Musharraf and was held in custody until 2007, when he was evidently released.

Following the storming of the Lal Masjid mosque, HuJI was suspected of involvement in a number of high-profile terrorist attacks in Pakistan. These included, notably, two assassination attempts against Benazir Bhutto in 2007—the second of which proved successful—and the bombing of a Marriott hotel in Islamabad in 2008. At this time Akhtar moved to Waziristan, where under his auspices HuJI continued to foster links to Al Qaeda as well as the newly formed Tehrik-e-Taliban Pakistan (Pakistani Taliban). Until his death in June 2011, HuJI's operational commander, Ilyas Kashmiri, emerged as a top commander for joint operations conducted by his group, Al Qaeda, the Pakistani Taliban, and other Deobandi terrorist outfits. HuJI itself has been tied to an assault on the Pakistani Army's general headquarters in 2009, a plot to attack a Danish newspaper that had published offensive cartoons of the Prophet Muhammad, and the assassination of Khalid Khwaja, an ex-ISI squadron leader, in 2010 (the latter being claimed under the name Asian Tigers).

Despite these operations, HuJI's overall level of activity has declined in recent years as the group has been eclipsed by other terrorist organizations based in Pakistan. HuJI's current infrastructure in India is unknown at the present time, although its affiliate in Bangladesh, Harakat-ul-Jihad-Islami Bangladesh, is thought to retain a strong network in the country, particularly in the state of West Bengal.

BEN BRANDT

See also
Al Qaeda

References
"Harakat_ul-Ansar (Now Known as Harakar-ul-Mujahideen): Evolution of the Outfit." South Asia Terrorism Portal, http://www.satporg/satporgtp/countries/india/states/jandk/terrorist

_outfits/harakat_ul_ansar_or_harakat_ul_jehad_e_islami
.htm.

"Harakat-ul-Jihad-al-Islami." Investigative Project on Terrorism,
http://www.investigativeproject.org/profile/147.

"HuJI Chief behind EX-ISI Man's Killing?" *Times of India*, May 2,
2010.

Roul, Animesh. "HuJI Operations Expand beyond the Indian Subcontinent." The Jamestown Foundation, April 29, 2010, http://
www.jamestown.org/programs/gta/single/?tx_ttnews%5Btt
_news%5D=36327&cHash=77e57144d9.

Harethi, Qaed Salim Sinan al-, Drone Strike on

On November 3, 2002, the U.S. Central Intelligence Agency (CIA) engineered a targeted assassination of high-ranking Al Qaeda leader Qaed Salim Sinan al-Harethi as part of the ongoing Global War on Terror. The attack occurred in Yemen's northern province of Marib, about 100 miles east of the Yemeni capital of Sana'a, and was carried out using a Predator drone (a remote-controlled unmanned aerial vehicle). The drone fired an AGM-114 Hellfire air-to-surface missile into an automobile in which Harethi and five associates, believed to be lower-ranking Al Qaeda leaders, were riding. The missile strike killed all six people, including Harethi.

The Harethi drone strike was notable for several reasons. First, it marked the first known use of a Predator drone for a targeted killing outside Afghanistan; second, it was the first drone attack in Yemen; and third, it was the first occasion in which a U.S. citizen was killed by the U.S. government during the ongoing Global War on Terror. One of Harethi's associates who died with him was Kamal Derwish, an American citizen of Yemeni ancestry. The intended target of the attack, however, was Harethi and not Derwish. Harethi was a close confidante of Al Qaeda mastermind Osama bin laden and was believed to have been responsible for the October 12, 2000, attack against USS *Cole*. That assault had taken place in the Yemeni port of Aden and resulted in the deaths of 17 American sailors and the wounding of 39 others. He had been at the top of the CIA's kill list since that time. After the September 11, 2001, terror attacks on the United States, the U.S. government dramatically expanded its efforts to target and kill terror suspects such as Harethi.

The CIA, working with Edmund Hull, America's ambassador to Yemen at the time, had been planning the drone attack for some time. Indeed, it was Hull who helped gather intelligence on Harethi's whereabouts, and it was he who paid local tribesman in return for information on Harethi's location and activities. Yemen's government, however, was not pleased with the drone attack because Washington had not coordinated its efforts with Yemeni intelligence or military officials. Yemeni leaders were also angry that members of the George W. Bush administration had made the attack public, apparently in violation of an earlier agreement that the U.S. government would not claim responsibility for the drone assault.

The drone attack also created controversy in the United States because Darwish, who was among those killed, held U.S. citizenship. Darwish was by no means an altar boy, and American authorities had strong evidence that he had been operating an Al Qaeda sleeper cell outside Buffalo, New York. Nevertheless, some critics of the attack argued that Darwish's constitutional rights were abrogated because he was effectively killed by the U.S. government without being charged with any crime and without due process of law. Bush administration officials countered that Darwish was active as an enemy combatant against American interests, in a foreign country no less, and therefore had ceded any constitutional rights he might otherwise have enjoyed. Furthermore, the White House asserted that the president had broad latitude to wage the Global War on Terror, given to him by the U.S. Congress after the September 11, 2001, attacks, and that authority empowered him to engage in covert operations against Al Qaeda and other terrorist organizations anywhere in the world. U.S. drone attacks against terrorists and suspected terrorists rose steadily after the Harethi attack, and they accelerated even more rapidly under the Barack Obama administration.

PAUL G. PIERPAOLI JR.

See also

Unmanned Aerial Vehicles

References

Lumpkin, John J. "Al-Qaida Suspects Die in U.S. Missile Strike." Associated Press, November 5, 2002.

Lumpkin, John J. "U.S. Can Target American Al-Qaida Agents." Associated Press, December 3, 2002.

Volker, Franke C., ed. *Terrorism and Peacekeeping: New Security Challenges*. Westport, CT: Praeger, 2005.

Harrell, Gary L. (ca. 1951–)

U.S. Army general who served for three decades in various special operations forces, including as Delta Force commander during operations in Somalia. Gary L. Harrell is a Tennessee native who enrolled in the Reserve Officers' Training Corps at East Tennessee State University as a means to pay for college. He did not plan on a military career but found the duty enjoyable and challenging. Commissioned after graduation with a BS degree in December 1973, Harrell was assigned to the 82nd Airborne Division at Fort Bragg, North Carolina. He participated in the U.S. invasion of Grenada in 1983 as a member of the 82nd Airborne Division. He later completed ranger training and became a member of Delta Force. In 1989 he was a part of a team that rescued American Kurt Muse from a Panamanian prison during the U.S. invasion of Panama. Harrell also helped capture infamous drug lord Pablo Escobar in Colombia.

During Operation DESERT STORM in 1991, Harrell served with the Joint Special Operations Command and participated in the effort by special operations forces in western Iraq to locate and destroy Scud missiles used to attack Israel and Saudi Arabia. The effort was largely unsuccessful. Two years later Harrell was special assistant to the commander of the 1st Special Forces Operational Detachment-Delta (Airborne) in Somalia. During an attempt to capture warlords who were opposed to U.S. interests, two helicopters carrying U.S. Army Rangers were shot down. While a rapid-reaction force battled toward one crash site, the other crash site was threatened by Somali militiamen. A Delta Force team providing oversight to the second downed helicopter requested permission to land and protect the survivors. Harrell twice refused permission but reluctantly gave in on the third request. The two Delta Force members, knowing their possible fate, were eventually killed by the Somalis but saved the pilot of the downed helicopter. The incident and Harrell's participation in it are portrayed in the book and movie *Black Hawk Down*.

During the 2001 invasion of Afghanistan to overthrow the Taliban, Harrell—promoted to brigadier general on November 1, 2001—commanded the U.S. Army Special Forces. In June 2002 he became the commander of Special Operations Command Central, a position with responsibility for the Middle East and Iraq. As war with Iraq approached, Harrell was charged with planning and overseeing special operations forces in Iraq.

Unlike the 1991 Persian Gulf War, special operations forces were expected to play a major role. Harrell devised the plans that employed more than 20,000 special operations troops. General Tommy Franks, in charge of Operation IRAQI FREEDOM, was open to Harrell's proposals, as was Secretary of Defense Donald Rumsfeld.

Harrell's plan built on his experiences in the Persian Gulf War. The 5th Special Forces Group was charged with securing the largely uninhabited western desert of Iraq and protecting the left flank of the main invasion force as it approached Baghdad. Most Scuds had been launched from this area in 1991, and Harrell hoped that more troops on the ground might control the area. The special forces employed specially modified vehicles that allowed them to move rapidly across the desert. The operation was a success, and no missiles were launched during the war.

The second part of Harrell's plan included using the 10th Special Forces Group to work with Kurdish forces to provide a credible threat in northern Iraq. Turkey's refusal to allow American forces passage into Iraq forced U.S. planners to rely on special forces teams working with the Kurds to tie down Iraqi forces and capture Mosul and the vital oil fields. Special forces commanded by Colonel Charles Cleveland were completely successful in this. Using advanced weapons such as the Javelin fire-and-forget antiarmor missile, small teams were able to defeat much larger Iraqi regular forces.

Harrell was promoted to major general on November 1, 2004, and served as commander of the U.S. Army Special Operations Command at Fort Bragg. From April 2005 to March 2008 he was deputy chief of staff of operations, Joint Force Command Headquarters, the Netherlands. He retired from the army on March 6, 2008. Harrell then took a position as vice president of business development and integration for Pacer Health Corporation, a Miami-based owner-operator of acute care hospitals.

TIM J. WATTS

See also

Delta Force; IRAQI FREEDOM, Operation; Persian Gulf War; Somalia, Federal Republic of; United States Special Operations Command

References

Murray, Williamson, and Robert H. Scales Jr. *The Iraq War: A Military History*. Boston: Belknap, 2003.

Robinson, Linda. *Masters of Chaos: The Secret History of the Special Forces*. New York: PublicAffairs, 2004.

Hazmi, Nawaf al- (1976–2001)

One of the hijackers of American Airlines Flight 77, which crashed into the Pentagon on September 11, 2001. Nawaf bin Muhammad Salim al-Hazmi was born on August 9, 1976, in Mecca, Saudi Arabia. His father was a grocer, and his older brother was a police chief in Jizan. Hazmi became an Islamist militant at an early age, and as a teenager he traveled to Afghanistan. There he met Khalid al-Mihdhar. They subsequently joined Muslims in Bosnia fighting against the Serbs there in 1995. Then with his brother Salem al-Hazmi, Hazmi and Mihdhar returned to Afghanistan to fight with the Taliban against the Afghan Northern Alliance. In 1998 Hazmi traveled to Chechnya, where he took part in fighting with the Chechen rebels against the Russian Army. Returning to Saudi Arabia in early 1999, Hazmi decided to go to the United States with Mihdhar and his brother Salem al-Hazmi, where they easily obtained visas.

By 1999 Hazmi had been recruited by the Al Qaeda terrorist organization for a special mission. Original plans had called for him to become a pilot, but he lacked the necessary competency in English and the ability to pass pilot's training. He thus teamed with Mihdhar to provide logistical support for the September 11 plot. On September 11, 2001, Hazmi was among the 5 hijackers on board American Airlines Flight 77. He helped subdue the crew and provided security while the airliner was crashed into the Pentagon. All 5 hijackers, in addition to 64 passengers and crew, died that day when the aircraft crashed into the Pentagon; another 125 people died on the ground.

STEPHEN E. ATKINS

See also

Al Qaeda; Mihdhar, Khalid al-; September 11 Attacks

References

Graham, Bob. *Intelligence Matters: The CIA, the FBI, Saudi Arabia, and the Failure of America's War on Terror.* New York: Random House, 2004.

McDermott, Terry. *Perfect Soldiers: The 9/11 Hijackers; Who They Were, Why They Did It.* New York: HarperCollins, 2005.

Heavy Expanded Mobility Tactical Truck

Large heavy-duty, all terrain, single-unit vehicle employed by the U.S. armed forces, first put into service in 1982. The Oshkosh Truck Corporation manufactures the Heavy Expanded Mobility Tactical Trucks (HEMTTs). These 10-ton trucks are produced in a half dozen different models: a general-purpose cargo truck, some of which feature a small crane mounted in the rear; a tanker, used to refuel tactical fighting vehicles and helicopters; a tractor tow, which pulls the M1M-104 Patriot missile battery; a generator truck capable of producing 30 kilowatts of power with a crane capable of towing the MGM-31 Pershing missile erector launcher; and a heavy-duty recovery vehicle with a built-in lift-and-tow system, a winch, and a small crane. All HEMTTs are 8x8 vehicles, meaning that power is distributed to all eight wheels, giving them the ability to operate in extremely rugged terrain as well as in deep mud, sand, and snow. Their huge wheels carry low-pressure puncture-resistant tires. HEMTTs have a crew of two men. Currently there are some 13,000 HEMTTs in use, and they have become the tactical workhorses of the U.S. Army.

Depending on their model and design, HEMTTs are anywhere from 29.25 feet to 33.4 feet in length. All are 96 inches wide and have a 2-foot ground clearance; maximum fording depth is 4 feet. Vehicle curb weights (without cargo) range from 32,200 pounds to 50,900 pounds. The trucks are powered by a V-8 diesel engine manufactured by Detroit Diesel Alison. The HEMTT produces 450 horsepower at 2,100 revolutions per minute. Top speed is 57 miles per hour, predetermined by a governor; range on one tank of fuel is approximately 300 miles. The transmission is an Alison-made four-speed automatic with a single reverse gear. Brakes are air-activated internal expansion at all eight wheels. Mounted winches are capable of pulling 20,000–60,000 pounds. The most heavy-duty mounted crane is capable of lifting 14,620 pounds. Several models also include a self-recovery winch.

Affectionately known as the "Dragon Wagon," the HEMTT has repeatedly proven its mettle under combat situations, including those in Operation DESERT STORM and Operation IRAQI FREEDOM. The HEMTT frequently accompanies fast-moving units, typically led by the M1 Abrams tank, and also fulfills countless roles in logistical support, refueling, and cargo hauling. Several key weapons systems, including the Patriot missile, are often towed by HEMTTs. The M978 model serves as a highly mobile 2,500-gallon fuel tanker. A low-end general-purpose HEMTT (M977 or M985) costs approximately $140,000.

PAUL G. PIERPAOLI JR.

See also

M1A1 and M1A2 Abrams Main Battle Tanks; Patriot Missile System; Vehicles, Unarmored

References

Braulick, Carrie A. *U.S. Army Tanks.* Cottage Grove, MN: Blazers, 2006.

Kaelberer, Angie P. *U.S. Army Humvees.* Cottage Grove, MN: Blazers, 2006.

Hekmatyar, Gulbuddin al-Hurra (1948–)

Former leader of the Islamic Party of Afghanistan (Hezb-e-Islami Afghanistan), prime minister of Afghanistan (1993–1994 and 1996–1997), and key figure in the Afghan jihad against the Soviet occupation (1979–1989). Born sometime in 1948 to a Kharuti Pashtun family in the Imam Saheb district of Kunduz Province in northern Afghanistan, Gulbuddin al-Hurra Hekmatyar attended the Mahtab Military School in Kabul. Fluent in Dari (Farsi), Urdu, Arabic, English, and Pashto, he was expelled within two years because of his political activities.

From 1970 to 1972 Hekmatyar attended the engineering school at Kabul University, although he was once more prevented from completing his studies because of his involvement in illicit political activity. Implicated in the murder of Saydal Sukhandan, a member of the pro-China Shola-e-Jawedan Movement, Hekmatyar was sentenced to two years in jail by the government of King Zahir Shah. Hekmatyar was freed from prison following a 1974 coup executed by the king's cousin, Mohammad Daud Khan.

Hekmatyar's interest in religious-political ideologies emerged early. As a high school student he had been a member of the communist People's Democratic Party of Afghanistan, and later, as a student at Kabul University, his communist ideology was influenced by an extremist version of Islam nurtured through his membership in the Muslim Youths Movement (Nahzat-e-Jawanane Musalman). Although initially a leftist, Hekmatyar later became a disciple of the Egyptian author, socialist, and intellectual Sayyid Qutb and the Muslim Brotherhood movement.

Following his release from jail in 1974, Hekmatyar sought refuge in the Pakistan border city of Peshawar, accompanied by Burhanuddin Rabbani, Qazi Muhammad Amin Waqad, and a number of other jihadi leaders. Although members of the Muslim Youths Movement, the radical leaders nevertheless broke into competing factions and parties, and with the support of Pakistani prime minister Zulfiqar Ali Bhutto, Hekmatyar established Hezb-e-Islami Afghanistan in 1976.

Also known as Hezb-e-Islami Gulbuddin (HIG), the movement was led by Hekmatyar and fellow jihadi leader Mawlawi M. Younus Khalis until 1979, when the two leaders parted ways and the new Hezb-e-Islami Khalis faction constituted a countergroup to HIG. A significant ideological dichotomy inherent in the split resided in Khalis's conservative and traditional clerical approach, in contrast to Hekmatyar's more youthful and ideological activist stance. While Khalis walked away with the preponderance of the movement's most skilled commanders, HIG continued to dominate the Afghan resistance against the Soviets, with support from Pakistan. The movement drew the majority of its membership from ethnic Pashtuns, and its ideology was influenced by the Muslim Brotherhood and the Sunni

Pakistani theologian and political philosopher Abul Ala Mawdudi.

Advocating the notion that sustainable development and stability in Afghanistan could be achieved only through sharia (Islamic law), throughout the 1980s and early 1990s the movement garnered substantial financial and arms support from Arab and Western countries, including Saudi Arabia, Pakistan, and the United States. Most notably, Hekmatyar received antiaircraft Stinger missiles from the U.S. government through Pakistan's Inter-Services Intelligence, with which he facilitated the Afghan jihad against Soviet forces. Currently, the nonviolent faction of HIG is a registered political party in Afghanistan, led by Abd al-Hadi Arghandiwal, and is thought to be in decline.

During the Soviet occupation, Hekmatyar ascended to new heights of power. This posed a substantial threat to Dr. Mohammad Najibullah, the former chief of the Afghan government's security service, Khedamat-e Etelea'at-e Dawlati, and the last president of the communist Democratic Republic of Afghanistan (1987–1992). Despite Najibullah's attempt to neutralize the threat posed by Hekmatyar by offering him 95 percent control of the regime, Hekmatyar refused, and in 1992 Najibullah's government was overturned by the leader of the Afghan National Liberation Front, Sebghantullah Mujadeddi, who then transferred power within two months to the leader of Jameat-e-Islami.

While Hekmatyar anticipated an easy transition to power, the Jabalurseraj Agreement, signed on May 25, 1992, enabled the strategic garrisons in Kabul to be seized by Tajik leader Ahmad Shah Masoud, Abdul Ali Mazari of the Hazaras, and Uzbek leader Abul Rashid Dostum. Left out of the city, Hekmatyar's forces shelled Kabul mercilessly in February 1993 before Hekmatyar joined a coordination council (Shora-e-Hamahangi) with Dostum and Mazari against President Burhaniddin Rabbani. Hekmatyar served as prime minister during 1993–1994 and 1996–1997. With HIG weakened, Hekmatyar nevertheless kept up his rabid anti-American rhetoric while capitalizing on the weaknesses of his enemies, most notably through the exhortation of militants in Pakistan to attack American interests there rather than fighting across the border.

Hekmatyar was not always anti-American. During the 1980s the U.S. Central Intelligence Agency (CIA) had provided him and his allies with hundreds of millions of dollars in weapons and ammunition to help them battle the Soviet Army during its occupation of Afghanistan. In 1985 the CIA even flew Hekmatyar to the United States, and the agency considered him to be a reliable anti-Soviet rebel. Contrastingly, in the post-9/11 period, Hekmatyar coordinated numerous attacks against U.S. and North Atlantic Treaty Organization troops in Afghanistan while calling on Pakistani militants to attack U.S. targets from across the border. More recently, Hamid Karzai's government has extended a peaceful—if not controversially tentative—hand toward Hekmatyar in hopes of coaxing him to join its side. However, assertions by the former governor of Nooristan province, Tamim Nooristani, that Hekmatyar alongside Pakistani and Afghan Taliban fighters took part in a series of deadly attacks against U.S. soldiers forced Hekmatyar into deep hiding. It is believed that since 2008 Hekmatyar has shuttled between the remote mountainous areas of Pakistan and Afghanistan. He is considered one of the main leaders of the Afghan insurgency, but since 2010 he has exhibited some interest in negotiating with the Afghan government in hopes of achieving reconciliation among Afghanistan's warring factions.

K. LUISA GANDOLFO

See also

Afghanistan; Afghanistan War; Afghanistan Warlords; Dostum, Abd al-Rashid; Muslim Brotherhood; Taliban

References

Appleby, Scott. *Fundamentalism and the State: Remaking Polities, Economies, and Militance.* Chicago: University of Chicago Press, 1996.

Emadi, Hafizullah. *Politics of the Dispossessed: Superpowers and Developments in the Middle East.* Westport, CT: Greenwood, 2001.

Friedman, Norman. *Terrorism, Afghanistan, and America's New Way of War.* Annapolis, MD: Naval Institute Press, 2003.

Giraldo, Jeanne K., and Harold A. Trinkunas. *Terrorism Financing and State Responses: A Comparative Perspective.* Stanford, CA: Stanford University Press, 2007.

Helicopters

See Aircraft, Helicopters

Hersh, Seymour Myron (1937–)

Controversial Pulitzer Prize–winning journalist and author who in 2004 was among the various sources who publicized the mistreatment of Iraqi prisoners at Abu Ghraib and has been a vocal critic of the Iraq War. Seymour Myron Hersh was born in Chicago on April 8, 1937. His parents were Jewish immigrants from Eastern Europe, and he grew up in a working-class inner-city neighborhood.

Hersh graduated from the University of Chicago in 1959 and began his long journalism career as a police reporter in Chicago, working for the City News Bureau. Not long after, he joined United Press International (UPI) and by 1963 had become a UPI correspondent covering both Washington, D.C., and Chicago. Hersh soon earned a reputation as a hard-driving investigative reporter. In 1968, he served as Senator Eugene McCarthy's press secretary during his unsuccessful bid for the 1968 Democratic presidential nomination. After that, Hersh became a reporter based in Washington, D.C., for the *New York Times.* It was here that he became internationally renowned for his investigative reporting.

In November 1969, it was Hersh who first revealed the story of the March 1968 My Lai Massacre in Vietnam, perpetrated by U.S. soldiers against South Vietnamese civilians. His scoop also included the bombshell that the Pentagon had engaged in a purposeful campaign to cover up evidence of the massacre to ensure that it did not become public knowledge. For his reporting of the incident and its aftermath, Hersh received the Pulitzer Prize in International Reporting for 1970. That same year he published a well-read book on the subject, the first of many books he would author.

Hersh made it his business to seek out stories that he knew would be hard to break and that would generate a maximum amount of attention. In 1986, three years after a Korean Air Lines Boeing 747 jetliner was blasted out of the sky by Soviet jet fighters, Hersh published a book in which he alleged that the incident—coming as it did at the height of the renewed Cold War—was caused by Soviet stupidity and provocative U.S. intelligence operations that had been sanctioned by the Reagan administration. Later, Hersh's conclusions were somewhat vindicated by the subsequent release of classified government documents. Hersh's critics on the Right, however, were outraged by his allegation that the tragedy had been brought about by U.S. policy.

Hersh continued his investigative reporting, often working independently of any publication or news agency so he could be free to pursue those stories that most interested him. He did, however, develop a long-standing relationship with the *New Yorker* magazine, for which he has frequently provided articles and opinion pieces. In August 1998, Hersh once more drew the ire of the political establishment by blasting the Clinton administration for authorizing bombing a suspected chemical weapons factory in Sudan, which Hersh concluded was in fact an important pharmaceutical-manufacturing facility. The bombing was in retaliation for the bombings of U.S. embassies by Al Qaeda terrorists, who were believed to be operating in Sudan.

The Iraq War, which began in March 2003, drew Hersh's attention and scrutiny. Since that time, he has launched numerous in-depth investigations into various events and developments in Iraq and into the Bush administration's interest in pursuing regime change against Syria and Iran. In the spring of 2004, Hersh published a series of articles illuminating the extent of the prisoner abuse scandal in Iraq's Abu Ghraib prison. This unleashed a torrent of media attention, the release of photos showing prisoner abuse, and a major congressional investigation. Hersh also alleged that prisoners had been tortured in other holding facilities, including those in Afghanistan and at Guantánamo Bay, Cuba. That same year he also wrote that the invasion of Iraq in 2003 had been based on faulty intelligence about Iraq and that Vice President Dick Cheney and Secretary of Defense Donald Rumsfeld had purposely misused prewar intelligence to manufacture a justification of war. Hersh was intensely disliked by the George W. Bush administration, and some military analysts were not permitted to cite him. Richard Perle, a leading neoconservative and frequent adviser to the Bush White House, termed Hersh a journalistic "terrorist." In March 2007 Hersh excoriated the Bush administration's surge strategy, alleging that it would only embolden Sunni extremists in Iraq.

Beginning in January 2005, Hersh began publishing a series of articles in which he alleged that the U.S. government was clandestinely preparing to launch preemptive air strikes against suspected nuclear weapons facilities in Iran. The Bush administration denied that such operations were being contemplated but did not deny that contingency plans existed. In 2006, Hersh wrote that the United States was preparing to use a bunker-busting bomb against Iranian nuclear facilities. This provoked a vehement denial from the White House and the Pentagon. President Bush termed Hersh's allegations "wild speculation." In late 2007, Hersh drew the ire of many Democrats when he asserted that Senator Hillary Clinton's hawkish views on Iran were related to the large number of donations her presidential campaign had received from American Jews.

Following the use of chemical weapons by Syrian government forces in August 2013 during the civil war in that country (2011–present), Hersh charged that President Barack Obama in a televised address to the American people had "omitted important intelligence" and also "presented assumptions as facts" and that the Syrian government was not the only agency in Syria with access to sarin.

Hersh has sharply criticized both Democratic and Republican administrations. In 1997 he was criticized in some circles for a book he published on President John F. Kennedy, both for its evidentiary value and its dubious allegations that Kennedy had been married before he wed Jacqueline Bouvier and that the president had a long-standing relationship with Chicago mob boss Sam Giancana.

PAUL G. PIERPAOLI JR.

See also

Abu Ghraib; Bush, George Walker; Chemical Weapons and Warfare; Cheney, Richard Bruce; Obama, Barack Hussein, II; Rumsfeld, Donald; Syrian Chemical Weapons Agreement; Syrian Civil War; Torture of Prisoners

References

Hersh, Seymour. *Chain of Command: The Road from 9/11 to Abu Ghraib.* New York: HarperCollins, 2004.

Lewis, Justin. *Shoot First and Ask Questions Later: Media Coverage of the 2003 Iraq War.* New York: Peter Lang, 2005.

Hester, Leigh Ann (1982–)

Army National Guardsman and the first woman to earn the Silver Star for valor in combat in 60 years, since World War II. Born in Bowling Green, Kentucky, in 1982, Leigh Ann Hester later moved to Nashville. A varsity basketball and softball player in high school, she joined the Kentucky National Guard in April 2001 and was assigned to the 617th Military Police Company in Richmond, Kentucky, which was later deployed to Iraq.

At midday on March 20, 2005, Hester was patrolling with her unit in Humvees, providing security for a supply convoy of about 30 trucks near the town of Salman Pak south of Baghdad, when the convoy came under attack by about 50 insurgents. The insurgents attacked the convoy with assault-rifle and machine-gun fire and rocket-propelled grenades. In the ensuing 90-minute firefight, Hester participated in a dismounted flanking counterattack against the insurgents, helping with hand grenades and rifle grenade rounds to clear two trenches of insurgents. Hester personally shot and killed 3 insurgents with her M-4 carbine.

At the same time that Hester was awarded the Silver Star, her squad leader, Staff Sergeant Timothy F. Nein, was also awarded the Silver Star for his role in the same engagement. Another woman, Specialist Ashley J. Pullen, a driver, received the Bronze Star Medal. The battle reportedly resulted in the deaths of 27 insurgents and the capture of 7 others.

Hester left the army in 2007 and worked as a civilian law enforcement officer in Nashville, Tennessee, but she rejoined the military in 2010.

SPENCER C. TUCKER

See also

Vehicles, Unarmored; Women, Role of in Afghanistan and Iraq Wars

References

Shane, Leo, III. "Female Soldier Awarded Silver Star." *Stars and Stripes,* June 18, 2005.

Tyson, Ann Scott. "Soldier Earns Silver Star for Her Role in Defeating Ambush." *Washington Post,* June 17, 2005.

High-Mobility Multipurpose Wheeled Vehicle

Multipurpose wheeled vehicle used by the U.S. armed forces. The High-Mobility Multipurpose Wheeled Vehicle (HMMWV, popularly called the Humvee) has been in service since 1983. A commercial, civilian version was successfully marketed as the Hummer. The Humvee first saw service in Operation JUST CAUSE in Panama in December 1989. It has seen extensive service in Iraq and Afghanistan since the 1991 Persian Gulf War.

Since the invention of the internal combustion engine, the world's militaries have developed and used a wide variety of wheeled and tracked vehicles to transport personnel and cargo and to serve as platforms for weapons and other uses. During World War II the most common wheeled utility vehicle was the jeep. Developed for the U.S. Army, the jeep had various official designations and was a small .25-ton truck with four-wheel drive for off-road capability. It served through the 1970s with many changes over time. The jeep's limited capacity and high center of gravity, which resulted in numerous rollovers, led the army to develop other wheeled vehicles, such as the six-wheel-drive 1.5-ton M-561 Gamma Goat and the M-715, a 1.25-ton truck. The army also procured commercial trucks such as the .75-ton Dodge, designated the M-880. In 1975 and 1976 the army tested the commercial CJ-5 Jeep, the Dodge Ram Charger, the Chevrolet Blazer, and the Ford Bronco. Funding cuts in the post–Vietnam War era and the need for a platform for the TOW (tube-launched, optically tracked, wire-guided) missile led the army to consider other options, such as the Cadillac Gage Scout, various dune buggies, and the Combat

U.S. Air Force security police patrol an air base flight line in an M998 High Mobility Multipurpose Wheeled Vehicle (Humvee) mounting an M-60 machine gun during Operation DESERT STORM. (U.S. Department of Defense)

Support Vehicle (CSV) dedicated to the TOW mission. The plan was to produce 3,800 CSVs, but Congress scrapped that program in 1977, deeming that vehicle too limited.

In 1980 Congress approved the development of the Humvee, with the objective of producing 50,000 1.25-ton four-wheel drive vehicles to replace the multiplicity of vehicles, many worn out by years of use, in the army inventory. This was a breakthrough, as up to this time the army had opted for vehicles of varying sizes and carrying capacities. In 1981, three contractors were asked to bid on the Humvee: Chrysler Defense, Teledyne Continental, and AM General, whose parent company, American Motors, had purchased Kaiser-Jeep in 1969. All three produced prototypes for testing, which was done at Aberdeen Proving Ground, Maryland, and Yuma, Arizona, in 1982. The AM General model, nicknamed the "Hummer" as a play on the military designation and thought to be catchier than "Humvee," won.

The first production contract in 1983 was for 55,000 vehicles to be produced over five years, a number later raised to 70,000 vehicles. The U.S. Army received 39,000, the U.S. Marine Corps received 11,000, and the remainder went to the U.S. Air Force and the U.S. Navy. By 1995 more than 100,000 Humvees had been produced. Production would double by 2005 for both U.S. and foreign sales. American Motors began marketing the Hummer commercially in 1983, and the brand is still marketed by General Motors.

Designated the M-998, the Humvee four-wheel-drive vehicle weighs 5,200 pounds; measures 15 feet long, 7.08 feet wide, and 6 feet high (reducible to under 5 feet); and is powered by a 150-horsepower, 378-cubic-inch V-8 diesel engine. Its ground clearance of more than 16 inches and four-wheel drive make the Humvee an effective off-road carrier. Its 25-gallon fuel tank allows for a range of 350 miles at speeds up to 65 miles per hour. It can ford water up to 2.5 feet deep and double that with a deepwater-fording kit. It can climb a 60 percent incline and traverse a 40 percent incline fully loaded. Its very wide stance and low center of gravity make it difficult to turn over.

Humvees replaced several military vehicles and became the platform for many tasks. In addition to the Humvee's basic configuration as a truck with more than a ton of carrying capacity, there are variants that function as an ambulance, a TOW-missile platform, a machine-gun or grenade-launcher platform, a prime mover for towing a 105-mm howitzer, and a shelter carrier. Some variants are equipped with a winch on the front that provides additional capabilities, especially self-recovery. The Humvee can be delivered to the battlefield by helicopter. The weight of the vehicle can be reduced by using versions without roofs or with canvas roofs and sides. The Humvee has been reconfigured and manufactured in what the military calls M-A1 and M-A2 versions.

Not designed to be an armored combat vehicle, the Humvee in its original configuration posed serious problems in the Afghanistan War and the Iraq War. The military had already been exploring how to armor Humvees in light of experience in the peacekeeping mission in the Balkans in the 1990s. The canvas roofs and sides of some models offered no protection from small-arms fire, and the metal versions were little help against roadside mines. The solutions were not simple, but there have been several programs to alleviate this serious hazard in the M-1114 and M-1151 up-armored variants.

The up-armored vehicle entered service in combat areas, and armor kits were made available for installation in the theater of operations. The basic upgrade in armament was a 2,000-pound kit that added steel plating and ballistic-resistant windows. The steel plating under the vehicle was designed to absorb an 8-pound explosive. The kit for in-theater installation weighs about 750 pounds. More than 10,000 Humvees saw service in the Iraq War, and as the Humvee's mission expanded, changes were made in engine power, transmission, suspension, and engine cooling. While some changes can be made in theater, many have been done at depot level in the United States, as Humvees are modified for deployment or repaired after combat damage. Combat also produces vehicle wear seven times that in peacetime. This fact, the loss of 250 Humvees in combat, and the aging of the inventory stresses the ability of the military to maintain readiness and prepare for future challenges. In 2007, the U.S. Marine Corps decided to start replacing Humvees in combat with Mine-Resistant Armor Protected vehicles, and in 2012 the U.S. Army stated that the Humvee was "no longer feasible for combat."

DANIEL E. SPECTOR

See also

Vehicles, Unarmored

References

Cordesman, Anthony H., and Abraham R. Wagner. *The Lessons of Modern War*, Vol. 4, *The Gulf War*. Boulder, CO: Westview, 1996.

Green, Michael, and Greg Stewart. *HUMVEE at War*. St. Paul, MN: Zenith, 2005.

Scales, Robert H. *Certain Victory: The U.S. Army in the Gulf War*. Washington, DC: Brassey's, 1994.

Thompson, Loren B., Lawrence J. Korb, and Caroline P. Wadhams. *Army Equipment after Iraq.* Arlington, VA: Lexington Institute, Center for American Progress, 2006.

Zaloga, Steven J. *HMMWV, Humvee, 1980–2005: U.S. Army Tactical Vehicle.* Oxford, UK: Osprey, 2006.

Holbrooke, Richard Charles Albert (1941–2010)

U.S. diplomat, assistant secretary of state (1977–1981 and 1994–1996), ambassador to the United Nations (UN) (1999–2001), and diplomatic troubleshooter. Richard Charles Albert Holbrooke was born in New York City on April 24, 1941, and graduated from Brown University in 1962. Inspired by President John F. Kennedy's call for public service, Holbrooke entered the U.S. Foreign Service. He served in the Republic of Vietnam, first in the Agency for International Development there and then as a staff assistant to U.S. ambassadors Maxwell Taylor and Henry Cabot Lodge. Holbrooke returned to Washington in 1965 to be a member of a Vietnam study group in the National Security Council.

Holbrooke was next a special assistant to Undersecretaries of State Nicholas Katzenbach and Elliot Richardson before joining the U.S. delegation to the Paris Peace Talks in 1968. Holbrooke also drafted a volume of what became known as the Pentagon Papers, which traced the escalating U.S. involvement in Vietnam. During 1969–1970 he was a visiting fellow at the Woodrow Wilson School at Princeton University.

At his own request, in 1970 Holbrooke became the director of the Peace Corps in Morocco. He left government service two years later to become the managing editor of *Foreign Policy* magazine. Holbrooke was also a contributing editor to *Newsweek* magazine.

In 1976, Holbrooke left his publishing positions to become a foreign policy adviser to Democratic Party presidential candidate Jimmy Carter. Following Carter's victory, Holbrooke became assistant secretary of state for East Asian and Pacific Affairs, a post he held from 1977 to 1981. During his tenure, in 1978 the United States established full diplomatic relations with the People's Republic of China. Holbrooke was also very much involved in the resettlement of hundreds of thousands of Southeast Asian refugees in the United States.

In 1981 Holbrooke became vice president of Public Strategies, a consulting firm in Washington, D.C. He also became a consultant to the investment firm Lehman Brothers, which led to him becoming managing director at Lehman Brothers. At the same time, he was a principal author of the bipartisan Commission on Government and Renewal, sponsored by the Carnegie Foundation.

In 1992 during the presidency of Bill Clinton, Holbrooke was a candidate to be ambassador to Japan. When that post went to former vice president Walter Mondale, Holbrooke was a surprise pick to be ambassador to the Federal Republic of Germany. He held that position until 1994, when he returned to the United States to become assistant secretary of state for European and Canadian affairs. He served in that capacity until 1996, the first individual in U.S. history to be an assistant secretary of state for two different areas of the world. While assistant secretary, Holbrooke led the effort to enlarge the North Atlantic Treaty Organization.

In 1995 Holbrooke was the principal figure in putting together the Dayton Peace Accords that ended the wars in Bosnia and Croatia. Upon leaving the State Department in 1996, he joined Credit Suisse First Boston, becoming its vice chairman. President Clinton asked him to be a special envoy to the Balkans as a private citizen, and Holbrooke worked on a pro bono basis to try to resolve crises over Cyprus and Kosovo.

During 1999–2001, Holbrooke was U.S. ambassador to the UN. During his tenure he brokered a deal with that body whereby the United States agreed to pay back dues in return for a reduction in future annual dues. He also secured a UN resolution that recognized HIV/AIDS as a threat to global security, the first time that body had so designated a public health issue. Upon leaving the UN, Holbrooke became the key figure in what is now the Global Business Coalition on HIV/AIDS, Tuberculosis, and Malaria, which seeks to mobilize the world business community to deal with pressing health issues. At the same time, he continued his involvement with a wide variety of organizations and found time to speak on foreign affairs issues. Holbrooke is also the author of numerous articles and several books, including the acclaimed *To End a War* (1998), which details the efforts to end the fighting in Bosnia. He has been nominated for the Nobel Peace Prize on seven occasions.

During the 2004 presidential campaign, Holbrooke served as a foreign policy adviser to Democratic Party candidate John Kerry. Holbrooke filled the same position for Senator Hillary Rodham Clinton when she ran for the Democratic presidential nomination in 2008. When she lost the nomination, he served in the same position for Barack Obama. In an article in the September–October 2008 issue of *Foreign Affairs,* Holbrooke said that the new government would need to reestablish the reputation of the United States in the world. He also called U.S. policy in Afghanistan a failure and listed four main problem areas: the tribal areas of northwestern Pakistan, the drug lords who dominate Afghanistan, the national police, and an incompetent and corrupt Afghan government.

On January 22, 2009, Obama appointed Holbrooke as special representative for Afghanistan and Pakistan. Holbrooke was not able to secure any diplomatic breakthroughs and found himself at odds with President Hamid Karzai. Holbrooke died at George Washington University Hospital in Washington, D.C., on December 13, 2010, from complications of a torn aorta.

Spencer C. Tucker

See also
Afghanistan War; Karzai, Hamid; Obama, Barack Hussein, II; Pakistan

References
Clifford, Clark, and Richard Holbrooke. *Counsel to the President: A Memoir.* New York: Random House, 1991.

Holbrooke, Richard. "The Next President: Mastering a Daunting Agenda." *Foreign Affairs* 87(5) (September–October 2008): 2–24.

Holbrooke, Richard. *To End a War.* New York: Random House, 1998.

Holland, Charles R. (1946–)

U.S. Air Force general. Charles R. Holland was born in 1946 and graduated from the U.S. Air Force Academy in 1968. He went on to earn an MS degree in business management from Troy State University in 1976 and an MS degree in astronautical engineering from the Air Force Institute of Technology at Wright-Patterson Air Force Base, Ohio, in 1978. He also attended the Industrial College of the Armed Forces in 1986.

Holland held a series of flight-oriented positions and was also increasingly responsible for command posts. As a command pilot, he accumulated more than 5,000 flying hours in more than 100 combat missions during the Vietnam War. In the 1991 Persian Gulf War, Holland commanded the 1550th Combat Crew Training Wing, headquartered at Kirtland Air Force Base, New Mexico.

On May 20, 1993, Holland was promoted to brigadier general and became deputy commanding general of the Joint Special Operations Command (Fort Bragg, North Carolina). In June 1995 Holland began serving as commander, Special Operations Command–Pacific, a post he held until 1997. Promoted to major general in 1997, he headed the Air Force Special Operation Command (Hurlburt Field, Florida) until August 1999. Until October 2000 Holland was vice commander, U.S. Air Forces in Europe; he was promoted to lieutenant general in November 1999.

In October 2000 Holland became commander, headquarters, U.S. Special Operations Command (SOCOM), MacDill Air Force Base, Florida, a position he held until his retirement in October 2003. Holland was promoted to full general (four-star rank) in December 2000. As commander of SOCOM, Holland was a forceful spokesperson for the need to augment and improve U.S. special operations forces in order to allow a rapid response to any military contingency. His advocacy proved prescient after the September 11, 2001, terrorist attacks, and his efforts to bolster SOCOM aided rapid victories in Afghanistan in 2001 and the overthrow of the Saddam Hussein regime in Iraq in 2003.

Holland was an ardent proponent of the Bell/Boeing CV-22 Osprey, the controversial tilt-rotor, multimission, vertical takeoff and landing aircraft. Since May 2004, Holland has been on the board of directors of a number of corporate and nonprofit organizations.

Paul G. Pierpaoli Jr.

See also
United States Air Force, Afghanistan War; United States Air Force, Iraq War; United States Special Operations Command

References
Boyne, Walter J. *Beyond the Wild Blue: A History of the U.S. Air Force, 1947–2007.* 2nd ed. New York: Thomas Dunne Books, 2007.

Pushies, Fred J. *U.S. Air Force Special OPS.* Osceola, WI: Zenith, 2007.

Hollande, François Gérard (1954–)

President of France. François Gérard Georges Nicolas Hollande was born on August 12, 1954, in Rouen, France. His father was a doctor, and his mother was a social worker. When he was 13, Hollande and his family moved to Paris. Hollande earned a degree in political science from Institut des Sciences Politiques, then secured a business degree from l'Ecole des Hautes Etudes Commerciales. After that he attended the prestigious French finishing school for the business and political elite, L'Ecole National d'Administration, graduating in 1980.

Hollande became involved with university-level politics while a student. He campaigned for former president

François Mitterrand in 1974 and eventually joined the French Socialist Party (Parti Socialiste, PS) in 1979. After completing his studies, Hollande immediately secured a position as a civil servant in the Court of Audits, France's quasi-judicial government body charged with overseeing financial and legal audits of all public institutions and most major private businesses. In the early 1980s, he was appointed a junior economic adviser in Mitterrand's government. In 1988, Hollande was elected to the National Assembly as a representative from the Corrèze region. Although he briefly lost this seat in the early 1990s, he regained it in 1997. That same year, he replaced Lionel Jospin as leader of the PS. Hollande remained at the helm of the PS for more than a decade, finally stepping down in 2008 after the party's poor turnout in 2007 elections. In addition to his leadership role in the PS, he also served as mayor of Tulle from 2001 to 2008. Hollande remained in the political limelight on a regional level, however. In 2008 almost immediately after leaving the PS, he was elected to head the general council in the Department of Corrèze in southwestern France. He held this post until his election as president of France in 2012.

Hollande was not viewed as the PS's initial choice as its presidential candidate in the 2012 elections. However, he gained the inside track following multiple sexual abuse scandals involving former PS favorite Dominique Strauss-Kahn in May 2011. Hollande topped the ballot in the primary elections. He officially launched his presidential campaign in January 2012. His campaign agenda included touching on hard-hitting economic reforms such as a renegotiation of the European Union's fiscal austerity pact and instituting a sharp tax increase on the wealthiest French citizens. Perhaps most important, however, was his low-key contrast to his opponent: the fiery, conservative incumbent president Nicolas Sarkozy. Hollande was considered the "anti-Sarkozy"—a politician who would seek consensus and moderation.

Although critics panned Hollande for having a vague campaign platform and a general lack of charisma, on April 22, 2012, he defeated Sarkozy by just over 1 percent of the vote in the first round of presidential elections. Hollande received nearly 52 percent of the vote in the runoff elections on May 6 and was inaugurated as president of France on May 15, 2012.

Hollande's election was viewed as a victory for those opposed to severe economic cuts in the name of austerity, an effort led by Sarkozy and German chancellor Angela Merkel to confront the eurozone crisis currently threatening European Union countries. Hollande has argued for a mix of cuts and economic growth measures, views expected to change the dynamic in European politics.

Hollande's tenure in office has not been a happy one. The French economy has lagged, and his popularity has plummeted as a result (in November 2014, it was an astonishing 12 percent). His promises to cut back on France's foreign military interventions (he pledged an early withdrawal of French troops from Afghanistan) have been offset by Operation SERVAL, the January 2013 French military intervention in Mali that turned back Muslim extremists on track to take over that entire African country. Hollande has committed French forces to the fight against the Islamic State of Iraq and Syria (ISIS), sending aircraft to participate in bombing ISIS targets, and he has urged a stronger stance by the West against the Syrian regime of Bashar al-Assad. Hollande has also supported sanctions against Russia for President Vladimir Putin's actions in Ukraine and has taken the difficult financial decision of at least suspending delivery of two $1 billion assault landing ships constructed under contract by France for Russia.

TAMAR BURRIS AND SPENCER C. TUCKER

See also

Assad, Bashar al-; Islamic State in Iraq and Syria; Syrian Civil War

References

Brizzi, Riccardo, and Gabriel Goodliffe. *La Francia di Hollande*. Bologna, Italy: Il Mulin, 2013.

Michel, Richard. *François Hollande: L'inattendu*. Paris: Archipel, 2011.

Raffy, Serge. *François Hollande: Itinéraire Secret*. Paris: Fayard, 2011.

Ruet, Stephane. *François Hollande*. Paris: Le Cherche midi, 2012.

Wall, Irwin M. *France Votes: The Election of François Hollande*. Bastingstoke, UK: Palgrave Macmillan, 2014.

Hormuz, Strait of

Narrow body of water that connects the Persian Gulf to the Gulf of Oman and the Indian Ocean. The Strait of Hormuz is bounded in the north by Iran and on its south by the United Arab Emirates (UAE) and the Sultanate of Oman. The waters of the Strait of Hormuz are predominately within the claimed territorial waters of these three nations because the United Nations Convention on the Law of the Sea defines territorial waters as 12 nautical miles from shore. At its narrowest point the strait is 21 nautical miles wide, but there are islands throughout its length, most of which belong to Iran. The strait is designated as an international shipping lane. As such, ships are allowed to transit it under the rules of "innocent" or "transit" passage, which permit maritime traffic in key straits that separate international bodies of water.

Because of its location, the Strait of Hormuz is considered a strategic choke point. About 20 percent of world oil shipments transit the strait on any given day aboard commercial tankers. The key nation in this regard is Iran, whose largest port and naval base, Bandar Abbas, is located at the northernmost tip of the strait.

Iran has fortified several islands—the Tunb Islands and Abu Musa—that dominate the strait. Abu Musa in particular has long been a source of conflict between Iran and the UAE, especially since Iran's occupation of it in the early 1970s.

The Strait of Hormuz has always been a significant factor in modern wars. During World War II, it was the key conduit for American Lend-Lease aid through Iraq and Iran to the Soviet Union. Since then, the strait has been the chief avenue for U.S. seaborne trade into the Persian Gulf region and oil out of it. The strait became even more an issue after the 1979 Islamic Revolution in Iran, which deposed pro-U.S. Mohammad Reza Shah Pahlavi. After that, the United States began to station a number of warships in the Persian Gulf to protect U.S. interests in the region.

Near the end of the 1980–1988 Iran-Iraq War, Iran attempted to close the strait by mining it to deprive Iraq and other Persian Gulf states of their oil revenues. The United States responded by reflagging oil tankers and forcibly reopening the strait in Operation ERNEST WILL. Not long after, the United States used the strait as the main conduit for sea-supplied military matériel in support of Operations DESERT SHIELD (1990) and DESERT STORM (the Persian Gulf War, 1991). Thereafter, the United States maintained a strong naval presence in the region, to include at least one aircraft carrier battle group and often several.

Most recently, the strait was critical to the maritime power projection of Operation IRAQI FREEDOM, the 2003 Anglo-American–led invasion of Iraq. Without access to the Strait of Hormuz, the United States and other Western powers would be severely limited in influencing events in the Middle East. U.S. policy makers in particular continue to keep a wary eye on the Strait of Hormuz, especially given Iran's nuclear ambitions and the often harsh rhetoric coming from its rightist leaders.

JOHN T. KUEHN

See also

Iraq, History of, 1990–Present; IRAQI FREEDOM, Operation; Iran; Oil; United Arab Emirates

References

Bowden, Mark. *Guests of the Ayatollah: The First Battle in America's War with Militant Islam.* New York: Atlantic Monthly, 2007.

Marolda, Edward, and Robert Schneller. *Shield and Sword: The United States Navy and the Persian Gulf War.* Annapolis, MD: U.S. Naval Institute Press, 2001.

Hospital Ships

Unarmed and clearly marked ships with comprehensive medical facilities that operate near combat zones and have the capacity to take aboard and treat large numbers of casualties brought in by medical evacuation (medevac) helicopters. The only dedicated hospital ships currently in operation with the U.S. Navy are the two large vessels of the Mercy class. USNS *Mercy* (T-AH-19) entered naval service in 1986; its sister ship, the *Comfort* (T-AH-20), was commissioned the next year. Dimensions are length, 894 feet; beam, 105.75 feet; and draft, 33 feet. Speed is 17.5 knots with a range of 13,400 nautical miles at 17.5 knots. Crew complement (reduced operating status in home port) is 16 civilian and 58 U.S. Navy support/communications (6 officers and 52 enlisted); active deployed is 61 civilian, 58 navy, and 1,100 medical/dental personnel.

Originally built at San Diego as the civilian tankers SS *Worth* and SS *Rose City*, these two ships were converted during 1984–1986 and 1985–1987, respectively. They entered service with the Military Sealift Command (MSC) as the largest hospital ships in the world. The *Mercy* is based on the U.S. West Coast at San Diego, and the *Comfort* is based at the East Coast port of Baltimore, placing their potential for combat or humanitarian medical support within range of critical need areas, whether nearby or overseas. Both ships are maintained in a state of readiness known as reduced operating status within the MSC by caretaker crews when not deployed but can be fully staffed, outfitted, and supplied within five days when called on to proceed to a battle zone or the site of a disaster.

Each ship has 1,000 hospital beds, 80 of which are designated for intensive care, and the level of onboard care matches or outdoes that of a respectable land-based hospital with an extensive surgical center, albeit one with an exceedingly large trauma component. There are 12 operating theaters, a 50-bed triage area, 4 radiological units and a CT installation, a burn unit, a full medical laboratory, a blood bank, and a pharmacy as well as the onboard capacity to generate oxygen and distill 75,000 gallons of freshwater each day. When the ships are activated, medical personnel aboard the *Mercy* generally are drawn from the naval medical center at Oakland, California, while Bethesda Naval Hospital in Maryland furnishes medical crews to the *Comfort*. The majority of patients and casualties are typically airlifted by helicopter to each ship's large helipad, but there is also a limited ability to accept casualties from boats alongside when weather and sea state allow. Maximum ingest is staked at 300 patients per day if half or more of that number require surgery, and the turnaround rate averages five days aboard the facility prior to discharge and return to action or medevac to the United States for further treatment.

Despite their great size, both the *Mercy* and *Comfort* experience some limitations stemming from their original design as tankers, most notably in the internal transfer of patients. The impenetrable transverse bulkheads that once kept the oil cargo's wave action deep in the ship to a minimum now require the use of an awkward up-and-over technique when patients on lower-level wards need to be shifted forward or aft.

The two ships were activated and served in the Persian Gulf during Operations DESERT SHIELD and DESERT STORM and returned to the United States in late March 1991. In 1994, the *Comfort* was called to Jamaica and Guantánamo Bay to support and treat Haitian and Cuban refugees. The *Comfort* joined the July 1998 NATO Partnership for Peace exercise Baltic Challenge 1998 and arrived in New York within six days of the terrorist attacks in New York on September 11, 2001, to augment regional hospitals' trauma capacities. From January to June 2003, the *Comfort* deployed in support of Operation IRAQI FREEDOM, during which the medical staff treated a great number of Iraqi civilians and prisoners of war as well as troops from the U.S. and coalition forces. The *Mercy* deployed in response to the destruction and health crisis resulting from the South Asian earthquake and tsunami on December 26, 2004, attending to some 200,000 victims. In 2006 it undertook a five-month humanitarian deployment to the Philippines and the South Pacific, while the *Comfort* spent four months of 2007 in the Caribbean and Latin America, treating nearly 100,000 patients in need of basic vaccinations, eye care, and dental work.

Hospital ships' medical capabilities have been regularly augmented by the facilities aboard U.S. amphibious assault ships of the Tarawa (LHA-1) class, which include medical facilities and a 300-bed capacity, and the newer Wasp (LHD-1) class, each with 600 beds.

As the *Mercy* and *Comfort* edge closer to retirement, the thought of building or converting similar replacement vessels has in recent year been overtaken by the U.S. Navy's preference for streamlining its auxiliary and support forces. The Maritime Prepositioning Force (MPF) has moved from concept to partial reality, including MSC cargo vessels that are kept in forward deployment and stocked with equipment, provisions, fuels, and matériel with which to supply all U.S. armed forces moving into an area. A current plan calls for the construction of MPF ships that would incorporate features of flagships, landing ships, supply ships, and fully equipped hospital ships.

GORDON E. HOGG

See also

Military Sealift Command; United States Navy, Iraq War

References

Baker, A. D. *The Naval Institute Guide to Combat Fleets of the World: Their Ships, Aircraft, and Armament.* Annapolis, MD: Naval Institute Press, 1995.

Polmar, Norman. *The Naval Institute Guide to the Ships and Aircraft of the U.S. Fleet.* 18th ed. Annapolis, MD: Naval Institute Press, 2005.

Saunders, Stephen, ed. *Jane's Fighting Ships, 2002–2003.* Coulsdon, Surrey, UK: Jane's Information Group, 2002.

Houthi, Hussein Badr al-Din al- (?–2004)

Yemeni political and religious leader. Hussein Badr al-Din al-Houthi was the charismatic leader of a Yemeni political movement that has opposed the national government. The members of Houthi's movement are drawn from the Zaydi Shia sect, which constitutes some 45–50 percent of Yemen's population. Followers of the Houthi movement, as it came to be called, are estimated at 30 percent of the population.

Between 1993 and 1999, Houthi was a member of parliament representing the Al-Haqq Party. In 1992, a movement known as the Shabab Mu'minin (Believing Youth) developed, apparently to counter growing Salafist influence and assert a new Zaydi identity. Houthi led this movement until 1997, when it split.

Following the U.S. invasion of Iraq in 2003, some members of the Zaydi community protested strongly against the U.S. occupation of Iraq and the Yemeni government's close ties with the United States. Houthi was identified as a leader of these protests. Since the attack on the U.S. Navy destroyer *Cole* in Aden in October 2000, the United States had become concerned about the growth of Al Qaeda in Yemen, and the Yemeni government took great strides to combat the Houthi movement, characterizing it as a deviant and terrorist group like Al Qaeda and claiming that it had links to Iran and Libya, which were never firmly established.

Houthi portrayed his movement as primarily seeking social justice and basic human, political, and religious rights. His movement did not call for an end to the Saleh government but did oppose the Saleh government's alliances with the United States and the manipulation of Salafi or Wahhabist elements in Yemen by that government. Houthi held that the government encouraged those groups but oppressed the Zaydis. Houthi's movement represented a challenge from within the Shia elite, for Houthi was a sayyid, a descendent of the Prophet Muhammad with roots in the Zaydi imamate that had dominated northern Yemen until the establishment of a Yemeni republic in 1962.

The Houthi Rebellion, also known as the al-Sadah Conflict, took place in northern Yemen about 150 miles from Sanaa. In 2004, armed fighting among Houthi's followers broke out against the Yemeni government there. The Yemeni government employed force to crush the movement, which continued after Houthi's death in September 2004. Afterward the movement came under the leadership of Abd al-Malik al-Houthi, his brother; Yusuf Madani, his son-in-law; and Abdullah Ayedh al-Razami. It also came under the spiritual leadership of Badr al-Din al-Houthi, his father.

Following 82 days of fighting in 2004 and after some 1,500 troops and civilians were killed and thousands had fled their villages, Yemeni government forces killed Sheikh Houthi in Jarf Salman, a village in the Marraan mountains in Sadah, on September 10, 2004. Fighting broke out again in March 2005. Some 400 persons were killed within two weeks, hundreds of locals were detained, hundreds of religious schools and religious summer camps were closed, and the government ordered that 1,400 charities be closed. Intermittent fighting has continued thereafter.

SHERIFA ZUHUR

See also

Al Qaeda in the Arabian Peninsula; *Cole,* USS, Attack on; Global War on Terror; Salafism; Yemen

References

Carapico, Sheila. *Civil Society in Yemen: The Political Economy of Activism in Modern Arabia.* Cambridge: Cambridge University Press, 2007.

Dresch, Paul. *A History of Modern Yemen.* Cambridge: Cambridge University Press, 2008.

Hill, Ginny. "Yemen: Fear of Failure." Chatham House Briefing Paper. London: Royal Institute of International Affairs, 2008.

Knickmeyer, Ellen. "In Yemen, a Mostly Concealed Sectarian Fight Endures." *Washington Post,* June 7, 2008, A09.

Human Shields

The term "human shield" can refer to civilians who are forced by military or paramilitary forces to precede them in an attack. More recently, the media and others began using the term to refer to a person or group of people who are voluntarily or involuntary positioned at or near a potential military target as a means to deter enemy fire or attack. States and military establishments have often claimed that their opponents have employed civilians as human shields in order to explain civilian casualties resulting from military action.

A potential enemy may choose not to use force against the employers of the shield for fear of harming the person or persons who form the shield. A potential attacker's inhibition regarding the use of force depends on various considerations, such as fear for his or her own security, societal norms, the inclination to abide by international law forbidding attacks on civilians during an armed conflict, fear of negative international or national public opinion, or a close affiliation with the person or group of people forming the shield.

Human shields are similar to hostages, but there are important differences. In contrast to hostages, who are invariably taken involuntarily, human shields might be civilian volunteers utilized by a government at a particular site to deter an enemy from attacking it. The term also refers, however, to the involuntary use of civilians to shield combatants during attacks. In such incidents, the civilians are forced to move in front of the soldiers in the hope that the enemy force will be reluctant to attack, or if it does so and the civilians are killed, this might have propaganda value.

When there is a case of deliberate seizure of civilians to act as human shields, in most cases once the threat is over the seized are released. Usually, no ransom is involved. Historical records indicate that human shields have been used by state authorities, nongovernmental organizations, and terrorists alike.

The use of human shields is expressly prohibited by the Geneva Convention of 1949 and the Additional Protocols of 1977. Article 28 of the Fourth Geneva Convention states that "The presence of a protected person may not be used to render certain points or areas immune from military operations." Article 3 of the Geneva Convention also forbids the taking of hostages. Furthermore, the Additional Protocols expanded the prohibitions. Protocol II, Part IV, Article 13, states that "The civilian population and individual civilians shall enjoy general protection against the dangers arising from military operations. . . . [They] shall not be the object of attack . . . unless and for such times as they take a direct part in hostilities."

Despite attempts to prevent the use of human shields through the development of international law during the second half of the 20th century, the use of human shields was recorded and discussed in the context of several conflicts, mainly in the 1991 Persian Gulf War, the Bosnian conflict of 1992–1995, the Kosovo War (1999), the Iraq War (2003–2011), and the ongoing Israeli-Palestinian conflict.

Both in Bosnia in 1995 and in Kosovo in 1999, human shields were used extensively by the Serbs. In the war in Bosnia, Bosnian-Serb armed units chained captured United Nations (UN) soldiers to potential North Atlantic Treaty Organization (NATO) air-strike targets. This strategy was effective in paralyzing the UN military forces' operations in Bosnia in May 1995. The nations participating in the UN operation refused to support the use of force against Serbian military targets, as their soldiers' lives were in jeopardy. In 1999, Serbian forces compelled civilian Kosovars to remain near Serb military bases to deter NATO from bombing the bases.

Iraqi dictator Saddam Hussein's regime used human shields of both Westerners and Iraqi civilians on several occasions during the 1990s and right up to the Anglo-American–led invasion of Iraq in March 2003 to safeguard potential military targets. After Iraq's armed forces occupied Kuwait on August 2, 1990, the Iraqi government held dozens of foreign nationals as human shields in strategic locations. To emphasize that human shields were in place, the Hussein regime released videos showing the human shields, some of them interacting with Hussein himself. Only after coming under intense international pressure did the Iraqi government allow these individuals to leave the country. The last human shields left Iraq by December 1991, several weeks before the beginning of Operation DESERT STORM.

In November 1997, a crisis developed between Iraq and the UN concerning weapons inspection in the country. There have been charges that the Iraqi government then encouraged hundreds of civilians to move into palaces and other strategic locations in order to deter attacks there.

Human shields were used again in Iraq in early 2003 but this time by antiwar protesters. The human shield operation was termed the Human Shield Action to Iraq, and it deployed several hundred Western volunteers to potential civilian strategic targets such as water and power plants and a communications center.

With the start of Operation IRAQI FREEDOM on March 20, 2003, many of the volunteers left the country, but approximately 100 remained. The Human Shield Action to Iraq claimed that none of the strategic facilities to which it

deployed volunteers were bombed while human shields were present.

In contrast to the examples given above, which emphasize the use of human shields by only one side in a conflict, during the Israeli-Palestinian conflict both sides have employed human shields. There are records of Palestinians wanted by the Israeli government using civilians as a shield to prevent the Israel Defense Forces (IDF) from firing at them. This tactic was repeated when leaders of Hamas—an Islamic Palestinian political faction that has controlled the Gaza Strip since June 2007—encouraged the Palestinian civilian population to gather near potential Israeli Air Force targets. Hamas also launched rockets on Israeli towns from civilian centers in Gaza. This practice was also reportedly employed by Hezbollah fighters during their war with Israel in July and August 2006, when they fired Katyusha rockets at Israel from civilian centers and fortified their positions inside villages. The Israelis also charged during the 2014 Israeli-Gaza conflict that Hezbollah had used the same tactics, placing rockets in our near schools and mosques.

Beginning in 2002, records kept by the Israeli human rights group B'Tselem indicate that some IDF units used Palestinian civilians as human shields during their operations in order to prevent Palestinian terrorists from firing at them. In these instances, the IDF forced persons held as hostages to precede them into buildings and certain areas. This practice was outlawed by the Israeli Supreme Court in October 2005. Nevertheless, since then and on several occasions, human rights groups have recorded the use of Palestinian civilians as human shields by IDF units. In some cases, the IDF took disciplinary measures against its officers who employed this practice.

CHEN KERTCHER

See also

Global War on Terror; Hussein, Saddam; IRAQI FREEDOM, Operation; Persian Gulf War

References

Ezzo, Matthew V., and Amos N. Guiora. "A Critical Decision Point on the Battlefield—Friend, Foe, or Innocent Bystander." *U of Utah Legal Studies Paper* 8(3) (2008): 91–115.

Gross, Emmanuel. "Use of Civilians as Human Shields: What Legal and Moral Restrictions Pertain to a War Waged by a Democratic State against Terrorism?" *Emory International Law Review* 16 (2002): 445–524.

Skerker, Michael. "Just War Criteria and the New Face of War: Human Shields, Manufactured Martyrs, and Little Boys with Stones." *Journal of Military Ethics* 3(1) (2004): 27–39.

Husaybah, Battle of (April 17, 2004)

Battle fought on April 17, 2004, near the Iraqi town of Husaybah, close to the Syrian border, involving marines of the U.S. I Marine Expeditionary Force. The 14-hour battle occurred concurrently with the First Battle of Fallujah (April 4–May 1, 2004), an operation by the United States to capture the city of Fallujah, also known as Operation VIGILANT RESOLVE. From Husaybah, the insurgents had been attempting to launch an offensive against U.S. forces to divert resources from the attack against Fallujah. The insurgent force numbered about 300 and was operating from positions in the vicinity of the former Baath Party headquarters in Husaybah. U.S. forces numbered 150.

On April 17, the insurgents drew the Americans from their base on the outskirts of Husaybah with a roadside bombing and then with a mortar assault. When the marines retaliated, they encountered an ambush during which they were hit with small-arms and machine-gun fire. The marines then called in reinforcements. The resulting street fighting lasted the entire day and late into the night, with the marines having to advance block by block to clear buildings of insurgents. During the night, Bell AH-1 Cobra helicopter gunships also attacked insurgent positions in the city.

The American forces defeated the insurgents after fierce fighting. Five marines were killed and 9 wounded in the fight. The insurgents suffered an estimated 150 killed in action, an unknown number of wounded, and 20 captured. The insurgent losses represented more than 50 percent of their original strength.

RICHARD B. VERRONE

See also

Fallujah, First Battle of

References

Murray, Williamson, and Robert H. Scales Jr. *The Iraq War: A Military History.* Cambridge, MA: Belknap, 2005.

Ricks, Thomas E. *Fiasco: The American Military Adventure in Iraq.* New York: Penguin, 2006.

West, Bing. *No True Glory: A Frontline Account of the Battle for Fallujah.* New York: Bantam, 2006.

Hussein, Qusay (1966–2003)

Iraqi government and military official and son of Iraqi dictator Saddam Hussein. At the time of the U.S.-led invasion of Iraq in March 2003, Qusay Hussein was considered the second most powerful man in Iraq and the likely successor to his father. Qusay Hussein was born in Tikrit, Iraq, on May

Qusay Hussein, former Iraqi president Saddam Hussein's youngest son, listens to a speech by his father on May 17, 2001. (AP Photo)

17, 1966, the second son of Saddam Hussein and Sajida Talfah. As Arab custom dictates, Saddam Hussein's elder son, Uday, was the most prominent and was raised as his father's successor. Although out of the limelight, Qusay Hussein remained loyal to his father to the point of even imitating his dress and trademark mustache.

While Uday Hussein proved to be mentally unstable and a flamboyant sexual sadist whose antics embarrassed the ruling family, Qusay was much more reserved. Complying with his father's wishes, in 1987 he married the daughter of Mahir Abd al-Rashid, an influential military commander. The marriage produced four children. Although possessing numerous mistresses, Qusay Hussein portrayed himself as a devoted family man.

Qusay Hussein's loyalty and patience eventually bore dividends. When Uday's behavior became more erratic in the late 1980s, Saddam Hussein began to turn more to his second son. For example, Qusay was granted broad authority in crushing the Shiite Muslim and Marsh Arab uprisings following Iraq's defeat in the 1991 Persian Gulf War. He responded ruthlessly, using torture and executing entire families believed to be disloyal to the regime.

As Uday's position declined, Qusay began to emerge as the likely successor to his father. For his role in crushing the 1991 rebellions, Saddam entrusted Qusay with command of the Special Security Organization, including Internal Security and the Presidential Guard. In his role as security head, Qusay oversaw Iraqi's chemical, biological, and nuclear programs. He was also responsible for the repression of opponents of his father's regime. It is believed that Qusay, with his father's approval, had a hand in the attempted assassination of Uday on December 12, 1996.

Clearly Saddam Hussein's favorite, Qusay was named "caretaker" in the event of Saddam's illness or death and given command of the elite Republican Guard. Possessing no formal military training, Qusay refused to accept advice from more experienced commanders. None dared to question his orders for fear of the consequences, however. The dismal performance of the Republican Guard in failing to slow the American-led invasion in 1991 is often blamed on the lack of military experience of Qusay and his advisers.

Following the terror attacks of September 11, 2001, foreign pressure on Iraq began to increase, and the United States began preparing for a second invasion of Iraq, this time to topple the Hussein regime. Saddam Hussein and his sons temporarily rallied in the face of the overwhelming military force gathering to confront them. On March 18, 2003, U.S. president George W. Bush called on Saddam Hussein and his sons to leave the country, a demand that was rebuffed.

Following the invasion on March 20, 2003, Qusay Hussein went into hiding. On July 22, 2003, Qusay, his 14-year-old son Mustapha, Uday, and their bodyguard were cornered in Mosul. During the course of a four hour firefight, all were killed. Following identification, the bodies were buried in Awja.

ROBERT W. MALICK

See also

Hussein, Saddam; Hussein, Uday; Iraq, History of, 1990–Present; IRAQI FREEDOM, Operation; Marsh Arabs; Persian Gulf War; Republican Guard; Shia Islam

References

Balaghi, Shiva. *Saddam Hussein: A Biography*. Westport, CT: Greenwood, 2006.

Bengio, Ofra. "How Does Saddam Hold On?" *Foreign Affairs* (July–August 2000): 90–103.

Bennett, Brian, and Michael Weisskopf. "The Sum of Two Evils." *Time*, June 2, 2003, 34.

Thomas, Evan, and Christopher Dickey. "Saddam's Sons." *Newsweek*, October 21, 2002, 34.

Woods, Kevin, James Lacy, and Williamson Murray. "Saddam's Delusions." *Foreign Affairs* (May–June 2006): 2–16.

Hussein, Saddam (1937–2006)

Iraqi politician, leading figure in the Baath Party, and president of Iraq (1979–2003). Born on April 28, 1937, in the village of Awja, near Tikrit, to a family of sheepherders, Saddam Hussein attended a secular school in Baghdad and in 1957 joined the Baath Party, a socialist and Arab nationalist party. Iraqi Baathists supported General Abd al-Karim Qasim's ouster of the Iraqi monarchy in 1958 but were not favored by President Qasim.

Wounded in an unsuccessful attempt to assassinate Qasim in 1959, Hussein subsequently fled the country but returned after the 1963 Baathist coup and began his rise in the party, although he was again imprisoned in 1964. Escaping in 1966, Hussein continued to ascend through the party's ranks, becoming second in authority when the party took full and uncontested control of Iraq in 1968 under the leadership of General Ahmad Hassan al-Bakr, a relative of Hussein's. The elderly Bakr gradually relinquished power to him so that Hussein eventually controlled most of the government.

Hussein became president when Bakr resigned, allegedly because of illness, in July 1979. A week after taking power, Hussein led a meeting of Baath leaders during which the names of his potential challengers were read aloud. They were then escorted from the room and shot. Because Iraq was rent by ethnic and religious divisions, Hussein ruled through a tight web of relatives and associates from Tikrit, backed by the Sunni Muslim minority. He promoted economic development through Iraqi oil production, which accounted for 10 percent of known world reserves. Hussein's modernization was along Western lines, with expanded roles for women and a secular legal system based in part on sharia and Ottoman law. He also promoted the idea of Iraqi nationalism and emphasized Iraq's ancient past, glorifying such figures as Kings Hammurabi and Nebuchadnezzar.

Before assuming the presidency, Hussein had courted both the West and the Soviet Union, resulting in arms deals with the Soviets and close relations with the Soviet Union and France. He was also instrumental in convincing Mohammad Reza Shah Pahlavi of Iran to curb his support of Iraqi Kurds. Hussein's efforts to take advantage of the superpowers' Cold War rivalry, including rapprochement with Iran, fell apart with the overthrow of the shah in the 1979 Iranian Revolution. The shah's successor, Ayatollah Khomeini, a radical fundamentalist Muslim, bitterly opposed Hussein because of his Sunni background and secularism.

After a period of repeated border skirmishes, Iraq declared war on Iran in September 1980. Hussein's

Iraqi president Saddam Hussein fires a rifle in Baghdad on November 20, 2000, to begin events on this day demonstrating Iraq's commitment to liberating Jerusalem from Israeli rule. (AP Photo/Jassim Mohammed)

ostensible dispute concerned a contested border, but he also feared Iran's fundamentalism and its support for the Iraqi Shia Muslim majority. Initial success gave way to Iraqi defeats in the face of human-wave attacks and ultimately a stalemate. By 1982 Hussein was ready to end the war, but Iranian leaders desired that the fighting continue. In 1988 the United Nations (UN) finally brokered a cease-fire, but not before the war had devastated both nations. The war left Iraq heavily in debt, and Hussein requested relief from his major creditors, including the United States, Kuwait, and Saudi Arabia. He also sought to maintain high oil prices. His efforts were in vain; creditors refused to write off their debts, and Kuwait maintained a high oil output, forcing other oil-producing nations to follow suit.

Hussein responded by declaring Kuwait a "rogue province" of Iraq. He was also enraged by Kuwaiti slant-drilling into Iraqi oil fields. Hussein's demands became more strident, and after securing what he believed to be U.S. acquiescence, he ordered Iraqi forces to attack and occupy Kuwait on August 2, 1990. Hussein miscalculated the U.S. reaction. President George H. W. Bush assembled an international military coalition, built up forces in Saudi Arabia (Operation

DESERT SHIELD), and then commenced a relentless bombing campaign against Iraq in January 1991. The ground war of February 24–28, 1991, resulted in a crushing defeat of Iraqi forces. Although Hussein withdrew from Kuwait, coalition forces did not seek his overthrow; he remained in power, ruling a nation devastated by two recent wars.

Hussein retained control of Iraq for another decade, during which he brutally suppressed Kurdish and Shia revolts, relinquished limited autonomy to the Kurds, acquiesced to the destruction of stockpiles of chemical weapons, and pursued a dilatory response to UN efforts to monitor his weapons programs. Convinced—wrongly as it turned out—that Hussein had been building and stockpiling weapons of mass destruction, President George W. Bush asked for and received authorization from Congress to wage war against Iraq. U.S. and coalition forces invaded Iraq in March 2003. Coalition forces took Baghdad on April 10, 2003, and captured Hussein on December 14, 2003, to be brought to trial on charges of war crimes and crimes against humanity.

On November 5, 2006, the Iraqi Special Tribunal found Hussein guilty for the deaths of 148 Shiite Muslims in 1982 whose murders he had ordered. That same day, he was sentenced to hang. Earlier, on August 21, 2006, a second trial had begun on charges that Hussein had committed genocide and other atrocities by ordering the systematic extermination of northern Iraqi Kurds during 1987–1988, resulting in as many as 180,000 deaths. Before the second trial moved into high gear, however, Hussein filed an appeal, which was rejected by the Iraqi Supreme Court on December 26, 2006. Four days later on December 30, 2006, the Muslim holiday of 'Id al-Adha, Hussein was executed by hanging in Baghdad. Before his death, Hussein told U.S. Federal Bureau of Investigation interrogators that he had misled the world to give the impression that Iraq had weapons of mass destruction in order to make Iraq appear stronger in the face of its enemy, Iran.

DANIEL E. SPECTOR

See also

Iraq, History of, 1990–Present; IRAQI FREEDOM, Operation; Kurds

References

Bengio, Ofra. *Saddam's Word: Political Discourse in Iraq.* New York: Oxford University Press USA, 1998.

Karsh, Efraim. *Saddam Hussein: A Political Biography.* New York: Grove/Atlantic, 2002.

Miller, Judith, and Laurie Mylroie. *Saddam Hussein and the Crisis in the Gulf.* New York: Times Books, 1990.

Wingate, Brian. *Saddam Hussein: The Rise and Fall of a Dictator.* New York: Rosen, 2004.